AFTER ENRON

At the end of the twentieth century, it was thought by many that the Anglo-American system of corporate governance was performing effectively and some observers claimed to see an international trend towards convergence around this model. There can be no denying that the recent corporate governance crisis in the US has caused many to question their faith in this view. This collection of essays provides a comprehensive attempt to answer the following questions: first, what went wrong—when and why do markets misprice the value of firms, and what was wrong with the incentives set by Enron? Secondly, what has been done in response, and how well will it work—including essays on the Sarbanes-Oxley Act in the US, UK company law reform and European company law and auditor liability reform, along with a consideration of corporate governance reforms in historical perspective. Three approaches emerge. The first two share the premise that the system is fundamentally sound, but part ways over whether a regulatory response is required. The third view, in contrast, argues that the various scandals demonstrate fundamental weaknesses in the Anglo-American system itself, which cannot hope to be repaired by the sort of reforms that have taken place.

After Enron

Improving Corporate Law and Modernising
Securities Regulation in Europe and the US

Edited by
John Armour
and
Joseph A McCahery

·HART·
PUBLISHING

OXFORD AND PORTLAND, OREGON
2006

Published in North America (US and Canada) by
Hart Publishing
c/o International Specialized Book Services
920 NE 58th Avenue, Suite 300
Portland, OR 97213-3786
USA
Tel: +1 503 287 3093 or toll-free: (1) 800 944 6190
Fax: +1 503 280 8832
Email: orders@isbs.com
Website: www.isbs.com

Hart Publishing, 16C Worcester Place, Oxford, OX1 2JW
Telephone: +44 (0)1865 517530 Fax: +44 (0) 1865 510710
Email: mail@hartpub.co.uk
Website: http://www.hartpub.co.uk

British Library Cataloguing in Publication Data

Data Available

ISBN 13: 978-1-84113-531-1
ISBN 10: 1-84113-531-3

Typeset by Forewords, Oxford
Printed and bound in Great Britain by
TJ International, Padstow, Cornwall

Acknowledgements

We are grateful to the authors for agreeing to contribute their material to this collection. Several of the chapters have previously been published as articles, and where the copyright is not held by the authors, we are also grateful to the publishers for permitting us to reproduce their material. In particular, we acknowledge the permission of the American Bar Association (Chapters 3 and 7); Sage Publications (Chapter 4); Oxford University Press (Chapters 6 and 14); the Asser Press (Chapters 9 and 15); Blackwell Publishing (Chapter 10); *Theoretical Inquiries in Law* (Chapter 11); Cambridge University Press (Chapter 16) and the *University of Pennsylvania Journal of International Economic Law* (Chapter 17).

We gratefully acknowledge financial support from the Anton Phillips Fund. We owe a large debt of gratitude to James Risser and Mel Hamill for their excellent work in editing the chapters, and are most grateful to Richard Hart and his colleagues at Hart Publishing for their patience in responding to the inevitable delays in a project of this sort.

Contents

List of Contributors

JOHN ARMOUR is a Senior Lecturer in the Faculty of Law, and Research Associate in the Centre for Business Research, at the University of Cambridge.

LUCIAN ARYE BEBCHUK is William J. Friedman and Alicia Townsend Friedman Professor of Law, Economics, and Finance, Harvard Law School.

BERNARD BLACK is Haydn W. Head Regents Chair for Faculty Excellence and Professor of Law at the University of Texas Law School and Professor of Finance at the Red McCombs School of Business, University of Texas.

WILLIAM W. BRATTON is Professor of Law at the Georgetown University Law Center.

BRIAN CHEFFINS is S.J. Berwin Professor of Corporate Law in the Faculty of Law at the University of Cambridge.

JOHN C. COFFEE, JR. is Adolf A. Berle Professor of Law at Columbia University and Director of the Center on Corporate Governance at Columbia University Law School.

JAMES D. COX is Brainerd Currie Professor of Law at the Duke University School of Law.

PAUL DAVIES is Cassel Professor of Commercial Law at the London School of Economics.

SIMON DEAKIN is Robert Monks Professor of Corporate Governance in the Judge Business School, Acting Director of the Centre for Business Research, and Yorke Professorial Fellow in the Faculty of Law at Cambridge University.

LUCA ENRIQUES is Professor of Business Law at the University of Bologna, Faculty of Law, and ECGI Research Associate.

GUIDO FERRARINI is Professor of Law at the University of Genoa and the Centre for Law and Finance.

EILÍS FERRAN is Professor of Law in the Faculty of Law at the University of Cambridge.

RONALD J. GILSON is Meyers Professor of Law and Business at Stanford Law School and Stern Professor of Law and Business at Columbia Law School.

PAOLO GIUDICI is Professor of Law at the Free University of Bozen and Centre for Law and Finance.

GÉRARD HERTIG is Professor of Law and Economics, Eidgenössische Technische Hochschule Zürich.

KLAUS J. HOPT is Professor of Law and Director of the Max Planck Institute for Foreign Private and Private International Law in Hamburg.

MICHAEL KLAUSNER is Professor of Law at Stanford Law School.

SUZANNE J. KONZELMANN is Reader in Management at Birkbeck College, University of London and Research Associate at the Centre for Business Research, University of Cambridge.

REINIER KRAAKMAN is Ezra Ripley Thayer Professor of Law at Harvard Law School.

DONALD C. LANGEVOORT is Professor of Law at Georgetown University Law Center.

JOSEPH A. MCCAHERY is Professor of Corporate Governance at the University of Amsterdam Center for Law and Economics.

RICHARD C. NOLAN is a Fellow of St. John's College and Senior Lecturer in Law at the University of Cambridge; he is also a Barrister at Erskine Chambers, Lincoln's Inn, London.

DAVID A. SKEEL, JR. is S. Samuel Arsht Professor of Corporate Law at the University of Pennsylvania Law School.

Introduction

After Enron: Improving Corporate Law and Modernising Securities Regulation in Europe and the US

JOHN ARMOUR[*] and JOSEPH A McCAHERY[**]

URING THE 1990s, US stocks led the world in the greatest bull market in history. On 24 March 2000, the S&P 500 Index peaked at a record high of 1,527.47, up a dizzying 500 per cent on ten years earlier (Standard & Poor, 2006). For much of this period, the Enron Corporation was one of Wall Street's darlings. It was a member of an elite club of 'new economy', growth-driven firms whose stocks were at the forefront of the market's spectacular rise. Acclaimed as 'America's most innovative company' by Fortune magazine for each of the years from 1996 to 2001, Enron is, however, best remembered for what happened *after* the stock market had peaked. Whilst many 'new economy' stocks started to fall, Enron's continued to rise for a while, seemingly defying gravity (Fortune, 2001). But in the autumn of 2001, Enron tumbled spectacularly from grace. Revelations of widespread accounting fraud and other misconduct by senior executives spiralled the firm into what was then the largest bankruptcy in history. Enron's demise was soon followed by scandals at a number of other 'new economy' stars, such as Worldcom, Tyco, Adelphia and Global Crossing. This wave of accounting fraud shook investors' faith in stock markets and by 9 October 2002, the S&P 500 had fallen by over 50 per cent from its record high. Many asked whether something was not profoundly wrong with the US system of corporate governance.

Several things had gone wrong at Enron. Its top executives had

[*] Faculty of Law and Centre for Business Research, Cambridge University.
[**] Professor of Corporate Governance, University of Amsterdam Center for Law and Economics, and Professor of International Business Law, Tilburg University Faculty of Law. We are grateful to Brian Cheffins for helpful comments on earlier drafts. The usual disclaimers apply.

engaged in aggressive accounting manipulations in an effort to boost the company's stock price. They were motivated, at least in part, by a desire to maximise the value of their stock options. The company's auditors had been persuaded to become complicit in earnings misstatements by the corrosive effect of valuable consulting contracts, which were in management's gift. Moreover, analysts at several investment banks, supposedly offering independent advice, were tainted by conflicts of interest arising out of their firms' involvement in Enron's financing. As a result, Enron's share price was artificially inflated for a considerable period of time.

Because the revelations of misconduct came on the back of a stock market fall, Enron's shareholders suffered heavy losses. One of the worst-hit groups—and least able to afford it—were the company's employees, whose pension plans had been heavily invested in the firm as an 'incentive' measure. Particularly egregious, in many people's eyes, was the fact that Enron executives had started to sell their shares in the company by mid-2001, when it was clear that trouble was unavoidable, whereas the terms of employees' pension schemes prohibited them from doing so. These factors gave the scandal a particularly intense political salience.

The US Congress responded very rapidly. On 30 July 2002, less than nine months after Enron filed for bankruptcy, the Public Company Accounting Reform and Investor Protection Act of 2002 was passed.[1] The new legislation, known universally as the 'Sarbanes-Oxley' Act after its two sponsors, was intended to restore public confidence in stock markets. In the main, it sought to restore the integrity of the audit process by strengthening oversight of the accounting profession. However, the Act also put in place a number of measures designed to counter failures in corporate governance. These include requiring CEOs and CFOs to certify, on pain of criminal penalties, their firms' periodic reports and the effectiveness of internal controls; the imposition of obligations on corporate lawyers to report any evidence of suspected violations of securities law; the prohibition of corporate loans to managers or directors; restrictions on stock sales by executives during certain 'blackout periods;' and requiring firms to establish an audit committee comprised of independent directors, of which at least one member must be a 'financial expert.'

For a short while after the American scandals broke, European observers might have been forgiven for experiencing a hint of *schadenfraude*. Continental Europeans had frequently been lectured on the virtues of the Anglo-American 'outsider' model of corporate governance, and on how the globalisation of capital and product markets would supposedly force the abandonment of their 'insider' model in order to remain

---

[1] Sarbanes-Oxley Act of 2002, Pub L No 107-204, 116 Stat 745.

competitive (see Hansmann and Kraakman, 2001). In the immediate aftermath of Enron, some Europeans were heard to wonder whether the insider system might not have advantages after all: at least it seemed to be immune from stock market-driven scandals (see Enriques, 2003).

Any complacency was short-lived. In late 2002—little more than a year since the Enron scandal had broken—news began to emerge that something was seriously amiss at Parmalat, the Italian dairy-produce conglomerate. As this and other earnings misstatement scandals—such as those at the Dutch retail giant Ahold and the French engineering firm Alstom—unfolded over the next year, any illusion of European immunity was shattered. It did not take the European Commission long to respond. They had already, in spring 2002, asked their High-Level Company Law Expert Group to prepare a report elaborating any necessary EU legislation in the field of corporate governance. In May 2003, the Commission announced a number of initiatives, including an Action Plan for the modernization of company law and plans for the reform of the statutory audit (European Commission, 2003a, 2003b). These proposals are finding their way onto the statute book at varying speeds.

In the UK, Marconi, a firm that had won stock market plaudits for its acquisition-led expansion into new economy businesses during the 1990s, suffered a dramatic fall into the hands of its creditors during the second half of 2001. The UK's corporate community held their collective breath, because memories of scandals at Polly Peck, BCCI and Maxwell in the early 1990s were still vivid. Although Marconi turned out to have been a case of management error, rather than fraud, the UK was spurred into renewed reflection on whether its corporate governance system was functioning effectively. As it happened, a large-scale reform of English company law, following the independent Company Law Review commissioned by the DTI, had been announced well before the Enron scandal broke (see Arden, 2003). Whilst preparations for these reforms were continuing, the government ushered in a number of corporate governance-related initiatives, including the controversial Higgs Report on the role and effectiveness of non-executive directors (Higgs, 2003), and the Smith Report on audit committees (Financial Reporting Council, 2003a), both of which were implemented through a revision to the UK's non-statutory Combined Code on Corporate Governance (Financial Reporting Council, 2003b).

The series of corporate scandals on both sides of the Atlantic and the energetic reform activity it engendered around the world provoke a multitude of questions, many of which are explored in more detail by the contributions in this volume. First, reflection is prompted about the extent to which capital markets price stocks 'efficiently'—that is, take into account all publicly-available information about firms. Some investors were suspicious about Enron's artificially high stock price, even before its bubble burst (Fortune, 2001). If such investors might have viewed selling it short as an opportunity for profit, why did it not fall more quickly? Do capital markets behave less rationally than had previously been imagined?

Secondly, we might investigate the ways in which, if at all, the US and European scandals differed both from each other, and from other corporate scandals that have occurred in history. Are corporate scandals, and knee-jerk legislative responses to them, a cyclical process, forming an inevitable corollary to stock market bubbles? Did the pattern of misconduct in Europe differ significantly from that in the US, reflecting underlying differences in systems of corporate governance, or are all the scandals best characterised as sharing certain basic commonalities?

Thirdly, and perhaps most obviously, questions arise about the legislative prescriptions for reform. In the US context, was the Sarbanes-Oxley Act sufficient, or indeed necessary, to remedy the problems? What should be done about issues concerning shareholder rights, accounting regulation and board structure? The reforms in the European context not only provoke reiterations of these questions, but also raise an additional group of issues. The EU is characterised by a much greater degree of both political and economic diversity than is the US. This calls for examination both of the appropriateness of particular substantive measures as pan-European reforms, which must cater to this diversity, and of the political feasibility of reform programmes. The post-Enron era has seen renewed energy in European company law and capital markets reform, which in turn prompts reflection on the degree of success with which these new measures have surmounted the political obstacles.

Parts I–IV of this collection address these four groups of issues in turn.

PART I: STOCK MARKETS AND INFORMATION

Whilst it was clear that executives at Enron—and perhaps to a greater extent, at Tyco and Worldcom—had engaged in outright manipulation of their accounts, many observers expressed surprise that this had not been picked up by the markets before the summer of 2001. This was because the accounts contained a number of gaps, which, it has been argued, ought to have lead seasoned investors to conclude well before then that there was something unnatural about the stock's continued rise. The quest to understand why they did not do so forms the stepping-off point for the chapters in Part I of this collection.

From the mid 1970s until the late 1990s, the orthodox view amongst finance scholars was that capital markets priced securities 'efficiently'. The first tenet of this view, which is known as the Efficient Capital Markets Hypothesis (ECMH), posits that price-sensitive information is impounded in stock prices (Fama, 1970). Numerous 'event studies' have shown empirically that companies' stock prices do in fact react almost instantaneously to significant events affecting their performance. These tend to confirm the so-called 'semi-strong' form of the ECMH, namely that securities prices take into account all *publicly available* information about the firms issuing them (see Malkiel, 1992).

If the finance orthodoxy is correct, then what went wrong at Enron was purely a matter of the manipulation of disclosure. If markets take into account all publicly available information, then it should not be surprising that if price-sensitive information is concealed, a company such as Enron should have—for a limited period at least, until the market discovers what is going on—an over-inflated stock price.

Enron, however, provides a seeming puzzle for adherents to the finance orthodoxy. Many of the irregularities in its accounts were not concealed, or at least not with any real efficacy. The notes to the company's accounts dropped very large hints about the over-engineering of its finances. The surprising thing, if the finance orthodoxy is correct, is not that the company ultimately failed, but that this publicly-available information seems to have been ignored.

Since the mid 1990s, however, an alternative framework for understanding stock markets, known as 'behavioural finance', has emerged (e.g. Shleifer, 2000). The name reflects the way in which this view starts from empirical studies of investor behaviour, as opposed to axiomatic postulates of rationality. Such studies show that investor behaviour differs markedly from what would be 'rational' in a range of circumstances. However, proponents of the traditional perspective have responded with a series of explanations consistent with the rationality axioms (e.g. Fama, 1998).

Part I contains two chapters that consider the extent to which the behavioural finance view might call for a reappraisal both of claims that capital markets are 'efficient' and of perceptions about how best to regulate them. In so doing, they each consider whether investor irrationality might help to explain what happened at Enron. Chapter 1, by Ronald Gilson and Reinier Kraakman, is a reprise to an influential earlier article, 'The Mechanisms of Market Efficiency' by the same authors (Gilson and Kraakman, 1984). The earlier paper sought to offer an account of the institutions that facilitate the informational efficiency of capital markets. The authors argued that arbitrageurs act as an important conduit for the reflection in stock prices of information available only to a subset of investors. The arbitrageurs would follow the trading activities of well-informed investors, such as corporate insiders, and any unusual activity would thereby be rapidly picked up by the market.

In Chapter 1, Gilson and Kraakman review the same terrain in light of developments in finance theory. Their analysis focuses on institutional limitations, such as regulatory and market restrictions on short selling, which make arbitrageurs less effective at transmitting negative information about corporate performance into stock prices than positive information. For such restrictions to impede market efficiency does not necessitate any assumption that investors behave irrationally. However, the presence of a substantial number of irrational investors ('noise traders') in the marketplace compound these problems by introducing 'noise trader risk'—that is, a risk that an arbitrageur will suffer loss on an 'informed' position because that information is ignored by noise traders. Moreover, where the irrationality consists of a general bias in a particular direction, then this may generate a 'momentum effect'—that is, a change sustained only by virtue of a previous change—for particular stocks, or for the market in general. It may become rational for arbitrageurs to trade *with*, rather than against, the momentum effect—that is, if a large number of investors are behaving irrationally by ignoring information about fundamentals, it becomes rational to ignore that information too. Gilson and Kraakman suggest that a sudden influx of uninformed investors would be a good proxy for the existence of 'bubbles' in the market. However, such a momentum effect requires a continuous stream of new investors to sustain it, and at a certain point, will come to an end. This echoes old wisdom that the time to sell investments in a bubble market is the moment at which everyone else has entered the market, and so there will be no fresh money to prop it up—or as Joseph Kennedy is famously reputed to have said: 'when the shoe-shine guy starts giving you stock tips, it's time to get out of the market.'

In Chapter 2, Donald Langevoort considers more directly the ways in which various behavioural biases might impact on the ECMH. He focuses on biases such as 'loss aversion'—which can lead investors to sell winning stocks too quickly (so as to avoid the risk of suffering a loss) but to delay selling losing stocks too long (in a desire to avoid crystallising a loss), and 'cognitive conservatism', which leads people to change their views in response to new information more slowly than would be consistent with rationality. However, both effects are subject to change under particular circumstances. Loss aversion has been shown to be significantly reduced in the light of recent experience—that is, gamblers are more confident when 'on a roll'. The salience, representativeness or availability of new information may dramatically affect the way in which people react to it—under certain circumstances they may overreact, rather than react conservatively. The problem with many of these findings—as Langevoort clearly recognises—is that they are highly contingent, making prediction difficult, and the task of a policymaker—who must work with generalities—very complex. Without taking a position on the question whether behavioural analysis better predicts market movements than traditional 'rationality' assumptions,

Langevoort teases out implications for a variety of different aspects of market regulation—including 'fraud on the internet', fair disclosure and insider trading.

Both chapters suggest that even if information was publicly available—or could readily have been extrapolated—about Enron's true position, the market might have failed to respond to it as quickly as might have been expected, owing to irrationality on the part of investors, institutional limitations, or both. This implies that what went wrong was more than just the manipulation of disclosure by Enron's executives.

PART II: CORPORATE SCANDALS IN HISTORICAL AND COMPARATIVE CONTEXT

The chapters in Part II draw on experiences of corporate scandals from both history and different financial systems. In Chapter 3, David A Skeel, Jr suggests lessons that might be learned from history about the causes—and consequences—of corporate scandals. The compensation packages granted to Enron's top executives gave them extremely high-powered incentives to focus on the share price. This contributed to their willingness to misstate the financial affairs of the company so as to please analysts and investors. Skeel compares this with the behaviour of errant executives in two previous rounds of US corporate scandals—that of Jay Cooke, who engineered the finances of the Northern Pacific Railroad during the 1860s until its spectacular collapse in 1873; and that of Samuel Insull, who built a vast empire of electricity companies in the 1920s, which imploded amid allegations of fraud in 1932. Skeel argues that in each case, the problems were caused by a combination of a culture in which risk-taking by executives was linked to reward, with excessive competition. These encouraged managers to take ever-increasing gambles. Each time round, some executives responded to these pressures by manipulating the corporate form in order to inflate returns artificially.

In each case, such manipulation permitted a few executives to obtain very high returns from wrongdoing that impacted negatively on the lives of many individuals. Thus when the wrongdoing came to light, scandals—popular outrage—followed. As a result, there was a populist demand for a response, which in each case took the form of legislation designed to ensure that the particular malpractices which had occurred would not be repeated: the cessation of federal subsidies to railways in the 1870s; the Securities Acts of 1933 and 1934, and the Sarbanes-Oxley Act in 2002. Skeel then reflects on the link between interest group politics and the regulation of corporate behaviour in the US. For most of the history of the corporate form, managers have been the dominant interest group: they have at their disposal corporate resources that can be used to lobby politicians in an effective and concentrated manner. Thus, on the whole, the legal environment within which public companies operate has a tendency to respond to managers' preferences. Yet for brief periods following the scandals that have occurred intermittently throughout the history of the corporate form, populist outrage compels legislatures to enact manager-constraining legislation.

Skeel's account is thus sympathetic to the widely-held view that Sarbanes-Oxley Act was a 'knee-jerk' response to populist pressure. It is doubtful whether this piece of legislation, passed as quickly as it was, can have been adequately thought through. It is hardly surprising, therefore, that it has drawn widespread criticism from commentators who argue, alternatively, that it is either unnecessary, or insufficient, to address the underlying problems. Precisely which reforms, if any, *would* lead to the smoother functioning of market-based corporate governance is of course a highly contentious question. A troubling suggestion, exemplified by Simon Deakin and Suzanne Konzelmann's contribution in Chapter 4, is that Sarbanes-Oxley is merely a response to the *symptoms* of a deeper malaise in a system of corporate governance that focuses too closely on 'shareholder value' (see also Bratton, 2002).

As is well-known, companies listed in the US and UK are said to operate within an 'outsider' system of corporate governance (e.g. Berglöf, 1997; Bratton and McCahery, 2002). The most important distinguishing feature is that share ownership is dispersed, with no single blockholder being able to exert significant control over the company. The principal goal of corporate governance is understood in terms of rendering managers of such companies accountable to their dispersed shareholders. The fear is that managers would otherwise tend to prefer their own interests, to the detriment of shareholders. Since the mid-1980s, an orthodox view in Anglo-American corporate governance, based largely on the traditional finance perspective, has been that the best way to render managers of public corporations accountable to stockholders has been to give them incentives to focus on the share price, for example through the threat of hostile takeovers (Easterbrook and Fischel, 1991). If markets impound all publicly available information about corporate performance, then the market price will give the most reliable indicator of the extent to which managers are pursuing the shareholders' interests. Thus many of the mechanisms of corporate governance employed in Anglo-American public companies during the 1990s have equated shareholders' interests with the pursuit of higher stock prices.

Yet, as Deakin and Konzelmann argue, giving executives powerful incentives—both positive, in the form of lucrative remuneration packages, and negative, in the form of threats of hostile takeover—that are linked to a single benchmark—share price—creates a powerful and counter-productive temptation to manipulate indicators. This criticism is complemented by the perhaps more fundamental point that the use of 'accountability to share price' as a proxy for 'accountability to shareholders' rests on the assumption that capital markets are, to a large degree, informationally efficient. To the extent that they are not, as was contemplated by the contributions in Part I, then the share price might not reflect shareholders' long-term interests (Singh *et al*, 2005). Consequently, tying managers' conduct to share price maximization might result in misallocations of resources.

Deakin and Konzelmann view the Enron scandal as a demonstration of the failure of 'shareholder value' as a guiding principle for business, and argue for a return to a more pluralistic view of the ambitions of corporate entities. Placing less emphasis on accountability to shareholders would not only reduce incentives to 'massage' figures, but would also make it easier for firms to commit to 'partnership' arrangements with employees. What would be lost in accountability, it is argued, would be more than made up for through the increased effort devoted to productive activity rather than signal manipulation. The characteristic feature of most of the world's corporate governance systems—that is, apart from the US and the UK—is that the ownership of shares in listed companies is concentrated in the hands of blockholders. Systems following this pattern are said to have an 'insider' model of corporate governance, in contrast to the Anglo-American 'outsider' model. Under an insider system, there need be little regulatory concern about rendering managers accountable to shareholders, as the blockholder will control the managers, who will clearly be accountable to them. Hence it is possible for the corporate governance framework explicitly to promote a pluralistic approach.

A drawback with the foregoing argument is that whilst many corporate governance systems—especially those in continental Europe—already embrace such pluralism, Parmalat and the other European collapses have amply demonstrated that such systems enjoy no special immunity from scandal. The Parmalat scandal, recounted by Guido Ferrarini and Paolo Giudici in Chapter 5, forcefully drove home the point that the incentive and opportunity to commit fraud is not limited to any particular system of governance, geographic region, industry, or size of company. As is the case with many large continental European firms, Parmalat was controlled by members of its founding family. Its failure was a classic case of fraud carried out by the family-controlled managers to enrich family members and private companies controlled by the family trust.

There were some clear commonalities between the Enron and Parmalat scandals. First, both involved self-interested executives manipulating corporate assets for the benefit of themselves and their associates. Secondly, as Ferrarini and Giudici explain, auditor failure appears to have contributed materially to both scandals.

Despite these similarities, there were also significant differences. Although both Enron and Parmalat involved accounting misstatements, John Coffee argues in Chapter 6 that each involved characteristically divergent forms of misconduct, reflecting differences in the underlying systems of corporate governance. In outsider systems, managers are most likely to be tempted to inflate the share price, as happened in the various cases of earnings misstatements in US public companies. In insider systems, on the other hand, the concern is less with manipulating the share price, and more with the diversion of corporate assets into the hands of blockholders—as appears to have been at the heart of Parmalat's woes. One implication of Coffee's chapter is that we should not assume that legal reforms which are matched to the problems of outsider governance regimes will necessarily also work in an insider system. For example, it might be asked how effective attempts to make boards of directors more 'independent', recently popular in Anglo-American corporate governance, would be if transplanted into an 'insider' system where top managers are in any event controlled by a blockholder.

Another important difference between corporate governance systems, which has received considerable recent attention in the economic literature, concerns the appropriate *mode* of regulation. That is, the ways in which rules governing corporate behaviour are created and enforced. One provocative strand of work has focused on generic differences between civil and common law countries, arguing that the common law (associated with Anglo-American systems) is more readily adaptable to changes in market conditions, and less susceptible to harmful political interference (e.g. La Porta *et al*, 2000; Beck *et al*, 2002). Whilst a binary division between 'civil law' and 'common law' seems overly simplistic, it is nevertheless becoming clear that differences in the creation and enforcement of regulation may matter at least as much in corporate governance as the content of the substantive rules themselves. This point is forcefully made in this collection by Ferrarini and Giudici (Chapter 5), who explain that the substantive rules regarding auditor liability in Italy were, at the time the misdeeds occurred at Parmalat, actually more stringent than the post Sarbanes-Oxley regime in the US. Yet these rules nevertheless failed to prevent large-scale auditor failure. Ferrarini and Giudici argue that this was because of weaknesses in the rules' enforcement. In Italy, as in much of continental Europe, the regulation of corporate governance rules relies heavily on public enforcement to render the substantive rules effective as a deterrent. The authors contrast this with the US, where private enforcement plays a much more significant role. To be sure, the US system, which relies heavily on class action litigation, does not result in perfect deterrence (see Pritchard, 2005). But Ferrarini and Giudici's argument is that, as a general matter, private parties have more reliable incentives to enforce than do public prosecutors, whose efficacy may be sidelined by rent-seeking activities.

Thus, whilst auditor failure was at the heart of both the US and European scandals, there were significant differences, which in turn might require different responses—both in terms of the substance and the mode of regulation—to prevent a recurrence. In light of these differences, the US and European regulatory responses are considered separately, respectively in Parts III and IV of the book. The UK, which shares many of the features of the US system of corporate governance, yet is subject to the same EU rules as continental Europe, is considered at appropriate points in both.

PART III. EVALUATING REGULATORY RESPONSES: THE US AND UK

The five chapters in Part III of the book consider various reforms, both actual and proposed, that have been prescribed in the Anglo-American context. At the core of this discussion must necessarily be the Sarbanes-Oxley Act. As we have seen, it is easy to criticise the speed with which the US legislation was rushed through Congress. A widely-held view is that it lead to provisions that are costly and ineffective, inserted to appease populist demand rather than as genuine solutions to the underlying problems. Moreover, acting in haste may have lead Congress to overlook more effective regulatory techniques.

Those who consider that capital markets function efficiently tend to criticise Sarbanes-Oxley as unnecessary and unjustified (Ribstein, 2005; Romano, 2005). The new rules create significant compliance costs for public companies, which critics claim are far greater than any countervailing benefits (Jain and Rezaee, 2005). The market, it is said, responded to the misdeeds at Enron even without the new legislation. Market forces punished the company's executives—and consequently, the auditors and analysts who had compromised themselves—through reputational sanctions. Enron, on this account, was not an example of market *failure*, but of the market *functioning*, by removing a 'bad apple'.

Another group of commentators criticise the recent reforms for what was omitted. This perspective differs from the 'efficient markets' critique in that its adherents have less faith in the ability of capital markets to impound price-sensitive information, and commensurately greater belief in the ability of regulatory intervention to improve on market outcomes. On this view, the Congressional error was largely in omitting to include provisions which were necessary to resolve the underlying problems: for example, in relation to shareholder rights (Bebchuk, Chapter 7, this volume), accounting regulation (Cox, Chapter 9, this volume), board structure (Kraakman, 2004), and the use of stock options to compensate executives (Johnson *et al*, 2003).

It is probably too soon to reach a final conclusion as to which of the foregoing positions is closer to the truth, as the answer depends in part upon the view taken about the efficiency of capital markets—itself an area in which, as the essays in Part I evidence, no settled position currently exists. In reaching an answer, however, it is necessary to understand not just the weaknesses of the legislation that was passed, but also the relative merits of various proposals that have been offered by critics in the second camp. To this end, the five chapters that comprise Part III consider three regulatory mechanisms that are at the core of the post-Enron reform debate: (i) strengthening shareholder rights; (ii) the reform of accounting regulation and (iii) increasing the role played by non-executive (or 'outside') directors. Some, but not all, of these were significantly reformed by Sarbanes-Oxley, and each has featured prominently in policy debates about corporate governance since Enron on both sides of the Atlantic. Considering the actual or potential merits of these various mechanisms provokes thought about the extent to which, if at all, regulatory intervention may be capable of remedying the problems exemplified by Enron.

A. Strengthening Shareholder Rights

In 'outsider' systems of corporate governance, the notion of 'shareholder rights' is often used to refer to the extent to which shareholders, if they are so minded, are able to exercise 'voice' within the firm to keep managers in check—sometimes referred to as 'antidirector rights' (see La Porta *et al*, 1997, 1998). It encompasses not only positive entitlements by shareholders to elect (or remove) the board, veto (or authorise) certain types of transaction and the like, but also correlative restrictions on management's ability to entrench themselves against shareholder decisions (for example, through defences capable of blocking a takeover bid). A number of recent empirical studies have reported correlations between various indices of 'shareholder rights' and share prices (Gompers *et al*, 2001; Bebchuk *et al*, 2004; Larcker *et al*, 2005). Of particular significance is a link between mechanisms by which managers are able to entrench themselves—for example, through takeover defences, staggered boards and the like—and weaker corporate performance.

In the US, most of corporate law is formulated at the state, rather than the federal, level. The Sarbanes-Oxley Act, being federal, is an important exception. US corporations are free to select their state-level governing law by changing their state of incorporation, something which Sarbanes-Oxley did nothing to change. ILucian Bebchuk has argued that because share ownership in US listed companies is widely dispersed, managers of listed companies have too much influence over decisions to reincorporate (Bebchuk, 2005; 2006). He claims that as a result, firms will tend to be steered towards legal regimes that entrench managers and disenfranchise shareholders, which the empirical evidence suggests may, over time, have a negative impact upon firm values. In Chapter 7, Bebchuk proposes a partial solution: federal rules facilitating shareholder access to the ballot box for board elections, which would limit the extent to which managers could entrench themselves.

The problem of managerial entrenchment is one that is peculiar to 'outsider' systems of corporate governance. This is because where listed firms are controlled by blockholders, the problem becomes one of blockholder, rather than managerial, entrenchment. It is therefore interesting to contrast the case of the US with that of the UK, the only other country in which share ownership is typically widely dispersed. Perhaps surprisingly, there are considerable differences in the extent to which the two countries permit managerial entrenchment: the UK is significantly more restrictive than the US. UK directors are mandatorily subject to the threat of dismissal by a simple majority of the shareholders in general meeting.[2] Strong pre-emption rights and market hostility to dual class voting stock disable managers from using such structures to perpetuate their control (Ferran, 2003). Moreover, the UK's City Code, written and implemented by the self-regulatory Panel on Takeovers and Mergers, gives much greater control to shareholders over the conduct of takeover bids than they enjoy under the more manager-friendly doctrines under Delaware law (Armour and Skeel, 2005).

One possible explanation for this divergence in outcomes is that the relatively weaker position of US shareholders results from a 'race to the bottom' in US corporate law. The UK's corporate law, based in a unitary jurisdiction, has for most of its history not faced any pressure from regulatory competition, a force which in Bebchuk's view has been responsible for degrading shareholder rights in the US. However, this explanation provokes further questions, suggesting that it may only be part of the story. Much of the UK's regulatory regime for public companies has developed out of self-regulatory or 'soft law' codes promulgated by stock market institutions, as opposed to legislation. Paul Davies (Chapter 12), argues that the use of 'soft law' has been useful to the UK government in overcoming managerial lobbying, because the government retains thinly-veiled bargaining power from the (unexercised) threat to resort to legislation. Such techniques have also been used in the US: for example, in response to Enron, both the New York Stock Exchange and NASDAQ have recently introduced new rules

---

[2] UK Companies Act 1985 s 303.

regarding board structure. Regulatory competition does not explain why such codes have historically not been more extensively deployed in the US to reinforce shareholder rights. Rather, this may be because the federal securities acts of the 1930s—a populist response to an earlier set of corporate scandals—pre-empted self-regulation by mandating the SEC to approve stock exchange listing rules (Armour and Skeel, 2005).[3] Of course, shareholder enfranchisement may still be advanced, within this framework, through changes to SEC rules, and it is a proposal of this variety that is made by Bebchuk in Chapter 7.

B. The Reform of Accounting Regulation

Arguably the most fundamental of the Sarbanes-Oxley reforms has been the tightening of controls on auditors. The basic problem, to which the Act responds, is that of managerial influence over auditors. Whilst a concern with reputation would supposedly encourage auditors not to be too soft on management, such effects have been considerably under-mined in recent years by the growth in the provision of non-audit services by accountants to their audit clients. These have provided the large accountancy firms with an ever-increasing share of their revenues, and in so doing have given their corporate clients a powerful, and not readily visible, lever with which to encourage the auditor to agree with management's own preferred statement of the company's position. In extreme cases, this may provide enough of an incentive to auditors to sign off where not just aggressive accounting, but downright fraud, has been taking place (Coffee, 2002, 2004).

In response, the Sarbanes-Oxley Act has mandated the creation of a new accounting regulator, the Public Companies Accounting Oversight Board, with whom firms auditing US-listed public companies must register. The Act has also required public companies to channel auditor appointment and oversight through an audit committee, comprised of independent directors; required CEOs and CFOs, on pain of criminal penalties, to certify the veracity of financial statements; mandated quin-quennial rotation of audit partners at accounting firms; and prohibited the offering by audit firms of a range of specified nonaudit services. However, some argue that the problems with US audit practices go deeper, and consequently are not remedied by the Act. Chapters 8 and 9 consider two such claimed problems: the heavy reliance on rules, rather than principles, in US accounting practice, and the oligopolistic structure of the US accounting industry.

---

[3] Recently, the trend in the UK has been away from self-regulation, as with the Financial Services Authority taking control of the Listing Rules from the London Stock Exchange in 2000.

It has been argued by some that one of the factors that facilitated Enron's balance sheet manipulation was the 'rules-based' structure of US GAAP (generally accepted accounting principles). The US GAAP is often contrasted with 'principles-based' systems such as UK GAAP or the IASB's guidelines, which involve more generally-worded, open-ended norms, the application of which, it is said, requires a greater level of professional judgement by accountants. The criticism levelled at US GAAP is that a system in which accounts are audited primarily for compliance with a body of rules, depends for its integrity on the comprehensiveness of the rulebook employed. Any body of accounting rules will have loopholes, which in a rules-based system then lend themselves to exploitation by companies seeking to manipulate their earnings. On the other hand, it is argued that a principles-based system, which requires professionals to exercise their judgement more frequently instead of passively standing behind the rule book, would lead to less of this sort of 'gaming' behaviour.

William Bratton disputes this argument in Chapter 8. In Bratton's view, Enron was really a case of 'old-fashioned fraud', rather than sophisticated, aggressive accounting. Moreover, he suggests that US GAAP is in reality more principles-based than many of the proponents of 'principles' seem to realise. In practice, the demand for rules appears to have been fuelled not by companies wishing to be assured of loopholes to exploit, but rather by accountants facing competitive pressures, because rules foster certainty and help to lower the fees auditors need to charge to insure themselves.

In Chapter 9, James Cox argues that the highly concentrated structure of the US accounting industry allows firms to coordinate on price and strategy, and contributed to the profession's weaknesses. Such concentration may have facilitated the development of the accounting firms' consultancy businesses, and the conflicts of interest with audit to which these gave rise. Moreover, he suggests that the industry's concentration is also likely to undermine the effectiveness of the Sarbanes-Oxley reforms. He reports preliminary findings on the Act's operation, which do not suggest that it has made a significant difference. Because the accounting profession around the world is dominated by the same 'Big Four' firms, the implications of Cox' argument are not limited to the US.

C. The Board of Directors

Corporate boards and the closely-related role of independent directors have been amongst the most important areas of reform. In the US, the Sarbanes-Oxley Act has mandated the creation of audit committees by public companies. These must be staffed by independent directors, at least one of who must be a 'financial expert'. In addition, new NYSE and NASDAQ rules require that public company boards comprise a majority of independent directors. These developments mirror those in the UK, where the use of independent non-executive directors has been a central part of the governance of listed companies since the introduction of the Cadbury Code in 1992, following scandals in the early 1990s. Post-Enron, the UK's Higgs Review (Higgs, 2003) has seen a further, 'incremental', strengthening of the rules relating to non-executives, (Davies, Chapter 12, this collection).

The thinking behind these reforms is that independent non-executive directors may be able to act as champions of shareholders' interests, and a check on egregious fraud, by ensuring that proper procedural steps are taken. However, there is considerable debate about the best way to give such directors appropriate incentives to perform their function. One oft-cited mechanism for encouraging attentiveness is the threat of legal liability. However, liability risk may have side-effects that actually outweigh any benefits generated by deterrence. Fear of too much liability, leading directors to behave in an excessively risk-averse fashion, may be just as likely to compromise directorial judgement as lack of independence.

In Chapter 10, Bernard Black, Brian Cheffins and Michael Klausner focus on the *actual*, rather than perceived, risk of outside director liability. While it is often assumed that the liability risk for directors varies across countries, depending on the mechanics of civil procedure and the structure of the legal profession, Black, Cheffins and Klausner show that this picture is misleading. Rather, a range of other factors affect both the likelihood of a lawsuit being brought and the amount which a director who was found liable might need to pay from his or her own pocket. For example, in systems where the frequency of lawsuits against directors is high, so too is the incidence of directors and officers' (D&O) insurance. Once these various factors are taken into account, it appears that independent directors around the world face a very similar—and uniformly low—level of real liability risk. One interpretation of this finding might be that high, real levels of liability exposure are counter-productive, and consequently parties 'contract out' by using insurance in systems where such risks would otherwise be run.

Another way to incentivise non-executive directors would be for them to be, or be appointed by, the holder of a significant block of shares in the company. However, a director with a significant shareholding, whilst having strong incentives, may not be as independent as an individual wholly without ties. This in turn provokes thought about the proper scope of non-executives' role. Some suggest that non-executives should be viewed as capable of playing an active part in the formulation of business strategy, by bringing outside experience to strengthen the board's capabilities, and a valuable network of contacts. Others see non-executives as performing a role akin to board-level auditors of decision-making processes—asking questions, and putting a check on any misconduct by executives. Whilst these two functions are not necessarily mutually exclusive, they may sometimes be in tension, and their implications for the desirability of director share ownership may cut in different directions.

In resolving the foregoing issue, the Sarbanes-Oxley Act strongly prioritises independence, at least for audit committee members (Chandler and Strine, 2003). The Act prohibits them from receiving any compensation from the company on whose audit committee they serve, other than in their capacity as a board or committee member. Moreover, they may not hold a controlling stake, or be appointed by a person who holds (either alone or in concert with others) a controlling stake in the company. 'Control' is determined by a factual test, although there is a 'safe harbour' provision that ownership of less than 10 per cent of any class of voting equity securities will not count as control.

In contrast to the mandatory rules used in the Sarbanes-Oxley Act, the UK's Combined Code regulates these issues using a 'comply or explain' mechanism. That is, listed firms are required either to comply with the Code's requirements, or to explain to investors why they have not done so. In Chapter 11, Richard Nolan reviews the UK position, and describes the changes that were implemented following the Higgs Review of the Role of Non-Executive Directors (Higgs, 2003). The Higgs Review sought to reconcile both lines of thinking about non-executives' role, a compromise that Nolan criticises. In Nolan's view, the Review's recommendations, which were subsequently incorporated into the UK's Combined Code, would have been clearer and more effective had they focused solely on the goal of ensuring the independence of non-executives. This would avoid any possibility of conflict of interest, and incentives to monitor effectively could be generated not only by the threat of legal liability, but also by reputational concerns. The latter might in turn be strengthened by drawing such directors from pools of professionals which have strong reputational bonds for independence anyway.

It seems plausible that one 'model' of non-executives' role might not be appropriate for all types of company. Interestingly, one empirical study (Lasfer, 2002) finds that compliance with the UK Combined Code's provisions in respect of independent non-executive directors is positively associated with stock price performance for companies in mature industries, but is actually *negatively* associated with performance for smaller, high-growth companies. His interpretation is that for high-growth companies, strategic guidance and networking functions—associated with non-independent directors—are relatively more valuable inputs from the board, whereas in mature industries, it is relatively more useful to have genuine outsiders who will ask searching questions of managers, particularly about what will be done with free cash flow. The foregoing suggests that—as Nolan argues—what seems most appropriate is perhaps not mandatory legislation on board structure, but rather a framework which promotes reflection upon the use of outside directors and disclosure of the practices which have been adopted. To this end, the UK Combined Code's 'comply or explain' framework seems preferable to the mandatory rules adopted in the US.

PART IV. REFORMING EU COMPANY LAW AND
SECURITIES REGULATION

Part IV of the collection considers the particular issues raised by modernising company law and securities regulation in Europe. In addition to difficulties generated by the issues that have proved controversial in the US, the European reform agenda faces several unique challenges. The most fundamental stems from the fact that the EU encompasses a diversity of systems of corporate governance. Most obviously, there is a divide between the UK's 'outsider' share ownership and the 'insider' share ownership of continental Europe, with a corresponding difference in the emphasis of regulation between rendering management accountable and keeping blockholders under control. Member states also differ systematically in the way in which their regulation is designed and enforced. Furthermore, following enlargement in 2004, the EU now contains several Eastern European economies in varying stages of transition. As a result, not only might the appropriate regulatory measures differ from state to state, but there are also likely to be severe political obstacles to wide-ranging European legislative reform.

A. The European Reforms

Given the foregoing, the scale and speed of the European-level response to Enron may seem surprising. In the spring of 2002, even before any problems had surfaced at Parmalat, the European Commission asked their High-Level Company Law Expert Group to prepare a report elaborating any necessary EU legislation in the field of corporate governance. In May 2003, the Commission were able to announce a number of initiatives, including an Action Plan for the modernisation of company law (European Commission, 2003a), the goal of which was to increase the transparency of intra-group relations and transactions with related parties and to improve disclosures about corporate practices. The Commission also launched plans for the reform of the statutory audit

(European Commission, 2003b). Then, in the wake of the Parmalat scandal, the Commission proposed additional measures mandating collective board responsibility for financial statements and regulating disclosure of related party transactions, including those between a company and controlling shareholders or top executives (European Commission, 2004).

In Chapter 12, Paul Davies offers an explanation for the speed of the response in Europe, and in the UK in particular. He argues that the breaking of the Enron scandal had the effect of neutralising a range of opposition to pre-existing reform initiatives, which were simply re-characterized (and in some cases extended) by advocates of the post-Enron measures. Although there are echoes of Skeel's account (Chapter 3) of how populist pressure generated by corporate scandals can upset the ordinary balance of power between interest groups, several other factors contributed to the rapid progress of the reforms. First, the EU was in 2002 engaged in difficult negotiations with the US over the proposed extraterritorial reach of the Sarbanes-Oxley Act. Crucial to the strength of the EU's position was the existence of a set of safeguards for European investors that could credibly be said to be equivalent to those in the US. Secondly, the imminent accession to the EU of 10 new countries leant a 'now or never' quality to proposals. And thirdly, the stirring for the first time within the EU of regulatory competition in company law, following the ECJ's landmark 1999 ruling in *Centros*,[4] may have added further pressure towards the achievement of consensus at the European level over minimum standards, at least in the eyes of those who fear that unbounded regulatory competition may lead to a 'race to the bottom'.

The blueprint for the Commission's Company Law Action Plan was the report delivered by the Commission's High Level Expert Group in December 2002. In Chapter 13, Klaus Hopt, a leading member of the Expert Group, explains how the Group approached its task and the thinking behind its conclusions. The Group were much exercised by the problems of ensuring that the reforms would be appropriate for both the diversity of corporate ownership structures and regulatory enforcement techniques that are employed throughout the EU. The essence of their response, as Hopt explains, was to focus on identifying those reforms for which a *European*-level (as opposed to member state level) rule was strictly necessary and appropriate. These were the core—or common denominator—rules which, in the Group's view, would be necessary to ensure good governance in any of the member states, regardless of national diversity. At the same time, much attention was also paid to ensuring that appropriate regulatory instruments were chosen. Together,

[4] Case C-212/97, *Centros Ltd v Erhvervs-og Selskabssyrelsen* [1999] ECR I-1459, [2000] Ch 446.

this produced a package of reforms intended to comprise the 'minimum necessary' for European legislation.

Perhaps unsurprisingly, a number of similar issues to those discussed in Part III, in the Anglo-American context, were identified as priorities by the Group. Shareholder rights—in particular, rights to vote on executives' remuneration packages, and to block defensive tactics in the face of a takeover bid—were seen as core features of the reform programme.[5] It is worth noting that such rules are essentially 'antidirector' in character, and may therefore be thought to be of less significance for systems in which insider ownership is common. In such systems, a majority shareholder would of course control the vote. This is reflected in the way in which these issues were ultimately implemented—voting on directors' remuneration took the form of a non-binding Commission Recommendation, and the ban on defensive tactics, implemented as part of the Takeover Directive, contains an opt-out provision for member states (or individual companies).

Turning to the role of auditors, the Group focused in particular on the usefulness of having an audit committee comprised of independent directors to channel communications between the company and its auditors as a key strategy for overcoming potential conflicts of interest between audit and non-audit work. As Davies explains in Chapter 12, the Commission's reforms in this area, which have now yielded a proposed Directive (European Commission, 2004) have also included a number of changes clearly inspired by Sarbanes-Oxley, including mandating collective responsibility of the board for financial statements; mandatory rotation of audit partners or audit firms; the barring of 'business relationships' between audit firm and customer which 'might compromise' the auditor's independence, and the strengthening of disclosure rules relating to auditors.

A particularly important issue for the High-Level Group concerned the role and structure of the board of directors, the relevant proposals for which have now been incorporated into a Commission Recommendation.[6] Hopt explains in Chapter 13 that their proposals for independent directors were designed to be capable of complementing both UK-style unitary boards, and German-style two-tier boards with employee co-

---

[5] Both proposals have since been taken forward. The Commission Recommendation on fostering an appropriate regime for the remuneration of directors of listed companies (2004/913/EC, [2004] OJ L 385/55) indicates that shareholders should be given a say in the performance-related aspects of directors' pay, and the Takeover Directive (2004/25/EC, [2004] OJ L 142/12) includes a rule prohibiting target management from taking any action which may frustrate an actual or potential bid without the approval of the company's shareholders. However, the impact of this latter provision is significantly diluted by the availability of a national opt-out: see Chapter 15, discussed below, text to n 8.

[6] Commission Recommendation on the role of non-executive or supervisory directors of listed companies and on the committees of the (supervisory) board (2005/162/EC, [2005] OJ L 52/51).

determination: monitoring functions can be carried out by non-executive shareholder appointees or by employee representatives respectively. Moreover, independent directors are viewed as having a role to play in both outsider and insider owned companies, as safeguards against self-serving conduct by, respectively, managers and blockholders.

B. Developments in Regulatory Techniques

The Expert Group/Action Plan's philosophy of focusing legislative energies on core issues for which consensus might be achieved, and the greater use of non-binding Recommendations, can be seen as part of an emerging trend. European policymakers are becoming both more sensitive to the different capabilities of various regulatory techniques both to overcome political obstacles and to achieve regulatory goals. The last four contributions to the collection consider three examples of this new thinking in operation, followed by a pessimistic assessment of the impact of more traditional harmonization techniques.

The ECJ's jurisprudence in *Centros* and subsequent cases has opened up, for the first time, a degree of regulatory competition in European company law.[7] In Chapter 14, John Armour considers the possibilities for harnessing regulatory competition as a means of mutual learning by regulators, whilst nevertheless permitting continued diversity of national company law regimes. This would be appropriate in fields where no European consensus has emerged. Whilst regulatory competition has traditionally been feared in Europe as leading to a 'race to the bottom', Armour argues that this need not be the case, provided that sufficient safeguards are in place to ensure that relevant constituencies are able to participate in a firm's decision to reincorporate, protections he suggests may be better catered for in the EU context than has hitherto been the case in the US.

Two other major areas of recent European reform in relation to companies have concerned takeovers and securities markets. As well as being of enormous substantive significance for the development of European corporate governance, the processes by which these reforms have been effected evince two distinct further regulatory techniques. The Takeover Directive,[8] following a lengthy political roadblock, was

---

[7] To date, this has only been with regard to incorporations. However, remaining barriers to competition for reincorporations appear to be falling swiftly with the advent of the Tenth Directive on Cross-Border Mergers (Parliament and Council Directive 2005/56/EC on cross-border mergers of limited liability companies, [2005] OJ L 310/1), and the recent extension by the ECJ of its *Centros* jurisprudence to mergers (C-411/03, *Reference for a Preliminary ruling from the Landgericht Koblenz in proceedings against SEVIC Sytems AG* [2006] OJ C 36/5). Together these will permit companies to change their registered office by the expedient of a cross-border merger into a shell company.

eventually passed in a form that permits member states, and individual firms, to opt into or out of key provisions. In Chapter 15, Gérard Hertig and Joseph McCahery argue that this 'menu of legal options' approach can overcome many of the difficulties of fitting a single legislative rule to diverse systems, and suggest that it might be used as a blueprint for future reforms. The beneficial effects may also include the development of a richer set of regulatory arrangements, offering the potential for mutual learning by firms and regulators and thereby leading to improvements in the quality of investor protection.

By contrast, the 'comitology' technique used in the new regulatory frameworks for the European securities market, considered by Eilís Ferran in Chapter 16, involves the delegation of legislative power to a committee of technocrats. In relation to securities markets, this is known as the 'Lamfalussy process', after the chairman of the committee of experts who recommended the current structure. Ferran's account concentrates on the mechanics of the process, discussing the cooperation between the Commission, Council and Parliament in the process, as well as the new Committees created under Lamfalussy, the consultation process and implementation of the new regime. Comitology, too, could provide a blueprint for future reform activity, seemingly permitting contentious issues to be placed outside the realm of political discussion by delegation to experts.

The three foregoing mechanisms—transforming political choices into market choices through regulatory arbitrage; preserving political choices through options in European legislation; and disguising political choices through devolution to a technocratic committee, each represent possible futures, and part of the probable future, of European company and securities law-making. They stand in stark contrast to the attempts at harmonization which were in vogue in previous decades. In Chapter 17, Luca Enriques examines the weaknesses of this mode of law-making, arguing that it has tended to fall foul of political opposition on all significant issues. This meant that, even in the early days of the European project, the body of EC company law which was made through traditional 'harmonizing' directives, which require member states to implement a particular regime or set of minimum standards, was only capable of proceeding by focusing on issues that were essentially trivial. It is to be hoped that the new techniques described above may yield greater success in the future.

---

[8] 2004/25/EC, [2004] OJ L 142/12.

CONCLUSION

An issue at the centre of this collection concerns the extent to which the differences between Anglo-American and continental European systems of corporate governance—outsider and insider systems respectively— have lead to differences in the nature of, and susceptibility to, corporate governance failures. The fact that failings have exposed in both types of system has tended to weaken the force of accounts that view Enron solely as a symptom of weaknesses of the Anglo-American system of corporate governance. At the same time, it has tended to strengthen the conviction of those who call for generalised regulatory solutions without regard to the underlying corporate governance context. Yet whilst some common weaknesses did indeed exist—in particular, the universal failure of auditors to function effectively—for which the same solutions may be appropriate, it is dangerous to regard the systems as otherwise equiv- alent, because both the causes of, and appropriate solutions for, recent failures are different.

So far as the US is concerned, it seems unlikely that a hastily-prepared populist measure such as Sarbanes-Oxley will break with history by definitively putting an end to corporate scandals. Even the relatively uncontentious measures concerning audit regulation seem to have been less successful than may have been hoped. And the corporate governance measures, which have drawn widespread criticism for the costs they impose on US public companies, betray a lack of thought on issues concerning board structure and shareholder rights. What is less clear, however, is the appropriate way forward on these issues. It seems plausible that for different firms, different constellations of board structure and shareholder rights may be appropriate. If that is the case, then US policymakers might do well to rethink their recent fondness for mandatory federal rules regarding corporate governance, and to consider some of the more flexible regulatory strategies that have been employed in the EU.

In Europe, the scandals have provided the impetus for surmounting political obstacles to the reform of corporate and securities law at the EU level. In rolling out their responses, European policy-makers faced the need to regulate a diversity of systems, and also a means of minimising the political cost of implementation. In response, they have begun to experiment with a range of new regulatory techniques, few, if any, of which rely upon traditional mandatory rules at the federal level. These include a mixture of non-binding recommendations, opt-in rules, delegation to committees of experts and the selective use of regulatory competition (coupled with procedural safeguards contained in federal rules). Whilst a considerable amount has been achieved, it remains to be seen how the highly complex regulatory architecture that has resulted will actually function.

By March 2006, the S&P 500 Index had crept back up to more than 1,300, little more than 10 per cent short of its peak in 2000. Some may view this as evidence that the crisis precipitated by Enron has been resolved. A reader of this collection should rightly view such an interpretation as simplistic. Our understanding of stock markets is actually rather less secure than had previously been imagined. Moreover, corporate scandals have tended to repeat themselves in history, following the bursting of market bubbles and provoking populist legislation which has failed to prevent future cycles of scandal. It is wise to regard current conclusions as no more than preliminary, and appropriate for prescriptions to be advanced with humility.

REFERENCES

Arden, Rt Hon Lady Justice Mary (2003), 'UK Corporate Governance After Enron' 3 *Journal of Corporate Law Studies* 269.

Armour, J. and Skeel, D.A., Jr (2005), 'Who Writes the Rules for Hostile Takeovers? The Peculiar Divergence of the US and the UK', Working Paper, University of Cambridge Faculty of Law/University of Pennsylvania Law School.

Bebchuk, L.A. (2005), 'The Case for Increasing Shareholder Power' 118 *Harvard Law Review* 833.

—— (2006), 'Letting Shareholders Set the Rules' 119 *Harvard Law Review* 1784.

Bebchuk, L.A., Cohen, A., and Ferrell, A. (2004), 'What Matters in Corporate Governance', Harvard Law School John M. Olin Discussion Paper No 491, available on www.ssrn.com .

Beck, T., Demirgüç-Kunt, A., and Levine, R. (2003), 'Law and Finance: Why Does Legal Origin Matter?' 4 *Journal of Comparative Economics* 653.

Berglöf, E. (1997), 'A Note on the Typology of Financial Systems' in K.J. Hopt and E. Wymeersch, *Comparative Corporate Governance: Essays and Materials* (Berlin: Walter de Gruyter), 151.

Bratton, W.W. (2003), 'Enron and the Dark Side of Shareholder Value' 76 *Tulane Law Review* 1275.

Bratton, W.W. and McCahery, J.A. (2002), 'Comparative Corporate Governance and Barriers to Global Cross Reference', in J.A. McCahery *et al* (eds), *Corporate Governance Regimes: Convergence and Diversity* (Oxford: OUP), 23.

Chandler, W.B. and Strine, L.E., Jr (2003), 'The New Federalism of the American Corporate Governance System: Preliminary Reflections of Two Residents of One Small State' 152 *University of Pennsylvania Law Review* 953.

Coffee, J.C. (2002), 'Understanding Enron: "It's About the Gatekeepers, Stupid"' 57 *Business Lawyer* 1403.

—— (2004), 'What Caused Enron? A Capsule Social and Economic History of the 1990s' 89 *Cornell Law Review* 269.

Easterbrook, F.H. and Fischel, D.R. (1991), *The Economic Structure of Corporate Law* (Cambridge: MA, Harvard University Press).

Enriques, L. (2003), 'Bad Apples, Bad Oranges: A Comment From Old Europe on Post-Enron Corporate Governance Reforms' 38 *Wake Forest Law Review* 911.

European Commission (2003a), *Modernising Company Law and Enhancing Corporate Governance in the European Union—A Plan to Move Forward*, COM(2003) 284 final 21 May 2003.

—— (2003b), *Reinforcing the statutory audit in the EU*, COM(2003) 286 final, [2003] *Official Journal* C236/2.

—— (2004), *Proposal for a Directive of the European Parliament and of the Council amending Council Directives 78/660/EEC and 83/349/EEC concerning the annual accounts of certain companies and consolidated accounts*, COM(2004) 725 final, 27 October 2004.

Fama, E.F. (1970), 'Efficient Capital Markets: A Review of Theory and Empirical Work' 25 *Journal of Finance* 383.

—— (1998), 'Market Efficiency, Long-term Returns, and Behavioural Finance' 49 *Journal of Financial Economics* 283.

Ferran, E. (2003), 'Legal Capital Rules and Modern Securities Markets—the Case for Reform, as Illustrated by the UK Equity Markets' in K. Hopt and E. Wymeersch (eds), *Capital Markets and Company Law* (Oxford: OUP), 115.

Financial Reporting Council (2003a), Audit Committees—Combined Code Guidance: A Report and Proposed Guidance by an FRC-Appointed Group Chaired by Sir Robert Smith (London: FRC).

—— (2003b), *The Combined Code on Corporate Governance* (London: FRC), available online at: http://www.frc.org.uk/combined.cfm.

Fortune (2001), 'Is Enron Overpriced?', *Fortune*, 5 March 2001.

Gilson, R. J. and Kraakman, R. (1984). 'The Mechanisms of Market Efficiency' 70 *Virginia Law Review* 549.

Gompers, P., Ishii, J., Metrick, A. (2001), 'Corporate Governance and Equity Prices', 118 *Quarterly Journal of Economics* 107.

Hansmann, H.B. and Kraakman, R. (2001), 'The End of History for Corporate Law' 89 *Georgetown Law Journal* 439.

Higgs, D. (2003), *Review of the Role and Effectiveness of Non-Executive Directors* (London: DTI).

Jain, P.K. and Rezaee, Z. (2005), 'The Sarbanes-Oxley Act of 2002 and Security Market Behavior: Early Evidence,' Working Paper May 2005, available at: www.ssrn.com.

Johnson, S.A., Ryan, H.E., and Tian, Y.S. (2003), 'Executive Compensation and Corporate Fraud,' Economics Working Paper, Louisiana State University, April 2003, available at: www.ssrn.com.

Kraakman, R. (2004), 'Disclosure and Corporate Governance: An Overview Essay,' in G. Ferrarini, K.J. Hopt, J. Winter and E. Wymeersch (eds), *Reforming Company and Takeover Law in Europe* (Oxford: OUP).

La Porta R., Lopez-de-Silanes F., Shleifer A. and Vishny R. (2000) 'Investor Protection and Corporate Governance' 58 *Journal of Financial Economics* 3.

Larcker, D.F., Richardson, S.F., and Tuna, A.I. (2005), 'How Important is Corporate Governance?', Working Paper, Stanford Graduate School of Business/ Wharton School, available at www.ssrn.com .

Lasfer, M. (2002), 'Board Structure and Agency Costs', EFMA 2002 London Meetings, available on www.ssrn.com.

Malkiel, B.G. (1992), 'Efficient Markets Hypothesis', in P. Newman *et al* (eds), *The*

New Palgrave Dictionary of Money and Finance Markets, Vol 1 (London: Macmillan), 739.

Pritchard, A. (2005), 'Should Congress Repeal Securities Class Action Reform' in W. Niskanen (ed.), *After Enron: Lessons for Public Policy* (New York: Rowman and Littlefield), 125.

Ribstein, L. (2005), 'Sarbanes-Oxley After Three Years', [2005] *New Zealand Law Review* 365.

Romano, R. (2005), 'Sarbanes-Oxley and the Making of Quack Corporate Governance,' 114 *Yale Law Journal* 1521.

Shleifer, A. (2000), *Inefficient Markets: A Guide to Behavioural Finance* (Oxford: Clarendon Press).

Singh, A., Glen, J., Zammit, A., Singh, A. and Weisse, B. (2005), 'Shareholder Value Maximisation, Stock Market and New Technology: Should the US Corporate Model be the Universal Standard?', University of Cambridge CBR Working Paper No 315, September 2005.

Standard & Poor (2006), S&P 500 Price Index data, www.standardandpoor.com (checked 14 April, 2006).

Part I
Stock Markets and Information

1

The Mechanisms Of Market Efficiency Twenty Years Later: The Hindsight Bias

RONALD J GILSON* AND REINIER KRAAKMAN**

I. INTRODUCTION

THIS IS A propitious time to revisit The Mechanisms of Market Efficiency (MOME) (Gilsen and Kraakman 1984).[1] We began that project some twenty years ago, as newly-minted corporate law academics[2] trying to understand what to make of a large empirical literature proclaiming the efficiency of the U.S. stock market. In an observation then offered as a simple description of the state of play, Michael Jensen (1978: 95) announced that 'there is no other proposition in economics which has more solid empirical evidence supporting it than the Efficient Market Hypothesis' (EMH). But if this were so, it seemed to us that it could not be because market efficiency was a physical property of the universe arising, like gravity, in the milliseconds following the big

* Meyers Professor of Law and Business, Stanford Law School, and Stern Professor of Law and Business, Columbia Law School.
** Ezra Ripley Thayer Professor of Law, Harvard Law School.
This chapter was previously published, as part of a symposium on the Mechanics of Market Efficiency, in (2003) 28 *Journal of Corporation Law* 715–742. We are grateful to Donald Langevoort and Hillary Sale for suggesting this symposium, and to the *Journal of Corporation Law*, the University of Iowa School of Law, and the Sloan Foundation for their support for the event. Participants at the symposium and a Columbia Law School corporate faculty workshop, as well as Bernard Black, Allen Ferrell, Jeffrey Gordon, Zohar Goshen, Samuel Issacharoff, and Michael Klausner provided perceptive comments on an early version of this chapter. The chapter is better for their contributions; the remaining failings belong to the authors. This chapter originated in a lecture given at the symposium and maintains some of the informality of that format..
[1] MOME is pronounced 'mommy'—an acronym meant to evoke a memory of warm maternal feelings.
[2] Gilson had joined the Stanford Law School faculty in 1979; Kraakman had joined the Yale Law School faculty in 1980. The project began while Gilson was a visiting professor at Yale Law School in 1982.

bang. Rather, the prompt reflection of publicly-available information in a security's price had to be the outcome of institutional and market interactions whose proper functioning necessarily depended on the character of those institutions.[3] Thus, MOME represented the efforts of two young scholars to understand the institutional underpinnings of the empirical phenomenon called market efficiency.

We concluded that the level of market efficiency with respect to a particular fact is dependent on which of a number of mechanisms— universally-informed trading, professionally-informed trading, deriv- atively-informed trading, and uninformed trading—operated to cause that fact to be reflected in market price. Which mechanism was operative, in turn, depended on the breadth of the fact's distribution, which in turn depended on the cost structure of the market for information. The lower the cost of information, the wider its distribution, the more effective the operative efficiency mechanism and, finally, the more efficient the market.

Revisiting this framework is particularly appropriate because we are now experiencing the early stages of a quite different framework for evaluating the efficiency of the stock market, also supported by a

---

[3] We should be clear at the outset that we are addressing here, and addressed in MOME, the phenomenon of informational efficiency. It is now commonplace to distinguish fundamental efficiency—that market price represents the best current estimate of the present value of the future cash flow associated with an asset—from informational efficiency, that is, the absence of a profitable trading strategy based on publicly available information. Although this is a longer discussion than is appropriate here, we remain sceptical of the analytical foundations of the distinction. A stock price is efficient with respect to a particular information set. The assertion that fundamental value differs from an informationally efficient market price must mean one of two things. Either the market is inaccurately assessing currently available information, in which case a profitable trading opportunity in fact exists (unless there is a breakdown in the arbitrage mechanism, see below text accompanying notes 24-34), or someone has additional, non-public, information (including a better asset pricing model) that demonstrates the inaccuracy of the current stock price—a circumstance that plainly does not call into question the market's semi-strong form efficiency. Operationally, the distinction is posed in terms of whether there is an institution other than the market whose estimates of current value we believe are systematically better than the market's (assuming private information is divulged). For example, do we imagine that an investment banker's fairness opinion is likely to be a better predictor? Compare the Delaware Supreme Court's unexamined commitment to the discoverability of fundamental value if one only asks an investment banker in *Smith v van Gorkom*, 488 A.2d 858 (Del. 1985) (failure of board to secure a fairness opinion was compelling evidence of violation of duty of care) with the Chancery Court's scepticism of investment bankers' valuation opinions in *Paramount Communications, Inc. v Time Inc.*, Fed. Sec. L. Rep. (CCH) P 94,514 (Del. Ch. 1989, aff'd 571 A.2d 1140 (Del. 1990)) (investment banker opinion reflecting 'a range that a Texan might feel at home on'). Or that a judge's estimate following evaluation of duelling expert reports is likely to be more accurate? If no existing institution will systematically better predict the fundamental value of a security on the available information, the distinction between informational efficiency and fundamental efficiency smacks of the Nirvana fallacy. Professor Allen (2003) advises that this analysis identifies us as 'epistemological materialists'. If we were choosing a label to dignify our effort, we'd lean toward calling it a pragmatic rejection of a Platonic form of fundamental value, but we appreciate Professor Allen's effort on our behalf.

growing number of empirical studies and also accompanied by an expansive description of the literature's reach by another respected Harvard economist.[4] The new framework is styled 'behavioral finance' and its ascent and market efficiency's descent is recounted by Andrei Shleifer (2000: 23): 'Whatever the reason why it took so long in practice, the cumulative impact of both [behavioural finance] theory and the evidence has been to undermine the hegemony of the EMH ...' Michael Jensen's 1978 statement of the empirical support for market efficiency is now proffered with a tone somewhere between irony and condescension.[5]

The movement from Jensen's to Shleifer's formulation over twenty years surely merits a reconsideration of the substance and implications of market efficiency for legal and public policy. Although no longer new to the academy,[6] in the end we remain convinced that how quickly and accurately the stock market reflects information in the price of a security is a function of the performance of institutions. In what follows we offer a brief, appropriately tentative assessment of the fit of behavioral finance with the framework developed twenty years ago in MOME, and an even briefer and more tentative evaluation of the policy implications arising from the behavioral finance framework.

In Part II, we put market efficiency in an intellectual context—as part of the shift of finance from description to applied microeconomics that also included the development of the Capital Asset Pricing Model and the Miller-Modigliani Irrelevancy Propositions, and ultimately gave rise to the award of three Nobel Prizes. Part III briefly recounts the MOME thesis, and Part IV describes the challenge of behavioral finance. In Part V, we offer our assessment of the central principles that drive behavioral finance and in Part VI evaluate how the MOME thesis stands up to the challenge. In Part VII we stick our necks out a little, offering some MOME-based predictions about where it is likely that behavioral finance will and will not have significant policy implications. Part VIII concludes.

---

[4] To be entirely accurate, Jensen was still at the University of Rochester at the time he wrote his now familiar assessment of market efficiency.

[5] See, e.g., Cunningham (2002: 773). ('[Jensen's statement] was not an overly broad claim at the time perhaps, but with the passing of the years and the emergence of newer studies, one continues to wonder whether the claim said more about the social sciences than it did about the EMH [efficient market hypothesis]').

[6] Much to our discomfort, one of the authors whose paper is included in this volume announced at the symposium that he was still in grade school when MOME was published.

II. PUTTING MOME IN AN INTELLECTUAL CONTEXT: THE RISE OF MODERN FINANCE

MOME was written in response to the first spill-over of finance into another discipline. Thus, to place MOME in its proper context we first need a snippet of intellectual history—a capsule account of the development of modern finance. The nature of that development set the stage for MOME and, we will argue, for the important recent work in behavioral finance.

A fair place to begin is 1960. The *Journal of Finance* was then only eight years old and, according to a popular historian of modern finance's early years, to that date had published no 'more than five articles that could be classified as theoretical rather than descriptive' (Bernstein 1992: 42).[7] Thus, it was hardly surprising that a generation of younger economists, intent on transforming finance into a mathematically rigorous branch of microeconomics, was focusing on developing theories that might explain description. Science involves empirically testing hypotheses, but formulating hypotheses requires an animating theory.

For present purposes, we will focus on three bodies of theory that arose in the period from the late 1950s to the early 1970s. These sought to state rigorously how capital assets are priced, whether a corporation's choice of which capital assets to issue affects the corporation's value, and whether the market price of capital assets reflects all available information concerning their value. These three familiar theories—the Capital Asset Pricing Model (Sharpe 1964), the Miller-Modigliani Irrelevance Propositions (Modigliani 1958; Miller and Modigliani 1961), and the Efficient Capital Market Hypothesis (Fama 1970)—shared a critical common methodology. The theories' rigor is achieved through an extensive set of perfect markets assumptions—in essence, rational investors, perfect information, and no transaction costs.

Start with the Capital Asset Pricing Model (CAPM). If one assumes that all unsystematic risk can be diversified away, what else but systematic risk could affect the price of capital assets? If investors need not bear unsystematic risk, then investors who do not bear it will require the lowest return (pay the highest price) for a capital asset, thereby setting the asset's price. CAPM simply takes the next step of identifying the systematic risk that matters to investors with the covariance of an asset's returns with those of the market—i.e., beta. Given these assumptions, CAPM is, in short, a tautology.

The Miller-Modigliani Irrelevance Propositions share the same conceptual structure. That the choice of a debt-equity ratio does not affect

---

[7] Bernstein's history, complete with personalities, is an entertaining account of the rise of modern finance.

firm value is, in Miller's words thirty years later, 'an implication of equilibrium in perfect capital markets' (Miller 1988: 99). Like CAPM, the perfect capital market assumptions result in the Irrelevance Propositions appearing tautological. Think of a simple T-diagram, with assets on one side and ownership interests—debt and equity—on the other. The balance sheet balances because of another tautology: the total value of the assets corresponds to the total ownership—debt and equity—interests. Why then should the divisions on the right side of the balance sheet—the manner in which ownership interests are divided—affect the left side of the balance sheet—that is, the value of the assets?[8] If for some reason debt or equity was mispriced, arbitrage would restore the proper relation, so that increasing the amount of lower cost debt would result in an offsetting increase in the cost of equity and vice versa.

The Efficient Capital Market Hypothesis (ECMH) also builds on perfect market assumptions. Commenting on Fama's 1970 seminal review article, William Sharpe stated: 'Simply put, the thesis is this: in a well-functioning market, the prices ...[of securities] will reflect predictions based on all relevant and available information. This seems almost trivially self-evident to most professional economists—so much so, that testing seems rather silly' (Sharpe 1970: 418). William Beaver made much the same point ten years later: 'Why would one ever expect prices not to "fully reflect" publicly available information? Won't market efficiency hold trivially?' (Beaver 1981: 32).

In addition to its prediction of the information content of stock prices, the ECMH also played a critical integrative role, providing the necessary link between asset pricing and capital structure choice through the medium of market prices. Both CAPM and the Modigliani-Miller propositions depend on an arbitrage mechanism for their proof: mispricing will be traded away. But for arbitrage to be triggered by mispricing, market prices must be reasonably informative. Thus, along this important dimension, the positive power of the three theories rises and falls together.

Despite their tautological character, all three theories generated a groundswell of angry response because, if one imagined that their predictions survived the release of their perfect market assumptions, each theory attacked the value of important participants in the capital market. CAPM called into question the value of highly paid portfolio managers—simply assessing the volatility of an asset relative to that of the market might not command the same rewards as firm specific

---

[8] Miller reports that even the tautological character of the propositions in a perfect capital market world was initially a difficult sell: 'We first had to convince people (including ourselves!) that there could be any conditions, even in a "frictionless" world, where a firm would be indifferent between issuing securities as different in legal status, investor risk and apparent cost as debt and equity' (Miller 1998: 100).

assessments of risk and reward. The Irrelevancy Propositions were even more offensive. Getting a corporation's debt-equity ratio right was a central function of chief financial officers (and their highly-compensated investment banker consultants); why pay people large amounts to engage in an activity that does not increase the value of the firm? The ECMH took the attack one step further, calling into question not only the value of chartists (marginalized by weak form efficiency), but fundamental analysis as well (marginalized by semi-strong form efficiency).

While it is tempting to dismiss the reaction of capital market professionals as simply turf protection, that would miss the deeply felt belief that all three theories' perfect market elegance did not reflect the world in which the professionals worked. What happens when the theories confronted the real world where information was costly and asymmetrically distributed, at least some investors were plainly irrational, and transactions costs were pervasive?

Thus, the transformation of finance into financial economics gave rise to a set of theorems that explained the operation of asset pricing and capital structure in perfect capital markets and evoked a predictable reaction from those whose function the theorems called into question. The next step, clear in hindsight but perhaps more murky at the time, was to find out the extent to which the real-world capital market worked the way the financial economics predicted.[9] This conflict—between the elegant world of perfect capital markets and the messy real world—defined the problem we addressed in MOME. We said that '[w]hat makes the ECMH non-trivial, of course, is its prediction that, even though information is not immediately and costlessly available to all participants, the market will act as if it were' (Gilson and Kraakman 1984:

[9] The extent to which CAPM, the Irrelevance Propositions, and the ECMH were originally proffered as perfect market theorems with the goal of framing a research agenda that would relax the perfect market assumptions to the end of understanding how real markets work and how real institutions respond to market imperfections is an interesting question. Plainly the authors came to understand their work in that fashion. Looking back at his and Modigliani's early work with the benefit of thirty years of the efforts of others to show what market imperfections falsify the Irrelevance Propositions, Merton Miller acknowledges that '[l]ooking back now, perhaps we should have put more emphasis on the other, upbeat side of the "nothing matters" coin: showing what doesn't matter can also show, by implication, what does' (Miller 1998: 100) (emphasis in the original). Sharpe himself acknowledged in his Nobel lecture that CAPM is compromised when there are institutional restrictions on short-selling (Sharpe 1990). And one of the authors, roughly contemporaneously with MOME, framed the role of business lawyers as that of transaction cost engineers, whose task was to craft a transaction structure that allowed the parties to act as if CAPM's perfect market assumptions were really true (Gilson 1984). This recognition of the value of perfect market theorems to understanding the messy real world surely will remind legal academics of the Coase theorem, Ronald Coase's seminal demonstration, which also formed the basis for the award of a Nobel Prize in Economics, that in a world without transaction costs, the allocation of liability is irrelevant (Coase 1960). There, however, Coase was explicit in his motivation: to demonstrate that precisely because the world was messy, the study of transaction costs should be the centre of the scholarly agenda. Allen (2003: 552) nicely makes this point.

552). Thus, in MOME, we proposed 'a general explanation for the elements that lead to—and limit—market efficiency' (*ibid.*: 553).

III. THE MOME THESIS

Beginning in the 1980s, a growing empirical literature challenged the predictions of the 1960s perfect market theorems, and in turn gave rise to a reassessment of the underlying theory. The Mechanisms of Market Efficiency was one such effort at explanation and reassessment. The principal focus of the MOME thesis was a concept that we termed 'relative efficiency.' By this we meant that particular information might be reflected in real—as opposed to ideal—market prices more or less rapidly (or, in our terminology, with more or less relative efficiency). The more quickly that prices re-equilibrated to reflect new information, the more closely they behave 'as if' they were set by the theorist's ideal of a market populated exclusively by fully-informed traders. Thus market efficiency, as we saw it, concerned how rapidly prices responded to information, rather than whether they responded 'correctly' according to the predictions of a particular asset pricing model such as CAPM.[10] By the early 1980s, a large body of empirical work demonstrated that price responded extremely rapidly to most public and even 'semi-public' information—too rapidly to permit arbitrage profits on most of this information. By and large, then, the public equities market appeared to be semi-strong form efficient, meaning that relative efficiency was high for public information. But how was this possible, given that most traders were likely to be uninformed about the content of much of this information?

We addressed this question on two levels. On the level of the capital markets, MOME proposed that four mechanisms work to incorporate information in market prices with progressively decreasing relative efficiency. First, market prices immediately reflect information that all traders know, simply because this information necessarily informs all trades, just as perfect markets theorists assumed ('universally-informed trading'). Secondly, information that is less widely known but nonetheless public, is incorporated into share prices almost as rapidly as information known to everyone through the trading of savvy professionals ('professionally-informed trading'). Thirdly, inside information

---

[10] Put another way, our view was that prices responded 'correctly' to information to the extent that they responded rapidly. The only meaningful sense in which market prices can ever be said to be inefficient with respect to widely available information is that they have not yet responded fully—although they will sometime. As we discuss, above note 3, we are sceptical of the utility of distinguishing between this concept of informational efficiency of price and 'fundamental' efficiency.

known to only a very few traders would find its way into prices more slowly, as uninformed traders learned about its content by observing tell-tale shifts in the activity of presumptively-informed traders or unusual price and volume movements ('derivatively-informed trading'). Finally, information known to no one might be reflected, albeit slowly and imperfectly, in share prices that aggregated the forecasts of numerous market participants with heterogeneous information ('uninformed trading').[11]

In retrospect, the four market mechanisms that we introduced to sketch the institutional reality behind the rapid incorporation of public and semi-public information into share price seem stylised themselves. Subsequent research into the structure of trading markets reveals yet another level of micro-trading mechanisms at play in the channelling of information in prices, including the critical role played by market makers.[12]

Our concern, however, was not with the microstructure that underlies the mechanisms of market efficiency, but rather with the larger institutional framework of the market that regulated the distribution of information among traders, and hence determines which market mechanism incorporates information into price. Simply put, MOME's second claim was that cost determines the distribution of information in the market, and that this cost of information, in turn, depends on the market institutions that produce, verify, and analyse information —ranging from the *Wall Street Journal* to the exhaustive research of the best professional investors. While every step in the institutional pathways that channel information into price bears on the relative efficiency of market price, none are as important as the institutions that determine the transaction costs of acquiring and verifying information in the first instance.

IV. THE CHALLENGE OF BEHAVIORAL FINANCE

In finance itself, the empirical literature challenging the perfect market theorems soon gave rise to a reassessment of the underlying theory. With respect to the Irrelevance Propositions, a focus on the imperfections in the market for information stimulated a series of explanations of how capital

---

[11] Uninformed trading is the least efficient of the four market mechanisms, precisely because the true content of information is unknown and, as a result, price 'averages' the partial information and opinion of all investors democratically. But this does not imply that we believed that market efficiency generally depends on the views of the average investor (see Stout 2003). On the contrary, three of the four market mechanisms depend on the possession of information, and two are devices by which the views of informed traders enter price, even when these knowledgeable investors are a minority in the market.

[12] See, e.g., Mahoney (2003).

structure could matter if information was costly and asymmetrically distributed. If corporate managers had private information concerning the corporation's future prospects, and if bankruptcy is costly to managers, then exposing the corporation to a greater risk of bankruptcy either by paying dividends or maintaining a higher debt to equity ratio could credibly signal that information to the market and thereby influence the price of the corporation's securities (Holstrom and Tirole 1989). Correspondingly, capital structure could also function as an incentive: an increased risk of bankruptcy resulting from a more leveraged capital structure provides an incentive for managers, for whom bankruptcy would be costly, to work even harder.[13]

The Capital Asset Pricing Model always had problems when attention shifted from theory to empirical testing. First, it was not clear that CAPM could be tested at all. CAPM predicts a linear relationship between a stock's systematic risk and returns on the market portfolio. While the market portfolio is operationally defined as a securities index like the S&P 500, the market portfolio theoretically consists of all investment assets, including non-tradable assets such as human capital. If the investigator cannot specify how the proxy for the market portfolio differs from the real but unobservable market portfolio, it is difficult to evaluate empirical results concerning how accurately CAPM predicts stock prices. Either a good prediction or a bad prediction may be the result of using an incomplete proxy for the market portfolio.[14] A second problem arises out of the integrative role played by the ECMH. CAPM predicts how prices should be set. If observed prices are different from predicted prices, it could mean that CAPM is wrong, but it could also mean that the ECMH is wrong.

Conceptual problems aside, the empirical results were not kind to CAPM. In the end, a security's beta does not predict its return very well. Two categories of evidence are especially relevant here. First, studies show that asset pricing models with multiple factors in addition to systematic risk do a better job of predicting prices. Fama and French, for example, find that they can better predict market prices with a three-factor pricing model that includes company size and book-to-market ratio in addition to systematic risk (Fama 1993; Fama and French 1996). More generally, the Arbitrage Pricing Model abandons the effort to determine nondiversifiable risk factors on the basis of a priori economic reasoning. Instead, the APM specifies that prices are a linear function of factors derived from the data itself, which may include what appear to be measures of, perhaps, liquidity or inflation.[15]

---

[13] Interestingly, Michael Jensen himself draws on this literature to explain why the capital structure of LBO association portfolio companies is not irrelevant (1989: 61).

[14] See Roll (1977: 130).

[15] See Ross (1976) (advancing the arbitrage model of capital asset pricing).

Secondly, the CAPM's empirical failures appear to exhibit certain empirical regularities. The literature identifies a number of what are styled 'anomalies,' that is, persistent evidence of higher than predicted returns based on publicly available information. Consistent with the joint test problem, these results seem to be inconsistent both with CAPM and with the ECMH. Such anomalies include the tendency of small companies to earn higher than predicted returns; the seeming existence of a 'January effect,' in which much of the abnormal returns to smaller firms occurs during the first half of January; the 'weekend effect,' in which stock returns are predictably negative over weekends; and the 'value effect,' in which firms with high earnings-to-price ratios, high dividend yields, or high book-to-market ratios earn higher than predicted returns.[16]

A variety of explanations have been offered for the empirical discrepancies. Some explain the data as the result of incorrect asset pricing models.[17] Others note that the studies revealing the anomalies are sensitive to the particular empirical techniques used (Fama 1998), or demonstrate that at least some of the anomalies disappear or are dramatically reduced in size following their announcement in the literature, thus suggesting that markets learn, although not necessarily quickly.[18]

These more particularized problems with the link between perfect capital market theories and empirical reality have had their most significant impact, however, with respect to the ECMH. Here, in a movement called behavioral finance, an alliance of cognitive psychologists and financial economists have taken direct issue with the perfect market foundations of modern finance in general and the ECMH in particular. As discussed above, the core theories of modern finance assume that investors are fully rational (or that the market acts as if they are), and that markets are efficient and transactions costs small so that professionally-informed traders quickly notice and take advantage of mispricing, thereby driving prices back to their proper level. Behavioral finance takes issue with both these premises, arguing that many investors are not rational in their financial decision-making, that there are observable directional biases resulting from departures from rational decision-making, and that significant barriers prevent professional

---

[16] For recent surveys of the empirical findings, see Barberis and Thaler (2003); Schwert (2003).

[17] Suppose that it is difficult to diversify one's human capital and that human capital is especially sensitive to economic downturns, so that individuals bear an undiversifiable risk. Investors then will desire to hold more financial assets that fare better in bad times, for which value oriented characteristics are a proxy. See Fama (1993); Fama and French (1996); Cochrane (2003).

[18] See, e.g., Schwert (2003); Rubenstein (2001).

traders from fully correcting the mistakes made by less than rational investors.[19]

The criticism of the rationality premise builds on an important literature growing out of work by cognitive psychologists Daniel Kahneman and Amos Tversky, which uses decision-making experiments to show how individuals' cognitive biases can lead them systematically to misassess an asset's value.[20] The list of biases has grown impressively with time, and includes overconfidence, the tendency of individuals to overestimate their skills; the endowment effect, the tendency of individuals to insist on a higher price to sell something they already own than to buy the same item if they do not already own it; loss aversion, the tendency for people to be risk averse for profit opportunities, but willing to gamble to avoid a loss; anchoring, the tendency for people to make decisions based on an initial estimate that is later adjusted, but not sufficiently to eliminate the influence of the initial estimate; framing, the tendency of people to make different choices based on how the decision is framed such as whether it is framed in terms of the likelihood of a good outcome or in terms of the reciprocal likelihood of a bad outcome; and hindsight, the tendency of people to read the present into assessments of the past.[21]

Individuals whose decisions are subject to one or more of these biases, referred to in the literature as 'noise traders,' will then make investment decisions that deviate from those that theory would predict of rational investors. Lee, Shleifer, and Thaler's clever effort to explain the discount often associated with closed-end mutual funds, one of the long-standing phenomena that conflicts with the ECMH, aptly illustrates the potential for such misguided investors to influence price efficiency (Lee, Shleifer, and Thaler 1991).[22] When an investor sells shares in a closed-end mutual

---

[19] Among a large number of surveys by economists, see Shleifer (2000); Barberis and Thaler (2003). Among legal commentators, see Langevoort (this volume, ch. 2) for a careful discussion. Cunningham (2002) presents the behavioral case more aggressively.

[20] For a collection of their early work, see Kahneman, Slovic, and Tversky (1982). Barberis and Thaler (2003), and Hirschliefer (2001), provide recent finance-oriented surveys. Daniel Kahneman's receipt of the 2002 Nobel Prize in Economics for this body of work is dramatic evidence of these psychologists' impact on economics. Because of his untimely death, Amos Tversky was not eligible to share in the Nobel Prize award. The symposium, *Empirical Legal Realism: A New Social Scientific Assessment of Law and Human Behavior*, 97 Nw. U. L. Rev. 1075 (2003), considers the impact of the literature on a variety of matters of legal concern.

[21] The hindsight bias is our current favorite example. In 2002, Lawrence Cunningham described the state of the ECMH literature in the mid-1980s: 'Among the legal scholars, the EMH became so dominant that two leading corporate law teachers [Gilson and Kraakman] announced that it was the context in which to discuss markets ...' (Cunningham 2002: 773) (emphasis in the original). When we first presented MOME at the symposium in connection with which it was published, Gilson had been teaching for four years, Kraakman for three. We self-servingly choose to interpret the comment as hindsight bias.

[22] We note that the econometrics in this article gave rise to a heated debate. See Chen, Kan, and Miller (1993a) (discounting Lee *et al.*'s attempt to solve the discounts on the closed-end funds puzzle); Chopra, Lee, Shleifer, and Thaler (1993) (supporting their earlier paper over

fund, she receives whatever a buyer is willing to pay, rather than a proportionate share of the fund's net asset value, as she would if she redeemed her interest in an open-end mutual fund. Because the net assets of a closed-end fund are observable, the ECMH predicts that the stock price of a closed-end fund should reflect its net asset value. In fact, closed-end funds systematically (but not uniformly) trade at a discount from their underlying asset value, a serious problem for the claim that stock prices generally are the best estimate of a security's value. In the one case where we can actually observe underlying asset value, stock price diverges from it (Kraakman 1988).

Lee, Shleifer, and Thaler blame this phenomenon on noise traders, whose views about value, perhaps because of some combination of the litany of cognitive biases, plainly ignore the value in their primary market of the securities held by the closed-end fund. Using individual, non-professional investors as a proxy for noise traders—should we all take this personally?—the authors note that institutions hold only a very small percentage of closed-end mutual fund shares, leaving individual investors as the central clientele for this type of investment.

Importantly, however, the presence of noise traders alone is insufficient to result in inefficient market prices. Two other elements are necessary. First, the biases held by the noise traders must be more or less consistent; otherwise, at least some of the biases will, in effect, regress out.[23] Secondly, arbitrageurs must be unwilling to police the resulting price inaccuracies. Under perfect capital market assumptions, fully informed traders with unlimited access to capital immediately pounce on mispriced securities. If arbitrageurs were available to trade against the noise traders, then their action would suffice to return prices to their efficient level. In the case of closed-end mutual funds, however, the absence of institutional investors in this niche limits the extent of corrective arbitrage, and prices retain an irrationality component.

This limited arbitrage condition is critical to the behavioral finance perspective,[24] and the problem is more general than the simple case of closed-end mutual funds. Limits on arbitrage fall into four general categories: fundamental risk; noise trader risk; institutional limits, both

Chen *et al.*'s criticism); Chen, Kan, and Miller (1993b) (reaffirming their point that Lee *et al.*'s sentiment index does not work). Recent analysis of UK closed-end funds suggests that the amount of noise trading does not explain the size of discounts on particular funds, but that variations in retail investor demands for funds—a different index of small investor sentiment—does explain changes in aggregate fund discounts over time. See Gennill and Thomas (2002).

[23] Andrei Shleifer and Lawrence Summers acknowledge this condition: 'These demand shifts [trading resulting from noise traders' irrational views] will only matter if they are correlated across noise traders. If all investors trade randomly, their trades cancel out ...' (Shleifer and Summers 1990: 23).

[24] See, e.g., Shleifer and Summers (1990: 24).

regulatory and incentive; and the potential that even professional traders may be subject to cognitive biases.

The problem of fundamental risk simply reflects the fact that, unless hedged, the arbitrageur has a position in the stock of a particular company that is exposed to loss from a change in that company's fortunes. This can be avoided by holding an offsetting position in a substitute security. However, substitutes may not be available and in all events will be imperfect. Barberis and Thaler (2003) offer the illustration of an arbitrageur who believes that Ford is underpriced. To hedge the risk associated with purchasing Ford, the arbitrageur simultaneously shorts GM. But this strategy only provides a hedge against bad news in the automobile industry generally; it does not hedge against firm-specific bad news about Ford (and to the extent that bad news for Ford is good news for GM, it may actually increase firm-specific risk). The arbitrageur must therefore expect a higher return to offset her basis risk, which in turn reduces arbitrage activity and lowers market efficiency. The result is much like Grossman and Stiglitz's now familiar point that informationally efficient markets are impossible because full efficiency eliminates the returns to the very activity that makes the market efficient, with the result of an 'equilibrium degree of disequilibrium' (Grossman and Stiglitz 1980: 393).

The impact of noise trader risk on arbitrage effectiveness reflects the same mechanism as operative with respect to fundamental risk but differs in the mechanism's trigger. With respect to fundamental risk, the arbitrageur must be compensated for the risk that she will have accurately estimated the probability distribution concerning future economic performance, but that the ultimate realization turns out unfavorable to her position. With respect to noise trader risk, the uncertainty concerns neither the accuracy of the arbitrageur's analysis, nor even the realization. In addition to this fundamental risk, the arbitrageur also bears the risk that noise traders will continue to be irrational, therefore maintaining, or even increasing, the mispricing. Since the arbitrageur will also have to be compensated for the risk that noise traders' continued confusion will adversely affect the value of their rational bets, the required return goes up and level of activity goes down, resulting in a cost-driven level of market inefficiency.[25]

Institutional limits on arbitrage reflect barriers to arbitrageurs trading away information inefficiencies that result not from market risk, but from the structure of the institutions through which the arbitrageurs act. For our purposes, these limits fall into two categories: regulatory and market constraints on the mechanisms of arbitrage, and the structure of

---

[25] See DeLong, Shleifer, Summers, and Waldman (1990); Shleifer and Summers (1990).

arbitrageurs' incentives. Each category operates to restrict the extent to which arbitrage can correct mispricing.

Regulatory restrictions on arbitrage are directed at short sales, undertaken by an arbitrageur when she believes the market price of a security is higher than its efficient price. In a short sale, the arbitrageur sells a security she does not own. To accomplish this, she must first find an existing owner of the overpriced security who is willing to lend the security to the arbitrageur. The borrowed stock is then sold, the arbitrageur betting that the price of the security will fall before the security must be purchased to repay the loan.[26]

Securities Exchange Act Rules 10a-1 and 10a-2 provide the basic regulatory framework. Rule 10a-1, the 'uptick test,' generally prohibits a short sale at a price below the security's last reported price, and Rule 10a-2 restricts activities by broker-dealers that could facilitate a violation of the uptick rule.[27] The idea behind the prohibitions, dating to aftermath of the stock market crash of 1929, is to prevent 'speculators' from driving down the price of a stock by continuing to sell stock below the market price (Macey, Mitchell, and Netter 1989). The difficulty with the rule is simply the obverse of its asserted benefit. Short-selling, through its information-revealing properties, pushes stock prices to a lower, more efficient level; to the extent that the uptick rule actually succeeds in restricting arbitrage, the level of market efficiency suffers.[28]

Market restrictions on short-selling involve both limits on the demand side—the parties who can engage in short-selling—and on the supply side—the costs and availability of shares to borrow to affect a short sale. While the Securities Exchange Act 316(c) restricts short-selling by officers, directors, and large shareholders of publicly traded companies, the more serious demand constraint is voluntary; a recent SEC study reports that only some 43 per cent of mutual funds were authorized by their charters

[26] Securities Exchange Act of 1934 Rule 3b-3 defines a short sale as any sale of a security that the seller either does not own or is closed by delivery of a borrowed security. For a transactional account of the steps in a short sale, see D'Avolio (2002).

[27] More fully stated, an exchange-listed security may be sold short only (1) at a price above the immediately preceding reported price ('plus tick'), or (2) at the last sale price if it is higher than the last different reported price ('zero-plus tick'). For NASDAQ listed securities, NASD Rule 3350 prohibits NASD members from effecting short-sales when the best bid displayed is below the preceding best bid for the security. See SEC (2003); Macey, Mitchell, and Netter (1989).

[28] Powers, Schizer, and Shubik (2003: 40) collect the substantial body of literature showing that restrictions on short sales inflate prices. The authors also point out that the tax law imposes an additional cost on short-selling by effectively denying profits from a short position the more favorable capital gains rate accorded profits from long positions. On 22 October 2003, the SEC proposed for comments a new Regulation SHO that would modernize and replace Rules 10a-1 and 10a-2. In addition to substantially reducing the bite of the uptick rule, the new regulation would adopt a pilot program that authorizes the SEC to choose 300 of the 1000 largest US stocks for which restrictions on short-selling would be suspended for two years, following which the performance and volatility of these shares would be compared to that of stocks subject to the new regulation.

to sell short (SEC 2003: 108). During the six-month period ending 30 April 2003, only approximately 2.5 per cent of registered investment companies (236 out of some 9000) actually engaged in short-selling. Because 79 per cent of mutual funds report that they do not use derivatives (Koski and Pontiff 1999), it is unlikely that the charter restrictions are being avoided through the use of synthetic securities (Chen, Hong, and Stein 2002: 172).

   Market restrictions on the supply side relate to the lending market for the securities that must be borrowed for a short sale to be made. Preparation for a short sale begins with a request that the arbitrageur's broker find a lender for the shares that are to be sold. The universe for potential lenders includes the broker itself if it has an inventory of the desired stock, or institutional investors, including pension funds, insurance companies, and index funds, all of whom have long-term strategies that are unlikely to be negatively affected by liquidity constraints resulting from securities lending. The arbitrageur transfers collateral to the lender in the amount of 102 per cent of the value of the borrowed securities, typically in cash. The lender then pays interest to the arbitrageur on the cash collateral, termed the rebate rate, and has the right to call the loan at any time. If the loan is called at a time when the shares have risen in value, the arbitrageur will be forced to close her position at a loss unless another lender is found. Additionally, SEC Regulation T requires that the arbitrageur post a margin of 50 per cent of the borrowed securities' value in additional collateral.

   In general, the lending market available to short sellers for large issuer securities is broad and deep. Large cap stocks are generally easy and cheap to borrow, with the great majority requiring loan fees of less than 1 per cent per year (D'Avolio 2002: 273). In contrast, borrowing smaller cap stocks with little institutional ownership may be difficult and expensive.[29] As many as 16 per cent of the stocks in the Center for Research in Security Prices file may be impossible to borrow. These companies are quite small, in total accounting for less than 1 per cent of the market by value, with most being in the bottom decile by size and typically trading at under $5.00.

   Recent theoretical and empirical work suggests that it is more costly to borrow a stock the greater the divergence of opinion in the security's value. The logic reflects the fact that those who do not lend the security forego the price they would have received for its loan. Thus, those holding a stock must value it more highly than those who lend it by an amount in excess of the loan fee. The greater the divergence of opinion concerning the stock's value, the higher the loan fees, yielding the

---

[29] The discussion in the text is based on accounts of the short-sale process in Jones and Lamont (2002); Geczy, Musto, and Reed (2002); Duffie, Gârleanu, and Pedersen (2002).

perverse result that the transaction costs of arbitrage increase in precisely the circumstance when the activity is most important.[30]

Consistent with significant market limits on arbitrage, short interest in securities is generally quite small. A recent study reports that over the period 1976 through 1993, more than 80 per cent of listed firms had short interests of less than 0.5 per cent of outstanding shares, and more than 98 per cent had short interests of less than 5 per cent (Dechow *et al.* 2001), a level consistent in magnitude with earlier assessments (Jones and Lamont 2002: 212). And consistent with a significant impact on market efficiency from limited arbitrage, the empirical evidence 'is broadly consistent with the idea that short-sales constraints matter for equilibrium stock prices and expected returns' (Chen, Hong, and Stein 2001: 201). The problem, however, is with the magnitude of the costs. If the stock of all but small, non-institutional stock is readily available for borrowing, the regulatory and market-imposed transaction costs of short-selling seem too small to account for the limited amount of short-selling we observe and for its impact on pricing. A recent study of the impact of short-selling constraints concluded that

> An interesting question that our work raises, but does not answer, is this: why do short-sale constraints seem to be so strongly binding? Or said slightly differently: why, in spite of the high apparent risk-adjusted returns to strategies involving shorting, is there so little aggregate short interest in virtually all stocks? ...[W]e are skeptical that all, or even most of the answer has to do with ...specific transaction costs (Chen, Hong, and Stein 2001: 201).[31]

The structure of arbitrageurs' incentives may provide the identity of the dark matter of the short-sale universe—the source of constraints that the transaction costs of short-selling do not explain. Recent work highlights a number of incentive problems, including a more realistic account of arbitrageurs' goals and the agency costs of arbitrage.

The first problem is that we have, to this point, operated on a quite naïve framing of the goal of arbitrageurs. In effect, we have treated arbitrageurs as a kind of market-maker whose role is to police the efficiency of prices and whose efforts will be compromised to the extent that regulatory and transaction costs make short-selling costly. In fact, however, arbitrageurs have a quite different goal: to make money. This, in turn, suggests that arbitrageurs act not only on a difference between a

[30] Chen, Hong, and Stein (2001) and D'Avolio (2001) present empirical evidence and a review of the literature.

[31] D'Avolio (2002: 303) reaches a similar conclusion: 'While specialness [high loan fees] and recall risk could be onerous for many mid- to small-sized stocks, they cannot explain low short interest among S&P 500 stocks. To fully understand the observed reluctance, researchers must explore less explicit measures of short seller costs and risks—ones that extend beyond the loan market.'

stock's market price and its fundamental value, but also on a difference between a stock's current market price and its future market price, regardless of the relation between its future market price and its fundamental value. Here the idea is simply that if overly optimistic noise traders are in the market, shorting the stock is not the only way to make money. Instead, one can profit by anticipating the direction of the noise traders' valuation error, and taking advantage of that error through long, not short, positions with the goal of selling the shares to noise traders at a higher future price. The result may be to drive up the price of already overvalued stocks, and to prolong the length and increase the extent of bubbles.[32]

The second problem is the agency costs of arbitrage, arising from, as Andrei Shleifer has nicely put it, the fact that 'brains and resources are separated by an agency relationship' (Shleifer 2001: 89). To see this, keep in mind that arbitrage positions are made based on ex ante expectations, but the gain realized depends on ex post outcomes. The two may differ because of either the arbitrageur's skill in identifying mispricing or because of fundamental or noise trader risk; that is, an investment may fail either because of bad judgment or because of bad luck.

For an arbitrageur trading for her own account, we can presume the explanation for a failed investment is observable. But now assume that the arbitrageur is instead an investment professional whose capital is raised from institutional investors and who receives a portion of the profits—the arbitrageur runs a hedge fund. Because the initial ex ante assessment of the portfolio investment is not observable to the fund investor, the investor then may use the investment's ex post outcome as a proxy of the arbitrageur's skill, with the effect of exposing the arbitrageur's human capital to both fundamental and noise trader risk because the fund investor may mistakenly treat a loss that really results from bad luck as evidence of bad judgment. Arbitrageurs thought to have 'bad judgment' will have difficulty raising new funds. This potential, in turn, will cause the arbitrageur to reduce her risk by taking more conservative positions. Importantly, the personal risk to the arbitrageur increases as the importance of arbitrage as a means to correct market price increases. The greater the disagreement about a stock's price, the greater the bad luck risk that the arbitrage position turns out badly and, hence, the greater risk to the arbitrageur's human capital.[33]

---

[32] See, e.g., DeLong, Shleifer, Summers, and Waldman (1990) (discussing the possibility that noise traders follow positive feedback strategies—buy high, sell low); Bulow and Klemperer (1994) (arguing that because buyers can choose when to buy, markets are extremely sensitive to new information); Shleifer (2000: ch. 6).

[33] This approach is that of Shleifer and Vishny (1997). In structure, the agency model should be familiar. In a somewhat different form, it has provided the economic basis for the business judgment rule: because courts and juries will find it difficult to distinguish between director decisions that result in bad outcomes because of bad judgment or because of bad luck,

This interaction between noise trader risk and the agency costs of arbitrage can plausibly lead to bubble-like conditions. Once noise traders enter the market in large numbers, the risk to arbitrage increases, which in turn results in an independent reduction in the level of arbitrage. This reduction, one might imagine, is more or less linear. More important, the presence of a market driven by noise traders has the potential to create a kink in the arbitrage supply curve, when the potential profits from momentum trading exceeds the potential profit from short-selling. From this perspective and extrapolating from Lee, Shleifer, and Thaler's treatment of closed-end mutual funds, one might consider a sharp increase in the number of individual investors in the market as a pre-bust signal of a bubble. This assessment turns on its head the familiar anecdotal observation that when individuals get into the market the professionals get out: when individuals enter the market in large numbers, professionals find something to sell them.

A final potential limit on arbitrage looks back to the psychological biases that may underlie the noise trader phenomenon. To this point, we have treated arbitrageurs as if they still met the perfect rationality assumption of traditional theory—even if they are responding to the presence of noise traders or frictions in the incentive structure they face, they do so rationally. In the end, however, even professional traders are people. Maybe they are subject to cognitive biases as well; that is, the existence of irrational professional traders may be a limit to arbitrage.

The issue whether some or all of the cognitive biases are hard-wired or can be diminished by education or experience is a contested subject whose review is far beyond our ambition here. For present purposes, we note only that when the studies place individuals in a position where the goal is to make money, the cognitive biases seem to disappear quickly.[34] And because the organization has the capacity to shape the traders' incentives so that the goal is clear, the potential for learning to occur and be reinforced is significant. Thus, for our purposes, we will treat professional traders as rational actors in responding to the incentives that they face.

---

imposing liability on directors will result in conservatism to avoid the cost of the legal system making a mistake in assessing causation. See also Gilson and Black (1996: 866–68) (arguing lawyers provide too conservative advice when clients use bad outcomes as a proxy for bad judgment).

[34] In a helpful and balanced assessment of the literature, Mark Kelman notes: '[V]iolations of rationality precepts seem to disappear rather quickly when people have the opportunity to make decisions again. [Especially] ...when those who will have the chance to repeat the decisionmaking process are rewarded if they behave the way rational choice theorists believe the normative decisionmaker should behave, and are penalized if they do not' (Kelman 2003: 1380). See also List (2003) (providing experimental evidence that experience significantly eliminates the endowment effect).

V. A TENTATIVE ASSESSMENT OF THE BEHAVIORAL FINANCE PRINCIPLES

Assessing the contribution of behavioral finance to the market efficiency debate even on the tentative basis we have in mind here, as well as avoiding some of the shrillness that has been associated with the debate, requires that we be quite clear both about the aspect of market efficiency we have in mind, and which of the two behavioral finance principles—investor irrationality and limits on arbitrage—is doing the heavy lifting. From our perspective, evidence that some investors sometimes systematically deviate from rational decision-making is not a revelation. Roughly coincident with the publication of MOME, one of us published a text on *The Law and Finance of Corporate Acquisitions* that contained a lengthy excerpt from a survey article by Amos Tversky and Daniel Kahneman, to our knowledge the first time their work appeared in corporate law teaching materials (Gilson and Black 1986: 99–112). What makes the market efficiency claim non-trivial is that prices are said to be efficient despite the fact that perfect market assumptions do not hold. Investor irrationality on the part of some investors, like information costs and transaction costs, affects relative efficiency. Irrationality takes on special meaning only if its impact on the incorporation of information into price differs from that of other market imperfections. Otherwise, limits on arbitrage should command the most attention (including, of course, those limits that are linked to investor irrationality).

A. The Investor Irrationality Principle

Despite the body of experimental evidence supporting persistent decision-making biases in some portion of the population, we are sceptical that this phenomenon will be found, generally, to play a significant role in setting aggregate price levels. Start with the familiar complaint that the sheer number of biases that have been identified, together with the absence of precision about which bias, or combination of biases, are operative in particular circumstances, leaves too many degrees of freedom in assigning causation. For example, the psychology literature has been proffered to support giving a target board of directors more discretion to undertake defensive action—cognitive biases may cause the shareholders to make the wrong decision (Lipton and Rowe 2002).[35] But what bias can be predicted to operate in this setting? If one imagines the endowment effect is at work on target shareholders, then

---

[35] Perhaps this is what the Delaware Supreme Court means by 'substantive coercion.'

they may require too high a price for their stock, and mistakenly let a good offer pass. Alternatively, if one imagines that the shareholders are loss averse, and if they anchor the measure of their loss by the premium offered, they may fear the risk of losing the existing premium more than they value the chance of a still higher offer.[36] One cannot help but be reminded of Karl Llewellyn's famous demonstration that for every canon of statutory interpretation there is an equal and opposite canon, leaving one in search of a meta principle that dictates when one or the other applies (Llewellyn 1950).[37]

Indeed, this indeterminacy concerning the incidence and interaction of the variety of cognitive biases raises the possibility that biases could not be shown to influence aggregate price levels even if they did. Here the concern echoes that raised by Richard Roll with respect to testing CAPM—if one cannot observe the market portfolio, one cannot assess the extent to which one's proxy differs from it. If one cannot observe which biases are operative and their interaction, one may not be able to assess whether a market price reflects any bias at all (Roll 1977).

To be sure, the indeterminacy criticism is overstated in the sense that it applies the ambitions of economics to cognitive psychology. It is unlikely that this body of work will lead to models like arbitrage pricing, which would aspire to estimate what biases apply in particular circumstances and their coefficient—the weight each bias has in the ultimate decision. As Mark Kelman stated recently:

> [T]he fact that one recognizes the existence of hindsight bias may make it somewhat more plausible that decision makers are not perfectly rational in general or, a touch more narrowly, in assessing the probability of events. However, its existence does not make it any more likely that they are subject to any of the other particular infirmities of reasoning …that behavioural researchers have identified But the fact that a vice does not quite close does not mean it is

---

[36] Of course, this framing of the problem depends on when the shareholders switch their reference point from the market price to the offered price. This quandary has real world importance. Those who backpack in the Sierra Nevada Mountains know that black bears suffer from the endowment effect. The park rangers' standard advice about what to do when a bear enters your camp looking for food is to throw stones at it, bang pans, and otherwise aggressively seek to chase the bear away. That advice changes, however, if the bear actually gets your food. At that point, the food instantly becomes part of the bear's endowment, and one can be hurt trying to take the food away. For those of us who are somewhat skittish about large animals with sharp teeth, the precise point when the endowment effect kicks in and triggers the possibility of violently expressed loss aversion is awfully important.

[37] This type of indeterminacy or 'degrees of freedom' criticism is voiced in Zwiebel (2002). To some extent, the 'equal and opposite' criticism is exaggerated. Take two familiar and competing homilies—'the early bird gets the worm' and 'look before you leap.' If each is plainly dominant in a particular domain (and hence their status as a homily), the indeterminacy problem concerns only the areas where the two domains overlap.

without value in addressing more general, as opposed to more precise, problems' (Kelman 2003: 1350).[38]

For the purpose of evaluating the role of irrationality in setting prices, however, this criticism is important. It means that the simple presence of cognitive biases has no necessary implications for prices at all. Indeed, we cannot dismiss the possibility that the price effects of offsetting biases, on a single individual or across individuals, regress out in significant respect and thereby reduce the pressure on arbitrage, that is, on the mechanisms of market efficiency.

The same analysis also suggests circumstances where investor irrationality should be a matter of real concern. When a single bias extends across most noise traders, the price effect will not regress out, leaving a much heavier burden on arbitrage. And the problem will increase more than monotonically as the number of infected noise traders increases. As the volume of irrational trades increases, a point is reached where the arbitrageur's most profitable strategy shifts from betting against the noise traders to buying in front of them, with the goal of exploiting the noise traders' mistake by selling them overvalued stock. In other words, increasing numbers of similarly mistaken noise traders serve to turbo-charge the price impact of their mistake. A sharp increase in the participation of individual investors is a powerful indication that they share a common bias—the likelihood that a coincidence of different biases all lead to increasing participation at the same time seems small. Thus, a spike in individual trading, Lee, Shleifer, and Thaler's proxy for noise trading, may serve as a limited predictor of price bubbles.

Where do we come out, then? Very tentatively, we suggest that noise trading—or investor irrationality—is likely to matter to price episodically. Under conditions of 'normal trading,' the arbitrage mechanism will suffice to cabin the eddies of bias in noise trading, and the extent to which irrationality influences price will be set by other constraints on arbitrage including transaction costs and the costs of information. However, circumstances of abnormal trading—when a spike in the number of individual investors suggests that noise traders will share a common mistaken belief—will give rise to a shift in arbitrageur strategy that drives prices further from efficiency. On these occasions, arbitrage constraints on price are relaxed, and the effects of cognitive biases on prices are likely to be of significantly greater magnitude than cost-based deviations from perfect market conditions.

Thus, our attention will focus on arbitrage limits in assessing the

---

[38] It is important to stress that the fact that research in cognitive psychology does not solve problems in economics is no criticism of psychology literature. Interdisciplinary scholarship encounters its own 'limits on arbitrage'—other disciplines have their own agendas as the overlap between disciplinary areas of interest is only partial.

impact of behavioral finance on the market efficiency debate. However, this emphasis does not mean that the bias literature does not usefully speak to matters of financial market concern. Rather, we expect that it will have its greatest impact on circumstances when the concern is not with aggregate price effects, but with the behavior of individual investors. As we will discuss in more detail in Part VI, we may care a great deal if individuals systematically make poor investment decisions with respect to their retirement savings, especially with the growing shift from defined benefit to defined contribution pension plans, even if their mistakes do not affect price levels at all. Put differently, we may care what happens to the people whose mistakes are regressed out.

B. Limits on Arbitrage

In contrast to our scepticism that cognitive biases will have a significant influence on relative market efficiency other than episodically (when the number of individual investors spikes and their biases therefore likely coincide), we are quite sympathetic to concerns that agency and incentive problems constrain the professionally-informed trading mechanism continuously, even in times of normal trading. MOME's relative efficiency concept, following Grossman and Stiglitz (1980), builds on the idea that the cost of information limits the effectiveness of professionally-informed trading—it has to pay to be informed. Agency and incentive problems between, for example, hedge funds and their investors and between hedge funds and their portfolio managers, pose the same kind of tradeoff—it has to pay to reduce these costs.[39]

That said, the recent literature identifying the limits on arbitrage[40] closes a fascinating circle of intellectual history. As we described in Part I, the late 1950s and early 1960s gave rise to a wave of models that described the workings of segments of the capital market under perfect market conditions: asset prices were a function only of systematic risk; capital structure did not affect firm value; and informationally efficient markets policed these relationships through arbitrage. Almost from the beginning, the Irrelevancy Propositions were attacked for the extent to

[39] Models of herd behavior, for example, reflect this phenomenon. See, e.g., Zwiebel (1995) (demonstrating how outside concerns may deter managers from taking innovative actions); Scharfstein and Stein (1990) (examining forces that can lead to herd behavior). Michael Klausner has suggested that agency limits on arbitrage might temper our view with respect to the uptick rule, see above text accompanying note 27, because such limits could lead to mispricing short of the large, sharp price movements associated with crashes and bubbles. While resolving this point requires more attention than is possible here, we would start by distinguishing between the uptick rule, which affects small movements in price and therefore also impacts useful arbitrage, and current breakers, which because they are triggered only by large price movements, exclude much 'normal' arbitrage from their operation.
[40] See above text accompanying notes 21–34.

which their assumptions differed from the observed world, and for the fact that observed capital structures displayed regularities. The parallel rise of agency and information economics then provided a conceptual structure to order how deviations from perfect market assumptions rippled through corporate finance. The limits on arbitrage literature extends this project to the joined-at-the-hip subjects of asset pricing and market efficiency. The circle closes.

But why all the fanfare? Precisely because it does not depend on the presence of cognitive biases, the limits on arbitrage literature seems to be very useful, but entirely straightforward steps in the project of moving from a perfect market extreme null hypothesis to the messy world where transaction costs are positive, agents are disloyal, and information is costly and unevenly distributed.[41] We thought we had signed on to this project twenty years ago although, as we confess in the next Part, we were painfully naïve about the level of frictions affecting the professionally-informed trading mechanism. But if this is behavioral finance, then it began with Grossman and Stiglitz. The fanfare seems to us a little late.

VI. HOW WELL DOES MOME STAND UP TO BEHAVIORAL FINANCE? GOOD NEWS AND BAD

If, as we claim, MOME is a precursor of some aspects of modern behavioral finance, it is only fair to ask how well MOME's focus on the distribution and cost of information stands up to behavioral finance today. The answer, we believe, is mixed. The good news is that the central categories of MOME, including the market mechanisms and the concept of relative efficiency, are consistent not only with the established

---

[41] A recent paper nicely distinguishes between explanations for pricing anomalies that focus on limits to arbitrage as opposed to cognitive bias (Phalippou 2003). One familiar anomaly is the tendency of value stocks to outperform growth stocks. See above text accompanying notes 15–18. Taking their expected sides, Fama and French argue that the value effect results from an imperfect asset pricing model, see Fama and French (1996); Fama (1993), while Lakonishok, Shleifer and Vishny (1994) argue that 'value strategies produce higher returns because they bet against strategies followed by most investors, who may extrapolate past earnings growth too far into the future, assume trends in stock prices, or equate a good investment with a well-run firm irrespective of prices,'—a cognitive bias explanation. Phalippou provides a third explanation that focuses attention on limits on arbitrage. Because approximately half of the value-effect results from underperformance by growth stocks, not overperformance by value stocks, an investor would have to short growth stocks in order to capture the differential. The problem is that some one-half of the most overvalued growth stocks are so small as to have little institutional ownership and therefore could not be borrowed and, it follows, could not be shorted. As to the other one-half of the value differential, Phalippou argues that it results from a small number of stocks with markets so illiquid that efforts to take a significant position would have moved the price of the stock. As we have suggested, limits on arbitrage, rather than cognitive biases, are doing the heavy lifting.

empirical findings of behavioral finance but with some of its more promising models as well. The bad news is that back in the early 1980s, we greatly underestimated the institutional obstacles to the production and rapid reflection of information in share prices.

A. The Good News

The good news about MOME extends to both fact and theory. On the empirical side, proponents of both rational markets and behavioral finance agree that many of the long-term pricing anomalies that cut against the efficiency of market prices largely disappear when analysts control for company size.[42] These disappearing anomalies include, for example, the underpricing of IPOs and seasoned equity offerings. The size-related character of these anomalies is good news because it is precisely what MOME would predict on the assumption that the size of the float is a critical determinant of the amount and quality of information about issuers, and the relative efficiency with which this information is reflected in market prices. The reasoning is simple. Small issuers have a limited following among analysts and other professional investors, in part because there is little profit to be made by researching issuers whose size restricts the potential gains. As a result, less information is produced, verification of information is more costly, and net returns available to investors and securities traders are lower as a result (Gilson and Kraakman 1984: 635–42).

Size, analyst coverage, and the attendant availability can account for pricing anomalies of other sorts as well. On the theory side, an important model developed by Hong and Stein (1999) explains momentum trading and skewness in stock prices on the basis of the slow diffusion of private information through the economy.[43] Traders without access to private information rationally treat price movements as a proxy for the injection of new information, which explains momentum trading as well as sudden reversals in price, when traders discover they have already overshot share value. In support of this model, Hong, Lim, and Stein (2000) present evidence that momentum trading in shares is particularly

---

[42] See Fama and French (1996); Barbaris and Thaler (2003).

[43] Arguing that if information diffuses gradually, prices will under-react in the short-term.

[44] This account of momentum trading is closely related to the mechanism of 'price decoding,' as described in Gilson and Kraakman (1984: 574–79). A related finding is that the share prices of small and poorly-followed issuers have a positive skew relative to prices of larger companies. Bad information takes longer to enter share prices for smaller firms, possibly because managers of these firms are able to dribble bad news out more slowly than can managers of widely followed firms. Good news is generally announced immediately (Chen, Hong, and Stein 2001).

strong among small firms and firms that attract little interest among analysts.[44]

B. The Bad News

If recent models of the production and diffusion of information confirm the continuing relevance of MOME's analysis, our original account of market mechanisms and the institutional production of information suffered from what might be termed 'naiveté bias.' We implicitly underestimated the institutional complexities that attend the production, processing, and verification of market information, as well as its reflection in share prices. Some aspects of our naiveté were discussed earlier in this essay: in particular, the legal and institutional limitations on arbitrage, including the agency problems that afflict institutional investors—such as the role of incentive structures in encouraging herding behavior by fund managers at the expense of fund investors.

But even more important than underestimating the limits on the arbitrage mechanism, we failed to appreciate the magnitude of the incentive problems in the core market institutions that produce, verify, and process information about corporate issuers. As the Enron cohort of financial scandals demonstrated, lucrative equity compensation has had the side effect of creating powerful incentives for managers to increase share prices. Usually, we suppose, managers respond by creating additional value for shareholders. But sometimes they respond by feeding distorted information to the market—or even by lying outright, as in recent cases such as WorldCom and HealthSouth Corporation.[45] Similarly, recent scandals demonstrate that we also were too sanguine about the role of the institutions that we termed 'reputational intermediaries'—the established investment banks, commercial banks, accounting firms, and law firms that use their reputations to vouch for the representations of unknown issuers, and so reduce the information costs of investors (Gilson and Kraakman 1984: 604–5, 619–21). As the example of Arthur Andersen's relationship to Enron demonstrated all too clearly,[46] misaligned incentives and intra-organizational agency problems limit the ability of even the largest reputational intermediaries to police the accuracy of their clients' representations. Finally, we were naïve about the role of security analysts, and particularly those employed by the investment banks on the sell-side of the market.[47] These analysts, it appears, often acted as selling agents for the client-issuers of the

---

[44] See, e.g., Franks *et al.* (2003).

[45] See, e.g., Franks *et al.* (2003); Coffee (2002).

[46] See Gilson and Kraakman (1984: 601) (suggesting securities analysts work unambiguously to reduce the processing costs of information for the market).

institutions that employ them.[48] Or, put differently, an investment bank's reputation among issuers is likely to matter more to it than its reputation among the lay investors who rely on its analysts' reports.

In sum, on every dimension of information costs—the costs of producing, verifying, and processing valuation data—we confess error by implication, not about the roles of the institutions that supply information to the market, but about how well they perform their roles. The point is perhaps too obvious today to merit elaboration, but the market cannot be more efficient than the institutions that fix quality and cost of valuation information permit. That, after all, was MOME's principal point.

VII. THE FUTURE OF BEHAVIORAL FINANCE: RESEARCH AND POLICY IMPLICATIONS

We have argued that the binding constraints on market efficiency arise, either from institutional limitations or the interaction of the arbitrage mechanism with cognitive biases—not from the widespread existence of cognitive biases alone. There are implications of this view for future research as well as the formulation of regulatory policy.

A. Future Research

We will not fully understand the import of psychological distortions on the functioning of the capital market until we first understand the institutional limitations on the production and distribution of valuation information. The well-documented list of cognitive biases that motivates much of behavioral finance allows so many degrees of freedom that the framing of testable predictions about real world financial markets is difficult. Fruitful hypotheses will require not only an understanding of cognitive biases but, even more importantly, an understanding of the market processes that screen, channel, dampen, or amplify the biases of traders to produce observed market behavior.

In pursuing this research agenda, the most fruitful topics of investigation are likely to be market frenzies and crashes, such as the 1987 market crash and the recent internet bubble, rather than well-documented pricing anomalies such as the closed-end fund discount or the underpricing of IPOs. The evidence suggests that the traditional anomalies—the usual suspects—can be comfortably explained within the MOME framework as a function of institutional limitations on the operation of the mechanisms of market efficiency in the course of 'normal

---

[48] See, e.g., Franks *et al.* (2003).

trading,' including limitations on the ability of informed traders to engage in arbitrage. We know much less about the institutional and psychological underpinnings of bubbles and crashes. On one hand, the attractions of—psychological hypotheses are greatest for explaining such unusual or violent market behavior. As we suggested in Part V, above, the price effects of cognitive pathologies are likely to be episodic: associated with bias, surges of individual trading, and extraordinary breakdowns in the arbitrage mechanism. This scenario fits nicely with the periodic appearance and demise of market bubbles. On the other hand, there is a competing body of literature pointing to institutional pathologies that can generate seemingly irrational market disturbances even without the help of noise traders.[49] If the study of market institutions teaches anything, it is that not every instance of collective irrationality is necessarily rooted in individual irrationality.

B. Policy Implications

Given the limits of our knowledge at the moment, it is useful to ask about the policy implications that follow from the progress that behavior finance has made or is likely to make in the foreseeable future. These implications, it seems to us, fall into two categories: those in which behavioral finance holds promise for guiding regulatory policy and those in which it does not.

1. Where Behavioral Finance Can Guide Reform

We see two principal areas where behavioral finance is likely to have policy implications in the near term. One lies on the institutional side. Given the importance of limitations on the arbitrage mechanism that we have emphasized thus far, regulators should clearly seek to reduce legal and institutional barriers to arbitrage. Thus, the SEC should consider removing the uptick rule and margin requirements that burden short-selling,[50] as well as campaigning against the lingering taint that makes institutional investors such as mutual funds reluctant to pursue short-selling strategies. Far from being suspect, short-selling actually confers a positive externality on the entire market by speeding the reflection of unfavorable information in share prices. In addition, behavioral finance may support temporary interventions in the market, such as trading halts, when market behavior suggests a surge of biased trading that threatens to destabilize arbitrage. We hesitate to make this

---

[49] See, e.g., Chen, Hong, and Stein (2001); Rubenstein (2001); Bulow and Klemperer (1994).
[50] See above text accompanying notes 27–28.

prediction too forcefully, however, as there is still much work to be done in parsing out the psychological and institutional roots of market frenzies.

We are far more confident about a second area in which behavioral finance might eventually inform regulatory policy: the protection of individual investors. The possible consequences for policy involve paternalistic responses to cognitive bias. As we argued above, three conditions must be met for psychological distortions to affect share prices: (1) cognitive biases must be pervasive (as most commentators believe they are); (2) they must be correlated (because otherwise they are offsetting); and finally, (3) the arbitrage mechanism must fail with respect to their effects. Notice, however, that cognitive bias can injure investors even if it has no effect whatsoever on share prices, i.e., conditions (2) and (3) are not met.[51] Perhaps the best example is the employee who, as a result of limited knowledge or cognitive bias, misallocates investment in a 401k plan by failing to diversify her investments, or assumes a level of risk inappropriate to her age and retirement aspirations. As Howell Jackson points out, the rise of defined contribution and voluntary investment plans has shifted discretion over retirement savings from professional traders to individual 'lay' investors, who are often noise traders as well (Jackson 2003).[52] It might well be, then, that we would be wise to limit the investment discretion of these employee-investors, precisely in order to prevent them from harming themselves. Such limitations might be mandatory for government-sponsored or tax-favored retirement plans: for example, an inflexible diversification requirement. Alternatively, these limitations might take the form of what one group of authors has termed 'asymmetric paternalism,' i.e., default rules that sophisticated investors can avoid but that are binding on unsophisticated investors who are more likely to make costly errors as a result of cognitive bias or bounded rationality (Camerer 2003).

2. The Limits of Behavioral Finance as a Policy Tool

Once we leave the easy cases of short-selling restrictions, obvious market frenzies, and undiversified retirement savings, the legal implications of behavioral finance for corporate and securities law become much murkier for the simple reason that we know little about both the extent and nature of cognitive bias among traders or the interaction of cognitive bias with the institutions that generate information and the mechanisms that reflect it in price (including, above all, the arbitrage activity of sophisticated investors). We therefore find ourselves largely in agreement

---

[51] Issacharoff (1988) puts forward similar criteria in assessing the application of the cognitive bias literature to law and economics more generally.

[52] See above text accompanying notes 27–28.

with Donald Langevoort's assessment of the implications of behavioral finance for securities regulation, which, no doubt over-simplifying, we would summarize as, 'not much so far, although lawmakers should stay tuned to current research and keep an open mind' (this volume, ch. 2). Indeed, we would go one step further, to caution against the use of behavioral finance to advance policy agendas that it cannot possibly support. We close this essay with the cautionary example of a policy debate in which behavioral finance is sometimes said to have important implications when in fact it does not.

3. The Takeover Debate and the Limits of Behavioral Finance

The example we have in mind is the claim that is sometimes made in debates over takeovers that investor irrationality demonstrates the wisdom of vesting discretion over the decision to defend against hostile takeovers in the hands of managers rather than shareholders.[53] We find this claim unpersuasive for several reasons that nicely illustrate the limits of cognitive psychology in setting basic corporate policy. In the first place, market efficiency has a limited role in the takeover debate. The primary policy tradeoff is between the absence of strong form efficiency—the possibility that managers have information about the corporation's value the market lacks, which is the reason for giving management discretion to defend—and the possibility of managerial agency cost, the reason for giving the decision to shareholders. This one comes out in favor of shareholder decision-making because target management can always ameliorate the failure of strong form efficiency by disclosing its information if takeover decision-making is allocated to shareholders,[54] while allocating authority to management does nothing to ameliorate the agency cost problem.[55]

It is at this point that the cognitive bias component of behavioral finance comes into play: the balance may shift if, despite disclosure, shareholders will predictably reject target managers' advice because of one or another cognitive bias.[56] Of course, given the range of cognitive biases one cannot entirely reject this possibility. As we suggested above,

---

[53] For the most recent rematch—it may feel to some like Rocky XXX—see, for example, Gilson (2002a) (analysing the use and development of Unocal); Lipton and Rowe (2002); Gilson (2002b) (replying to Lipton and Rowe's response to the author's analysis of the fifteen-year history of Unocal); Lipton (2002) (discussing the evolution of the law of corporate takeover); Bebchuk (2002) (arguing that boards should have no veto power against takeover bids after shareholders' choice is ensured).

[54] The problem cannot be completely eliminated by disclosure because target management may have difficulty establishing the credibility of its disclosure of information suggesting a higher target value.

[55] See Gilson (2002b: 42).

[56] Perhaps this is the unarticulated justification for the Delaware Supreme Court's concern that shareholders will be subject to 'substantive coercion.'

some biases predict that shareholders will tender too readily while others predict an unwarranted reluctance to tender.[57] In the context of the allocation of takeover decision-making between managers and shareholders, however, the critical point is that cognitive bias analysis be applied on a bilateral or comparative basis.

This concern grows out of the fact that the experimental literature is largely unilateral in its focus. The experiments are concerned only with whether a particular decision-maker is subject to a cognitive bias, not whether one competing decision-maker is more impaired than another. But when cognitive bias is invoked to allocate authority among competing decision-makers, the analysis must be bilateral; the potential biases of the decision-makers must be compared. In our context, the question is: whether managers' or shareholders' decisions are likely to be more distorted?

The comparison seems to us to favor allocating decision-making authority to shareholders. First, it is simply unclear which, if any, biases are likely to apply to individual shareholders when they must choose whether to accept a hostile offer. Moreover, the outcome of the takeover is likely to be determined by the decisions of institutional investors, who are less likely to be subject to cognitive biases (but may be subject to institutional influences). The shareholders critical to the outcome of a hostile takeover look little like the noise trader clientele of closed-end mutual funds.[58] Finally, the market for corporate control operates, to an extent, as a backstop in case cognitive biases nonetheless cause target shareholders to tender into too low an offer. The ubiquity of competing bidders emerging in response to an underpriced offer can save the shareholders from their biases.

On the other side, one can imagine a range of biases that may influence target managers to resist a hostile takeover even when the transaction is in the shareholders' best interests. A reaction to cognitive dissonance may cause managers to respond to an offer that calls into question their performance and competence by deriding the bidder's motives and promising a brighter future if only the shareholders have patience. Managers may genuinely believe their claims, but behavioral finance suggests that their assessment may be driven by a cognitive bias (Gilson 2002b: 46).[59] This effort at dissonance reduction may, in turn, be exacerbated by the overconfidence bias—managers' vigorous defence may be encouraged by a biased assessment of their own skills. Other examples are possible, but the point by now should be clear: when

---

[57] See above text accompanying notes 35–37.

[58] See above text accompanying note 22.

[59] Put differently, where self-interest and cognitive bias move in the same direction, one might expect the build-up of significant momentum.

cognitive bias analysis is invoked to illuminate the choice between two decision-makers, its application must be bilateral.

In all events, we conclude that the cognitive bias element of behavioral finance is unlikely to change the trade off between agency costs and strong form market inefficiency that we believe supports allocating the choice whether a hostile takeover goes forward to shareholders. To be sure, by highlighting the possibility of good faith but systematically misguided defensive action, the cognitive bias analysis does serve to give richness to the explanation for target managers' behavior that agency theory's simple self-interest paradigm lacks.[60] But this useful insight reinforces, rather than undercuts, an allocation of decision-making authority to shareholders.

VIII. CONCLUSION

So where does our retrospective leave us? Twenty years further, we think, along the road leading from elegant models of the workings of the capital market in a frictionless world, to an understanding of how the market operates in a world where information is costly and unevenly distributed, agents are self-interested, transactions costs are pervasive, and noise traders are common. The nature of this more realistic understanding is beginning to take shape, and it can be described in a single word: messy. There are a lot more moving parts with, as a result, a much larger number of interactions to understand. Models will be necessarily partial, illuminating particular interactions but far short, and without the ambition, of a unified field theory. That said, we come away with some confidence in a number of themes, some that were explicit in MOME, some that we missed, and others that reflect an assessment of the likely contribution of cognitive psychology to our understanding of how the capital market functions.

---

[60] To be sure, one can create a model in which this outcome may be different. For example, Andrei Shleifer and Robert Vishny proffered a model in which takeover activity in the 1970s, 1980s, and 1990s can be explained by market inefficiency. The model, however, makes some extreme assumptions. First, the market is assumed to be dramatically inefficient, either badly over or undervaluing a company's stock, while managers are assumed to be completely rational and understand precisely the way in which the market is inefficient and are also able to predict the long-term value of their companies and the companies they purchase. Next, the managers are assumed to maximize their personal objectives given their own time horizons. In effect, the model requires both market inefficiency and enormous agency costs (Shleifer and Vishny 2001). An effort to test empirically the Shleifer and Vishny model presents interesting results (Dong, Hirschleifer, Richardson, and Teoh 2003). While the paper's econometrics and results are too complicated to discuss in detail here, we note that the results are consistent both with some level of market irrationality and with a combination of bidder management agency behavior serving as a correcting signal of strong form inefficiency. In either event, the outcome does not speak in favor of allocating decision-making authority to target management.

First, as was explicit in MOME, we believe that understanding the structure of institutions is central to understanding the operation of the capital market. MOME's shortcoming was the failure to drill deeply enough into the incentive and agency structure of important market institutions like those through which arbitrage is carried out. To the large extent that behavioral finance is composed of applying agency information and incentive analysis to capital market institutions, it promises to deepen our understanding of how the capital market operates in the real world.

Secondly, we are sceptical that the new focus on cognitive biases in the end will explain very much about price formation, except in circumstances in which the biases of investor biases both coincide and give rise to increased participation. Thus, we expect that this component of behavioral finance will have a limited role in the market efficiency debate. In contrast, this literature can be quite important in circumstances where we care about the consequences of biased decision-making on the decision-makers themselves, independent of whether aggregate price levels are affected. Reform efforts directed at individuals' decisions with respect to pension investments, as with 401k, provide a good example.

Our final theme is one of balance. When cognitive psychology is used to analyse issues relating to the allocation of decision-making between competing parties, the application must be bilateral and comparative. Demonstrating one party's cognitive bias merely begins the analysis; to complete the analysis this bias must be compared to those of alternative decision-makers. As we suggested in our analysis of the application of cognitive bias analysis to tender offers, the fact that shareholders may have a bias in deciding whether to tender does not demonstrate that managers should have the power to block an offer. Rather, the shareholders' bias must be compared with those biases that affect management.

Twenty years after publication, we remain comfortable with the analytic framework that animates MOME. We should have been more sceptical of market institutions then, but scepticism grows with age.

REFERENCES

Allen, W.T. (2003), 'Securities Markets as Social Products: The Pretty Efficient Market Hypothesis', 28 *J. Corp. L.* 565.

Barberis, N. and Thaler, R. (2003), 'A Survey of Behavioural Finance', in *Handbook of the Economics of Finance* (George Constantinides, Milton Harris & Rene Stulz eds.) (Amsterdam/Boston: Elsevier/North-Holland).

Beaver, W. (1981), 'Market Efficiency', 56 *Acctng. Rev.* 23.

Bebchuk, L.A. (2002), 'The Case Against Board Veto in Corporate Takeovers', 69 *U. Chi. L. Rev.* 973.

Bernstein, P.L. (1992), *Capital Ideas: The Improbable Origins of Modern Wall Street* (New York: Free Press).

Bulow, J. and Klemperer, P.D. (1994), 'Rational Frenzies and Crashes', 112 *J. Pol. Econ.* 1.

Camerer, C., *et al.* (2003), 'Regulation for Conservatives: Behavioral Economics and the Case for "Asymmetric Paternalism"', 151 *U. Pa. L. Rev.* 1211 (2003).

Chen, J., Hong, H., and Stein, J. (2001), 'Forecasting Crashes: Trading Volume, Past Returns, and Conditional Skewness in Stock Prices', 61 *J. Fin. Econ.* 345.

Chen, N., Kim, R. and Miller, M. (1993a), 'Are Discounts on Closed-end Funds a Sentiment Index?' 48 *J. Fin.* 795.

Chen, N., Kim, R., and Miller, M. (1993b), 'Yes, Discounts on Closed-end Funds are a Sentiment Index: A Rejoinder', 48 *J. Fin.* 890.

Chen, N., Hong, H. and Stein, J. (2002), 'Breadth of Ownership and Stock Returns', 66 *J. Fin. Econ.* 171.

Chopra, N., Lee, C.M.C, Shleifer, A. and Thaler, R. (1993), 'Yes, Discounts on Closed-End Funds are a Sentiment Index', 48 *J. Fin.* 801.

Coase, R. (1960), The Problem of Social Cost, 3 *J.L. Econ.* 1.

Cochrane, J.H. (2003), 'New Facts in Finance', in *Handbook of the Economics of Finance* (George Constantinides, Milton Harris & Rene Stulz eds.) (Amsterdam/Boston: Elsevier/North-Holland).

Coffee, J.C. (2002), 'Understanding Enron: "It's About the Gatekeepers, Stupid"', 57 *Bus. Law.* 1403.

Cunningham, L.A. (2002), 'Behavioural Finance and Investor Governance', 59 *Wash. & Lee L. Rev.* 767.

D'Avolio, G. (2002), 'The Market for Borrowing Stock', 66 *J. Fin. Econ.* 271.

Dechow, P.M., Hutton, A.P., Meulbroek, L., and Sloan, R.G. (2001), 'Short-Sellers, Fundamental Analysis, and Stock Returns', 61 *J. Fin. Econ.* 77.

DeLong, J.B., Shleifer, A., Summers, L., and Waldman, R. (1990), 'Noise Trader Risk in Financial Markets', 98 *J. Pol. Econ.* 703.

—— (1990), 'Positive Feedback Investment Strategies and Destabilizing Rational Speculation', 45 *J. Fin.* 379.

Dong, M., Hirschleifer, D., Richardson, S., and Teoh, S.H. (2003), 'Does Investor Misvaluation Drive the Takeover Market', (EFA 2003 Annual Conference Paper No. 652; Dice Center Working Paper No. 2003-7) available at http://www.ssrn.com/abs=393021 (last visited 1 Aug. 2005).

Duffie, D., Gârleanu, N. and Pedersen, L.H. (2002), 'Securities Lending, Shorting, and Pricing', 66 *J.Fin. Econ.* 307.

Fama, E. (1970), 'Efficient Capital Markets: A Review of Theory and Empirical Work', 25 *J. Fin.* 283.

—— (1993), 'Common Risk Factors in the Return on Bonds and Stocks', 33 *J. Fin. Econ.* 3.

—— (1998), 'Market Efficiency, Long-Term Returns, and Behavioural Finance', 49 *J. Fin. Econ.* 283.

Fama, E. and French, K. (1996), 'Multifactor Explanations of Asset Pricing Anomalies', 51 *J. Fin.* 55.

Franks, R. *et al.* (2003), 'Scandal Scorecard: Executives on Trial', *Wall St. J.*, Oct. 3, at p. 1.

Geczy, C.C., Musto, D.A., and Reed, A.V. (2002), 'Stock are Special Too: An Analysis of the Equity Lending Market', 66 *J. Fin. Econ.* 241.

Gilson, R.J. (1984), 'Value Creation and Business Lawyers: Legal Skills and Asset Pricing', 94 *Yale L. J.* 23.

—— (2002a), 'Unocal Fifteen Years Later (and What We Can Do About It)', 26 *Del. J. Corp. L.* 491.

— (2002b), 'Lipton & Rowe's Apologia for Delaware: A Short Reply', 27 *Del. J. Corp. L.* 37.

Gilson, R.J. and Black, B. (1985), *The Law and Finance of Corporate Acquisitions* (Westbury, NY: Foundation Press).

Gilson, R.J., and Kraakman, R. (1984), 'The Mechanism of Market Efficiency', 70 *Va. L. Rev.* 549 (1984).

Grossman, S. and Stiglitz, J. (1980), 'On the Impossibility of Informationally Efficient Markets', 70 *Am. Econ. Rev.* 393.

Hirschliefer, D. (2001), 'Investor Psychology and Asset Pricing', 56 *J. Fin.* 1533.

Holstrom, B. and Tirole, J. (1989), 'The Theory of the Firm', in 1 *Handbook of Industrial Organization* 63 (Schmalansee & Willig eds.) (Amsterdam/Boston: Elsevier/North-Holland).

Hong, H., and Stein, J.C. (1999), 'A Unified Theory of Underreaction, Momentum Trading, and Overreaction in Asset Markets', 54 *J. Fin.* 2143.

Hong, H., Lim, T., and Stein, J. (2000), 'Bad News Travels Slowly: Size, Analyst Coverage, and the Profitability of Momentum Strategies', 55 *J. Fin.* 265.

Issacharoff, S. (1998), 'Can There Be a Behavioural Law and Economics', 51 *Vand. L. Rev.* 1729.

Jackson, H. (2003), 'To What Extent Should We Rely on the Mechanisms of Market Efficiency: A Preliminary Investigation of Dispersion in Individual Investor Returns', 28 *J. Corp. L.* 671.

Jensen, M. (1978), 'Some Anomalous Evidence Regarding Market Efficiency', 6 *J. Fin. Econ.* 95.

—— (1989), 'The Eclipse of the Public Corporation', *Harv. Bus. Rev.*, Sept.–Oct.

Jones, C.M. and Lasmont, O.A. (2002), 'Short-sale Constraints and Stock Returns', 66 *J. Fin. Econ.* 207.

Kahneman, D., Slovic, P., and Tversky, A. (1982), *Judgment Under Uncertainty: Heuristics and Biases* (Daniel Kahneman, Paul Slovic & Amos Tversky eds.) (Cambridge: CUP).

Kelman, M. (2003), 'Law and Behavioural Science: Conceptual Overviews', 97 *Nw. L. Rev.* 1347.

Koski, J.L. and Pontiff, J. (1999), 'How are Derivatives Used? Evidence from the Mutual Fund Industry', 54 *J. Fin.* 791 (1999).

Kraakman, R. (1988), 'Taking Discounts Seriously: The Implications of "Discounted" Share Prices as an Acquisition Motive', 88 *Col. L.Rev.* 891.

Lakonishok, J., Shleifer, A., and Vishny, R.M. (1994), 'Contrarian Investment, Extrapolation and Risk', 49 *J. Fin.* 1541.

Langevoort, D.C. (2002), 'Taming the Animal Spirits of the Stock Market: A Behavioural Approach to Securities Regulation', 97 *Nw. U. L. Rev.* 135.

Lee, C., Shleifer, A., and Thaler, R. (1991), 'Investment Sentiment and the Closed-End Fund Puzzle', 46 *J. Fin.* 75.

Lipton, M. (2002), 'Pills, Polls, and Professors Redux', 69 *U. Chi. L. Rev.* 1037.

Lipton, M. and Rowe, P. (2002), 'Pills, Polls and Professors: A Reply to Professor Gilson', 27 *J. Corp. L.* 1.

List, J.A. (2003), 'Does Market Experience Eliminate Market Anomalies', 118 *Q. J. Econ.* 41.

Llewellyn, K.N. (1950), 'Remarks on the Theory of Appellate Decision and the Rules or Canons About How Statutes are to be Construed', 3 *Vand. L. Rev.* [ ].

Macey, J.R., Mitchell, M., and Netter, J. (1989), 'Restrictions on Short Sales: An Analysis of the Uptick Rule and its Role in View of the October 1987 Stock Market Crash', 74 *Cornell L. Rev.* 799.

Mahoney, P.G. (2003), 'Market Microstructure and Market Efficiency', 28 *J. Corp. L.* 541.

Miller, M.H. (1988), 'The Modigliani-Miller Propositions After Thirty Years', 2 *J. Econ. Perspec.* 99.

Miller, M.H. and Modigliani, F. (1961), 'Dividend Policy, Growth, and the Valuation of Shares', 34 *J. Bus.* 411.

Modigliani, F. and Miller, M.H. (1958), 'The Cost of Capital, Corporation Finance, and the Theory of Investment', 48 *Am. Econ. Rev.* 655.

Phalippou, L. (2005), 'Institutional Ownership and Valuation Ratios', (EFA 2004 Maastricht Meetings Paper No. 3804), available as ssrn.com/sol3/papers.cfm?abstract_id=360760).

Powers, M., Schizer, D., and Shubik, M. (2003), 'Market Bubbles and Wasteful Avoidance: Tax and Regulatory Constraints on Short Sales', notes 35 & 40, Working Paper (available at http://ssrn.com/abstract=391020),

Roll, R. (1977), 'A Critique of Asset Pricing Theory's Tests', 4 *J. Fin. Econ.* 129.

Ross, S. (1976), 'The Arbitrage Pricing Theory of Capital Asset Pricing', 13 *J. Econ. Theory* 341.

Rubenstein, M. (2001), 'Rational Markets: Yes or No? The Affirmative Case', *Fin. Analysts J.*, May–June, at 15.

Scharfstein, D. and Stein, J. (1990), 'Herd Behaviour and Investment', 80 *Am. Econ. Rev.* 465.

Schwert, G.W. (2003), 'Anomalies and Market Efficiency', in *Handbook of the Economics of Finance* (George Constantinides, Milton Harris & Rene Stulz eds.) (Amsterdam/Boston: Elsevier/North-Holland).

SEC (2003), 'Implications of the Growth of Hedge Funds', Staff Report to the United States Securities and Exchange Commission 41 (Sept.).

Sharpe, W. (1964), 'Capital Asset Prices: A Theory of Market Equilibrium Under Conditions of Risk', 19 *J. Fin.* 425.

Sharpe, W.F. (1970), 'Discussion', 25 *J. Fin.* 418.

—— (1991), 'Capital Asset Prices with and without Negative Holdings' (Dec. 7).

Shleifer, A. (2000), *Inefficient Markets*.

—— (2000), *Inefficient Markets: An Introduction to Behavioral Finance* (Oxford: Clarendon Press).

Shleifer, A, and Summers, L. (1990), 'The Noise Trader Approach to Finance', 4 *J. Econ. Perspec.* 19.

Shleifer, A. and Vishny, R. (1997), 'The Limits of Arbitrage', 52 *J. Fin.* 35.

—— (2001), 'Stock Market Driven Acquisitions' (National Bureau of Economic Research Working Paper No. 8439).

Stout, L. (2003), 'The Mechanisms of Market Efficiency: An Introduction to the New Finance', 28 *J. Corp. L.* 635.

'The Symposium on Empirical Legal Realism: A New Social Scientific Assessment of Law and Human Behaviour', 97 *Nw. L. Rev.* No. 2 (2003),

Tversky, A. and Kahneman, D. (1974), 'Judgment Under Uncertainty: Heuristics and Biases', 185 *Science* 1124.

Zwiebel, J. (1995), 'Corporate Conservatism, Herd Behaviour and Relative Compensation', 103 *J. Pol. Econ.* 1 (1995).

—— (2002), 'Review of Shleifer's Inefficient Markets', 40 *J. Econ Lit.* 1215 (2002).

2

Taming the Animal Spirits of the Stock Markets: A Behavioural Approach to Securities Regulation

DONALD C LANGEVOORT[*]

[Our decisions] to do something positive . . . can only be taken as a result of animal spirits . . . and not as the outcome of a weighted average of quantitative benefits multiplied by quantitative probabilities.

—Keynes (1936: 131).

T HE RECENT ENRON bankruptcy is one of those rare events that brings corporate and securities law close to sustained public attention.[1] It has shaken confidence that the prevailing legal norms work as well as we want, or that the marketplace imposes the kind of discipline we have assumed. Among its many puzzles is one about the stock markets. How was the market for such a widely-followed stock so easily fooled, especially when (in hindsight, at least) warning signs about obscure accounting, risk-shifting, and self-dealing practices were visible?

To a sceptic about the stock markets, the Enron debacle comes as no surprise. It was an issuer-specific stock bubble, different from countless predecessors only in terms of its size and the political attention it gained. The market fell in love with the company and, like many lovers, was far too slow to realize that the object of devotion was cheating. Keynes's

* Professor of Law, Georgetown University Law Center. Work on this chapter was supported by the Georgetown-Sloan Program on Business Institutions. Many thanks to Mitu Gulati, Kim Krawiec, Bill Bratton, Frank Partnoy, Claire Hill, and workshop participants at Boalt Hall, the University of San Diego, the University of Iowa, and the Australian Corporate Law Teachers Association for helpful comments. This chapter was previously published in (2002) 97 Northwestern University Law Review 135–187.

[1] A fairly good description of the key events underlying the rapid demise of Enron can be found in the Report of the Special Committee of the Board of Directors, chaired by University of Texas Law School Dean William Powers. See Enron Corp. (2002); BNA (2002a). For academic commentary, see Gordon (2002) and Bratton (2002).

animal spirits were at work. The ones with the explaining to do are the believers in market efficiency, especially those whose faith is so strong in its miraculous healing powers that they think legally mandated disclosure has little role to play in investor protection.[2]

It is much too early to judge whether any plausible rational explanation is available as to Enron in particular, though no doubt some will be offered. Instead, this chapter seeks more general answers in the increasingly sophisticated debate over the validity of the efficient market hypothesis (EMH), the most venerable tenet of financial economics and a staple of contemporary legal analysis. In the form most often invoked by legal academics, the EMH teaches that the prices of the stocks of actively traded companies, like Enron, rapidly adjust to reflect the rational expectations generated by all available information as it becomes available. Stocks are consistently 'rationally' priced, in other words. But faith in the EMH among economists has been weakening for some time.[3] That is not new news; by the mid-1980s, the notion of market efficiency was already under attack by finance scholars of considerable prominence.[4] Since then, however, the battle has turned into something akin to a siege. Critics are still increasing in visibility and numbers and seldom does an edition of one of the best finance journals appear without at least one or two major papers offering theoretical or empirical claims inconsistent with strong views of efficiency. Yet, the orthodox EMH adherents are far from dead and still claim sizable numbers on their side.[5] As often happens with long sieges, if we look closely we see a good bit of intermarrying occurring as scholars quietly redefine efficiency or inefficiency in a way that mediates between the two camps.[6]

---

[2] See, e.g., Easterbrook and Fischel (1984).

[3] For a good current articulation, see the debate between Kothari (2001) and Lee (2001). Economists test for market efficiency largely by assessing speed of adjustment of stock prices to new information (so-called 'informational efficiency'). The assumption of the rationality of stock prices underlying the adjustment is harder to test. See below note 17.

[4] For an extensive, but now somewhat dated, literature review, see LeRoy (1989). The work of Robert Shiller was (and still is) seminal in the critiques of market efficiency. For a collection of his early work, see Shiller (1989). I used this literature in my first look at the relevance of the efficiency debate to securities regulation. See Langevoort (1992). For another early effort in the legal literature, see Cunningham (1994).

[5] For the standard recent account, see Fama (1998). For a balanced and thoughtful review from the pro-efficiency side, see Rubenstein (2001); see also Kothari (2001). For a fairly neutral evaluation of the state of the literature, both rational and non-rational, see Campbell (2000).

[6] See Brav and Heaton (2002) (observing that the differences are small between what behavioral theories predict and what models based on rationality but incomplete information predict); Rubenstein (2001: 17–18) (taking a strong pro-efficiency view, but also stating that investors are systematically overconfident, which leads to much more disagreement and trading than that which would be produced in a perfectly rational world).

In this chapter, I will explore this debate, which—as Enron shows—is profoundly important to legal academics.[7] What I especially want to draw from is the most interesting development in the past decade from the EMH critics' camp. It is one thing to attack market efficiency simply by showing that empirical reality does not conform to its predictions or by offering explanations for the inconsistency. It is a more ambitious task, both empirically and theoretically, to build an alternative model of market pricing. If so-called irrational activity is simply random and unpredictable, then markets are nothing more than noisy.

However, if the nonrational properties of the securities markets reflect predictable behavioral tendencies—in other words, that the animal spirits that seemingly drive the markets are well grounded in cognitive and social psychology—then there is something more to say that might be useful to the task of securities regulation. While psychological explanations for market behavior have been offered since the early days of the critical finance literature,[8] the last few years have seen this field mature into a subject area with a name—'behavioral finance.'[9]

Securities regulation is an especially important subject in which to take measure of the behavioral claims, for two reasons. First, as has been repeatedly said about the now-flourishing subject of behavioral law and economics, there is a natural difficulty in extending what is observed in artificial laboratory experiments to the real world, with its Darwinian incentive structure, rich institutional context, and opportunities for learning from experience.[10] Empirical testing for the presence of bias in most real economic settings is difficult, because we lack an extensive enough set of data. But as finance scholars have shown, one important characteristic of the financial markets is that they generate extensive data. Due to this transparency, behavioral finance is somewhat better positioned to test the real world impact of bias in market prices than research in more opaque economic settings. It is still not easy, but if empirical headway is to be made anywhere in behavioral law and economics, it is likely to be made here.

The second reason is found in the oft-repeated claim that the capital markets are the ideal settings for efficiency. They are liquid and transparent, and offer immense competitive rewards. If the capital markets are not efficient, it is difficult to imagine many other markets that

---

[7] For the classic law-oriented study of efficiency in the capital markets, see Gilson and Kraakman (1984).

[8] David Dreman (1979) was an early and persistent proponent of the psychology of investing as grounds for a contrarian investment strategy.

[9] For book-length treatments of behavioral finance, see Shleifer (2000); Shefrin (2000). Robert Shiller has focused again on behavioral theories in his recent book (Shiller 1999). For a readable and entertaining study of the history of risk analysis, particularly as it relates to the stock markets, touching on the behavioral materials, see Bernstein (1998: chs. 16–17).

[10] See Posner (1998); Arlen (1998). But see below note 29.

would be.[11] The securities markets (and securities regulation) are a natural crucible for the research agenda of behavioral law and economics generally.

Hence, I offer the following set of exercises in 'behavioral securities regulation.'[12] I cannot try to resolve, or even contribute much to, what still is a contested empirical battle. But we can try to think through how best to formulate securities law in the face of the increasing uncertainty. To this end, Part I begins by reviewing the critical literature from the last decade, taking stock of the main points of contention. Then, Part II turns cautiously to the normative problems. It is unsatisfying simply to say that if the critics of market efficiency are right, then those aspects of securities law (or securities law scholarship) that rely on strong efficiency claims are wrong. That may be so, but the point is unlikely to be of much interest to those unpersuaded by the assumption. Positive strategies for regulation are hard to craft precisely because the alternative behavioral theories in the literature are so tentative.

To finesse this problem, I take a slightly different path. One of the initial appeals of the once-upon-a-time new genre of law and economics was not so much that it led to clear-cut normative solutions, but rather that it offered thought-provoking new ways of looking at problems. This article is in that same spirit. There are many vexing problems in securities law that might benefit from consideration of fresh possibilities, which generate new lines of thinking if not obvious answers. Judges and regulators often make bets with their behavioral predictions. What follows is simply the case for factoring psychology into the odds.

Part III explores internet securities fraud. There have been celebrated allegations of people moving markets through brief chat room postings that, at first glance, defy explanation. The most obvious intuition, extreme gullibility on the part of investors, is possible but unlikely. Here, I consider the role of a particular cognitive bias, overconfidence, in order to develop a more plausible story of what was going on, reorienting how we might respond.

Part IV examines securities analysts and the phenomenon of 'selective disclosure'—companies secretly giving inside information to analysts. Conventionally, this practice engenders a battle between efficiency and

---

[11] See Hogarth and Reder (1986: S199–200).

[12] For other behavioral securities regulation work dealing largely with market pricing, see Thompson (1997); Bainbridge (2000). In addition to this focus on behavioral finance, the research agenda in behavioral securities regulation attends to a number of issues unrelated to market efficiency. For example, the research agenda explores the behavior of corporate managers in making disclosure decisions, see Langevoort (1997), and stockbroker-customer sales interactions, see Langevoort (1996). I apologize, by the way, to those psychologists who object to the term 'behavioral' in this context—claiming that it refers to the now largely abandoned research program associated with B.F. Skinner—and believe that 'cognitive' is the better word. See Rachlinski (2000: 740). They are right, but the behavioral label has stuck in both law and finance.

fairness. But a large body of work has emerged within the critical finance literature about analyst biases which, if we take it seriously, changes the nature of this battle. More subtly, however, the debate explicitly reintroduces into securities regulation doubts about the rationality of individual investors. If cognitive biases really exist and are more pronounced among individuals than institutions, this says something about how markets should be designed and structured.

Finally, Part V explores open-market securities fraud and how we might rethink both our definition of 'materiality' and the way we devise remedies when markets are less than rational or efficient. The payoff here is that a vision of even mildly inefficient markets can help us see just how fruitless the current approach to remedies truly is.

I. THE INEFFICIENCY HYPOTHESIS AND BEHAVIOURAL FINANCE

The research agenda for critics of market efficiency proceeds in a series of steps. The initial step is the foundation—empirical studies that demonstrate that the markets are not behaving in accordance with the predictions of the efficient market hypothesis. The second step entails the creation of alternative models or theories of stock price behavior, with some explanation of why they might generate more plausible predictions than the efficiency account. Here is where psychology sometimes comes into play—to the extent that the new models are based on fairly sophisticated understandings of how human beings act, their plausibility increases.[13] Empirical testing can then determine which models fit the data better. These alternative theories, in turn, focus on two distinct questions. First, what forces drive stock prices out of line with rational expectations? Secondly, why doesn't rational arbitrage[14] promptly bring prices back to the rational expectations equilibrium? This introductory section does not undertake an exhaustive overview of any of these steps. Reviews of each are now readily available in the finance literature, including some book-length treatments.[15] My aim here is simply to describe some of the more intriguing and well-supported ideas from what I will refer to as the inefficient market hypothesis (IMH) literature

---

[13] See Shleifer (2000: 10–11). For a comprehensive survey, see Hirshleifer (2001). For a brief survey, see Daniel and Titman (1999: 28).

[14] Arbitrage is the process by which informed traders buy or sell in such a way as to eliminate any mispricing caused by uninformed trading. For example, when a stock becomes overvalued because uninformed traders are bidding it up, informed traders would sell, hence moving the price back to its rational expectations equilibrium.

[15] See above note 9.

that might inspire a constructive theory of behavioral securities regulation.[16]

A. Evidence Against Market Efficiency

The Sunday, 3 May 1998 edition of the *New York Times* carried a front-page story about EntreMed, a biotechnology company with licensing rights to an exciting medical breakthrough. As a result of this conspicuous media attention, EntreMed's stock price rose dramatically and stayed at the higher valuation, as did (to a somewhat lesser degree) the prices of related biotech stocks. What is puzzling about this phenomenon is that the *Times* article contained absolutely no 'new news': everything in it had already been said, albeit with less prominence, in earlier stories in the *Times* and in widely-respected scientific publications.

Most people, including many in the investment industry, would hardly be surprised by the possibility that media attention alone can drive stock prices. To conventional financial economists and their many followers in the legal community, however, this is implausible because old news (i.e., no news) cannot have a sustainable stock price impact. The EMH states that stock prices promptly impound all available information. Under most formulations of the EMH, this impoundment reflects market participants' rational expectations, so that stock prices are 'fundamentally' efficient.[17]

A number of important conclusions follow from a belief in fundamental efficiency. Most importantly, once new information is impounded in the stock price, subsequent price movements must stem from some new or different information, as there is no basis for inferring the direction or magnitude of future price movements simply from the observation of past movements. More generally, the EMH states that it will be impossible to make money on any sustained basis by trying to discover 'undervalued' or 'overvalued' stocks, unless one expects repeatedly to be the first to discover or infer new, heretofore nonpublic information.[18] Very few people have the experience, contacts, resources

[16] To avoid undue repetition, I will concentrate on work published since my review of this literature (Langevoort 1992).

[17] A distinction between informational and fundamental efficiency is often mentioned. Most tests of market efficiency emphasize speed of adjustment (informational efficiency), without purporting to demonstrate that the adjustment is based on rational expectations. By and large, economic theory—or different sorts of empirical tests—is invoked to justify the further step that the adjustment is rational. As such, mere informational efficiency is not necessarily inconsistent with the view that stock prices can over- or under-react to information. See Lev and deVilliers (1994).

[18] A somewhat more realistic appraisal is that markets have a high (but not perfect) degree of efficiency: the residual inefficiency is that which makes it profitable for analysts and other professional investors to stay in business. See Grossman and Stiglitz (1980).

and skill to hold that expectation reasonably. The vast majority of us should be passive investors, holding risk-adjusted portfolios designed to seek normal market returns and minimize our trading costs.

The EntreMed story—recently explored by two Columbia economists in their field's leading journal—is but one of many efficiency-defying anomalies that have been unearthed since the late 1970s by finance researchers (Huberman and Regev 2001).[19] There are scores of such anomalies, which have provoked spirited debates as to whether they truly are violations of the EMH, or whether instead there might be some explanation that preserves the validity of the theory. What is impressive in the case against market efficiency is not the strength of any individual claim, but their aggregate weight. As one proponent of market efficiency conceded recently, '[t]he weight of paper in academic journals supporting anomalies is now much heavier than the evidence to the contrary' (Rubenstein 2001: 15). If far from dead, market efficiency is at least more contestable than ever.

There are many interesting anomalies. Some of the first doubts about the EMH arose out of observations that stock markets are more volatile and generate more trading volume than the EMH would predict. Theoretically, a rational person would hesitate to trade aggressively against the prevailing consensus without private access to nonpublic information, but such trading occurs with extraordinary frequency. In fact, many significant market swings occur without any obvious new information—the market 'break' of 1987 being one of the more closely examined.[20]

There are also puzzling studies of individual stocks and industries. The EntreMed example is one, and Enron will likely soon be another. Likewise, a recent study shows that much of the price movement in the Massmutual Corporate Investors closed-end fund is due to investors mistakenly confusing its ticker symbol (MCI) when they respond to information released by MCI Communications (MCIC).[21] The recent technology stock 'bubble' provides many more examples.[22]

For our purposes, however, the most interesting work is that which challenges the primary prediction of the EMH: that prices promptly and rationally impound all available information, so that subsequent price

---

[19] This article aims to rule out all plausible rational explanations for what happened. In securities regulation, the frequency of insider trading cases in which people steal advance copies (or trade with knowledge) of forthcoming publications that will mention individual issuers favorably or unfavorably is further testimony to the belief that publicity alone can influence stock prices. e.g., *US v Carpenter*, 791 F.2d 1024 (2d Cir. 1986) (*Wall Street Journal's* 'Heard on the Street' column); *US v Libera*, 989 F.2d 586 (2d Cir. 1993) (*Business Week* advance copies).

[20] e.g., Stiglitz (1990: 17). See generally Partnoy (2000).

[21] See Rashes (2001).

[22] See Ofek and Richardson (2001); see also below text accompanying notes 87–92.

movements are independent of their antecedents. A large body of research rejects this prediction and finds ample evidence of 'momentum' in stock prices; price moves in one direction or another are frequently followed by a continuation in that direction, without any 'new news' to justify that trend.[23] Unfortunately for those who seek simplicity, this momentum can take two very different forms. First, especially with the case of newly-publicized accounting data, there is a slow, but sustained adjustment of the price.[24] Thus, it takes some time for the stock price to 'drift' to a level that reflects the information in question. In such an instance, the market price underreacts to the information. Secondly, there is a quick, but excessive reaction to the new information, sending the price to a level that is either too high or too low. Eventually, the price reverts to a more reasonable value. This phenomenon is referred to as the overreaction hypothesis, called 'positive feedback' trading when describing the creation of price bubbles.[25]

These are both important observations, because they suggest that at any given time, a stock price will often not be identical to rational expectations about its fundamental value. Important conclusions flow from this concept for both corporate and securities law, and we shall examine a few of these shortly. However, it is important not to overstate the evidence. One of the drivers in the market efficiency debate is the search for investment strategies that consistently deliver above-average, risk-adjusted returns. Such strategies, according to the EMH, do not exist apart from the repeated discovery of new material information. If over- or underreaction could be keyed with some predictability to an observable triggering event, then a profitable investment strategy would be present. Investors should bet against the trend when overreaction is likely, but bet with the trend when underreaction is indicated. To date, some contrarian strategies have been identified that would have, at least during the time-period under observation, delivered superior returns.[26] But there is no compelling evidence that simple strategies along these lines remain exploitable on a sustained basis. Some of the more moderate supporters of market efficiency point to this lack of evidence as definitive proof that gradually someone will discover and eliminate whatever anomalies might exist, so that the market is at least 'long-term' efficient.[27] Critics, in turn, reply that the absence of obviously profitable investment strategies simply reflects the highly situational nature of things like over- and underreaction. Their unpredictability in terms of both extent and duration renders it too difficult to exploit these anomalies consistently

---

[23] See, e.g., Hong *et al.* (2000); Chan *et al.* (1996).
[24] See Bernard and Thomas (1989).
[25] See, e.g., Shleifer (2000: ch. 6).
[26] See Grundy and Martin (2001); Jegadeesh and Titman (2001).
[27] See, e.g., Campbell (2000: 1557–58).

without bearing excessive risk. Somewhere in the middle of these views are finance theorists like Fischer Black, a Nobel Prize winner, who conjectured early in the debate (Black 1986) that stock prices simply wander within a range that varies from roughly half their fundamental value to twice that value—nothing approaching a faithful vision of efficiency, but not entirely removed from it either.

B. The Psychology of Market Price Movements

Behavioural finance is an effort to build new and different models of stock price behavior that better fit the observable data. The element of psychology in such models proceeds from the assumption that important forms of human behavior are unlikely to be 'washed out' in the financial markets as conventional economists have long assumed. Large numbers of so-called noise traders and investors buy and sell stock. If their cognitive biases are systematic enough, they will have an impact on prices that others do not arbitrage away. Thus, the models are constructed by reference to the many sorts of biases that have been identified in the explosion of work on investor judgment and decision-making that has occurred over the last thirty years or so.[28]

As with the literature about stock price anomalies, the research connecting psychology and finance has become too voluminous to catalogue here.[29] Commentators have considered virtually every well-recognized bias some way or another, as well as some less obvious ones. Finance scholars, for example, have found evidence that moods triggered by good or bad weather can affect stock prices on a given day.[30] However, I want to concentrate on four biases on which finance scholars have built the most visible and sustained research efforts, with special emphasis on the last bias—the phenomenon of investor over-confidence.

The first of these biases, and the one with the most distinguished pedigree in the cognitive bias literature, is loss aversion. People appear to approach risk-taking differently depending on the framing of the choice before them. When evaluating a potential gain, people exhibit a strong degree of risk aversion. But if prompted to see the choice as one of trying to avoid a loss of that which is currently possessed, people tend to be more risk-seeking. Thus, there could be differences in investors' risk-taking approaches in buying versus selling stocks. We might expect

[28] See Kahneman and Riepe (1998). In addition to the finance studies on which we will focus, there has been an explosion in laboratory studies that seek to replicate features of the financial markets. See, e.g., Ganguly *et al.* (2000).

[29] See Hirshleifer (2001).

[30] See Saunders (1993); Hirshleifer (2001: 1560).

people to hold on to their losing stocks too long, and sell their winners too readily.[31]

A prominent behavioral model incorporates loss aversion with an interesting twist. Drawing on prior work sometimes described as the 'house money effect,' Barberis, Huang, and Santos argue that one's degree of loss aversion will vary depending on recent prior performance (Barberis *et al.* 2001).[32] If one has recently enjoyed gains, 'possession' effects do not operate as strongly; people are willing to take considerable risks with 'found money.' On the other hand, when one has suffered recent losses, people are reluctant to gamble much unless it is necessary to preserve what they have left. This suggests that after a run up in prices, people become more aggressive—one reason why we might observe greater volatility than traditional models might suggest.

The next two biases seem to present opposing tendencies (Barberis *et al.* 2001).[33] Cognitive conservatism is an extremely robust behavioral construct showing that people change their views slowly even in the face of persuasive evidence. In other words, people cling as long as possible to what they previously believed. This bias could be the basis for the underreaction phenomenon described earlier. However, under some circumstances, this tendency is reversed, as new information has an excessive effect on judgment, prompting overreaction. This could be explained by the 'representativeness' effect, under which people's attentions are distracted from the baseline. Much work in psychology and finance tries to reconcile these conflicting tendencies.[34] One possible reconciliation relates the new information to the pattern of prior news events. Another centres on the salience of the new information.[35] When the investor receives the new information in a particularly dramatic way, for example, it might be overweighted; when it is presented normally, it is not, so that cognitive conservatism controls the process of inference. Salience would explain the EntreMed story. The ever-increasing volume of media coverage of investment information—on the internet, cable TV, and in the financial press—means that some stories will gain substantial saliency, while others will be buried under a heavy load of other information.[36]

While media attention is a well-recognized influence, many IMH scholars contend that the most underexplored aspect of behavioral

---

[31] See Odean (1998a); Shefrin and Statman (1985).

[32] See also Barberis and Huang (2001).

[33] See Shleifer (2000: 128–30).

[34] See Hong and Stein (1999); Nicholas Barberis *et al.* (1998); Michaely *et al.* (1995). For work in the options market, see Poteshman (2001).

[35] See Klibanoff *et al.* (1999).

[36] In addition, increases in demand—for whatever reason—may themselves start bandwagon effects, even if no other information is conveyed. See Shiller (1999: 60–2).

finance is informal social contact among investors.[37] It is very likely that investors affect each other not simply by trading, but through conversations, including internet-based talk,[38] and other forms of social influence.[39] Hence, it is possible that further research will be able to document an 'epidemiology' of investor behavior—tracking the contagion of excitement or panic within embedded communities of traders. That research eventually may help us understand better, if not predict, why information becomes overweighted in some circumstances while similar information is underweighted in others.

Although loss aversion, cognitive conservatism, and representativeness are mainstream subjects in behavioral finance, the last of our four has gained a particularly high level of prominence in recent years: the phenomenon of investor overconfidence. In an oft-repeated quotation in the finance literature, De Bondt and Thaler state that 'perhaps the most robust finding in the psychology of judgment is that people are overconfident' (De Bondt and Thaler 1995: 385-6). People have a strong tendency to have greater faith in their intuitions and judgments than the evidence warrants.[40] They put too much weight on their privately-acquired information or inference, and calibrate poorly even when they realize the presence of some uncertainty. This bias has a comparative dimension to it: people are overconfident in their skills vis-a-vis others. Indeed, far more than fifty per cent of a sampling of active investors will rate themselves as above average as compared to their peers at the task of investing.[41] Notably, there is an interesting gender element at work here: overconfidence is dominantly a male trait.[42]

This bias of investor overconfidence is a popular subject of study among economists, including some conventional ones,[43] for a few reasons. First, much observable economic behavior seems hard to explain except by reference to a hubris hypothesis. The volume of corporate takeover activity is an example, as winning bidders consistently pay high premiums for what often turn out to be unprofitable acquisitions.[44] Secondly, there is an interesting evolutionary story behind the bias, which

[37] See Shiller (1999: 153–62); Hirshleifer (2001: 1552–53, 1577); Shiller and Pound (1989). For some early efforts in this direction, see Baker (1984); Klausner (1984). See generally Ellison and Fundenberg (1995).

[38] See below Part III.

[39] Of substantial relevance here is work on rumours among investors. See DiFazio and Bordia (1997).

[40] See Odean (1998b). For a review of the psychology literature, see Griffin and Varey (1999). For a linking of overconfidence with corporate disclosure policy, see Langevoort (1997).

[41] See Moore *et al.* (1999: 97). Interestingly, the authors demonstrate that people overrate their past performance, as well as their future prospects.

[42] See Barber and Odean (2000a).

[43] See Rubenstein (2001: 17–18).

[44] See Roll (1986); see also Camerer and Lovallo (1999).

appeals to economists.[45] Illusions of control and overoptimism are associated with a variety of positive outcomes: greater willingness to take risk, more persistence in the face of adversity, etc. One can readily see why being unrealistically confident, within moderation, can lead to greater success, even if it also leads to more mistakes as well. Those who bear greater risk are compensated for it, on average. Indeed, when they are also beneficiaries of a streak of good luck, we might expect that highly successful people—an important group in the world of investing—might be particularly infused with hubris.[46]

Finally, and most importantly, there is an increasing body of empirical evidence that directly supports investor overconfidence as an important trait. In what became a widely-reported study, Barber and Odean (2000) studied the investment performance of a large number of online brokerage accounts, which are held by those who think they can make their own trading decisions without the assistance of a stockbroker as adviser and have been the fastest growing segment of the brokerage industry over the last few years. What the researchers found is that the rate of trading increased once the accounts were established, especially after an initial spurt of good performance (or good luck). Notwithstanding this increasing volume of trading, overall average performance lagged behind what a more passive, well-diversified trading strategy would generate. Not surprisingly, almost all of the lag could be traced to the costs (e.g., commissions) associated with active trading. The authors state their conclusion simply: 'Overconfident investors will overestimate the value of their private information, causing them to trade too actively and, consequently, to earn below-average returns' (*ibid.*: 800).

Overconfidence is notably dynamic in character. Another long-recognized trait in human behavior, 'biased self-attribution,' is the tendency to take credit for positive results, but externalise blame for bad results. This tendency is one reason that people learn poorly from experience, as people are not willing to recognize that their failures stem from a lack of competence or skill. As a result, people will attribute a streak of good luck as skill and will attribute a run of losses to bad luck or someone else's fault. Thus, when prices rise and investors gain from that alone, their investment decisions are readily self-characterizable as talent, which in turn will promote even more aggressive trading. Downswings will not have a comparable cautionary influence.[47] In recent years, academics have developed several different behavioral finance models on overconfidence and biased self-attribution. Perhaps the best known is by

---

[45] For a formalization of this idea, see Benabou and Tirole (2002). For applications in the financial markets, see Kyle and Wang (1997); Benos (1998).

[46] See Gervais and Odean (2001).

[47] Obviously, there are many parallels here with gambling behavior. See Statman (2002). For a legal discussion linking these two phenomena, see Gabaldon (2001).

Daniel, Hirshleifer, and Subrahmanyam (1998), who explicitly use a dynamic model that assumes that overconfident traders overreact to private informational signals but underreact to those which are public. This allows them to reconcile the observed underreaction and overreaction phenomena.[48]

C. The Limits of the Smart Money: Arbitrage and Advice

The behavioral models discussed above only predict that cognitive biases systematically affect the decision-making of some investors, and that these biases could potentially affect stock prices. But these models do not, for the most part, address what has long been the economists' trump card: 'smart money' forces in the market are likely to counter. This countering takes two main forms. First, and far and away the most important, smart money will arbitrage away any noisy price movements that have no fundamental rationality. Secondly, sophisticated institutions will offer investment advice and analysis to the unsophisticated in a way that will 'de-bias' many of them. Each of these, not surprisingly, has received substantial attention in the IMH literature.

1. Arbitrage

The standard EMH argument states that if irrational price moves were to occur, rational investors would quickly see that the stock has become over- or undervalued vis-a-vis its fundamentals and trade accordingly. This contrarian trading would promptly move back the price to its rational expectations level.

Yet, the literature critical of market efficiency has built a substantial case against the likelihood of fully effective arbitrage on two main fronts.[49] First, there are significant limits on the ability to arbitrage away an inflated price because the principal technique needed to do so—short-selling—is both legally and practically difficult.[50] Secondly, if neither the extent nor the duration of the irrational impulses can be determined with accuracy ex ante, then arbitrage is a very risky bet to make. The irrationality may persist for some time. For a variety of reasons, the smart money will hesitate to make this bet and may sometimes prefer an alternative strategy, such as playing the momentum game by buying in the face of an irrational price increase, so long as the

---

[48] See also Bloomfield *et al.* (2000).

[49] See Shleifer (2000: 13–16); Shleifer and Vishny (1997). For a perspective integrating overconfidence and the arbitrage problem, see Daniel *et al.* (2001).

[50] This is not to say that short-selling is not at least partially effective as a counter to noise trading. See Dechow *et al.* (2001); Macey *et al.* (1989).

buying occurs early enough and the investor is disciplined enough to sell before the noise traders do.[51] That strategy, too, is risky, but may result in the higher expected payoff. The consequence is that the price swing is exacerbated, not countered.

Somewhat more aggressively, some behavioral critics have also cast doubts on the rational decision-making of professional investors, an idea that shall be explored in more depth below in our discussion of the investment analyst. Notably, there is substantial evidence of herding by professionals.[52] However, whether psychological reasons provide a better explanation for such evidence, as opposed to an explanation reflecting the skewed economic incentives faced by portfolio managers (thereby raising a conventional agency cost problem),[53] remains a challenging question. Most accounts emphasize rational limitations more than the irrational and assume that institutions exploit noise trader biases, albeit incompletely.[54]

2. Investment Analysts

Investment analysts have long been identified in both law and economics as a strong positive force in market efficiency. Analysts are paid (handsomely) to do investment research, and fall into two rough categories. 'Buy-side' analysts work for institutional investors, like mutual funds and pension funds, as part of a portfolio management team. Their success in investment analysis redounds solely to their private clients. 'Sell-side' analysts work for brokerage firms and typically publish their guidance publicly. The public nature of their estimates and recommendations is meant to influence the retail segment of the investing public. Various services, such as First Call, aggregate sell-side analyst advice in the form of consensus estimates and recommendations, so that savvy investors can get a sense of either agreement or dispersion from a broad range of analysis.

Because buy-side advice is private, one can only observe its effects by examining the performance of the large institutional investors who, by law, must make performance data available to their investors or beneficiaries. While much of this research shows that institutional investors, on average, underperform market indices, so that the large sums of money spent on analysis are essentially wasted, this is not necessarily an argument against market efficiency. To the contrary,

---

[51] See Shleifer (2000: 174).
[52] See Scharfstein and Stein (1990); Wermers (1999). For a behavioral view, see DeLong *et al.* (1991).
[53] See Chevalier and Ellison (1999).
[54] See Gompers and Metrick (2001); Nofsinger and Sias (1999).

proponents usually offer it as part of the EMH case.[55] Most commonly, this wastefulness is seen as an agency-cost issue, however, not evidence of the cognitive biases of buy-side managers.[56] The one point of relevance here involves the incentives of portfolio managers. To the extent that these managers are evaluated on a periodic basis against their peers, they have less of an incentive to take long-term risky bets against the direction of the market. As noted earlier, this agency-cost problem is often cited as one reason that smart money arbitrage is less powerful than might otherwise be expected.[57]

Research has focused more on sell-side analysts because their recommendations are publicly available.[58] The 1990s were not kind to analysts, in the finance literature at least. Prior to that point, there was a strong assumption that analysts and their employers had such strong reputational incentives that they could not afford to be anything but diligent and unbiased in their research. If so, investors would be justified in following analyst recommendations, supporting their role as efficiency-drivers.[59]

But a decade of work, both empirical and theoretical, has taken issue with this conclusion. Some studies are explicitly behavioral. A number of researchers offer evidence of analyst overconfidence,[60] as well as other biases.[61] But as noted above, researchers have mainly emphasized agency-cost problems. The primary concern involves conflicts of interest. Multi-service investment banks make considerable amounts of money from corporate finance activities for issuer clients. The analysts might thus be pressured to be unduly favorable to current or potential clients, with the revenue from those tasks outweighing the reputational risk from the biased advice.[62] After Enron and related scandals, Congress and securities regulators became sufficiently concerned about this particular conflict such that they added new layers of rules to counteract it and they brought enforcement actions where the evidence indicated serious distortion in the way recommendations were formulated.[63] Even when investment banking conflicts are not present, a second concern arises involving the analysts' access to information. The easiest and most

[55] e.g., Rubenstein (2001: 20–21).
[56] Indeed, recent evidence shows that mutual funds do pick stocks reasonably well, but that the costs charged to their customers remove all the abnormal return. See Wermers (2000).
[57] See sources cited above note 53.
[58] See, e.g., Easterwood and Nutt (1999); Womack (1996); Chopra (1998).
[59] Though as just observed, any assessment that sell-side analyst recommendations have investment value is itself an IMH point. The EMH postulates that what analysts learn is impounded in market price before the recommendations are made public.
[60] See Hirshleifer *et al.* (1994); Hilary and Menzly (2001).
[61] See Fisher and Statman (2000: 72).
[62] e.g., Michaely and Womack (1999); Carleton *et al.* (1998). For a sociological perspective, see Hayward and Boeker (1998).
[63] See BNA (2002b: 1624).

reliable source of nonpublic information is through private contacts with issuer officials, and the insider trading laws were for a long time at least ambiguous as to whether such contacts were lawful. Because of the ambiguity, the enforcement risk was minimal. Under those circumstances, it would be rational for the analyst to trade off some skewing of the advice in a positive direction in order to keep channels of communication open.[64]

Having identified these two kinds of conflicts, the researchers' task becomes one of evaluating empirically the actual performance of the analysts. Superficially, at least, one glaring concern emerged: in the aggregate, buys substantially outnumbered sells, with the imbalance becoming more pronounced throughout the decade. The presence of an investment banking relationship did indeed exacerbate the bias. As a whole, the analyst community was heavily pushing technology stocks up through the time the technology bubble deflated. Yet, in all fairness, the empirical data is not entirely critical.[65] At least prior to the market downturn in 2000,[66] aggregate analyst recommendations would have resulted in mildly profitable results for investors vis-a-vis other investment benchmarks.

A particularly interesting study, for our purposes, is a 'clinical' dissection by Bradford Cornell (2001) of analyst behavior with respect to Intel Corporation before and after 21 September 2000, when the company announced lower than expected third quarter earnings. The stock price dropped 30 per cent, erasing $120 billion of market value. Prior to the announcement, the consensus recommendations had been strongly on the buy side. After the announcement, when the stock price was much lower, a fair number of analysts shifted to the sell side. This occurrence was perplexing, because the earnings announcement was of relatively small fundamental significance with respect to the company's long-term financial circumstances. It would be odd, then, that a company stock that was worth buying at $60 should, on that news alone, be sold at $43.

Cornell tests whether the reported information could, using standard tools of fundamental investment analysis, justify the drop in stock price, much less the shift to sell recommendations. He concludes not, and he is disturbed by the fact that the recommendations done both before and after gave no indication that discounted cash flow analysis was even relevant to the advice. If analysts in the Intel situation were not performing such analyses, what were they doing? Cornell suggests that analyst recommendations reacted to recent stock price performance rather than anticipated changes in the company's fundamentals. As he postulates, a series of good news announcements and upward price

---

[64] See Lim (2001).
[65] See Barber *et al.* (2001a).
[66] On the 2000 downturn, which analysts failed badly to anticipate, see Barber *et al.* (2001b).

movements leads to an escalation of buy recommendations, until bad news occurs and the price drops. That price drop causes a shift in recommendations. If this notion is accurate, then there is relatively little added value in the recommendations. And if these recommendations nonetheless influence investor behavior, it would tend to exacerbate stock price volatility (Cornell 2000: 134).[67]

Cornell's qualifier with respect to this last point is important. The fact that there are biases or methodological flaws in the recommendations of sell-side analysts does not in itself suggest that they influence investors. If investors are smart enough to anticipate the biases or the flaws, they will discount or ignore the recommendations. The recent frenzy of concern by regulators about analyst conflict of interests rests on the assumption that analysts are influential, especially with their earnings forecasts. Empirically, however, we have to be more cautious.[68] Without trying to resolve this at least partially open question, we should simply take note of where it leaves us. If there is an influence, this kind of work gives reason for concern. If there is little or no influence, then sell-side analysts should forfeit the privileged position that law and economics have heretofore given them. This is an issue to which we shall return in Part IV.

II. FIRST STEPS TOWARD BEHAVIOURAL SECURITIES REGULATION

Lawyers and policy-makers cannot hope to resolve the academic dispute over market efficiency reflected in the foregoing finance scholarship. However, they cannot avoid it either. If lawmakers simply assume that the markets are strongly efficient or inefficient, then we face a serious risk of error if the assumption turns out to be inaccurate. So far as the pro-efficiency risk is concerned, there may not be all that much to worry about in current law. As I have previously shown, surprisingly few important rules or principles of securities law depend strongly on market efficiency, notwithstanding some strong rhetoric to the contrary. The rules or principles most closely identified with the EMH, such as the fraud-on-the-market theory or the SEC's simplified Form S-3 and shelf registration procedures for public offerings, can be justified whether the markets are efficient or not.[69]

The faith in efficiency provides real bite when considering the regulation not undertaken because of doubts that it is necessary. To return to Enron and the subject of earnings management, for example, one could

---

[67] See also Bulkey and Harris (1997).
[68] On this possibility that analysts have a significant influence, see Hirst *et al.* (1995). Investor credulity also is suggested in Teoh *et al.* (1998).
[69] See Langevoort (1992: 876–86).

justify a restrained posture that tolerates a high degree of accounting cosmetics if one thinks that the market consistently sees through the make-up.[70] Academics, in particular, have advocated the most aggressive deregulation on efficiency grounds.[71] In response, critics of efficiency have a fairly obvious task. Behavioural finance can be invoked as a counterweight, to demonstrate the costs and risks of these kinds of proposals under an arguably more realistic view of how markets behave.[72]

But as noted at the beginning of this article, this task, though surely important, is unsatisfying for two reasons. First, due to the siege-like state of the debate, neither side is inclined to concede the underlying empirical assumptions of the other. A behavioral criticism, however sophisticated, can be deflected simply by responding that the empirical case for rejecting the EMH has not yet been established.[73] There is also the familiar point that even if the case for efficiency has been partly undermined by the data, the IMH theorists still lack a widely accepted, tractable theory of their own on how markets do behave. In this sense, the behavioral research is at most a defence against strong efficiency-driven theories than a positive vision of how regulation should be designed or evaluated, and thus underwhelms.

In what follows, then, I will try a different tack. One of the contributions of the behavioral finance research is that it may help us explain otherwise puzzling marketplace behavior, even if it does not yield clear-cut answers on the appropriate response. The payoff here is that this literature may point us in directions that we might not otherwise have considered. While this is my main aim, we will also take note of a new kind of exploitation of the IMH research. As conventional economics did twenty-five years ago,[74] behavioral finance has begun to seep from academia to real-life policy discussions. This reliance by policy-makers offers an opportunity for those of us sympathetic to the IMH agenda to take the measure of this seemingly friendly fire and see whether the citations to the research are fair and supportable. To this end, we now turn to three specific examples that connect behavioral finance to hard issues in securities law: fraud on the internet, the controversy over the analyst's role in the markets, and redefining fraud-on-the-market.

[70] See Hill (1997) (explaining how these cosmetics might and might not fool investors).
[71] See Romano (1999); Choi and Guzman (1998). The common element of these proposals is that the markets 'price' risk rationally and precisely, so that investors are fully compensated for the risk they bear. Although the IMH literature does not, so far as I know, address this pricing claim directly, the natural implication is that noisy markets will wash out pricing precision. Moreover, highly salient risks (or nonsalient ones) may themselves be the subject of market misperception.
[72] e.g., Prentice (2002).
[73] e.g., Romano (1999: 2366 n.17).
[74] See Derthick and Quirk (1985: 246).

III. FRAUD ON THE INTERNET

The emergence of the internet as an economic and cultural phenomenon in the 1990s disoriented securities regulation in a number of ways.[75] First, it created a new communications medium for the dissemination of information and opinion about financial matters. Individuals could establish websites, or participate in discussions on existing ones, in a way that created worldwide visibility for such information. Popular sites attracted extensive attention. This 'democratization' of investment-related information supposedly wrested control from the established institutional sources of advice and analysis that had theretofore dominated the financial media.

The second major change related to the trading process. Formally, brokers always operated as gatekeepers to the exchanges; direct trading by the investor public was not practicable, and certainly not encouraged. A retail customer had to communicate with a broker, and brokerage firms used this opportunity to practice the arts and science of salesmanship.[76] But the internet created a chance for online brokers like Charles Schwab and Datek to emerge and offer customers online trading capacity at very low cost. These firms succeeded by convincing investors that they had the power to make their own trading decisions without the need for extensive professional advice.[77]

These first two changes were closely related: the explosion in web-based investment information operated as a substitute for brokerage firm guidance, supporting (if not inflating) the sense of confidence for the retail investor.[78] Web-based execution mechanisms became the basis for the phenomenon of 'day-trading,' in which retail investors devoted nearly all their time to investing and mimicking the behaviors of professional traders by seeking to profit from very short-term price movements.[79]

The third change was different, but still part of a unified story. Internet-based issuer companies became extraordinarily popular investments in the 1990s, rising in valuation well beyond what conventional fundamental investment analysis could apparently justify.[80] Firms with no positive net income, or even a near-term hope of such, achieved market capitalizations in the billions of dollars, with increasingly elevated stock prices until the popping of the 'tech bubble' in 2000. Although institutional investors traded in technology stocks throughout

---

[75] For interesting perspectives, see Stout (1997); Frankel (1998); Hass (1998); Prentice (1999).
[76] See Langevoort (1996a).
[77] See SEC (1999a).
[78] See Barber and Odean (2001).
[79] See Bradley (2000); Gabaldon (2001: 238).
[80] See Ofek and Richardson (2001); Cornell (2001: 73).

the period, the available data suggests that retail investors held larger portions of tech stock compared to the more heavily institutional holdings in other kinds of industries.[81]

For our purposes, the performance of technology stocks in the 1990s is noteworthy mainly because of the research attention that it generated. For example, both during and after the growth of the bubble, many critics pointed to the high valuations as evidence of market inefficiency: How could a rational market price the shares of unprofitable start-up companies so highly? A recent survey of both new and existing evidence by two self-described believers in market rationality finds 'a strong circumstantial case against market prices reflecting fundamentals in the [i]nternet sector' (Ofek and Richardson 2001). Some of the examples in this literature border on amusing, if not sad. During the height of the frenzy, simply changing a firm's name to an internet moniker (e.g., adding '.com' to the name) produced a 53 per cent abnormal return over the subsequent five-day period.[82] In another well-known example, 3Com sold a 6 per cent stake in its Palm subsidiary, which exclusively makes Palm Pilots, in a transaction that promptly produced an estimated $53 billion market capitalization for Palm. Yet, at the same time, the total market capitalization of 3Com was approximately $28 billion, which could make sense only if the market was valuing the remainder of the 3Com assets as, essentially, a basket of liabilities.[83]

The Intel example recounted in the previous section is another example. Cornell's analysis suggests not so much that the market overreacted when Intel's price dropped by 38 per cent on minimally important bad news, but rather that Intel's stock price was already much too high before the news. To be sure, supporters of the EMH have not thrown in the towel in the face of evidence like this,[84] but concede that they have work to do.

The single legal issue I want to explore here emerges from the confluence of these three developments posing a problem that delves deep into the heart of what securities law is (or should be) all about, although it appears admittedly in a world far from efficient markets. It involves a case that gained extensive media attention,[85] including a segment on the television news program 60 Minutes and a cover story in the New York Times Magazine by celebrated author Michael Lewis (2001: 26).[86]

---

[81] See Hand (2000).

[82] See Cooper *et al.* (2001).

[83] See Lamont and Thaler (2001).

[84] See, e.g., Schwartz and Moon (2000); Hall (2001).

[85] See Schroeder and Simon (2000).

[86] Lewis is well known for his book, *Liar's Poker* (Lewis 1989), a recounting of his experience as a Salomon bond trader before becoming a writer.

In late 2000, a young New Jersey teenager was the subject of an enforcement action by the SEC for 'internet fraud.' He consented to a settlement, disgorging some, but far from all of his hundreds of thousands of dollars in trading profits.[87] The accused teenager, Jonathan Lebed, allegedly bought stock in small, thinly-traded high-tech companies. He then would make multiple postings on various investment websites, under different web addresses, extolling these stocks. Lebed's postings were fairly consistent. He would provide some basic, presumably accurate information about the company in question. The hype, in bold and billed with exclamations, would be phrased in recommendations like 'next stock to gain 1000 per cent,' or 'the most undervalued stock ever.' Occasionally, he predicted something like a 50 per cent price gain in a day or two. In any case, Lebed, according to the SEC, amassed a sufficient presence on the internet such that online investors would buy the stock, causing its price to rise. Lebed would then sell out.[88]

Assuming these facts, what did Lebed do that was unlawful? There are two possibilities that the SEC pursues in these kinds of cases. One is to claim that the person has gone into the business of giving investment advice, which is illegal absent registration with the SEC and creates a fiduciary-like duty vis-a-vis one's advisees. The difficulty with this tack is that 'mass media' advisory services are exempt from the definition of investment adviser, in part due to First Amendment concerns.[89] The SEC has tread gently in the internet area, recognizing under the Investment Advisers Act both the constitutional and practical difficulties of trying to sanction persons who give out investment advice on websites when the SEC clearly could not penalize comparable activity in a newspaper or magazine, or on radio or television. Because Lebed did not have his own website, this route was not available.

So, the claim was a more conventional one of simple 'fraud and manipulation,' and here the fragility of the SEC's case becomes visible. For a fraud case, the SEC must establish that the defendant made a materially false or misleading statement, with scienter.[90] Materiality is generally defined by reference to an objective standard, requiring that the information misrepresented be of sufficient importance that a reasonable

---

[87] *SEC v Lebed*, 73 S.E.C. 741 (20 Sept. 2000). For a survey of the SEC's enforcement position in this area, with extensive reference to the Lebed case, see Walker and Levine (2001).

[88] While Lebed became the celebrity, he was only one of a number of people accused of similar activities (including a set of Georgetown University law students). See *SEC v Colt*, 71 S.E.C. 1951 (2 Mar. 2000).

[89] See *Lowe v SEC*, 472 U.S. 181 (1985) (establishing a broad definition of exemption for bona fide financial publishers); see also Neuborne (1989); *SEC v Park*, 99 F. Supp. 2d 889 (N.D. Ill. 2000) (showing an SEC victory in this setting).

[90] See *Ernst & Ernst v Hochfelder*, 425 U.S. 185 (1976) (establishing scienter requirement).

investor would likely attach significance to it.[91] Were it to litigate a case like Lebed's, the SEC might well have a difficult time showing that anything that the teenager said could possibly have been treated as both true and significant by any reasonable person. The fact that a pseudonymous person on a website says, even repeatedly, that he thinks that a stock is poised to gain an immense amount does not by itself convey any seemingly reliable information. In other areas of antifraud litigation under the securities laws, the courts have dismissed claims involving far more substantive assertions of general optimism even when made by corporate insiders as immaterial as a matter of law.[92]

One response to this concern would be to say that materiality should be measured by its actual impact, not some idealized theory of reasonableness, and in the SEC's view, enough investors relied upon what Lebed said in fact that it moved the market price. We will turn later to whether this approach is sound as a matter of law, an inquiry that will take us directly into the world of behavioral finance. But the first question is whether the factual claim of causation is even plausible. It is doubtful that the Commission did any econometric work to demonstrate that Lebed's postings actually moved the price, especially in a case that was settled so quickly. Hence, one possibility here is that the SEC itself confused coincidence with causation. Perhaps Lebed's purchases and postings reacted to some other information (e.g., some price move that he observed), and the subsequent price increase was due to the delayed impoundment of that information rather than anything he said. He might simply have identified the early stages of momentum-driven bubble. A recent aggregate-data study of internet postings was unable to identify significant cause-and-effect relationships between postings and price changes generally, suggesting that the SEC perhaps was responding more to the media attention to the phenomenon than careful empirical analysis.[93]

---

[91] See *TSC Indus. v Northway, Inc.*, 426 U.S. 436, 449 (1976) (defining materiality).

[92] Even high-level executives of issuers are given freedom to make inflated claims about their companies, so long as there are no specific factual misstatements. See below text accompanying notes 180–182 (discussing the so-called 'puffery' defence). The SEC apparently believes that unfounded predictions of price movements either are exempt from this treatment, which is unlikely, or could be treated as half-truths—in other words, incomplete and misleading disclosure—because of the omission of defendants' intent to sell shortly after the recommendation. See Walker and Levine (2001: 413). As to the latter, the only authority for imposing anything remotely approaching such a duty can be drawn from the treatment of securities professionals, who owe a different level of obligation to the public. See *Park*, 99 F. Supp. 2d 889. Absent such a predicate, the half-truth doctrine in fact provides very little support for the SEC's claim. See Langevoort (1999a: 101).

[93] See Tumarkin and Whitelaw (2001). The authors look at aggregate data to disprove the claim that there is a high incidence of message posting in advance of increased trading volume.

That said, however, I think that there is substance to the SEC's concern with Lebed's conduct. But we need a much more plausible story about how those postings could in fact have affected the market price. Here is where behavioral finance can help, if used carefully. I want to avoid the reductionist argument that because the behavioral literature demonstrates that investors often do not act rationally, we can simply presume the kind of gullibility that would lead people to trust in Lebed's predictions as solid investment analysis. The cognitive biases that are the stuff of behavioral finance are mental shortcuts, not abject stupidity. To be sure, wishful thinking among investors is commonplace, but is actually fairly challenging to exploit.[94] Moreover, we must remember that the category of direct 'victims' is mainly the online investor community. Studies of online investors have shown some lack of insight, but hardly extreme foolishness.[95] Indeed, it is fair to assume that those technologically adept enough to establish online investment accounts and navigate the financial sites on the internet have somewhat greater sophistication than other segments of the investor community. The SEC's theory of causation remains dubious if all we can do is point to bounded rationality.[96]

But the behavioral literature offers a more focused possibility for explaining the causation puzzle, if not for making the Commission's legal case easier. Imagine Lebed simply as a focal point—a salient voice on the financial internet. How the salience came to be is difficult to ascertain. Most likely, he was initially lucky in predicting some stock moves, and others noticed correlations. The psychological literature suggests that people overattribute 'hot hands' to skill rather than luck,[97] but I do not want to push this notion too far. At least as likely is the possibility that that others simply perceived the saliency of what he had to say and predicted that others would follow the advice, i.e., that the market price would therefore move up. If these investors believed that they could get in early on this game and sell before the crowd, they might well choose to buy. And if enough people chose to play this game on similar reasoning, a self-fulfilling prophecy would result: the buying activity of the game players, if no one else, would be enough to cause the thinly-traded stock price to jump. As to who wins the game, it would be those with good—or better yet, lucky—inclination to sell out. In a sense, we would come full

[94] Stockbrokers often work carefully and diligently to exploit customer biases such as wishful thinking or self-serving inference. See Langevoort (1996a).

[95] See Barber and Odean (2001). Indeed, their study shows that aside from trading costs, the stock picking abilities of the on-line investor community is respectable. See Barber and Odean (2002).

[96] While I am sceptical that this particular event deceived anyone, I do not doubt that other forms of publicity can fraudulently move prices by taking advantage of investor biases. See below text accompanying notes 183–184.

[97] See Gilovich (1991: 75–87).

circle to Keynes's famous analogy of stock market behavior to entrants in a newspaper contest who try to predict what others will consider the most beautiful baby picture—everyone trying to outguess everyone else.[98]

A strong rationalist, or especially a conventional game theorist, would object that this is a fool's game. If everyone were thinking similarly, there would be no reason to expect a predictably consistent winner. The game would unravel quickly. But here is where the behavioral literature makes its clearest contribution. There are two possibilities to consider. One is that there is a second group of traders wholly unaware of Lebed or his game, who trade on the momentum generated by the initial response, jumping onto the bandwagon.[99] Lebed's immediate audience might not think that they can out compete one another, but might expect to beat the second-stage momentum traders.

The more likely possibility is that the immediate audience does not see the fool's game in the first place. Recall that the one cognitive bias that seems to have the greatest resonance in behavioral finance is overconfidence. People, especially younger males, overrate their own skills and readily confuse luck with ability. Work by Barber and Odean shows this overconfidence to be an especially strong trait among online traders, and that the bias does not easily wash out via the school of hard knocks. They note that the internet, with its overabundance of information, strengthens the illusion of control.[100] Especially in a bull market, there is much in the way of good fortune to confuse with brains, leading to a surprising persistence of biased belief. One can readily see how more traders would think that they could win Lebed's game than the statistical odds would indicate. They keep on playing.

To me, this latter story is far more plausible than one based on fraudulently induced reliance by the website participants on Lebed as a credible source of fundamental investment advice. If so, however, the hole in the SEC's fraud case simply widens. We are now telling a causation story where there is no deception at all. The traders are all simply overconfident in their ability to win a contrived trading game. If some website participants also convinced themselves that Lebed was a good stock picker because they saw an illusory correlation, it is still hard to identify any affirmative misrepresentation or omission that falsely created such a belief with which the teenager could be charged.

[98] See Piron (1991).
[99] Of course, Lebed's own purchases may have had an upward influence on the price, itself operating as a signal to the momentum traders that was then simply reinforced by the postings. So far as the law of fraud is concerned, however, he had no duty to others to disclose either the purpose or effect of his trading. Such a duty, generally, arises only when there is a fiduciary-like relationship between the parties. See *US v Chiarella*, 445 U.S. 222 (1980).
[100] See Barber and Odean (2001: 46); see also Barber and Odean (2000).

At the same time, this account might also justify the SEC's concern with the phenomenon, albeit under a different theory. If Lebed promoted the kind of game-playing I've suggested, it might be roughly analogised to another teenage game: drag racing. Lebed sponsored a contest that caused other actors to engage in a highly competitive trading race, with the predictable risk of a crash at the end. The participants knew what they were doing, albeit overconfident with respect to their safety. Putting aside concern for the physical safety of the youths involved in a real drag race, the concern here is one of externalities. The reckless race takes over the streets, causing sensible people to travel elsewhere or not at all. So too, a reckless trading race pre-empts the trading market for the stock in question, displacing any legitimate buying activity that might otherwise have taken place. That stock's trading market (and perhaps those of similarly situated stocks) is temporarily destabilized. If that result is what Lebed was promoting, it was economically dysfunctional even if it was not fraudulent.

This is why I find myself sympathetic to the SEC's intervention, if it is factually sound (i.e., the Commission can indeed demonstrate causation in fact) and if the SEC can unearth a persuasive legal theory to support it. The initial place to search for doctrinal possibilities is the law of manipulation. Manipulation is a term of art that refers to a set of practices that seek 'improperly' to move market prices up or down to serve the self-interest of the manipulator.[101] The term is often described by reference to its opposite: manipulation is conduct that deprives investors of prices set by the free interplay of supply and demand.[102] While these definitions are notoriously ambiguous, one can readily see their potential relevance to the internet trading scenario. Like the drag race, the irrational trading game allegedly set in motion by Lebed distorted the trading market of the stocks in question for a short period of time, depriving other investors of fair access.

Most manipulation is effected through trading, of course, often involving fictitious transactions. We should pause here to note the vigorous literature in both law and economics over whether, absent some evidence of fraud, manipulative trading is even plausible in the first place. Ross and Fischel wrote a seminal article claiming that attempts at manipulation are inevitably self-defeating, partly because it is so hard to move prices by trading in widely-traded stocks, at least, and partly because it is irrational to assume that one can successfully sell out without defeating the scheme once the price has moved (Ross and Fischel

---

[101] See generally Cox *et al.* (2001: 691–700). For the SEC's view as applied to the Internet, see Starr and Herman (2001).

[102] See, e.g., *Sullivan & Long, Inc. v Scattered Corp.*, 47 F.3d 857 (7th Cir. 1995) (Posner, J.); *US v Hall*, 48 F. Supp. 2d 386, 387 (S.D.N.Y. 1999).

1991). Others have criticized their argument, which depends heavily on market efficiency theory, on conventional economic grounds.[103] Behavioural finance gives ample reason to suspect that trade-based schemes can succeed by triggering positive momentum-trading activity by others. Noise traders often confuse past price moves with future profit opportunities—this is what 'positive feedback' trading is all about.[104] With respect to thinly-traded stocks, especially, there is little reason to doubt their viability as a profitable strategy.

But Lebed's activity did not involve fictitious trading. Nor, as we have seen, was there likely any conventional fraud. This seems to pose a problem, because the Supreme Court has said that deception is necessary in any manipulation case.[105] Here, the behavioral insights lead us to a question that I suspect securities regulation ought to confront head on: should it be deemed manipulative deliberately to say or do something designed to take advantage of heuristic thinking by investors, thereby at least temporarily destabilizing the market price, even if the investor response was in some sense 'irrational?' In an IMH world, opportunities to exploit the judgment biases of investors abound, and we are likely to observe efforts in this direction with some frequency. Assuming that such a scheme and its harmful effect can be shown as a matter of fact, 'manipulation' in terms of both statutory intent and history[106] is a sensible label to attach. Unlike fraud, manipulation is concerned less with the immediate victim than the integrity of the market.[107]

To be sure, this market integrity approach rings of what is a justifiably controversial theory in the law of manipulation: that it is unlawful simply to trade for a bad purpose, i.e., simply to move the stock price for some selfish motive.[108] When stretching a doctrinal construct like this, we do need to ask whether imposing an elastic standard will do more harm than good. Subjective intent is hard to fathom; why someone traded or said or did something is difficult to prove. Hence, attempts to convict a trader for trading with a bad purpose will lead to a high frequency of prosecutorial

---

[103] See Thel (1994).

[104] See above notes 33–48.

[105] See *Schreiber v Burlington N., Inc.*, 472 U.S. 1 (1985).

[106] See Thel (1990; 1988). Thel demonstrates that Congress intended in the securities laws to allow the Commission to treat as manipulative any speculative activity that distorts stock prices.

[107] Later, we will consider whether the concept of fraud should itself be revised to address the exploitation of investor biases, even if seemingly unreasonable. See below text accompanying notes 188–198.

[108] See *Markowski v SEC*, 274 F.3d 525 (D.C. Cir. 2001); *US v Regan*, 937 F.2d 828 (1991); *US v Mulherin*, 938 F.2d 364 (2d Cir. 1991) (recognizing and applying this theory *arguendo*, while questioning its viability). Indeed, we might refocus our attention away from Lebed's postings to his earlier purchases, which arguably had no rationale except to commence the game of exploitation.

and judicial error. This, in turn, raises the prospect of chilling legitimate behavior.[109]

To that end, those familiar with the psychology literature might even wonder whether Lebed had the requisite state of mind to be liable under this approach. He claimed that he conducted some rudimentary inquiry into the companies he hyped. I suspect that as his success grew, he might have deluded himself into thinking that he had skills as a stock-picker. While he was also aware of the games he was setting in motion and the likelihood of overreaction by others, he might have honestly denied that his only purpose was to move the stock prices artificially in a direction that suited his interest. Indeed, people are adept at rationalizing their actions and beliefs.[110] Perhaps Lebed thought that these really were undervalued stocks, and that he was engaged in bona fide publicity of socially useful information using the only medium at his disposal. After all, it can hardly be unlawful for the owner of recently acquired securities to publicize his research, even if the effect of the publicity (if credible) is to raise stock prices excessively.[111]

Thus, I concede that the pursuit of internet-based speech under an expansive manipulation theory leads to something of a quagmire for securities regulation. Aggressive policing here will be costly, and not necessarily accomplish all that much in light of the inevitably noisy nature of trading in thinly-traded stocks. Maybe we should analogize this setting to Las Vegas casinos and leave those who choose to play to the inevitable consequences of facing bad odds. On the other hand, to stay out of the swamp simply invites more opportunistic destabilizing activity by people like Lebed. There is no easy solution.

But final resolution of the right policy is beyond what I am trying to do here. At least for the moment, it is enough to have shown how an understanding of behavioral finance (particularly the phenomenon of investor overconfidence) is useful to shed light on what would otherwise seem a hopeless puzzle—how Jonathan Lebed's words might really have moved the stock markets and why it is at least worth worrying about. Our thinking has advanced, if only to see more clearly the difficulty of the problem.

---

[109] See Fischel and Ross (1991). Illustrative of this point, courts concede that it is not manipulation to trade even though it is foreseeable that one's acts will have an impact on price. Manipulation requires that impact on price is the sole or dominating purpose behind trading.

[110] See Langevoort (2000).

[111] More specifically, the practice of front-running—buying in advance of a recommendation—is potentially sanctionable through a variety of legal and self-regulatory strategies. See, e.g., *SEC v Blavin*, 557 F. Supp. 1304 (E.D. Mich. 1983), *aff'd*, 760 F.2d 706 (6th Cir. 1985); Lowenfels and Bromberg (1991: 331–35). As a general matter, however, most front-running problems can be cured by adequate disclosure at the time of the recommendation. As noted earlier, see above note 99, it is possible to find a duty to disclose on the part of securities professionals, but not as easy when non-professionals are involved.

IV. THE ANALYSTS' PRIVILEGE

Our second puzzle is an older one in securities regulation and takes us right to the heart of the efficiency debate. As the law of insider trading developed in fits and starts over the last forty years, it quickly became clear enough that corporate insiders cannot trade for their own accounts in their own company's stock. Nor can they favor their friends or family by 'tipping' them so that they can profit, or sell the information to those to whom it is valuable. These prohibitions are built on fiduciary principles, particularly the duty of loyalty. Insider trading and tipping are self-serving rather than motivated by a desire to benefit the issuer, the owner of the confidential information. When the Supreme Court drew this line in the famous *Dirks* case,[112] it said that when insiders pass information on to others without acting selfishly, there is no taint for insider trading purposes.

So articulated, this rule seems to confer an important privilege on one class of persons who regularly seek nonpublic information from corporate insiders—investment analysts.[113] Although motivations can be complicated, executives will generally give inside information to an analyst because the insider genuinely believes that the company's interests will be served by the selective disclosure. Companies want analyst coverage and want analysts to help them tell their stories to investors. When, as is predictable, company executives have an optimistic view of the company's prospects,[114] they want analysts to share those views. Face-to-face meetings with one or a handful of analysts, at which executives convey private information, have long been considered as a means of good investor relations. Under the insider-trading test articulated above, this practice was at least arguably (perhaps even probably) lawful. Indeed, the court in *Dirks* articulated the fiduciary breach test in part precisely to avoid a chill on analyst activity, which in the spirit of the early 1980s it praised as an essential contribution to marketplace efficiency.[115]

Efficiency-minded academics have naturally been delighted with the analysts' privilege, but the SEC has not been so pleased. For a long time, it expressed chagrin with the apparent unfairness of the result, and on

---

[112] *Dirks v SEC*, 463 U.S. 646 (1983). In addition to regulating insider and tippee trading, the securities laws also address—under a separate analytical structure—the trading in a company's stock while in possession of information entrusted to the trader by some other source. See *US v O'Hagan*, 521 U.S. 642 (1997).

[113] For a celebration of the analysts' role, see Fischel (1984). Prior to *Dirks*, the place of investment analysts in the insider-trading doctrine was far less secure. See *SEC v Bausch & Lomb, Inc.*, 565 F.2d 8, 9 (2d Cir. 1977).

[114] See Langevoort (1997).

[115] *Dirks*, 463 U.S. 646 at 658–59.

one occasion, sought to circumvent it via an enforcement action.[116] In 2000, the Commission became considerably more assertive in this area by adopting new Regulation FD ('Fair Disclosure').[117] Regulation FD does not regulate analysts directly. Rather it prohibits senior executives of publicly-traded issuers from privately disclosing material nonpublic information to any of a carefully defined class of persons, most notably investment analysts. The rule has infuriated the securities industry in particular, igniting a controversy that still continues to pervade efforts at repeal or significant modification. It has also displeased many in the issuer and legal communities.

This opposition to Reg FD has a distinctly self-serving potential to it: the securities industry lost a lucrative privilege and wants it back, and insiders are naturally concerned about a new source of potential liability. But the issue of the analysts' privilege poses a legitimately difficult policy question. Putting aside the awkward doctrinal structure that gave rise to the analysts' privilege in the first place, the standard argument in its favor is that private contacts contribute to marketplace efficiency, which in turn redounds to the benefit of all investors as well as the public interest through the efficient allocation of economic resources.[118] This contribution comes in two ways. First, corporate executives may be more willing to release information if they can do it privately, rather than publicly. They can be more nuanced and forthcoming because they are dealing with sophisticated listeners and can speak without attribution.[119] If so, more useful information makes its way into the market. Secondly, analysts will have a greater incentive to do research if they can ask sensitive questions privately and profit from their discoveries than if any material information they elicit has to be visible to and thus shared with other analysts and the public.[120] For smaller issuers, a promise of special access may be needed to make coverage worthwhile to the analyst in the first place.

The main empirical attack on Reg FD, therefore, has been cast in terms of the likely adverse efficiency consequences that stem from the adoption of the rule (BNA 2001a). Predictably, one claim is that less information will now be made available by issuers. The second is that either research quality or analyst following will diminish, especially for smaller

---

[116] For a supportive review of the SEC's position, see Langevoort (1990). In *SEC v Stevens*, [1991] 23 *Sec. Reg. & L. Rep.* (BNA) 439 (S.D.N.Y. 1991), the Commission alleged that the insider's tip was motivated by his own reputational interests.

[117] Securities Act Release No.33-7881, 17 CFR 243.100-243.103 (Aug. 15, 2000).

[118] See Fox (2001).

[119] Corporate executives may be willing to talk to analysts about more confidential matters, or ones where they wish not to be identified as the source.

[120] In large part, concern over materiality drives the debate. There is no bar, in Reg FD or the law of insider trading, against giving immaterial information to analysts, even if it helps them piece together the mosaic from which profitable insights are gleaned. But because materiality is a fuzzy definition, a legal prohibition may chill all contacts.

companies. A third is one not anticipated above: that market volatility will increase. This last prediction is of particular interest to us because it has an explicit behavioral tint. The idea here is that if all sensitive disclosure is forced into public channels, then noise traders will compete with the professionals in defining the all-important initial reaction to the news. The overconfidence and lack of sophistication that so many retail investors bring to this task will result in mindless and erratic price movements only partially countered by the smart money investors. In other words, the teachings of behavioral finance counsel against Reg FD. To this end, for example, a Securities Industry Association document (SIA 2001) prepared after the adoption of the rule claims that:

> The barrage of unorganised data is simply too much for investors, most of whom have neither the time nor the inclination to sort through the data and perform quality analysis of their own. Investor behavior was beginning to indicate information overload even prior to Reg. FD, as evidenced by behavioral finance studies that illustrate an inability to process ever growing informational inputs.

The question is whether this expression of concern for the unsophisticated investor is legitimate or just a form of rent-seeking by the industry. If it is legitimate, what is the right modification to an initiative like Reg FD? Before considering that claim, however, we need to put the Reg FD debate in context.

A. Fairness

The SEC's primary justification for Reg FD is rooted in concerns over fairness, not efficiency. The SEC's stance, despised by most economics-oriented academics,[121] is that giving the issuer's managers the ability to play favorites among recipients of information confers an unfair advantage on those connected with large institutions compared to the average retail investor. The behavioral risk is that the perception of unfairness by individuals or others who expect to be disadvantaged might lead those individuals to withdraw from the equity markets, resulting in loss of depth and liquidity.

This claim has received an impressive amount of unkind attention in the academic literature. My narrower interest is in whether anything in the research in behavioral finance or economics helps much on this particular point. There is a strong temptation to invoke a body of literature that shows, fairly robustly, that people will often eschew their

---

[121] See, e.g., Manne (1966); Carlton and Fischel (1983). But see Schepple (1993: 123 note 3).

own immediate self-interest in order to spite someone else who is treating them unfairly.[122] The laboratory tests that demonstrate this behavior typically take the form of bargaining games where one party is given the right to split a sum of money, keeping some and offering the rest to the other party. The only condition on these tests is that the other party must accept what is offered. If she does not, neither party gets anything. The results seem fairly clear: unless a reasonable amount is offered to the other party, she will frequently reject the offer and take nothing, thereby becoming worse off.

Yet, I doubt that this finding gets us very far on the selective disclosure issue. First of all, note that the fairness research does not say that equal sharing is necessary to get players to agree. Rather, there is simply some tipping point where what is offered is sufficiently unfair that the person will abstain. There is also probably some point at which investors' sense of fairness could become so offended by a legal or economic practice that it leads to withdrawal. But it is unlikely that selective disclosure resonates anywhere near this strongly. Indeed, the long-standing increase in retail investor participation in the U.S. markets at a time when selective disclosure was a notorious practice indicates otherwise. The second point to make is that other behavioral traits, such as over-optimism or the illusion of control, tend to counterbalance perceptions of unfair disadvantage. Retail investors who think themselves smarter than average will play in the markets even against structurally induced odds.

In sum, I think that all that behavioral economics offers in support of the 'fairness' argument is that some set of legal or social institutions— law or norms—must guarantee a threshold level of confidence in the fairness of the system. That threshold need not be a high one, however, and it is not clear that any particular prohibition (even against insider trading generally)[123] must necessarily be part of it. With respect to selective disclosure to analysts, the normative argument should probably move to more substantive grounds.

B. The Criticism

The more substantive grounds begin with the empirical questions noted earlier. Will a ban on selective disclosure cause more or less information to be imparted by issuers, or have no perceptible effect? The behavioral literature offers little direct help on this question. We can, of course, use behavioral literature to predict that highly salient forms of legal risk will produce excessive issuer caution, especially when there is a high level of

---

[122] See Rabin (1993); Loewenstein (2000).
[123] See Black (2001: 803) (stating insider trading regulation is important, but not necessarily crucial).

ambiguity regarding the meaning of the prohibition in question. The adoption of Reg FD produced a barrage of publicity, mostly from lawyers, that might prompt such an effect. But if so, this phenomenon is likely just a temporary one. In fact, the SEC carefully designed Reg FD to minimize the threat of sanction,[124] and the SEC is unlikely for political reasons to pursue cases where issuer officials have acted in good faith (BNA 2001b). If the marketplace pressure is strong enough, executives will adjust the rule and disclose what analysts want short of clear-cut violation of the law.[125] If the SEC does not take an unusually aggressive enforcement posture, in other words, the fear-induced chill is likely to be minimal.

The bigger empirical question involves the effect on market efficiency. If sell-side analysts on balance produce more accurate stock prices, their claim to a privilege is bolstered considerably. But if there are serious doubts about that, then Reg FD is more appealing. And here is where the explosion of finance literature critical of analysts in the 1990s becomes important. Although a distinctive part of the IMH literature, most of this criticism deals with conflicts of interest as opposed to cognitive bias. There is a good deal of support from psychology for the proposition that these conflicts most often play out unconsciously; in other words, the pecuniary incentive leads the analyst to see things differently than she would otherwise so that the bias is not bad faith.[126] But so far as effects are concerned, awareness is not the important issue.

Again, the conflicts come in a variety of forms. First, analysts may bias their analysis and recommendations in order to please managers of the issuer. This distortion may accomplish two things. Positive recommendations may generate more business for the corporate finance department of an analyst's employer, who would then compensate the analyst for business brought into the firm.[127] Also, positive recommendations will create better and deeper access to private information, as insiders can be expected to favor those analysts over ones who adopt a more negative posture.[128] A separate conflict arises when analysts personally own stock in the companies they recommend. They may be overly bullish, especially at times when they are considering selling the stock.[129] There is empirical and theoretical support for all these concerns, some of which were cited in passing by the SEC in its rule making. So far as recommen-

---

[124] The SEC carefully drafted the rule to avoid creating any liability in a private right of action—one of the few rules in the securities laws with such an exclusion.

[125] For a study (admittedly, partially funded by the SEC) surveying preliminary evidence and finding no harmful effects from Reg FD, see Heflin *et al.* (2001).

[126] See above notes 60–61.

[127] See sources cited above note 63.

[128] See Lim, (2001). I have expressed this concern with specific application to the selective disclosure debate. See Langevoort (1990).

[129] See Opdyke (2001).

dations are concerned, for instance, the presence of an investment banking relationship plainly leads to a higher incidence of buy recommendations on average than if there is no such relationship.[130]

While recommendations are important, the more closely-watched task that analysts perform is making short-term quarterly earnings estimates. Forward-looking estimates are more useful in valuing a security than simple extrapolations from historic performance data, and hence add value to what is known in the markets.[131] But the finance literature has identified both conflicts of interest and forecasting imperfections. The conflicts are the same as noted earlier, but play out somewhat differently. Managers naturally want to beat analyst expectations, or at least meet them. The market punishes them and their company's stock for falling short of consensus forecasts, even if only by a small bit. In contrast to the optimistic bias preferred in recommendations, managers do not want too much optimism in the short-term forecast, because that sets the bar too high. Hence, the bias, so far as business-getting incentives are concerned, frequently leads analysts to be overly conservative in order to please managers.[132] There is also some literature on earnings forecasting that indicates that some cognitive biases may infect the process. For instance, overconfidence grows with past success: analysts on a hot streak tend to become more aggressive in their subsequent forecasts, with a higher than average likelihood of inaccuracy, in comparison to their peers.[133]

Accuracy aside, there is also concern about the analysts' undue emphasis on short-term earnings forecasts. While these forecasts offer significant information, they are far from the fundamental investment analysis that the sell-side is supposed to be undertaking. Cornell's study of the Intel stock drop is instructive.[134] His concern was largely that analysts were primarily following short-term performance data in their stock recommendations, to the exclusion of long-term fundamental analysis. This problem, coupled with undue attention to earnings forecasts, created an environment in which the analyst community may have contributed to mispricing rather than helped to correct it, until the company itself introduced a note of caution.[135]

---

[130] See, e.g., Machaely and Womack (1999).

[131] See Brown and Rozeff (1978).

[132] This desire to meet consensus forecasts is part of the phenomenon of earnings management. Managers and analysts would negotiate forecasts that permitted managers to meet or beat expectations, while not overly compromising the analysts' reputations. Managers would exercise discretion in financial reporting to assure that the numbers come out right. See Hill (1997); Hong *et al.* (2000); Collingwood (2001). In many ways, Reg FD was designed to prevent this from happening, and some preliminary reports suggest success along these lines. See Edmonstron (2001).

[133] See above note 60; see also Jacob *et al.* (1999); Mikhail *et al.* (1997).

[134] See above text accompanying notes 66–67.

[135] In addition to relaying forecasts and recommendations, a third role that analysts play is as interpreters of complex information. They simplify and evaluate information, using skills

The critical literature on sell-side analyst behavior, then, runs fairly deep. As with efficiency studies generally, this criticism is not dispositive, and sell-side analysts are still deemed a positive rather than a negative force in marketplace efficiency by many economists and finance scholars. A widely-publicized study by some well-known behavioral economists demonstrates that at least up until the technology bubble burst of 2000, analyst recommendations were reasonable predictors of positive performance: net of trading costs, at least, a trading strategy of following consensus recommendations immediately, would beat market indices by a statistically significant amount. This suggests that, on average, analyst recommendations have investment value, a story seemingly inconsistent with the criticisms recounted above (Barber *et al.* 2001a).[136] This research should be a caution to anyone wanting to indict the analyst community on a wholesale basis. The unanswered question here is whether the analyst recommendations themselves, rather than any information discovered by the analysts, may be what moves the prices and generates the positive abnormal returns. If the mere presence of a highly publicized buy recommendation causes retail investors to demand more of the security, and arbitrage and other countervailing forces do not counter the demand, the recommendation becomes a self-fulfilling prophecy.[137] It could be the equivalent to the Times front page story about EntreMed, where the saliency of what retail investors naively treat as positive news is the force that drives the price of the stock to a higher level. Consistent with this—although other explanations as well—the research also showed that any delay in responding to changes in the consensus recommendations (e.g., trading a day or two later) washed away most of the profitability of this strategy.

C. The Policy Debate

1. Bias

With this background from the IMH literature, we can return to the question of whether Reg FD furthers or detracts from investor welfare.

that most investors lack. Here again, the literature is not entirely supportive. For a detailed case study of the difficulties analysts had in interpreting the United Airlines employee buy-out, see Gilson (2000).

[136] Once trading costs were taken into account, the gains largely disappeared. Interestingly, this result was put forth as evidence of stock market inefficiency, because the EMH predicts that public recommendations will necessarily occur after the market adjusts to incorporate any new information that might lead to alterations in those recommendations.

[137] See Logue (1986); Jegadeesh *et al.* (2002). Building on our analysis of the online trading phenomenon in Part III, I think it is at least possible that highly salient recommendations are primarily a focal point, causing a trading frenzy among those seeking to anticipate the likely reactions of others and becoming a self-fulfilling prophecy.

Recall that the strongest claim against Reg FD is that it removes a useful predicate to the efficiency of the stock market, leaving it less calibrated and more volatile. The literature critical of sell-side analysts does not prove that their net effect is bad, but it does muddy the waters considerably about both the direction and magnitude of their contribution. If permitting selective disclosure invites managers to skew disclosure to a greater extent than if it is banned, then there could be a palpable benefit to the rule.

Criticism of Reg FD has come from many quarters. In the academic literature, a number of major articles have recently taken it to task. Goshen and Parchomovsky (2001), for example, have developed an elegant theory of 'negative property rights' that they would allocate to professional investors and their analysts in order to promote marketplace liquidity and efficiency. Though they would theoretically prefer a norm of non-discrimination among analysts, they treat selective disclosure as a necessary practice for their system of rights, at least for smaller issuers. Differently, Choi (2002) argues that discretion over selective disclosure presumptively ought to be given to the issuer because it can most efficiently internalize the mix of costs and benefits that disclosure produces.[138]

Surprisingly, both articles ignore the extensive finance literature on analyst conflicts and significantly downplay the risks that their proposed allocation of entitlements might lead to either skewed disclosure or biased advice.[139] True, the analyst bias literature does not establish the presence of abusive selective disclosure as such. But both theory and observation do establish: (1) a motive on the part of managers to cause analysts to skew both their forecasts and advice, and for analysts to respond in kind; (2) the opportunity to use selective disclosure as a form of currency; and (3) the existence of some degree of analyst bias in fact. While Reg FD may not neutralize these biasing incentives completely, we cannot say either that the risk is simply anecdotal or that the ban on selective disclosure will have no influence on biases in forecasts and

---

[138] Choi elaborates his point with respect to a theory of insider trading in his paper with Ian Ayres, a scholar also explicitly critical of Reg FD. See Ayres and Choi (2001).

[139] To be fair, neither scholar focuses particularly on the sell-side—both seem to work from the assumption that the main virtue from investment analysis comes from the actions of the buy-side. Choi's thesis, for example, is designed at least in part to encourage the formation of close monitoring relationships between the firm and a single block shareholder, or a small group of investors. See Ayres and Cramton (1994: 1062–63). However, neither makes any distinction among kinds of analysts, and any such effort would be unworkable. Many sell-side analysts also provide private research to clients, for example. In the political debate, at least, there is little appetite for a special privilege for the buy-side, because that so closely resembles classic insider trading—especially when the buy-side analyst represents a dominant shareholder who could influence the control of the firm.

recommendations.[140] There are ample grounds to believe that the most direct consequence of a ban on selective disclosure is that the more skilled analysts will gain a clearer comparative advantage over the unskilled, who were the ones most likely to trade bias for access in order to compete. If so, the incentive structure is improved, not compromised, and bias diminished.

Nor should we assume that state law fiduciary duties can be invoked to prevent any cases of abuse that happen to arise. Even putting aside the practical enforcement questions,[141] the business judgment rule alone renders it difficult as a matter of state corporate law to delve into subtle questions like these. To restate a brief behavioral point, in the eyes of an optimistic executive there is very little difference between rewarding the analysts who have been the most upbeat and a good faith desire to 'get the true story' out to the investing public. It is not easy to separate out deliberate deception from optimistic bias, which may make courts reluctant to police this area under the rubric of fiduciary responsibility. If there is inadequate policing, however, the likelihood of disclosure bias increases. While Enron is only an anecdote at this point, it at least underscores the importance of this line of inquiry.[142]

Criticism of Reg FD is premature unless it addresses this risk. Without knowing more about analysts' biases than the research currently permits, however, it is hard to say much more than to make two points. First, at the very least, there is a heretofore largely ignored but distinctly rational basis for justifying Reg FD by reference to the skewing potential of selective disclosure. Secondly, the over-romanticized case for an 'analysts' privilege,' at least on the sell-side, has evaporated.

2. Noise

The securities industry has more recently offered a different criticism of Reg FD. In contrast to the academics, the industry repeatedly claims that it opposes selective disclosure and only opposes the SEC's initiative because of its adverse effect on market efficiency.[143] Reg FD allegedly interferes with efficiency in the ways noted earlier, e.g., by reducing the

[140] Choi gives far more weight than Goshen and Parchomovsky to the problem of abusive selective disclosures but proposes only alternative ways of dealing with them. For example, Choi suggests that analysts could be given a right not to be cut off from information once granted. While theoretically appealing, perhaps, this proposal cannot be accomplished within the framework of the securities laws as currently formulated.

[141] State law lacks a public surveillance or enforcement capacity, leaving the matter simply to the private shareholder-plaintiff. See Bainbridge (1999: 1622–4).

[142] As noted earlier (see above note 63), Enron and related scandals did lead Congress, the SEC, the self-regulatory agencies, and state authorities to act against analysts based on these kinds of conflicts.

[143] See, e.g., SIA (2001: 3).

quantity and quality of issuer-generated information and by inducing excessive reluctance by managers to submit to one-on-one interviews with analysts. Again, these hypotheses present empirical questions outside the scope of our inquiry here. What is more intriguing is the securities industry's contention that analysts play a necessary role as 'buffers' against the noise-trading propensities of the retail investor, the point on which they cite behavioral finance research. In essence, the industry's claim is as follows. When issuers comply with Reg FD, they present new data directly to the full range of interested persons. Overconfident retail investors will react in unsophisticated ways to the unvarnished information for a time, adding excess volatility to the stock price. On the other hand, allowing analysts access and the opportunity to massage the information in advance of its public release means that the price will adjust more steadily in the right direction. The market can be conditioned, and hence reduce its vulnerability to shock, panic or undue exuberance.

Putting aside yet unanswerable empirical questions, such as whether there indeed is more volatility after public announcements under Reg FD,[144] there is an obvious retort here. If there is reason to doubt the objectivity of sell-side analysis, then the pre-release 'massaging' of information is of questionable value. There might be a good bit of analyst-tolerated 'spin' mixed in with the fundamental analysis. Or if Cornell's fears are well founded, there may be too little fundamental analysis in the first place. Whether the retail investor really is able to sort through the various analyst views well enough to gain better perspective is not all that clear.[145]

Having said this, however, we should pause to reflect on where this line of thinking is taking us, for there is an ideological issue lurking here. The behavioralists are right that the more emotions and cognitive biases of noise traders adversely affect market prices the more noise traders can be construed as 'bad guys' (Hong and Stein 1999).[146] Good public policy

[144] A pre-Reg FD study comparing companies that voluntarily open access to analyst conference calls to those that do not found that volatility did increase during open conference calls. See Frankel *et al.* (1999).

[145] Indeed, at heart the claim here seems to be that smooth price movements reflecting new information are better than sharp ones. On close inspection, this idea itself is shaky. To the extent that smart money investors are picking off the less savvy in advance of the public disclosure, the smoothness comes at a price that is not particularly appealing. Recall that critics of the ban on insider trading have long claimed that markets would be less volatile were insiders able to trade, see, e.g., Manne (1966) but their position is one now largely rejected. Similarly, we are quite tolerant of sharp breaks in some noteworthy instances—such as the merger deal that is successfully kept confidential until the announcement. Dramatic market swings in response to 'new news' are a known risk of investing.

[146] Hong and Stein describe this as a 'negative externality' imposed by noise traders. This view assumes that professional investors demonstrate a higher degree of rationality, a point with which most behavioral finance scholars—even those that point out the suboptimal behaviors which institutions sometimes exhibit—would agree.

would then be to eradicate these biases if possible, or at least neutralize their social and economic influence, as Lynn Stout (1995) has suggested.[147] That is why there is some bite to the SIA's argument, putting aside the specific concern about analyst biases, and this is the deep concern about where the behavioral literature leads us: if accurate, it invites regulation that privileges the savvy and treats unsophisticated traders as economic undesirables.[148]

Politically, such regulation is impossible to advocate openly. Both Congress and the SEC have a strong interest in the support of the retail investor community and the presence of strong public markets. Indeed, in some ways, a fair amount of what the Commission does, especially the Division of Corporation Finance's review and comment on registration statements, is in the name of making disclosure 'accessible' to the average investor. That sentiment has led to the creation of an awkward myth-story in which probably few have deep faith.[149] In this story, the typical retail investor is very much an earnest and rational person, but with bounded capacity. He wants a substantial amount of government-mandated disclosure and evaluates it fairly carefully in making his investment decision so long as it is packaged properly (e.g., in 'plain English'). To be sure, some investors actually do this. But the Commission has never studied investor behavior deeply enough to say, publicly at least, what percentage of investors read or understand these documents, or what influence the fundamental analysis-oriented disclosure has on their investment decisions. I suspect that it does not really want to know[150] for fear that the myth-story might have to give way to a vision of retail investors somewhat more in keeping with the predictions of the behavioralists.

Nor could it stomach the antidemocratic implication of these predictions. The Commission's main 'brand message' is about its role in empowering retail investors as a class. This message brings us back specifically to Reg FD. I have come gradually to believe that insider-trading regulation in the United States is only loosely related to any direct investor protection strategy.[151] As said earlier, the fairness ideology only

---

[147] Stout questions market efficiency in light of a host of factors, leading her to doubt the desirability of encouraging—much less romanticizing— the growth of the public marketplace for securities.

[148] Steve Choi, in a separate article, has sensed this and thus proposes to put some kinds of trading off limits to unsophisticated investors (Choi 2000). While I have doubts about the practicability (political and otherwise) of this proposal, it does have the virtue of intellectual coherence if we take the noise trader threat seriously.

[149] See Langevoort (1999b).

[150] See Kripke (1979: 189–20).

[151] See Langevoort (1992). I do not mean to say that insider-trading regulation is not economically justifiable, but rather that the nature and substance of the regulation extends beyond what is immediately necessary. I would agree with the many scholars who believe that insider-trading controls of some sort are an efficient response to the adverse selection

requires a set of norms and institutions, including but not limited to law, that credibly promises a threshold level of fairness. Quite likely, even wholesale federal deregulation of the insider trading laws could occur without undermining this foundation, because the other institutions are strong enough. At the very least, selective disclosure regulation is unnecessary from this standpoint. However, for a large number of reasons, insider-trading regulation has become the most visible advertisement for American-style securities regulation, effectively attracting public support because of its sharp, resonant egalitarian appeal. The SEC has invested a fair portion of its resources in building this brand message, and would no more let its trademark be compromised than would Coca-Cola or Anheuser-Busch. The main problem with selective disclosure is that, emotionally or intuitively, it is so visibly inconsistent with the rhetoric of retail investor empowerment. The growing publicity surrounding issuers' practices of granting preferential access to sell-side analysts introduced a level of static that interfered too much with the Commission's campaign. We would run too far afield were we to explore whether this kind of influence activity by the SEC is socially good or bad.[152] The point here is simply that research showing that non-rational trading behavior is more than the province of a marginal segment of the retail investor community is potentially destabilizing.[153]

However, our analysis should not simply dwell on the political. An interesting question is whether there are unexpected behavioral costs to the SEC's myth-story apart from what might turn out to be excessive regulation from a purely efficient standpoint. The risk here is that the message of empowerment may contribute not simply to investor confidence, but to overconfidence. Henry Hu (2000) has argued correctly that the SEC's cheerleading for broad public participation in the securities markets implicitly overstates both the safety and promise of equity securities vis-a-vis other forms of savings and investment. This over-statement leads to investor overconfidence insofar as capital allocation is concerned. Similarly, it seems plausible that steps like Reg FD can

problem and the potential for wider bid-ask spreads from market makers and specialists. And perhaps that applies to selective disclosure as well. As I have said before, however, it is hard to find more than passing attention to these issues in the SEC's formulation of its policy.

[152] Without delving deeply into this question, I suspect that insider-trading regulation helps the SEC gain the resources necessary to fight less salient, but more pernicious, forms of securities fraud and wrongdoing.

[153] The securities industry is unlikely to push too hard with a privileging claim either, even though it might like the FD policy consequences of its acceptance. In terms of revenue generation, overconfident investors are the broker's best friends: they are inclined to trade often, and are susceptible to well-crafted influence techniques. So, too, are the financial media. Investor empowerment is a key theme in the growth of specialty magazines, websites and cable financial news channels, as well as a lucrative set of products delivered by the mainstream media. In other words, the media happily promotes the Commission's message.

contribute to a false sense of competitiveness on the part of retail, which in turn can lead to excessive trading and investment of time and resources in what is likely an unprofitable effort.

Once more, we cannot take the behavioral research farther than it currently goes. We do not have settled empirical data that tells us about the 'relative rationality' of retail investors compared to institutions or permits us to evaluate how serious the risk of inefficiency caused by noise trader activity really is. But it does seem likely that as we come to know more about investor behavior and its impact on stock prices, judgments about what constitutes optimal securities regulation are subject to considerable dislocation. The Reg FD debate may not be the best example due to the agency-cost problems relating to the analysts' filtration role. These same issues reappear more subtly in a set of issues about the relative merits of public versus private markets as tools of capital formation. Much of how the SEC has set the rules relating to both corporate finance and market regulation has been influenced by the desire to keep the public securities markets the dominant place for trading. There has been growing pressure, however, to allow for 'institution'-only or 'accredited investor'-only markets that would be subject to far less regulation, thereby efficiently lowering the cost of capital. We see this pressure exhibited in the structure of the Rule 144A exemption and how the private placement rules are drafted, resulting in financing techniques that have no mandatory disclosure requirements so long as the investors are wealthy enough.[154] The Commission has refused to make it too easy for limited access markets to flourish, fearing that these markets could gradually pre-empt the public markets on which its political fortunes so heavily rest. But if encouraging limited access markets were truly to increase the likelihood of stock price efficiency by excluding noise traders, then it is not necessarily good policy to discourage them. Perhaps unexpectedly, behavioral finance deserves some voice in this discussion.

V. OPEN-MARKET FRAUD

A. Fraud-on-the-Market Lawsuits

In securities regulation, the influence of the EMH has been most visible in fraud-on-the-market lawsuits, where a class of plaintiffs who bought or sold securities claims that the issuer and its associates lied to the investing public and thus distorted the stock price. Each class member

---

[154] For a useful study of the 'deregulated' offering environment for large-scale capital raising, see Jackson and Pan (2001).

seeks recovery for out-of-pocket damages. These lawsuits have become controversial because of fears about plaintiffs' attorney abuses, generating reactive legislation in the form of the Private Securities Litigation Reform Act of 1995.[155]

Famously, the Supreme Court invoked the EMH in *Basic, Inc. v Levinson*,[156] in which the Court created a presumption of reliance for almost all investors simply upon a showing that the securities were traded in an 'efficient' market, and that there was a material misrepresentation or actionable omission. For a conservative court, this ruling exhibited an oddly progressive use of economic theory in securities law, which expanded the scope of issuer liability considerably and which even some notable economics-oriented scholars applauded.[157] As I have shown elsewhere, however, the EMH is unnecessary to justify the Court's approach, and potentially confusing.[158] The roots of the fraud-on-the-market presumption have less to do with economic theory than practical case management.[159] One can readily justify the presumption as the only workable way to facilitate private litigation in this area, substituting causation in place of reliance. In this sense, the IMH literature does not indicate much need to rethink the doctrine.[160]

A second notorious usage of the EMH in fraud-on-the-market litigation is the so-called 'truth on the market' defence.[161] Unlike the presumption of reliance, this defence is no case management tool. This doctrine states that once the defendant shows that the allegedly misrepresented or omitted information was actually known to the 'smart money' segment of the marketplace, a court will presume that the fraud was impounded rationally into the stock price so that even those allegedly deceived by an identifiable lie were not injured. No harm, no foul. Given the strong presumption of the EMH, this doctrine falls if the EMH falls. Much of the IMH literature purports to demonstrate that stock prices adjust more slowly to news, and in particular bad news, than the EMH predicts.[162] The notion of stock price drift with respect to earnings information is the best example, but the literature is filled with others.

---

[155] Compare Grundfest (1994) with Seligman (1994). For more on the legislation, see, e.g., Cox (1997); Yablon (2000).

[156] 485 U.S. 224 (1988).

[157] See, e.g., Fischel (1989). For some critics from the conventional law and economics side, see Macey and Miller (1990); Mahoney (1992).

[158] See Langevoort (1992: 892-903). It is confusing in that there is no clear-cut articulation of what the plaintiff is presumed to be relying on. If it is that the stock price is 'correct' (i.e., a strong use of the EMH), then the presumption seriously overcompensates to the extent that large numbers of traders are instead assuming that they can beat the market; if it is simply that the market is undistorted by fraud, then that has little to do with the EMH.

[159] See Note (1982).

[160] Of course, one could devise substitute reliance standards.

[161] See, e.g., *In re Apple Computer Sec. Litig.*, 886 F.2d 1109 (9th Cir. 1989); *Wielgos v Commonwealth Edison*, 892 F.2d 509 (7th Cir. 1989).

[162] See above notes 24–26.

Under the IMH approach, a messier, arguably fruitless factual inquiry is necessary to try to determine whether there has in fact been an adjustment to the news at any given point in time.

That brings us to the third use of the EMH, which I want to explore here. If we assume prompt rational adjustment to new information, then measuring damages in fraud-on-the-market seems easy, at least conceptually. The standard out-of-pocket measure of damages asks the court to determine the difference between the price the plaintiff paid for the stock (or sold it at) and the fair value at the time of the transaction.[163] The latter figure is a hypothetical one. But economists have persuaded lawyers that fair value can be calculated with relative precision by examining the abnormal return on the stock the day the truth finally came out and 'backing' that measure to the date of the fraud.[164] To be sure, this approach can in practice become very complicated, especially if there are suspicions that the truth leaked out to the market over time, or if other material events were simultaneously affecting the stock price. Even under the standard methodology, each side's calculations can differ wildly.[165] But the principle is clear enough.

On the other hand, if we assume that market prices underreact or overreact to information, or both, so that the adjustment time lengthens, the measurement difficulties become obvious. Event study methodology can still be utilized to test for whether or when adjustment has occurred—i.e., abnormal returns disappear—over substantial periods of time. In fact, empiricists critical of stock price efficiency measure precisely this in their efforts to demonstrate inefficiency. But with respect to any one firm at a given period of time, the longer the potential period of adjustment, the more likely it is that noise and the presence of other information will render the calculations imprecise and perhaps unusable. The ability of the econometrics to guide judicial, much less jury-based, fact-finding toward a meaningful measure of damages, or to test rigorously the 'truth on the market defence,' becomes increasingly doubtful.[166]

The more interesting question is whether the IMH offers something beyond methodological deconstructionism that might help move settlement negotiations to a meaningful end. Here, I want to examine two

[163] See Cox *et al.* (2001: 793-6).

[164] e.g., Cornell and Morgan (1990); Fischel (1982).

[165] See Alexander (1994); Cone and Laurence (1994).

[166] I hesitate to push this point too far as a doctrinal matter because judicial calculations of damages in fraud-on-the-market class actions are so rare today that the doctrinal question is almost hypothetical. If cases approach anywhere near the liability stage, they are almost always settled. On the other hand, the calculations play a substantial role in the settlement negotiations, setting at least the boundaries for discussions. Assuming that the merits matter to some extent, compare Alexander (1991) with Seligman (1994), thinking through the conceptual problem of how to fashion the out-of-pocket award is still significant.

positive claims about damage calculations that others have presented in law review articles, both of which draw explicitly from some of the literature we have been examining. The first is an article by a practicing lawyer specializing in defending class actions, William Fisher, who contends that aggregate damages in fraud-on-the-market cases should be reduced to reflect what he calls the 'analyst-added premium' (Fisher 1997). In essence, Fisher's claim is that analysts are often an independent cause of a large portion of inflated stock prices, separate from any fraud by the issuers. That portion should be deducted from what the issuer owes the defrauded investors. The second article is one that has actually had a policy impact already: Baruch Lev and Meiring deVilliers (1994) claim that short-term stock market overreaction in response to bad news is so likely that damages should be measured by reference to the 'levelled off' price after the truth has been told. Congress cited their article in 1995 as justification for capping damages by reference to the mean price over a ninety-day period after disclosure of the truth.[167]

1. The Analyst-Added Premium

We begin with Fisher, who believes that investors obsess about analysts' earnings forecasts, and that these forecasts are often erroneous. According to Fisher, when the error is on the high side, the stock price is inflated. When the company fails to meet this excessive forecast, the price drops significantly. Fisher wants to create a deduction from the damages owed to the extent that the issuer's fraud did not cause the analyst-added premium. The most obvious example of such premium would be when the analysts were hyping the stock before the misrepresentation or omission. The doctrine Fisher invokes to justify this is loss causation; the idea, well enshrined in securities litigation, that only losses proximately caused by the fraud itself are recoverable by plaintiffs.[168] In other words, he wants to deduct losses that would have occurred regardless of the fraud.

In evaluating Fisher's claim, we must keep our eyes on something very important. An illustration may help. Suppose a stock is trading at thirty at a time when management knows some unpublicised bad news. On 1 July, they make a fraudulent misstatement touching on that same news and the price rises to thirty-two.[169] On 1 September, the truth is discovered, and the market drops by twelve, so that the price is now at

---

[167] See Thompson (1996).

[168] See, e.g., *AUSA Life Ins. Co. v Ernst & Young*, 206 F.3d 202 (2d Cir. 2000); Cox *et al.* (2001: 761-71); Merritt (1988); Gabaldon (1990).

[169] For simplicity, assume that these price movements have been adjusted to remove general market influences.

twenty. A suit is brought by those who bought the issuer's stock between 1 July and 1 September.

The crucial loss causation question, assuming that the issuer had told the truth on 1 July instead of lying, is whether that candour would have immediately triggered the full stock price drop to twenty. If so, then the plaintiffs who bought after that date should recover the full measure of damages, without any deduction, because they would have bought at twenty (or not at all) and avoided the entire loss. Fisher (1997: 60-61) understands this reasoning, but wants to make it a fact question whether the stock price really would have dropped so far. Would analysts have in fact downgraded their estimates and recommendations, or instead have kept optimistically propping the stock up? I am far less sanguine than he is that this is a constructive idea. Recall from our prior discussion of analyst bias that analysts' predictions and recommendations may well be motivated by a desire to curry favor with management, and may be responsive to subtle nudges by managers that may fall short of the current legal definition for when the company bears responsibility for what analysts say. Perhaps, then, the analysts would front for the company by remaining optimistic, but if so, that is not good reason to absolve the company from liability. Moreover, the assumption of continued analyst favor is hardly a safe one. Also keep in mind the phenomenon Cornell described in his Intel study (Cornell 2001), where analysts may have moved the price up mindlessly, but corrected the price fairly rationally once reality set in as a result of Intel's disappointing earnings report. My sense is that surprising bad news from a company is often likely to lead to a correction, and if so, plaintiffs should recover under the standard measure. Even more bothersome is Fisher's suggestion for resolving this fact question: testimony from the analysts' themselves regarding how much their forecasts would have changed had management told the truth. If the currying favor phenomenon is real, this testimony is likely to be pro-issuer.

Thus, Fisher's argument for an 'analysts-added premium' deduction is not convincing, at least the way he frames it. However, I suspect that he could have made a far more powerful case by taking the doctrine of loss causation more seriously. If the right legal standard is to compare the plaintiffs' situation had there been no fraud rather than had the truth been told, then the measure of damages in our hypothetical might well be two rather than twelve. If the issuer had simply remained silent, neither lying nor revealing the truth, many of the plaintiffs would have bought anyway, except for those who specifically relied on the misstatement as the reason to buy. They would have suffered the drop of ten in any event when the truth later came out.

This alternate perspective is logical. There is no general duty to disclose bad news: the permissible alternative to lying often is simply to remain silent. If so, this alternative would normally lead to the situation noted above: 'bad news' injury for most plaintiffs even had there been no fraud. If we ignore this, we significantly overcompensate the plaintiff class in a fraud-on-the-market lawsuit. To avoid this overcompensation, in turn, we would want to deduct Fisher's analysts-added premium, but only because all of the portion of the drop that reflects the discovery of the truth (as opposed to the discovery of the fraud) should be deducted. All we would look for is the price impact of the specific misstatement and then perhaps add to the damages the portion of the drop reflecting the reputational penalty imposed by the market upon discovering the issuer's dishonesty.

While there is a fairly compelling conceptual basis for this approach, there are powerful practical reasons counselling against it. Note that the backwards induction method cannot be used under the second approach, because it uses the total stock price drop as its baseline. This method would have to focus on the time of the misstatement and would have to seek to discover the abnormal returns associated with the given misstatement.[170] More seriously, there is the difficult causation problem of determining whether, if the lie had not been told, the truth may still have come out earlier than it did. Most corporate lies are cover-ups, and the lulling potential is real. The conventional approach obviates the need for this inquiry. Additionally, we might add the concern that the alternate approach may not create enough damages to operate as enough of a deterrent to open-market securities fraud, given the problems of detecting wrongdoing in the first place.[171]

So this revised approach is another quagmire, which may be why the problem has been largely ignored, notwithstanding its underlying difficulty.[172] But that leaves in place the overcompensation concern, which exists even if markets are efficient but becomes all the more compelling when we take the IMH literature into account. Assume that psychological forces and analysts' biases combine to cause significant mood swings in stock prices. A streak of good corporate fortune leads to an inflated valuation until some exogenous shock causes a correction. The inflation makes the managers nervous, and they issue false publicity to hide some danger signs that begin to appear and buy time for a

---

[170] I am not skilled enough to compare the two techniques rigorously, but I suspect that whatever the difficulties associated with backwards induction, they are compounded significantly when there is no observable correction to use as a guide.

[171] See Georgakopoulos (1995). There is very little doubt that courts have devised fairly large damage awards in fraud-on-the-market cases that operate as a deterrent, given how difficult and costly these actions are to mount.

[172] At first glance, academics seem to be aware of the problem. See, e.g., Cornell and Morgan (1990: 908–11). Nonetheless, there is no proposed solution in the literature, and much of the writing on the subject simply assumes that the backwards induction methodology is sound.

turnaround. But the truth then comes out, and there is a large stock price decline.

Under these circumstances, there is no good reason to impose the full range of manic repricing damages on the issuer, for the reasons Fisher suggests. Two considerations add clarity to this idea. First, any award against the issuer or settlement is funded directly or indirectly out of the issuer shareholders' pockets, as the fraud-on-the-market litigation system is premised almost exclusively on a system of vicarious liability.[173] Secondly, investors tend to be, directly or indirectly, diversified in their investments and are just as likely to gain a windfall from issuer 'fraud-on-the-market' as to end up a loser.[174] Under these circumstances, then, there is very little reason to use the class action device as what is essentially an insurance system against market mood swings.[175]

The foregoing seems so obvious to me that I wonder why, notwithstanding Fisher and a few others, there has not been more concern raised about it by either policy-makers or litigants. I would venture a guess that one unexpected cost of strong faith in the EMH is that it has blinded people to the remedial flaws in this litigation system. This faith in the EMH makes too many questions seem too easily resolvable through the magic of econometrics. The more irrationality there is in the markets, the harder we have to work to find remedial solutions that are fair and reasonable.

2. Panic Damages

Lev and deVilliers's arguments have a similar thrust, albeit with a different starting point. While Lev and deVilliers do not make any strong psychology-based claims and indeed take pains not to be overly critical of rational actor accounts of stock market behavior, they put themselves squarely on the IMH side of the efficiency debate (Lev and deVilliers 1994: 19–22). Like many others, they distinguish between two different notions of efficiency: informational and fundamental. The latter is the standard understanding invoked by strong EMH proponents. Fundamental efficiency refers to prices that at all times conform to a consensus rational expectation about fundamental value. By contrast, in their view, informational efficiency assumes only that prices promptly respond to

---

[173] See Arlen and Carney (1992).

[174] See Easterbrook and Fischel (1985).

[175] To me, the goal of class action securities litigation is deterrence of managerial misconduct—compensation is of far less importance than is often thought, given the pocket-shifting nature of the process and the immense legal fees that tax each litigation-induced transfer. A much more sensible system would take all the foregoing reliance and causation issues off the table and fashion remedies in private litigation that simply reflect a penalty for the misconduct, with the amount adjusted upward to reflect the difficulty of detecting it. See Langevoort (1996b); see also Alexander (1996).

news, without any claim of close coupling with fundamental value. Thus, informationally-efficient markets can be quite volatile, and prices can overreact to news. The authors take a fairly moderate view here, estimating that reversion to something approximating fundamental efficiency typically occurs within a few days for larger issuers, and a week or two for smaller ones.

Lev and deVilliers's claim is that individuals are likely to overreact upon the announcement of bad news that corrects some prior misrepresentation. Their simple solution is thus to wait some relatively short period of time before assessing the price that is used as the baseline for the backwards induction described earlier. In turn, this approach allows the stock price to stabilize from its 'panic.' Lev and deVilliers contend that panic-based damages operate as an inappropriate award of consequential damages. Like Fisher, their point in this regard is that even had there been no fraud, and the truth told at an earlier point in time, there still would have been a panic reaction to it. Hence, the reaction is not properly part of actual damages.

This last claim is the interesting one and strikes me as plausible, if not obviously correct. Before addressing it, however, note a problem that illustrates the risks of applying the IMH literature prematurely to policy formulation. Lev and deVilliers invoke a fairly moderate proxy for speed of adjustment. The literature is far less clear that adjustment occurs as quickly or predictably as they suggest. Were it clear that an overreaction and bounce-back occur quickly in reaction to bad news, there would be very exploitable profit opportunities, and we would expect the phenomenon to disappear. In fact, the literature suggests that underreaction is actually more common in response to bad news (Hong and Stein 1999), especially for smaller issuers, and adjustments occur somewhat more slowly. If the IMH predictions are less consistent, developing a coherent doctrinal rule is harder.

This notion aside, the authors' immediate point is fairly persuasive.[176] The overreaction levels off fairly quickly in their view. If this bounce-back is an empirical regularity, then we should not use the excessive short-term response to the news as the baseline for backwards induction. Doing so would be the equivalent of saying that had the truth been told at

---

[176] What Congress did with Lev and deVilliers's suggestion is very different from their proposal, but simply illustrates the biases of the political process. Using a 90-day mean as a floor in terms of recovery is surely a ham-fisted solution. Imagine that the stock price is at 30 when the news is announced, and quickly falls to 20. Over the next three months, the stock market rallies, and the issuer's stock moves back up to 29 without any significant abnormal performance vis-a-vis the market as a whole after the first week. Plainly, this results in undercompensation. Congress 'forgot' to treat the 90-day mean as simply the starting point for backwards induction, as Lev and deVilliers (1994) had recommended, and instead turned it into a cap on damages.

the time of the fraud, the excessive reaction would have lasted throughout the class period.

B. Irrational Reactions, Materiality and the Puffery Defence

A harder question lurks in Lev and deVilliers's analysis, which is raised by the invocation of 'consequential damages' thinking. Suppose management makes a misleading announcement of good news: say, a pharmaceutical discovery. Such news, aided by media hype, significantly increases the company's stock price. Later, there is disappointment, and the stock price drops. In contrast to our earlier examples, here we will assume that the announcement was the sole significant cause of the entire price increase, and none of the subsequent decline reflects any pre-fraud bad news. In an action by buyers, should we allow a defence that the market overreacted to the news and limit the recovery to what a 'reasonable' market, devoid of animal spirits, would have done?

There are two possibilities. One is that the falsity was material but that noise traders overreact to it, pushing the price higher than it should rationally go. Here, a court might entertain the argument that the reliance was unreasonable. There is some indirect doctrinal support for so doing in a long series of cases dealing with face-to-face transactions, where courts deprive plaintiffs of recovery on grounds that their reliance was extremely unreasonable (i.e., reckless).[177] Widespread belief in the EMH has largely precluded recognition of this possibility in open market cases; the IMH invites us at least to consider it.[178]

The other possibility is that the false good news would not have triggered any reaction by reasonable investors at all but would have moved the noise traders. Here, we revisit the notion of materiality, which as we have already seen, is a crucial concept in securities regulation conventionally defined by reference to what might likely be of

---

[177] See, e.g., *Royal Am. Managers, Inc. v IRC Holding Corp.*, 885 F.2d 1011 (2d Cir. 1989).

[178] It is probably best here to distinguish between wrong and remedy. In a world of hype and overreaction, an excessive market response to news is a foreseeable consequence of a false statement. Familiar tort principles dictate that what is foreseeable is presumptively intended, and this principle should suffice to establish the wrong. To make this point clear, imagine that the falsity was designed specifically to move the stock price to a point that made profitable some executive compensation grants. The defendants were counting on the overreaction effect in styling the misinformation. A remedy in full makes sense when this kind of self-serving manipulative purpose can be shown. On the other hand, there are many cases where the overreaction is to information that was disseminated without such a purpose. A false press release makes claims about a company product mainly to influence some other audience (e.g., retailers or customers), not harm investors. See Langevoort (1999a). Investors say they were misled. Recalling the primacy of deterrence over compensation in open market cases, it would be worth considering whether an overreaction defence could be applied here, because it might be a useful corrective to the overcompensatory bias currently built into the law.

significance to the 'reasonable investor.' Recall that in our discussion of internet fraud, we saw this definition as a possible constraint,[179] but then invoked an insight from behavioral finance to explain what might have happened there that did not depend on extreme gullibility on the part of those who see the chat room messages. In the securities fraud context, there are many more instances where the same kind of question is posed: Is the test for materiality satisfied in cases where market participants seemingly respond in a heuristic fashion to a falsehood by defendants? If not, a powerful defence is created. If something is immaterial, people are free to lie about it without any liability at all.

Although there are numerous instances where this might arise, I want to begin by exploring a very popular defence in class action securities litigation: the so-called 'puffery' defence.[180] Courts today frequently dismiss cases on the grounds that all the management did when it spoke was generally express optimism about the firm's prospects. This action, courts say, is inherently nonactionable, even if the managers at the time knew that things were not as positive as represented. Most courts have justified this holding on the grounds that reasonable investors simply do not rely on such statements.[181] In a more extended analysis, Judge Posner has stated that investors anticipate optimism from managers and interpret it appropriately. If managers were instead mandated actually to tell the exact truth, he says, investors would be misled into believing that things were far worse than they really are.[182]

Here, we run into the ever-troublesome distinction between the normative and the descriptive. My focus is first on the latter: is it clear that typical investors do not rely on puffery? There is little research that studies this specifically, and so many judges are guessing.[183] As before, I want to avoid the reductionism of confusing cognitive bias with mere foolishness, which could justify reliance on just about anything. However, we can tell a story that comes closer to capturing what is occurring in these kinds of cases—one that cautions that too easy a dismissal on materiality grounds is unwarranted.

These cases almost always arise in a setting in which a company has had a very visible streak of success. For example, suppose that after a company develops and markets a new product or negotiates a lucrative contract, the stock price rises accordingly. Then, allegedly, the company discovers problems, in the form of technical glitches or cancels orders that

---

[179] See above text accompanying notes 91–92.

[180] See O'Hare (1998).

[181] e.g., *Lasker v New York State Elec. & Gas Co.*, 85 F.3d 35 (2d Cir. 1996); *Raab v Gen. Physics Corp.*, 4 F.3d 286 (4th Cir. 1993).

[182] *Eisenstadt v Centel Corp.*, 113 F.3d 738, 746 (7th Cir. 1997).

[183] To be sure, one could say that there is a normative dimension here and that judges are saying that investors should not rely on these things, whether or not they do in fact. For a discussion of judicial heuristics in this area, see Bainbridge and Gulati (2002).

they keep secret from the market. The company's public expressions remain optimistic, without including specific false statements that would render such expressions fraudulent. If we focus on those statements in isolation, we can see why an efficiency-minded court might doubt any significant incidence of reliance by any but the most gullible of investors. After all, who buys simply because management brags about how things are going? In context, however, this story becomes much more complicated. It is important to go back to the set of facts that originally gave rise to the optimism—the good news and the price rise. As we have seen, behavioral finance suggests that investors do extrapolate too readily and see in past success too much likelihood of future gains. Indeed, prospective future gains are probably the impetus for continued buying activity among investors, especially if analysts are also recommending the stock or estimating continued earnings growth. From this perspective, the continued statements of optimism would be non-events, and courts might be justified in discounting their significance alone as part of a fraud case. But I think there is more to it, as illustrated by the EntreMed experience. If managerial hype succeeds in gaining media attention, it will draw a higher level of investor attention to the company and its past success, prompting the kinds of heuristic reasoning that causes investors to buy the company stock.[184] In other words, as in the internet fraud story in Part III, the salience of such hyped optimistic information sets the stage for harmful behavioral reaction, whether or not the substance of those statements is deceptive in and of itself.

Given this description, how should the law respond? The conservative inclination would be to declare that any such behavioral reaction is irrational or gullible enough not to deserve legal protection.[185] Such a response could refer to the doctrine of materiality to argue that such weak-minded thinking does not rise to the level of reasonableness, so that no legal wrong ever occurred. When animal spirits roam the markets, however, this rationale strikes me as dangerous for the same reason identified in our discussion of chat-room fraud. In terms of commonplace investor behavior, a hands-off legal approach would only invite a high incidence of exploitation. Here again is the conundrum that securities law will have to face up to: the higher the incidence of heuristics-driven investor behavior, the more expansive the definition of materiality has to become unless we are willing to tolerate the distortions that occur when savvy people take advantage of those heuristics. I suspect that courts to date have implicitly assumed efficiency or that noise trader influence is

---

[184] See Shleifer (2000: 129) ('When a company has a consistent history of earnings growth over several years, accompanied as it may be by salient and enthusiastic descriptions of its products and management, investors might conclude that the past history is representative of an underlying earnings growth potential.').

[185] On the politics of reliance on psychological explanations, see Tetlock (2000).

small. If so, a fairly strict definition of materiality in open-market cases works.[186] If not, then these courts have made a bad bet.

My preference here is to keep the definition materially tied to what is commonplace or normal, whether we admire the behavior or not. If what we want is some semblance of market price integrity (i.e., unmanipulated markets), we have little other choice. With respect to puffery in particular, courts should treat a general expression of optimism as if it were a half-truth and inquire into the circumstances of its making. If the publicity appears to be a deliberate effort by company managers to attract investor attention to the company's past successes, courts should treat it as misleading. The same result would follow, without the need to resort to much in the way of investor psychology, if the communicative content of the general statements was an expression that nothing from the recent reported past has changed.[187] As before, courts could treat some such expressions as material by reference to predictable investor heuristics, but still exercise restraint on the private remedies side when plaintiffs' investment judgments fell too far short of the rational ideal.

A concrete example of all this has arisen amid the controversy associated with an SEC staff accounting bulletin (SAB 99) on the subject of earnings manipulation.[188] The most important question in the bulletin involved the company that makes a tiny upward adjustment in reported earnings (perhaps less than one per cent) in order to meet analyst expectations for a particular quarter. The bulletin provides that the small amount is material because the market treats it as important, punishing companies that fall short. Fundamentally, it is hard to imagine how a reasonable investor would treat that data as significant. It is possible that the SEC is assuming an irrational overreaction here. But there are other possibilities, too. If we follow Cornell's story, the small shortfall may actually operate as a wake-up call, rationally correcting what had heretofore been an irrationally inflated valuation. Or, unexpected shortfalls may simply be salient focal points, triggering a cascade of selling simply in anticipation of similar actions by others—i.e., the overconfidence-driven story I put forth earlier to explain some kinds of internet fraud. Whatever the causal explanation, IMH thinking suggests that we define materiality in terms of likely market behavior, heuristic or not.

---

[186] For a thoughtful and highly contextual consideration of materiality, see Brudney (1989).
[187] See Langevoort (1999a).
[188] Staff Accounting Bulletin No. 99, 64 Fed. Reg. 45150 (1999). For an application of SAB 99 in the litigation context, see *Ganino v Citizens Utils. Co.*, 228 F.3d 154 (2d Cir. 2000).

CONCLUSION

The route toward a behaviorally-sophisticated form of securities regulation is a slow one, and I have tried here not to jump too far ahead of the available empirical evidence. To me, that evidence presents a fairly strong case for the presence of significant market inefficiencies. But it is not dispositive and leaves open to question both the specific directions that the inefficiency takes and the magnitude of the deviations. For now, the most valuable use of that evidence may well be in the form that I have followed here: using the IMH and behavioral literature to explore such possibilities as the overconfidence-induced drag race on the internet, the subtle nature of analyst biases, or the bloating of liability in fraud-on-the-market cases when stock prices exhibit manic-depressive symptoms. These examples can help us think through difficult problems outside the box of conventional theories of investor behavior. In formulating strategy in the face of an admittedly imperfect under-standing of the stock markets, we can at least consider hedging our bets.

To the extent that the behavioral insights point in any particular regulatory direction, they are more likely than not to be pro-regulatory. That is, the IMH evidence weakens the comparative appeal of marketplace discipline vis-a-vis the possibility of regulatory correction. With respect to earnings management of the sort typified by Enron, for example, we should be less confident of the market's ability to see through the financial cosmetics. What is less obvious, however, is the extent to which these same insights also call into doubt some cherished pro-regulatory strategies. Essentially, if we deliver better transparency to investors, will they use it effectively? The SEC's myth-story about investors carefully perusing the details of regulation-mandated disclosure documents gives way to an image of sustained investor overconfidence and self-serving inferences. An investor convinced that he has skilfully spotted a trend and can ride the momentum for a while is not going to be moved by a clearer, 'plain English'[189] disclosure about the risks a company faces. People with an inflated view of their investment capacities don't necessarily want the help of regulation offers. Even fraud-on-the-market remedies—a beloved regulatory intervention with a wide base of academic support—look less appealing in the light shed by inefficiency accounts of stock price movements.

This is disorienting, for sure. Unless we are prepared to isolate the noise trader—in the direction of Steve Choi's interesting, but politically fanciful proposal for licensing investors[190]—securities regulation is left to serve as the market's therapist, seeking to de-bias investors from all their

[189] 1933 Act Rule 421(d), 17 CFR § 230.421(d).
[190] See above note 148.

dangerous propensities. In contrast to some others who have suggested this role,[191] I doubt that the government can accomplish this well, or that the intended audience has much inclination to learn.

Of course, we could be rescued from all this complexity if the empirical siege is broken and efficiency regains the upper hand. Perhaps investors are really better learners than the critics think, or smart money forces powerful enough to moderate most of the harmful effects of the average investors' cognitive limits. Critics of efficiency cannot be so wedded to their contrarian visions that they deny this possibility. If efficiency is indeed the better description of marketplace behavior, then we thankfully have less to worry about. But we should not commit to that account simply because it offers the more comforting solutions or is politically more palatable. And the lesson of Enron is hardly encouraging.

Those involved in securities regulation, then, need to look harder at the evidence in both directions and, in fact, help generate more of it. Neither the SEC nor academics have spent enough time on detailed field studies of investor behavior, so we lack a solid sense of how decisions occur or what social dynamics are at work that might drive market prices.[192] In-depth interviews and survey data would take us in this direction, as would more laboratory studies on investor behavior. Somewhat more conventionally, it would also be helpful to know the relative balance between individual and institutional trading—something roughly measurable by reference to trade size—when prices are on their way up compared to when they reach their top and start coming back down. In other words, who ends up winning or losing from stock-price gyrations? The data developed during discovery in fraud cases like Enron might be of special interest along these lines. We cannot be too confident about our behavioral predictions one way or the other until much more of this kind of work is done.

In the meantime, however, we should at least prepare for the possibility that further research may lead us down a darker road than on the one we have been. Enron may prove to be a large contributor along these lines. Enron's story rings true with so many of the IMH predictions: a momentum play fed by accounting illusions that worked largely because investors, and maybe many of the company's senior executives, wanted to believe them; analysts who let their desire for Enron's business cloud their judgment; a manic-depressive crash that came only once reality became too stark to ignore. If that story helps push us to a new realism in securities regulation that displaces undue faith in market efficiency, it will be a small payoff amid all the damage.

---

[191] See, e.g., Fanto (1998).

[192] See above notes 36–39. Interestingly, Finland offers a particularly rich data set on individual investment decisions. See Grinblatt and Keloharju (2000).

REFERENCES

Alexander, J.C. (1991), 'Do the Merits Matter?: A Study of Settlements in Securities Class Actions', 43 *Stan. L. Rev.* 497.

Alexander, J.C. (1994), 'The Value of Bad News in Securities Class Actions', 41 *UCLA L. Rev.* 1421.

Alexander, J.C. (1996), 'Rethinking Damages in Securities Class Actions', 48 *Stan. L. Rev.* 501.

Arlen, J. (1998), 'The Future of Behavioural Economic Analysis of Law', 51 *Vand. L. Rev.* 1765.

Arlen, J.H. and Carney, W.J. (1992), 'Vicarious Liability for Fraud on Securities Markets: Theory and Evidence', *U. Ill. L. Rev.* 691.

Ayres, I. and Cramton, P. (1994), 'Relational Investing and Agency Theory', 15 *Cardozo L. Rev.* 1033.

Ayres, I. and Choi, S. (2001), 'Internalizing Outsider Trading', available at http://papers.ssrn.com/sol3/papers.cfm?abstract_id=277580 (last visited 15 Jan. 2005).

Bainbridge, S. (1999), 'Insider Trading Regulation: The Path Dependent Choice Between Property Rights and Securities Fraud', 52 *SMU L. Rev.* 1589.

—— (2000), 'Mandatory Disclosure: A Behavioural Analysis', 68 *U. Cin. L. Rev.* 1023.

Bainbridge, S. and Gulati, G.M. (2002), 'Judging Shortcuts: How Do Judges Maximize? (The Same Way Everybody Else Does—Boundedly): Rules of Thumb in Securities Fraud Opinions', 51 *Emory L.J.* 83.

Baker, W. (1984), 'The Social Structure of a National Securities Market', 89 *Am. J. Soc.* 775.

Barber, B. and Odean, T. (2000a), 'Trading Is Hazardous to Your Wealth: The Common Stock Investment Performance of Individual Investors', 55 *J. Fin.* 773.

—— (2000b), 'Boys Will Be Boys: Overconfidence and Common Stock Investment', 116 *Q.J. Econ.* 261.

—— (2001), 'The Internet and the Investor', 15 *J. Econ. Persp.* 41.

—— (2002), 'Online Investors: Do the Slow Die First?', 15 *Rev. Fin. Stud.* 455.

Barber, B., *et al.* (2001a), 'Can Investors Profit from the Prophets? Consensus Analyst Recommendations and Stock Returns', 56 *J. Fin.* 531.

—— (2001b), 'Prophets and Losses: Reassessing the Returns to Analysts' Stock Recommendations', available at http://papers.ssrn.com/sol3/papers.cfm?abstract_id=269119 (last visited 15 Jan. 2005).

Barberis, N., *et al.* (1998), 'A Model of Investor Sentiment', 49 *J. Fin.* Econ. 307.

—— (2001), 'Prospect Theory and Asset Prices', 66 *Q.J. Econ.* 1.

Barberis, N. and Huang, M. (2001), 'Mental Accounting, Loss Aversion and Individual Stock Returns', 56 *J. Fin.* 1247.

Benabou, R and Tirole, J. (2002), 'Self-Confidence and Personal Motivation', 117 *Q.J. Econ.* 871.

Benos, A. (1998), 'Aggressiveness and Survival of Overconfident Traders', 1 *J. Fin. Mkts.* 353.

Bernard, V. and Thomas, J. (1989), 'Post-Earnings Announcement Drift: Delayed Price Response or Risk Premium?', 27 *J. Acct. Res.* 1.

Bernstein, P.L. (1998), *Against the Gods: The Remarkable Story of Risk* (New York: John Wiley & Sons).

Black, B. (2001), 'The Legal and Institutional Preconditions for Strong Securities Markets', 48 *UCLA L. Rev.* 781.

Black, F. (1986), 'Noise', 41 *J. Fin.* 529.

Bloomfield, R., *et al.* (2000), 'Under-reactions, Over-reactions and Moderated Confidence', 3 *J. Fin. Mkts.* 113.

BNA (2001a), 'Industry Participants Want SEC To Issue Guidance on Regulation FD', 33 *Sec. Reg. & L. Rep.* 637 (30 Apr. 30).

—— (2001b), 'Pitt Concurs in Staff Views on Good Faith Reg FD Compliance', 33 *Sec. Reg. & L. Rep.* 1206 (20 Aug.).

—— (2002a), 'Enron Internal Probe Finds Abuses; Board Claims No Knowledge', 34 *Sec. Reg. & L. Rep.* 246 (11 Feb.).

—— (2002b), 'Regulators Join Together To Resolve Analyst IPO Cases', 34 *Sec. Reg. & L. Rep.* 1622, 1624 (7 Oct.).

Bradley, C. (2000), 'Disorderly Conduct: Day Traders and the Ideology of "Fair and Orderly Markets"', 26 *J. Corp. L.* 63.

Bratton, W.W. (2002), 'Enron and the Dark Side of Shareholder Value', 76 *Tulane L. Rev.* 1275.

Brav, A. and Heaton, J.B. (2002), 'Competing Theories of Financial Anomalies', 15 *Rev. Fin. Stud.* 575.

Brown, L.D. and Rozeff, M.S. (1978), 'The Superiority of Analyst Forecasts as Measures of Expectations: Evidence from Earnings', 33 *J. Fin.* 1.

Brudney, V. (1989), 'A Note on Materiality and Soft Information Under the Federal Securities Laws', 75 *Va. L. Rev.* 723.

Bulkey, G. and Harris, R. (1997), 'Irrational Analysts' Expectations as a Cause of Excess Volatility in Stock Prices', 107 *Econ. J.* 359.

Camerer, C. and Lovallo, D. (1999), 'Overconfidence and Excess Entry: An Experimental Approach', 89 *Am. Econ. Rev.* 306.

Campbell, J.Y. (2000), 'Asset Pricing at the Millenium', 55 *J. Fin.* 1515.

Carleton, W., *et al.* (1998), 'Optimism Biases Among Brokerage and Non-Brokerage Firms' Equity Recommendations: Agency Costs in the Investment Industry', 27 *Fin. Mgmt.* 17.

Carlton, D. and Fischel, D (1983), 'The Regulation of Insider Trading', 35 *Stan. L. Rev.* 857.

Chan, L., *et al.* (1996), 'Momentum Strategies', 51 *J. Fin.* 1681.

Chevalier, J. and Ellison, G. (1999), 'Career Concerns of Mutual Fund Managers', 114 *Q.J. Econ.* 389.

Choi, S. (2000), 'Regulating Investors, Not Issuers: A Market-Based Proposal', 88 *Cal. L. Rev.* 279.

—— (2002), 'Selective Disclosures in the Public Capital Markets', 35 *U.C. Davis L. Rev.* 533.

Choi, S. and Guzman, A. (1998), 'Portable Reciprocity: Rethinking the International Reach of Securities Regulation', 71 S. *Cal. L. Rev.* 903.

Chopra, V. (1998), 'Why So Much Error in Analysts' Earnings Forecasts?', 54 *Fin. Analysts J.* 66.

Collingwood, H. (2001), 'The Earnings Game: Everyone Plays, Nobody Wins, *Harv. Bus. Rev.* (June, at 65).

Cone, K. and Laurence, J. (1994), 'How Accurate Are Estimates of Aggregate Damages in Securities Fraud Cases?', 49 *Bus. L.* 505.

Cooper, M. *et al.*, (2001), 'A Rose.com by Any Other Name', 56 *J. Fin.* 2371.

Cornell, B. (2001), 'Is the Response of Analysts to Information Consistent with Fundamental Valuation? The Case of Intel', *Fin. Mgmt.*, (Spring, at 113).

Cox, J.D. (1997), 'Making Securities Fraud Class Actions Virtuous', 39 *Ariz. L. Rev.* 497.

Cox, J.D., *et al.* (2001), *Securities Regulation: Cases and Materials* (3d edn.) (New York: John Wiley & Sons).

Cunningham, L. (1994), 'From Random Walks to Chaotic Crashes: The Linear Genealogy of the Efficient Capital Market Hypothesis', 62 *Geo. Wash. L. Rev.* 546.

Daniel, K. and Titman, S. (1999), 'Market Efficiency in an Irrational World', *Fin. Analysts J.*, (Nov.-Dec., at p.28).

Daniel, K., *et al.* (1998), 'Investor Psychology and Security Market Under-and Overreactions', 53 *J. Fin.* 1839.

—— (2001), 'Overconfidence, Arbitrage and Equilibrium Asset Pricing', 56 *J. Fin.* 921.

De Bondt, W. and Thaler, R. (1995), ' Financial Decisionmaking in Markets and Firms: A Behavioural Perspective in Finance', *Handbook of Operations Research and Management Science* (R. Jarrow *et al.* eds.), Vol 9 (Amsterdam: Elsevier Science).

Dechow, P.M., *et al.* (2000), 'Short-sellers, Fundamental Analysis and Stock Returns', 61 J. Fin. Econ. 77.

DeLong, B., *et al.* (1991), 'The Survival of Noise Traders in Financial Markets', 64 *J. Bus.* 1.

Derthick, M. and Quirk, P. (1985), *The Politics of Deregulation* (Washington: Brookings Institute Press).

DiFazio, N. and Bordia, P. (1997), ' Rumor and Prediction:Making Sense (But Losing Dollars) in the Stock Market', 71 *Org. Behav. & Hum. Decision Processes* 329.

Dreman, D. (1979), *The New Contrarian Investment Strategy* (New York: Random House).

Easterbrook, F. and Fischel, D. (1984), 'Mandatory Disclosure and the Protection of Investors', 70 *Va. L. Rev.* 669.

—— (1985), 'Optimal Damages in Securities Cases', 52 *U. Chi. L. Rev.* 611, 642.

Easterwood, J. and Nutt, S. (1999), 'Inefficiency in Analysts' Earnings Forecasts: Systematic Misreaction or Systematic Optimism?', 54 *J. Fin.* 1777.

Edmonstron, P. (2001), 'Shhh! Focus on Whisper Numbers Fades as Pundits Sidestep the Informal Targets', Wall St. J., (26 July, at C1).

Ellison, G. and Fundenberg, D. (1995), 'Word of Mouth Communication and Social Learning', 110 *Q.J. Econ.* 93.

Enron Corp. (2002), Special Investigative Comm. of the Bd. of Dirs.: Report of Investigation (on file with author).

Fama, E. (1998), 'Market Efficiency, Long-Term Returns and Behavioral Finance, 33 *J. Fin. Econ.* 3.

Fanto, J. (1998),'We're All Capitalists Now: The Importance, Nature, Provision and Regulation of Investor Education', 49 *Case W. Res. L. Rev.* 105.

Fischel, D. (1982),'Use of Modern Finance Theory in Securities Fraud Cases', 38 *Bus. L.* 1.

—— (1984), 'Insider Trading and Investment Analysts: An Economic Analysis of Dirks v SEC', 13 *Hofstra L. Rev.* 127.

—— (1989),'Efficient Capital Markets, the Crash and the Fraud on the Market Theory', 74 *Cornell L. Rev.* 907.

Fischel, D. and Ross, D. (1991),'Should the Law Prohibit Manipulation in Financial Markets?', 105 Harv. L. Rev. 503.

Fisher, K. and Statman, M. (2000), 'Cognitive Biases in Market Forecasts', *J. Portfolio Mgmt.*, (Fall, at p.72).

Fisher, W.O. (1997), 'The Analyst-Added Premium as a Defense in Open Market Securities Cases', 53 *Bus. L.* 35.

Fox, M. (2001),'Regulation FD and Foreign Issuers: Globalization's Strains and Opportunities', 41 *Va. J. Int'l L.* 653.

Frankel, R., *et al.* (1999), 'An Empirical Examination of Conference Calls as a Voluntary Disclosure Medium', 37 *J. Acct. Res.* 133.

Frankel, T. (1998), 'The Internet, Securities Regulation, and the Theory of Law', 73 *Chi.-Kent L. Rev.* 1319.

Gabaldon, T. (1990), 'Causation, Courts and Congress: A Study of Contradiction in the Federal Securities Laws', 31 *B.C.L. Rev.* 1027.

—— (2001),'John Law, with a Tulip, in the South Seas: Gambling and the Regulation of Euphoric Market Transactions', 26 *J. Corp. L.* 225.

Ganguly, A., *et al.* (2000), 'Do Asset Market Prices Reflect Traders' Judgment Biases?', 20 *J. Risk & Uncert.* 219.

Georgakopoulos, N. (1995), 'Fraud, Markets and Fraud-on-the-Market: The Tortured Transition of Justifiable Reliance from Deceit to Securities Fraud', 49 *U. Miami L. Rev.* 671.

Gervais, S. and Odean, T. (2001), 'Learning To Become Overconfident', 14 *Rev. Fin. Stud.* 1.

Gilovich, T. (1991), *How We Know What Isn't So* (New York: Free Press).

Gilson R.J. and Kraakman R. (1984), 'The Mechanisms of Market Efficiency', 70 *Va. L. Rev.* 549.

Gilson, S. (2000), 'Analysts and Information Gaps: Lessons from the UAL Buyout', *Fin. Analysts J.*, (Nov.-Dec., at 82).

Gompers, P. and Metrick, A. (2001), 'Institutional Investors and Equity Prices', 116 *Q.J. Econ.* 229.

Gordon, J.N. (2002), 'What Enron Means for the Management and Control of the Modern Business Corporation: Some Initial Reflections', 69 *U. Chi. L. Rev.* 1233.

Goshen, Z. and Parchomovsky, G. (2001), 'On Insider Trading, Markets and "Negative" Property Rights in Information', 87 *Va. L. Rev.* 1229.

Griffin, D. and Varey, C. (1999), 'Towards a Consensus on Overconfidence', 65 *Org. Behav. & Hum. Decision Processes* 227.

Grinblatt, M. and Keloharju, M. (2000), 'The Investment Behaviour and Performance of Various Investor Types: A Study of Finland's Unique Data Set', 55 *J. Fin. Econ.* 43.

Grossman, S. and Stiglitz, J. (1980), 'On the Impossibility of Informationally Efficient Markets', 70 *Am. Econ. Rev.* 393.

Grundfest, J. (1994), 'Disimplying Private Rights of Action Under the Federal Securities Laws: The Commission's Authority', 107 *Harv. L. Rev.* 961.

Grundy, B. and Martin, J.S. (2001), 'Understanding the Nature of the Risks and the Sources of the Rewards to Momentum Investing', 14 *Rev. Fin. Stud.* 29.

Hall, R.E. (2001), 'Struggling To Understand the Stock Markets', 91 *Am. Econ. Rev.* 1.

Hand, J.R.M. (2000), 'Profits, Losses and the Non-Linear Pricing of Internet Stocks', available at http://papers.ssrn.com/sol3/papers.cfm?abstract_id=204875 (last visited 15 Jan. 2005).

Hass, J. (1998), 'Small Issue Public Offerings Conducted over the Internet: Are They Suitable for the Retail Investor?', 72 S. *Cal. L. Rev.* 67.

Hayward, M.L.A. and Boeker, W. (1998), 'Power and Conflicts of Interest in Professional Firms: Evidence from Investment Banking', 43 *Admin. Sci. Q.* 1.

Heflin, F., *et al.* (2001), 'Regulation FD and the Financial Information Environment', available at http://papers.ssrn.com/sol3/papers.cfm?abstract_id= 276768 (last visited 15 Jan. 2005).

Hilary, G. and Menzly, L. (2001),'Does Past Success Lead Analysts To Become Overconfident?', at http://papers.ssrn.com/sol3/papers.cfm?abstract_id= 261476 (last visited 15 Jan. 2005).

Hill, C. (1997), 'Why Financial Appearances Might Matter: An Explanation for Dirty Pooling and Some Other Types of Financial Cosmetics', 22 *Del. J. Corp. L.* 121.

Hirshleifer (2001), 'Investor Psychology and Asset Prices', 56 *J. Fin.* 1533.

Hirshleifer, D., *et al.* (1994), 'Security Analysis and Trading Patterns When Some Investors Receive Information Before Others', 49 *J. Fin.* 1665.

Hirst, E., *et al.* (1995), 'Investor Reactions to Financial Analysts' Research Reports', 33 *J. Acct. Res.* 335.

Hogarth, R. and Reder, M. (1986), 'Perspectives from Economics and Psychology', 59 *J. Bus.* S185.

Hong, H. and Stein, J. (1999), 'A Unified Theory of Underreaction, Momentum Trading and Overreaction in Asset Markets', 54 *J. Fin.* 2143.

Hong, H., *et al.* (2000), 'Bad News Travels Slowly: Size, Analyst Coverage and the Profitability of Momentum Strategies', 55 *J. Fin.* 265.

Hu, H.T.C. (2000), 'Faith and Magic: Investor Beliefs and Government Neutrality', 78 *Tex. L. Rev.* 777.

Huberman, G. and Regev, T. (2001), 'Contagious Speculation and a Cure for Cancer: A Nonevent that Made Stock Prices Soar', 56 *J. Fin.* 387.

Jackson, H. and Pan, E. (2001), 'Regulatory Competition in International Securities Markets: Evidence from Europe in 1999', 56 *Bus. L.* 653.

Jacob, J., *et al.* (1999), 'Expertise in Forecasting Performance of Security Analysts', 28 *J. Acct. & Econ.* 51.

Jegadeesh, N. and Titman, S. (2001) 'Profitability of Momentum Strategies: An Evaluation of Alternative Explanations', 56 *J. Fin.* 699.

Jegadeesh, N., *et al.* (2002), 'Analyzing the Analysts: When Do Recommendations Add Value?', available at http://papers.ssrn.com/sol3/papers.cfm?abstract_id=291241 (last visited 15 Jan. 2005).

Kahneman, D. and Riepe, M. (1998), 'Aspects of Investor Psychology', 24 *J. Portfolio Mgmt.* 52.

Keynes, J.M. (1936), *A General Theory of Employment, Interest and Money* (Cambridge: CUP).

Klausner, M. (1984), 'Sociological Theory and the Behaviour of Financial Markets', in Adler, P. and Adler, P. (1984), *The Social Dynamics of Financial Markets* (vol. 2: 57).

Klibanoff, P., *et al.* (1999), 'Investor Reaction to Salient News in Closed-End Country Funds', 53 *J. Fin.* 673.

Kothari, S.P. (2001), 'Capital Market Research in Accounting', 31 *J. Acct. & Econ.* 105.

Kripke, H. (1979), *The SEC and Corporate Disclosure: Regulation in Search of a Purpose* (New York: Law and Business Inc.).

Kyle, A. and Wang, F.A. (1997), 'Speculation Duopoly with Agreement To Disagree: Can Overconfidence Survive the Market Test?', 52 *J. Fin.* 2073.

Lamont, O.A and Thaler, R.H. (2001), 'Can the Market Add and Subtract? Mispricing in Tech Stock Carve-Outs', available at http://papers.ssrn.com/sol3/papers.cfm?abstract_id=384240 (last visited 15 Jan. 2005).

Langevoort, D.C. (1990), 'Investment Analysts and the Law of Insider Trading', 76 *Va. L. Rev.* 1023.

—— (1992), 'Theories, Assumptions and Securities Regulation: Market Efficiency Revisited', 140 *U. Pa. L. Rev.* 851.

—— (1996a), 'Capping Damages for Open Market Securities Frauds', 38 *Ariz. L. Rev.* 641.

—— (1996b), 'Selling Hope, Selling Risk: Some Lessons for Law from Behavioural Economics About Stockbrokers and Sophisticated Customers', 84 *Cal. L. Rev.* 627.

—— (1997), 'Organized Illusions: A Behavioural Theory of Why Corporations Mislead Stock Market Investors (and Cause Other Social Harm)', 146 *U. Pa. L. Rev.* 101.

—— (1999a), 'Half-Truths: Protecting Mistaken Inferences by Investors and Others', 52 *Stan. L. Rev.* 87, 101.

—— (1999b), 'Rereading Cady Roberts: The Ideology and Practice of Insider Trading Regulation', 99 *Colum. L. Rev.* 1319.

—— (2000), 'Taking Myths Seriously: An Essay for Lawyers', 74 *Chi.-Kent L. Rev.* 1569, 1575–77.

Lee, C.M.C. (2001), 'Market Efficiency and Accounting Research', 31 *J. Acct. & Econ.* 233.

LeRoy, S.F. (1989), 'Efficient Capital Markets and Martingales', 27 *J. Econ. Lit.* 1583.

Lev, B. and deVilliers, M. (1994), 'Stock Price Crashes and 10b-5 Damages: A Legal, Economic and Policy Analysis', 47 *Stan. L. Rev.* 7.

Lewis, M. (1989), *Liar's Poker* (New York: Penguin).

—— (2001), 'Jonathan Lebed's Extracurricular Activities', *N.Y. Times Mag.*, (25 Feb., at 26).

Lim, T. (2001), 'Rationality and Analysts' Forecast Bias', 56 *J. Fin.* 369.

Loewenstein, G. (2000), 'Emotions in Economic Theory and Economic Behaviour' 90 *Am. Econ. Rev.* 426.

Logue, D. (1986), 'Discussion: Discrete Expectational Data and Portfolio Performance' 41 *J. Fin.* 713.

Lowenfels, L. and Bromberg, A. (1991), 'Securities Market Manipulations: An

Examination and Analysis of Domination and Control, Front-Running and Parking', 55 Alb. L. Rev. 293.

Macey, J., *et al.* (1989), 'Restrictions on Short Sales: An Analysis of the Uptick Rule and Its Role in the 1987 Stock Market Crash', 74 Cornell L. Rev. 799.

Macey, J. and Miller, G. (1990), 'Good Finance, Bad Economics: An Analysis of the Fraud on the Market Theory', 42 *Stan. L. Rev.* 1059.

Mahoney, P. (1992), 'Precaution Costs and the Law of Fraud in Impersonal Markets', 78 *Va. L. Rev.* 623.

Manne, H. (1966), *Insider Trading and the Stock Markets* (New York: Free Press).

Merritt, A. (1998), 'A Consistent Model of Loss Causation in Securities Fraud Litigation: Suiting the Remedy to the Wrong', 66 *Tex. L. Rev.* 469.

Michaely, R., *et al.* (1995), 'Price Reactions to Dividend Omissions: Overreaction or Drift?', 50 *J. Fin.* 573.

Michaely, R. and Womack, K. (1999), 'Conflict of Interest and the Credibility of Underwriter Analyst Recommendations', 12 *Rev. Fin. Stud.* 653.

Mikhail, M. *et al.*, (1997), 'The Development of Expertise: Do Security Analysts Improve Their Performance with Experience?', *J. Acct. Res.* 131.

Moore, D.A., *et al.* (1999), 'Positive Illusions and Forecasting Errors in Mutual Fund Investment Decisions', 79 *Org. Behav. & Hum. Decision Processes* 95.

Neuborne, B. (1989), 'The First Amendment and Government Regulation of the Capital Markets', 55 *Brook. L. Rev.* 17.

Nofsinger, J. and Sias, R. (1999), 'Herding and Feedback Trading by Institutional and Individual Investors', 54 *J. Fin.* 2263.

Note (1982), 'The Fraud on the Market Theory', 95 *Harv. L. Rev.* 1143.

—— (1990), 'Fraud on the Market Cases', 37 *UCLA L. Rev.* 883.

Odean, T. (1998a), 'Are Investors Reluctant To Realize Their Losses?', 53 *J. Fin.* 1775.

—— (1998b), 'Volume, Volatility, Price and Profit When All Traders are Above Average', 53 *J. Fin.* 1887.

Ofek, E. and Richardson, M.P. (2001), 'DotCom Mania: A Survey of Market Efficiency in the Internet Sector', available at http://papers.ssrn.com/sol3/papers.cfm?abstract_id=268311 (last visited 15 Jan. 2005).

O'Hare, J. (1998), 'The Resurrection of the Dodo: The Unfortunate Re-emergence of the Puffery Defense in Private Securities Fraud Actions', 59 *Ohio St. L.J.* 1697.

Opdyke, J. (2001),'Many Analysts Found to Invest in Companies They Covered', *Wall St. J.*, (1 Aug., at C1).

Partnoy, F. (2000), 'Why Markets Crash and What Law Can Do About It', 61 *U. Pitt. L. Rev.* 741.

Piron, R. (1991), 'Correspondence—Keynes as a Noise Trader', 5 *J. Econ. Persp.* 215.

Posner, R. (1998), 'Rational Choice, Behavioural Economics and the Law', 50 *Stan. L. Rev.* 1551.

Poteshman, A.M. (2001), 'Underreaction, Overreaction and Increasing Misreaction to Information in the Options Market', 56 *J. Fin.* 851.

Prentice, R. (1999), 'The Future of Corporate Disclosure: The Internet, Securities Fraud and Rule 10b-5', 47 *Emory L.J.* 1.

—— (2002), 'Whither Securities Regulation? Some Behavioural Observations Regarding Proposals for Its Future', 51 *Duke L.J.* 1397.

Rabin, M. (1993), 'Incorporating Fairness into Game Theory and Economics', 83 *Am. Econ. Rev.* 1284.

Rachlinski, J. (2000), 'The New Law and Psychology: A Reply to Critics, Skeptics and Cautious Supporters', 85 *Cornell L. Rev.* 739.

Rashes, M. (2001), 'Massively Confused Investors Making Conspicuously Ignorant Choices (MCI-MCIC)', 56 *J. Fin.* 1911.

Roll, R. (1986), 'The Hubris Hypothesis in Corporate Takeovers', 59 *J. Bus.* 197.

Romano, R. (1999), 'Empowering Investors: A Market Approach to Securities Regulation', 107 *Yale L.J.* 2357.

Rubenstein, M. (2001), 'Rational Markets: Yes or No? The Affirmative Case', *Fin. Analysts J.*, (May-June, at 15).

Saunders, E. M. (1993), 'Stock Prices and Wall Street Weather', 83 *Am. Econ. Rev.* 1337.

Scharfstein, D. and Stein, J. (1990), 'Herd Behavior and Investment', 80 *Am. Econ. Rev.* 465.

Schepple, K.L. (1993), 'It's Just Not Right: The Ethics of Insider Trading', 56 *Law & Cont. Probs.* 123.

Schroeder, M. and Simon, R. (2000), 'Teenager in Stock-Fraud Case Kept $500,000 in Profits', *Wall St. J.*, (20 Oct. at C1).

Schwartz, E. and Moon, M. (2000), 'Rational Pricing of Internet Companies', 56 *Fin. Analysts J.* 62.

SEC (1999), 'Special Study—On-Line Brokerages:Keeping Apace of Cyberspace', [1999-2000 Transfer Binder] *Fed. Sec. L. Rep.* (CCH) P 86,222 (22 Nov.).

—— (1999), 'Staff Accounting Bulletin No. 99', 64 *Fed. Reg.* 45150.

—— (2000), 'Securities Act Release No.33-7881', 17 CFR 243.100-243.103 (15 Aug.).

Securities Industry Association (2001), 'Costs and Benefits of Regulation Fair Disclosure', available at www.sia.com. [ ] (last visited 15 Jan. 2005)

Seligman, J. (1994), 'The Merits Do Matter', 107 *Harv. L. Rev.* 438.

Shefrin, H. (2000), *Beyond Greed and Fear: Understanding Behavioral Finance and the Psychology of Investing* (Oxford: OUP).

Shefrin, H. and Statman, M. (1985), 'The Disposition to Sell Winners Too Early and Ride Losers Too Long: Theory and Evidence', 40 *J. Fin.* 777.

Shiller, R.J. (1989), *Market Volatility* (Cambridge: MIT Press).

—— (1999), *Irrational Exuberance* (Princeton: Princeton University Press).

Shiller, R.J. and Pound, J. (1989), 'Survey Evidence on Diffusion of Interest and Information Among Investors', 12 *J. Econ. Behav. & Org.* 47.

Shleifer, A. (2000), *Inefficient Markets: An Introduction to Behavioural Finance* (Oxford: Clarendon Press).

Shleifer, A. and Vishny, R. (1997), 'The Limits of Arbitrage', 52 *J. Fin.* 35.

Starr, J. and Herman, D. (2001),'The Same Old Wine in a Brand New Bottle: Applying Traditional Market Manipulation Principles to Internet Stock Scams', 29 *Sec. Reg. L.J.* 236.

Statman, M. (2002), 'Lottery Players/Stock Traders', *Fin. Analysts J.* (Jan.-Feb., at p. 14).

Stiglitz, J. (1990), 'Symposium on Bubbles—Introduction', 4 *J. Econ. Persp.* 13.

Stout, L. (1995), 'Are Stock Markets Costly Casinos?: Disagreement, Market Failure and Securities Regulation', 81 *Va. L. Rev.* 611.

—— (1997), 'Transactions Costs and Investor Welfare: Is a Motley Fool Born Every Minute?', 75 *Wash. U. L.Q.* 791.

Teoh, S.H., *et al.* (1998), 'Earnings Management and the Long-Run Market Performance of Initial Public Offerings', 53 *J. Fin.* 1935.

Tetlock, P. (2000), 'Cognitive Biases and Organizational Correctives: Do Both Disease and Cure Depend on the Politics of the Beholder?', 45 *Admin. Sci. Q.* 293.

Thel, S. (1988), 'Regulation of Manipulation Under Section 10(b): Securities Prices and the Text of the Securities Exchange Act of 1934', *Colum. Bus. L. Rev.* 359.

—— (1990), 'The Original Conception of Section 10(b) of the Securities Exchange Act', 42 *Stan. L. Rev.* 385.

—— (1994), '$850,000 in Six Minutes: The Mechanics of Securities Manipulation', 79 *Cornell L. Rev.* 219.

Thompson, R. (1996), 'Simplicity and Certainty in the Measure of Recovery Under Rule 10b-5', 51 *Bus. L.* 1177.

—— (1997), 'Securities Regulation in an Electronic Age: The Impact of Cognitive Psychology', 75 *Wash. U. L.Q.* 779.

Tumarkin, R. and Whitelaw, R. (2001),'News or Noise?Internet Postings and Stock Prices', *Fin. Analysts J.*, (May-June, at 41).

Walker, R and Levine, D. 'You've Got Jail: Current Trends in Internet Securities Fraud', 38 *Am. Crim. L. Rev.* 405 (2001).

Wermers, R. (1999), 'Mutual Fund Herding and the Impact on Stock Prices', 54 *J. Fin.* 581.

Wermers, R. (2000), 'Mutual Fund Performance: An Empirical Decomposition into Stock Picking Talent, Style, Transaction Costs and Expenses', 55 *J. Fin.* 1655.

Womack, K. (1996), 'Do Brokerage Analysts' Recommendations Have Investment Value?', 51 *J. Fin.* 137.

Yablon, C. (2000), 'A Dangerous Supplement? Longshot Claims and Private Securities Litigation', 94 *Nw. U. L. Rev.* 567.

Part II
Corporate Scandals in Historical and Comparative Context

3

Icarus and American Corporate Regulation

DAVID A SKEEL, JR*

W HEN THE AMERICAN corporate scandals hit—Enron, then
Global Crossing, Adelphia, and finally WorldCom—two of the
most frequently asked questions were: have there ever been
corporate scandals of this magnitude in America before?; and if so, are
there any similarities between today's scandals and the scandals of the
past? The first question was easily answered: yes, there certainly were
major scandals before Enron and WorldCom. The second turns out to be
much more subtle; and it goes to the heart of America's peculiar two track
mode of corporate governance, with its division of authority between
federal and state regulation. To a remarkable extent, American corporate
regulation has proceeded scandal by scandal.

To appreciate the links between scandal and regulation, it is useful to
begin by briefly describing two historical scandals—scandals long
forgotten by most Americans yet central to much of the discussion that
follows. (The scandals are described in much more detail in Skeel (2005)
61 *Business Lawyer* 155–77). In the 1860s, Philadelphia banker Jay Cooke
was probably the most famous businessman in America. At the outset of
the Civil War, he pioneered a revolutionary new strategy for selling
government debt—a strategy that relied on extensive advertising and
door-to-door sales of the bonds—which he used to raise millions of
dollars for the Union cause. Buying government debt, he argued,
wrapping his appeals in the flag, 'would strike terror to the rebels and
greatly help' the war effort. After the war, he used the same technique to
finance the nation's second transcontinental railroad, the Northern
Pacific. But Cooke got in over his head, continuing to throw money at the

* S. Samuel Arsht Professor of Corporate Law, University of Pennsylvania. I am grateful
to Bill Bratton, Joe McCahery, and Robert Prentice for helpful comments. This chapter was
previously published in (2005) 60 *Business Lawyer* 155–177. The permission of the American
Bar Association to republish is gratefully acknowledged.

railroad even when everyone else (including his own partners) had concluded it was too risky, and acquiring more and more of the railroad's stock. Like Ken Lay of Enron in our own era, Cooke had close ties to the American president, Ulysses S. Grant; in fact, Grant was staying at Cooke's Philadelphia house the night before Cooke, the railroad, and Cooke's bank came crashing down, ushering in a depression known as the Panic of 1873.

Fast forward sixty years to the 1920s. Samuel Insull—a Chicago electricity magnate who had started out serving as Thomas Edison's right hand man—was a business superstar known to millions in Chicago and beyond as a yachtsman and benefactor who built a forty-two floor building to house the Chicago Civic Opera Company. Like Bernie Ebbers and WorldCom, Insull embarked on a relentless expansion program in the 1920s, acquiring electricity companies and other businesses as far away as Maine. To disguise the empire's increasingly precarious finances, Insull, like Enron, erected an elaborate holding company structure that included several parent corporations and a maze of subsidiaries, some of which had substantial assets and some of which didn't. When the empire came crashing down in 1932, it was described by some as the 'biggest business failure in the history of the world'; (McDonald 1962: vii) and it inspired one of Franklin Roosevelt's most famous campaign speeches, a call for action against the 'Ishmael or Insull whose hand is against every man's' (Roosevelt 1938: 755).

With each of these scandals, as with our most recent corporate collapses, the high-flying businessmen at the heart of the scandals were not alone. Cooke and Insull personified a breakdown in accountability that pervaded all of American corporate and financial life. Indeed, Insull's lawyers successfully defended him in his 1934 criminal trial by, as his biographer puts it, portraying Insull as 'an infirm and aged sometime public benefactor persecuted for the sins of his generation' (McDonald 1962: 319).

As devastating as they have been, the massive scandals also have a crucial silver lining; in each case, public outrage has forced lawmakers to step in. This pattern, as it turns out, lies at the heart of American corporate governance. For the past century, American corporate regulation has consisted of periodic, dramatic regulatory interventions by federal lawmakers after a major scandal, together with more nuanced ongoing regulation by the states.

The first two parts of this chapter will try to explain how and why this pattern emerged. I start by describing how scandals have inspired nearly all of our most important federal regulation of corporate and financial life. I then turn to the very different role played by the states, focusing most extensively on Delaware, the nation's de facto regulator of state corporate law.

After exploring America's two-track regulatory structure, I consider the implications of the current regulatory framework. This final part assesses the likely effectiveness—that is, the merits—of the recent Sarbanes-Oxley Act and other recent governance reforms; considers the mode of American regulation—in particular, the reliance on federally imposed, mandatory rules, in contrast to the more norms-based approach used for important issues such as takeover regulation in England; and concludes by briefly considering the scope of American corporate law and the role of corporate ethics.

I. ICARUS EFFECT SCANDALS AND FEDERAL REFORM

Each of America's great corporate scandals, from Jay Cooke's 1873 collapse to the 2002 corporate scandals, can be traced to the confluence of the same three general factors. I refer to these factors elsewhere as 'Icaran,' and to the scandals that they have made possible as 'Icarus Effect' scandals (Skeel 2005). Icarus, for those who may have forgotten their Greek mythology, was a boy who was given wings made of wax and feathers by his father. Although Icarus was warned not to fly too close to the sun, he became intoxicated with his new-found powers, flew higher and higher and, when the wax holding the feathers in place melted, fell to his death.[1]

The first of the three factors—and the one that most closely fits the Icarus theme—is risk-taking. Although we tend to associate risk-taking with the garages and Silicon Valley coffee shops where the newest innovations are percolating, it also can be found in the boardrooms of America's largest corporations. To rise to the top of the corporate ladder, an executive must win 'probationary crucibles' at each step on the way up (Jackall 1988: 40). The executives who succeed tend to be self confident and willing to take risks. The takeover wave of the 1980s magnified this tendency by creating more managerial mobility than ever before, as new managers were brought in to run target companies; and even companies that hadn't been taken over searched for charismatic CEOs.[2]

The structure of managerial compensation further reinforced the incentive to take risks. Much of the $14.7 million that the average CEO of an S&P 500 firm took home in 2000 came from stock options, which reward risk, since options are all upside and no downside: they promise a big payoff if the company's stock price goes up, but there's no cost to the

---

[1] Interestingly, in some accounts of the Icarus myth, Icarus is also warned not to fly too low, in order to avoid the spray from the sea's waves. In this version, as with executive risk-taking, there are dangers in both directions.

[2] This tendency, and the attention lavished on celebrity CEOs, is explored in detail in Khurana (2002).

CEO if she gambles with the company's business and the stock price plummets (Bebchuk and Fried 2004).

Risk-taking isn't necessarily a bad thing, of course. Much of American corporate governance is designed to encourage managers to take appropriate risks.[3] But if risk-taking—and perhaps more importantly, financial manipulation—isn't reigned in, it has catastrophic consequences.

The second factor is competition. Competitive markets also are good, but they too can reinforce managers' incentives to take risks. Americans have long rebelled against concentrated economic power, in favour of industries with a multitude of competing companies. In this kind of marketplace, a marketplace where monopolies like Microsoft are the exception rather than the rule, the success of a business innovator attracts competitors. If an innovative company's profits are eroded by the influx of competitors, its managers may be tempted to respond by taking increasingly misguided and even illegal risks, or disguising their precarious finances, as they attempt to replicate their early success.

The final factor is manipulation of the corporate form. The ability to tap huge amounts of capital in enterprises that adopt the corporate form, together with the large number of people whose livelihood depends in one way or another on the business, means that an Icaran executive who takes excessive or fraudulent risks may jeopardize the financial lives of thousands of employees, investors, and suppliers of the business. The corporate form itself can also multiply the opportunities for mischief. By permitting corporations to hold the stock of other corporations in the late nineteenth century, lawmakers gave corporate managers the ability to tuck some of the assets of a business in one corporate entity and other assets elsewhere.[4] This corporate smoke and mirrors figured prominently in the collapse of Samuel Insull and other utility empires in the 1930s, and it was equally central to Enron's managers' efforts to keep investors in the dark as they ratcheted up the gas company's risks.

American business history can be seen—at its simplest level—as an ongoing cat-and-mouse game between regulators, whose job is to reign in excesses in the three areas just described; and business leaders, who push

---

[3] Since shareholders can diversify their investments, they benefit if managers are willing to take risks that have a positive net present value for the company. Encouraging sensible risk taking has long been one of the principal justifications for the business judgement rule, which discourages second-guessing of managerial decision-making. See, e.g., *Joy v North*, 692 F.2d 880 (2d Cir. 1982). The problem comes when executives begin taking risks that have a negative net present value. Historically, these gambles have all too often been accompanied by deceptions that are designed to disguise from investors the risks being taken.

[4] New Jersey led the way, passing a corporate law statute in 1889 that permitted corporations to own stock in other corporations (thus reinforcing a 1888 court decision). See, e.g., Skeel (2005: 63).

back against regulatory strictures in order to promote flexibility and innovation.

Under ordinary circumstances, business leaders usually have the upper hand, due to the relentless logic of interest group politics. Corporate managers are intensely interested in the regulatory landscape and they are backed by the coffers of the corporation itself. They also are well organized, through groups such as the Chamber of Commerce and the Business Roundtable. Although ordinary Americans have a great deal at stake overall, their stake is far more thinly spread. Even now, when more than half of all Americans own stock, most of us have a relatively small overall stake in corporate America. As a result, ordinary Americans are much less likely than corporate managers to focus on the contours of corporate regulation; and even when they do, collective action problems interfere with their efforts to translate their concerns into effective regulation.[5] Mobilization is costly, and ordinary Americans generally do not have enough at stake to justify a campaign for reform.

The influence of managers is reflected both in state lawmaking and in the legislation that is enacted by Congress. In the 1990s, for instance, business leaders pushed through two separate federal reforms that were designed to make it harder to bring securities law claims again companies that are alleged to have made misstatements to the markets.[6]

But corporate scandals instantly transform the political calculus. The outrage provoked by a wave of corporate scandals galvanizes public opinion in favour of sweeping corporate reforms that simply would not be possible in a more placid corporate and financial environment. America's most important corporate regulations have always been enacted in the wake of stunning Icarus Effect collapses.[7]

Consider the regulatory implications of the most dramatic waves of scandal, in the 1870s, the 1930s, and the early 2000s. When Jay Cooke collapsed in September 1873, capping a series of railroad scandals that also included a colourful battle over the Erie Railroad (which was dubbed the 'Scarlet Woman of Wall Street' because of the blatant corruption

---

[5] The literature on collective action is enormous. The well-spring is Olson (1971), which explores in detail the political disadvantage large diffuse groups have as compared to small groups whose members have a significant stake. The literature is surveyed in Skeel (1997a: 647).

[6] See Private Litigation Reform Act of 1995, Pub. L. No. 104-67, 109 Stat. 737 (1995)(imposing enhanced pleading requirements and providing more protection for forward-looking information); Securities Litigation Uniform Standards Act of 1998, Pub. L. No. 105-353, 112 Stat 3227 (1998)(preventing most securities fraud class actions from being pursued in state court).

[7] The pattern outlined in the text is similar to the interest group transformation described in North (1971). Bratton and McCahery (2004) characterise the same dynamic as bringing the median voter's perspective to the fore.

engaged in by both sides)[8] and massive self-dealing by the managers of
the Union Pacific Railroad, Congress and the states responded by cutting
off the subsidies that had been used to finance the railroads. In
Pennsylvania, lawmakers amended the state constitution to prohibit the
state from authorizing any political subdivision 'to obtain or appropriate
money for ... any corporation, association or individual' (Pinsky 1963:
279). This and similar statutes in other states were, in a sense, an early
effort to limit corporate influence over the political process.

As challenges to the abuses of the railroads percolated through the
judicial system, the courts also helped to reshape the regulatory
environment. In response to the self-dealing contracts that the managers
of the Union Pacific had used to siphon large amounts of money to
themselves, the Supreme Court adopted a per se rule prohibiting
corporations from entering into any contract with their own managers.[9]

The 1873 crisis also transformed American politics. Prior to the 1873
Panic, Populism had been a diffuse movement of farmers and small
merchants in the south and west. The panic launched the Populists onto
the national stage,[10] and would eventually contribute to railroad rate
regulation—through the enactment of the Interstate Commerce Act of
1887—and federal regulation of antitrust issues under the Sherman Act of
1890.

The corporate scandals at the outset of the New Deal inspired another
major wave of corporate reforms.[11] After campaigning on a promise to
clean up corporate America, Franklin D. Roosevelt and the New Deal
reformers enacted a broad array of sweeping reforms that still provide
the principal infrastructure of American corporate and market regulation.
First came the securities acts of 1933 and 1934, which introduced
extensive new disclosure requirements and antifraud provisions, and
established the Securities and Exchange Commission to police the
securities markets.[12] Secondly, in order to break the grip that J.P. Morgan
and a handful of other Money Trust banks had on American corporate
finance, the New Deal reformers prohibited banks from engaging in both

[8] The Erie battle pitted one group of railroad robber barons, headed by Cornelius
Vanderbilt, against another, which included Jay Gould, Jim Fisk, and Daniel Drew. Both sides
obtained favourable rulings from sympathetic New York judges, and both bribed the New
York legislature. The battle is colourfully recounted in Gordon (1988).

[9] See, e.g., *Wardell v Union Pacific Railroad Co.*, 103 US 651, 658 (1880). The gradual erosion of
this rule is described in Marsh (1966). Interestingly, the recent Sarbanes-Oxley reforms have
reintroduced the per se prohibition with respect to loans by a company to its executives.

[10] The Populist ascendancy was reflected in the 1874 elections, which shifted control of
Congress to the Democratic Party. See, e.g., Skeel (2005: 46).

[11] The New Deal reforms described in this paragraph are discussed in detail in Skeel (2005:
ch. 3).

[12] Although the original proposal called for the Federal Trade Commission to oversee the
securities market, influential Senator Carter Glass objected, ostensibly due to concerns about
regulatory independence. See, e.g., Seligman (1982: 97–99).

investment and commercial banking.[13] Finally, the New Dealers completely restructured the utilities industry, simplifying its structure by prohibiting the managers of utilities from setting up the kind of complicated holding company structures that Insull and his peers had used to mislead investors.

Most recently, we have Enron and WorldCom to thank for the Sarbanes-Oxley Act of 2002, the recent stock exchange reforms, and Eliot Spitzer's settlement with the securities industry.[14] The Sarbanes-Oxley Act focused most extensively on the accounting industry and on the responsibility of top corporate executives. With accounting, the most glaring problem was a pervasive conflict of interest: the auditors of the nation's largest companies usually provided (or sought to provide) consulting services as well; this gave the auditors a huge disincentive to conduct a tough audit, for fear that an unhappy client might direct its consulting business elsewhere. (At Arthur Andersen, the poster child for this problem, second-guessing Enron would have jeopardized roughly $25 million a year in consulting business.)[15] The corporate responsibility reforms address this concern by prohibiting the Big Four accounting firms from providing consulting services to their audit clients[16]; the reforms also established a new, more independent accounting regulator.[17] Turning to corporate executives, the law's most controversial provision requires every public company to establish an internal control system designed to make sure that every part of the business provides accurate financial information.[18] The CEO and CFO are required to certify its periodic financial statements, and to report on the company's internal control system.[19] These reforms—which I'll discuss further in the final part of the chapter—were so clearly inspired

[13] This legislation, the Glass-Steagall Act of 1933, lasted until 1999, when it was largely repealed.

[14] For good overviews and analysis of the Sarbanes-Oxley Act, see, e.g., Cunningham (2003); Ribstein (2002). References to the Sarbanes-Oxley Act will be cited hereafter as 'SOA.' As discussed in more detail in Part III(A), below, the New York Stock Exchange and NASDAQ added a series of 'independence' requirements. The boards of directors of listed firms must have a majority of independent directors, and they must have independent compensation and nomination committees.

[15] For a good discussion of the conflict, see Coffee (2002). One recent empirical study concludes that companies whose auditors also performed significant amounts of consulting services for the same client were not significantly more likely to later restate their financial results. Other evidence suggests that consulting business did distort the auditing process, however, and even auditors whose firm did not provide substantial consulting business for a client may well have been influenced by the prospect that consulting opportunities might increasingly come their way.

[16] SOA § 201.

[17] SOA §§ 101–9 (establishing Public Company Accounting Oversight Board consisting of five independent members, two of whom are to be certified public accountants).

[18] SOA § 404.

[19] SOA § 302.

by the recent scandals that they might well be called the Future Enron Prevention Act.[20]

Scandals also have served as the lightening rod for more targeted reforms. In the 1940s, Richard Whitney, head of the New York Stock Exchange, was discovered to have embezzled several million dollars from the exchange. The outrage provoked by his misbehaviour enabled SEC chairman William O. Douglas to orchestrate a major restructuring of the exchange.[21] In the early 1970s, the Watergate investigators uncovered evidence that many of America's leading corporations had set aside slush funds for bribing foreign officials. Congress responded to the widespread anger by enacting the Foreign Corrupt Practices Act, which forbids companies from paying foreign officials.[22]

Each of these reforms followed the same pattern as the more pervasive legislation in the 1930s and in 2002: a shocking scandal galvanizes attention, neutralizing the influence that corporations have under ordinary circumstances; Congress (or, in the case of the Whitney scandal, regulators) quickly responds by enacting reforms that are demanded by ordinary Americans. It is these reforms that provide the federal regulatory infrastructure for the decades that follow.

II. SMOOTHING THE SKIDS: DELAWARE AND STATE REGULATION

For the past seventy years, nearly all of the scandal-based reforms have come from federal lawmakers and regulators. How, then, do the states fit into the regulatory picture? In the beginning, the states handled nearly all of corporate law, because they were the ones who doled out corporate charters. But the state role shifted sharply at the end of the nineteenth century. Since then, the states' regulatory role has looked quite different from the federal interventions described in Part I.

The key period in early American business history—the moment when the federal and state roles shifted toward the modern pattern—came in the 1880s and 1890s, with the emergence of the so-called 'corporate trusts'. In 1882, John D. Rockefeller bought out all of his significant competitors in the oil industry and assembled them into the corporate behemoth known as Standard Oil. After Rockefeller successfully cobbled together his giant trust, the trust strategy was employed in one industry

[20] The emphasis on Enron is particularly evident in provisions such as a whistle-blowing provision that requires the audit committee to establish a hotline for complaints such as those raised by Sherron Watkins at Enron: SOA § 301(m)(4).
[21] The Whitney scandal and the stock exchange reforms it facilitated are described in Seligman (1982: 167–79).
[22] See, e.g., Bratton and McCahery (2004: 45–47).

after another.[23] By the end of the decade, roughly 100 different trusts had already been formed. The trusts were not America's first large-scale corporations; this honor belonged to the railroads, as we have seen. But with the trusts, big business seemed to be coming of age.

The emergence of large-scale corporations met with serious resistance at both the state and federal levels. Many states had maximum capital limitations, which were designed to keep corporate growth in check.[24] State Attorneys-General also challenged expansion, particularly by railroads, as ultra vires—that is, as not within the corporation's power.[25] In 1890, Congress entered the fray by enacting the Sherman Act, which prohibited any 'contract, combination in the form of trust or otherwise, or conspiracy, in restraint of trade or commerce;' as well as 'any attempt to monopolize' trade or commerce.

The most important ally of Rockefeller and his peers in the battle over corporate size and concentration was New Jersey.[26] In 1889, New Jersey enacted a revolutionary new corporate law statute that, among other things, explicitly authorized corporations to own stock in other corporate entities.[27] Since acquiring the stock of other companies in an industry was one strategy for setting up a trust, the New Jersey statute served as a welcome mat for large corporations. The managers of many of the largest corporations, including Rockefeller, quickly made their way to New Jersey, thus setting the stage for a major clash between state corporate regulation and the Sherman Act.

The crucial battle came in an 1895 case called *E.C. Knight*, which involved the Sugar Trust run by the notorious Havermeyer family.[28] Havermeyer's American Sugar Company had assembled 97 per cent of the nation's sugar refining capacity by purchasing the stock of all of its substantial competitors. The Pennsylvania Attorney-General challenged the Sugar Trust under the Sherman Act, arguing that it operated as a restraint of trade. Although it is hard to imagine a more complete

---

[23] Because a corporation could not own the stock of other corporations, Rockefeller initially could not simply buy the stock of his competitors. To circumvent this limitation, he set up a trust arrangement. The shareholders of the constituent companies retained their stock, but ceded voting authority to a trust controlled by Rockefeller. See, e.g., Skeel (2005: 59–60).

[24] In Massachusetts, for instance, mechanical, mining, and manufacturing corporations were prohibited from having more than one million dollars in capital. See, e.g., Blair (2003: 389 note 3).

[25] In the 1870s and 1880s, many of these state challenges were successful. The battles are described in detail in Horwitz (1992: 82–86).

[26] In a famous muck-raking article, Lincoln Steffins (1905: 43) recounted how prominent corporate attorney James Dill persuaded New Jersey's governor that providing corporation-friendly laws could be a major source of revenue for New Jersey.

[27] New Jersey followed up with additional changes in 1896 that gutted the ultra vires doctrine by permitting corporations to define their business extremely broadly, and largely eliminated 'watered stock' challenges by making directors' assessment of the value received for stock dispositive. For further discussion, see, e.g., Skeel (2005: 63).

[28] *US v EC Knight Co*, 156 US 1 (1895).

monopoly, the Supreme Court rejected the Sherman Act claim. According to the Court, the American Sugar Company's purchase of its competitors' stock affected only manufacturing, not commerce, and thus did not amount to a restraint that interfered with trade or commerce.[29]

The *Knight Sugar* case was long viewed as evidence that the Supreme Court catered to the whims of big business. But the reality was more complicated. Late nineteenth-century conservatives worried about giant corporations—which they feared would lead to a form of private socialism—at least as much as liberals did. In a brilliant 1979 article, Charles McCurdy (1979) argued that the Supreme Court actually sought in its *Knight Sugar* decision to preserve a role for state regulation of large-scale American corporate enterprises. Vigilant state regulators, he pointed out, could have continued to challenge corporate combinations like the Sugar monopoly on ultra vires grounds. The states declined to take up this invitation, however, for at least three reasons.

The first was financial. Since state Attorneys-General had relatively little funding, the cost of taking on well-heeled corporate defendants probably chilled at least some state challenges.

Secondly, even if the Attorneys-General had adequate funding, their challenges might have proved to be pyrrhic victories. Rather than prospering if regulators challenged the emergence of an industry colossus, many of the local businesses that were preserved would have been too weak to survive.

Over time, another factor loomed largest of all, and came to define the state role in corporate regulation. By the late nineteenth century, American business had become increasingly mobile, thanks to the advent of railroads, the telegraph, and other new forms of communication and transportation. If a state developed a reputation for aggressively policing the large corporations located within its borders, the corporations might move elsewhere. As political scientists Jacob Hacker and Paul Pierson have argued, the threat of relocation gave businesses structural power (Hacker and Pierson 2002: 290). As a result, even states that weren't competing to offer business-friendly corporate laws were reluctant to pursue policies that confronted big business head on. It was this political reality that laid the groundwork for the role that state lawmakers still play in contemporary corporate law.[30]

[29] There was nothing about the purchase of the stock of a sugar plant, the Supreme Court reasoned, that necessarily interfered with trade or commerce. The court categorised this as a decision that involved manufacturing. An agreement that directly undermined the competitive conditions of the market, by contrast—such as a price-fixing agreement—would qualify as interfering with commerce, and thus would violate the Sherman Act.

[30] Notice that this argument is somewhat different from the standard focus in the charter competition literature on the fact that the state of incorporation governs the internal affairs of the corporations it charters. The structural power that the corporations have would remain even if the internal affairs doctrine were reversed, since it stems from a company's physical presence in the state. For a somewhat similar intuition, see Folk (1968: 418–19).

The states' abandonment of the fight against corporate combinations shifted the campaign against corporate monopoly from the states to Congress and federal regulators. Two decades later, a trust-busting campaign led by Teddy Roosevelt would firmly establish federal regulators as the principal guardians of competition in American industry.[31] One effect of the transition to federal oversight (which we will revisit later) was to separate antitrust issues from the rest of corporate law.

The core terms of internal governance are still regulated by the states. Until 1913, New Jersey was the Liberia of corporate law, the clear winner in the competition to persuade large corporations to fly under the state's flag. But New Jersey dropped out of the picture in 1913, due to the presidential aspirations of Woodrow Wilson.[32] Delaware took over and has made sure that it will not repeat its forerunner's mistake.[33]

Whereas federal law provides the market infrastructure, regulates disclosure, and deputizes the principal outside watchers, state corporate law focuses on the internal affairs of the corporation—in particular, on the relations among shareholders, managers, and directors. This includes everything from fiduciary duty and shareholder voting rights, to the standards for effecting mergers and other transactions. Although Delaware has been the most important corporate law regulator since 1913, the moment that defined Delaware's current pre-eminence came in 1967, when Delaware passed a major overhaul of its general corporation law. Spearheaded by Samuel Arsht, who is viewed by many as the father of Delaware corporate law, the 1967 reforms permitted cashout mergers for the first time and expanded corporations' right to indemnify their directors against liability claims (Roe 2003).[34]

---

[31] Roosevelt's campaign against the corporate trusts, which began with a Sherman Act challenge in 1902 to the Northern Securities Corporation that had been formed by J.P. Morgan, is described in Skeel (2005: 68–69).

[32] While serving as president of Princeton, Woodrow Wilson ran a successful campaign for governor of New Jersey on a platform calling for more stringent regulation of corporations. As his US presidential campaign geared up, he began promoting a group of laws known as the Seven Sisters that were designed to re-invigorate state antitrust enforcement in New Jersey. The Seven Sisters were enacted as Wilson awaited his presidential inauguration. For a more detailed discussion of Delaware's displacement of New Jersey as the state of choice for major corporations, see, e.g., Grandy (1989); Kirk (1984).

[33] Among the provisions Delaware has put in place to discourage a sudden shift in the focus of its corporate laws are requirements that changes to its corporate laws be passed by a two-thirds supermajority and that its judgeships be divided between the two political parties. Delaware's most important commitment, however, is the fact that the state relies on its chartering business for roughly 20% of its revenues. Roberta Romano (1993) has labeled the commitment that stems from Delaware's dependence on its corporate revenue the 'genius' of American corporate law.

[34] Perhaps I'm getting a little carried away here—I have Arsht's family to thank for the chair that I hold at the University of Pennsylvania. But by any yardstick, Arsht was a major player in the 1967 amendments, and in promoting the revisions. Bratton and McCahery (2004: 21–22) note that the portion of Delaware's revenues that came from chartering had dropped to 7% as of the early 1960s, but that Delaware's success in attracting corporations soared after the 1967 reforms.

For the past thirty years, since former SEC chair William Cary threw down the gauntlet in a law review article (Cary 1974), the $64,000 question in American corporate law—at least among corporate law academics—has been: does Delaware's pre-eminence reflect a race to the top in state corporate regulation, or a descent to the muck at the bottom? The titans in the debate have been Roberta Romano (1993), who views states' competition to attract charters as the 'genius' of corporate law; and Lucian Bebchuk (1992), who contends that Delaware caters to the desires of a corporation's managers at the expense of its shareholders. Not surprisingly, the answer is almost certainly somewhere in the middle: Delaware is sensitive to managers' interests, but market pressures force it to take shareholders concerns into account as well.

The most important recent development in the debate is an emphasis on the effect that the threat of federal intervention has on Delaware oversight.[35] It has long been apparent—and candidly acknowledged even by Delawareans—that Congress's shadow has a way of concentrating Delaware's attention. As a campaign for federal incorporation legislation led by Ralph Nader and others gathered steam in the 1970s, Delaware ratcheted up its scrutiny of freezeout mergers that cash out a company's minority shareholders[36]; after the corporate scandals broke three years ago, Chief Justice Norm Veasey signaled that the Delaware courts were likely to start casting a colder eye on managerial compensation packages.[37] Although the observation that Delaware keeps a wary watch on developments in Washington D.C. is not new, at least one prominent scholar argues that this is a principal driver of corporate law—that rumours of state charter competition, and that Delaware regulates the most important issues, are greatly overstated (Roe 2003).

The threat of federal intervention is important, but focusing too much on Congress's episodic jolts can distract us from the crucial role that Delaware plays in corporate regulation. Start with the Delaware legislature. Although Delaware's courts get the headlines, the legislature continuously revises the general corporation law to adjust to changes in the business environment. Most of the changes draw little notice— changes such as permitting shareholder meetings to be held on the

[35] The emphasis on Congress's role can be seen as growing out of another major recent strand in the charter competition debate—the argument that charter competition looks more like a Delaware monopoly than like true competition. See, e.g., Kahan and Kamar (2002).

[36] See, e.g., Drexler (1994: 596–97). Delaware's decision in *Paramount v Time*, 571 A.2d 1140 (Del. 1989) is also viewed by many as having been influenced by rumblings in Washington—in particular, concerns that Congress might pass antitakeover legislation if the takeover market were not slowed down.

[37] See, e.g., 'What's Wrong with Executive Compensation', *Harv. Bus. Rev.*, Jan. 2003, at 5, 11–12 (Veasy remarks at roundtable): 'I would urge boards of directors to demonstrate their independence...not only as a guard against the intrusion of the federal government but as a guard against anything that might happen to them in court from a properly presented complaint'.

internet[38]—but they are crucially important to minimizing unnecessary friction between business and regulation. A Delaware corporation that plans to engage in a merger or other major corporate transaction knows exactly what to expect. In this respect, Delaware offers more clarity, more certainty, than any other state; this certainty can translate to significant cost savings.[39]

The most dramatic issues are usually resolved in Delaware's courts. When Marty Lipton first dreamed up the poison pill, or when takeover bidders challenged target directors' use of takeover defenses, the issues were thrashed out in the particularized context of a judicial challenge, not as a general policy debate. An obvious difficulty with resolving corporate issues through the courts is that business is constantly and rapidly changing. There is no guarantee that Delaware's judges will get cases quickly enough to adapt the existing regulatory structure to new conditions. As former chief justice Norm Veasey is fond of saying, the judges are like clams in the water—they must wait for what comes along.[40]

The Delaware courts, with an occasional assist from the legislature, have developed several ingenious strategies for—to continue the metaphor—keeping the water swirling. First, as even Delaware's critics concede, the Delaware court system is remarkably efficient. There are a total of ten judges on the two courts, and at both the Chancery and Supreme Court levels, cases are decided extraordinarily quickly.[41] Secondly, to further encourage the parties to bring their cases in a Delaware court rather than elsewhere, Delaware makes it extremely easy to establish jurisdiction.[42] Delaware's courts also have been notably generous in awarding attorneys' fees to plaintiffs' lawyers, which encourages attorneys to file their litigation in Delaware.[43]

In addition to keeping the water swirling, Delaware also makes the most of the cases that come its way, through a tendency I have referred to elsewhere (Skeel 1997b: 163–65) as the 'moral dimension' in the caselaw (and which my colleague Ed Rock (1997: 1016) calls 'preaching'). Even when they find that directors have not breached their duties, Delaware's

[38] Del. Code Ann. tit. 8, § 211(a)(2).
[39] This point has sometimes been obscured by the emphasis in recent scholarship on the opacity of Delaware law on controversial issues such as takeovers. See, e.g., Kamar (1998).
[40] See, e.g. Gapper (2005: 19).
[41] See, e.g., Skeel (1997b: 160).
[42] Under Del. Code Ann. tit. 10, § 3114, Delaware directors are deemed to consent to personal jurisdiction in Delaware. Section 3114 was drafted days after the Supreme Court struck down the prior jurisdictional provision in *Shaffer v Heitner*, 433 US 186, 214–17 (1997).
[43] For a criticism, particularly in the context of freezeout mergers, see Weiss and White (2005).

judges often point out deficiencies in their performance and use the critique to signal the court's expectations as to appropriate directorial oversight going forward.[44] In this way, Delaware's judges engage in a continuous dialogue with corporate America.[45]

Painting with a very broad brush, then, American corporate law consists of two parallel and interlocking systems, state corporate law and the federal over- and underlay.[46] Congress has tended to intervene crisis by crisis, following years of relative silence with dramatic intervention in the crucible of a wave of major corporate scandals. Delaware and other states regulate in a more continuous fashion, generally promoting flexibility and innovation.

III. THE ROAD AHEAD: GOOD, BAD AND POINTS IN BETWEEN

America's peculiar two-track regulatory system, with its allocation of responsibilities between Congress and the states, is hardly inevitable. Even before the Nader campaign in the 1970s, there were several serious efforts to federalize corporate law, first under Teddy Roosevelt in the early twentieth century, and then again during the New Deal.[47] Also, the existing allocations of authority are not stable. The recent corporate responsibility reforms—with their independence and compliance program requirements, which move well beyond the traditional federal focus on disclosure and policing fraud—intrude deeply into the traditional domain of state corporate law oversight. And even before the recent reforms, the overlaps between federal insider-trading and mis-disclosure actions, on the one hand, and state fiduciary duty litigation, on the other, have been steadily increasing.[48]

What should we make of the two-track system that American history and politics have given us? Let me conclude by offering three sets of observations about the way that corporate law is made and enforced in the United States.

---

[44] Eisenberg (1993) has characterised this tendency in terms of a difference between the (high) standard of conduct and the (more lax) standard of review articulated by Delaware's judges.

[45] In recent years, Delaware's judges have also got the word out through frequent speeches and appearances at corporate law conferences. For a long list of recent articles by Delaware judges, see Kahan and Rock (2004: 23 note 100).

[46] The SEC obviously also helps to develop the contours of American corporate law. The boundaries of SEC oversight are set by congressional legislation, but the SEC plays an ongoing role in articulating the standards for proxy voting and on other issues.

[47] The initiatives are described in Skeel (2005: 71–72); Seligman (1982: 205–9).

[48] See, e.g., Thompson and Sale (2003).

A. Crisis Legislation Comes with No Guarantees

The first lesson our history teaches is that crisis legislation comes with no guarantees. Each of the major waves of corporate scandal has reflected a breakdown in American corporate and financial life. The silver lining has been the overwhelming pressure on lawmakers to pass structural reform. But the fact that Congress steps into the fray doesn't necessarily mean that Congress will solve the problems revealed by the corporate collapse.[49]

The remarkable success of the New Deal reforms may have made us too optimistic in this respect. The securities acts and banking reforms of the 1930s greatly enhanced the transparency of the American securities markets and replaced the Wall Street banks with a new set of 'watchers'—companies' auditors and, in time, the securities analysts who covered them.

The recent Sarbanes-Oxley Act and the new stock exchange rules that accompanied it, by contrast, are more of a mixed bag. As noted earlier, many of the new rules are aimed at the accounting industry, including provisions that forbid the Big Four firms from providing consulting services to their audit clients; and others that set up a new independent oversight board for the accounting industry.[50] These are the best of the new reforms, a welcome (though partial) solution to the conflicts that bedeviled the accounting industry during the 1990s.[51]

At the other end of the spectrum, the stock exchanges have salted their listing rules with a spate of new independence requirements, starting with the obligation that listed companies have a majority of independent directors on their boards. Most firms won't be hurt by these requirements, and many might be helped, but the existing empirical data suggest that the changes won't make much of a difference.[52] Delaware's judges rightly complain, moreover, that these provisions run roughshod over state lawmakers' traditional authority over internal governance issues.[53] The new standards for directorial independence create a danger that boards will be subject to different definitions of independence in different

[49] For a much stronger version of this point, see Ribstein (2003). Unlike my analysis, which suggests that post-scandal reforms are often necessary, Ribstein argues that bubble laws frequently stifle economic growth.

[50] See above notes 14–20 and accompanying text.

[51] In my own view, Congress should have gone still further, and required that the stock exchanges rather than the companies themselves select the company's auditor. The problem with permitting the company to select its auditor—even when a independent audit committee does the selecting—is that the auditor inevitably views the company as its client. For a more detailed discussion, see Skeel (2005: 188–89).

[52] See, e.g., Romano (2005); Black (1998: 463).

[53] For a good statement of this concern by a corporate law scholar, see, e.g., Bainbridge (2003).

contexts—one standard for stock exchange listing, another for state fiduciary duty oversight.

By far the most controversial reform is SOA § 404, a new requirement that companies establish an internal control system.[54] Corporate America is complaining bitterly about the cost of putting the required controls in place, which for some companies amounts to millions of dollars a year.[55] If the expense assures that accurate financial information is produced at every level of the company, the cost will be worth it. And costs are likely to decline once the compliance programs are put in place—the largest expense is the cost of getting the program up and running in the first instance. But the efficacy of the new programs remains to be seen. There is a risk that the new requirements will simply add up to more internal bureaucracy—that companies will hire a new internal compliance officer and essentially keep doing what they were doing before. There is also a risk that companies will focus narrowly on the financial compliance called for by the reform, while ignoring other kinds of potential misbehaviour within the firm.[56]

A major question raised by the fact that the reforms reach far into the heart of traditional corporate governance functions is whether these rules should apply to non-American companies.[57] The commitment to comply with American disclosure obligations has traditionally been an important benefit to European companies of listing on the American exchanges. But the new reforms mandate a 'one size fits all' approach on governance issues for which there is not a single, optimal approach for every firm. The most sensible way to apply the new rules to non-US companies would be to treat them as disclosure obligations, rather than as mandatory rules. European companies should be required to disclose the independence (or not) of their directors and the nature of their internal controls. But they shouldn't be forced to adopt a US-style structure as the price for listing shares on US markets.[58]

---

[54] In addition to the company's obligation to establish and report on its 'internal control structure and procedures...for financial reporting,' the auditor is required to 'attest to, and report on, the assessment made by the management of the issuer.' SOA § 404(b). The auditor attestation requirement has dramatically increased the costs of recent audits.

[55] See, e.g., Fernandez (2005).

[56] Congress also indulged its penchant for moralistic criminal legislation by adding a slew of new corporate crimes to the criminal code, and ratcheting up the penalties for others. I have criticised these provisions elsewhere. Skeel and Stuntz (2006).

[57] The SEC has delayed implementation of § 404 for foreign companies, as well as small- and mid-sized American firms. But as of this writing, the Commission takes the position that foreign companies eventually will be required to fully comply. See, e.g., Donaldson (2005: A14).

[58] Many foreign companies that are currently listed on US exchanges are considering delisting in order to avoid the new mandates. Under the securities laws, companies are required to continue complying unless they have less than three hundred US shareholders. For an argument that this requirement should be relaxed if the company makes a reasonable buyout offer to its US shareholders, see Pozen (2004: 17).

Much more troublesome than the reforms that Congress passed were the ones it did not. Congress did almost nothing to address two of the most obvious problems highlighted by the corporate scandals. The first is runaway compensation, and in particular, the perverse incentives created by injecting huge amounts of stock options into executives' pay.[59] Options are a one way ratchet, with an unlimited upside but little downside for executives who pump the company's stock price.[60] Second is the risk to employees whose retirement plans are now invested in the stock market. At the least, employees should be required to diversify their investment, to prevent a reprise of the financial devastation suffered by Enron and WorldCom employees whose retirement accounts were loaded with company stock. Lawmakers also need to give more serious thought to the need to provide at least limited protection for the funds that investors have in market-based pension plans.[61]

In Delaware, the principal legacy of the scandals seems to be the newly emerging good faith duty and the possibility that Delaware will subject directorial compensation to closer scrutiny in the future. It is important to note that this response to the scandals has come in Delaware's courts, rather than through a statutory reform effort. This is significant for at least two related reasons. First, because the judicial process takes time, even in Delaware, the principal cases are being decided long after the initial outrage at the scandals has passed. As a result, there is much less pressure for a radical response now.[62] Secondly, Delaware's fiduciary duty jurisprudence has a self-correcting quality. It is open-ended enough so that the courts can incorporate new concerns without dramatically altering its precedent.[63]

In short, in the 2000s, as in the 1930s, the most dramatic reforms have come from Congress because Congress faces intense public pressure to address breakdowns in corporate America. The shortcomings of the

[59] For more detailed discussion of the compensation problem, see, e.g., Skeel (2005: 152–54); Bebchuk and Fried (2004). A new study by Kees Cools (2005) found that the best predictors of whether a company was likely to be required to restate its financials in the 1990s were the amount of options-based compensation it provided its executives, the amount of media attention the company received, and the percentage increase in its average earnings targets.

[60] Under an Internal Revenue Code provision put in place in 1993—ironically, in an effort to curb managerial compensation—companies are permitted to deduct a maximum of one million dollars per year of compensation for each executive as a business expense. The deduction is lost for amounts in excess of one million dollars. But Congress excluded stock and stock options from the ceiling, which encourages companies to use these forms of compensation rather than cash.

[61] Several possible insurance strategies are discussed in Skeel (2005: 212–14).

[62] The waning sense of outrage may be part of the explanation for the Delaware Chancery Court's recent decision in the *Disney* case, which found no liability despite an almost complete lack of oversight of CEO Michael Eisner's decision to give Michael Ovitz $140 million in termination benefits. *In re Walt Disney Shareholder Litigation* (Del. Ch. 9 Aug. 2005).

[63] For an extended analysis of this attribute of Delaware corporate law, see Kahan and Rock (2004). See *also* Griffith (2005).

recent reforms vividly illustrate the point made at the outset of this section—that the pressure Congress faces to act after a scandal does not guarantee that the reforms that are passed will be ideal. But each of the great corporate scandals has reflected a breakdown in corporate oversight, which suggests, at the least, that Congress is likely to be aiming at the right target when it steps in. As a result, scandal reforms generally will make things better rather than worse overall, which is a fair assessment of the recent reform efforts.

B. A Road Not Taken: England's Informal Regulation of Takeovers

This brings us to a second lesson: the mode of regulation. We tend to take it as given in the United States that corporate law will be regulated through the legislative thunderbolts from Congress that set the mandatory parameters of corporate law, together with case-by-case adjudication in Delaware and the federal courts. But if we look across the Atlantic at England we see a very different regulatory strategy, despite the broad similarities in our approach to corporate life. Let me briefly describe our contrasting regulation of the archetypal corporate event of our era: takeovers.

In the United States, the emergence of takeovers in the 1950s and 1960s was attended by two pieces of landmark corporate legislation. Delaware enacted the 1967 amendments to its General Corporation Law which, as we have seen, authorized cashout mergers and significantly expanded companies' right to indemnify their directors. A year later, Congress passed the Williams Act amendments to the securities laws, which require that tender offers be held open for at least twenty days and that everyone who tenders receives the same price for their shares.[64] Ever since, the Williams Act has regulated the structure of tender offers, and Delaware has handled takeover challenges as fiduciary duty issues to be resolved on a case-by-case basis in the courts.

England started in the same place, but adopted a dramatically different style of regulation. When corporate raiders threatened to take their challenges to the courts in the late 1950s, the London Stock Exchange, the investment banks, and the institutional shareholders took matters into their own hands, devising an informal Takeover Code to regulate takeovers.[65] Although the Bank of England was closely involved—the 'Governor's eyebrows' directed the process, as the Brits

[64] For analysis of the Williams Act in the immediate aftermath of its passage, see, e.g. Note (1969); Comment (1971).

[65] John Armour and I discuss these developments in detail in a new article (Armour and Skeel 2005). The most detailed existing account of the origins of the Takeover Code is Johnston (1980).

like to say—the Takeover Code relies on norms-based self regulation rather than mandatory rules. The UK Takeover Code is far more shareholder-oriented than the US approach—target directors are forbidden from using defenses, for instance, and shareholders must be given equal treatment. This shareholder orientation was used, quite intentionally, to pacify bidders who might otherwise pursue their grievances in the courts.[66]

This history has important implications for a prominent current debate in the American corporate law literature. In important recent work, Lucian Bebchuk has developed a shareholder choice model for takeovers and other corporate law issues (Bebchuk 2005). Bebchuk argues that this shareholder choice model should be implemented through mandatory federal regulation. Whether or not one is persuaded by Bebchuk's shareholder choice model,[67] there is a striking, thus far unnoticed irony in his proposal: the very regulatory strategy he endorses—mandatory, top-down federal intervention—is precisely the reason that informal, norms-based regulation never emerged in the United States.

To understand the irony, recall that the securities acts of 1933 and 1934 installed the SEC as regulatory cop and gave the SEC control over the stock exchanges, in order to break the grip that J.P. Morgan and other Wall Street banks had over American finance and to diminish the role of the New York Stock Exchange. Federal Regulation also sharply curtailed the ability of banks, insurance companies, and other institutional creditors to hold substantial blocks of stock in American corporations.[68] The overall effect during the New Deal was to clean up the markets. But pervasive, top-down federal intervention also foreclosed the possibility of norms-based self-regulation as a regulatory strategy.[69] By neutralizing investment banks and shareholder groups, Congress quite accidentally

---

[66] See, e.g., Armour and Skeel (2005).

[67] In response to the shareholder choice model, several commentators have argued that there may be good reasons to give discretion to the managers of a takeover target, rather than leaving the takeover decision to shareholders. Somewhat similarly, Arlen and Talley (2003) argue that, if managers are prohibited from resisting takeovers, they may thwart takeovers in other ways. Kihlstrom and Wachter (2003) argue that managers may 'manage to the market,' making investment decisions they know are suboptimal, but shareholders don't, in order to satisfy market pressures. Kahan and Rock (2003) have suggested that managers may have better information as to whether a takeover auction (which shareholder choice requires) or a negotiated sale will bring the highest price in a sale.

[68] The political economy of these restrictions is the principal focus of Roe (1994).

[69] This effect may have been reinforced by the traditional hostility to influence by financial institutions in American corporate governance: see Roe (1994). The one place self-regulation has remained in place to some extent is with the New York Stock Exchange and other self-regulatory organisations. But stock exchange regulation is a very imperfect proxy for shareholder interests, and it is significantly circumscribed in the US by SEC authority over the exchanges. For a defense of stock exchange regulation, as contrasted with the SEC, see Mahoney (1997); for a critique, see Kahan (1997).

left more room for corporate managers to influence the regulatory process.[70]

There's probably too much water under the bridge to shift to a self-regulatory approach in the United States, despite the huge stock ownership stakes now held by institutional investors. But the divergent histories of the United States and United Kingdom have important implications for contexts as diverse as the European Union, on the one hand, and emerging economies, on the other.[71] The principal moral is quite simple: although mandatory regulation and reliance on a central regulator like the SEC can play an important role, it also can crowd out self-regulatory alternatives. The Delaware courts have counteracted many of the problems of a mandatory approach by providing a remarkably efficient judicial response to fiduciary duty litigation. But it is a response that bears managers' fingerprints, rather than truly reflecting the interests of shareholders. In countries that depend more on centralized regulators and less on the judicial system, moreover, and thus are not likely to replicate Delaware's quasi-legislative judicial process, the mandatory approach could prove highly inefficient. In these environments, the government might do well to pressure shareholder representatives to adopt a non-legal code of conduct, as with the UK takeover panel, rather than setting up a powerful SEC-style regulator.

C. Corporate Ethics and the (Narrow) Scope of Corporate Law

The final implication of the historical evolution of American corporate governance lies in the contemporary scope of corporate law. Over the last century, the domain of American corporate law has steadily shrunk. Antitrust, labor law, and environmental regulation—all of which are integral to corporate life—were each separated from corporate law at various points in the twentieth century.[72] In America, corporate law now means internal governance issues such as fiduciary duties and decision-making on fundamental transactions, and not much else. This balkanization is also reflected in the academic world, where most corporate law scholars do not specialize in areas like environmental or employment law.

---

[70] John Armour and I have developed this point in more detail elsewhere: see Armour and Skeel (2005).

[71] Takeovers are the subject of the EU's Thirteenth Directive, which has been under consideration for many years. For a critical assessment of the most recent proposal, see McCahery and Renneboog (2003).

[72] One could add corporate reorganisation to this list, too. See, e.g., Skeel (2001) (describing the severing of corporate reorganisation from corporate and securities practice in the 1930s, and the partial reintegration in the 1980s and 1990s).

Although the narrow scope of corporate law is in many respects a historical accident, as we have seen, it has had profound implications for American corporate governance. Limiting the field of inquiry to the agency relations among shareholders, directors, and officers has reinforced the emphasis on the profit-making role of corporations. Corporate managers can't ignore their employees or environmental obligations, but the regulatory structure treats these concerns as peripheral to the core functions of corporate governance.

This emphasis on profits, and on shareholders as the managers' principal constituency has a tremendous upside benefit: it provides an appropriate focus for managerial decision-making.[73] But the narrow scope of corporate law may also have abetted some of the excesses of the 1990s. The prevailing ethos of the bubble years assumed that managers, directors, and shareholders were (and should be) motivated entirely by self-interest.[74] Managers were encouraged to focus solely on the company's stock price not just by the structure of corporate law, but also by compensation arrangements that relied on stock options as the principal form of executive pay. Unfortunately, the relentless appeal to self-interest—narrowly defined in terms of stock price—too often forced basic ethical considerations out.

IV. CONCLUSION

What would it take to bring a healthier focus to American corporate life? Let me conclude by offering three simple suggestions. The first is to reform the regulatory rules that contributed to the corporate scandals, as discussed earlier.[75] So long as the tax code rewards companies for compensating their executives with stock options rather than cash, there will be structural pressures for managers to continue focusing narrowly on stock price. Altering the regulatory incentives that encouraged misbehaviour should therefore remain a top priority.

The second is to insist on a broader perspective on corporate law, one that looks beyond the narrow confines of shareholder, director and

---

[73] And conversely, expecting managers to focus on a broader range of constituencies could actually undermine their accountability, as noted below. As will quickly become clear, I do not share Milton Friedman's famous view that 'there is one and only one social responsibility of business—to use its resources and engage in activities designed to increase its profits [for shareholders]' Friedman (1962: 133; 1970: 33). But I agree that managers should view the company's shareholders as their primary constituency.

[74] For a postmortem critique of the assumption that 'people are selfish, constantly calculating to their own advantage, with no thought of others,' see Shiller (2005: A25).

[75] See above notes 59–61 and accompanying text.

manager relations.[76] I don't mean to suggest that directors' fiduciary duties should encompass not only shareholders, but also employees, suppliers and other constituencies, as advocates of a 'team production' approach to corporate law have proposed (Blair and Stout 1999). The problem with inviting directors to abandon their focus on shareholders is that directors who are told to be loyal to many constituencies are too likely to prove loyal to none. The effect—as we saw with the 'other constituency' statutes enacted during the takeover wave of the 1980s—is to give the directors unfettered discretion, since nearly any decision they wish to make can be defended as benefiting one or more constituencies.[77] But policy-makers and corporate scholars need to pay greater heed to areas like labor law, antitrust or campaign finance that often do not even figure in our discussions of corporate regulation. Although directors' principal internal responsibility is to the company's shareholders, the company's compliance with its obligations to employees, creditors and other third parties should be central to our assessment of corporate performance.[78]

Third is simply integrating ethics into the existing emphasis on self-interest, starting with our law and business school classrooms and continuing into corporate life itself. There are many reasons to believe that simply announcing a policy of ethical behaviour will not by itself change the ethical tone of the company. If compensation and promotion practices are closely tied to bottom line performance measures, they will undercut the company's code of ethics by signaling that the code is simply window dressing. Corporate ethics also requires that executives practice what they preach. '[I]t probably is necessary,' as Don Langevoort puts it, 'that senior management display in their own actions the sort of other-regarding behaviours they want to see from their agents' (Langevoort 2002)). Only if the company's values are reflected in the executive suite and in the expectations created throughout the firm will the recent emphasis on ethics prove more than a temporary fad.

The lessons just described are not a cure-all that will end corporate misbehaviour and single-handedly usher in a new, permanent era of corporate and financial health. For better or worse, the historical cycle of periodic waves of Icarus Effect scandals followed by a federal regulatory response is part of the inevitable push and pull of American business. In

[76] A fascinating recent article that takes a similar perspective is Winkler (2004). Winkler argues that if we construe corporate law broadly to include the full range of regulation that comprises the 'law of business,' it is not nearly so narrowly focused on shareholders' interests as is often believed.

[77] For an early, influential discussion of this problem, see Berle (1931).

[78] An important contribution of the recent book *The Anatomy of Corporate Law* is to reintroduce these kinds of considerations into the analysis of corporate law (Kraakman *et al* 2004). As noted above, Adam Winkler (2004) has also argued for a broader conception of the 'law of business.'

the name of flexibility and innovation corporate leaders push back against the regulatory constraints imposed in the aftermath of scandal (a process now well underway, as reflected in the continuing debates over Sarbanes-Oxley's internal controls requirement) and technological advances create new challenges for reining in abuses that stem from the combination of risk-taking, competition, and opportunities for misuse of the corporate form. But whether the next round of corporate scandals comes later or soon depends in no small part on how fully regulators and businesses respond to what we have learned from the most recent breakdown in American corporate and financial life.

REFERENCES

Arlen, J. and Talley, E. (2003), 'Unregulable Defenses and the Perils of Shareholder Choice', 152 *U. Penn. L. Rev.* 577.

Armour, J. and Skeel, D. (2005), 'Who Regulates Takeovers and Why? The Peculiar Divergence of US and UK Takeover Regulation' (unpublished manuscript).

Armour, J., Cheffins, B., and Skeel, D.A., Jr. (2002), 'Corporate ownership structure and the evolution of bankruptcy law: lessons from the UK', 55 *Vand. L. Rev.* 1699.

Bainbridge, S. (2003), 'The Creeping Federalization of Corporate Law', 26 *Regulation* (2003).

Bebchuk, L.A. (1992), 'Federalism and the Corporation: The Desirable Limits on State Competition in Corporate Law, 105 *Harv. L. Rev.* 1437.

Bebchuk, L.A. (2005), 'The Case For Increasing Shareholder Power, 118 *Harv. L. Rev.* 833.

Bebchuk, L and Fried, J. (2004), *Pay Without Performance: The Unfulfilled Promise of Executive Compensation* (Cambridge: HUP).

Berle, Jr., A.A. (1931), 'Corporate Powers as Powers Held in Trust', 44 *Harv. L. Rev.* 1049.

Black, B.S. (1998), 'Shareholder Activism and Corporate Governance in the United States, in 3 *The New Palgrave Dictionary of Economics and the Law* 459 (Peter Newman ed.)(New York: Palgrave MacMillan).

Blair, M.M. (2003), 'Locking In Capital: What Corporate Law Achieved or Business Organizers in the Nineteenth Century', 51 *UCLA L. Rev.* 387.

Blair, M.M. and Stout, L.A. (1999), 'A Team Production Theory of Corporate Law', 85 *Va. L. Rev.* 247.

Bratton, W.W. and McCahery, J.A. (2004), 'The Content of Corporate Federalism', ECGI Law Working Paper, 23/2004.

Cary, W.L. (1974), 'Federalism and Corporate Law: Reflections Upon Delaware', 83 *Yale L.J.* 663.

Coffee, J.C. (2002), 'Understanding Enron: It's About the Gatekeepers, Stupid', 57 *Bus. Law.* 1403.

Comment (1971), 'Section 13(d) And Disclosure of Corporate Equity Ownership', 119 *U. Pa. L. Rev.* 853.

Cools, K. (2005), Presentation at Good Governance Conference (Amsterdam, 6 Apr.).

Cunningham, L.A. (2003), 'The Sarbanes-Oxley Act: Heavy Rhetoric, Light Reform (And It Just Might Work)', 35 *U. Conn. L. Rev.* 915.

Davis, L.E. and North, D.C. (1971), *Institutional Change and Economic Growth* (Cambridge: CUP).

Donaldson, W. (2005), 'We've Been Listening', *Wall St. J.*, 29 Mar. at A14.

Eisenberg, M. (1993), 'The Divergence of Conduct and Standards of Review in Corporate Law', 62 *Ford. L. Rev.* 437.

Fernandez, B. (2005), 'Firms Surprised by the Cost to Keep Ledgers Honest', *Phila. Inq.*, 13 Apr. at A1, A6.

Folk, E.L. (1968), 'Some Reflections of a Corporation Law Draftsman', 42 *Conn. Bar J.* 409.

Friedman, M. (1962)(2nd edn 1982), *Capitalism and Freedom* (Chicago: Univ. of Chi. Press).

Friedman, M. (1970), 'A Friedman Doctrine—The Social Responsibility of Business is to Increase its Profits', *N.Y. Times*, 13 Sept. (Magazine) at 33.

Gapper, J. (2005), 'Capitalist Punishment', *FT Mag.*, 29 Jan. at 16.

Gordon, J.S. (1988), *The Scarlet Woman of Wall Street: Jay Gould, Jim Fisk, Cornelius Vanderbilt, The Erie Railway Wars, and the Birth of Wall Street* (New York: Weidenfeld & Nicolson).

Grandy, C. (1989), 'New Jersey Corporate Chartermongering, 1875–1929', 49 *J. Econ. Hist.* 677.

Griffith, S. (2005), 'Good Faith Business Judgment: A Theory of Rhetoric in Corporate Law Jursprudence', 55 *Duke L.J.* 1.

Hacker, J.S. and Pierson, P. (2002), 'Business Power and Social Policy: Employers and the Formation of the American Welfare State', 30 Pol. & Soc. 277.

Horwitz, M.J. (1992), *The Transformation of American Law, 1870-1960: The Crisis of Legal Orthodoxy* (Oxford: OUP).

Jackall, R. (1988), *Moral Mazes: The World of Corporate Managers* (New York: OUP).

Johnston, A. (1980), *The City Take-Over Code* (Oxford: OUP).

Kahan, M. (1997), 'Some Problems with Stock Exchange-Based Securities Regulation', 83 *Va. L. Rev.* 1509.

Kahan, M. and Kamar, E. (2002), 'The Myth of State Competition in Corporate Law', 55 *Stan. L. Rev.* 679.

Kahan, M. and Rock, E. (2003), 'Corporate Constitutionalism: Antitakeover Charter Provisions as Precommitment', 152 *U. Penn. L. Rev.* 473.

Kahan, M. and Rock, E. (2004), 'Our Corporate Federalism and the Shape of Corporate Law' (Unpublished Manuscript).

Kamar, E. (1998), 'A Regulatory Competition Theory of Indeterminacy in Corporate Law', 98 *Colum. L. Rev.* 1908.

Khurana, R. (2002), *Search for a Corporate Savior: The Irrational Quest for Charismatic CEOs* (Princeton: PUP).

Kihlstrom, R.E. and Wachter, M. (2003), 'Corporate Policy and the Coherence of Delaware Takeover Law', 152 *U. Penn. L. Rev.* 523.

Kirk, III, W.E. (1984), 'A Case Study In Legislative Opportunism: How Delaware Used the Federal-State System to Attain Corporate Pre-Eminence', 10 *J. Corp. L.* 233.

Kraakman, R. *et al.* (2004), *The Anatomy of Corporate Law* (Oxford: OUP).

Langevoort, D.C. (2002), 'Monitoring: The Behavioural Economics of Corporate Compliance With Law', *Colum. Bus. L. Rev.* 71.

Mahoney, P.G. (1997), 'The Exchange as Regulator', 83 *Va. L. Rev.* 1453.

Marsh, H. (1966), 'Are Directors Trustees? Conflict of Interest and Corporate Morality', 22 *Bus. L.* 35.

McCahery, J.A. and Renneboog, L. (2003), 'The Economics of the Proposed European Takeover Directive' (Centre for European Policy Studies).

McCurdy, C.W. (1979), 'The *Knight Sugar* Case of 1895 and the Modernization of American Corporation Law', 53 *Bus. Hist. Rev.* 304.

Mcdonald, F. (1962), *Insull* (Chicago: Univ of Chi. Press).

Note (1969), 'Cash Tender Offers', 83 *Harv. L. Rev.* 377.

Olson, M. (1971), *The Logic Of Collective Action* (Cambridge: HUP).

Pinsky, D.E. (1963), 'State Constitutional Limitations on Public Industrial Financing: An Historical and Economic Approach', 111 *U. Pa. L. Rev.* 265.

Pozen, R. (2004), 'How To Break Free From an American Listing', *Fin. Times*, 13 Feb. at 17.

Ribstein, L.E. (2002), 'Market vs. Regulatory Responses to Corporate Fraud: A Critique of the Sarbanes-Oxley Act of 2002', 28 *J. Corp. L.* 1.

Ribstein, L.E. (2003), 'Bubble Laws', 40 *Houston L. Rev.* 77.

Rock, E.B. (1997), 'Saints and Sinners: How Does Delaware Corporate Law Work?', 44 *Ucla L. Rev.* 1009.

Roe, M.J. (1994), *Strong Managers, Weak Owners* (Princeton: Princeton University Press).

Roe, M.J. (2003), 'Delaware's Competition', 117 *Harv. L. Rev.* 588.

Romano, R. (1993), *The Genius of American Corporate Law* (Washington: ALI Press).

Romano, R. (2005), 'The Sarbanes-Oxley Act and the Making of Quack Corporate Governance', 114 *Yale L.J.* 1521.

Roosevelt, F.D. (1938), 'New Conditions Impose New Requirements Upon Government and Those Who Conduct Government', in *The Public Papers and Addresses of Franklin D. Roosevelt* (Samuel I. Rosenman ed.) (New York: Random House).

Seligman, J. (1982), *The Transformation of Wall Street: A History of the Securities and Exchange Commission and Modern Corporate Finance* (Boston: Houghton Mifflin).

Shiller, R.J. (2005), 'How Wall Street Learns to Look the Other Way', *N.Y. Times*, Feb. 8, at A25.

Skeel, D.A. (1997a), 'Public Choice and the Future Of Public Choice-Influenced Legal Scholarship', 50 *Vand. L. Rev.* 647.

Skeel, D.A. (1997b), 'The Unanimity Norm in Delaware Corporate Law', 83 *Va. L. Rev.* 127.

Skeel, D.A. (2001), *Debt's Dominion: A History of Bankruptcy Law in America* (Princeton: Princeton University Press).

Skeel, D.A. (2005), *Icarus In The Boardroom: The Fundamental Flaws In Corporate America And Where They Came From* (New York: OUP).

Skeel, D. and Stuntz, W. (2006), 'Christianity and the (Modest) Rule of Law', *U. Penn. J. Const. L.* (Forthcoming).

Steffins, L. (1905), 'New Jersey: A Traitor State', 25 *McClure's Magazine*, May.

Thompson, R.B. and Sale, H.A. (2003), 'Securities Fraud as Corporate Governance: Reflections upon Federalism', 56 *Vand. L. Rev.* 859.

Veasy, N. (2003), 'What's Wrong With Executive Compensation', *Harv. Bus. Rev.*, Jan. , at 5 (Veasy Remarks at Roundtable)

Weiss, E.J. and White, L.J. (2005), 'File Early, Then Free Ride: How Delaware Law (Mis)Shapes Shareholder Class Action', 57 *Vand. L. Rev.* 1797.

Winkler, A. (2004), 'Corporate Law or the Law of Business?: Stakeholders and Corporate Governance at the End of History', 67 *L. & Contemp. Probl.* 109.

4

Corporate Governance after Enron: An Age of Enlightenment?

SIMON DEAKIN* AND SUZANNE J KONZELMANN**

T HE FALL OF Enron has again focused attention on the failure of
mechanisms of corporate governance to protect investor interests.
However, financial scandals of this kind are nothing new,
particularly in periods of 'correction' following stock market bubbles.
Moreover, there is no consensus on the wider implications of the Enron
affair. Three distinct positions might be taken. According to the first,
Enron's collapse simply tells us that the existing corporate governance
system is working. As the *Economist* put it (2002a), the unraveling of the
corporate scandals 'might actually be a reason to be more confident about
corporate America.' Enron's share price nose-dived once news of its
earnings restatements surfaced: 'what is interesting about Enron is not
the fact that the energy giant collapsed, but how fast the market brought
it down' (Benefits Canada 2002). Market sanctions, in the form of
reputational damage to its senior managerial team and to its auditors,
Arthur Andersen, served as an effective disciplinary device. Enron's
bankruptcy offers an appropriate lesson: 'in the drama of capitalism,
bankruptcy plays an essential part' (*Economist* 2001). On this basis, there
is nothing to be gained and much to be lost from wider reforms to the
corporate governance system.

The second point of view is more sceptical. It acknowledges that the
company's corporate governance exhibited serious failures of
monitoring, which can be traced back to conflicts of interest on the part of
board members and its auditors. Changes are needed: 'if corporate
America cannot deliver better governance as well as better audit, it will

† This chapter was previously published in (2003) 10 *Organization* 583–587. The
permission of Sage Publications to republish is gratefully acknowledged.
* Faculty of Law and Centre for Business Research, University of Cambridge.
** School of Management and Organisational Psychology, Birbeck University of London,
and Centre for Business Research, Cambridge.

have only itself to blame when the public backlash becomes both fierce and unpleasant' (*Economist* 2002b). This is the agenda that shaped the Sarbanes-Oxley Act which was passed by the US Congress in the summer of 2002. As a result, audit partners (although not audit firms) must now be rotated every five years and audit firms may not supply services to a company whose CEO and chief accounting officers were employed by the auditor and took part in an audit of the issuer within the preceding year. In addition, the Act imposes tighter standards on the certification of annual and quarterly reports by CEO and other leading officers; requires the reimbursement of gains from stock options if earnings are retrospectively restated; prohibits share sales by top officers during 'pension blackouts' of the kind which locked in the Enron workforce as its shares collapsed; prohibits loans to top corporate officers; imposes a duty to disclose 'on a rapid and current basis' additional information 'concerning material changes in the financial condition or operations of the issuer, in plain English' [sic]; and introduces a tighter definition of non-executive director independence. Thanks to its extra-territorial reach, the Act applies to overseas companies with a US stock exchange listing or holding US corporate debt.

The third view offers a radically different explanation for Enron's fall. It holds that Enron's business model exemplifies the pathology of the 'shareholder value' system which became dominant in Britain and America in the 1980s and 1990s (Bratton 2002). The company's focus on short-term stock price appreciation, in part the result of the share options granted to senior management, was the cause of its downfall. It was this which led to the use of 'special purpose entities' to conceal debts and artificially inflate the value of the company's stock. In pursuing an 'asset light' strategy at the expense of long-term growth, the company placed itself at risk of implosion once the business cycle turned down, as happened in the course of 2001. From this perspective, the fate of Enron is less important than the future of the business model which it came to represent. Unless the regulatory framework is adjusted to make this model unattractive, it will only be a matter of time before the same approach is tried again.

We believe that this third interpretation of events goes to the heart of the matter, and explains why the Enron case, more than any of the other corporate scandals, has given rise to concern. If we are to take this view seriously, nothing less than a fundamental rethinking of corporate governance practices and procedures is required. Above all, corporate governance must no longer confine its analysis to the relationship between managers, boards and shareholders. The narrowness of this focus is a major contributing factor to the present round of corporate scandals of which Enron is the most emblematic.

The case for shareholder value as the lodestar of corporate governance was made by financial economists in the early 1980s as a means of minimizing agency costs arising from the separation of ownership and control. Contrary to what is often supposed, it did not derive from legal conceptualizations of the duties of company directors. These tend (still) to be framed in open-ended terms which provide management with considerable discretion in balancing the interests of different stakeholder groups. However, a norm of shareholder primacy gained ground in the 1980s in the American and British systems, principally as a result of the rise of the hostile takeover as the basis of the 'market for corporate control.' In the 1990s, this was reinforced by the growing influence and power of institutional investors (principally the pension funds). Novel accounting metrics, measuring corporate performance by reference to 'economic value added' and 'return on capital employed', expressed the new philosophy very clearly, as did the linking of managerial pay to stock price movements through the use of share options. The composition of the senior managerial class itself began to change, as companies increasingly prized financial skills and deal-making above organizational ability and applied professional knowledge.

The implications for employees were far-reaching: restructuring and downsizing, once thought to be a sign of corporate weakness, became instead the source of share price gains. How far these gains were made as a result of improved efficiency in the use of productive resources, and how far they represent the effects of particular accounting conventions, remains hotly debated. What is not in dispute is that these changes put the post-war 'social contract' between labour and management under unprecedented strain.

Enron simply took the logic of shareholder value to its extreme. Its aggressive approach to mergers and acquisitions, the unique 'rank and yank' system of employee appraisal, and the sheer scale of the stock options granted to senior managers, may have marked it out from its rivals. But in its essential respects, the path followed by Enron was no different from that being pursued by many other apparently successful companies during this period. This explains the wider, negative stock market response to the revelation that Enron's strategy was built on sand.

If Enron's fall was the inevitable consequence of its rise, the question of what comes next is a pressing one. Tinkering with rules on conflicts of interests is unlikely to be the answer. There is already a substantial body of regulation on this issue, but Enron shows that it does not prevent serious corporate collapses. It is now clear that Enron's senior managers committed various legal wrongs even before the point at which its shares began to decline as part of the general response, during 2001, to the end of the dot com boom. However, although the contracts made with the special purpose entities involved 'self-dealing' of the kind which is closely scrutinized by corporate and securities law, these arrangements may well have passed tests of adequate disclosure. While board members may have been mistaken, with the benefit of hindsight, in waving through these deals, it does not necessarily follow that individual directors thereby breached the duty of care they owed to the company; the protective 'business judgment rule' insulates directors from liability for decisions taken in good faith. Breaches of fiduciary duty, or worse, may emerge in due course as litigation continues. The wider question is whether existing corporate governance mechanisms are sufficient to deal with the true mischief which Enron represents.

Enron teaches that a regime based on disclosure can only take us so far. An alternative reform would be to restore to managers something of the autonomy which company law once sought to provide them with. This is not as counter-intuitive as it might seem. In the United Kingdom, the recent governmental review of company law proposed that company boards should aim to achieve 'enlightened shareholder value' (Company Law Review Steering Committee 2001). According to this notion, it is by balancing the interests of the different stakeholder groups in such a way as to promote cooperation between them, that the board can best advance the long-term interests of the shareholders. This also implies a redefinition of the shareholder interest. The ultimate beneficiaries of pension funds and insurance policies have a long-term interest in the sustainability of the system, a point which is being taken on board by a small but growing number of fund managers who regard the break-up strategies of the 1980s and 1990s with scepticism and seek to engage actively with management to promote long-term growth.

The argument that managers should be accountable to shareholders alone, leaving other economic and social interests to protect themselves through the interplay of market forces, is at the root of present difficulties in the Anglo-American systems of corporate governance. It is not too late to revise this point of view, which is both more recent in origin and less institutionally embedded than is generally supposed. But if Enron's fall is to usher in a new age of enlightenment, a profound reassessment of current orthodoxies is required.

REFERENCES

Benefits Canada (2002), 'Governance in Shreds' 26(5), 50.
Bratton, W.W. (2002), 'Enron and the Dark Side of Shareholder Value' 76 *Tulane Law Review* 1275.
Company Law Review Steering Committee (2001), *Modern Company Law for a Competitive Economy: Final Report Volume 1* (London: DTI).
Economist (2001), 'Wasted Energy', 8 Dec, Leader.
—— (2002a), 'Another Scandal, Another Scare', 29 June.
—— (2002b), 'The Lessons from Enron', 9 Feb, Leader.

5

Financial Scandals and the Role of Private Enforcement: The Parmalat Case

GUIDO FERRARINI* AND PAOLO GIUDICI**

I. INTRODUCTION

T
HE PARMALAT SCANDAL has been described by the Securities and Exchange Commission (SEC) as 'one of largest and most brazen corporate financial frauds in history.'[1] Coming soon after the Enron and WordCom scandals, it offers a good opportunity to compare governance failures on both sides of the Atlantic. The *Parmalat* case epitomizes the most important problem traditionally associated with continental European governance structures, namely a controlling shareholder that exploits the company rather than monitoring its managers. Parmalat's governance structure was openly deficient, unlike Enron's, which apparently was well designed. Despite this deficiency, Parmalat enjoyed an investment grade credit-rating, and was able to

* University of Genoa, Centre for Law and Finance.
** Free University of Bozen and Centre for Law and Finance. A draft of this paper was presented at the Harvard Law School/ETH Zurich conference 'EU Corporate Law Making: Institutional Structure, Regulatory Competition, and Regulatory Strategies' in October 2004. The authors are grateful to Gérard Hertig, Mark Roe, Donald Langevoort, and other conference participants for helpful comments. Drafts of this paper were also presented at a Yale Law School Alumni Meeting in New Haven, CT in October 2004; a meeting of the Associazione Via Isonzo in Milan in October 2004; and at a seminar at the Institute of Law and Finance (ILF), University of Frankfurt in January 2005. The authors are grateful to Theodore Baums, Andreas Cahn, Carmine Di Noia, Jon Macey, Katharina Pistor and other seminar participants for helpful suggestions. Special thanks to Bruno Cova (former General Counsel of Parmalat's Extraordinary Administration), Lucie Courteau and Justin Rainey. The authors acknowledge research assistance by Liliana Emer, Gian Giacomo Peruzzo and Andrea Zanoni.

[1] *Securities and Exchange Commission v Parmalat Finanziaria SpA*, Case No. 03 CV 10266 (PKC) (S.D.N.Y.), Accounting and Auditing Enforcement Release No. 1936/30 Dec. 2003.

borrow increasing amounts of capital from investors. With the benefits of hindsight one could be tempted to argue that capital markets were inefficient because they did not take into proper consideration Parmalat governance's flaws. However, a more plausible assertion would be that they discounted the perceived risk and heavily relied on gatekeepers.

Thus, once again, as in many sudden financial collapses of recent times, attention is focused on the gatekeepers' role. Two large networks of auditors (Grant Thornton International and Deloitte Touche Tohmatsu) failed to detect the frauds. Grant Thornton's Italian partners are also suspected of having orchestrated them. Some first-ranking international banks allegedly assisted Parmalat's senior managers in structuring and executing complex financial transactions aimed at concealing Parmalat's true situation. In the face of due diligence reviews and top-firms' legal opinions, the market was never openly warned. As John Coffee pointed out with reference to Enron (Coffee 2002, 2004a), it seems clear that Parmalat is another tale of the corporate governance deficiencies of undeterred gatekeepers.

As we show, Italian substantive rules cannot be blamed for what occurred in Parmalat. Indeed, we argue that the existing Italian substantive rules that have been in place during last decade were sufficient and, somewhat surprisingly, were even stricter than those in the United States. If gatekeepers were undeterred, it is not due to Italian substantive law, but rather the enforcement regime.

When 'enforcement' is discussed in Continental Europe, this typically means *public* enforcement. The Parmalat scandal has affected a country that relies heavily on public enforcement and essentially dislikes the whole concept of private vindication of the public interest. Yet the Italian capital markets watchdog, Consob, only commenced its investigations after the market had signalled, in late 2002 to early 2003, that something was wrong at Parmalat. The market knew something that Consob did not. Thus, the Parmalat scandal should discourage any idea that more regulation and public supervision of markets can prevent major frauds. The reaction both at Italian and European levels, nevertheless, is in the direction of more regulation and public enforcement, even though the idea of a European public regulator equivalent to the SEC seems not to be a priority on the EU's agenda. However, the Italian public learned from the mass-media shortly after Parmalat's collapse that civil actions were being launched, at a speed unthinkable for Italy, by class-action lawyers in the United States, and that those actions could also involve unsuspecting Italian investors. Class actions were no longer an ingredient of a John Grisham novel. This news gave impetus to a discussion (albeit ill-conceived) concerning the introduction of class-action mechanisms in Italy, conducted in the mass-media and at a political level as a side-issue of the main topic concerning new regulation in response to the scandal. Indeed we assert (strange as it may sound in a study devoted to one of the most significant criminal scandals in Europe's recent history) that the whole framework of civil procedure is one of the main problems in Italy. In reaching this conclusion, we also rely on the pattern of litigation that has followed the Parmalat collapse. It confirms both Lord Denning's dictum that '[a]s a moth is drawn to the light, so is a litigant drawn to the United States'[2] and the modern trends of litigation in the mass tort[3] and antitrust areas, which led to the recent US Supreme Court decision in the *Hoffmann La Roche v Empagran* case.[4] Indeed, whenever it has been possible, both Parmalat's Extraordinary Commissioner (Mr Bondi, who acts on behalf of the company and its creditors) and investors have brought civil actions in the United States, escaping the jurisdiction of Italian courts. We argue that this pattern cannot be understood if it is considered simply as a form of 'forum shopping' based on the search for the most convenient substantive rules, because it is mainly motivated by the array of weapons that US civil procedure offers plaintiffs in complex cases regarding collective interests. Accordingly we argue, drawing from similar conclusions reached by one of us with reference to the problem of private enforcement of cartels in Europe, that the balance between public and private enforcement must be reconsidered and that the whole framework of civil procedure has to be reviewed in Italy. As far as possible, cyclical bursts of criminal proceedings should be replaced by the continuous, low level pressure of private suits, in order to keep deterrence working on a day-by-day basis.

While advocating the modernisation of civil procedure in continental Europe along the US model, we do not claim that US securities law and regulation are in all respects superior to their homologues in Europe. The fact that serious financial scandals recently plagued US capital markets may be taken as evidence of deficiencies affecting US corporate law and securities regulation and their enforcement. As we note below, the limits of law and enforcement concerning gatekeepers in general presumably contributed to the recent wave of corporate frauds in the United States and no doubt determined a substantial amount of re-regulation through legislative reforms. Yet the Italian and European experiences show that

[2] *Smith Kline & French Lab. Ltd v Block* [1983] 2 All ER 72, 74 (CA). This passage is quoted by Carrington (2004: 1420).
[3] One of the most remarkable examples being the action brought by the Republic of India against the Union Carbide Corporation for the Bhopal tragedy in 1984. See Carrington (2004: 1420).
[4] In *Hoffmann La Roche v Empagran*, 124 S. Ct. 2359, the US Supreme Court limited the subject jurisdiction of US antitrust law, holding that it is not reasonable to apply it to a price-fixing conduct that affects both customers outside and within the United States, when the adverse foreign effect is independent from any domestic adverse effect.

deficiencies as to private enforcement may have materially contributed to the recent scandals in Europe, and led aggrieved investors—and Parmalat's Extraordinary Administrator—to seek relief in US courts. Therefore, the reference to US institutions in the area of private enforcement, like class actions and discovery rules, appears to be justified despite the failures of US law recently shown by Enron and similar scandals. As we argue in this chapter, the design of substantive rules needs to be balanced by appropriate enforcement mechanisms. In Italy, the substantive rules concerning gatekeepers, while reflecting high standards of behaviour, are not matched by corresponding rules of civil procedure that offer an appropriate setting for mass claims and complex litigation.

This chapter proceeds as follows. In Part II we briefly trace Parmalat's history from its rise in the late-1960s to its collapse in December 2003. We describe the frauds, the criminal proceedings that followed the collapse, and the civil actions that have been brought in the United States by investors and Parmalat's Extraordinary Commissioner. Part III is devoted to Parmalat's governance record and its gatekeepers. In particular, we show that gatekeepers in Italy are substantially undeterred, not because of substantive rules, but because of poor enforcement. The 'law the books', as we point out with reference to auditors, is even more severe than common law.

Part IV considers the causes of underenforcement and the reason why the *Parmalat* case is generating litigation in the United States, but not in Italy (or in Europe). Further, we explain why deterrence must rely also on private enforcement and consider the advantages, from a European perspective, of class actions. We emphasize the role of discovery rules, and their interplay with pleading rules, and explain the absence of derivative actions in Italy. Finally, we turn to the interplay between public and private enforcement, to show that this interplay is missing and that the most significant junction between private gatekeepers and the public watchdog is totally ill-suited in Italy because the watchdog relies on the wrong gatekeeper.

II. A SHORT HISTORY OF PARMALAT

A. Parmalat

Calisto Tanzi was the heir to a dynasty of food traders based in Collecchio, Parma. At the end of the 1960s, Mr Tanzi entered the milk market, taking advantage of the continuous packaging process developed by Tetra Pak,[5] and Parmalat started its expansion into the dairy industry. During the 1970s the Parmalat trademark became popular thanks to high-profile sponsorship in the world of sport. In the same decade, Parmalat started its penetration of Latin American markets. The 1980s was a period of further expansion: Parmalat consolidated its position as a world leader in the dairy market and extended into other food markets, such as bakery products, tomato sauces, and fruit juices. Mr Tanzi became very well known for his Catholic fervour and his political connections with Christian Democrats leaders. In particular, he was considered to be a close friend of Ciriaco De Mita, the powerful leader of the ruling Christian Democrat party during the 1980s. Parmalat built one of its factories in Nusco, a small town in southern Italy whose principal claim to fame is that it is Mr De Mita's home town.

Allegedly the influence of politicians is one of the reasons why Mr Tanzi ventured into the television market during the 1980s. Odeon TV, the channel he bought through a family shield, recorded terrible results and was sold in 1989 to a company of the Sasea Group managed by Mr Florio Fiorini.[6] Odeon TV went bankrupt and Tanzi, who had guaranteed Odeon TV debts, had to pay out huge amounts of money. During the criminal investigations into the Parmalat collapse it came to light that this money was actually provided by Parmalat.[7] This was probably one of the first large cases in which Parmalat money was used to cover Mr Tanzi's debts in other business areas.

Following the TV fiasco, at the end of the 1980s Parmalat was a large international group in financial turmoil. Through a complex financial transaction, Coloniale s.r.l. (the Tanzi family's company holding Parmalat's shares) used its controlling stake as non-cash consideration in the raising of capital of a listed company, Finanziaria Centro Nord, which was to become Parmalat Finanziaria. Through the financial transaction, Coloniale kept a controlling stake of around 51 per cent in Parmalat Finanziaria, which became the listed holding of a group formed by fifty-eight companies, of which thirty-three were based outside Italy, with a group turnover of around ITL 1,100 billion (€560 million). The most

---

[5] For references to Tetra Pak's competitive advantage in the packaging of liquid and semi-liquid foods see the EC Commission decision in *Elopak Italia Srl v Tetra Pak* (No. 2), 24 July 1991, (1992) O.J. L72/1, at para 11 *et seq*.

[6] Mr Fiorini was later to become famous worldwide because he was an associate of Mr Parretti, who was at the centre of the Hollywood studio Metro-Goldwyn-Mayer saga. Mr Fiorini and Mr Parretti were the dominant figures of the Swiss Sasea group of companies, which were vehicles of massive frauds and collapsed in 1992, with a financial scandal that, amongst other things, rocked Credit Lyonnais's lending policy. Some accounts of the scandal can be read in the UK case *Sasea Finance Ltd (in liquidation) v KPMG (formerly KPMG Peat Marwick McLintock)* [2000] 1 All ER 676, [2000] 1 BCLC 236.

[7] Fausto Tonna's confessions to the prosecutor, mentioned by Gabriele Franzini (2004: 25) and by Capolino, Massaro, and Panerai (2004: 41).

significant of these companies was Parmalat SpA, the main operating company.

In the 1990s, the Parmalat Group (hereinafter, Parmalat) launched a new international acquisition campaign, which was particularly intense in South America. The group turnover was ITL 4,300 billion (€2.4 billion) in 1995 and ITL 5,464 billion (€2.8 billion) in 1996. Around 45 per cent of the turnover was generated in Latin America. The multinational group was a lucrative client for investment banks, Chase Manhattan Bank in particular. The group became very active on the capital market, issuing waves of bonds on the Euromarket.

Meanwhile, Parmalat had diversified into professional football, buying Parma Calcio (Parma's soccer club), the well-known Brazilian club Palmeiras, and a Chilean club named Audax Italiano. The group started a massive sponsorship plan in Latin America. Parma Calcio was handed to Mr Tanzi's son Stefano, who became the club's president in 1996. One of Mr Tanzi's main rivals in the dairy-product market—Sergio Cragnotti—was also involved in the football market. A former manager of the Ferruzzi Group who had been involved in the criminal proceedings that followed the collapse of the Ferruzzi family's empire,[8] Cragnotti was the main shareholder and manager of Cirio, as well as owner of Lazio, one of Rome's two football clubs. Cirio was to go bankrupt in 2003, in a financial scandal involving banks accused of having covered their debt exposure by dumping Cirio bonds onto retail investors.[9]

Mr Tanzi also entered the tourism market in the 1990s. Through many transactions and acquisitions, the tourism firm of the Tanzi family, HIT, reached a turnover of ITL 1,000 billion (€550 million), generating a mountain of losses and debt. Stefania, Calisto Tanzi's daughter, was in charge of the business.

At the end of the decade the Parmalat Group was still expanding. Between 1998 and 2000 it purchased around twenty-five companies. Amongst them, in 1999 Parmalat bought Eurolat, the diary business of the Cirio group, in a deal that is now under investigation also in consideration of the role played by Banca di Roma, a bank heavily involved in the Cirio financial crisis.

The trend continued at the beginning of the new millennium. Parmalat was continuously issuing bonds. In November 2000 Standard and Poor's rated Parmalat with a BBB- grade (the lower level of investment grade). Following the problems experienced by Latin American economies (with Argentina's default in December 2001)[10] and the default of the fellow

[8] The Ferruzzi Group went almost bankrupt in 1993, with a criminal and political scandal that led its CEO, Mr Raul Gardini, to commit suicide. The Group was successfully restructured by a five-bank committee: Penati and Zingales (1997).

[9] For a review of the Cirio scandal see Onado (2003).

[10] The problems raised by Argentina's default in the Italian market are discussed by Consob (2004a).

food manufacturer Cirio in November 2002, Parmalat's cost of capital increased. Yet the group was still pursuing its apparent strategy of holding a huge amount of cash to be used in mergers and acquisitions whilst financing its cash needs through bonds.

At the end of 2002 Parmalat Finanziaria SpA was the listed holding of a multinational food group made up of more than 200 companies spread around fifty countries. The group was a world leader in the markets of milk, dairy products, and beverages. It operated 139 industrial plants and totalled more than 36,000 employees (Consob 2004b), with a consolidated turnover of €7.6 billion (Bank of Italy 2004: 10). Parmalat Finanziaria was still controlled by Coloniale SpA, the instrument of the Tanzi family that held around 51 per cent of the share capital (Parmalat 2003). Parmalat's 2002 last quarterly report showed €3.35 billion in cash and equivalents; Parmalat Group's assets amounted to €10 billion and its liabilities €7.17 billion. Amongst these liabilities was €1.5 billion in bond debt, launched through 31 different issues. At the beginning of 2003 Parmalat was back on the Mib30 index, the index of the 30 largest Italian companies in terms of market capitalisation.

B. The Collapse

The most distinctive feature of Parmalat's financial reports was the concurrently high level of cash and debt. Its disclosure policy was characterized by its management's opaque and arrogant approach towards analysts and investors, similar to Enron's.[11] However, Parmalat was not a 'faith' stock.[12]

In October 2002 the group launched a bond issue of €150 million with Banca Akros and UBM acting as lead underwriters, and in November a new bond issue by Parmalat Soparfi—its Luxembourg subsidiary—followed, with a value of €200 million and Morgan Stanley Limited acting as the only bookrunner (Parmalat 2002). These issues alerted the market. In a report titled 'Putting a Focus on Debt', Unicredit Banca Mobiliare's (UBM's) analysts recommended 'accumulate' but wrote:

> As for the debt refinancing issue, we argue that, post-Cirio and owing to the higher risk perception following the instability in South America, refinancing expiring debt at a reasonable cost has become harder. Moreover the Group has shown no intention to use its €3.3 billion cash pile. This point would need to be accurately assessed with the management, which, however, continues to remain unapproachable. (UBM 2002)

[11] For accounts of Enron's opaque financial statements and arrogance, see Bratton (2002: 1281).

[12] Asset managers considered Enron a 'faith' stock Bratton (2002: 1340); Gordon (2002: 1236).

Parmalat management's arrogance was a recurring theme in the reports. A Merrill Lynch report of the previous day had a much more straight-forward tone. The report, entitled 'The Straws that Break the Camel's Back', downgraded Parmalat from 'buy' to 'sell'. The analyst wrote:

> The key issue which continues to perplex us is why the group continues to tap the market for relatively small, yet often quite complex debt issues, when its cash pile continues to rise. (Merrill Lynch 2002: 8)

Indeed, the analyst's estimate was that Parmalat's raising money on a BBB- credit rating compared to an implied rate on cash and equivalent of 5.2 per cent had generated a ninety basis point loss on the spread. Thus, the first conclusion was that 'the group is *prima facie* losing money by running a high level of total debt and total cash'. The second conclusion was that problems could be hidden: 'this need for re-financing raises questions as to the underlying cash generation of the group'.

All the other analysts remained apparently unconcerned. For instance, Euromobiliare's report dated 23 January 2003 referred to a 'Debt Mountain … Under Control' and defended Parmalat's strategy on tax considerations. The unconcerned analysts considered the strategy to be theoretically sound, even though they had no clear picture of how it could work, since Parmalat did not disclose sufficient information and the group structure was terribly complex.[13]

Notwithstanding analysts' apparent support, the market became more suspicious of Parmalat's behaviour, clearly evidenced by rumours concerning a new bond issue at unfavourable conditions in February 2003, which hit the company. As an analyst wrote in March 2003,

> November 2002–February 2003 period saw Parmalat's price fall by 45 per cent, following the announcement of bond issues …. In our view, market speculation on debt sustainability and accounting procedures, strongly denied by a company press release, combined with poorly-timed group communication, accentuated the market reaction. (UBS Warburg 2003).

The new issue was officially cancelled. On 6 March 2003 Assogestioni, the Italian asset management association, wrote a letter to Parmalat, Consob, and Borsa Italiana, denouncing the lack of transparency of the group. As a reaction, Parmalat organized a meeting in Milan on 10 April 2003, during which Mr Tanzi announced that the Group's CFO, Mr Tonna, had resigned and that a new CFO, Mr Ferraris, was in charge. The market reacted positively and the price soared after the February downturn.

---

[13] On the failure of institutional investors and securities analysts to understand structured transactions even when these transactions are duly disclosed see Schwarcz (2004). On the information overload issue, see Paredes (2003).

Meantime, Parmalat denounced market manipulation and related abuses concerning its stock to Consob, the Italian watchdog, also mentioning that Lehman Brothers and other investment banks were asserting in private talks with clients that Parmalat's reports were false. Consob started to investigate.

Parmalat's new CFO, Mr Ferraris, had assured investors that it would only use cash to repay the Group debt. However, in June it was discovered that Parmalat, assisted by Morgan Stanley, had privately placed a new bond issue, wholly undersigned by Nextra, the asset manager of Banca Intesa group. The real amount of all pending bonds was still a mystery. When questioned, Parmalat replied that it had bought back some of its own bonds, as an Italian newspaper reported on 7 July 2003, but the numbers did not match.[14] Following the article, Consob forced the company to be more explicit, but at this stage any communication would raise more problems than it solved. The watchdog started to apply strong pressure on Parmalat Finanziaria's statutory auditors and external auditors, Deloitte. Subsequently, Deloitte announced that it could not give a 'fairness opinion' of the true value of Parmalat's open ended mutual fund Epicurum, which was recorded as cash equivalent by Parmalat Finanziaria for a book value of €497 million; Deloitte also disclosed the existence of a complex currency swap transaction with the fund. On 31 October, Consob wrote to Parmalat, their statutory auditors and their external auditors, requesting more information. Parmalat replied that the participation in Epicurum would be sold immediately. In the meantime, another discovery was made: the existence of an unreported complex contract between a Swiss subsidiary (Geslat) and a company constituted by Citigroup and named *Buconero*, the Italian equivalent of 'Black Hole'. This news caused an uproar in the market.

On 8 December 2003 Parmalat informed the market that Epicurum was unable to liquidate Parmalat's interest. The same day a bond was expiring and Parmalat declared that it could not pay it. S&P downgraded Parmalat's bonds to junk bond status. The next day, during a desperate attempt to sell the company to American investors, Mr Tanzi admitted in private that the company's records were false. On 11 December, the share price collapsed. Consob asked Grant Thornton, the auditor of a Cayman Islands company named Bonlat, which held a bank account with Bank of America where all €3.95 billion of Parmalat's group cash was supposedly deposited, to investigate whether Parmalat's statement concerning the bank account was true. Bank of America replied that the document confirming the bank account was a forgery. In the meantime Parmalat's management completed the destruction of the relevant company's

---

[14] 'Affari e Finanza', *La Repubblica*, mentioned by Franzini (2004).

documentation and hardware containing evidence of the fraud. Criminal investigations started. On 27 December 2003 Parmalat SpA was declared insolvent. The same day Mr Tanzi was jailed. On the 8 January 2004 it was the turn of Parmalat Finanziaria: the group's insolvency procedure started and Mr Enrico Bondi, a renowned manager, was appointed as Extraordinary Commissioner.

From 5 December 2002 to the 17 November 2003, only one analyst (from Merrill Lynch) had issued sell recommendations, amongst those posting reports on the Italian Stock Exchange website.

With the benefit of hindsight, Parmalat reveals some features common to firms that have faced catastrophic financial failures: massive growth—a 'nova effect', as Geoffrey Miller (2004) writes—questionable accounting and accountants, poor underlying performance, political connections, a dominating shareholder, complex corporate structures, and operational mystery. In contrast with other bankrupt firms, however, Parmalat's governance structures did not appear to be well designed or state-of-the-art.[15]

C. The Fraud and the Criminal Proceedings

When jailed, the managers (and, in particular, Mr Tonna, the most deeply involved) immediately cooperated with prosecutors and explained what had happened. Basically, all Parmalat's financial statements had been false for a long time, although it is not yet clear from exactly when. Both the poor performance of the core business and the exceptional amount of cash siphoned off by the Tanzi family over the years, when combined with the terrible results of the tourism business and the other activities of the Tanzi family (e.g., the football business), had created a mountain of debt that went out of control.

Indeed, the first analysis shows that from 1990 up to the collapse, the Parmalat Group consumed €14.2 billion of financial resources, generating an operating income of €1.1 billion; €13.2 billion was advanced by banks. The figure also includes €5.3 billion in interest and fees. Around 80 per cent of bank finance was provided by non-Italian groups. €3.8 billion was used for acquisitions. €2.3 billion was used for unknown, unreported transactions (Oddo: 2004a).[16]

As far as the technical means used to conceive the fraud, they were extremely basic. Parmalat hid losses, overstated assets or recorded

[15] See below, para III.A.1. Miller (2004: 451) observes that collapsed firms usually had well designed or even state-of-the-art corporate governance structures.
[16] Oddo (2004a) quoting the Extraordinary Commissioner's report.

non-existent assets, understated its debt, and diverted company cash to Tanzi family members.[17]

In order to hide losses, Parmalat had used various wholly-owned entities, amongst which the most significant was Bonlat, the Cayman Island subsidiary of the Group in its final five years, and the holder of the Bank of America's false account. Typically, uncollectible receivables were transferred from the operating companies to nominee entities, where their real value was hidden. Fictitious trades and financial transactions were organized to offset losses of operating subsidiaries and to inflate assets and incomes. Securitization schemes based on false trade receivables and duplicate invoices were recurrently used to finance the group.

Parmalat understated its debt through different fraudulent schemes. It recorded non-existent repurchases of bonds. It sold receivables falsely described as non-recourse, in order to remove the liabilities from the records. It mischaracterized debt or, simply, did not record it.

Funds were diverted to Tanzi family members and their private companies. A recurrent scheme was to record the payments as receivables and then move the false receivables through the web of the offshore entities in order to disguise their true nature. Allegedly, the Tanzi family also channelled repayments for quantity discounts made by Tetra Pak at the end of each year into a bank account held by a company wholly controlled by the family. The funds were used by the family as spending money. In order to understand the dimension of this misappropriation, it is worth noting that Parmalat was Tetra-Pak's third largest customer worldwide. The Extraordinary Commissioner of Parmalat has alleged that for the period from 1995 to 2003 the discount payments reached an average of around US $15 million per year.

Needless to say, some of the gatekeepers assisted management with implementing and devising this scheme. The role of the auditors and Parmalat's lawyer attracted attention after the collapse, and they were immediately arrested.

Prior to 1995, Mr Maurizio Bianchi and Mr Lorenzo Penca were providing auditing services to Parmalat's companies through Hodgson Landau Brand S.a.S. In 1995 they moved to Grant Thornton, Parmalat's principal auditor since 1990. Under Italian law, every nine years auditors must rotate. It is alleged that both men well knew all the frauds and were concerned that Deloitte, the new auditor, could discover them at the start of its term. Accordingly, they suggested the constitution of a Cayman Islands company, Bonlat, with the contribution of the fictitious assets of other offshore companies (mainly Zilpa and Curcastle). Grant Thornton would continue to audit Bonlat as secondary auditor of the group. Indeed

---

[17] See SEC, First Amended Complaint, 27 July 2004.

it was Grant Thornton that established Bonlat (Ansa/Bloomberg 2004). Bonlat became the group's principal waste basket and Mr Bianchi and Mr Penca helped Parmalat's managers to conceal the losses and the debt until the end of 2003. The two men are to appear in January 2005 before the Criminal Court of Milan in a fast-track procedure (*giudizio abbreviato*) typically asked for by defendants with little chance of success who at best can hope for a reduced conviction. This special procedure is part of the criminal proceedings started in Milan concerning market abuses, false financial reports and obstacles placed in the way of the watchdog's inquiry. These proceedings concern twenty-seven defendants, amongst which Parmalat's management and statutory auditors,[18] partners of the audit firms and bankers, the audit firms and some banks (Oddo 2004b: 33).[19] With regards to the bankruptcy criminal offences, the investigation seems to be nearing an end and the trial phase of the Parma proceedings is expected to start in 2005. Also these investigations involve Parmalat's managers, statutory auditors, partners of the audit firms and bankers, the audit firms and some banks.

Parmalat's lawyer, Mr Zini, was a Milan-based attorney who had worked in the well-known law firm of Pavia Ansaldo and established, in 2000, his own law firm, Zini & Associates. The latter was basically a Parmalat captive, since the large majority of its turnover was generated by the dairy group. Allegedly, Zini was the legal mind behind Parmalat's complex web of companies and transactions. He became known to the mass media during the group's final month as the legal representative of the infamous Epicurum fund, held by Bonlat. He also was immediately jailed after the collapse. He is facing charges in the Milan trial and is the subject of investigation in Parma.

D. Civil Actions

The Parmalat scandal is generating a flurry of civil litigation. In early January 2004, US class action lawyers sued a group of defendants amongst which were Tanzi, Tonna, Zini, and the auditors. The news that only a few days after Parmalat's insolvency a class action had been started in the United States, allied to rumours that Italian investors might benefit from it, fuelled the debate concerning the introduction of class action-like mechanisms in Italian civil procedure. In the same period the

[18] On statutory auditors see below, section III.C.

[19] Both the audit firms and the banks are involved because they are subject to special administrative fines (which in fact have a quasi-criminal nature) in the course of the criminal proceedings concerning their partners, managers, employees, under the D. Lgs. (Legislative Decree) of 8 June 2001 No. 231, a law that has created two types of corporate liability: the first in the form of vicarious liability; the second in the form organizational fault, see Gobert and Punch (2003: 108–13).

SEC brought an action against Parmalat. The action was settled at the end of July 2004. Parmalat's Commissioner agreed to comply with extensive provisions concerning corporate governance and shareholder participation, which were also an important part of its restructuring plan in Italy, as well as cooperating with the SEC investigation in the Parmalat case.

In August 2004 Parmalat's Commissioner sued Grant Thornton in the United States and Italy as well as the Swiss Association of Deloitte Touche Tohmatsu, and members and affiliated firms (Deloitte & Touche USA LLP, Deloitte & Touche LLP and Deloitte & Touche SpA). The Commissioner pointed out that the international affiliations and relationships of Grant Thornton and Deloitte were a core issue of the audit services they sold to Parmalat and therefore that as members of an integrated network they are to be held liable for damages as agents or joint venturers. The Commissioner held that both networks failed to properly audit Parmalat's companies and their related party transactions.

Subsequently, the Commissioner started an action in the United States against Citigroup, its subsidiary Citibank and other subsidiaries, and a further action against Bank of America. The Commissioner alleges that Citigroup structured Parmalat's securitization program knowing that Parmalat's management was using the program to increase Parmalat's cash flow artificially by double-counting its receivables, and that Citigroup structured many equity investments (amongst which the infamous Buconero transactions) that actually were disguised loans. The latter charge was also brought separately against Bank of America.[20]

In October 2004, asset managers acting as lead plaintiffs filed a class action in the United States against the two banks, the auditors and former management, in an action based on similar arguments as those presented by Parmalat and aimed at redressing damages suffered by investors and, particularly, by those investors that had sold Parmalat's shares and bonds and could not therefore take advantage of the Commissioner's actions.

In Italy more than 7,000 investors joined as civil claimants the criminal trial that started in Milan in October 2004. This number subsequently grew to 40,000. Such a number was unprecedented in Italy and highlighted the differences existing between class-action mechanisms and individual participation to legal proceedings. Also Parmalat and Consob joined the proceedings as civil claimants against the individual defendants. Consob's position is, in particular, controversial, because the securities watchdog's right to claim damages as a civil party acting on behalf of investors is far from clear under Italian law.

---

[20] Citigroup, as well as Bank of America, has been involved in the US financial scandals. For a review see Fanto (2004: 20 *et seq.*).

As far as we know, no other liability actions have been started in Italy. There are civil proceedings started by the Commissioner before the Court of Parma, but they seek to nullify under insolvency law transactions entered into by the banks and the company prior to its insolvency declaration.

E. Political Reactions to the Parmalat Scandal in Italy and in the EU

The Parmalat scandal is the subject of political debate concerning the distribution of powers amongst Italian supervisors. The Bank of Italy was attacked for not having screened Parmalat's issues on the bond market under Article 129 of the Consolidated Banking Law. It was also criticised for failing to discover the true nature of the information provided by Parmalat regarding its debt, given that the Bank of Italy manages the so-called 'Centrale Rischi', a data bank that classifies bank debts. The Governor of the Bank of Italy replied that the banking supervisor has no power to screen bond issues and to evaluate the financial soundness of industrial groups and that the data classified in the 'Centrale Rischi' have limited informational value when a large part of the group finance comes from foreign lenders (Bank of Italy 2004). Consob, the capital markets supervisor, claimed that access to the data of the 'Centrale Rischi' would have provided essential information and required more resources and more powers to conduct investigations and to sanction wrongdoers (Consob: 2004a).

The Italian Parliament created a joint committee for the analysis of the Parmalat collapse and the drafting of a new law concerning capital markets, a sort of Italian Sarbanes-Oxley Act. After almost a year, no legislation has been produced. In particular, the debate concerning the distribution of powers between the Bank of Italy and Consob is ongoing. A side issue of the Parmalat scandal is the political debate concerning class actions, as it did not go unnoticed that investors took action in the United States, whereas in Italy nothing happened until the criminal trial in Milan had begun. This debate has been presented in the Italian mass media and sometimes also in Italian law journals as a panacea for all the problems affecting investors' protection under Italian civil procedure.[21] Needless to say, the class-action mechanism can offer an explanation to investors' actions that have been brought in the United States, but cannot explain why also Parmalat acted in the United States and did not seek to fight against Grant Thornton, Deloitte, Citigroup, and Bank of America in its local jurisdiction. Thus, the Italian political debate is misconceived and

---

[21] For some references cf. De Nicola (2004a; 2004b); Zoppini (2004); Giussani and Zoppini (2004).

will not lead to any significant advance in the solution of the problems affecting Italian civil justice.

At the European level, following the European Parliament resolution on corporate governance and supervision of financial services (concerning the Parmalat case) dated 12 February 2004,[22] the EC Commission adopted on 27 September 2004 a communication addressed to the Council and the European Parliament. The communication points out that transparency, supervision, and oversight have to be improved, especially as far as tax havens are concerned, and law enforcement has to be strengthened through increased cooperation amongst agencies and public prosecutors. The communication stresses the need for further regulation concerning auditors, corporate advisors, analysts, rating agencies, and money-laundering. Interestingly, private enforcement is not at issue in the communication.[23]

F. Market Effects of the Parmalat Scandal

In the wake of the Parmalat scandal, Consob launched a wide-ranging investigation concerning bond issues. Listed companies were required to provide additional information, auditors adopted a stricter approach and some cases of insolvency were probably accelerated.

The effect of the Parmalat scam on the bond market has been quite significant. According to a report from Fitch Ratings, the number of Italian companies accessing the bond market is collapsed. More than half of the overall amount of new issues relates to two single companies, Telecom Italia, the telecommunications operator, and Autostrade, the motorway operator.[24] These two issuers complied with best international market practices and were able to issue bonds notwithstanding the financial scandals. Other companies exited the market and turned their attention back to the loan market.[25]

---

[22] The text of the resolution is available at: http://www.europa.eu.int/eur-lex/en/com/cnc/2004/com2004_0611en01.pdf (last visited 2 Aug. 2005).

[23] The Parmalat scandal has also influenced the Commission in the drafting of the proposal for a directive on statutory audits of annual accounts and consolidated accounts and amending Council Dirs 78/660/EEC and 83/349/EEC (http://europa.eu.int/comm/internal_market/auditing/officialdocs_en.htm). On its side, the International Organization of Securities Commissions (IOSCO) established a task force in February 2004 addressed at coordinating a response to the financial frauds. See IOSCO's website at http://www.iosco.org/news.

[24] One of us is independent director of both companies.

[25] We have drawn this information from newspaper coverage of the Fitch Report. See Simensen (2004).

III. CORPORATE GOVERNANCE AND GATEKEEPERS

A. The Board of Directors

1. Parmalat's Board

The Milan Stock Exchange's listing rules require listed companies to illustrate their corporate governance system. Those companies that have decided not to follow the Corporate Governance Code's recommendations, issued by Borsa Italiana in 1999 and amended in 2002, have to justify this choice. The Code recommends the appointment of independent directors, a concept which is loosely defined and frequently misunderstood in practice.

If Enron's board 'was a splendid board on paper, fourteen members, only two insiders,' (Gordon 2002: 1242) Parmalat's board was basically the opposite. In its first report, dated 2001, Parmalat declared that four of its thirteen directors were independent, but did not mention the relevant names. It gave the names in 2002. As far as 2003 is concerned, amongst Parmalat's thirteen directors, eight were executives: they were Calisto Tanzi (CEO) and his son Stefano, his brother Giovanni, his nephew Paola Visconti, the company's CFO Fausto Tonna and the top managers Luciano Del Soldato, Alberto Ferraris, and Francesco Giuffredi. The CFO was also a member of the three-member audit committee. The other committee members were Mr Francesco Giuffredi (another executive) and Mr Luciano Silingardi. Amongst the five non-executive directors, three were qualified as independent directors by the report. The most significant was Luciano Silingardi. He and Tanzi had been close friends since school and Silingardi had been Tanzi's accountant before being appointed, through Tanzi's and his own political connections, president of Cassa di Risparmio di Parma (the local bank that was to be one of Parmalat's most reliable banking partners) and, later on, of the foundation that controls the bank. The other two independents were Mr Paolo Sciumè, allegedly one of Tanzi's lawyers and a member of many boards, amongst which Mediolanum,[26] and Mr Enrico Barachini, he also a member of many boards, amongst which the boards of two subsidiaries of the Banca Popolare di Lodi group, another significant banking partner of Parmalat.[27]

The situation was similar as far as previous boards were concerned. It is clear that during Parmalat's history non-executive directors had never supervised managers. One should ask why they did not have enough

---

[26] Mediolanum's main shareholder was at the time the Prime Minister of Italy, Mr Silvio Berlusconi. See information published in Consob's database at: www.consob.it.

[27] Directors disclose their appointments following the Italian Stock Exchange's corporate governance code (Art. 1.3).

incentives to monitor. There are probably many answers. At least one of the three directors who were qualified as independent by Parmalat was not truly so. They accepted procedures that were clearly inadequate (recall Mr Tonna's role as member of the audit committee). The complexities of the group's structure and finance required a great amount of work and financial understanding, and they were not prepared to dig into Parmalat's intricate business. They probably relied on Mr Tanzi. One could still wonder why they were not afraid of lawsuits. US commentators discuss the role of lawsuits on corporate governance. It is hotly debated whether shareholders' derivative actions and securities class actions are proper incentives for management. The issue is complicated by D&O insurance, which in any case protects directors' out-of-pocket liability. However, Italy offers a completely different set of circumstances. To date, there have been no significant lawsuits against the directors of a solvent company and, more important, virtually no cases of securities actions against a solvent company and its directors. As a consequence, D&O insurance is an unimportant issue[28]; and there are even questions whether directors' civil liability is absolute or not.[29] Directors face lawsuits only from bankruptcy receivers. Since they are well protected against a negative court decision, they tend to obtain a very favourable position when a settlement is discussed. Criminal investigations are not particularly effective and sanctions are probably inadequate. In short, unless the company goes bust, there is nothing the directors should be afraid of. Thus, Parmalat's story (like Enron's) is about gatekeepers.

Yet probably the most interesting question is whether the market was actually discounting Parmalat's poor governance. We will briefly deal with this matter further on in this chapter.[30]

B. External Auditors

1. Gatekeepers' Role

The term 'gatekeeper' is used to refer to outside professionals who provide verification or certification services to investors (Coffee 2004a: 308-9).[31] Before the financial scandals that culminated in the Enron case, it was believed that market incentives could be sufficient to induce gatekeepers to screen against fraud and improper disclosure by their

---

[28] One writer has recently covered the issue: Franco Bonelli (1998: 151).

[29] Tombari (1999: 180). On absolute liability see Kraakman (1984: 876–87).

[30] See below, sections III.C.3 and III.D.2.

[31] Cf. Kraakman (1986). Professor Kraakman's definition of gatekeepers is broader than Professor Coffee's (2004a: 308–9).

clients. A classic example of how market forces should have worked was offered by auditors, by far the most important class of gatekeepers. Auditors are reputational intermediaries that receive a far smaller benefit than do their clients from the operations they certify. Since they share none of the gains of fraud (or just a small fraction of it) and are exposed to a large fraction of the risk (in the form of reputation disruption and also legal liability), they have all the proper incentives to monitor their clients efficiently and stop or denounce wrongdoings. Accordingly, they are easier to deter than their clients (Coffee 2004: 308; Kraakman 1984: 891). One of the best-known judicial expressions of this straightforward belief in market efficiency was Frank Easterbrook's position in the *DiLeo v Ernst Young* case.[32]

The fact that auditors as well as other gatekeepers are paid by their clients was not an actual issue for the paradigm, for two related reasons. First, it was thought there is no price a gatekeeper can accept for the disruption of its reputation. Secondly, firms face significant costs when they fire a gatekeeper (think once again of an auditor), because the market interprets the decision as a signal of hidden problems within the firm. Accordingly, gatekeepers can credibly offer a collective service to investors and creditors even though they are paid by companies. The belief was severely hit by the American corporate scandals.

2. Corporate Governance Problems within the Audit Organization

During the 1990s the big auditing firms learned how to use auditing services as an entry-point into the more lucrative market of consulting services (Coffee 2004a: 321). Auditing companies became involved in tax-planning services, management services, corporate finance services, legal services. For instance, it is well known that in Europe the Big Five tried to enter into the lucrative transactional legal business that was starting to be dominated by London firms and, to a lesser extent, by US law firms that had decided to go global. Prior to its own collapse following Enron's insolvency, Andersen's affiliated law firm had successfully gained a position in the Italian legal market. Just to offer an example, it was the legal advisor of a signficant securitization offering involving state-owned real estate assets.[33]

---

[32] *DiLeo*, 901 F.2d at 629. For a classic statement of this position see also Goldberg (1988: 312). For an intermediate course that considers too heavy-handed gatekeepers' liability regime and, at the same time, ineffective the private contractual solutions that Professor Goldberg considers as the best approach towards gatekeepers, see Choi (1998), proposing a 'self-tailored liability system.' Professor Choi has developed this proposed framework: see below notes 34 and 38.

[33] The 'SCIP' securitization program.

The involvement in non-audit services offered audited companies a weapon. They could now discipline their auditors in a way that could remain undetectable, through the threat of the reduction of the non-audit services. Clients were in a position to adopt an effective 'tit-for-tat' strategy,[34] to which auditors were exposed because of agency problems concerning their partners' incentives (Partnoy 2001: 500).[35] Partners' fees are related to the overall volume of revenues that their clients generate. Accordingly, partners do not want to make their clients unhappy, because in the short term this would affect their earnings. Enron generated one per cent of Arthur Andersen's whole turnover, but was the main client of David Duncan, the Houston partner of the auditing firm, who accepted a lowering of the auditing standards and thus of Andersen's reputational asset in order to protect and increase his own revenues. In such situations corporate governance within the audit firm becomes crucial. When internal control is not effective, the problem can be disruptive, as it was for Andersen.[36] Thus, the usual corporate governance problem is simply shifted from the issuer to the gatekeeper (Macey and Sale 2003).[37] With reference to auditors, some scholars also point out that the limited liability structure of auditing companies had impaired the previous monitoring role of partners, typical of a regime of vicarious liability for each other's professional negligence (*ibid.*: 1170–72, 1180–81). In a world where 'equity-based compensation constituted approximately two-thirds of the median annual compensation of chief executives of large public corporations' and where managers had large incentives to 'inflate the stock price of their company through premature revenue recognition or other classic earning management techniques,' corporate managers had significant incentives to lure auditors' partners or to discipline them by means of stick-and-carrot strategies affecting non-audit services (Coffee 2004a: 327–28).

Yet, one could still question why rational auditors put their clients in a position where the latter could condition the quality of the former's original core business. Apart from behavioral biases affecting auditors, it is suggested that the market bubble had a role. Indeed, euphoric investors do not rely upon the collective services offered by gatekeepers as cautious investors do (*ibid.*: 323–24). Thus, in an overconfident growing market the value of reputation (an asset that generates revenues that are collectively paid by investors and firms' creditors through the audited firm) decreases and the value of consulting services offered to the firm increases. In short, the Enron case and the following scandals indicate

---

[34] See Gordon (2002); Coffee (2002; 2004a); Bratton (2002); Choi (2003: 293).

[35] Considering, in particular, underwriters and independent auditors.

[36] See Gordon (2002); Coffee (2002).

[37] As the two authors point out at p. 180, 'Andersen suffered an internal corporate governance failure of epic proportions.'

that a corporate governance problem led gatekeepers to relax their professional standards.[38]

The story is not yet complete. If reputation was not enough to keep gatekeepers on the right track, in theory legal liability should still have had some deterrence effect. As Professors Coffee and Partnoy in particular have pointed out, however, auditors and other gatekeepers experienced in the United States a progressive reduction of civil liability risk during the 1990s, because of new statutes (e.g., the Private Securities Litigation Reform Act of 1995, and the Securities Litigation Uniform Standard Act of 1998) and new judicial trends (e.g., the Supreme Court's decisions in the *Lampf, Pleva* and in the *Central Bank of Denver* cases) that decreased the exposure to securities class actions. Indeed, in the wake of the financial scandals one of the most provocative issues in the US legal academic arena seems to be the one concerning gatekeepers' liability, an issue that has not been touched by the Sarbanes-Oxley Act. Auditors are the most significant targets of this debate,[39] which cannot ignore the fact that the audit market is concentrated: the 'Big Four'—Deloitte & Touche, Price Waterhouse Coopers, Ernst & Young, and KPMG—audit the majority of listed companies worldwide (*Economist* 2004).

3. Auditors and Parmalat

Grant Thornton was Parmalat's auditor through the first half of 1999. According to Italian law, auditors are appointed for three years and can be re-appointed twice. After nine years, they have to be changed. In 1998, the duty to appoint new auditors created a significant problem for both Grant Thornton and Parmalat, which feared that the new auditors could discover the true purpose of the offshore entities. Allegedly, Mr Bianchi and Mr Penca used the Grant Thornton network to create a new shield, the infamous Bonlat, that could be certified by Grant Thornton, acting as secondary auditor, with the new auditor acting as primary auditor. Accordingly, if the primary auditor was not too strict, Bonlat could be used as a waste basket that was out of the primary auditor's direct control. Should such accusations be confirmed by the courts, it would be clear that Grant Thornton's internal controls were totally lacking. Consob

---

[38] For a general review of institutional failures concerning security market intermediary institutions see Choi (2004). In the Enron case the US global office of Arthur Andersen drew affiliates underwater. In the *Parmalat* case it remains to be seen whether local shielding will be able to resist the Commissioner's action and, at the same time, to protect the reputation of Grant Thornton's and Deloitte's global trademarks. In this case, corporate shielding would offer another argument about the corporate governance problem of international auditors, since it would become clear that, in a catastrophic scenario, reputation is effectively at stake only when the US offices are in trouble.

[39] See Partnoy (2001; 2004); Coffee (2004; 2004a); Cunningham (2004); Hamdani (2003); Oh (2004).

has already cancelled the company through which Grant Thornton operated in Italy (Grant Thornton SpA, renamed Italaudit SpA following the Parmalat scandal) from the register of the certified auditors (entitled to audit listed companies),[40] after having ascertained that the Italian entity of the Grant Thornton network did not follow adequate audit procedures (Consob 2004b). In 2002 Grant Thornton audited on a mandatory basis fifteen listed companies (amongst which were Parmalat and Cirio) and financial intermediaries. In particular, Grant Thornton audited Cirio's first quarter 2002 consolidated financial report and Mr Bianchi was the partner in charge of the audit.[41] Since Cirio's default became apparent in November 2002, no doubt someone linked Cirio to Parmalat through the Grant Thornton connection. Perhaps it was chance, but the first serious warning to the market concerning Parmalat's financial situation occurred in December 2002.[42] Needless to say, since Grant Thornton is not in the top league of auditing services, it would be interesting to know how much of Grant Thornton's income was generated by Parmalat and if and how the Parmalat scandal will affect the Grant Thornton trademark. As far as we know, there are no publicly-available data on the issue, at least in Italy.[43]

The Italian member firm of Deloitte Touche Tohmatsu (Deloitte & Touche SpA), the world's number two accounting firm, was appointed as Parmalat's primary auditor in 1999. Deloitte Touche Tohmatsu had been already involved in consulting services for Parmalat. For instance, it is reported that the appraisal concerning a controversial transaction announced in December 1999 and involving Parmalat's main Brazilian unit had been prepared by Deloitte's corporate finance arm many months earlier in July 1998. Some evidence shows that Deloitte's network was involved in non-audit services to Parmalat even after Deloitte's appointment in 1999. Another transaction investigated because of Deloitte's apparent lax attitude concerns the member office in Malta and, particularly, a large intercompany loan between Parmalat Capital Finance Ltd, a special-purpose vehicle controlling Bonlat, and the latter (Bloomberg 2004). Indeed the Maltese-registered office of Parmalat Capital Finance was Deloitte's office. The related party transaction between Parmalat Capital Finance and Bonlat would appear to be just one of many (Parmalat 2004).

Deloitte's story with Parmalat raises some issues that seem to be similar to the ones raised by the Enron affair. Allegedly, a Brazilian

---

[40] See below, note 52.

[41] Therefore, it would be interesting to explore whether an 'illicit market' in 'pliable gatekeeping' was in place. Illicit markets in gatekeeping are discussed by Kraakman (1986: 66–68).

[42] See above, section II.B.

[43] However, in December 2004, Grant Thornton 'reported full-year global revenues of US $2.1bn—an increase of 12 per cent compared with 2003' (Parker 2004).

auditor who was unconvinced by information provided by the Italian parent was removed from the Parmalat account thanks to heavy lobbying in Deloitte's US global headquarters by the Italian Deloitte member firm (Kapner 2004). The Commissioner, Mr Bondi, alleges that the Italian firm acted in the same way in other similar situations.

Deloitte's firm in Luxembourg audited Parmalat Soparfi SA. Financial information services have reported that Deloitte:

> wrote in three separate reports that the unit's directors hadn't supplied enough evidence to support book values they put on stakes held in two other Parmalat units (Bloomberg 2004a).

With the benefit of hindsight it seems that the problem could have offered an early warning about Parmalat's management attitude.

For a five-year period Deloitte certified Parmalat's statements. It is not clear whether it was the market turmoil that started in February 2003 to force Deloitte to take more care, or the action of the Italian watchdog that followed the incredible complaint lodged by Parmalat in March 2003. It seems clear, however, that Deloitte had never asked GT to explain how the existence of the huge cash pile held by Bonlat in the New York account had been checked. Deloitte were also the auditors of Cirio and had audited that company's 2001 statements, those impugned by Consob in January 2003.[44]

4. Do Italian Rules Facilitate Audit Failures?

According to some in the media, Grant Thornton and Deloitte's failures can be attributed to lax Italian auditing rules. We do not agree. The issue is one of enforcement, not substantive rules.[45]

(a) Primary Auditor Liability.   A common view about the Parmalat scandal holds that it was caused also by lax Italian rules concerning the relationship between the primary auditor and secondary auditor. However, there were national auditing standards reflecting the international ones that govern the situation[46] and at least one very significant court case in which the primary auditor has been considered liable because of the lack of controls over the activity of the secondary auditor. The case was decided by the Milan Tribunal on 21 October 1999 and concerned,

---

[44] With its decision No. 14488 dated 25 March 2004 Consob disqualified for a two-year period Mr Stefano Baudo, Deloitte's partner in charge of Cirio (www.consob.it).

[45] For an overview of the main issues discussed at an international level with reference to auditor standards, see Ebke (2004).

[46] The Italian auditing standards basically incorporate the International Standards on Auditing (ISAs) and International Standards on Assurance Engagements (ISAEs) issued by IAASB, available at www.ifac.org.

amongst other issues, the liability of the Ferruzzi group's primary auditor (Price Waterhouse SpA) in connection with reports certified by a secondary auditor not directly appointed by the primary auditor.[47] The court applied the national auditing standards and held that the primary auditor cannot accept without criticism the work of the secondary auditor and certify the consolidated accounts, but has a duty (when it decides to avail itself of the secondary auditor's work) to check the procedures followed by the secondary auditor and to access the documentation used by the latter. Accordingly, the emphasis on relaxed Italian auditing standards is misplaced.

(b) Independence.   As far as independence is concerned, Italian rules are very strict. Auditing companies must have an exclusive activity in order to be recorded by Consob in the register of auditors entitled to certify listed companies' financial reports (Art. 6 Legislative Decree No. 88/92, referred to by Art. 161 Consolidated Financial Services Act (CFSA)). Any provision in the company's statute concerning non-audit services makes the company non-eligible. The sole advisory service that the registered auditor can offer concerns the accounting systems (*organizzazione contabile*) of the audited company.

The appointed auditor must be independent (Arts. 160–62 CFSA). Before hiring the auditor, the shareholders' meeting must receive the statutory auditors' opinion (Art. 159 CFSA).[48] Consob's rule provides that this opinion must expressly consider the independence issue. This system gives responsibility for the hiring and the compensation of the auditor to the shareholders' meeting, creating a situation, in companies dominated by a controlling shareholder (as Parmalat was), similar to the one that existed before the SOA in US public companies, in which the auditors were appointed by management.

Supervision of independence after hiring is in the hands of Consob. The watchdog can ask for information, inspect the business premises of the auditor and ask for information from partners, directors, statutory auditors, CEO of the audited company. It can also indicate the auditing principles to be followed by registered auditors. When 'serious' breaches of the rules are ascertained, the public supervisor can order the auditor not to use the services of the involved partner for a period of up to two years, or order the auditor to decline new appointments for a period of one year. When breaches of rules are 'particularly serious' or the auditor has lost the prerequisite required in order to be recorded in the register (exclusive statutory objects and technical qualification), Consob may

---

[47] Below, note 70.

[48] Statutory auditors are the members of an internal board of auditors which until the recent reform of Italian company law was mandatory. See Ferrarini, Giudici, and Stella Richter (2005).

cancel the name of the auditor from the registry. Accordingly, disqualification is the main administrative remedy (Art. 163 CFSA).

Typically, the problem arises when rules are to be enforced. In order to circumvent independence criteria, international auditors have organized their activity through a network of companies that are formally independent from the auditing entity but are actually linked through participation agreements. Italian scholars and practitioners never really challenged these participation agreements as serious impediments to independence.[49] Consob followed this pattern and never launched an attack on the non-audit services offered by the auditors' networks, in spite of the fact that auditors openly market themselves as global multifunctional brands.

Moreover, it is clear that the watchdog supervision on auditors was very lax due to a lack of resources. More generally, owing to a detection policy that was too heavily dependent on statutory auditors' complaints,[50] Consob never followed a proactive law enforcement approach,[51] but always punished auditors after a problem in the audited companies had arisen.[52]

(c) Liability Rules.   Probably the most striking difference between the United States and continental Europe concerns the level of private enforcement. Italy is no exception. Yet, the 'law on the books' is, once again, very strict. There are no doubts whatsoever that auditors are liable for damages.

Prior to the February 2004 amendment to the Consolidated Financial Services Act, this conclusion could be drawn from the civil law of obligations and, even though implicitly, from Art. 164 CFSA, stating that:

> The persons responsible for an audit and the employees who performed the audit shall be liable, jointly and severally with the auditing firm, for injury to the hiring company and third parties as a result of non-fulfilment of their duties or illicit actions.

The rule recognizes a civil liability of the auditing firm towards the audited firm, its creditors and investors, posing a regime of joint liability with individual auditors and employees.

---

[49] See Balzarini (1999: 1898, 1901).

[50] See below, section III.C.4.

[51] On the role of regulators as proactive enforcers see Pistor and Xu (2002; 2003: 963–64). On SEC's failures to act as a proactive enforcer see Kroger (2005: 64).

[52] Italaudit SpA (previously Grant Thornton SpA) was cancelled from the Registry on the 28 July 2004 (Consob's resolution No. 14671). Mr Bianchi was disqualified for the audit services rendered to Cirio in 2002 with Consob decision No. 14480 dated 23 March 2004. Two days later it was Mr Baudo's turn for the audit services rendered by Deloitte to Cirio in 2001, see Consob decision No. 14488 dated 25 March 2004.

The new Art. 164 (1) as amended in February 2004 explicitly foresees liability towards the audited firm and the creditors, through a combined reference to Arts. 2407 and 2394-bis Civil Code: the insolvency liquidator and the extraordinary commissioner of a large insolvent company (like Parmalat) are entitled to bring actions against the directors, the statutory auditors and the audit firm, cumulating both the company's and the creditors' actions.

As noted, this liability regime can also be inferred by general rules concerning contractual obligations and tort. More specifically, as for the nature of the auditing firm's liability, it clearly is contractual when the company is suing. It must be pointed out that Italian scholars hold that the auditors cannot raise defences of *in pari delicto*, contributory negligence or fault, and unclean hands, because the auditors' function is to monitor the managers through the auditing processes: a party whose duty is to monitor cannot escape liability by asserting that the monitored party concurred in the damage, since the gatekeeper was rewarded in order to prevent managers' misbehaviour (Bussoletti 1985: 352; Casadei 2000: 149).[53] The only court decision that dealt with the issue also rejected these kinds of defences.[54] The rationale is probably clearer if one recalls that under Italian law auditors are appointed by shareholders[55]: also under Italian law, therefore, one can assert—as the House of Lords did in *Caparo Industries Plc v Dickman*—that auditors' reports are intended to enable shareholders to question the management of the company.[56]

Auditors are also liable towards creditors and investors. The nature of this liability is discussed in the legal literature, as a part of the wide debate concerning the nature of prospectus liability and, more in general, liability for pure economic loss.[57]

The main differences between a contractual action and an action in tort concern time limitation and burden of proof. If the action is in tort, the plaintiff has to show that the auditor intended to cause damages or at least was *in culpa*, while if the action is contractual the onus is on the auditor to escape liability through a due diligence defence (even though some scholars assert that when the contract concerns duties and not specific results, the burden of proof lies on the plaintiff's shoulders).[58] Under both regimes of liability, auditors are jointly and severally liable with companies, directors and statutory auditors, depending on which party claims damages. If it is the company (typically, through its

---

[53] A different view is expressed by Montalenti (2004: 316), who considers applicable standards of comparative negligence, imputing to the company the managers' wrongdoings.

[54] Turin Tribunal, 18 settembre 1993, *I.F.C. Istituto Fiduciario Centrale v KPMG*, I/2 Giur. it. 655 (1994).

[55] Above, section III.B.4.b.

[56] *Caparo Industries plc v Dickman and others*, [1990] 2 AC 605.

[57] See Portale (1982: II, 1169); Ferrarini (1986: 49; 1997: 203 *et seq.*).

[58] For references cf. Barcellona (2003: 20–21).

liquidator or insolvency trustee) or a creditor who claims damages, the negligent audit firm is jointly and severally liable with negligent directors and statutory auditors. If investors claim damages, the company can also be held liable, since towards innocent third parties the directors acted on behalf of the company, which accordingly is responsible for their misstatements.[59]

The framework that we have depicted is very strict. These are severe liability rules indeed, even more so than those applied in the United States, where the 'imputation' defences that we have mentioned are routinely invoked and can be effective.[60] As far as investor protection is concerned, they are also more severe than the ones adopted under common law, where the problem of proximity between the auditor and the investor[61] is treated in a way that may appear narrow viewed from Italy, where in contrast tort liability for pure economic loss is admitted by scholars and courts adopting more relaxed standards. Thus, Italian rules are very favourable to plaintiffs. Parmalat's action in the United States against the auditors cannot be understood by mere reference to 'law on the books,' because Italian substantive rules governing auditors' liability are severe.[62]

(d) Private Enforcement.   Case analysis of the published court decisions shows that any discussion concerning the legal risk associated with the auditing profession in Italy (and thereby the level of deterrence) misses the target if it relies upon 'law on the books'. The first published decision concerning auditors' liability is dated 1992. The law journals have reported, as far as we know, only nine cases concerning auditor liability, for a total of eleven published decisions. These cases can be classified as follows.

[59] Cassation Court, 14 Jan. 1987, No. 183, II Dir. Fall. 319 (1987), asserting that the shareholder is not a third-party and cannot sue the company together with the directors under Art. 2395 Civil Code; Rome Tribunal, 27 Aug. 2004, not yet published.

[60] For a recent overview, cf. Swanson (2004).

[61] In England one of the leading cases is *Caparo Industries plc v Dickman and others*, [1990] 2 AC 605; in the United States the leading case is *Ultramares Corp. v Touche*, 255 N.Y. 170, 174 n.e. 441 (1931). For recent overviews, cf. Anand and Moloney (2004: 247); Witting (2000); Swanson (2004).

[62] Since Parmalat's action against Deloitte and Grant Thornton in the United States cannot be explained on the grounds of liability rules, one could still wonder whether Italy offered a less friendly environment as to the Extraordinary Commissioner's claim that the audit firms of the network are to be considered agents one for the other (or joint venturers with one another) in their auditing of Parmalat entities. Even though a comparison between the chances of success in the United States (if any) with the chances of success in Italy (if any) would require a thorough investigation of legal doctrines that is beyond the scope of this chapter, our general impression is that a claim of this nature might also be attempted under Italian law, despite the absence of precedents on the issue. Needless to say, the establishment of a network liability would affect the governance of auditor networks. If the actions against parent companies and networks in the United States are successful, audit networks will have to reflect on their governance systems and possibly adopt more transparent group structures.

Two cases concern actions by purchasers of controlling stakes claiming that the price paid in an acquisition was overvalued because of financial misstatements or omissions that the auditor should have detected (*BPM Leasing v KPMG*)[63] or claiming that the auditor's appraisal of the true equity value of the target company was wrong (*Carraro v Arthur Andersen*).[64] In the acquisition context we find also the unsuccessful claim against the auditor of a controlling shareholder that had sold the shares at a certain price but, later on, had to give back part of the price as it was discovered that some receivables were in fact not recoverable (*Efim v Coopers & Lybrand*).[65] The fourth case (*Efim v Reconta Ernst & Young*) concerns an action brought by a state-owned controlling shareholder against the auditor with reference to the unreported losses of a subsidiary,[66] and the fifth case regards the successful claim of a company that had sued its auditors, directors and statutory auditors because it had entered into a null and void contract as a result of which it had paid consultancy fees. In this case (*Alumix v Reconta Ernst & Young*), the court held that the company would have not paid the illegal fees had the auditors properly screened the relevant contract.[67] Potential defences of *in pari delicto*, contributory negligence or fault, and unclean hands, were not considered by the decision. As far as creditors' actions are concerned, in the *I.F.C.* and *I.M.F.* cases the liquidator of an insolvent financial intermediary successfully recovered damages suffered by the bankrupt intermediary's investors and creditors.[68] The typical situation of US securities litigation appears in the last two cases, the *FIN.GE.M.* case, regarding the successful action of a sophisticated investor who had bought on the market Ferfin's shares (Ferfin was a listed company of the bankrupt Ferruzzi)[69] relying on the information contained in the prospectus, whose financial statements were audited by Price Waterhouse,[70] and the *Lugli* case, regarding the unsuccessful claim of a plaintiff who alleged to have relied on the data contained in the balance sheet 1992 with reference to purchases effected during 1994.[71]

[63] Milan Tribunal, 18 June 1992, *Banca Popolare di Milano, Bipiemme Leasing v KPMG*, I Giur. it. 1 (1993).

[64] Cassation Court, 18 July 2002, n. 10403, *Arthur Andersen v Carraro*, 1 Foro it. 2147 (2003); Milan Court of Appeal, 7 July 1998, *Carraro v Arthur Andersen*, 10 Soc. 1171 (1998).

[65] Milan Tribunal, 18 Oct. 1999, *Efim v Coopers & Librand*, I Giur. it. 570 (2000).

[66] Milan Tribunal, 30 April 2001, *Efim v Reconta Ernst & Young*, II Banca borsa 320 (2003).

[67] Rome Tribunal, 26 April 1999, *Alumix v Reconta Ernst & Young*, 10 Soc. 1232 (1999).

[68] Turin Tribunal, 18 Sept. 1993, *I.F.C. Istituto Fiduciario Centrale v KPMG*, I/2 Giur. it. 655 (1994); Turin Court of Appeal, 30 May 1995, *KPMG v I.F.C. Istituto Fiduciario Centrale*, II Giur. comm. 492 (1996); Milan Court of Appeal, 27 March 2001, *KPMG v Istituto Milanese Fiduciario*, II Banca borsa 319 (2003).

[69] Above, note 10.

[70] Milan Tribunal, 21 Oct. 1999, *FIN.GE.M. v Price Waterhouse and other defendants*, I Giur. it. 554 (2000).

[71] Milan Court of Appeal, 7 July 2000, *Lugli and others v Ria & Mazars s.a.s.*, II Banca borsa 320 (2003).

Needless to say, the numbers are striking. Maybe there are some unreported cases. Clearly there have been settled cases. Nevertheless, it seems evident that private enforcement of auditor liability is very weak, unless one optimistically believes that reputational incentives are so strong in Italy as to make private litigation unimportant.

5. Administrative and Criminal Sanctions

We have mentioned Consob's powers as far as administrative sanctions ('disqualification') are concerned. Needless to say, auditors can also commit criminal offences, when they wilfully state false information in order to enrich themselves and with the specific intention of deceiving the readers (Art. 2624 Civil Code). The prison term can vary, up to a maximum of four years. However, imprisonment terms are usually very short, and the auditor would in any event benefit from the large array of alternative criminal sanctions aimed at avoiding imprisonment.

C. Statutory Auditors

1. The Collegio Sindacale

In Italian joint-stock companies (*società per azioni*—SpA) a board of statutory auditors (*collegio sindacale*) is seen to have monitoring tasks (Arts. 2397 *et seq.*). Traditionally, the board of auditors was entrusted with the audit of the company's accounts. However, the board of auditors has never been efficient in discovering mismanagement and frauds, a task which was subsequently transferred to outside auditors leaving to statutory auditors general monitoring duties. The traditional view in Italy is that statutory auditors are usually complacent because they are appointed by controlling shareholders. In a corporate governance system characterized by concentrated ownership, in which managers are often the company's controlling shareholders and directors are in general closely related to them, statutory auditors are appointed on the basis of friendship with controlling shareholders or professional ties. Usually statutory auditors are professional accountants (*commercialisti*, who in the Italian tradition are experts in accounting, tax and company law matters). Indeed, firms often appoint as auditor the controlling shareholder's personal professional accountant, or a professional accountant the managers worked with in the past or still work with, or a partner of a professional firm offering its services to the management. This professional is appointed as chairman of the board and informally indicates the two other professionals to be appointed as members of the board. Thus, the board approaches problems with a consultant's rather than a monitor's attitude.

2. Statutory Auditors in Italian Listed Companies

In order to strengthen the controls of listed companies, the auditing activity was passed on to external auditors in 1975.[72] After the reform concerning listed companies that took place in 1998 (Consolidated Financial Securities Act (CFSA)), statutory auditors' monitoring functions are limited to two areas. First, they supervise the company's compliance with the relevant laws and statutes. Secondly, they monitor the management of the company, with particular regard to the compliance with standards of good management and the adequacy and functioning of the company's organizational and management structure (Art. 2403 (1)). Needless to say, this monitoring role is still affected by the fact that statutory auditors are appointed by controlling shareholders. In order to limit the inherently complacent attitude of statutory boards, the CFSA mandated that listed companies introduce clauses in their articles of association that enable minority shareholders to appoint a statutory auditor (Art. 148.2 CFSA). The introduction of this right was obviously a source of considerable debate. Lawmakers clearly wanted to offer minority shareholders an access to boards in order to prevent the establishment of lax auditing procedures by statutory auditors. One suspects also that one purpose was to provide minority shareholders with access to relevant information. Companies complained that a minority shareholder with no significant stake in the company could have appointed an inexperienced or malevolent statutory auditor, thereby creating an atmosphere of distrust and conflict in the board room. Scholars and courts accommodated both arguments, holding that the rule is addressed to institutional shareholders and minority shareholders possessing a significant stake in the company. Therefore, all Italian listed companies have inserted a threshold in their articles of association, allowing minority shareholders to appoint a statutory auditor only if they represent a significant percentage (usually, from 0.5 to 5 per cent) of the voting rights.

3. Funds and the Minorities' Statutory Auditor in Parmalat

Something very strange happened in the case of Parmalat. As noted by

[72] The company law reform extends a similar regime to non-listed companies by subjecting their accounts to the audit of either an individual registered auditor or a registered auditing company; however, in the case of non-listed companies which do not publish consolidated accounts the articles of association can reserve the audit of the accounts to the board of statutory auditors provided that its members are all registered auditors (Art. 2409-bis).

many commentators, Italian fund management firms have been curiously untouched by Parmalat's insolvency, in contrast with foreign asset managers (Funds International 2004). Moreover, only eight out of 166 pension funds were invested in Parmalat at the time of its collapse (COVIP 2004). Clearly the national asset managers had spotted problems early on.[73] Apparently, the role of the auditor appointed by the minority shareholders could help to explain the circumstance.

Parmalat's articles allowed minority shareholders representing at least 3 per cent of the voting rights to appoint a statutory auditor. In 1999 institutional investors were successful in appointing a statutory auditor to Parmalat's board. However, at the end of her three-year term in 2002 the minority-appointed auditor informed the institutional investors that she was not available for re-appointment. It is rumoured that her decision was construed by the industry as an alarm signal. As a consequence, many funds sold Parmalat shares and thus at the general meeting of 2002 institutional investors were not able to reach the required threshold and therefore could not appoint a statutory auditor for the minority shareholders.

If confirmed, this account would add credibility to the idea that well before the end of 2002 information concerning Parmalat's problems was buried in the market.

4. Adverse Selection At Work

We have outlined that in Italy statutory auditors are generally considered unreliable gatekeepers because they are often professionals appointed by controlling shareholders and are frequently complacent figures rather than investigative ones. Lack of independence exposes them to 'tit-for-tat strategies' similar to the ones analyzed with reference to external auditors.

However, there are two further issues that make the Italian corporate governance structures peculiar. First, statutory auditors do not fit the 'market incentives' account of the gatekeepers' role. It is worth recalling that the traditional market theory of gatekeepers was based on the following reasoning: any gatekeeper can be easily deterred because she shares none of the gains of fraud (or just a small fraction of it) and is exposed to a large fraction of the risk (in the form of reputation disruption and also legal liability). Accordingly, she has all the incentives to monitor the company efficiently and stop or denounce wrongdoings, even though it is the company that pays her. Of course, the theory

---

[73] It should be noted that this is not COVIP's explanation. COVIP's chairman explains the circumstance praising the regulatory constraints concerning pension funds' investments: COVIP (2004).

assumes that the gatekeeper enjoys a wide reputation and has at least some assets pledged, in the form of company capital or partners' unlimited liability. However, a statutory auditor has only his own personal assets, which can be easily covered in order to make any negative judgment difficult to enforce.[74] Most important, his reputation is usually limited to a restricted circle of persons, among which usually are the shareholders and managers who appoint him. Accordingly, the reputation argument can be reversed. The statutory auditor builds up his own reputation among a small social circle that appreciates professional skills and cooperative behaviour more than the inquisitive side of an independent and effective gatekeeper. In short, adverse selection is at work as far as statutory auditors are concerned.

Secondly, the Italian financial watchdog (Consob) has publicly stated that it relies heavily on statutory auditors to detect frauds and launch investigations.[75] Clearly Consob's reliance on statutory auditors as its 'eyes and ears' in market supervision is a passive approach that relies on the wrong detectives, so ultimately eroding the quality of public enforcement. This passive approach is based on a very narrow reading of the law emphasizing that statutory auditors have a duty to whistle-blow to Consob on all corporate wrongdoings found in their monitoring activities. However, a different interpretation of the law would be preferable, assigning to the Securities Commission a proactive role with limited reliance on statutory auditors, who should rather be subject to intense scrutiny by Consob as to the performance of their monitoring duties.

D. Other Gatekeepers

1. Investment Banks and Universal Banks

Other gatekeepers are underwriters and other financial intermediaries whose services are used to gain reputation, attorneys, and analysts. The arguments offered to explain why auditors' reputation is not enough to

---

[74] On the judgment-proof problem, see Shavell (2004: 230).

[75] The Report of the Chairman of Consob to the Parliamentary Commission states as follows: 'In this institutional setting it is to be pointed out that the relevant rules, included in the Consolidated Financial Services Act of 1998, assign a fundamental role to internal corporate governance, primarily to the board of statutory auditors. This body is bound to timely disclose to Consob the wrongdoings found in the company's management ant to report on the meetings and the enquiries made, trasmitting all relevant documents. The underlying philosophy of the Consolidated Financial Services Act is that the internal monitoring body of the company is better placed than a third party to timely spot possible wrongdoings of the managers and report the same to public authorities such as Consob and public prosecutors.' (Consob 2004b).

grant efficient auditing services can be extended to other reputational intermediaries. Incentives concerning career advancement within banks and large law firms create an agency problem, which can be exacerbated by a euphoric bull market. In the absence of efficient internal controls and effective deterrence, reputation is no longer an asset to be preserved at any cost.

Underwriters can be held liable if the prospectus contains a material misrepresentation or omission and a due diligence defence cannot be established. In the first Italian case concerning prospectus liability, the underwriting bank was held liable for not having conducted reasonable investigation of the accuracy of the prospectus drafted by the issuer in connection with a bond placement.[76] However, this case is today still the only significant decision on the issue. Again, deterrence through private enforcement is virtually absent in Italy.[77] Parmalat's Commissioner actions against the bankrupt company's investment banks are the first massive civil action against investment banks as gatekeepers concerning an Italian group. It is no coincidence, however, that the most significant actions taken by Parmalat's Extraordinary Commissioner started in the United States against Citigroup and Bank of America.

In the recent Italian financial scandals banks have been under attack, in the media and in the courts, for the breach of rules of conduct governing their activity as investment brokers. Allegedly, banks advised their clients to buy Cirio bonds, knowing that the proceeds would be used, as agreed with the issuer, to repay the food group's bank loans. Moreover, many banks advised their clients to buy high interest bonds, such as those issued by Argentina, Cirio, or Parmalat, which were not suitable to their clients' portfolios. The public uproar, the activism of consumer associations that fuelled investors' litigation (even though not comparable to US class-action litigation), and investigations carried out by the capital markets supervisor and criminal prosecutors forced the most exposed banks to open settlement discussions with their clients. This situation shows another typical pattern of the Italian (and probably European) enforcement system. When great cases explode, criminal prosecutors step in and investigations end up in the hands of criminal judges. The Ferruzzi case created a huge criminal investigation at the beginning of the 1990s. The Cirio and the Parmalat cases did the same in the new decade. As we have noted, no significant civil litigation lies in the middle of the

---

[76] See Milan Trib., 11 Jan. 1988, II Giur. Comm. 585 (1988); Milan Court of Appeal, 2 Feb. 1990, II Banca borsa 734 (1990); Ferrarini (1993: 289).

[77] Usually underwriters also take the role of sponsors in the listing of a company. The rules of the Italian Stock Exchange demand companies to use a financial intermediary in the process of listing. The financial intermediary has to take responsibility in connection with the company's compliance to listing rules and corporate information rules. As yet there is not a single case concerning sponsor's liability.

cyclical explosion of criminal scandals and the ensuing response on the part of the politicians.

2. *Attorneys and Analysts*

Transactional attorneys are routinely involved in financial transactions and securities placements. In Italy most of the important players are the Italian offices or affiliates of top London or US law firms. They are usually involved in due diligence, transactional engineering, drafting of prospectuses and contracts, and compliance. They are very well paid for their role, 'as if' liability were attached to the gatekeeper's position they take. However, no single case concerning attorney liability in financial market transactions has yet been published.

As far as analysts are concerned, Consob's regulation affects research disclosure.[78] Analysts' reports prepared for general circulation have to be posted in the stock exchange's website.[79] As we noted, one analyst only posted negative reports from 5 December 2002 to 17 November 2003.[80] Nevertheless, no investigations comparable to those conducted by the Attorney-General of the State of New York, Eliot Spitzer, have been launched after the Parmalat affair: Italy has not benefited from any competition among regulators in this field.[81] Analysts' behaviour in the Parmalat case raises many questions. A thorough investigation would be needed in order to understand whether the 'buy' and 'hold' recommendations were motivated by conflicts of interest. Indeed there is also a serious possibility that the market was already discounting Parmalat's poor governance, as analysts' reports took into consideration Parmalat's opaque management and financial structure. In defence of the unconcerned analysts that continued to issue 'buy' or 'hold' recommendations, one could point out that there was a large valuation gap between Parmalat and its competitors and, as a consequence, Parmalat seemed to be cheap. Further research in this area is needed.[82]

---

[78] It is arguable whether an analyst's civil liability can be established in tort, and under what conditions: Mazzoni (2002).

[79] Art. 69 Consob Regulation No. 11522/1998.

[80] See above, para II.B.

[81] For an example of beneficial competition among regulators see below, para III.D.4. The competition between Spitzer and the SEC has been analyzed by Macey (2004). See also Kroger (2005: 65), writing that: 'Spitzer is successful, and the SEC is not, because Spitzer is able to gather intelligence about market problems in an effective manner and then prioritize and attack those problems swiftly.'

[82] Analysts have been the target of much debate after the Enron collapse: amongst the others, Kroger (2005: 38–45) (discussing analysts' debacle with reference to Enron) and (*ibid.*: 55–56) (commenting on the wake of litigation affecting analysts after Enron); Macey (2004b); Choi and Fisch (2003).

3. Another Example of Weak Enforcement of Capital Markets Law: the SCI Case

We think that the numbers of published cases concerning gatekeepers' liability offer evidence of a weak level of enforcement, even if one takes into consideration the size of the financial market involved. Though not relating to gatekeepers, one further example can be added to the picture regarding private enforcement in securities markets. The first case concerning civil liability arising from insider trading has only recently been decided in Italy. It involved a group of banks that were negotiating, as large creditors, the rescue of a small listed company on the edge of insolvency. When negotiations came to a halt the banks, separately and massively, sold their shares before any information had been passed onto the market. The court held them liable for damages in tort. However, damages were not calculated using a 'fraud-on-the-market' theory, but adopting 'fairness' criteria more favourable to the defendants.[83] Damages are another area where European courts are very prudent.

4. The Sai-Fondiaria Saga

An account of the poor record in the enforcement of Italian capital market law would not be complete without any reference to the *Sai-Fondiaria* saga, a well-known case of elusion of mandatory takeover rules that started in summer 2001. At the beginning of 2002 Sai, a large insurance company, was stuck in a situation were it had promised (acting in concert with Mediobanca) to buy a large stake in Fondiaria, another large insurance company, but could not purchase the shares because this would have triggered mandatory takeover rules (pursuant to Arts. 106 and 109 CFSA). In order to elude the problem, Sai and Mediobanca used five intermediaries (among which J.P. Morgan and Commerzbank), which bought the stake that Sai should have purchased. The five intermediaries claimed to have acted independently, i.e., not in concert, notwithstanding the large premium they were paying on the shares; in spite of these declarations, they were immediately and ironically renamed 'The White Knights' by the financial press (Oddo and Sabbatini: 2002).[84] Following the White Knights' intervention, Consob received many complaints but succinctly dismissed them without any further investigation, asserting that there was no evidence of a running action in concert between Sai (and its five White Knights) and Mediobanca. After this decision Sai's and Fondiaria's shareholders agreed a merger and soon after Sai bought

---

[83] Milan Tribunal, 14 Feb. 2004, *Matteini v Intesa, Unicredit and other banks*, I Foro it. 1567 (2004).

[84] The article starting as follows: 'Non uno ma ben tre cavalieri bianchi sono giunti in soccorso della Sai' [Not one, but three white knights arrived to help Sai].

the White Knights' stake in Fondiaria. As a consequence the antitrust authority opened a proceeding in order to ascertain whether the concentration would create a dominant position in the insurance market, taking into consideration Mediobanca's influence over Sai, Fondiaria, and Generali. Two days later an inspection was ordered in the offices of Mediobanca, Premafin (Sai's controlling shareholder), Sai, Fondiaria, Generali, Compagnia Fiduciaria Nazionale, and Interbanca. The existence of secret, unwritten agreements was confirmed by the inspectors.[85]

The *Sai-Fondiaria* case is another tale of poor enforcement. Fondiaria's minority shareholders had to rely on complaints lodged to the financial supervisor, who did not take any active role. If it had not been for another agency, the antitrust authority, the elusion would have remained undisclosed. Up to now only a few large Fondiaria blockholders have sued the concerting parties, successfully claiming damages suffered because of the elusion of the mandatory rules.[86] In the absence of any class-action mechanisms, dispersed shareholders' rights have not been taken to courts.

IV. VINDICATING THE PUBLIC INTEREST: ENFORCEMENT IN THE EUROPEAN CONTEXT

A. The Current Italian Discussion Concerning Class Actions

In the wake of recent financial scandals and an antitrust case involving a massive cartel in the motor insurance market (Giudici 2004), the Italian public has discovered that it is difficult to deter substantial wrongdoings through private actions, in the absence of effective aggregation mechanisms. Existing (ineffective) mechanisms are based on the role of consumer associations, which have no standing in actions to recover damages and can only obtain cease or desist orders to protect consumers' interests. The news that only a few days after Parmalat's insolvency a class action had been started in the United States against individuals and investment banks, as well as rumours that Italian investors might be positively affected by it, gave a strong impulse to the debate concerning the introduction of class action-like mechanisms in Italian civil procedure.

Indeed, an insolvency procedure such as that of Parmalat is probably

---

[85] In a scenario completely reshaped by the results of the antitrust watchdog analysis, an administrative court declared the Consob's decision to be null and void and ordered Consob to re-evaluate the case. For further details see Consiglio di Stato, 13 May 2003, No. 4142, Giur. It. 2107 (2004), with comment of Eva Desana, *Opa obbligatoria 'da concerto occulto': alcune osservazioni a margine della vicenda Sai-Fondiaria.*

[86] Milan Tribunal, 26 May 2005, *Promofinan v Fondiaria-Sai s.p.a.*, not yet published.

the only mechanism of collective action in Italian private law, since the liquidator, as we have already pointed out, is entitled to sue the gatekeepers in order to get compensation for the company's and creditors' losses. It is clear that the collective action of an insolvency liquidator usually comes too late, and not all the liquidators adopt the aggressive approach Mr Bondi is meritoriously following: after all, also liquidators are public servants and may face problems of incentives.

The dominant impression concerning Italy is that private enforcement is underdeveloped because courts are extremely slow and inefficient.[87] This is undoubtedly true, but it is not the only reason why securities law, as well as antitrust law and consumer protection law, are under-enforced. The motor insurance case in antitrust and the *Parmalat* case in capital market law show that it is essential for a modern civil liability system to be able to vindicate collective interests, otherwise under-enforcement creates incentives to adopt socially-inefficient behaviours such as horizontal cartels and market frauds. As we will point out, however, even American-style class actions would not change the pattern of Italian private enforcement. Private enforcement cannot be ameliorated without revolutionary changes to the whole civil procedure system, since the current Italian system is simply not suited to disputes concerning the protection of investors' diffuse interests.

Since one of the most striking differences between the US and European scandals concerns the pattern of litigation, the problem of private enforcement in Italy (and Europe) needs to be set in context.[88]

B. The Interplay between Private and Public Enforcement: Theory

From a welfare economics perspective, where civil remedies are not seen in terms of compensation and corrective justice, liability systems and government regulations have to establish optimal levels of deterrence. The dimensions of legal intervention are different. Professor Shavell (2004: 572–75) has classified the methods of legal intervention using three fundamental dimensions: (i) time of intervention (intervention before acts are committed, after acts but before harm, after harm); (ii) form of intervention (i.e., sanctions); (iii) parties entitled to bring actions (public *v*

---

[87] For a recent investigation see Marchesi (2003). With reference to corporate courts it has been pointed out that Italian judges have a formalist approach, do not possess basic notions of corporate finance, accounting and business administration, do not have experience in handling complex cases and, moreover, have a deferential attitude towards corporate insiders: Enriques (2002).

[88] One of us has investigated the issue with reference to antitrust enforcement; the following paragraphs draw from Giudici (2004).

private enforcement). Needless to say, these dimensions are closely connected.

As far as securities frauds are concerned, non-monetary fines (e.g., imprisonment) are needed because, moral considerations apart, the level of the private benefits that can be achieved through fraud is so high that civil suits cannot be sufficient to deter the violator, since his assets will never be sufficient to redress the social cost of his action.

In order to prevent fraud, mandatory disclosure is also needed. A system of mandatory disclosure has to rely on a public enforcer, able to intervene when a company is seeking to hide information and able to:

> verify the veracity of the number disclosed', an action that 'a private interme-
> diary can only do ... through a lawsuit, an avenue which is very slow and
> expensive (Zingales 2004).

Monetary civil fines (administrative fines, in continental Europe) are also usually associated with public enforcement of mandatory disclosure.

In theoretical terms some scholars argue that public enforcement offers two advantages. First, it allows better control in setting the optimal monetary or non-monetary sanction in accordance with the theory of deterrence, because a single public enforcer can take into proper consideration social cost and the probability of detection when deciding punishment. Damages awarded in private litigation can be unrelated both to the social cost and the *ex ante* probability of detection of the violation, and when used together with administrative or criminal fines may alter the optimal (even though purely theoretical) level of deterrence. Secondly, public enforcers usually have stronger investigative powers and are equipped to discover information that private parties cannot uncover. This aspect is not only related to the need to control interferences in private life, but also to the economies of scale and scope that can be necessary to create an efficient system of identification and apprehension of violators (Shavell 2004: 580–81).

However, as far as the first point is concerned, no public body can realistically calculate on a case-by-case basis the social cost of wrongdoings; and it is in any event impossible to assert *ex ante* the probability of detection if the actual level of diffusion of wrongdoing is unknown. In such a situation, there are at least three strong arguments against a system that relies entirely on the public enforcement of law. First, in the real world public agencies are not usually the most efficient enforcers because they cannot have access to the widespread information that private parties naturally possess (*ibid.*: 578–79). As we have seen, the Parmalat story is a case in point. Secondly, they lack adequate financial resources to investigate all potential wrongdoers and to pursue all pending investigations with the same unrestricted vigour.[89] Thirdly, the public agency can face agency costs in the same form of auditors and other gatekeepers, because the public servant could be 'amenable to payoffs,' as Professor Easterbrook has written.[90] The 'revolving door' between public and private jobs, i.e., the incentive to be not too harsh with some wrongdoers in view of potential future employment with them in the private sector,[91] and political influence are very easy examples of the nature of these payoffs, if one does not want to mention bribery, the extreme form of payoff.[92]

For all these reasons private parties are provided with economic incentives to report wrongdoings, in the form of damages, restitution, bounties or any other form of monetary reward whatsoever (Shavell 2004: 578–79; Kraakman 1986: 60–61).[93] Accordingly, even though the private incentive to bring suit remains:

> fundamentally misaligned with the social optimal incentive to do so, and the deviation between them could be in either direction, (Shavell 2004: 391)

---

[89] In favour of private Attorneys-General it is argued, for instance, that they ensure enforcement as they are 'not wholly dependent on the current attitudes of public enforcers': Coffee (1983: 227); Morrison (2004: 20 *et seq.*), reviewing the arguments in favour and against private Attorneys-General.

[90] With reference to the public prosecutor in antitrust cases, Professor Easterbrook writes: 'Unable to capture the benefits of his work, he would tend to shirk. He might seek to maximize something other than allocative efficiency. He also would be amenable to payoffs, perhaps in the indirect form of future employment (the "revolving door" between public and private jobs) or support for future political campaign' (Easterbrook 1985: 454). See also Glaeser, Kessler, and Piehl (1999).

[91] Doubts concerning the existence of such an 'agency problem' affecting regulators have been recently raised by Professor Langevoort, who argues as follows: 'Two problems, however, make this problematic. First, the broad consensus among officials needed for significant action makes it hard for one or a handful of officials to push policy in the direction of a particular interest. Secondly, the dominating strategy for opportunistic officials may be instead to create some new body of regulation that is dense and difficult to interpret or apply, and upon departure claim the rents associated with expert informational advantage.' (Langevoort 2004).

[92] Glaeser, Johnson, and Shleifer (2001: 853) adopt a different approach and reach different conclusions, asserting that regulators are more aggressive enforcers than courts; however, in their analysis the authors 'focus on the inquisitorial legal system of civil law countries, where the judge must himself undertake an investigation into the facts of the situation and the law' (*ibid.*: 856). Generally speaking, this preliminary assumption is wrong as far as private enforcement is concerned, since also in the so-called 'inquisitorial legal systems' facts have to be submitted to the Court by the litigants. Indeed all the emphasis on the differences existing between adversary and inquisitorial models is, as a well-known specialist of the field has written, 'meaningless' :Taruffo (2002: 80).

[93] It must be noted that civil law countries such as Italy have never adopted *qui tam* legislation or citizen-suit provisions, enlisting citizens in law enforcement (on the subject, from a US perspective, see DePoorter and De Mot (2004)). Accordingly, in countries like Italy private incentives are always in the form of damages. Usually the right to claim damages is associated to violations of public regulation specifically constructed (in order to grant the action) as instruments to protect private interests also.

it is nonetheless advisable to have a certain level of private enforcement pressure. If one wants to add to these arguments considerations of corrective justice, it is clear that the issue is not whether or not private actions should have a role in securities law enforcement. Rather, the problem is, in effect, that of reaching a balance between private and public enforcement and creating formal or informal effective mechanisms for coordinating the roles of the two institutional frameworks (litigation and regulation), as is usual in fields where there is a cumulative effect of both (Viscusi 2002: 3).[94]

C. Class Actions

In civil procedure law the most significant device to aggregate damaged parties is the class suit. When private interests are widespread, the violator could avoid costs because each victim's injury is too small to warrant suit (Fleming *et al* 2001: 643). If each victim's injury is significant, independent actions create duplicative litigation. The main regulatory instrument that can be used to aggregate victims' interests and create economies of litigation scale, thereby enforcing mass claims through the liability mechanism and the action of private parties is the class suit. Since class actions require lawyers to find potential cases and launch expensive, complex multi-parties suits, and attorneys compete to be vested with the right to prosecute all the aggregate claims, the class suit is by definition a lawyer-driven litigation. That creates, once again, a well-studied agency problem: an attorney's interest can conflict with those of his or her clients.

> The lawyer for the class will be tempted to offer to settle with the defendant for a small judgment and a large legal fee, and such an offer will be attractive to the defendant, provided the sum of the two figures is less than the defendant's net expected loss from going to trial (Posner 2003: 586).

Securities litigation class actions faced strong criticism in the 1990s. Securities class suits were perceived to be 'epidemic' and too frequently based on 'frivolous' claims aimed at coercing companies to settle in order to avoid disproportionate legal costs, especially in the form of discovery costs. What Jennings *et al* (1998: 1250) describe as 'the increasing disenchantment for much of the public with the class action (and possibly with private enforcement of law in general)' led to the PSLRA,[95] designed to curtail class actions in securities litigation. A rich body of empirical research is now investigating the actual effects of the PSLRA on securities

---

[94] For a recent analysis of the interplay and overlap of SEC public enforcement proceedings and private enforcement of securities regulation, cf. Cox and Thomas (2003).
[95] See above, para III.B.2.

litigation (Choi 2004a). Nevertheless, class actions still exist and are increasing in the wake of the corporate scandals, notwithstanding the PSLRA and the many proposals to repeal it.[96]

From a European perspective, it must be noted that the US debate concerning the defects of the class-action mechanisms and the pros and cons of the PSLRA tends to develop its arguments from a situation where class action exists: the issue is how to control their defects and, particularly, the agency problem created by the attorney-class relationship (Macey and Miller 1991). As far as we know, nobody has seriously suggested the repeal of class actions. Indeed, a liability system cannot operate when there are mass damages and there is no effective aggregating device, because it leads to under-deterrence unless a very efficient public alternative is at work. However, an efficient public enforcement system cannot exist because of the three problems we have pointed out. Italy is a case in point. The result is strong under-enforcement. This conclusion is supported by empirical research concerning the control premium of transactions in Italy, which show that private benefits of control are very high and correlate this fact with a weak legal system that, as we have shown, is not weak in substance, but in enforcement (La Porta *et al* Vishny 1997; 1998; 1999; Shleifer and Vishny 1997; Djankov *et al* 2003; La Porta *et al* 2003). The introduction of class action-like mechanisms is deemed to be a forced step to improve the liability system in many European countries. England has recently enacted new instruments that permit the pooling of separate claims against one defendant,[97] and in Germany it is debated how to introduce class action devices.[98]

D. Further Advantages of Class Actions: Breaking Down Social Networks

We would like to advance a further argument in favour of class actions. It is well known that economic systems with low enforcement of legal rights tend to survive thanks to social networks.[99] Conversely, strong social networks may limit the adoption of liability rules for dispute resolution and, hence, limit the positive externalities related to the development of a rule of law. We think that the literature on class actions no longer considers the positive effect that class action grants as an

[96] For a discussion see Pritchard (2003).
[97] For references, see Black and Cheffins (2004: 26–27).
[98] See the Federal Government proposal of law at http://www.bmj.bund.de/media/archive/798.pdf On the issue see also Baums and Scott (2003).
[99] See, also for further references, Dixit (2004: 12–14); de Mesquita and Stephenson (2003); Posner (2000); North (1994).

instrument to break down social networks that usually, in small financial markets, hinder law enforcement. In a market where collective interest cannot be aggregated, only large creditors or blockholders can seriously face the cost of litigation in order to recover damages. However, large creditors and blockholders are usually members of a social and professional network that would have to sue members of their own club, a choice that can have a negative outcome in a repeated game. It is common experience in a country like Italy to see economic actors not enforcing their rights in order to avoid peer entanglement and the deterioration of some of their 'club relationships.' When lawyers are vested with the power to drive litigation, interpersonal links between plaintiff and defendant could be more easily broken and the rule of law could be more easily established.

[handwritten margin note: Are the lawyers part of that group in Italy?]

E. Attorneys' Fees

Contingency fees are deemed to be essential to the development of the entrepreneurial lawyer, who is the driving force of private enforcement, especially in the case of mass tort claims enforced through class suits (Zingales 2004). The point is relevant, even though it seems to be over-emphasized (at least when it refers to well-grounded actions). Contingency fees are probably necessary; however, they are not sufficient to ignite more effective forms of private enforcement.

Under the 'American Rule', applied in the United States, a prevailing plaintiff does not normally recover from the loser its litigation expenses. However, the plaintiff can enter into a contingent fee arrangement with its lawyer, by means of which in case of defeat he is liable for nothing but court costs and the lawyer's out-of-pocket disbursements; if he wins or settles, his lawyer takes a significant fraction of the recovery (usually one-third) (Fleming, Hazard and Leubsdorf 2001: 51). Accordingly, lawyers can finance plaintiffs' actions. It must be noted that, under a contingency fee arrangement, redress of damages is never complete because the lawyer takes part of the recovery and the loser does not contribute.

European countries usually adopt the 'English rule', i.e., the rule under which a prevailing party recovers her attorney's fees from the loser. Under this rule, the plaintiff's attorney could in theory still finance the action, with the loser paying the final sum. In this situation, however, the final sum cannot be negotiated in advance by the plaintiff and her lawyer, because it is a cost that the loser has to face. Accordingly, it is regulated by the law and fixed by the court. If the regulation and the court were able to take into consideration all the costs faced by the plaintiff's lawyer in terms of monitoring, identification of the case, financing of the case through her work etc., and the plaintiff's lawyer were allowed to renounce any advanced payment of fees before the case is ended, the 'English rule' could also be more effective than the 'American rule,' for the loser would pay an amount of money closer to the social cost of his action (redress plus damaged party's legal expenses). Once again, the problem is in the application of the rule, not in its nature or quality. The English rule fails because its effectiveness depends on a form of public enforcement. Indeed, the regulator and the court have no information about the true costs of the plaintiff's attorney. Paternalism embedded in the European culture also influences the outcome. Italian courts quite often shift away from a rigid application of the rule and do not require the losing defendant to pay the actual amount of a plaintiff's litigation costs. A rule adopted to offer full redress to the damaged party ends up chilling lawyers' activism as 'general private attorneys.'

Not all claims, however, have crystal-clear chances of success at the start of the civil action. The English rule is clearly unfavourable to risk averse plaintiffs, as it puts on the party—and not on her more informed lawyer—the risk of a negative outcome. From an Italian perspective, however, it has to be observed that courts, which do not apply rigidly the English rule, quite often do not require the losing plaintiff to pay the defendant's litigation costs (or the full amount) when the plaintiff's action had some grounds and the defendant has 'deep pockets'. Thus, the chilling effect of the English rule on risk averse plaintiffs is not to be overemphasized in Italy.

F. Access to Information: Discovery Rules

In order to start any enforcement action, information is needed. If a private party is directly involved in a deal, as in a standard breach of contract situation, she probably possesses relevant information. If an investor wants to start actions against a gatekeeper on the basis of a very preliminary set of information, things obviously become more complex.

Civil procedure law approaches the problem of access to information in various ways. The most radical approaches are no discovery and broad discovery. English Civil Procedure Rules 1998 and US Federal Rules of Civil Procedure allow extensive recourse to discovery.[100] The broadest range of discovery measures is offered by Rule 26 Federal Rules Civil Procedure in the US Federal system (Stürner 2001). Even after the recent amendments aimed at containing discovery (Marcus 2001; Rowe 2001; Stempel and Herr 2001), they can still impress, if not shock, any

---

[100] English compulsory disclosure rules are analyzed by Matthews (2001: 10–11), who briefly covers the main differences between England and the United States.

continental European lawyer. Parties can not only access documents held by their opponents, but they can also inspect offices with detective-like powers that are simply inconceivable in continental Europe (at least, as far as Italy, Germany, and France are concerned). The discovery phase is the core of litigation and, as Professor Hazard has pointed out, 'a procedural institution perhaps of virtually constitutional foundation' (Hazard 1998: 1694). Since roughly 95 per cent of all civil cases are resolved without trial, pre-trial discovery is 'the trial' (Taruffo 2002: 80).

It is highlighted in the American literature that certain types of claims such as discrimination claims would not have been possible without broad discovery granted to plaintiffs (Marcus 1998: 751). Cases where discovery is also an essential tool in the hands of plaintiffs are negligence torts, product liability claims, environmental degradation cases, antitrust, and securities regulation cases (Stempel 2001: 603 *et seq.*)

Italian procedural rules allow broad discovery in a very limited and defined set of marginal cases. When reading a book on Italian civil procedure it may appear that access to the documents held by the other party can be obtained through a court order. The problem is that the party does not know exactly what documents his opponent has, and the court cannot grant any disclosure order unless a document is specifically indicated. Moreover, if the party obliged to discover the document does not comply, the court can only consider this issue when deciding on the merits. The same is true for German and French laws. Hence, discovery is virtually absent. Given the lack of efficient discovery rules, investor action against mass wrongdoings is virtually impossible in Italy as it is in the rest of Europe, unless information is gathered by public authorities.[101]

G. Interplay between Pleading Rules and Discovery Rules

The information situation at the beginning of the 'game' is also influenced by the pleading rules. Basically, two different systems of pleading exist: 'fact pleading' and 'notice pleading'. As has been noted,

> Fact pleading requires a full statement of all material facts from the beginning of the pleading process; notice pleading requires only that the party against which the pleading is directed is given notice of the nature of the claim (Priestly 2001: 842).

---

[101] The role of discovery in private litigation is stressed by many articles in the European literature on private antitrust enforcement: see Giudici (2004: 1180); Mestmäcker (2000). In the Italian literature on civil procedure law the analysis of discovery rules has been conducted by Professor Dondi (1985, 2003). For a general review concerning Civil Law countries see Huang (2003).

Needless to say, the former system assumes that the plaintiff is in possession of all relevant information, while the latter expects that litigation is also a way of discovering and accessing information.[102] The US Federal and English systems are based on notice pleading.[103] Civil law is generally based on fact pleading mechanisms.

Common law and civil code systems are on opposing ends of the spectrum as far as pleading and discovery are concerned. It could be argued that this difference is based on opposite conceptions of what private civil litigation is about. Many American scholars assert that in common law jurisdictions the promotion of justice is seen as a value at stake, whereas this is not true in civil law jurisdictions (Subrin 1998; Clermont and Sherwin 2003).[104] This assertion is contested by leading comparativists.[105] Nevertheless, it is clear that, at least in the United States, the process enhances the vindication of the public interest in a more effective way than in civil law countries (Cappelletti 1989; Kotz 2003). In the absence of notice pleading and discovery rules, in Europe any serious hope that investor claims could take a significant role in the enforcement of securities law is ungrounded.[106]

H. Derivative Actions

In a highly publicized attempt to develop private enforcement as a tool to influence companies' corporate governance, the CFSA introduced in 1998 derivative suits by minority shareholders into Italian law (Art. 129

[102] Fleming, Hazard, and Leubsdorf (2001: 181): 'Imposing on a plaintiff a requirement that the claim be articulated in detail means that only claimants who have access to such detail are in a position to state a claim.'

[103] We are aware of PSLRA heightened pleading, and we understand that notice pleading could be a sort of myth: cf. Fairman (2003). Nevertheless, we are interested in notice pleading as a pleading model functional to the discovery mechanism.

[104] Clermont and Sherwin argue that the search of truth characterizes the American process.

[105] Professor Taruffo does not think that the American civil procedure is especially oriented to the search of truth: see Taruffo (2003), criticizing Clermont and Sherwin (2002). Since discovery is one of the core issues of the debate, Professor Taruffo argues (2003: 676) that 'one may wonder whether the American discovery, with its well known abuses, is really aimed at the search of truth or if its real purpose is not that of exerting pressures on the adverse party in order to achieve a forced settlement or of fishing for evidence that is needed to set up a case, although such evidence will not be presented at trial.' In his fundamental book on justice, Professor Damâska (1986: 131–34) debates how discovery could fit a pure conflict-solving process (i.e., purely adjudicative). He does not suggest that the search of truth lies at the heart of discovery rules.

[106] Needless to say, introduction of discovery would raise litigation costs and in 'loser pays' systems that would considerably increase the risk to a plaintiff in initiating a private Attorney-General lawsuit against large firms with deep pockets, whereas in the United States the defendant is not reimbursed by the plaintiff for the cost of the defendant's lawyers. See Marcus, Redish and Sherman (2002, 100–6); Fleming, Hazard and Leubsdorf (2001: 48–53). From an Italian perspective, however, the difference between the English Rule and the American Rule should not be overemphasized for the reasons mentioned at section IV.E.

CFSA).[107] Many problems affected the new system, which has been recently introduced as a standard rule (Article 2393-bis) also in the general law of joint-stock companies (*società per azioni*). However, the most significant hindrance is probably the lack of discovery. In the absence of any instrument allowing the plaintiff to access information in the hands of the defendant company, and with 'fact pleading' rules still governing plaintiffs' actions, derivative actions have had no effect on Italian corporate governance. As far as we know, there are no significant cases of suits started by minority shareholders in a derivative-suit context up to now. Accordingly, derivative suits have not changed the pattern of a legal system where managers (appointed by controlling shareholders or controlling coalitions) are sued by insolvency liquidators only. Needless to say, liquidators do possess all relevant information needed to sue managers, since they have access to all the company's documents.

There was the hope that the statutory auditor appointed by minority shareholders would have helped in the diffusion of information needed to start legal proceedings, but that simply did not happen. Of course, there are further explanations concerning the lack of derivative actions. An obvious explanation lies in the absence of incentives to establish lawyer-driven actions. Another explanation regards the size of Italian listed companies.[108] In any event, we think that the absence of discovery rules is the most significant weakness of Italian derivative suits, and the reason why they will never be really effective in monitoring ex post managers' and controlling shareholders' conducts.

I. Interplay between Public and Private Enforcement in Italy

It must be noted that class actions and discovery rules are not the only institutional designs that could be framed to sort out the problems of collective action and access to information. Theoretically, an alternative institutional design could be to have a public agency vested with the power to investigate and make (autonomously or before a court) a factual finding in favour of private parties seeking individual redress before civil courts.[109] In such a system, the public enforcer would create economies of scale and scope, and the general problem of access to information by the agency would be resolved as private parties would have strong incentives to report. Otherwise, a *partie civile* mechanism could be foreseen in administrative actions conducted by the agency, following the

---

[107] This move is discussed by Enriques (2002: 780).

[108] See Choi (2004b), discussing the size of South Korea's companies.

[109] For similar institutional designs, even though in the course of a completely different analysis, see Damâska (1986: 160–64).

model of criminal proceedings in some continental European countries, like France and Italy (Cappelletti 1989: 287–78).

The Italian law system (as well those of the other countries in continental Europe, as the antitrust experience shows) is unfriendly to this interplay between public and private enforcement; moreover, problems affecting public watchdogs' incentives are always ready to resurface.

1. Incentives to Report

Incentives granted to private parties to report wrongdoings are low. The watchdog receives many complaints every year, but the vast majority are too vague to establish an action without launching a specific investigation. In complex matters investors have to seek professional advice to draft a readable, persuasive complaint. However, professional advice is costly. Moreover, the investor has no costless control of the administrative proceeding. If the authority decides not to pursue a case, the complainant should seek judicial review of the decision. As usual, however, cost issues chill any attempt to pursue the matter any longer. Since the watchdog faces funding problems and cannot investigate all potential cases, the watchdog has to select cases. Case selection can be contaminated by the usual corporate governance problem, which a private attorney would not face at this stage. Moreover, as we have noted, the Italian watchdog case selection policy is affected by a misplaced reliance on the cooperative approach of statutory auditors.

2. Role of the Authority's Factual Finding

Italian public action is not equivalent to discovery. Consob and the Bank of Italy do not provide a private investor with information needed to offer evidence concerning his own claim. A special rule concerning confidential information acquired in the course of public enforcement actions forces investors to use only the general factual findings mentioned in the final decision taken by the authority, thereby denying access to any further information that could help in establishing a case against a wrongdoer. A well-known case concerned the Sai-Fondiaria affair, where Consob's decision denying the existence of a duty to launch a compulsory takeover bid was motivated so succinctly that investors could not understand the evidentiary basis of the decision.[110] Even though the watchdog pursues the case and offers in its administrative decision sufficient evidentiary basis for an independent civil action by the damaged party, the factual findings contained in the public authority's

---

[110] Above, section III.D.4.

decision can be considered by the civil court, but are not sufficient evidence. In theory, the investor should be able to offer independent evidence of the asserted facts, an insurmountable burden of proof in the absence of discovery rules, even though sometimes courts relax the burden of proof requirements.[111]

All these problems show that the system is not designed to offer a real interplay between public and private enforcement. In any event, when accessible information is sufficient to establish a prima facie case against the wrongdoers, duplicative litigation would be nevertheless unavoidable, in the absence of class-action mechanisms; legal costs would also be too high to justify an independent legal action, because lawyers are not entitled to renounce to partial, advanced payment of their fees and the 'English rule' is not strictly applied (and, in any event, it cannot be effectively applied).

J. Criminal Prosecutions

Finally, we briefly consider criminal proceedings. When private parties join criminal proceedings as investors are currently doing in the *Parmalat* case, they can benefit from the evidence offered by the prosecutors and can minimize the burden of persuading the court (a burden that in any event stays with the prosecutor). The absence of the weapons that we have briefly analyzed (class actions, discovery rules, and notice pleading) becomes less important in damage claims for economic loss lodged in criminal proceedings. This explains why the Milan criminal proceedings concerning Parmalat have gathered a considerable bundle of civil claims. However, civil claimants' compensation depends on conviction. In criminal actions the standard of proof is different, because proof beyond a reasonable doubt is required, whereas in civil cases proof-standards are more relaxed—even though, at least in Italy, they are usually stricter than the standard of preponderance of the evidence.[112] It must also be considered that gatekeepers can be liable under civil law for frauds committed by managers and yet be innocent under criminal law as their negligent behaviour does not necessarily amount to crime. In short, the

---

[111] Standards of proof in Italy, as in many civilian countries, are sometimes oblivious both in civil and in criminal litigation. As far as civil litigation is concerned, see Taruffo (2003). In criminal law the principle that proof must be beyond a reasonable doubt has been stressed, with reference to causation, in a recent case by Cassation Court, Joint Meeting (*Sezioni Unite*), 11 Sept. 2002 No. 30328, *Riv. it. dir. e proc. pen.*, 2002, 1133 *et seq.*, commented by Stella (2002).

[112] In a newspaper article, Professor Federico Stella (2004) has pointed out that criminal prosecutions are a weak instrument for the vindication of widespread economic interests, since the burden of proof in criminal proceedings has to be beyond any reasonable doubt; accordingly, the author has pointed out that, in order to be effective in the vindication of the public interest, civil procedure has to rely on a standard of preponderance of evidence.

Parmalat case is special and one should not indulge in the belief that criminal law offers sufficient deterrence against market frauds. In fact, public enforcement in Europe is increasingly dissatisfied with criminal enforcement and adopts models of administrative enforcement, as has always been the case for antitrust in Europe.

V. CONCLUSION

The Parmalat scandal raises the well-known gatekeepers' problem with respect to auditors, lawyers and financial intermediaries. It also confirms the low level of law enforcement in Italy, which might typify continental Europe as a whole. Yet, the problem does not lie with the substantive rules concerning corporate governance and gatekeepers' standards of behaviour. The Italian system has been influenced by corporate governance debates and has sought to respond to the demands of modernization by acting on substantive rules. The problem is that there was no serious effort to reshape the enforcement system. The result is underenforcement.

Europe's unfriendly approach to private enforcement of collective interests has to be reconsidered. An astonished Italian public learned from the mass media shortly after Parmalat's collapse that civil actions were being launched, at a speed unthinkable for Italy, and in the United States, by a public agency (SEC) and by class-action lawyers. Similarly, Parmalat's reorganization procedure brought its three main legal suits in the United States, one against Citigroup, the other against Grant Thornton and Deloitte, the third against Bank of America, claiming large amounts of money. On the contrary, in Italy the vindication of the public interest, driven by a liquidator with the highest reputation who is doing an excellent job, is currently in the hands of criminal and civil courts which are ill-equipped to deal with complex litigation concerning capital market frauds and masses of claimants seeking to recover damages.

As a result, global issuers and gatekeepers are mainly exposed to the US private enforcement system with its plaintiff-friendly weaponry: class actions and entrepreneurial lawyers, notice pleading rules, and aggressive discovery. The efficient US private enforcement system (as well as 'intra-brand' competition in the form of the SEC versus Eliot Spitzer rivalry), forces public enforcers to be faster and more reactive than their European counterparts. We conclude that Italy (Europe) has to upgrade and rebalance its public and private enforcement mechanisms in order to increase deterrence and weaken the role of secretive practices, political accountability, and social networks. It is clear that private enforcement cannot be improved without revolutionary changes to the whole civil procedure system, since the present system is ill suited for disputes concerning the protection of diffuse interests. Moreover, formal and effective mechanisms for coordinating the roles of the two institutional frameworks (litigation and regulation) have to be created. In the meantime, the United States will exercise an increasing role in the public and private enforcement of securities laws also with respect to foreign global issuers.

POST-SCRIPT

The political response to the Parmalat scandal was idle when another scandal hit Italy: the BPI affair, concerning an alleged concert action orchestrated by Banca Popolare Italiana (BPI) in order to gain control of Banca AntonVeneta, defeating a bid by ABN Amro. This scandal was eventually to bring down the Bank of Italy's Governor, Mr Antonio Fazio, who was accused of favouring BPI and, in particular, its chief executive, Mr Gianpiero Fiorani. The latter had allegedly launched (with a cohort of conspirators) large insider trading operations when his own bank undertook large capital markets transactions. The Italian parliament, under pressure again and close to the end of its term, enacted a new law (28 December 2005, no. 262) that can be seen as an Italian equivalent of the Sarbanes-Oxley Act.

The law addresses many of the issues raised by the Parmalat scandal. Private placements face new limits, aimed at inhibiting the resale of bonds to investors, as controversially occurred with Cirio and Parmalat bonds. Consob's powers of inspection and sanction have been reinforced. Listed companies have to provide more precise information about their compliance with the Italian Exchange code of best practice and at least one director has to be appointed by minority shareholders. This appears an over-reaction to the ease with which some listed companies declared compliance with the code of best practice, especially with reference to the appointment of independent directors. Consob is asked to adopt rules to make more effective the appointment of a statutory auditor by minority shareholders. The CEO and the CFO have to certify the truthfulness of the issuer's financial reports. The board, the CEO and the financial officer have to sign the financial statements of any subsidiaries established in off-shore countries specified by the Ministry for the Economy. This appears to be an over-reaction to Parmalat's use of off-shore shields. The rules concerning auditors were intensively re-drafted. Non-audit services offered to the audit client by members of the auditor's network are now explicitly forbidden. Administrative fines were reinforced, as well as criminal sanctions.

As predicted, private enforcement is not a significant issue in the law. To be sure, the law tries to promote derivative suits, by reducing the shareholding required to start an action to 2.5 per cent of the share capital; moreover, statutory auditors are empowered to sue the directors. However, the main structural problems analysed in our paper remain untouched, as well as our conclusions.

REFERENCES

Anand, A. and Moloney, N. (2004), 'Reform of the Audit Process and the Role of Shareholder Voice: Transatlantic Perspectives', 5 *European Business Organization Law Review* 223.

Ansa/Bloomberg (2004), 'Parmalat: Thornton registrò Bonlat', interview with Ian Johnson, partner of Grant Thornton, 13 January 2004.

Balzarini, P. (1999), 'Commento all'art. 161 TUF', in P. Marchetti and L.A. Bianchi (eds.), *La disciplina delle società quotate, II* (Milano: Giuffrè), 1929.

Bank of Italy (2004), Report of the Governor of the Bank of Italy to the Parliamentary Commission, 27 January 2004.

Barcellona, E. (2003), *Responsabilità da informazione al mercato: il caso dei revisori legali dei conti* (Torino: Giappichelli).

Baums, T. and Scott, K.E. (2003), 'Taking Shareholder Protection Seriously? Corporate Governance in the United States and Germany', Stanford Law and Economics Olin Working Paper No. 272; ECGI - Law Working Paper No. 17/2003.

Black, B. and Cheffins, B. (2004), 'Outside Director Liability Across Countries', Stanford Law School Working Paper No. 266.

Bloomberg (2004a), *Bloomberg News*, 16 March 2004.

Bloomberg (2004b), *Bloomberg News*, 10 February 2004.

Bonelli, F. (1998), 'L'art. 129 Legge Draghi: l'azione sociale di responsabilità esercitata dalla minoranza dei soci, e l'assicurazione contro i rischi incorsi nella gestione', in F. Bonelli *et al.* (eds), *La riforma delle società quotate* (Milano: Giuffrè).

Bratton, W.W. (2002), 'Enron and the Dark Side of Shareholder Value', 76 *Tulane Law Review* 1275.

Bussoletti, M. (1985), *Le società di revisione* (Milano: Giuffrè).

Capolino, G., Massaro, F. and Panerai, P. (2004), *Parmalat. La grande truffa* (Milano: Milano Finanza).

Cappelletti, M. (1989), *The Judicial Process in Comparative Perspective* (Oxford: Clarendon Press).

Carrington, P. (2004), 'The American Tradition of Private Law Enforcement', 5 *German Law Journal* 1413.

Casadei, D. (2000), *La responsabilità della società di revisione* (Milano: Giuffrè).

Castronovo, C. (1997), *La nuova responsabilità civile* (Milano: Giuffrè).

Choi, S. (1998), 'Market Lessons for Gatekeepers', 92 *Northwestern University Law Review* 916.

Choi, S.J. (2004a), 'A Framework for the Regulation of Securities Market Intermediaries', 1 *Berkeley Business Law Journal* 1.

Choi, S.J. (2004b), 'Do the Merits Matter Less After the Private Securities Litigation Reform Act?', UC Berkeley Public Law Research Paper No. 558285; USC CLEO Research Paper No. C04-11; USC Law School, Olin Research Paper No. 04-16.

Choi, S.J. (2004c), 'The Evidence on Securities Class Actions', UC Berkeley Public Law Research Paper No. 528145

Choi, S.J. and Fisch, J.E. (2003), 'How To Fix Wall Street: A Voucher Financing Proposal for Securities Intermediaries', 113 *Yale Law Journal* 269.

Clermont, K.M. and Sherwin, E. (2002), 'A Comparative View of Standards of Proof', 50 *American Journal of Comparative Law* 243.

Coffee, J.C. (1983), 'Rescuing the Private Attorney General: Why the Model of Lawyer as Bounty Hunter Is Not Working', 42 *Maryland Law Review* 215.

Coffee, J.C. (2002), 'Understanding Enron: "It's the Gatekeepers, Stupid"', 57 *Business Lawyer* 1403.

Coffee, J.C. (2004a), 'Gatekeeper Failure and Reform: The Challenge of Fashioning Relevant Reforms', 84 *Boston University Law Review* 301 (also published in G. Ferrarini, K. Hopt, J. Winter and E. Wymeersch (eds.), *Reforming Company and Takeover Law in Europe*, (Oxford: Oxford University Press), 455).

Coffee, J.C. (2004b), 'Partnoy's Complaint: A Response', 84 *Boston University Law Review* 377.

Consob (2004a), Audizione informale sulla diffusione in Italia di obbligazioni pubbliche argentine, 27 April 2004 (available atwww.consob.it).

Consob (2004b), Report of the Chairman of Consob to the Parliamentary Commission, 27 January 2004.

COVIP (Commissione di Vigilanza sui Fondi Pensione) (2004), Report of the Chairman to the Parliamentary Commission, 29 January 2004 (available at http://www.covip.it).

Cox, J.D. and Thomas, R.S. (2003), (with the Assistance of Dana Kiku), 'SEC Enforcement Heuristics: An Empirical Inquiry', 53 *Duke Law Journal* 737.

Cunningham, L.A. (2004), 'Choosing Gatekeepers: The Financial Statement Insurance Alternative to Auditor Liability', 52 *UCLA Law Review* 413.

Damâska, M.R. (1986), *The Faces of Justice and State Authority. A Comparative Approach to the Legal Process* (New Haven and London: Yale University Press).

de Mesquita, E.B. and Stephenson, M. (2003), 'Legal Institutions and the Structure of Informal Networks', Harvard Law School, Discussion Paper No. 419, 04/2003.

De Nicola, A. (2004a), 'Lotta di "class"', *Il Sole 24 Ore*, 17 March 2004.

De Nicola, A. (2004b), 'Se Roma fa la balia', *Il Sole 24 Ore*, 20 October 2004.

DePoorter, B. and De Mot, J. (2004), 'Whistle Blowing', George Mason University School of Law Working Paper No. 04/56).

Dixit, A.K. (2004), *Lawlessness and Economics. Alternative Modes of Governance* (Princeton: Princeton University Press).

Djankov, S., La Porta, R., Lopez-de-Silanes, F., and Shleifer, A. (2003), 'Courts', 118 *Quarterly Journal of Economics* 453.

Dondi, A. (1985), *Effettività dei provvedimenti istruttori del giudice civile* (Padova: Cedam).

Dondi, A. (2003), 'Questioni di efficienza della fase preparatoria nel processo civile statunitense (e prospettive italiane di riforma)', *Rivista Trimestrale di Diritto Procedurale Civile* 161 .

Easterbrook, F. (1985), 'Detrebling Antitrust Damage', 28 *Journal of Law and Economics* 445.

Ebke, W.F. (2004), 'Corporate Governance and Auditor Independence: The Battle of the Private Versus the Public Interest' in G. Ferrarini, K. Hopt, J. Winter, and E. Wymeersch (eds.), *Reforming Company and Takeover Law in Europe* (Oxford: Oxford University Press).

Economist (2004), 'Called to Account—The future of auditing', 20 November 2004.

Ellickson, R.C. (1994), *Order Without Law: How Neighbours Settle Disputes* (Cambridge, MA: Harvard University Press).

Enriques, L. (2002), 'Do Corporate Law Judges Matters? Some Evidence From Milan', 3 *European Business Organization Law Review* 765.

Fairman, C.M. (2003), 'The Myth of Notice Pleading', 45 *Arizona Law Review* 987.

Fanto, J.A. (2004), 'Subtle Hazard Revisited. The Corruption of a Financial Holding Company by a Corporate Client's Inner Circle', 70 *Brooklyn Law Review* 7.

Ferrarini, G. (1986), *La responsabilità da prospetto. Informazione societaria e tutela degli investitori* (Milano: Giuffrè).

Ferrarini, G. (1993), 'Sollecitazione del risparmio e quotazione in borsa' in G.E. Colombo and G.B. Portale (eds.), *Trattato delle società per azioni*, 10** (Torino: Utet).

Ferrarini, G., Giudici, P., and Stella Richter, M.(2005), 'Italian Company Law Reform: Real Progress?', 69 *Rabels Zeitschrift* 658.

Franzini, G. (2004), *Il crac Parmalat* (Roma: Editori Riuniti).

Funds International, 'Parmalat Collapse Leaves Most Scars on US Fund Managers', 31 October 2004.

Giudici, P. (2004), 'Private Antitrust Law Enforcement in Italy', 1 *Competition Law Review* 61.

Giussani, A. and Zoppini, A. (2004), 'Tutela del risparmio e mercati finanziari: una ricetta italiana per la "class action"', 27 *Guida al Diritto* 11.

Glaeser, E., Johnson, S., and Shleifer, A. (2001), 'Coase Versus the Coasians', 116 *Quarterly Journal of Economics* 853.

Glaeser, E.L., Kessler, D.P., and Piehl, A.M. (1999), 'What Do Prosecutors Maximize? An Analysis of the Federalization of Drug Crimes' Stanford Law John M. Olin Working Paper No. 170.

Gobert, J. and Punch, M. (2003), *Rethinking Corporate Crime* (Cambridge: Cambridge University Press).

Goldberg, V.P. (1988), 'Accountable Accountants: Is Third-Party Liability Necessary?', 17 *Journal of Legal Studies* 295.

Gordon, J.N. (2002), 'What Enron Means for the Management and Control of the Modern Business Corporation: Some Initial Reflections',69 *University of Chicago Law Review* 1233.

Hamdani, A. (2003) 'Gatekeeper Liability', 77 *Southern California Law Review* 53.

Hazard, G. (1998), 'From Whom No Secrets Are Kept', 76 *Texas Law Review* 1665.

Huang, K.-C. (2003), *Introducing Discovery into Civil Law* (Durham, NC: Carolina Academic Press).

James, F., Hazard, G.C. and Leubsdorf, J. (2001), *Civil Procedure* (New York: Foundation Press).

Jennings, R.W., Marsh, H., Coffee, J.C., and Seligmann, J. (1998), *Securities Regulation. Cases and Materials*, 8th ed. (Westbury, NY: Foundation Press).

Kapner, F. (2004), 'Parmalat Probe Focuses on Deloitte's Italian Office', *Financial Times* (London Edition), 10 April 2004, 1.

Kotz, H. (2003), 'Civil Justice Systems in Europe and the United States', 13 *Duke Journal of Comparative and International Law* 61.

Kraakman, R.H. (1984), 'Corporate Liability Strategies and the Costs of Legal Controls', 93 *Yale Law Journal* 857.

Kraakman, R.H. (1986), 'Gatekeepers: The Anatomy of a Third-Party Enforcement Strategy', 2 *Journal of Law Economics and Organization* 53.

Kroger, J.R. (2005), 'Enron, Fraud and Securities Reform: An Enron Prosecutor's Perspective', 76 *University of Colorado Law Review* 57.

La Porta, R., Lopez-de-Silanes, F., and Shleifer, A. (2003), 'What Works in Securities Law?', NBER Working Paper No. 9882 (available at: http://www.nber.org/papers/W9882.pdf).

La Porta, R., Lopez-de-Silanes, F., Shleifer, A., and Vishny, R.W. (1997), 'Legal Determinants of External Finance', 52 *Journal of Finance* 1131.

La Porta, R., Lopez-de-Silanes, F., Shleifer, A., and Vishny, R.W. (1998), 'Law and Finance', 106 *Journal of Political Economy* 1113.

La Porta, R., Lopez-de-Silanes, F., Shleifer, A., and Vishny, R.W. (1999), 'Corporate Ownership Around the World', 54 *Journal of Finance* 471.

Langevoort, D.C. (2004), 'Structuring Securities Regulation in the European Union: Lessons from the U.S. Experience', Georgetown Public Law Research Paper No. 624582.

Macey, J. (2004), 'The U.S. Experience: Wall Street in Turmoil: State-Federal Relations in U.S. Regulation of Corporations and Market Post-Eliot Sptizer', paper for the symposium on 'Changes of Governance in Europe, Japan, and the U.S.: Corporations, States, Markets, and Intermediaries', Berlin, 9–11 September 2004.

Macey, J. and Miller, G. (1991), 'The Plaintiffs' Attorney's Role in Class Action and Derivative Litigation: Economic Analysis and Recommendations for Reform', 58 *University of Chicago Law Review* 1.

Macey, J. and Sale, H.A. (2003), 'Observations on the Role of the Commodification, Independence, and Governance in the Accounting Industry', 48 *Villanova Law Review* 1167.

Macey, J. (2004), 'Efficient Capital Markets, Corporate Disclosure, and Enron', 89 *Cornell Law Review* 394.

Marchesi, D. (2003), *Litiganti, avvocati e magistrati. Diritto ed economia del processo civile* (Bologna: Il Mulino).

Marcus, R.L. (1998), 'Discovery Containment Redux', 39 *Boston College Law Review* 747.

Marcus, R.L. (2001), 'The 2000 Amendments to the Discovery Rules', *Federal Courts Law Review* 1.

Marcus, R.L., Redish, M.H., and Sherman, E.F. (2002), *Civil Procedure. A Modern Approach* (St. Paul, Minn.: West Group).

Matthews, P. and Malek, H.M., (2001), *Disclosure* (London: Sweet & Maxwell).

Mazzoni, A. (2002), 'Osservazioni in tema di responsabilità civile degli analisti finanziari', 1 *Analisi giuridica dell'economia* 209.

Merrill Lynch, 'The Straws That Break The Camel's Back', posted on the Italian Stock Exchange website (www.borsaitalia.it), 5 December 2002.

Mestmäcker, E.-J. (2000), 'The Commission's Modernization of Competition Policy: A Challenge to the Community's Constitutional Order', 1 *European Business Organization Law Review* 401.

Miller, G.P. (2004), 'Catastrophic Financial Failures: Enron and More', 89 *Cornell Law Review* 423.

Montalenti, P. (2004), *La società quotata* (Padova: Cedam).

Morrison, T. (2004), 'Private and Attorneys General and the First Amendment', Cornell Law School Research Paper No. 04-017.

North, D.C. (1990), *Institutions, Institutional Changes and Economic Performance* (Cambridge: Cambridge University Press).

Oddo, G. (2004a), 'Il cappio delle commissioni', *Il Sole 24 Ore*, 21 July 2004.

Oddo, G. (2004b), 'Parmalat, indagini alla svolta', *Il Sole 24 Ore*, 7 December 2004.

Oddo, G., Sabbatini, R. (2002), 'Fondiaria, Sai trova un tris di acquirenti', *Il Sole 24 Ore*, 3 February 2002.

Oh, P.B. (2004) 'Gatekeeping', 29 *Journal of Corporation Law* 735.

Onado, M. (2003), 'I risparmiatori e la Cirio: ovvero, pelati alla meta. Storie di ordinaria spoliazione di azionisti e obbligazionisti', 3 *Mercato Concorrenza Regole* 499.

Paredes, T.A. (2003), 'After the Sarbanes-Oxley Act: the Future Disclosure System: Blinded by the Light: Information Overload and Its Consequences for Securities Regulation', 81 *Washington University Law Quarterly* 417.

Parker, A. (2004), 'Revenue growth at Grant Thornton' News Digest, *Financial Times* (London Edition) 14 December 2004, 1.

Parmalat (2002), Parmalat press release, 14 November 2002.

Parmalat (2004), Parmalat press release, 29 July 2004.

Partnoy, F. (2001), 'Barbarians at the Gatekeepers?: A Proposal for a Modified Strict Liability Regime', 79 *Washintgon University Law Quarterly* 491.

Partnoy, F. (2004), 'Strict Liability for Gatekeepers: A Reply to Professor Coffee', 84 *Boston University Law Review* 365.

Penati, A. and Zingales, L. (1997), 'Efficiency and Distribution in Financial Restructuring: The Case of the Ferruzzi Group', Center for Research in Security Prices Working Paper No. 466.

Pistor, K. and Xu, C. (2002), 'Law Enforcement Under Incomplete Law: Theory and Evidence from Financial Market Regulation', London School of Economics and Political Science Working Paper No. Te/02/332.

Pistor, K. and Xu, C. (2003), 'Incomplete Law', 35 *New York University Journal of International Law and Politics* 931.

Portale, G. (1982), Informazione societaria e responsabilità degli intermediari, in *L'informazione societaria*, Atti del Convegno di Venezia (Milano: Giuffrè).

Posner, E.A. (2000), *Law and Social Norms* (Cambridge, MA: Harvard Univ. Press).

Posner, R. (2003), *Economic Analysis of Law*, 6th ed. (New York: Aspen Publishers).

Priestley, L.J. (2001), 'Transnational Civil Procedure, - Fact Pleading v. Notice Pleading: its Significance in the Development of Evidence', 4 *Revue de Droit Uniforme* 841.

Pritchard, A.C. (2003), 'Should Congress Repeal Securities Class Action Reform?', 471 *Policy Analysis* 1.

Rossi, A. (1985), *Revisione contabile e certificazione obbligatoria* (Milano: Giuffrè).

Rowe, T.D. (2001), 'A Square Peg in a Round Hole? The 2000 Limitation on the Scope of Federal Civil Discovery', 69 *Tennessee Law Review* 13.

Schwarcz, S.L. (2004), 'Rethinking the Disclosure Paradigm in a World of Complexity', 2004 *University of Illinois Law Review* 1.

Shavell, S. (2004), *Foundations of Economic Analysis of Law* (Cambridge, MA: Belknap Press).

Shleifer, A., and Vishny, R.W. (1997), 'A Survey of Corporate Governance', 52 *Journal of Finance* 737.

Simensen, I. (2004), 'The Spectre of Parmalat Still Haunts Market Italian Bonds', *Financial Times* (London Edition), 10 December 2004.

Stella, F. (2004), 'Quando l'azione civile tutela più del processo penale', *Corriere della Sera*, 6 February 2004.

Stempel, J.W. (2001), 'Politics and Sociology in Federal Civil Rulemaking: Errors of Scope', 52 *Alabama Law Review* 529.

Stempel, J.W. and Herr, D.F. (2001), 'Applying Amended Rule 26(B)(1) in Litigation: The New Scope of Discovery', 199 *Federal Rules Decisions* 396.

Stürner, R. (2001), 'Transnational Civil Procedure: Discovery and Sanctions Against Non-Compliance', 4 *Revue de Droit Uniforme* 871.

Subrin, S.N. (1998), 'Fishing Expeditions Allowed: The Historical Background of the 1938 Federal Discovery Rules', 39 *Boston College Law Review* 691.

Swanson, R.P. (2004), 'Accountants' Liability: Theories of Liability', American Law Institute—American Bar Association Continuing Legal Education ALI—ABA Course of Study, 20–21 May, 2004.

Taruffo, M. (2002), *Sui confini* (Bologna: Il Mulino).

Taruffo, M. (2003), 'Rethinking the Standards of Proof', 51 *American Journal of Comparative Law* 659.

Tombari, U. (1999), 'L'assicurazione della responsabilità civile degli amministratori di società per azioni' 52 *Banca borsa e titoli di credito* 180.

UBM (Unicredit Banca Mobiliare), 'Putting a Focus on Debt', posted on the Italian Stock Exchange website (http://www.borsaitalia.it), 6 December 2002.

UBS Warburg (2003), statement posted on the Italian Stock Exchange website (http://www.borsaitalia.it), 4 March 2003.

Viscusi, W.K. (2002), *Regulation through Litigation* (Washington D.C.: Brookings Institute).

Witting, C. (2000), 'Justifying Liability to Third Parties for Negligent Misstatements', 20 *Oxford Journal of Legal Studies* 615.

Zingales, L. (2004), 'The Costs and Benefits of Financial Market Regulation', ECGI - Law Working Paper No. 21/2004.

Zoppini, A. (2004), 'Tutela dei consumatori—I limiti della class action approvata dalla Camera', *Il Sole 24 Ore*, 28 July 2004.

6

A Theory of Corporate Scandals: Why the US and Europe Differ

JOHN C COFFEE, JR*

CORPORATE scandals, particularly when they occur in concentrated outbursts, raise serious issues that scholars have too
long ignored. Two issues stand out: First, why do different types
of scandals occur in different economies? Secondly, why does a wave
of scandals occur in one economy, but not in another, even though
both economies are closely interconnected in the same global economy
and subject to the same macro-economic conditions? This brief essay will
seek to relate answers to both questions to the structure of share
ownership.

Conventional wisdom explains a sudden concentration of corporate
financial scandals as the consequence of a stock market bubble. When the
bubble burst, scandals follow, and, eventually, new regulation.[1]
Historically, this has been true at least since the South Seas Bubble,
and this hypothesis works reasonably well to explain the turn-
of-the-millennium experience in the United States and Europe.
Worldwide, a stock market bubble did burst in 2000, and in percentage
terms the decline was greater in many European countries than in
the United States.[2] But in Europe, this sudden market decline was
not associated with the same pervasive accounting and financial
irregularity that shook the US economy and produced the
Sarbanes-Oxley Act in 2002. Indeed, financial statement restatements are

* Adolf A. Berle Professor of Law, Columbia University and Director, Center on Corporate
Governance, Columbia University Law School. This chapter was previously published in
(2005) 21 *Oxford Review of Economic Policy* 198–211. The permission of Oxford University
Press to republish is gratefully acknowledged.

[1] For a pre-Sarbanes-Oxley review of the last 300 years of this pattern, see Banner (1997).
[2] See Holmstrom and Kaplan (2003: 9) (showing that from 2001 through December 31, 2002,
the U.S. stock market returns were negative 32 per cent, while France was negative 45 per cent
and Germany negative 53 per cent).

rare in Europe.[3] In contrast, the United States witnessed an accelerating crescendo of financial statement restatements that began in the late 1990s. The United States General Accounting Office (GAO 2002: 4) has found that over 10 per cent of all listed companies in the United States announced at least one financial statement restatement between 1997 and 2002. Later studies have placed the number even higher.[4] Because a financial statement restatement is a serious event in the United States that, depending on its magnitude, often results in a private class action, an SEC enforcement proceeding, a major stock price drop, and/or a management shake-up, one suspects that these announced restatements were but the tip of the proverbial iceberg, with many more companies negotiating changes in their accounting practices with their outside auditors that averted a formal restatement.

While Europe also had financial scandals over this same period (with the Parmalat scandal being the most notorious),[5] most were characteristically different than the US style of earnings manipulation scandal (of which Enron and WorldCom were the iconic examples). Only European firms cross-listed in the United States seem to have encountered similar crises of earnings management.[6] What explains this difference and the difference in frequency? This short essay will advance a simple, almost self-evident thesis: Differences in the structure of share ownership account for differences in corporate scandals, both in terms of the nature of the fraud, the identity of the perpetrators, and the seeming disparity in the number of scandals at any given time. In dispersed ownership systems, corporate managers tend to be the rogues of the story, while in concentrated ownership systems, it is controlling shareholders who play the corresponding role. Although this point may seem obvious, its corollary is less so: The *modus operandi* of fraud is also characteristically different. Corporate managers tend to engage in earnings manipulation, while controlling shareholders tend to exploit the private benefits of control. Finally, and most importantly, given these differences, the role of gatekeepers in these two systems must necessarily also be different.[7] While gatekeepers failed both at Enron and Parmalat, they failed in characteristically different ways. In turn, different reforms may be

---

[3] Although they have been rare in the past, FitchRatings (2005), the credit ratings agency, predicts that they will become common in Europe in 2005, as thousands of European companies switch from local accounting standards to International Financial Reporting Standards, which are more demanding.

[4] See Huron Consulting Group (2003) (discussed in text at notes 10 to 11).

[5] For a detailed review of the Parmalat scandal, see Melis (2004) (http://ssrn.com/abstract=563223); Ferrarinni and Giudici, this volume, ch. 5.

[6] See text and notes, below at note 22.

[7] The term 'gatekeeper' will not be elaborately defined for purposes of this short essay, but means a reputational intermediary who pledges its considerable reputational capital to give credibility to issuers statements or forecasts. Auditors, securities analysts, and credit ratings agencies are the most obvious examples. See Coffee (2004a: 308–11).

justified, and the panoply of reforms adopted in the United States, culminating in the Sarbanes-Oxley Act of 2002, may not be the appropriate remedy in Europe.

Part I will review the recent American scandals to identify common denominators and the underlying motivation that caused the sudden eruption of financial statement restatements. Part II will turn to the evidence on private benefits of control in concentrated ownership systems. Patterns also emerge here in terms of the maturity of the capital market. Part III will advance some tentative conclusions about the differences in monitoring structures that are appropriate under different ownership regimes.

At the outset, it must be underscored that companies with dispersed ownership and companies with concentrated ownership co-exist in, all major jurisdictions.[8] Nonetheless, as much scholarship has demonstrated, the corporate universe divides into two basically alternative systems of corporate governance:

(1) *A Dispersed Ownership System*, characterized by strung securities markets, rigorous disclosure standards, high share turnover, and high market transparency, in which the market for corporate constitutes the ultimate disciplinary mechanism; and

(2) *A Concentrated Ownership System*, characterized by controlling blockholders, weaker securities markets, high private benefits of control, and lower disclosure and market transparency standards, but with a possibly substitutionary role played by large banks and non-controlling blockholders.[9]

This brief essay advances the modest proposition thai the role of gatekeepers also differs across these legal regimes and that gatekeepers, including even the auditor, arguably play a more central and critical role in the dispersed ownership system.

I. FRAUD IN DISPERSED OWNERSHIP SYSTEMS

While studies differ, all show a rapid acceleration in financial statement restatements in the United States during the 1990s. The earliest of these studies finds that the number of earnings restatements by publicly-held US corporations averaged roughly forty-nine per year from 1990 to 1997, then increased to ninety-one in 1998, and then soared to 150 and 156 in 1999 and 2000, respectively (Moriarty and Livingston 2001: 54). A later

---

[8] This has been demonstrated at length. See Porta *et al* (1999).
[9] For an overview of these rival systems, see Coffee (2001).

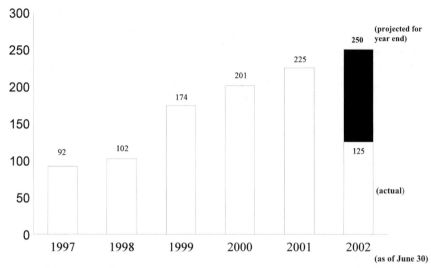

Figure 1: Total Number of Restatement Announcements Identified, 1997–2002

study by the United States General Accounting Office (GAO 2002) shows an even more dramatic acceleration, as set forth in Figure 1.

Even this study understated the severity of this sudden spike in accounting irregularity. Because companies do not uniformly report a restatement in the same fashion, the GAO was not able to catch all restatements in its study. A more recent, fuller study in 2003 by Huron Consulting Group shows the following results: in 1990, there were thirty-three earnings restatements; in 1995, there were fifty; then, the rate truly accelerated to 216 in 1999; to 233 in 2000; to 270 in 2001; and then in 2002, the number peaked at 330 (ten times the 1990 level).[10] On this basis, roughly one in eight listed companies restated over this period. An update this year by Huron Consulting shows that the number of restatements fell to 323 in 2003 and then rose again to 414 in 2004.[11] In any event, even if the exact number of restatements is disputed, the overall pattern of a hyperbolic rate of increase around the turn of the millennium persists across all studies.

Nor were these restatements merely technical adjustments. Although some actually increased earnings, the GAO study (2002: 5) found that the

[10] See Huron Consulting Group (2003: 4). The number of restatements fell (slightly) to 323 in 2003. *Ibid.* Not all these restatements involved overstatements of earnings (and some involved understatements). Still, the rising rate of restatements seems a good proxy for financial irregularity.

[11] See Huron Consulting Group (2005). If one wishes to focus only on restatements of the annual audited financial statements, excluding restatements of quarterly earnings, the numbers were: 2000: 98; 2001: 140; 2002: 183; 2003: 2006; and 2004: 253.

typical restating firm lost an average 10 per cent of its market capital-ization over a three-day trading period surrounding the date of the announcement. All told, the GAO estimated the total market losses (unadjusted for other market movements) at $100 billion for restating firms in its incomplete sample for 1997–2002 (GAO 2002:34).

Other studies have reached similar results. Studying a comprehensive sample of firms that restated annual earnings from 1971 to 2000, Richardson *et al* (2002: 4) reported a negative market reaction to the announcement of the restatement of 11 per cent over a three-day window surrounding the announcement. Moreover, using a wider window that measured firm value over a period beginning 120 days prior to the announcement to 120 days after the announcement, they found that restating 'firms lose on average 25 per cent of market value over the period examined and this is concentrated in a narrow window surrounding the announcement of the restatement' (Richardson *et al* 2002: 16). Twenty-five per cent of market value represents an extraordinary market penalty. It shows the market not simply to have been surprised, but to have taken the restatement as a signal of fraud. For example, in the cases of Cendant, MicroStrategy, and Sunbeam, three major US corporate scandals in the late 1990s, they found that 'these three firms lost more than $23 billion in the week surrounding their respective restatement announcements' Richardson *et al* 2002).

The intensity of the market's negative reaction to an earnings restatement appears to be greatest when the restatement involved revenue recognition issues (see Anderson and Yohn 2002). One study examining just the period from 1997 to 1999 found that firms in which revenue recognition issues caused the restatement experienced a market adjusted loss of –13.38 per cent over a window period beginning three days before the announcement and continuing until three days after the announcement.[12] Revenue recognition errors essentially revealed management not just to have been mistaken, but to have cheated, and the market reacted accordingly. Yet, despite the market's fear of such practices, revenue recognition errors became the dominant cause of restatements in the period from 1997 to 2002. The GAO Report (2002: 28) found that revenue recognition issues accounted for almost 38 per cent of the restatements it identified over that period, and the Huron Consulting Group study (2003: 4) also found it to be the leading accounting issue underlying an earnings restatement between 1999 and 2003.

The prevalence of revenue recognition problems, even in the face of the market's sensitivity to them, shows a significant change in managerial behavior in the United States. During earlier periods, US managements

---

[12] Anderson and Yohn (2002). This loss was measured in terms of cumulative abnormal returns (CAR). Where the cause of the restatement was reported as 'fraud,' the CAR rose to negative 19 per cent, but there were only a handful of such cases.

famously employed 'rainy day reserves' to hold back the recognition of income that was in excess of the market's expectation in order to defer its recognition until some later quarter when there had been a shortfall in expected earnings. In effect, managers engage in income-smoothing, rolling the peaks in one period over into the valley of the next period. This traditional form of earnings management was intended to mask the volatility of earnings and reassure investors who might have been alarmed by rapid fluctuations in earnings. In contrast, managers in the late 1990s appear to have characteristically 'stolen' earnings from future periods in order to create an earnings spike that potentially could not be sustained. Why? Although it had long been known that restating firms were typically firms with high market expectations for future growth, the pressure on these firms to show a high rate of earnings growth appears to have increased during the 1990s.

What, in turn, caused this increased pressure? To a considerable extent, it appears to have been self-induced—that is, the product of increasingly optimistic predictions by managements to financial analysts as to future earnings. But this answer just translates the prior question into a different format: why did managements become more optimistic about earnings growth over this period? Here, one explanation does distinguish the United States from Europe, and it has increasingly been viewed as the best explanation for the sudden spike in financial irregularity in the United States.[13] Put simply, executive compensation abruptly shifted in the United States during the 1990s, moving from a cash-based system to an equity-based system. More importantly, this shift was not accompanied by any compensating change in corporate governance to control the predictably perverse incentives that reliance on stock options can create.

One measure of the suddenness of this shift is the change over the decade in the median compensation of a CEO of an S&P 500 industrial company. As of 1990, the median such CEO made $1.25 million with 92 per cent of that amount paid in cash and 8 per cent in equity (Hall 2003: 23). But during the 1990s, both the scale and composition of executive compensation changed. By 2001, the median CEO of an S&P industrial company was earning over $6 million, of which 66 per cent was in equity (Hall 2003). Figure 2 shows the swiftness of this transition (Hall 2003).

To illustrate the impact of this change, assume a CEO holds options on two million shares of his company's stock and that the company is trading at a price to earnings ratio of thirty to one (both reasonable assumptions for this era). On this basis, if the CEO can cause the 'premature' recognition of revenues that result in an increase in annual

---

[13] For a fuller account of these various explanations, see Coffee (2004b).

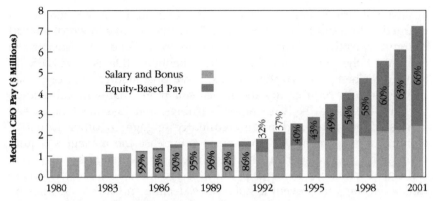

Figure 2: CEO Compensation at S&P Industrial Companies, 1980–2001

earnings by simply $1 per share, the CEO has caused a $30 price increase that should make him $60 million richer. Not a small incentive!

Obviously, when one pays the CEO with stock options, one creates incentives for short-term financial manipulation and accounting gamesmanship. Financial economists have found a strong statistical correlation between higher levels of equity compensation and both earnings management and financial restatements. One recent study by Efendi, Srivastava, and Swanson (2004) utilized a control group methodology and constructed two groups of companies, each composed of 100 listed public companies.[14] The first group's members had restated their financial statements in 2001 or 2002, while the control group was composed of otherwise similar firms that had not restated. What characteristic most distinguished the two groups? The leading factor that proved most to influence the likelihood of a restatement was the presence of a substantial amount of 'in the money' stock options in the hands of the firm's CEO. The CEOs of the firms in the restating group held on average 'in the money' options of $30.9 million, while CEOs in the non-restating control group averaged only $2.3 million—a nearly fourteen to one difference (Efendi *et al* 2004: 2). Further, if a CEO held options equaling or exceeding twenty times his or her annual salary (and this was the eightieth percentile in their study—meaning that a substantial number of CEOs did exceed this level), the likelihood of a restatement increased by 55 per cent.

Other studies have reached similar results. Denis, Hanouna, and Sarin (2005) find a significant positive relationship between a firm's use of option-based compensation and securities fraud allegations being leveled

---

[14] For an earlier similar study, see Johnson *et al* (2003).

against the firm.[15] Further, they find in their study of 358 companies charged with fraud between 1993 and 2002 that the likelihood of a fraud charge is positively related to 'option intensity'—i.e., the greater the amount of the options, the higher the likelihood (Denis *et al* 2005: 4). Similarly, Cheng and Warfield (2004) have documented that corporate managers with high equity incentives sell more shares in subsequent periods, are more likely to report earnings that just meet or exceed analysts' forecasts, and more frequently engage in other forms of earnings management. As stock options increase the managers' equity ownership, they also increase their need to diversify the high risk associated with such ownership, and this produces both more efforts to inflate earnings to prevent a stock price decline and increased sales by managers in advance of any earnings decline. In short, there is a 'dark side' to option-based compensation for senior executives: absent special controls, more options means more fraud.

At this point, the contrast between managerial incentives in the United States and Europe comes into clearer focus. These differences involve both the scale of compensation and its composition. In 2004, CEO compensation as a multiple of average employee compensation was estimated to be 531:1 in the United States, but only sixteen to one in France, eleven to one in Germany, ten to one in Japan, and twenty-one to one in nearby Canada. Even Great Britain, with the most closely similar system of corporate governance to the United States, had only a twenty-five to one ratio (Morgenson 2004: 1). But even more important is the shift towards compensating the chief executive primarily with stock options. While stock options have come to be widely used in recent years in Europe, equity compensation constitutes a much lower percentage of total CEO compensation (even in the United Kingdom, it was only 24 per cent in 2002).[16] European CEOs not only make much less, but their total compensation is also much less performance related.[17]

What explains these differences? Compensation experts in the United States usually emphasize the tax laws in the United States, which were amended in the early 1990s to restrict the corporate deductibility of high cash compensation and thus induced corporations to use equity in preference to cash.[18] But this is only part of the fuller story. Much of

[15] For an earlier study finding that the greater use of option-related compensation results in greater private securities litigation, see Peng and Roell (2004).

[16] See Ferrarini *et al* (2003: 7, note 21).

[17] Ferrarini *et al* (2003: 6–7) (noting that performance-related pay is in wide use only in the United Kingdom and that controlling shareholders tend to resist significant use of incentive compensation).

[18] In 1993, Congress enacted § 162(m) of the Internal Revenue Code, which denies a tax deduction for annual compensation in excess of $1 million per year paid to the CEO, or the next four most highly paid officers, unless special tests are satisfied. Its passage forced a shift in the direction of equity compensation. For a fuller account of this change, see Coffee (2004b: 274–75).

the explanation is that institutional investors in the United States pressured companies for a shift towards equity compensation. Why? Institutional investors, who hold the majority of the stock in publicly held companies in the United States, understand that, in a system of dispersed ownership, executive compensation is probably their most important tool by which to align managerial incentives with share-holder incentives. Throughout the 1960s and 1970s, they had seen senior managements of large corporations manage their firms in a risk-averse and growth-maximizing fashion, retaining 'free cash flow' to the maximum extent possible. Such a style of management produced the bloated, and inefficient conglomerates of that era (for example, Gulf & Western and IT&T). Put simply, a system of exclusively cash compensation creates incentives to avoid risk and bankruptcy and to maximize the size of the firm, regardless of profitability, because a larger firm size generally implies higher cash compensation for its senior managers.

Once the US tax laws and institutional pressure together produced a shift to equity compensation in the 1990s, managers' incentives changed, and managers sought to maximize share value (as the institutions had wanted). But what the institutions failed to anticipate was that there can be too much of a good thing. Aggressive use of these incentives in turn encouraged the use of manipulative techniques to maximize stock price over the short run. Although such spikes may not be sustainable, corporate managers possess asymmetric information, and anticipating their inability to maintain earnings growth, they can exercise their options and bail out.

One measure of this transition is the changing nature of financial irregularities. The Sarbanes-Oxley Act required the SEC to study all its enforcement proceedings over the prior five years (i.e., 1997-2002) to ascertain what kinds of financial and accounting irregularities were the most common. Out of the 227 'enforcement matters' pursued by the SEC over this period, the SEC has reported that 126 (or 55 per cent) alleged 'improper revenue recognition' (SEC 2003: 2). Similarly, the earlier noted GAO Study found that 38 per cent of all restatements in its survey were for revenue recognition timing errors. Either managers were recognizing the next period's revenues prematurely—or managers were simply inventing revenues that did not exist. Both forms of errors suggest that managers were striving to manufacture an artificial (and possibly unsustainable) spike in corporate income.

That managers were able optimistically to predict and prematurely recognize revenues in ways that ultimately compelled earnings restatements shows a market failure—particularly when the market penalty for premature revenue recognition was, as earlier noted, so Draconian as to result in a 25 per cent decline in market price on average.[19] Why did securities analysts accept such optimistic predictions and not discount them? Here, the evidence is that very few analysts downgraded public companies in the months prior to earnings restatements—even though short-sellers and insiders had recognized the likelihood of an earnings restatement.[20] Yet, while analysts and auditors may have been slow to recognize premature revenue recognition, considerable evidence suggests that short sellers were able to recognize the signals and profit handsomely by anticipating earnings restatements (Desai *et al* 2004).[21] The implications of this point are that smart traders could and did do what professional gatekeepers were insufficiently motivated to do: recognize the approach of major market collapses. In short, this is a story of 'gatekeeper failure' in that the professional agents of corporate governance did not adequately serve investors. In consequence, the Sarbanes-Oxley Act of 2002 understandably focused on gatekeepers and contained provisions regulating auditors, securities analysts and credit-rating agencies.

II. FRAUD IN CONCENTRATED OWNERSHIP REGIMES

The pattern in concentrated ownership systems is very different, but not necessarily better. In the case of most European corporations, there is a controlling shareholder or shareholder group. Why is this important? A controlling shareholder does not need to rely on indirect mechanisms of control, such as equity compensation or stock options, in order to incentivize management. Rather, it can rely on a 'command and control' system because, unlike the dispersed shareholders in the United States, it can directly monitor and replace management. Hence, corporate managers have both less discretion to engage in opportunistic earnings management and less motivation to create an earnings spike (because it will not benefit a management not compensated with stock options).

Equally important, the controlling shareholder also has much less interest in the day-to-day stock price of its company. Why? Because the controlling shareholder seldom, if ever, sells its control block into the public market. Rather, if it sells at all, it will make a privately negotiated sale at a substantial premium over the market price to an incoming, new controlling shareholder. Such control premiums are characteristically much higher in Europe than in the United States.[22] As a result, controlling shareholders in Europe do not obsess over the day-to-day market price

---

[19] See text above at note 15.

[20] See Griffin (2002) (reporting study of 847 companies sued in federal securities class actions between 1994 and 2001).

[21] For a similar study, see Efendi *et al* (2005).

[22] See Dyck and Zingales (2004); see also Nanora (2000).

and rationally do not engage in tactics to recognize revenues prematurely to spike their stock price. These two explanations—lesser use of equity compensation and lesser interest in the short-term stock price—explain at least in part why there were less accounting irregularities in Europe than in the United States during the late 1990s.

This generalization may seem subject to counter-examples. For example, some well-known European companies—e.g., Vivendi Universal, Royal Ahold, Skandia Insurance, or Adecco[23]—did experience accounting irregularities. But these are exceptions that prove the rule. All were US listed companies whose accounting problems emanated from US based subsidiaries or that had transformed themselves into American-style conglomerates (the leading example being Vivendi) that either awarded stock options or needed to maximize their short-term stock price in order to make multiple acquisitions.

Potentially, some of this disparity between Europe and the United States could be an artifact of less rigorous regulatory oversight of public companies in Europe or, alternatively, of the lesser litigation risk in Europe. Hence, European issuers might be less willing to restate their financial statements, even when they discovered a past error, because they did not expect regulatory authorities or the plaintiffs' bar to hold them accountable. While true to a point, the less demanding scrutiny given the financial statements of public issuers in Europe (particularly in the secondary market context where securities are not being issued) still does not supply a motor force or an incentive for financial manipulation. Even if European issuers could inflate their financial statements, they had less reason to do so. Finally, financial statement inflation can lead to the ultimate collapse of the corporate issuer when the market eventually discovers the fraud (as Enron and WorldCom illustrate). Here, European examples of similar collapses are conspicuously absent.[24]

Does this analysis imply that European managers are more ethical or

---

[23] Both the financial scandals at Adecco and Royal Ahold originated in the United States and, at least initially, centered around accounting at US subsidiaries. See Simonian (2004); McCoy (2005) (noting that Royal Ahold's accounting problems began at U.S. Foodservices, Inc., a subsidiary of Royal Ahold, where the US managers were compensated with stock options); Vivendi Universal can be described as a US-style acquisitions oriented financial conglomerate. See Johnson (2004).

[24] If one goes back far enough, one can certainly find examples of sudden financial collapse in Europe – for example, Metallgesellschaft in 1994. See Fisher (1995). But more recent examples are largely lacking. Also, Metallgesellschaft's financial distress seems to have been more the product of the negligent mishandling of derivatives than any fraudulent desire to inflate earnings. See also Edwards and Canter (1995). Such accounting scandals as have occurred in Germany – for example, the fraud at Klockner-Humboldt-Deuta or the collapse of the Jurgen Schneider real estate empire – involved longstanding frauds in which assets were overstated and liabilities understated with the apparent acquiescence of both auditors and sometimes the principal lending bank. The monitoring failures in these cases much more closely resemble Parmalat than Enron. Many of these failures are reviewed in Wenger and Kaserer (1998).

that European shareholders are better off than their American counterparts? By no means! Concentrated ownership encourages a different type of financial overreaching: the extraction of private benefits of control. Dyck and Zingales (2004) have shown that the private benefits of control vary significantly across jurisdictions, ranging from –4 per cent to +65 per cent, depending in significant part on the legal protections given minority shareholders.[25] While there is evidence that the market cares about the level of private benefits that controlling shareholders will extract,[26] the market has a relatively weak capacity to discern on a real-time basis what benefits are in fact being expropriated.

In emerging markets, the expropriation of private benefits typically occurs through financial transactions. Ownership may be diluted through public offerings, and then a coercive tender offer or squeeze-out merger is used to force minority shareholders to tender at a price below fair market value. These techniques have been discussed in detail elsewhere and in their crudest forms have been given the epithet 'tunneling' to describe them.[27] A classic example was the Bulgarian experience between 1999 and 2002, when roughly two-thirds of the 1,040 firms on the Bulgarian stock exchange were delisted, following freeze-out tender offers for the minority shares at below market, but still coercive, prices.[28]

In more developed economies, such financial transactions may be precluded. Instead, 'operational' mechanisms can be used: for example, controlling shareholders can compel the company to sell its output to, or buy its raw materials from, a corporation that they independently own. In emerging markets, growing evidence suggests that firms within corporate groups engage in more related party transactions than firms that are not members of a controlled group (see Ming and Wong 2003). In essence, these transactions permit controlling shareholders to transfer resources from companies in which they have lesser cash-flow rights to ones in which they have greater cash flow rights (Bertrand *et al* 2000).

Although it may be tempting to deem 'tunneling' and related opportunistic practices as characteristic only of emerging markets where legal protections are still evolving, considerable evidence suggests that such practices are also prevalent in more 'mature' European economies. Indeed, some students of European corporate governance claim that the dominant form of concentrated ownership (i.e., absolute.majority ownership) is simply inefficient because it permits too much predatory misbehaviour (Kirchmaier and Grant 2004b).

---

[25] See also Nenova (2000).

[26] See Ehrhardt and Nowak (2003).

[27] For the article coining this term, see Johnson *et al* (2000).

[28] See Atanasov *et al* (2005). These authors estimate that these transactions occurred at about 25 per cent of the shares' intrinsic value.

A danger lurks here in seeking to prove too much. If European corporate governance were as vulnerable to opportunistic behavior by controlling shareholders as some critics suggest, then one wonders why minority shareholders would invest at all and why even 'thin' securities markets could survive. Perhaps, the answer is that other actors substitute for the role that gatekeepers play in dispersed ownership legal regimes. For example, some argue that the universal banks, which typically hold large, but non-controlling blocks of stock as well as advancing debt capital, play such a protective role.[29] Others point to the impact of co-determination, which gives labor a major voice in corporate governance in some European countries that it lacks in Anglo-Saxon legal systems.[30] Still others point to cross-monitoring by other blockholders.[31] All these answers encounter problems, which need not be resolved in this brief essay. All that need here be asserted is that there is less reason to believe that gatekeepers – that is, professional agents serving share-holders but selected by the corporation – work as well in concentrated ownership regimes as in dispersed ownership regimes.

To understand this point, it is useful to examine the nature of the scandals that characterize concentrated ownership systems because they reveal a distinct and different pattern of gatekeeper failure. Two recent scandals typify this pattern: Parmalat and Hollinger. Parmalat is the paradigmatic fraud for Europe (just as Enron and WorldCom are the representative frauds in the United States). Parmalat's fraud essentially involved the balance sheet, not the income statement. It failed when a €3.9 billion account with Bank of America proved to be fictitious.[32] At least, $17.4 billion in assets seemed to vanish from its balance sheet. Efforts by its trustee to track down these missing funds appear to have found that at least €2.3 billion were paid to affiliated persons and shareholders.[33] In short, private benefits appear to have siphoned off to controlling shareholders through related party transactions. Unlike the

---

[29] This was once the consensus view. But more recently, skeptics have demonstrated that the universal banks in Germany have few representatives on the supervisory board, tend to do no more monitoring than banks in dispersed ownership regimes, and largely defer to the managing board's decisions. See Edwards and Fischer (1994).

[30] The impact of co-determination on corporate governance has been much debated. See, for example, Roe (1998).

[31] See Gorton and Schmidt (1996) who suggest the role of nonbank blockholders in monitoring the controlling shareholder.

[32] This summary of the Parmalat scandal relies upon the *Wall Street Journal's* account. See Galloni and Reilly (2004).

[33] Galloni and Reilly (2004). Parmalat's former CEO, Mr Tanzi, appears to have acknowledged to Italian prosecutors 'that Parmalat funneled about €500 Million to companies controlled by the Tanzi family, especially to Parmatour.' See Melis (2004: 6). Prosecutors appear to believe that the total diversions to Tanzi family-owned companies were at least €1500 million. *Ibid.*: at 6 note 2.

short-term stock manipulations that occur in the United States, this was a
scandal that had continued for many years, probably for over a decade.

At the heart of the Parmalat fraud, there was also a failure by its
gatekeepers. Parmalat's auditors for many years had been an
American-based firm, Grant Thornton, whose personnel had audited
Parmalat and its subsidiaries since the 1980s (Galloni and Reilly 2004: 10).
Although Italian law uniquely mandated the rotation of audit firms,
Grant Thornton found an easy evasion. It gave up the role of being
auditor to the parent company in the Parmalat family, but continued to
audit its subsidiaries (Galloni and Reilly 2004: 9–10). Among these
subsidiaries was the Cayman Islands-based subsidiary, Boulat Financing
Corporation, whose books showed the fictitious Bank of America account
whose discovery triggered Parmalat's insolvency (Galloni and Reilly
2004: 10).

The recent Hollinger scandal also involved overreaching by
controlling shareholders. Although Hollinger International is a Delaware
corporation, its controlling shareholders were Canadian, as were most of
its shareholders. According to the report prepared by counsel to its
independent directors, former SEC Chairman Richard Breeden, Hollinger
was a 'kleptocracy' (Hollinger 2004: 4). Its controlling shareholders
allegedly siphoned off more than $400 million from Hollinger—or more
than 95 per cent of the company's adjusted net income from 1997 to 2003
(Leonard 2004). On sales of assets by Hollinger, its controlling
shareholders secretly took large side payments, which they directed be
paid to themselves out of the sales proceeds (Leonard 2004). But bad as
the Hollinger case may be, little evidence suggests that Lord Black and
his cronies manipulated earnings through premature revenue
recognition. What this contrast shows is that controlling shareholders
may misappropriate assets, but have much less reason to fabricate
earnings. This does not mean that business ethics are better (or worse)
within a concentrated ownership regime, but only that the *modus operandi*
for fraud is different. The real conclusion is that different systems of
ownership encourage characteristically different styles of fraud.

III. GATEKEEPER FAILURE ACROSS OWNERSHIP REGIMES

Both ownership regimes—dispersed and concentrated—show evidence
of gatekeeper failure. The US/UK system of dispersed ownership is
vulnerable to gatekeepers not detecting inflated earnings, and
concentrated ownership systems fail to the extent that gatekeepers miss
(or at least fail to report) the expropriation of private benefits. A key
difference, of course, is that in dispersed ownership systems the villains
are managers and the victims are shareholders, while, in concentrated

ownership systems, the controlling shareholders overreach minority shareholders.

In turn, this raises the critical issue: can gatekeepers in concentrated ownership systems monitor the controlling shareholder who hires (and potentially can fire) them? Although there clearly have been numerous failures by gatekeepers in dispersed ownership systems, the answer for these systems probably lies in principle in redesigning the governance circuitry within the public corporation so that the gatekeeper does not report to those that it is expected to monitor. Thus, the auditor or attorney can be required to report to an independent audit committee rather than corporate managers. But this same answer does not work as well in a concentrated ownership system. In such a system, even an independent audit committee may serve at the pleasure of a controlling shareholder.

Indeed, some forms of gatekeepers common in dispersed ownership systems seem inherently less likely to be effective in a system of concentrated ownership. For example, the securities analyst is inherently a gatekeeper for dispersed ownership regimes. In concentrated ownership regimes, the volume of stock trading in its thinner capital markets is likely to be insufficient to generate brokerage commissions sufficient to support a profession of analysts covering all publicly-held companies. But even if analyst coverage in concentrated ownership regimes were equivalent to that in dispersed ownership systems, the analyst's predictions of the firm's future earnings or value would still mean less to public shareholders if the controlling shareholder remained in a position to squeeze out the minority shareholders.

Even the role of the auditor differs in a concentrated ownership system. The existence of a controlling shareholder necessarily affects auditor independence. In a dispersed ownership system, corporate managers might sometimes 'capture' the audit partner of their auditor (as seemingly happened at Enron). But the policy answer was obvious (and Sarbanes-Oxley quickly adopted it): rewire the internal circuitry so that the auditor reported to an independent audit committee. However, in a concentrated ownership system, this answer works less well because the auditor is still reporting to a board that is, itself, potentially subservient to the controlling shareholder. Thus, the auditor in this system is a monitor who cannot effectively escape the control of the party that it is expected to monitor. Although diligent auditors could have presumably detected the fraud at Parmalat (at least to the extent of detecting the fictitious bank account at the Cayman Islands' subsidiary), one suspects that they would have likely been dismissed at the point at which they began to monitor earnestly. More generally, auditors can do little to stop squeeze-out mergers, coercive tender offers, or even unfair related party transactions. These require statutory protections if the minority's rights are to be protected. In fairness, shareholders in a concentrated ownership system may receive some protection from other gatekeepers, including the large banks that typically monitor the corporation.

There is an important historical dimension to this point. The independent auditor arose in Britain in the middle nineteenth century, just as industrialization and the growth of railroads was compelling corporations to market their shares to a broader audience of investors.[34] Amendments in 1844 and 1845 to the British Companies Act required an annual statutory audit with the auditor being selected by the shareholders.[35] This made sense, because the auditor was thus placed in a true principal/agent relationship with the shareholders who relied on it. But this same relationship does not exist when the auditor reports to shareholders in a system in which there is a controlling shareholder.

Finally, even if the auditor is asked to report on the fairness of inter-corporate dealings or related party transactions, this is not its core competence. Other protections—such as supermajority votes, mandatory bid requirements, or prophylactic rules—may be far more valuable in protecting minority shareholders when there is a controlling shareholder.

This may explain the slower development of auditing procedures and internal controls in Europe. Potentially, there is a further implication for the use of gatekeepers in concentrated ownership economies. If the controlling shareholder can potentially dominate the selection of the auditor or other gatekeepers, then it becomes at least arguable that if the auditor is to serve as an effective reputational intermediary, it should be selected by the minority shareholders and report to them. This chapter will not attempt to design such an unprecedented system, but will smugly content itself with pointing out the likely inadequacy of alternative systems. The second-best alternative would appear to be according the auditor's selection, retention and compensation to the independent directors.

CONCLUSION

This article's generalizations are not presented as iron laws. 'Private benefits of control' can be misappropriated in a US public company, and recent illustrations include the Tyco and Adelphia scandals. Similarly, companies with dispersed ownership are now common (but still the minority) in Europe. Public policy needs, however, to start from the recognition that dispersed ownership creates managerial incentives to

[34] See Littleton (1988: 260–62).

[35] The 1844 amendment was to the Joint Stock Companies Act, (see 7 & 8 Vict., Ch. 110) (1844), and the 1845 amendment was to the Companies Clauses Consolidation Act (see 8 & 9 Vict., Ch. 16) (1845). For a more detailed review of this legislation, see O'Conner (2004).

manipulate income, while concentrated ownership invites the low-visibility extraction of private benefits. As a result, governance protections that work in one system may fail in the other. Even more importantly, different gatekeepers need to be designed into different governance systems to monitor for different abuses.

REFERENCES

[handwritten margin notes: 1) why not regs in EU? 2) why minority investment?]

Anderson, K.L. and Yohn, T.L. (2002), 'The Effect of 10K Restatements on Firm Value, Information Asymmetries, and Investors' Reliance on Earnings' (http://ssrn.com/abstract = 332380).

Atanasov, V., Ciccotello, C.S., and Gyoshev, S.B. (2005), 'How Does Law Affect Finance? An Empirical Examination of Tunneling in an Emerging Market', William Davidson Institute Working Paper Number 742 (http://ssrn.com/abstract=423506).

Banner, S. (1997), 'What Causes New Securities Regulation? 300 Years of Evidence', 75 *Washington University Law Quarterly* 849–55.

Bertrand, M., Mehta, P., and Mullainathan, S. (2000), 'Ferreting Out Tunneling: An Application to Indian Business Groups', MIT Dept. of Econ. Working Paper No. 00-28 (http://ssrn.com/abstract=246001).

Cheng, Q. and Warfield, T. (2004), 'Equity Incentives and Earnings Management' (http://ssrn.com/abstract=457840).

Coffee, J.C., Jr. (2001), 'The Rise of Dispersed Ownership: The Roles of Law and the State in the Separation of Ownership and Control', 111 *Yale Law Journal* 1–82.

—— (2004a), 'Gatekeeper Failure and Reform: The Challenge of Fashioning Relevant Reforms', 84 *Boston University Law Review* 301–64.

—— (2004b), 'What Caused Enron?: A Capsule Social and Economic History of the 1990s', 89 *Cornell Law Review* 269–309.

Denis, D.J., Hanouna, P., and Sarin, A. (2005), 'Is There a Dark Side to Incentive Compensation?' (http://ssrn.com/abstract=695583).

Desai, H., Krishnamurthy, S., and Venkataraman, K. (2004), 'Do Short Sellers Target Firms with Poor Earnings Quality?: Evidence from Earnings Restatements', (http://ssrn.com/abstract=633283).

Dyck, A. and Zingales, L. (2004), 'Private Benefits of Control: An International Comparison', 59 *Journal of Finance* 537–600.

Edwards, J., and Fischer, K. (1994), *Banks, Finance and Investment in Germany* (Cambridge: Cambridge University Press).

Efendi, J., Kinney, M.R., and Swanson, E.P. (2005), 'Can Short Sellers Predict Accounting Restatements?', AAA 2005 FARS Meeting Paper (http://ssrn.com/abstract=591361).

Efendi, J., Srivastava, A., and Swanson, E. (2004), 'Why Do Corporate Managers Misstate Financial Statements: The Role of Option Compensation, Corporate Governance and Other Factors' (http://ssrn.com/abstract=547920).

Ehrhardt, O. and Nowak, E. (2003), 'Private Benefits and Minority Shareholder

Expropriation (or What Exactly Are Private Benefits of Control)', EFA Annual Conference Paper No. 809, (http://ssrn.com/abstract=423506).

Ferrarini, G., Moloney, N., and Vespro, C. (2003), 'Executive Remuneration in the EU: Comparative Law and Practice' (ECGI Working Paper No. 09/2003).

FitchRatings (2005), 'Accounting and Financial Reporting Risk: 2005 Global Outlook,' 14 March.

Galloni, A. and Reilly, D. (2004), 'How Parmalat Spent and Spent', *Wall Street Journal*, 23 July.

GAO (2002), US Gen. Accounting Office, Pub. No. 03-138, *Financial Statement Restatements: Trends, Market Impacts, Regulatory Responses and Remaining Challenges* (Washington, D.C.: GAO).

Gorton, G., and Schmid, F. (1996), 'Universal Banking and the Performance of German Firms', National Bureau of Economic Research Working Paper No. 5453.

Griffin, P.A. (2002), 'A League of Their Own? Financial Analysts' Responses to Restatements and Corrective Disclosures' (http://ssrn.com/abstract=326581).

Hall, B.J. (2003), 'Six Challenges in Designing Equity-Based Pay', 15 *Accenture Journal of Applied Corporate Finance* 21–33.

Hollinger International (2004), 'Report of Investigation by the Special Committee of the Board of Directors of Hollinger International Inc'. (30 August), at 4.

Holmstrom, B. and Kaplan, S. (2003), 'The State of U.S. Corporate Governance: What's Right and What's Wrong', 15 *Accenture Journal of Applied Corporate Finance* 8–20.

Huron Consulting Group (2003a), 'An Analysis of Restatement Matters: Rules, Errors, Ethics, for the Five Years Ended December 31, 2002'.

—— (2003b), 'Annual Review of Financial Reporting Matters'.

—— (2005), Press Release, 'New Report by Huron Consulting Group Reveals Financial Restatements Increased at a Record Level in 2004' (19 January).

Johnson, J. (2004), 'Vivendi Probe Ends With Euro $1 Million Fine for Messier', *Financial Times*, 8 December at p. 31.

Johnson, S., La Porta, R., Lopez-de-Silanes, F., and Schleifer, A. (2000), 'Tunneling', 90 *American Economic Review* 22–7.

Johnson, S.A., Ryan, H.E., and Tian, Y.S. (2003), 'Executive Compensation and Corporate Fraud' (http://ssrn.com/abstract=395960).

Joint Stock Companies Act, (United Kingdom) (1844).

Kirchmaier, T. and Grant, J. (2004a), 'Financial Tunneling and the Revenge of the Insider System: How to Circumvent the New European Corporate Governance Legislation', (http://ssrn.com/abstract=613945).

—— (2004b), 'Corporate Ownership Structure and Performance in Europe', CEP Discussion Paper No. 0631 (http://ssrn.com/abstract=616201).

La Porta, R., Lopez-de-Silanes, F., Shleifer, A., and Vishny, R. (1999), 'Corporate Ownership Around the World', 54 *Journal of Finance* 471–517.

Leonard, D. (2004), 'More Trials for Lord Black', *Fortune*, 4 October, 42.

Littleton, A.C. (1988), *Accounting Evolution to 1900* (Tuscaloosa: University of Alabama Press).

McCoy, K. (2005), 'Prosecutors Charge Nine More in Royal Ahold Case', *USA Today*, 14 January, 1B.

Melis, A. (2004), 'Corporate Governance Failures. To What Extent is Parmalat a Particularly Italian Case?' (30 Sept. 2004) (http://ssrn.com/abstract=563223).

Ming, J.J. and Wong, T.J. (2003), 'Earnings Management and Tunneling through Related Party Transactions: Evidence from Chinese Corporate Groups', EAA 2003 Annual Conference Paper No. 549 (http://ssrn.com/abstract=42488).

Morgenson, G. (2004), 'Explaining (Or Not) Why the Boss Is Paid So Much', *New York Times*, 25 January , §3, 1.

Moriarty, G.B. and Livingston, P.B. (2001), 'Quantitative Measures of the Quality of Financial Reporting', *Financial Executive* (July/August) 53–4.

Nenova, T. (2000), 'The Value of Corporate Votes and Control Benefits: A Cross-Country Analysis', (http://ssrn.com/abstract=237809).

O'Conner, S.M. (2004), 'Be Careful What You Wish For: How Accountants and Congress Created the Problem of Auditor Independence', 45 *Boston College Law Review* 741–828.

Peng L. and Roell, A. (2004), 'Executive Pay, Earnings Manipulation and Shareholder Litigation' AFA Philadelphia Meetings (http://ssrn.com/abstract=488148).

Richardson, S., Tuna, I., and Wu, M. (2002), 'Predicting Earnings Management: The Case of Earnings Restatements' (http://ssrn.com/abstract=338681).

Roe, M.J. (1998), 'German Co-determination and German securities Markets', 1 *Columbia Business Law Review* 167–183.

SEC (2003), *Securities and Exchange Commission, Report Pursuant to Section 704 of the Sarbanes-Oxley Act of 2002* (Washington, D.C.: Securities and Exchange Commission).

Simonian, H. (2004), 'Europe's First Victim of Sarbanes-Oxley? Corporate Governance: Adecco was pilloried for its poor handling of U.S. Accounting Problems', *Financial Times*, 29 January, 14.

Part III
Evaluating Regulatory Responses:
The US and UK

7

The Case for Shareholder Access to the Ballot

LUCIAN ARYE BEBCHUK[*]

T HE SECURITIES AND Exchange Commission (SEC) last spring began a process of considering changes in the proxy rules that would require companies, under certain circumstances, to include in their proxy materials shareholder-nominated candidates for the board. Following an initial round of public comments, the SEC's Division of Corporation Finance recommended that the Commission propose for public comment rules that would provide such shareholder access (SEC 2003: 32–33). Although most of the comments received thus far by the SEC have been in favour of reform, The Business Roundtable, other business associations, and prominent corporate law firms and bar groups, have all expressed opposition to shareholder access.[1] Martin Lipton and

[*] William J. Friedman and Alicia Townsend Friedman Professor of Law, Economics, and Finance, Harvard Law School; Research Associate, National Bureau of Economic Research. This paper builds on the comment letter that I sent to the SEC on the subject of possible changes in the proxy rules (Bebchuk 2003a). I am grateful to Bob Clark, Marcel Kahan, Bob Pozen, B.J. Trach, and members of the Harvard corporate governance group for helpful discussions and suggestions. I also wish to thank Fred Pollock, Rob Maynes, and Wei Yu for their research assistance, and the John M. Olin Center for Law, Economics, and Business for its financial support. This chapter was previously published in (2003) 59 *Business Lawyer* 43–66. The permission of the American Bar Association to republish is gratefully acknowledged.

The chapter was largely finalized before the SEC's recent adoption of a formal rule proposal. In writing it, I therefore focused on analyzing the basic pros and cons of the shareholder access regime considered in the Commission's initial release and in the subsequent report of the SEC staff. I added in footnotes commenting on the concretization in the formal rule proposal of the triggering event idea generally put forward in the staff report.

[1] All letter comments are available at http://www.sec.gov/rules/other/s7103.shtml (last visited 2 Aug. 2005). Law firms and lawyer groups writing in opposition of shareholder access include the Association of the Bar of the City of New York (NYC Bar); the New York State Bar Association (NY Bar); the American Corporate Counsel Association (ACCA); Sullivan & Cromwell; and Wachtell, Lipton, Rosen, and Katz (Wachtell, Lipton). A comment letter that provided a detailed analysis of the different options, but refrained from taking a position, was submitted by the Task Force on Shareholder Proposal, American Bar Association (ABA) Section of Business Law. See NYC Bar (2002).

Steven Rosenblum put forward a forceful statement of the main concerns and objections expressed by opponents of shareholder access (Lipton and Rosenblum 2003). This chapter seeks to put forward the case for shareholder access and to address the wide range of objections raised by its opponents.

I begin by discussing why corporate elections need invigoration and how providing shareholder access would be a moderate step toward this goal. The main part of this chapter then examines in detail each of the objections that opponents of shareholder access have put forward. I conclude that they do not provide a good basis for opposing shareholder access. I also point out that the available empirical evidence is supportive of such reform. After concluding that the case for shareholder access is strong, I suggest that it would be desirable and important to adopt additional measures to make shareholders' power to replace directors meaningful.

I. THE NEED FOR INVIGORATING CORPORATE ELECTIONS

The recent corporate governance crisis highlighted the importance of good board performance. Reforming corporate elections would improve the selection of directors and the incentives they face. Some supporters of shareholder access have 'shareholder voice' and 'corporate democracy' as objectives. But the case for shareholder access does not depend on having such. My analysis below will focus on the sole objective of effective corporate governance that enhances corporate value. From this perspective, increased shareholder power or participation would be desirable if and only if such a change would improve corporate performance and value.[2]

The identities and incentives of directors are extremely important because the corporate law system leaves, and must leave, a great deal of discretion in their hands. Directors make or approve important decisions, and courts defer to these decisions. Among other things, directors have the power to block high-premium acquisition offers, as well as to set the compensation (and thus shape the incentives) of the firm's top executives.

How can we ensure that directors use their power well? In the structure of our corporate law, shareholder power to replace directors is supposed to provide an important safety valve. 'If the shareholders are displeased with the action of their elected representatives,' stresses the Delaware Supreme Court in *Unocal*, 'the powers of corporate democracy

---

[2] The objective of improved corporate performance (rather than increased shareholder voice) is one that my analysis shares with Lipton and Rosenblum (2003). We reach different conclusions, however, on whether shareholder access would serve this objective.

are at their disposal to turn the board out.'[3] In theory, if directors fail to serve shareholders, or if they appear to lack the qualities necessary for doing so, shareholders have the power to replace them. This shareholder power, in turn, provides incumbent directors with incentives to serve shareholders well, making directors accountable. As Chancellor Allen observed, '[t]he shareholder franchise is the ideological underpinning upon which the legitimacy of directorial power rests.'[4]

But the safety valve is missing. Although shareholder power to replace directors is supposed to be an important element of our corporate governance system, it is largely a myth. Attempts to replace directors are extremely rare, even in firms that systematically under perform over a long period of time. By and large, directors nominated by the company run unopposed and their election is thus guaranteed. The key for a director's re-election is remaining on the firm's slate. Whether the nomination committee is controlled by the Chief Executive Officer (CEO) or by independent directors, incentives to serve the interests of those making nominations are not necessarily identical with incentives to maximize shareholder value.

To be sure, shareholders who are displeased with their board can nominate director candidates and then solicit proxies for them. The costs and difficulties involved in running such a proxy contest, however, make such contests quite rare. The initiation of contests is severely discouraged by a 'public good' problem: those who run a proxy contest have to bear the costs themselves, but they would capture only a fraction of the corporate governance benefits that a successful contest would produce (Clark 1986: 390–96).[5]

Some opponents of shareholder access rely on the fact that, as the data put together by Georgeson Shareholder (2002) indicates, there were about forty cases of contested proxy solicitations in 2002 (Wachtell, Lipton 2003).[6] But a large fraction of the contests that year, as in preceding years, were conducted in the context of an acquisition attempt. Hostile bidders, for example, sometimes run a competing slate in order to overcome incumbents' opposition to an acquisition. Because hostile bidders have an interest in acquiring the target, the public good problem does not apply to them in the same way that it applies to challengers that seek to improve the firm's performance as a stand-alone entity.

I recently started a study of the cases of contested solicitations in the seven-year period 1996–2002, and the study's preliminary findings are

---

[3] See *Unocal Corp. v Mesa Petroleum Co.*, 493 A. 3d 946 (Del. 1985).

[4] *Blasius Industries, Inc., v Atlas Corp.*, 564 A.2d 651, 659 (Del. Ch. 1988).

[5] See Bebchuk and Kahan (1990: 1088–96). See also Bebchuk (2003b: 62–64) (Sarah Teslik, executive director of the Council for Institutional Investors, describes how the costs of launching a proxy contest discourage challenges).

[6] A list of all the cases of contested solicitation in 2002 is provided in Georgeson (2002).

provided in Table 1.[7] As the table indicates, the majority of the contested solicitations did not involve attempts to replace the board with a new team that would run the firm differently. About a quarter of the cases did not involve the choice of directors at all, but rather other matters such as proposed bylaw amendments. Among the cases that did focus on elections for directors, a majority involved a fight over a possible sale of the company or over a possible opening or restructuring of a closed-end fund. Contests over the team that would run the (stand-alone) firm in the future occurred in about 80 companies, among the thousands that are publicly traded, during the seven-year period 1996–2002.[8]

Furthermore, the firms in which the considered contests occurred were rather small. Of the firms in which such contests occurred, only ten firms had a market capitalization exceeding $200 million. The incidence of such contests for firms with a market capitalization exceeding $200 million was hence rather small—less than two a year on average.

Table 1: Contested Solicitations 1996–2002

Year	Contested Solicitations	Contests Not Over Election of Directors	Director Contests over Sale, Acquisition, or Closed-End Fund Restructuring	Director Contests Over Alternate Management Team
2002	38	5	19	14
2001	40	8	16	16
2000	30	6	17	7
1999	30	10	7	13
1998	20	1	6	13
1997	29	12	12	5
1996	28	11	8	9
Total	215	53	85	77

[7] See Bebchuk (2005). The starting point of the study was the data put together by Georgeson Shareholder (2000) listing all the contested solicitation cases in these seven years. Documents filed with the SEC and available on EDGAR were then examined to determine the subject of the contested solicitation and the characteristics of the target company. I am grateful to Rob Maynes and Fred Pollock for their research assistance help with this project.

[8] Because of the unavailability of some documents on EDGAR, it has not been possible thus far to classify six contests: four in 1996, one in 1998, and one in 1999. To be conservative, they were counted as contests over the team that will run the company as a stand-alone entity.

Maybe this
don't
want
+.((

Thus, the safety valve of potential ouster *via* the ballot is currently not working. In the absence of an attempt to acquire the company, the prospect of being removed in a proxy contest is far too remote to provide directors with incentives to serve shareholders. Confronting poorly performing directors with a non-negligible risk of ouster by shareholders would produce such incentives. Determining the optimal magnitude of the removal threat, and the optimal incidence of challenges to incumbent directors, is difficult. But there are strong reasons to doubt that this incidence is practically zero. The case for at least making the electoral threat viable, rather than negligible, is strong.

II. THE MODERATE PROPOSAL OF SHAREHOLDER ACCESS

Under the shareholder access regime being considered, companies would have to include candidates nominated by qualified shareholders in the proxy materials sent to shareholders prior to the annual meeting. Thus, the materials sent by the firm to voting shareholders would sometimes give them a choice between candidates nominated by the board and one or more candidates nominated by qualified shareholders. By making it unnecessary for shareholder nominees to incur the expenses associated with sending materials to shareholders and obtaining proxies from them, this access to the 'proxy machinery' would make it easier for shareholders to elect candidates other than those proposed by incumbent directors.

The proposal is a moderate step in the direction of invigorating elections. Indeed, as I explain below, stronger measures would be worth adopting. Several features combine to make the proposal a moderate step. First, the proposal would only apply to attempts to elect a minority of directors (a short slate). Secondly, even for such attempts, the proposal could reduce but would not eliminate the costs involved in an effective campaign for a shareholder-nominated candidate.

Thirdly, the proposal would limit access to the proxy machinery to 'qualified' shareholders or groups of shareholders that meet certain minimum ownership and holding requirements. Supporters of the shareholder access proposal suggest minimum ownership requirements, such as 3 per cent to 5 per cent, which could vary with firm size. The aim of these requirements is to screen nominations and allow only those whose support among shareholders is sufficient to indicate significant dissatisfaction with the incumbent directors. To this end, one could also disqualify shareholders who nominated a short slate that failed to get a certain set threshold of support (say, 25 per cent) from nominating another short slate for a certain period of time.

In addition, the SEC staff raised in its report a possible refinement of the access proposal that would further moderate a shareholder access regime (SEC 2003a). Qualified shareholders could be permitted to nominate a candidate only after the occurrence of 'triggering events' that suggest the need for shareholder nomination. Triggering events could include the approval of a shareholder proposal to activate the shareholder access rule or some other event indicating widespread dissatisfaction among shareholders.[9]

Requiring a triggering event would further moderate the effects of a shareholder access rule by limiting shareholder nominations to instances in which there is already strong evidence of widespread shareholder dissatisfaction. It would also provide boards with ample time to address shareholder concerns before shareholder nominations can be made.

Indeed, such a 'triggering events' requirement might make an access rule too weak in some cases. Suppose that, shortly after the annual election of a given company, substantial shareholder dissatisfaction arose due to certain board actions or disclosures. In such a case, if a triggering event in the form of prior shareholder vote were required, it would take two annual elections until a shareholder nominee could be elected to the board. The delay could significantly reduce the rule's effectiveness in facilitating desirable replacements quickly, as well as in supplying directors with incentives to serve shareholders. Indeed, such delay could make the rule ineffective in some of the cases where shareholder intervention might be most necessary.

Thus, if a triggering event were to be established, it would be worthwhile to provide a safety valve. In particular, it would be desirable to allow shareholder nomination even in the absence of a triggering event if support for the nomination exceeds an ownership threshold that is significantly higher than the threshold for nominations applying after the occurrence of a triggering event.[10]

It should be emphasized that the setting of threshold requirements for shareholder nominations would provide the SEC with a tool for ensuring that shareholder access works well. After the initial setting of the threshold, the SEC will subsequently be able to increase or lower the thresholds in light of the evidence. For example, if the ownership

---

[9] The formal rule proposal released by the SEC after this chapter was largely finalized proposes two triggering events: (i) a shareholder proposal (submitted pursuant to Rule 14a-8) to subject the company to a shareholder access regime wins a majority of the votes cast, and (ii) at least one of the board's nominees for directors receives 'withhold' votes from 35 per cent or more of the votes cast. See SEC (2003b).

[10] The formal proposal just released by the SEC proposes a threshold of 5 per cent ownership. See SEC (2003b). If this threshold were set for cases in which a triggering event occurred, it could also be established that a shareholder nomination could be made even without the prior occurrence of a triggering event if supported by, say, shareholders owning together 10–15 per cent of the company's stock.

threshold set initially were to produce a substantial incidence of nominations that fail to attract significant support in the annual meeting, the SEC would be able to raise the threshold to reduce the incidence of such challenges. The use of ownership thresholds that can be adjusted as experience accumulates, and the possible addition of a triggering event requirement, contribute to making the shareholder access proposal a rather moderate measure with relatively little risk.

Although the shareholder access proposal would be a rather moderate step in a beneficial direction, any introduction of shareholder access would constitute a significant departure from incumbents' long-standing control of the proxy machinery. Thus, the access proposal has naturally attracted some strong opposition. Below I consider each of the objections that have been raised by critics to determine whether any of them provides a reasonable basis for opposing shareholder access.

III. CLAIMS THAT INDEPENDENT NOMINATING COMMITTEES MAKE SHAREHOLDER ACCESS UNNECESSARY

Opponents of shareholder access argue that it is unnecessary because shareholders already have, or will soon have, substantial power to advance the candidacy of directors they support. In particular, they stress shareholders' ability to propose candidates to the firm's nominating committee (Business Roundtable 2003). This possibility, they argue, is especially important because pending stock exchange requirements would require all future nominating committees to be staffed exclusively by independent directors. Such committees, so the argument goes, would be open to shareholder input. Indeed, some critics of shareholder access suggest that, at most, concern about nominations should lead to the adoption of rules that encourage nominating committees to give adequate consideration to shareholder suggestions (Georgeson 2003: 3).

The critical question, of course, is whether nominating committees made of independent directors can be relied upon to nominate outside candidates whenever doing so would enjoy widespread support among shareholders. The answer to this question clearly depends on the directors' incentives and inclinations. By themselves, requirements that nominating committees comply with certain procedures or publish reports about their considerations can have only a limited effect.

Even if one accepts that nominating committees made of independent directors would do the right thing in many or most cases, independent nominating committees would not obviate the need for a safety valve. Director independence is not a magical cure-all. The independence of directors from the firm's executives does not imply that the directors are dependent on shareholders or otherwise induced to focus solely on shareholder interests.

Even assuming that the independence of the directors serving on the nominating committee would often lead to nomination decisions that would be best for shareholders, there would likely be some nominating committees that would fail to make desirable replacements of incumbent directors. Such failures might arise from private interest in self-perpetuation, because of cognitive dissonance tendencies to avoid admitting failure, or for other reasons. As long as such cases could occur, the safety valve of shareholder access would be beneficial.

Indeed, the cases in which shareholder access is needed are especially likely to be cases in which we cannot rely solely on the independence of the nominating committee. Suppose that there is a widespread concern among shareholders that a board with a majority of independent directors is failing to serve shareholder interests. It is precisely under such circumstances that the nominating committee cannot be relied on to make desirable replacements of members of the board or even of members of the committee itself—at least not unless shareholders have adequate means of applying pressure on the committee.

Having the possibility of shareholder nominations in the background might improve the performance of nomination committees. The threat of shareholder nomination of director candidates might induce the nomination committee to take shareholder suggestions seriously in those circumstances in which such shareholder-nominated candidates would be in a position to attract substantial support. In such a case, although a shareholder nomination might not actually take place, the possibility of shareholder nomination would play a beneficial role. The existence of an independent nominating committee, in short, does not at all obviate the need for shareholder access. Such access would not be made unnecessary, but rather would nicely complement the future operation of independent nominating committees.

IV. CLAIMS THAT SHAREHOLDER ACCESS WOULD HAVE NO PRACTICAL EFFECTS

Opponents of shareholder access also argue that, even assuming that at present shareholders have little practical ability to replace directors, shareholder access would not change this reality. A shareholder access regime, it is argued, would not lead to the election of shareholder-nominated directors because it would not eliminate the costs of running a dissident slate and institutional investors tend to be passive (ABA 2003: 11).[11]

Most money managers indeed cannot be expected to initiate or to sponsor a dissident slate. As Robert Pozen explains in an earlier work (Pozen 1994: 140) and more recently, mutual funds are at most 'reluctant activists' (Pozen 2003: 95). Among other things, money managers would not wish to devote management time to a contest over one firm's governance because they focus on trading and portfolio management, and they would wish to avoid any risk of litigation or company retaliation.

It is reasonable to expect, however, that when other shareholders nominate a dissident short slate whose success would likely raise share value, such money managers would vote for this slate. The past voting patterns of private money managers indicate that they commonly do not vote against management on social issues, but they do occasionally vote against management on takeover issues when management appears to be value-decreasing. This pattern indicates that, although shareholder access would not lead to the election of shareholder-nominated directors who run on a social agenda or represent special interests, it would occasionally lead to the election of such directors when incumbents' performance is especially poor and the election of these directors holds the promise of an increase in shareholder value.

It is important to stress that the benefits of a shareholder access regime should not be measured by the number of shareholder-nominated directors that would be elected. Most benefits can be expected to arise without shareholder nominations actually taking place. The benefits would arise chiefly from the effect that shareholders' greater power would have on the incentives of directors and nominating committees.

Finally, suppose that shareholder access would have only a small or even negligible effect on the viability of an electoral challenge and thus on the accountability of incumbents. Such a conclusion could justify consideration of more expansive reforms of corporate elections. It could not, however, provide a basis for some critics' strong opposition to the proposal. If shareholder access would not noticeably change the current reality in which directors face a negligible threat of removal, there is no reason to be fiercely opposed to it. To provide a basis for strong opposition, opponents must show that shareholder access, rather than being practically insignificant, would have significant practical consequences that would be undesirable overall. I now turn to arguments that shareholder access would have significant costs.

[11] The ABA letter states that '[n]ew mechanisms to increase on a routine basis shareholder participation in director selection will not be worth their costs because they will not likely result in significant numbers of shareholder-nominated directors being elected.'

V. POTENTIAL COSTS FROM THE OCCURRENCE OF CONTESTS

It is useful to distinguish between two types of costs that shareholder access could produce. One type, which I will discuss later on, would arise if shareholder-nominated directors were in fact elected. The other type, with which I shall begin, would arise from the mere occurrence of contests regardless of the outcome. Opponents of shareholder access name two ways in which the existence of contests would generate costs: (i) disruption and waste of resources caused by contested elections; and (ii) discouragement of potentially good directors from serving.

A. Disruption and Diversion of Resources

Critics paint a picture in which shareholder access would lead to a large-scale disruption of corporate management. They warn that, with shareholder access, contested elections would become the norm (NYC Bar 2003: 4). Each contested election, in turn, would be 'a tremendously disruptive event for [the] company' (Lipton and Rosenblum 2003: 83). Threatened managers and directors would launch 'a full-scale election contest, at least from the company's side, replete with multiple mailings, institutional investor road shows and full page newspaper fight letters' (ABA 2003: 11). Such contests would require the company to incur substantial out-of-pocket costs, wasting company resources. More importantly, they would divert management's effort and attention. The produced system of wide-scale elections, critics argue, 'would be very unhealthy for our nation's companies' (Wachtell, Lipton 2003: 2).

There is no reason, however, to expect full-scale contests to become the norm. Indeed, under a well-designed access regime, full-scale contests that attract much attention from incumbents would occur only in a small minority of companies, where performance would likely be poor and shareholder dissatisfaction widespread.

To begin, in companies that would be adequately governed without widespread dissatisfaction among shareholders, the election of the company's slate would be secure even if a qualified shareholder or shareholder group were to nominate a short slate. The past voting patterns of institutional investors clearly indicate that their voting *en masse* against management is the exception, occurring only in the presence of some strong reasons for doing so, rather than the norm. A shareholder nomination of a short slate, without broad shareholder dissatisfaction resulting from a poor record, would hardly require management to engage in a 'full-scale' election effort.

Let us suppose, however, that the mere nomination of a short slate, no matter how slim its chances of success, would lead management to make a significant campaigning effort. The considered concern would still be warranted, because a well-designed access regime would not produce shareholder nomination in most companies. The threshold requirements for making a nomination—as initially set and subsequently adjusted after experience is obtained—would ensure that shareholder nominations would not, as critics warn, become the norm.

Clearly, the incidence of shareholder nominations would depend on the threshold requirements set. Even in the absence of a triggering event requirement, a meaningful ownership requirement could substantially limit the incidence of contests. To be sure, if the requirements were set at a trivial level of ownership, nominations would likely become the norm. The higher the threshold, however, the lower the expected incidence of nominations. Indeed, if the minimum ownership required for nomination were set high enough, nominations would be exceedingly rare or even non-existent, and contests would remain as rare as they have been in the past.

If 0 per cent would open the gates too much, and 50 per cent would leave them practically closed, there would likely be some intermediate level of ownership requirement at which contests would become more frequent but would remain far from being the norm. And if the SEC's initial setting of the threshold level turned out to produce too many contests, it could simply be raised. Furthermore, if shareholder access were conditioned on a prior majority vote in favor of it, the incidence of shareholder nomination would be quite limited even if the ownership threshold for making nominations were placed at a low level.

Note that the small number of companies in which contests would occur in any given year would not be randomly drawn from the set of all companies. Rather, they would likely be companies with high shareholder dissatisfaction and sub-par performance. Although contests would of course involve some costs, these costs would be a price worth paying for a process that could improve corporate governance in companies where such improvement might well be needed.

To concretize the above discussion, there is no reason to assume that shareholder access would necessarily raise the incidence of contested elections (outside the acquisition context) from negligible (even among poorly performing firms) to pervasive across all firms. Suppose that the incidence of such elections would go up from practically non-existent to, say, fifty or 100 a year, about 0.5 per cent to 1 per cent of the publicly-traded firms, with those 100 presumably concentrated among the companies with the greatest and most widespread dissatisfaction. The presence of such elections would also have an effect in a large number of other companies, where nomination committees would be more attentive to shareholders, but without any contest occurring. Thus, in such a state of affairs, which an appropriate design of the shareholder access rule could produce, the disruption and resource diversion from the running of campaigns would be quite limited.

In short, critics concerned about contested elections becoming the norm should, at most, focus on ensuring that threshold requirements are set at levels that would not produce contests on a wide-scale basis. They should not argue for maintaining the current state of affairs in which such contests are practically non-existent outside the takeover context. This concern thus cannot justify a general objection to shareholder access.

Finally, and importantly, it should be stressed that the occurrence of actual contests in a small number of instances would hardly imply that the benefits of a shareholder access would be limited to this small number of companies. The presence of the shareholder access option might well operate to improve the selection and incentives of directors in many companies. Thus, while the costs and disruption from actual contests would be limited to a small number of cases each year, the benefits of having the shareholder access option would be system-wide.

B. Deterring Potential Directors from Serving

The occurrence of elections, opponents of shareholder access also argue, might deter some potentially good directors from serving on boards of publicly-traded companies (Lipton and Rosenblum 2003: 86–87). Shareholder access, it is argued, 'would dissuade from board service individuals who would be excellent directors but who are not prepared to stand for election in a contested election' (ABA 2003: 21).[12] Critics suggest that the increase in time commitment required by the Sarbanes-Oxley Act[13] already makes it 'more difficult for many companies to find well-qualified individuals willing to commit the time required to serve as a director,' and that shareholder access 'would likely exacerbate the retention and recruitment problem, resulting in an even smaller pool of well-qualified individuals willing to serve on corporate boards' (NYC Bar 2002: 6).

Clearly, any position would be more attractive (and, other things being equal, easier to fill) if the holder of the position were to be given complete security from removal. Firms elect not to grant most employees such security, however, even though doing so might well attract more job seekers and reduce the required level of compensation. In most cases, employers find that the benefits of retaining the power to replace

[12] See also NYC Bar (2002: 6) ('An Access Proposal ... is likely to create a disincentive for able candidates to seek, and for current members to continue with, board service.').
[13] Pub. L. No. 107-204, 116 Stat. 745 (2002).

employees—the ability to make desirable replacements and the provision of incentives to perform well—exceed its costs.

Because directors' use of their power and discretion can have major effects on corporate value, improving their selection and incentives is especially valuable. Thus, if shareholder access would improve director selection and incentives, that consideration should be given the most weight. Is there really no way to run the corporate system without the people at the very top of the pyramid not facing any risk of removal?

Note that, even with shareholder access, directors would face a rather small likelihood of removal relative to holders of other positions in the business world. Thus, it is far from clear that shareholder access would reduce the attractiveness of the well-paid and highly prestigious positions of directors. Even if shareholder access did make these positions somewhat less attractive, shareholders would be better off countering this effect with increased pay rather than with reduced accountability. Providing directors with complete job security as a means of attracting directors would be counterproductive.

VI. CLAIMS THAT SHAREHOLDER ACCESS WOULD PRODUCE WORSE BOARDS

I have thus far considered arguments that, regardless of the outcome, the mere existence of contests would harm companies and their shareholders. Critics also claim that, in those instances in which shareholder-nominated candidates would in fact be elected, additional costs would be imposed. In particular, critics claim that the election of shareholder-nominated candidates would (i) bring into the board 'special interest directors;' (ii) produce directors that would be less qualified and well chosen than the company-nominated candidates; and (iii) produce balkanized and dysfunctional boards.

A. 'Special Interest' Directors

Critics of shareholder access worry that it would facilitate the election of 'special interest' directors (NYC Bar 2002: 4–5; Lipton and Rosenblum 2003: 82–83). Although the candidates chosen by the company would act in the best interests of all shareholders, it is argued, those nominated by shareholders would be commonly committed to advance the views, social or otherwise, of a small fraction of shareholders.

Shareholder-nominated directors, however, would not be elected without majority support. To be sure, if a group with a special interest had enough shares, it could nominate a candidate. But such a candidate would have no meaningful chance of obtaining the majority of votes necessary to be elected. Given the tendency of most money managers to support management and have their sole focus on shareholder value, a special interest candidate would not be able to attract their votes.

In considering the concern about special interest directors, it is important to distinguish between the shareholder access regime and cumulative voting. With cumulative voting, a special interest candidate that appeals only to a minority of the shareholders might be elected. Shareholder access, however, would not represent any departure from a majoritarian approach to filling each and every slot on the board. Unlike cumulative voting, shareholder access would not enable any candidate to be elected without a majority support among shareholders.

It might be argued that, even if elected by a majority of the shareholders, shareholder-nominated directors would serve the interests of the group that nominated them because they would wish to be renominated (NY State Bar 2003). Interestingly, opponents making this argument are not willing to rely on the fact that elected directors have a fiduciary duty to serve the company and all of its shareholders—a fact to which they give much weight when assessing board nominations. In any event, to the extent that this issue is a significant concern, it could be addressed by stipulating that a shareholder-nominated candidate who was elected would appear automatically on the ballot in the next election. This provision would not ensure, of course, that this director would be re-elected. But it would ensure that the director's re-election would depend solely on how his contribution would be assessed by the majority of shareholders.

Finally, some critics believe that our experience with shareholder resolutions under Rule 14a-8 indicates that shareholder access would produce special interest directors (Lipton and Rosenblum 2003: 83). Because special interest groups dominate the Rule 14a-8 arena, it is argued, they are also likely to play a central role in the nomination of directors. This inference, however, is unwarranted. Experience with shareholder resolutions indicates that resolutions that focus on social or special interest issues uniformly fail to gain a majority, receiving little support from mutual funds. The only resolutions that gain such support are those motivated by enhancing share value through dismantling takeover defenses. This experience confirms the view that shareholder access would not lead to the election of special interest directors.

Indeed, our experience with Rule 14a-8 resolutions does not even suggest that special interest directors would often run under a shareholder access regime. The resolutions that focus on social or special interest issues have been commonly brought by groups with a very small ownership percentage, which would not qualify under the more demanding ownership requirements contemplated for shareholder nominations.

B. Bad Choices

Critics also argue that shareholder-nominated directors would not be as well-qualified as candidates selected by the board. Shareholder-nominated candidates, it is argued, would not be as well chosen as candidates selected by the board. Instead, shareholders would nominate candidates lacking the necessary qualifications and quality, candidates who 'would not likely be nominated by an incumbent board in the exercise of its fiduciary duties' (NYC Bar 2002: 5). The following concern expressed by The Business Roundtable (2003: 3) is typical:

> For instance, a nominating committee may determine to seek out a board candidate who has desired industry or financial expertise .... However, as a result of shareholder access to the company proxy statement, such a candidate might fail to be elected because of the election of a shareholder-nominated director who does not possess such expertise.

Some critics also worry that the election of shareholder-nominated candidates would lead to the company's non-compliance with various legal arrangements (e.g., NYSE or NASDAQ requirements to have a majority of independent directors). This particular problem could presumably be addressed by allowing the company not to include in the proxy materials candidates whose election would lead to company non-compliance with governing rules and listing arrangements. But the raising of this concern reflects critics' belief that shareholders electing a shareholder-nominated candidate would likely be making bad (or even stupid) choices.

Although opponents of shareholder access have little confidence in shareholder choices, they place a great deal of confidence in the choices made by nominating committees. One main reason given for this confidence is that independent directors have a fiduciary duty running to all shareholders. They can therefore be trusted to make the right choices, it is argued, unlike nominating shareholders who do not have the same duty to act in the best interests of the other shareholders of the corporation (Sullivan & Cromwell 2003: 3).

The question, however, is not whether nominating committees or qualified shareholders are better at selecting candidates. Granting that the former would commonly do a better job does not resolve the issue at hand. A shareholder-nominated candidate would be elected only with the support of a majority of the shareholders. Thus, the question is whether shareholders should ever be given a chance to prefer a shareholder-nominated candidate over a board-nominated candidate. There is little reason to expect that, in those occasions in which a majority of shareholders would choose a shareholder nominee over a board nominee, they would generally be making a mistake. As the US Supreme Court stated in *Basic Inc., v Levinson*, management should not 'attribute to investors a child-like simplicity.'[14]

First of all, if anyone has an interest to make choices that would be in the best interests of shareholders, the shareholders do. Even if nominating committees can be relied on to be solely concerned with shareholder interests most of the time, it is also possible that they would occasionally be influenced by other considerations. Accountability is important because the interests of an agent and principal do not always fully overlap. Shareholders, by definition, will always have an incentive to make choices that would serve shareholders.

Putting aside incentives, what about ability? Some critics stress that boards have better information and skills for selecting candidates for the board than do institutional shareholders (Lipton and Rosenblum 2003: 77). Assuming this to be the case, however, does not imply that shareholders should not have the option to choose differently from what the board recommends. Although institutional shareholders might not have the same skills and information, there is no reason to assume that they are unaware of the informational and other advantages possessed by the board and its nominating committee. Indeed, institutional shareholders usually display a substantial tendency to defer to the board. And they commonly would defer to the board's choices also under a shareholder access regime.

In some cases, however, the circumstances—including, for example, the past record of the incumbent directors and the characteristics of a shareholder-nominated candidate—might lead shareholders to conclude that they would be better off voting for a particular shareholder-nominated candidate. Of course, shareholders might not always get it right. But given that their money is on the line, shareholders naturally would have incentives to make the decision that would best serve their interests. And there is no reason to expect that choices they would make in favor of a shareholder-nominated candidate would likely be wrong.

The substantial presence of institutional investors makes such a paternalistic attitude especially unwarranted. Institutions are likely to be aware of the informational advantage of the board and its nominating committee, and they can be expected to make reasonable decisions on whether deferring to them would be best overall. Indeed, institutions can hardly be regarded as excessively reluctant to defer to management.

[14] 485 U.S. 224, 234 (1988) (quoting *Flamm v Eberstadt*, 814 F.2d 1169, 1175 (7th Cir. 1987)).

When circumstances convince shareholders to overcome their tendency to defer to management, there is little basis for a paternalistic view of their choices as misguided.

Critics also refer to 'confusion' as a reason that shareholders electing a shareholder-nominated candidate might make a bad choice. Shareholders would be confused, it is argued, as to which nominees are supported by the incumbent board and which are supported by shareholder proponents.[15] But surely this is a technical issue that can be addressed. It should be possible to ensure that the company's materials would indicate in absolutely clear and salient ways which candidates are nominated by the board and which (if any) by qualified shareholders.

C. Balkanization

Even if an elected shareholder-nominated director would be a good choice standing alone, opponents of shareholder access argue, the choice would likely be a bad one because of its impact on the directors as a team. Directors, it is argued, should work harmoniously and collegially with each other and with the firm's top executives. The election of a shareholder-nominated candidate, it is argued, would produce a balkanized, politicized, and dysfunctional board.[16]

It is far from clear that the election of a shareholder nominee would produce such division and discord. As explained, elected directors would be unlikely to represent special, parochial interests not shared by the other directors. Rather, they would be candidates with appeal to a majority of the shareholders, including in all likelihood most money managers, and with commitment to enhancing shareholder value. Other directors should not be expected to have legitimate reasons either to be on guard against such shareholder-nominated directors or to treat them with suspicion.

In any event, institutional investors presumably would be aware of whatever costs in terms of board discord might result from the election of a shareholder-nominated candidate. This possibility would be one of the considerations they would take into account, and it would weigh in favor of the board candidates. Shareholder-nominated candidates thus would be elected only when shareholders would conclude that, notwithstanding the expected effects on board harmony, there were reasons (rooted, for example, in the board's past record) making the election of some shareholder-nominated candidates desirable overall. When board

---

[15] See, e.g., Sullivan & Cromwell (2003: 5); see also ABA (2003: 21).
[16] See Lipton and Rosenblum (2003: 82–83) ; see also NYC Bar (2002: 5); Wachtell, Lipton (2003: 2).

performance is poor enough and shareholder dissatisfaction is strong enough that shareholders would likely elect a shareholder-nominated candidate, it would be a mistake to preclude such nominations to protect board harmony.

D. Other Potential Costs

(a) Costs to Stakeholders.   Some opponents argue that, even if shareholder access were to make directors more attentive to shareholder interests, it could well make them *too* attentive (Lipton and Rosenblum 2003: 87). The board, it is argued, should take into account not only the interests of shareholders but also the interests of other constituencies, such as creditors, employees, customers, and so forth. The board is supposed to balance all the competing interests of these groups. Permitting shareholders to nominate directors would put pressure on boards to focus on the interests of shareholders and neglect the interests of stakeholders.

It is far from clear, however, that insulating boards from shareholder nominations would benefit stakeholders. The interests of directors and executives are even less aligned with the interests of stakeholders than they are aligned with the interests of shareholders. Whereas directors often hold shares and options, they do not usually have any instruments that tie their wealth to that of bondholders or employees. And boards provide executive compensation schemes that are tied primarily to shareholder wealth.

Thus, there is no reason to expect that reduced accountability to shareholders would translate into increased attention to stakeholders. Limits on shareholder power thus should not be viewed as supporting the interests of stakeholders. Rather, it would enhance the unaccountable use of discretion by boards. By making directors accountable to no one and protecting them from removal even in the event of dismal performance, such limits would be costly to *both* shareholders and stakeholders.[17]

(b) One Size Doesn't Fit All.   To conclude our discussion of potential costs, let us consider the claim that the access proposal wrongly imposes the same arrangement on a large universe of companies that vary greatly in their characteristics and circumstances.[18] One size, it is argued, does not fit all. Even if shareholder access would be beneficial for many firms,

---

[17] For a general discussion of how stakeholder-based arguments do not provide a reasonable basis for limiting shareholder power, see Bebchuck (2003c: Part VI).

[18] See ABA (2003: 5) (noting 'the diversity that exists among the roughly 14,000 publicly-owned companies, which vary greatly in size, industry, complexity, resources, ownership and other circumstances').

there would likely be others for which it would have no beneficial effects or would even have adverse effects.

If valid, however, this argument would at most imply that the adopted SEC rule should leave firms free to opt out of the rule with shareholder approval. For example, the adopted rule could provide shareholder access unless, following the adoption of the access rule, shareholders vote to adopt a charter or bylaw provision that opts out of the shareholder access regime. Indeed, if shareholder access were conditioned upon a prior shareholder vote to provide shareholder access, then qualified shareholders would not be able to make nominations unless a majority of shareholders affirmatively opted into such an arrangement.[19]

Thus, the considered argument cannot provide a basis for general opposition to an SEC rule that facilitates shareholder access. The argument at most implies that such a rule should make opting out possible; it should either provide shareholder access as a default arrangement from which firms could opt out with shareholders' approval, or provide access as an arrangement into which shareholders would be able to opt.

VII. NOW IS NOT THE TIME

In addition to questioning whether shareholder access was ever desirable, opponents also argue that, given recent reforms, now is not the time to consider shareholder access. These reforms include the 2002 Sarbanes-Oxley Act and the pending new listing standards of the stock exchanges. Opponents suggest that 'any serious consideration of an Access Proposal ... should not take place until the scope and effect of initiatives already implemented are fully understood' (NYC Bar 2003: 3).[20] Given that it would take substantial time for companies to adjust fully to the reforms and for evidence about their effects to accumulate, these arguments imply that the shareholder access proposal should be shelved for at least several years.

---

[19] The formal rule proposal just released by the SEC enables shareholders to opt into a shareholder access arrangement by adopting a precatory resolution to this effect. See SEC (2003b). It should be noted, however, that the proposal would have companies subject to a shareholder access regime for only two years after the passage of such a precatory shareholder resolution. If one adopts the approach of letting shareholders make the choice, why not establish a shareholder access regime for a longer period of time if the adopted precatory resolution so specifies?

[20] See also ACAA (2003) ('Until the impact [of Sarbanes-Oxley Act] can more accurately be assessed, we believe it is appropriate to wait before making the proposed changes.'); Sullivan & Cromwell (2003: 2) ('Recent [c]orporate [g]overnance [r]eforms [s]hould [b]e [g]iven the [o]pportunity to [w]ork [b]efore [f]urther [s]teps [a]re [t]aken.'); Lipton and Rosenblum (2003: 94) ('[I]t seems only prudent to take the time to assess the impact of the far-reaching reforms we have just adopted.').

One reason given for such a delay is that, when feasible, it is preferable to have changes made gradually. Adopting many substantial changes simultaneously might be difficult and destabilizing for firms. And recent reforms, it is suggested, are already 'the most sweeping since at least the New Deal enactment of the basic federal securities laws' (ABA 2003: 10).[21]

Adding shareholder access to recent reforms would indeed produce a big change in corporate governance. But the magnitude of the changes should not dissuade us from making it. The changes might well be the most sweeping since the New Deal, but the crises of corporate governance and investor confidence that have precipitated them are the most severe since the New Deal. Even with the addition of shareholder access, the scale of reforms would not be disproportionate to the magnitude of perceived problems.

The other reason given for waiting until the consequences of recent reforms are fully understood is that these reforms might by themselves fully address the problems for which shareholder access is proposed. Because the pending changes in stock exchange listing requirements would place the nomination of directors in the hands of independent directors, critics argue, they would 'obviate the need for direct shareholder access to the issuer proxy statement' (Sullivan & Cromwell 2003: 3).

As explained earlier, the fact that directors are independent and selected by similarly independent directors does not by itself address all concerns about the selection and incentives of directors. It thus does not obviate the need for a safety valve: shareholders' ability to replace directors in the event of widespread dissatisfaction with the independent board and nominating committee. With shareholder access in the background, independent nominating committees can be expected to make choices that will commonly leave the shareholder access route unused. But the independent nominating committee is not a substitute for shareholder access.

VIII. THE EMPIRICAL EVIDENCE

Even if one believed that supporters of shareholder access had better arguments, opponents argue, significant changes should not be made without empirical evidence indicating that they would be beneficial overall (NY State Bar 2003: 2). Proponents of shareholder access, they suggest, have not shouldered the burden of providing such evidence.

---

[21] See also Lipton and Rosenblum (2003: 68) ('[Recent reforms] represent the most far-reaching set of new corporate regulation since the Securities Act of 1933 and the Securities Exchange Act of 1934.').

Requiring not only good policy reasons but also evidence that a change would be beneficial is a demanding test. In the case of many past reforms that proved to be beneficial, it would have not been possible to provide evidence that they would be beneficial before their adoption. In the case under consideration, however, there is nonetheless some solid empirical evidence that the direction in which the proposed reform would go—reducing incumbents' insulation from removal—would be beneficial.

A. The Costs of Insulation

There is substantial evidence that considerable insulation from removal via a takeover has adverse consequences on management performance and shareholder value. In a recent study Gompers, Ishii, and Metrick found a significant association between stronger anti-takeover protections—and more generally, stronger insulation of management from shareholder intervention—and lower stock market valuation (as measured by Tobin's Q).[22] According to their study, throughout the 1990s companies with stronger anti-takeover protection had a lower Tobin's Q, with the effect becoming more pronounced as the decade proceeded.[23]

Furthermore, in a current study, Alma Cohen and I investigate how the market value of publicly-traded firms is affected by protecting management from removal.[24] We find that staggered boards established by company charters are associated with a reduced market value. This reduction is economically significant, with a median of about 5 per cent of market value. We also find evidence consistent with charter-based staggered boards causing, and not merely reflecting, a lower firm value.

Studies have also identified the many ways in which insulation reduces corporate value. Studies by Bertrand and Mullainathan, as well as by Garvey and Hanka, found that anti-takeover statutes that provide strong protection from takeovers lead to increases in managerial slack.[25] Gompers, Ishii, and Metrick (2003) found that companies whose boards enjoy a wider array of insulating arrangements tend to have poorer operating performance—including lower profit margins, lower return on equity, and slower sales growth.

There is also evidence that greater insulation results in higher

[22] See Gompers, Ishii, and Metrick (2003: 144–45).

[23] This evidence is consistent with early evidence found by Morck, Shleifer, and Vishny (1989) on the association of managerial entrenchment with lower Tobin's Q.

[24] See Bebchuk and Cohen (2003).

[25] See Bertrand and Mullainathan (1999) (finding that the adoption of anti-takeover statutes weakened managers' incentives to minimize labor costs); Garvey and Hanka (1999: 520) (concluding that anti-takeover statutes 'allow managers to pursue goals other than maximizing shareholder wealth').

258   *Lucian Arye Bebchuk*

consumption of private benefits. Borokhovich, Brunarski, and Parrino (1997: 1515) found that firms with stronger anti-takeover defenses provide higher levels of executive compensation. Bertrand and Mullainathan obtained similar results for managers that are more protected due to anti-takeover statutes (1998). Gompers, Ishii, and Metrick found that firms with stronger takeover defenses are more likely to engage in empire-building (2003: 107).

Furthermore, a study by Coates, Subramanian and myself found that targets with strong takeover defenses, and in particular effective staggered boards, engage in value-decreasing resistance to hostile bids (Bebchuk *et al.* 2003: 24–25). Targets of hostile bids that have an effective staggered board are much more likely to remain independent both in the short run (twelve months) and in the long run (thirty months) even though remaining independent makes their shareholders much worse off both in the short run and in the long run. On average, the shareholders of targets of hostile bids that have staggered boards earn returns that are lower by more than 20 per cent.

To be sure, the empirical evidence discussed does not isolate the effects of giving or denying shareholders access to the corporate ballot. But the evidence indicates clearly that current levels of insulation are costly to shareholders and the economy. It thus provides general support for reforms that would reduce management's insulation, and providing shareholder access to the ballot would be a moderate step in this general direction.

B. The Effects of Independent Directors

There is also some relevant empirical work on the relationship between director independence and corporate performance. The results are somewhat mixed.[26] Some studies find evidence that boards with a majority of independent directors perform better on some dimensions of corporate decision-making.[27] Other studies find no evidence that such boards perform better.[28] There is no solid evidence of a systematic correlation between having a majority of independent directors and corporate value and performance.[29]

[26] For a detailed survey of this work, see Bhagat and Black (1999).
[27] See, e.g., Byrd and Hickman (1992: 219) (reporting that bidder returns are higher if firm has a majority of independent directors).
[28] See, e.g., Hanson and Song (2000) (finding no evidence that boards with a majority of independent directors make better divestiture decisions); Bebchuk, Coates, and Subramanian (2003: 17–18) (finding no evidence that target boards with a majority of independent directors are less likely to resist and defeat value-increasing bids).
[29] See Bhagat and Black (2001: 231).

The above work provides no basis for critics' suggestions that having nominating committees staffed by (board-nominated) independent directors would be sufficient to ensure adequate selection and incentives for directors. Although such composition of nominating committees might improve matters, it cannot be relied on to obviate the need for the safety valve of shareholder nomination.

Could opponents of shareholder access claim that the above evidence also casts doubt on the benefits of the election of shareholder-nominated directors? If the benefits of independent directors have not received clear empirical verification, it might be argued, there is no reason to provide shareholder nomination of director candidates. The aim of shareholder access, however, is not to increase the number of independent directors (a result that pending stock exchange reforms will produce in any case). Rather, shareholder access reform aims at improving the selection of independent directors and their incentives. Independent directors nominated by shareholders would likely be different, in both their identities and their incentives, than independent directors selected by boards under existing arrangements. Furthermore, studies about the effects that independent directors selected under current arrangements have do not capture the potential benefits that shareholder access would produce in terms of improved incentives for all directors. As explained, these benefits from reduced insulation and increased accountability might well constitute the biggest payoff from the shareholder access reform.

IX. BEYOND THE CURRENT SHAREHOLDER ACCESS PROPOSAL

The proposal for shareholder access, I have argued, is a moderate reform in the right direction. In fact, it is too *moderate*. While adopting it would be a step worth taking, additional measures are necessary to make shareholders' power to replace directors meaningful.

A. Beyond Access to the Company's Proxy Materials

To facilitate a shareholder-nominated short slate, it would be desirable to do more than require companies to include such slates in the proxy materials. To have a meaningful chance of success, nominees would have to incur expenses to make their case effectively to the shareholders. This is all the more true given that, whenever incumbents face a meaningful chance of losing, they will likely spend substantial sums on campaigning. A group of shareholders holding, say, 5 per cent of the shares might be unwilling to bear significant costs even if they believe that election of their nominee would enhance shareholder value (Clark 1986: § 9.5, at 389–94).

In an earlier article about the problem of costs in proxy contests, Marcel Kahan and I concluded that it would be desirable to reform the rules governing the financing of proxy contests (Bebchuk and Kahan 1990: 1135). We argued that such reforms are especially needed in cases—such as the case of a contest over a shareholder-nominated short slate—in which victory by shareholders would not provide them with control of the board. Under existing state corporate law, dissidents who gain control of the board in a proxy contest may reimburse themselves for the costs of their successful campaign. When control is not at stake, however, dissidents' success that improves the situation of the company would not produce a reimbursement of campaign costs. Accordingly, it would be desirable to ensure that, at least in the event that a challenger in such contests attracts substantial shareholder support, the company would bear some or all of the challenger's campaign costs.[30]

Thus, the SEC would do well to supplement a shareholder access rule with additional measures. In particular, the SEC should require that, if a nominee has sufficient initial support, companies will bear the costs of distributing to shareholders proxy statements by nominees who wish to have such materials distributed; companies would have the choice of either distributing such materials themselves or paying the challenger's reasonable expenses in doing so.[31]

The SEC could further require that, when a nominee has sufficient initial support, companies bear reasonable costs incurred in connection with the proxy process (e.g., legal fees necessary for preparing a proxy statement).[32] Such support could be made dependent upon sufficient success in the ultimate vote or on the level of initial support for the candidate.

The above measures could be opposed, of course, on the grounds that they would be costly to shareholders. Shareholders, it might be argued, should not bear the costs resulting from the decision of a group holding 5 per cent of the shares to nominate a director. As I explained above,

---

[30] The concern that the costs of running a short slate would remain too high even if companies were required to include shareholder nominations in the company's requirement is shared by Pozen (2003).

[31] In a recent symposium on corporate elections, Damon Silvers, associate general counsel of the AFL-CIO, stressed that, in the case of a large cap company, the costs of printing and postage for just the first mailing are a 'million dollar proposition,' and a serious contest might require more than one mailing. See Bebchuk (2003b: 84). Since the company will be sending materials to the shareholders anyway, including proxy statements by qualified shareholder-nominated candidates would cost somewhat less than for the candidates to do a separate mailing.

[32] Damon Silvers also noted that the costs of getting a mailing 'to the point where you can legally send it, meaning writing the documents and getting it through the SEC process is between 250,000 and 500,000 dollars, if it is not seriously contested.' See Bebchuk (2003b: 84).

however, an improved corporate elections process would be in the interests of companies and shareholders at large. Furthermore, the proposed additional measures would not require the expense of corporate resources on candidates whose chances of winning are negligible. Companies would be required to allocate resources only on the condition that a candidate has sufficient initial support and perhaps also on the condition that the candidate obtained sufficient support in the ultimate vote. The limited amounts that companies would have to spend under these measures would be a small price worth paying for an improved corporate governance system.

B. Beyond Short Slates

As I emphasized, there is a strong need to enhance shareholders' ability to exercise their theoretical power to replace directors. In a choice between the status quo and the proposal under consideration for facilitating short-slate nominations, the latter is clearly preferable. It would be even better, however, to go beyond the short-slate proposal and to facilitate also the possibility of shareholders' replacing all or most of the directors.

Providing shareholders with an effective power to replace a majority of the directors would have a greater payoff in terms of improving corporate governance than facilitating short slates only would have. The election of a new team can ensure a change when change is needed. And facilitating contests for control might provide directors with strong incentives to serve shareholder interests.

Interestingly, shareholders might sometimes be willing to vote for a full slate nominated by some qualified shareholders even though they would be reluctant to vote for a short slate (which would produce a more modest change). The reason for this is that, even when shareholders prefer a change in governance, they might sometimes feel that electing a short slate would lead to discord on the board without effecting sufficient change. In such a case, shareholders might not be willing to vote for a dissident short slate, but, if given the opportunity, they might be willing to vote to replace the incumbent directors with a dissident full slate.

Of course, there would be cases in which shareholders would be willing to vote only for a short slate but not a full slate. In many cases, for example, institutions would not wish to change the general management team, but would wish to add a director to address a particular corporate governance issue, such as executive compensation. Under a regime that facilitates both short-slate nominations and full-slate nominations, dissatisfied shareholders could choose to put forward a short slate or a full slate depending on which would seem more likely to address the problems they perceive in the firm's current board.

There are various ways in which contests for control could be facilitated to make the threat of replacement more meaningful than it is today. The SEC could permit shareholders that meet certain threshold requirements (e.g., ownership, holding, or triggering event requirements) to include an alternative full slate in the company's proxy materials. The SEC could also require that companies distribute to shareholders proxy statements made by such dissidents. The threshold requirements for full-slate nomination might be different (and, in particular, more stringent) than those for short-slate nomination. I plan to discuss measures to invigorate full-slate contests in future work. Here I wish only to point out the potential desirability of facilitating shareholder-nominated full slates.

CONCLUSION

Opponents of shareholder access have raised a wide range of objections to such reform. An examination of these objections, however, indicates that they do not provide a good basis for opposing a well-designed shareholder access regime. Such reform would contribute to making directors more accountable and would improve corporate governance. The proposed shareholder access arrangement would be a moderate step in a beneficial direction.

While this step is worth taking, we must recognize that it is not sufficient. We should adopt additional measures to make meaningful shareholders' power to replace directors. Such measures are necessary to make directors genuinely accountable to shareholders.

REFERENCES

ABA (2003), Charles Nathan, Co-Chair, Task Force on Shareholders Proposals, ABA Section of Business Law, to the SEC 11 (13 June 13) available at http://www.sec.gov/rules/other/s71003/aba061303.htm

Bebchuk, L.A. (2003), 'The Case for Empowering Shareholders' (Harvard Law School Working Paper), available at http://papers.ssrn.com/abstract=387940.

Bebchuk, L.A., ed. (2003), 'Symposium on Corporate Elections' Discussion Paper No. 448, Olin Center for Law, Economics, and Business, Harvard Law School, available at www.law.harvard.edu/programs/olin_center/corporate_governance/papers.htm.

Bebchuk, L.A. (2005), 'The Myth of Corporate Elections' (Work in Progress). See http://www.georgesonshareholder.com/html/index1.asp?id=t17.

Bebchuk, L.A. and Cohen, A. (2003), 'The Costs of Entrenched Boards' (Harvard Law School Working Paper), available at www.law.harvard.edu/faculty/bebchuk.

Bebchuk, L.A. and Kahan, M. (1990), 'A Framework for Analyzing Legal Policy Towards Proxy Contests', 78 *Cal. L. Rev.* 1073.

Bebchuk, L.A. *et al.* (2003), 'The Power of Takeover Defenses' (Harvard Law School Working Paper), available at http://www.nber.org/~confer/2003/si2003/papers/cf/bebchuk.pdf.

Bertrand, M. and Mullainathan, S. (1998), 'Executive Compensation and Incentives: The Impact of Takeover Legislation' (Nat'l Bureau of Econ. Research, Working Paper No. 6830), available at http://papers.nber.org/papers/W6830.

Bertrand, M. and Mullainathan, S. (1999), 'Is There Discretion in Wage Setting? A Test Using Takeover Legislation', 30 *Rand J. Econ.* 535.

Bhagat, S. and Black, B. (1999), 'The Uncertain Relationship Between Board Composition and Firm Performance', 54 *Bus. Law.* 921.

Bhagat, S. and Black, B. (2001), 'The Non-Correlation Between Board Independence and Long Term Firm Performance', 27 *J. Corp. L.* 231.

Borokhovich, K.A., Brunarski K.R., and Parrino, R. (1997), 'CEO Contracting and Antitakeover Amendments', 52 *J. Fin.* 1495.

Byrd, J.W. and Hickman, K.A. (1992), 'Do Outside Directors Monitor Managers? Evidence from Tender Offer Bids', 32 *J. Fin. Econ.* 195.

Clark, R.C. (1986), *Corporate Law* (Boston: Little, Brown & Co.).

Garvey, G.T. and Hanka, G. (1999), Capital Structure and Corporate Control: The Effect of Antitakeover Statutes on Firm Leverage, 54 *J. Fin.* 519.

Georgeson Shareholder (2002), Annual; Corporate Review, available at http://www.georgesonshareholder.com/pdf/02wrapup.pdf.

Gompers, P. Ishii, J. and Metrick, A. (2003), 'Corporate Governance and Equity Prices', 118 *Q. J. Econ.* 107, 144–45 (2003).

Hanson, R.C. and Song, M.H. (2000), 'Managerial Ownership, Board Structure, and the Division of Gains in Divestitures', 6 *J. Corp. Fin.* 55.

Lang, R.T., Co-Chair, Task Force on Shareholders Proposals, and Nathan C., Co-Chair, Task Force on Shareholders Proposals, ABA Section of Business Law, to the SEC 11 (13 June 2003), available at http://www.sec.gov/rules/others/s71003/aba061303.htm.

Lipton, M. and Rosenblum, S.A. (2003), 'Election Contests in the Company's Proxy: An Idea Whose Time Has Not Come', 59 *Bus. Law.* 67.

McKinnell, H.A. (2003), e-mail to Jonathan G. Katz, Secretary, SEC (June 13, 2003), available at http://www.sec.gov/rules/other/s71003/brt061303.htm.

Morck, R. *et al.* (1989), 'Alternative Mechanisms for Corporate Control', 79 *Am. Econ. Rev.* 842.

NY State Bar (2003), Michael J. Holliday, Chairman, Committee on Securities Regulation, Business Law Section of the New York State Bar Association, letter to SEC (13 June), available at http://www.sec.gov/rules/other/s71003/scrblsnysba061303.htm.

Pozen, R.C. (1994), 'Institutional Investors: Reluctant Activists', *Harv. Bus. Rev.*, Jan.–Feb., at 140.

Pozen, R.C. (2003), 'Institutional Perspective on Shareholder Nomination of Corporate Directors', 59 *Bus. Law.* 140.

Romanek, B. (2003), Chair, Corporate & Securities Law Committee, American Corporate Counsel Association, letter to John G. Katz, Secretary, SEC (13 June), available at http://www.sec.gov/rules/other/s71003/acca061303.htm.

SEC (2003), Proposed Rule: Director Nominations, Exchange Act Release No. 34-48626 (14 October 2003), available at http://www.sec.gov/rules/proposed/34-48626.htm.

SEC (2003), SEC Staff Report: Review of the Proxy Process Regarding the Nomination and Election of Directors (15 July), available at http://www.sec.gov/news/studies/proxyreport.pdf.

Silk, D.M. (2002), Chairman, Task Force on Potential Changes to the Proxy Rules, The Association of the Bar of the City of New York, letter to SEC (13 June), available at http://www.sec.gov/rules/other/s71003/tfpcprabny061303.htm.

Sullivan & Cromwell (2003), e-mail to Jonathan G. Katz, Secretary, SEC (13 June) available at http:// www.sec.gov/rules/other/s71003/sullivan061303.htm.

Wachtell, Lipton, Rosen & Katz (2003), Letter to Jonathan G. Katz, Secretary, SEC (11 June), at http://www.sec.gov/rules/other/s71003/wachtell061103.htm.

Wilcox, J.C. (2003), e-mail to SEC 3 (22 May), at http://www.sec.gov/rules/other/s71003/georgeson052203.htm.

8

Rules, Principles, and the Accounting Crisis in the United States

WILLIAM W BRATTON[*]

I. INTRODUCTION

AMERICAN EQUITY-HOLDERS AWOKE in 2002 to realize they no longer could trust corporate financial reports.[1] Their doubts extended beyond Enron and the Arthur Andersen firm[2] to a large set of companies with reputations for aggressive accounting. Entire sectors were implicated, finance and telecommunications most prominently. Securities issuers, oriented toward shareholder value enhancement by the corporate culture of the 1990s, had been adopting aggressive, even fraudulent treatments to enhance reported earnings, and their auditors had been doing nothing to stop them. The auditors had sold their independence in exchange for consulting rents. The Securities and Exchange Commission (SEC), some years before, had issued loud warnings about this dirty deal and its implications for reporting quality.[3] But nobody in the investment community had cared so long as money kept falling from the sky during the 1990s' bull market. Things were different in 2002. As equity-holders struggled in the worst bear market in a generation, diminished auditor independence triggered a crisis of confidence in corporate reporting. As audit failures piled up,[4] investors

---

* Professor of Law, Georgetown University Law Center. This chapter was previously published in (2004) 5 *European Business Organization Law Review* 7–36. The permission of the Asser Press to republish is gratefully acknowledged.

[1] See, e.g., Morgenson (2002).

[2] For a review of Enron disaster, see Bratton (2002a).

[3] See, e.g., Levitt (2000).

[4] The decline in compliance has not been limited to companies subject to enforcement actions, as *Cendant*: see *In re Cendant Corp. Sec. Litig.*, 109 F. Supp. 2d 235 (D.N.J. 2000). Investigations and criticisms touch reputable names such as Xerox: see Deutsch and Abelson (2001); Lucent: Romero (2001); American International, Coca Cola, and IBM: see Liesman (2002); and General Electric itself: see Kahn (2001); Silverman and Brown (2002: C16). The General

lost confidence in managers, market intermediaries, and auditors alike. Share prices suffered as a result.

The auditors responded by pointing a finger at US accounting's standard-setter, the Financial Accounting Standards Board (FASB), and the standards it articulates, Generally Accepted Accounting Principles (GAAP). The problem, said the auditors, was a shortage of rules. Auditors and reporting companies needed more guidance and regulators like FASB had failed to supply it. Joe Berardino, the managing partner of the Andersen firm, then under the gun for the audit failure at Enron and subsequent document-shredding, led this counter-attack. His firm's auditors, he said, had merely applied the rules. It followed that if there was a problem, it lay in the rules themselves, which permitted the off balance sheet financing arrangements that figured prominently in Enron's collapse. If something had gone wrong with the fairness of Enron's financial statements, then the rules ought to be rethought (Bernadino 2001). The burden to effect improvement lay on the FASB and the SEC rather than on the audit firms' own practices: to restore confidence, the SEC should supply 'immediate guidance' to public companies respecting disclosure of off-balance sheet transactions along with other transactional categories where Enron's financials had proved wanting, such as over the counter-derivative contracts and related-party transactions. In particular, the SEC should require issuers to provide more details respecting off balance sheet guarantees, commitments, and lease and debt arrangements that variously impact on credit ratings, earnings, cash flow, or stock price (Burns and Schroeder 2002).

The auditors, however, repeated an oft-heard refrain when they demanded more guidance from the standard-setters, and so failed to deflect the blame from themselves. Worse, voices from outside the accounting profession responded to the auditors' defense by singing the opposite tune: maybe the auditors had too much guidance; maybe the problem was not a shortage of rules on matters like off-balance sheet financing, derivative contracts, and leases, but an *excess* of rules. The critics charged that GAAP's exhaustive system of rules-based treatments had fostered a dysfunctional, check-the-box approach to compliance. Preparers and auditors applied the rules mechanically, ignoring the substance of the transactions being reported (Liesman 2002b; *Economist* 2002). The rules-based system of regulation, they alleged, fostered a culture of noncompliance in which regulated actors invested in schemes of rule evasion. Harvey Pitt, then the SEC chairman, led the charge against FASB and its rules (Pitt 2002: 5):

Accounting Office Report to the Chairman, Committee on Banking, Housing, and Urban Affairs, U.S. Senate, (GAO 2002) surveys public company restatements 1997 to 2002, showing marked increases across the period.

Present-day accounting standards are cumbersome and offer far too detailed prescriptive requirements for companies and their accountants to follow. We seek to move toward a principles-based set of accounting standards, where mere compliance with technical prescriptions is neither sufficient nor the objective.

Capitol Hill staffers, press commentators, and academics seconded Pitt in blaming the crisis on the rules and calling for principles-based accounting.

Even Wall Street joined the call for principles, in a rare moment of concurrence with the policy community. Of course, Wall Street's motivation lay in the association of principles-based accounting with the International Financial Reporting Standards (IFRS) issued by the International Accounting Standards Board (IASB) and selected for adoption by the European Commission.[5] The case for principles-based accounting overlaps the case for regulatory intervention to speed international securities market convergence, in particular SEC acceptance of financial reporting pursuant to IFRS. Principles-based accounting thus appeals to every intermediary on Wall Street anticipating more rents from foreign listing business.

The way thus prepared, the US Congress made its own call for principles when it enacted the Sarbanes-Oxley Act of 2002 (SOA),[6] the legislation that addresses the reporting crisis and attempts to restore confidence in the securities markets. SOA institutes a new regime of regulation of the accounting profession, following the standard regulatory strategy of delegating the task of filling in the new regime's terms to a new administrative agency, the Public Company Accounting Oversight Board (PCAOB) (SOA § 103(c)). On principles-based accounting, in contrast, SOA relies on the old agency, the SEC, ordering it to produce a study of the US accounting system that ascertains the extent to which it is principles-based (as opposed to rules-based) and reports on the length of time needed to achieve transition to a basis in principles (SOA § 108(d)).[7] The SEC Report (2003), which has appeared in due

[5] From 2005, listed companies in the EC were required to report under IFRS.
[6] Sarbanes-Oxley Act of 2002, Pub. Law. 107–204, 116 Stat. 745 (codified in scattered sections of 11, 15, 18, 28, and 29 U.S.C.).
[7] Sarbanes-Oxley Act s. 108 (d) provides as follows:
SEC. 108. ACCOUNTING STANDARDS.
...
(d) STUDY AND REPORT ON ADOPTING PRINCIPLES-BASED ACCOUNTING—
  (1) STUDY—
    (A) IN GENERAL—The Commission shall conduct a study on the adoption by the United States financial reporting system of a principles-based accounting system.
    (B) STUDY TOPICS—The study required by subparagraph (A) shall include an examination of—
      (i) the extent to which principles-based accounting and financial reporting exists in the United States;

course, confirms the relative superiority of principles-based over rules-based accounting and hands to FASB the job of a ground-up reconstruction of US GAAP.

This chapter enters a dissenting opinion. The dissent does not follow from a theoretical preference for rules over principles, however. In theory there need be nothing objectionable in an initiative that privileges principles over rules in the articulation of accounting standards (or, for that matter, any other regulation). Principles, or in lawyer's parlance 'standards,' lead to more responsive and flexible regulation. The lawmaker announces a broad-brush directive in the expectation that more particular instructions will derive from law to fact applications over time. Because the principle guides each application to fact, principles-based standards allow regulators to stay in closer touch with ultimate regulatory objectives even as they allow for variations in the facts of the cases. In contrast, rules-based systems tend toward formalism, even as they also tend to include statements of overarching principles. Whatever their motivating principles, exhaustively articulated rules that treat, categorize and distinguish complex transactions invite mechanical application. In practice, the statement of the rule can come to dominate both the wider regulatory purpose and the particulars of the given case. Problems result, since no system of rules ever can anticipate all future cases. Clever planners exploit the pattern of mechanical application, devising transactions that fit the pattern but evade the regulation's spirit. The US GAAP is justifiably famous for reliance on such rule-based treatments.

In the abstract, then, well-drafted principles may offer a better mode for articulating accounting standards. Unfortunately, the US reporting system's infirmities cannot be cured in the abstract. GAAP's rule-based treatments and the proposed move to principles must be evaluated in the process context in which preparers and auditors apply accounting principles. The process picture is not pretty. Professional standards have fallen to such a low estate that a near term shift to a principles-based

(ii) the length of time required for change from a rules-based to a principles-based financial reporting system;
(iii) the feasibility of and proposed methods by which a principles- based system may be implemented; and
(iv) a thorough economic analysis of the implementation of a principles-based system.
(2) REPORT—Not later than 1 year after the date of enactment of this Act, the Commission shall submit a report on the results of the study required by paragraph (1) to the Committee on Banking, Housing, and Urban Affairs of the Senate and the Committee on Financial Services of the House of Representatives.
S. 108(d) is coupled with § 108(a), which requires FASB and any other approved standards-setting body to adopt procedures assuring prompt consideration of new rules reflecting 'international convergence on high quality accounting standards.'

system would create a significant risk of unintended adverse consequences.

Management decides on accounting treatments and prepares financial reports. Auditors merely review these decisions.[8] It follows in theory that auditors should be the most independent and adversary of professionals, ready at all times to reject management's treatments as unfair or noncompliant. Unfortunately, in US practice, corporate clients have captured the loyalty of their auditors to a degree comparable to their capture of the loyalty of their lawyers. Multiple factors contribute to this compromise of the professional relationship. Prime among them are non-audit consulting rents, employment opportunities at clients, and audit industry concentration.[9] Now, had the Congress enacting SOA been serious about realigning auditor incentives and ameliorating their capture by the client interest, the statute would have prohibited all nonaudit forms of business consulting by audit firms. SOA, more cautiously, opts for gradual improvement through periodic professional review. It facilitates audit reform without assuring it, leaving it to the PCAOB and the SEC to address (or finesse) the problem of industry capture.

So long as management incentives respecting accounting treatments and auditor independence remain suspect, the US reporting system holds out no actor plausibly positioned to take responsibility for the delicate law to fact applications that are the hallmarks of principles-based systems. Principles, taken alone, do little to constrain rent-seeking behaviour. In a world of captured regulators, they invite applications that suit the regulated actor's interests. Rules, with all their flaws, better constrain managers and their compromised auditors.

Principles-based accounting may work well in other corporate governance systems or in the US system at some future time. But Congress and the SEC are moving too quickly in prodding FASB to move immediately to principles-based GAAP. Priorities here need to be ordered with more care. The incentive problems should be solved first through institutional reform that insulates the audit from the negative impact of rent-seeking and solves the adverse selection problems that otherwise impair performance of the audit function in the United States. SOA, with its blank-check agency delegation, merely starts the reform process without taking the concomitant and necessary step of reasserting professional standards. Broadbrush reformulations of rules-based GAAP should follow only when institutional reforms have succeeded.

[8] The leading discussion of the resulting incentive problem in the legal literature is Eisenberg (1975: 375). Eisenberg's critique continues to resonate today.

[9] The effects of industry concentration are a matter of debate. For the view that intense price competition among audit firms has contributed to low audit quality, see text accompanying note 36.

This chapter's subsequent sections proceed as follows. Part II traverses the US reporting crisis, situating the rules versus principles debate in the context of recent audit failures. The discussion shows that the wave of audit failures implicates principles-based GAAP much more than it implicates rules-based GAAP. A story about Enron much in circulation also is falsified. According to the story, Enron exemplifies the abuses of rules-based accounting under GAAP and demonstrates the need to move to principles. In reality, Enron violated whatever accounting standards got in its way, whether structured as rules or principles. Responsibility for the disaster does not lie at the door of the drafters of GAAP but at the door of those responsible for implementation and enforcement, Enron's managers and auditors. Part III explains why GAAP, which in fact is founded on principles, has evolved towards articulation in rules. The responsibility lies less with FASB, which has been operating as a responsive regulator, than with its constituents. The constituents, the preparers and auditors of financial statements, demand rules. Adverse selection problems in their professional relationships motivate the demands. Part IV compares rules and principles in the second-best world of US audit practice. Rules hold out cost savings and can enhance transparency. Principles make things simpler and enhance the comparability of financial statements across different firms. The problem is that principles presuppose an independent auditor who holds unmitigated professional power over the client and its treatment choices. In the absence of such an actor, the case for a principles-based regime rests on a false premise and holds out risks for audit quality. Part V concludes.

II. RULES, PRINCIPLES, AND AUDIT FAILURE

Proponents of principles-based accounting blame audit failures and reporting defalcations at firms like Enron and WorldCom on rules-based accounting and look to principles-based reformulations as a corrective tool. The rules, they say, are manipulated by managers, auditors, and consultants toward the end of reporting misstatement. A principles-based system, such as presently in effect in the United Kingdom and in IFRS, would be less manipulable and thus superior. No one challenges these assertions. But, as the discussion that follows shows, the charges are in significant part unfounded. This is not because GAAP contains no manipulable rules, for it does. Nor is this because the rules have not been manipulated, for they have been. It is because recent corporate scandals for the most part do not stem from rule manipulation. There is no persuasive causal connection between rule-based GAAP and recent, catastrophic audit failures. Enron, thought to be the prime case where corporate failure can be tied to rule exploitation, turns out to be much more a case of human pathology than of poor standard-setting.

A. Standard Setting and Audit Failure

According to the SEC's report (2003) under SOA on principles-based accounting, rules-based standards are characterized by 'bright line tests, multiple exceptions, a high level of detail, and internal inconsistencies.' A rules-based approach, moreover, seeks to supply a clear answer to every possible situation, thereby minimizing the need to apply professional judgment. According to GAAP's critics, this leads to transaction structuring and other strategic behaviour that undermines the quality of financial reporting (Schipper 2003: 61). Financials thus manipulated, while rule compliant, do not truly and fairly state the reporting company's income and financial position. Comparability suffers as a result: Reporting entities hewing to the same strict standard appear comparable on the faces of their financials when their arrangements in fact are dissimilar. Principles, say the critics, avoid this reporting pathology and lead to higher quality reporting; an effective system of accounting standards must build on principles and cannot be constructed entirely of rules.

The critics are right that effective accounting standards must have a basis in principles. Unfortunately for the line of criticism, however, GAAP exemplifies just such a system. GAAP is not comprised solely of rules, although some of its directives are indeed set out in elaborately stated rules replete with bright-line tests, multiple exceptions, and internal inconsistencies. But many GAAP standards are principles-based. Furthermore, a collection of broad and powerful principles stands behind the whole.[10] FASB, upon its inception in 1973, articulated GAAP's basic principles in a series of *Concepts Statements*,[11] collectively called the

---

[10] These are, according to a leading legal accounting text, historical cost, objectivity (or verifiability), revenue recognition, matching, consistency, full disclosure, and relevance (or fair value) (Herwitz and Barrett 2002: 67–70). The last principle on the list, fair value, lately has been growing in importance at the expense of the first two on the list, historical cost and verifiability: See FASB (1999a); Siegel (1996: 1839). Tension results—there is no way to have a system requiring verifiable numbers and at the same time offering fair value figures. That tension is being resolved in favor of fair value as GAAP moves away from a mandate that all reported numbers be hard numbers toward a system including many numbers that result from judgment calls but that in theory offer a better picture of the present value of the firm. Note that SOA § 108(a) directs FASB to prioritize the consideration of new rules reflecting 'emerging accounting principles and changing business practices.' This presumably means more movement to fair value treatments. The Congress overlooks the fact that the same movement certainly played a role in the accounting mess at Enron, where mark to market and fair value accounting of its derivative and energy contracts contributing mightily to suspicions about its earnings figures. See Partnoy (2003). Common sense indicates that we should readjust the balance in favour of verifiability, at least until the crisis has passed.

conceptual framework. This has ever since been the source of the objectives and concepts drawn on in the development of US accounting standards.[12] The overarching concept in the conceptual framework is 'decision usefulness'. It is in turn supported by the trio of relevance, reliability, and comparability.[13] Decision usefulness is achieved in the first instance through comparability. That is, similar things should be reported the same way by different firms and by each firm across time. The achievement of comparability in turn necessitates standard-setting. Relevance and reliability come into the framework at this point to assist the standard-setter in articulating requirements for recognition of income, measurement of assets and liabilities, and disclosure more generally (Schipper 2003: 62–63). As articulated within the conceptual framework, GAAP is explicitly principles-based, even as it contains many rules.

A critic might respond that other accounting systems manage to do as good a job as does US GAAP with materially greater reliance on principles than on rules. The UK regime often is held out at this point. As to auditing standards, the UK system does appear to be more principles-based than those in the United States.[14] But the picture is less clear with respect to the United Kingdom's substantive accounting principles. British accounting rests on eight Financial Reporting Standards, twenty-five Statements of Standard Accounting Practice, plus a thick supplementary literature. Much of this is as dense and rule-bound as US GAAP (Cunningham 2003: 915, 975–76). The same is true of IFRS (SEC 2003: § I.F.). One commentator, reviewing a number of systems for relative rule-based complexity, including those of the United States, the United Kingdom, and IFRS, found no obvious reason to distinguish US GAAP as a pathological outlier (Cunningham 2003: 976, note 291). All accounting systems mix rules and principles.

More importantly, there is no clear causal connection between rules-based US GAAP and recent high-profile reporting failures. Those who denounce GAAP for excessive reliance on rules cite a number of subject-matters. These core, rules-based regimes include accounting for derivatives and hedging activity, leasing, real estate sales, stock-based compensation arrangements, consolidation (or other recognition) of related entity financial assets and liabilities, and, prior to reforms

Other tensions come into the picture when we reference two modifying conventions— materiality, which lets the auditor disregard minor misapplications of the rules, and conservatism, which counsels understatement in case of doubt. Between historical cost, verifiability, and conservatism on the one hand, and fair value and materiality on the other, there is much room for good faith dispute about the best way to state a firm's results.

[11] For FASB's discussion of these in the context of the principles-based accounting movement of 2002, see FASB (2002b: 5–7).

[12] See FASB (1978).

[13] See FASB (1980).

[14] See Frost and Ramin (1996).

instituted in 2002,[15] mergers and acquisitions (SEC 2003: §§ I.G., II.B.). The General Accounting Office's (GAO) recent report of public company accounting restatements permits us to gauge the extent to which these rules-based subject-matter figures into the spate of accounting failures. Since accounting restatements presuppose audit failure, the GAO's compendium provides a roadmap to accounting's abused territories.

The GAO report (2002) shows that the annual number of restatements rose from ninety-two in 1997 to 225 in 2001. From 1997 to June 2002, the total number of restatements announced was 919. These involved 845 companies, amounting 10 per cent of all those listed on public exchanges in the United States. Issues involving revenue recognition, whether in respect of misreported or nonreported revenue, made up the largest group by subject-matter category, accounting for almost 38 per cent of the 919 restatements. The second largest group concerned cost- or expense-related issues, accounting for almost 16 per cent.[16] The GAAP revenue and cost recognition standards bearing on this 54 per cent majority group are for the most part principles-based—they are phrased in general terms and require significant exercises of judgment in their application (Herwitz and Barrett 2002: 449–62, 474–82).[17] WorldCom is the most famous recent case of these principles' opportunistic misuse. Over three years WorldCom shifted around $8 billion of line costs over to asset accounts, treating operating expenditures as capital expenditures, with earnings for the period of the shift increasing dollar for dollar. This age-old ruse for padding earnings implicated neither high-tech engineering nor manipulation of complex rules.[18] It was a bad faith application of a principle.

The remaining restatements cover a range of subject-matter, some of it rules-based, but most of it principles-based. On the rules-based side are restatements concerning merger and acquisition accounting and derivatives (GAO 2002).[19] More on the principles-based side lie restatements involving in-process research and development, related-party

---

[15] See FASB (2001) (ending pooling treatment for mergers).

[16] These types of restatements include instances of improper cost recognition, tax issues, and other cost-related improprieties that led to financial misstatements.

[17] The general principles are supplemented by industry specific rules. The door for this supplementation is opened by FASB Concepts Statement No. 5, which bases the revenue recognition standards on the closing practices of its time. FASB has a current project that looks toward a conceptual restatement. See Schipper (2003: 63).

[18] For description of this fraud, see Cunningham (2003: 934–36).

[19] Derivatives are a growth item on the list of restatements. Along with other securities-related restatements, they increased from 4.6% of restatements in 2001 to 12.4% of restatements in the first half of 2002. But the category is capacious, and includes errors and misstatements involving derivatives, warrants, stock options, and other convertible securities. Some of the standards in question are rules-based, while others are standards-based. Significantly, most involve fair value accounting.

transactions, loan-loss reserves and loan write-offs, asset impairment, inventory valuation, and restructuring activity.

There is a simple reason why rules-based subject-matters do not dominate the list of restatements: detailed rules hold out roadmaps both to GAAP compliance and the identification of GAAP noncompliance. Observers who disapprove of the rules-based treatments dislike the reporting destinations to which the roadmaps lead.[20] Since these destinations tend simultaneously to be favored by the managers of reporting companies, the managers happily comply with the rules. At the same time, a noncomplying issuer is more likely to confront an uncooperative auditor. Detailed rules hold out the benefit of enhancing transparency even as they can distort the overall story told by the report's bottom line. They make it easier to see what companies are doing, if only for the reason that the precise instructions narrow the room for differences of judgment.[21] Rules also ease verification. Detailed instructions provide a base of common assumptions and knowledge for both preparers and auditors. Differences in measurement decrease as a result. Noncompliance becomes more evident (Schipper 2003: 68). And the auditor who discovers noncompliance is more likely to refuse to let it pass given a rule. The rule provides it a clear-cut basis for justifying the refusal to the client, minimizing potential damage to the professional relationship. Since the rule makes noncompliance more visible, it also increases the risk of *ex post* enforcement respecting the preparer and the auditor both, further strengthening the auditor's resolve.

B. Enron and GAAP

Those who ascribe rules-based standards with a causal role in the accounting crisis point to Enron. At first glance the citation appears justified. Misleading accounting treatments of transactions between Enron and off-balance sheet entities lie at the scandal's core, and the applicable accounting standards are rules-based. Indeed, these rules' form over substance treatments are as notoriously arbitrary as any in US GAAP.

Criticism of these rules has been widespread for decades. Even FASB consistently has joined the critics. For two decades prior to 2001 it kept open a project inquiring into an alternative approach built on a principles-based definition of control.[22] Unfortunately for FASB, the

---

[20] See Nelson, Elliott, and Tarpley (2000) (showing that auditors pass on these treatments as GAAP compliant).

[21] As noted above, to the extent the rule strategic transaction design, comparability may be lost as dissimilar transactions receive common treatment. Schipper (2003: 67–68).

[22] See FASB (1999b).

business community, particularly the securitization industry, had come to rely on its mastery and manipulation of these rules, especially the labyrinthine set on transfers to off-balance sheet entities. The industry interests vociferously opposed reform. Exhausted by the opposition, FASB abandoned the project of substantive restatement as a failure even as the Enron scandal was breaking. Later, in the wake of the scandal, FASB's critics did an about-face, suddenly demanding principles-based reform. FASB responded by reviving the reform project, and has since produced a succession of Enron-responsive exposure drafts (FASB 2002a).[23] FASB's revived reform project amounts to a tacit admission of standard-setting failure. For all that appears, even the body responsible for GAAP agrees that its rules had a causative role in the company's collapse.

In acting out the role of a deficient lawmaker, FASB confirms the conventional wisdom circulating in the wake of Enron's collapse. This story follows from the assumption that a disaster of this magnitude never could have occurred had there not been a flaw in the rules. The story has it that Enron exploited technical rules governing Special Purpose Entities (SPE) in setting up and accounting for sham transactions. By carefully but cynically hewing to the rules, Enron managed materially to overstate its earnings. Had the rules been better drafted, Enron would have been forced to consolidate the results of the sham SPEs with its own results. Consolidation in turn would have deprived Enron of the opportunity to misstate its earnings.[24]

Generalizing from the story, rules-based GAAP's layers of precise instructions easily can be manipulated by clever and expensive accountants and lawyers. Had GAAP taken a principles-based approach, articulating general and substantive standards respecting the consolidation of related entities, there would have been no loophole through which the bad actors at Enron could have driven their fleet of sham SPE trucks.

The story is accurate in one respect: the rules respecting accounting for transactions with SPEs were badly drafted and incomplete. But in all other respects the story is nonsense. Enron, in fact, did not follow the rules. Had it done so, the substance of all of its questionable dealings with SPEs would have been disclosed in its financial statements. It follows that

[23] This draft deals with SPEs and would have caused the consolidation of Enron's LJM 1 and 2. It also increases the outside equity requirement to 10% for a residual class of SPEs that would have included those in question. A second initiative addresses disclosures of guarantees, on the purport that the present rules lack clarity. FASB (200b2).

[24] One finds this story casually mentioned as accepted wisdom in the pages of the *New York Times* at the end of 2002. See Eichenwald (2002) (quoting Professor Frank Partnoy as follows: 'Enron was following the letter of the law in nearly all of its deals. It is fair to say that the most serious allegations of criminal wrongdoing at Enron had almost nothing to do with the company's collapse. Instead it was the type of transaction that is still legal.').

the rules did not fail. The failure lay with actors at Enron and its auditor, Arthur Andersen. Failures at FASB played no role. FASB's implicit, after the fact, admission of a rule failure tells us more about its weakness as a political player than it does about the operation of GAAP.[25]

It is true that the SPE transactions at the heart of the Enron scandal emerged from an exhaustive and strategic planning process. It also is true that the transactions were designed to comply with the rules even as they exploited the rules' structural weaknesses. Under SFAS No. 140, issued in 2000, transfers of financial assets to SPEs are treated as sales by the transferor firm so long as, among other things, equity interests in the SPE are not returned as consideration for the assets transferred and the SPE gets control of the assets with the right to pledge or exchange them (FASB 2000). For the class of SPEs utilized in the Enron transactions, all the planner had to do was make sure that an outside equity investor in the SPE vehicle contributed capital at least equal to 3 per cent of the value of the financial assets transferred to the SPE vehicle by Enron.

It also is true that at the time Enron set up the critical 'LJM I' and 'LJM II' SPEs and entered into swap transactions with them, the transactions arguably complied with the rules. But, as subsequent investigations have detailed at length, the transaction structures had intrinsic flaws and went out of compliance with the 3 per cent rule very soon after the transactions closed (Powers *et al.* 2002: 98). Had Enron scrupulously followed the rules at that point, it would have been forced to consolidate the SPEs into its financials. Had the SPEs been consolidated, the outcomes of the swap transactions between Enron and the SPEs would have been eliminated from Enron's income statement with the result that Enron would not have been able to pump up its net earnings with revenues and gains from SPE transactions. But, of course, the financials were not consolidated and Enron overstated its earnings by $1 billion over five quarters. But such noncompliance does not result from the successful manipulation of flawed rules. Instead, like Parmalat's managers on the other side of the Atlantic, Enron's managers resorted to the old-fashioned expedient of concealment.

Enron's financials would have been out of compliance with GAAP even if the financials' treatment of its swaps with LJM had conformed to the rules on consolidation of financials. Consolidation was not the only compliance problem implicated by the LJM transaction structure. Under SFAS No. 57, contracts between Enron and the LJM SPEs were 'related party transactions.' This category includes transactions with a counterparty whose policies are so influenced by the first party as to

---

[25] Significantly, reporting companies and the big accounting firms (notably including Andersen and Enron: Simpson (2002)), vigorously opposed FASB's consolidation project, criticizing the FASB's draft as unworkable. See Burkholder (2002: 214, 215).

prevent one of the parties from fully pursuing its own interests. Given such a tie, special footnote descriptions of the transactions are required, including dollar amount impacts on reported earnings (FASB 1982: paras. 2, 24(f)). The footnote disclosures would have provided investors with the substantive equivalent of a set of consolidated reports. But, of course, Enron did not wish to make clear the truth respecting this component of its reported earnings, and its cooperative auditor failed to insist that it follow the rules on related party transactions.

An additional reporting failure figured prominently in Enron's final collapse. The straw that broke the camel's back, frustrated a last-ditch rescue plan, and forced the company to file for bankruptcy in December 2001 was Enron's last minute revelation of $4 billion of unreported contingent guarantees of obligations of unconsolidated equity affiliates. The revelation killed a bailout merger with Dynegy because the hidden $4 billion of obligations materially impaired Enron's financial condition and were about to come due (Bratton 2002a: 1320–25). As to these obligations GAAP holds out a clear instruction. To guarantee an equity affiliate's obligations is to take the disclosure treatment out of the parent-subsidiary or parent-investee context for treatment under the standards on contingent losses. Those standards call for disclosure. Under SFAS No. 5, loss contingencies are divided into three classes: probable, reasonably possible, and remote. Probable losses should be accrued as liabilities; reasonably possible losses should be disclosed in footnotes with information as to nature and magnitude; remote losses need not be disclosed. There is a separate rule for financial guarantees such as Enron's. With guarantees, even if the possibility of loss is remote, there must be footnote disclosure as to nature and amount.[26] Enron failed to make those disclosures because it was afraid that disclosure could trigger a rating agency downgrade to below investment grade status (Enron needed an investment grade rating to run its trading business and did everything it could to maintain one). This included material understatement of its obligations as guarantor. This amounts to another old-fashioned fraud by concealment. It comes as no surprise that, thus stated, Enron's financials did not comply with GAAP.[27]

---

[26] See FASB (1975: para. 5): 'The Board concludes that disclosure of [guarantees of indebtedness of others and others that in substance have the same characteristic] shall be continued. The disclosure shall include the nature and amount of the guarantee.' See also FASB (1981); Herwitz and Barrett (2002:. 617–20). Note that under SFAS No. 140, a separate recourse obligation against the transferor of an asset to an SPE in respect of reimbursement for losses on the underlying portfolio (as opposed to a derivative arrangement) continues to be treated under SFAS No. 5. That is, the transferor makes an ongoing assessment of the amount of the loss in its financials rather than adjusting the obligation to fair value and reporting it in income. Ernst & Young (2001: 29).

[27] And therefore were per se misleading for securities law purposes. See 'Administrative Policy on Financial Statements, Accounting Series Rel. No. 4', 11 *Fed. Reg.* 10,913 (S.E.C. 1938),

Contrary to the conventional wisdom, then, the central problem at Enron lay not with the rules themselves but with the company's failure to follow them. The Enron disaster stemmed not from the rules' structural shortcomings but from the corruption of Enron's managers and perverse financial incentives that inclined its auditor towards cooperation.

The conventional wisdom errs in a second respect as well. The story blames the complex rules on accounting for SPE transactions. It asserts that had FASB adopted a principles-based approach to consolidation of related entity financial statements, Enron would have been disabled from perpetrating its fraud. Unfortunately for the story, the complex rules governing SPEs in SFAS No. 140 applied in full only to mainstream transactions, like the securitization of pools of mortgages. Enron's SPE transactions did not flow in the mainstream governed by SFAS No. 140. They instead fell into a category of 'other' SPE transactions not covered in their entirety by FASB standard-setting. For transactions in the residual category, the critical requirement was a minimum outside equity investment. As to this the accounting firms used a 3 per cent rule of thumb, derived from a 1991 letter of the Chief Accountant of the SEC issued in respect of a lease transaction.[28] To read the 1991 letter is to see that the SEC required 3 per cent outside equity funding on the facts of the leasing case presented to it. The agency never intended to set 3 per cent as a one-size-fits-all, bright line test. During the 1990s, the SEC repeatedly pointed out to the accounting profession that no three per cent bright-line test existed and that the level of outside equity funding for a qualifying SPE in the residual category should follow from the nature of the transaction. In the SEC's view, the question was whether, on the facts of the case, sufficient outside equity capital had been invested to assure the SPEs independence.[29] The outside equity requirement was thus intended not as a rule but as a flexible principle to be applied in the circumstances. But, despite the agency's jawboning, the accounting profession nevertheless applied the principle as a 3 per cent bright-line rule. That rule-based 3 per cent was the operative assumption when Enron planned the LJM transactions.

A disturbing pattern of communicative breakdown and non-compliance emerges. A standard-setting agency articulates a principle and tells US auditors to apply it as such. The auditors instead bowdlerize the standard so that it operates as a check-the-box rule. At the level of practice, then, US auditors manufacture rules where rules do not exist. A

codified in 'Codification of Financial Reporting Policies, s. 101', reprinted in 7 *CCH Fed. Sec. L. Rep.* para. 72,921 (18 May 1988).

28   The GAAP authorities are EITF Topic D-14, 'Transactions Involving Special Purpose Entities', EITF 90–15, 'Impact of Nonsubstantive Lessors, Residual Value Guarantees and Other Provisions in Leasing Transactions', and EITF 96–21, 'Implementation Issues in Accounting for Leasing Transactions involving Special Purpose Entities'.

29   See Ragone (2000).

number of questions follow. Why do US auditors display a refractory preference for rules? What prevents auditors from applying standards as intended? Will the behaviour pattern persist under the new principles-based regime projected by GAAP reformers? Responses to these questions follow in Parts III and IV.

C. Summary

GAAP's form and content do need improvement and take some of the blame for the US accounting crisis. There can be no denying that practitioners often take advantage of GAAP's rule structures when they design aggressive treatments. Regulatory arbitrage—the practice of structuring an inappropriate transaction so it stays just within the bounds set by a rule[30]—clearly is widespread. But these rule-based aggressive treatments, which tend to involve structured finance, leases, and (until recently) pooled mergers, do not show up in large numbers on the list of recent restatements. The reason is that the rules make the treatments GAAP-compliant, even as many observers disapprove of the treatments.

The audit failures and restatements follow less from regulatory arbitrage than from strategic noncompliance—action under an interpretation of the law in conflict with the stated interpretation of the regulator (Malloy 2003). Neither rules nor standards prevent such conduct, and, as between the two, rules have the advantage in deterring it. Meanwhile, in every case of a restatement, GAAP by definition has proved adequate to the job of identifying the misstatement and providing corrective instructions. Under this analysis, the drafters of SOA were right in thinking that the absence of principles has contributed to the crisis but wrong in diagnosing the problem as legislative. This is not for the most part a problem concerning the relative merits of rules and principles in standard-setting. It is instead a problem of professional practice in a regulatory system made up of both. It is the auditors who need to get back to principles, taking seriously principles already governing the reporting system.

III. THE DEMAND FOR RULES

We have seen that US GAAP literally follows from general principles. Yet it has become more and more rules-based as articulated over time. This is not because its general principles no longer motivate particular GAAP standards, but because US accounting's constituents constantly and

---

[30] See Malloy (2003).

effectively register demands for tailored treatments. The propensity toward rules follows from a supply and demand dynamic between the standard-setter, FASB, the audit firms, and their management clients.

The demand for rules follows from auditing clients' constant desire for exception from rules. When an accounting principle articulates a treatment category and a set of reporting companies dislike the way the treatment applies to them, they (and their auditors) lobby for an exception. One means to the end of permitted deviation from the mandated treatment is a 'scope exception'—a rule that excludes stated transactions or items (Schipper 2003: 66–67). GAAP's complex derivative rules provide a good example, with their nine exceptions to the definition of derivative, several of which came into the rules solely for the purpose of reducing preparation costs. Alternatively, constituents request and attain 'treatment exceptions'—special rules for defined items or industry practices. Rules facilitating income-smoothing provide a prominent example. Having won their rule-based exceptions, the constituents then request detailed instructions respecting implementation. FASB responds, and GAAP becomes still more complex.

A. FASB: The Responsive Standard Setter

GAAP has very close formative ties to the profession that applies it, ties closer even than those between US legislatures and judges and the legal professionals who advise corporate clients. Government mandates dictate much of the advice lawyers give to clients. But the government, although heavily populated with lawyers, operates at arm's length from the legal profession. Accounting, in contrast, operates like a guild both at the legislative and at the professional level. Auditors apply law generated within their own profession, operating at closer quarters with the pertinent lawmaking institutions than do lawyers.

The governance structure of FASB demonstrates this proximity. At first glance it appears designed to prevent the large auditing firms from dominating the body that makes GAAP. Public accountants may fill no more than three of FASB's seven seats, with the remaining four seats being taken by two corporate executives, one financial analyst, and one academic (Herwitz and Barrett 2002: 154–56). On further consideration, however, the four to three split does not provide a credible guarantee against special interest influence. Auditors and corporate audit clients will have a community of interest on most hot button standard-setting issues. FASB, by coupling three auditors with two corporate executives, assures that this community of interest has a five-to-two voting advantage. FASB also is a very small shop, with a staff of only forty-five. For funding, it historically relied on the charitable support of the large audit firms, along with a trickle of revenues from publication sales.[31] Add all of this up, and the structure does not guarantee robust institutional independence for GAAP's standard-setter.

With this incentive problem in mind, let us revisit FASB's withdrawal of its two-decades-old project looking toward a substance-over-form approach to defining control and imposing consolidation.[32] Why did FASB give up? It seems unlikely that the decision followed from a jurisprudential commitment to rules-based accounting. More likely FASB abandoned the project because it expected a shift to a standard to trigger vociferous opposition from reporting companies and the large audit firms because it would have had a restraining effect on the structured finance. Securitization is a billion dollar industry. Auditing firms participate as consultants. Reporting companies securitize their assets to enhance their bottom lines. Market intermediaries draw enormous revenues from making the deals. To the extent that a new consolidation regime would have chilled deals by changing accounting treatments, all of these actors would have gone straight to the barricades to protect the status quo. FASB, after years of being greeted with threats from lobbyists and attack dog congressmen whenever it tried to improve anything, was entitled to be a little gun shy in the face of strong demand for the status quo respecting consolidation.

It should be noted that corporate managers do not have the power simply to dictate GAAP's terms. GAAP rule-makings are much contested, despite FASB's structural weakness and management's capture of the auditor interest. Indeed, FASB has conducted itself with admirable independence in recent years, taking positions opposed to those of management and the audit profession on key issues like the treatment good will arising in mergers and management stock options (Levitt 2002: 106–15). But FASB's structural weakness does bear on the rules-versus-principles choice in day-to-day standard-setting. When empowered constituents present FASB with a standard-setting problem or pose a question about a proposed standard, in either case asking for a solution in the form of a scope or treatment exception, they often get a sympathetic hearing.

US GAAP accordingly presents a cognisable capture problem. GAAP in many respects results from an internal conversation, with no institutional mechanism assuring that the public interest trumps the interests of audit firms and their clients in its promulgation. Asymmetries of information and methodological wherewithal aggravate the problem.

---

[31] Meanwhile, the Emerging Issues Task Force, which since 1984 has had the job of pronouncing on cutting-edge requests for advice on appropriate treatments, is a group populated almost entirely of representatives of the large firms (Herwitz and Barrett 2002: 157).

[32] See above, n. 22 and accompanying text.

GAAP is a body of law structurally shielded from outside inspection. Monitoring GAAP is difficult—to know what is going on respecting of substantive issues in accounting is to be a member of the guild in the first place.

Solidarity within the accounting profession aggravates the problem. This profession closes ranks when a major conflict breaks out between it and the rest of the economy. Among the multitude of talking heads from the business world that provided the US media with its sound bites during recent corporate crises, none were partners from the large auditing firms. Even as the rough and tumble world of public policy discussion suddenly occupied itself with GAAP and the audit profession, the audit firms stayed silent.[33] The silence hardly stemmed from disinterest. It instead served to preserve information asymmetry—the less said about audit practice outside the profession the better. Industry concentration augments accounting's professional solidarity. There remain only four firms left with the wherewithal to conduct audits of large capitalization companies. In a universe of four organizations, discipline is easily maintained.

The legal profession in the United States, with all its faults, displays no comparable solidarity. For every lawyer who closes ranks with a corporate client, there is another lawyer looking to bring suit against that first lawyer's client, or, alternatively, to get the legislature to authorize a lawsuit. When the corporation's lawyer goes to Capitol Hill to get the client protective legislation, the trial lawyers also are there, working the other side. When lawyers advocate for their clients in public, they are understood to be acting in a special role. Any representations they make on clients' behalf concerning the state of the law are greeted with scepticism. Indeed, critique usually is assured, for a second lawyer will be charged with articulating the opposing view.

Accountants operate differently as a profession; even as they have come more and more to resemble lawyers in playing an advocacy role for their clients. Whilst with lawyers the advocacy appears in briefs and memoranda of law, with accountants the advocacy merges into the numbers reported on the clients' certified financials. Readers of financial reports have not been on notice to bring scepticism to bear, at least until very recently. And those who do proceed cautiously get only indirect means within the reports' four corners with which to sort numbers influenced by advocacy from harder numbers uninfluenced by management's agenda. This does not go to say that financial reports always are taken at face value. In theory, Wall Street's financial analysts play the critical function. Unfortunately, in recent practice they too have

---

[33] We must put to one side Arthur Andersen's Joe Berardino, who publicly and unsuccessfully acted out the role of the CEO trying to quell an organizational conflagration.

lacked the incentive to criticize.[34] Nor can we assume that a vigorous critique will emanate from within the accounting profession, for it has no segment with a financial stake in articulating adversary positions. The entire burden of critique and correction has devolved on FASB, the SEC accounting office,[35] and a handful of academics.

B. Audit Firm Demands

Auditors are inclined toward cooperation with their clients and will tend to support their clients' reporting objectives. Competition for consulting business aggravates the inclination. Auditors also are disinclined to say no to their clients. It follows that before so doing they will seek the backing of a precise negative instruction in GAAP. The rule denudes the negative response to the client of any suggestion that the nay-saying stems from the auditor's own professional judgment. The external authority takes the blame. What the auditor seeks, the client demands. Under the prevailing relational pattern, audit clients balk at negative auditor demands absent a precise written justification: 'Show me where it says I can't do this' (SEC 2003: § III.I.). This professional dynamic generates a high demand for rules.

The profession's fear of enforcement entanglement strengthens the preference. With an open-ended principle, both the preparer and the auditor make a judgment respecting a law-to-fact application. Risk averse actors in this posture will be wary of second-guessing by regulatory authorities (SEC 2003: § I.C.). They fear that the good faith they bring to the principle's application will be unverifiable *ex post*. Principles, then, make it hard to minimize enforcement risk.

It follows that a high demand for rules could persist even in the wake of an across-the-board ban on nonaudit consulting. Recall that the 'check-the-box' allegation against rules-based GAAP can be restated in positive terms: Rules enhance verifiability, causing a decrease in differences in measurement and making non-compliance more evident. Now assume, as some assert,[36] that the audit firms engage in intense price competition (even as the number of firms equipped to audit large

[34] The incentive problem stems from underwriting and other rent streams flowing from the issuers of financial reports to the employers of analysts. It is not clear that the problem admits of an easy solution. Absent that corrupting rent flow, it is not clear that resources exist to support an adequate flow of critical analysis. Restating the point, reform implies a new pricing structure for the audit.
[35] The SEC had the power to impose accounting rules prior to SOA. See 15 U.S.C. ss. 77(a), 78m(b)(1) (1994). The SEC exercises its power only rarely, preferring to leave the job to FASB, acting under the threat of intervention should the SEC's preferences not be satisfied (Herwitz and Barrett 2002: 146).
[36] See Sunder (2003).

capitalization companies has decreased to four and quite apart from competition for consulting rents). Such price competition could come at the cost of audit quality. To see why, hypothesize the incentives of an audit partner under pricing pressure. Under Generally Accepted Auditing Standards, the audit process begins with an appraisal of the risk of compliance failure at the client. The auditor's professional judgment concerning the scope of the testing to be conducted in the course of the audit follows from this risk appraisal (Herwitz and Barrett 2002: 200–3). The scope of the testing in turn impacts on the audit fee—as the risk increases, more tests are needed, more time must be spent, and the fee rises. Rules recommend themselves over principles in a hard cash sense at this point in the scenario. Check-the-box verifiability gets the job done more quickly and predictably, making it easier to state a price in advance and lock in a profit on the engagement. Under a regime of principles, the preparer will have made fact sensitive applications of the standards, necessitating a more labor-intensive audit. With principles, unexpected, time-consuming problems also are more likely to arise. In sum, professional price competition, to the extent it exists, also fuels the demand for rules.

C. The Legal Profession Compared

US auditors, in demanding rules from their standard-setter, track the actions of US lawyers; and US GAAP, in evolving away from broad principles toward rules, tracks the evolution of US business law as a whole. Before telling their clients that a course of action is prohibited, lawyers also seek an explicit statutory bar or a case on all fours. Business law and lawyers no longer subscribe to the legal realists' view that fact specific adjudication under principles makes law more responsive.[37] As an example, compare the old Uniform Partnership Act,[38] drafted early in the twentieth century, with a Revised Uniform Partnership Act,[39] drafted at the end of the century. The former is a collection of short, general statements. The latter is a labyrinthine affair that reads like an attempt to answer every question that ever arose in this history of partnership governance. The evolution of the Uniform Commercial Code (UCC) and the cases thereunder over the last three decades has worked similarly. New legislative drafts of the UCC add layers of complications. Today's drafters no longer leave it to later case law to fill in the details. Instead they pursue the impossible dream of creating complete sets of

[37] See Bratton (2001: 737, 746).
[38] Uniform Partnership Act, 6 *ULA* 275 (1914).
[39] Revised Uniform Partnership Act, 6 *ULA* 1 (1997).

instructions, just like the accountants.[40] Meanwhile, courts applying the UCC have abandoned general ideas like liberal construction[41] and good faith (Bratton 2002b: 933–94).

Many reasons for business law's movement to rules can be suggested. Confidence in judicial decision-making has declined even as the expense of litigating questions of interpretation has risen. In commercial law contexts the scope of jury control over mixed law and fact questions expanded materially over the latter part of the twentieth century, destabilizing the expectations of business people. There also circulates a general notion that specific instructions import certainty that enhances economic welfare. Finally, lawyers, like auditors, turn to rules because they want to reduce risk both for themselves and their clients. A rule imports a safe harbour and control of future events where a standard does not.

To sum up, GAAP and business law have moved to rules simultaneously. Auditors, lawyers, and clients alike demand clear instructions, putting the burden of clarity on the lawmaker. They thereby relieve themselves of the burden of making judgments under uncertainty. Such judgments take time, cost money, and disrupt client relations. This is not a healthy development. But the fault lies neither in the proliferating rulebooks nor their drafters. The fault occurs at the point of demand: Drafters will continue to generate rulebooks until the demand ceases. Actors in practice will perceive the rulebooks to be inflexible and burdensome only with the cessation of the forces generating the demand.

D. Relative Merits of Rules and Principles: Ideal Conditions and Incentive Incompatibility

For the sake of argument, let us assume that the auditor-client demand for greater rule specificity ceases, freeing us to interrogate in a neutral policy space the question whether GAAP should be articulated in rules or principles. The result will depend on the inquiry's further assumptions. If an ideal professional environment is hypothesized, in which the auditor works unconstrained by pressures of time, price, and reputation, a strong case can be stated for a principles-based regime. But a plausible case can be stated for rules even under such ideal conditions. The case for rules strengthens materially in an imperfect institutional framework, such as that prevailing respecting the audit function in the United States.

---

[40] Compare the original UCC Art. 9 and the revised Art. 9 on the perfection and priorities of security interests, See UCC ss. 9-301–9-318 3A *ULA* 859-1037, 3B *ULA* 33-386 (1972); UCC ss. 9-301–9-342, 3 *ULA* 154-301 (2000).

[41] See Maggs (2000).

E. Cost Savings and Transparency

Rules-based accounting entails cost savings and enhances transparency. The cost savings follow from the nature of the subject-matter. Accounting standards govern homogenous, recurrent situations where the actors need *ex ante* instructions and have incentives to invest in compliance.[42] Such conditions tend to justify a rules-based approach. An across-the-board shift to principles would make sense only if the costs of constant revision of the rules to keep up with unintended applications due to faulty drafting and regulatory arbitrage outweighed the benefits of advance specification. GAAP does not appear to lie anywhere near that level of dysfunction. On this analysis, the indicated course of reform is incremental change. The standard-setter monitors the rules' operation looking to periodic amendment, adjusting categories so that reporting results follow from the rules' operative principles.[43]

Transparency imports a second justification for rules. Recall that rule compliance is more easily verified than principle compliance.[44] It follows that rules decrease the risk of audit failure even as they import inflexibility.

Rules enhance transparency for users of financial statements as well as for auditors. To see why, revisit the legal realists' case for principles over rules in respect of private law adjudication. That case presupposes that the law to fact application is explained and published in a judicial opinion. The reported cases give the practitioner an expanding body of fact sensitive applications, ever better articulating the standard's meaning. Over time, the accumulated case law offers the practitioners a level of certainty not dissimilar to that of a rulebook, even as the principle's flexibility is retained. Meanwhile, the cases (and thus the substance of the legal regime) are open for public inspection.

The ongoing rules-based articulation of GAAP by FASB and other public bodies works similarly.[45] But the application of open-ended accounting principles by reporting firms and auditors does not. Financial statements and footnotes are very summary documents. Decision-making about treatments goes on in a black box, evolving as a matter of practice amongst insiders.[46] There is no comparable moment of transparency

[42] See Kaplow (1992: 557, 570–77).

[43] The rule might be overinclusive; that is, it might bring inappropriate transactions into a given zone of treatment. A rule also might be underinclusive; that is, it might allow a transaction that should be included in a treatment category to be structured so as not to be included. See Sunstein (1995: 953, 995).

[44] See text accompanying n. 36 above.

[45] According to FASB, any bias toward rules in contemporary GAAP stems from exactly this sort of law-to-fact development process, as rules are rewritten to take into account different transactional facts and interpretive opinions accumulate. FASB (2002a: 3–4).

[46] The 3% rule applied to SPEs provides a good example, see above, text accompanying n. 28.

respecting the law-to-fact application. This diminishes the chance for outside evaluation. These law-to-fact decisions, meanwhile, are not made by judges empowered by the state. They come from the preparers—the regulated actors themselves—acting with an input of the auditor's professional review. And a professional, even one historically conceived to be in an adversary posture to its client, is in a materially different position from a judge. Adjudicatory authority imports absolute power to say no. The outside professional can only suggest no, on pain of giving up the client.

When confronting substandard financials, today's auditors are disinclined even to threaten to walk, much less actually to forego the rent flowing from the audit engagement. A serious incentive problem results, a problem that makes a move to flexible, open-ended principles ill advised at this time.

F. Flexibility and Professional Judgment

The case for principles-based accounting arises in large measure from the description of the perverse effects of rules. The principles case admits the force of the rules case but asserts that once rules come to dominate the accounting regime, cumulative perverse effects cause the disadvantages of rules to outweigh the advantages. The more detailed the set of exceptions, the greater the chance that essentially similar transactions receive different accounting treatments. Scope and treatment exceptions build inconsistencies into the standards, sacrificing the integrity of the underlying principles. Strategic behaviour results, as preparers seek to exploit the inconsistencies, designing compliant transactions that subvert the principles the rules supposedly effectuate. Meanwhile, the proliferating exceptions fuel additional demand for explication from the standard-setter. The responsive standard-setter finds itself attempting to articulate a treatment for every conceivable scenario. But the attempt always fails, for the goal of a perfect, exhaustive rulebook is unattainable (SEC 2003: § I.C.).

The case for principles at this point reverses the case for rules. Since the standard-setter cannot identify all pertinent business situations *ex ante*, it is not clear why exhaustive instructions should be held out as a goal in the first place, given that micro-level standard-setting always results in inconsistencies. The only party with all information respecting a given transaction is the reporting company itself. It follows that the company's preparer, operating in good faith, is more likely to derive an appropriate treatment when applying a principle than is a rulemaking standard-setter acting *ex ante*. With principles, company-specific knowledge and the regulatory framework interact flexibly and the regulation's purpose is more likely to be effectuated (SEC 2003: § I.D.).

Thus described, principles-based accounting not only permits but also requires exercises of professional judgment by auditors and actors at reporting companies (Schipper 2003: 61). Sir David Tweedie (2002), chairman of the IASB, stressed the importance of professional judgment in a principles-based system in his Congressional testimony:

> We favor an approach that requires the company and its auditor to take a step back and consider whether the accounting suggested is consistent with the underlying principle. This is not a soft option. Our approach requires both companies and their auditors to exercise professional judgment in the public interest. Our approach requires a strong commitment from preparers to financial statements that provide a faithful representation of all transactions and a strong commitment from auditors to resist client pressures. It will not work without these commitments.

Having heard the case for principles, we must return to the auditor-client relationship to inquire into the expected quality of professional judgments. If recent history is predictive, the prognosis is not good. Even as auditors have been disempowered with respect to their clients, so the clients have been guided by the short-term solicitude for their stock prices rather than fidelity to accounting principles. Proponents of principles seem to believe that reformulating rules into standards by itself solves these problems. But the belief is unfounded. The recent history of audit failure has been no respecter of principles. It will take more than a new approach to standard-setting to bring incentive compatibility to this compliance environment.

The SEC displays sensitivity to this problem in its SOA report on principles-based accounting (SEC 2003: § I.C.). The report's definition of an ideal principles-based standard makes an interesting comparison with Sir David Tweedie's approach:

> [T]he optimal principles-based accounting standard involves a concise statement of substantive accounting principles where the accounting objective has been incorporated as an integral part of the standard and where few, if any, exceptions or internal inconsistencies are included in the standard. Further, such a standard should provide an appropriate amount of implementation guidance given the nature of the class of transactions or events and should be devoid of bright-line tests. Finally, such a standard should be consistent with, and derive from, a coherent conceptual framework of financial reporting.

Where Tweedie lays the responsibility for law to fact determinations squarely on the regulated actors, the SEC hesitates. It takes a step back from the case for principles to endorse constituent demand for specificity.

It then shifts the burden back to the standard-setter to provide 'an appropriate amount of implementation guidance.' Bald statements of principles, says the SEC, provide users insufficient structure in which to frame their professional judgment. The 'principles' need to be 'defined specifically.' The SEC calls this an 'objectives-oriented' approach to principles-based standard-setting. As an exemplar, it holds out FASB's recent revision of the standard for mergers (SEC 2003: §§ I.C., I.E.).

The regime envisaged by the SEC appears to hold out the benefit of a decrease in the level of reporting detail. At the same time, comparability of treatment across different issuers would be enhanced. But the decrease in complexity implies a concomitant loss of transparency, since commonality of treatment obscures particulars in the economics of differing underlying transactions.[47] The SEC sees these as matters to be traded off by the standard-setter: '[T]he task of the standard-setter [is] to determine the trade offs among relevance, reliability, and comparability … in … an effort to find the "sweet spot"'(SEC 2003: §§ I.C., I.E.). Two additional SEC instructions to the standard-setter stand out: (1) economic substance should drive the development and scope of the standards, and (2) no scope and treatment exceptions should be conceded.

A question must be asked about the SEC's vision of accounting standards. How does the regime simultaneously articulate precise instructions and eschew all exceptions from its categories? So doing would amount to a considerable achievement. The drawing of lines is intrinsic to regulation. Line-drawing is what case law under principles is supposed to do. It is not at all clear that financial reporting principles differ from any other body of regulations in this regard. So, to the extent the SEC looks toward a new regime in which all standards mesh like the parts of a well-running machine, it is likely to be disappointed. Such perfect engineering is no more likely here than in any other regulatory context.[48] The search for 'sweet spots' is better consigned to sporting and other physical activities.

The SEC, in its search for a regime of broadly stated standards that incorporate no exceptions, might be better off abandoning the rubric of principles-based accounting. The system envisioned more accurately would be characterized as a one of tough, general rules.[49] Such a regime holds out advantages. For example, it presumably would prohibit whole classes of aggressive treatments tolerated in recent years, particularly those facilitating earnings management. But if this is the SEC's intent, a question arises: in the present political and institutional context how

---

[47] The comments in the text draw on FASB (2002a: 7).

[48] See FASB (2002a: 6).

[49] FASB's Proposal respecting Principles in effect warns audit firms and issuers of this when it points out that principles will mean more volatility in reported earnings figures (FASB (2002a: 7–8).

likely is it that reporting companies, their auditors, and their friends in Washington would permit FASB to use the rubric of principles-based accounting to usher in a new era of strict treatments? Even as the PCAOB takes steps to regulate the audit profession, the answer must be, very unlikely.

As a practical matter, then, the projected move to principles will have to be articulated in the form of general but flexible guidelines—what lawyers call 'standards.'[50] Choices of treatment will have to be made and the quality of preparer and auditor judgments will matter. The SEC warns that principles-based accounting implicates a more expensive, time-consuming audit process. The SEC anticipates that, in order to review preparer judgments, audit firms will have to hire expensive personnel with expertise in complex transactions. It also anticipates that active audit committee oversight and other strong enforcement agents will be required if the system is to work. Finally, it advises auditors and preparers to generate extensive paper records respecting treatment decisions so as to position themselves to defend their good faith (SEC 2003: § III.I.).

In effect the SEC asks users of financial statements to trust in the effectiveness of the PCAOB to create a compliance environment very different from the one prevailing—a wonderful new world of accounting. The question is not whether the regime it projects would be an improvement on the status quo; it would be. The question is whether the ideal world thus projected is feasible in practice without unintended effects in the form of poor professional judgments. It is too soon in the US reform process for an affirmative answer.

CONCLUSION

US GAAP, even as it has moved to rules, continues to contain many principles and holds out many choices of treatment. Independent auditors are supposed to make reference to the principles in filling in the inevitable gaps in the rules and in answering questions of interpretation under the rules. Such law to fact applications should with some frequency have been leading auditors to say no to aggressive treatments chosen by their clients. But such nay-saying has not been the practice. Application of principles in the manner contemplated requires exercises of judgment, exercises that captured auditors are disabled from making. Principles-based accounting only works when the actor applying it takes responsibility for its judgments.

---

[50] Kennedy (1976: 1685) offers the classic description of standards in American jurisprudence. America's principles-based accounting advocates would be well advised to read it.

The US accounting crisis stems less from the form of GAAP standards, whether rules- or principles-based, than from their application to fact and enforcement. The system's problems arise out of the professional relation between auditors and clients. It follows that SOA correctly prioritizes professional regulation in the form of the new PCAOB. It is less clear that rules-based GAAP should be a present law reform target. Until the enforcement mechanism works more reliably—and the PCAOB is only beginning to task of correction—a move to principles-based accounting could aggravate the crisis of confidence.

REFERENCES

Berardino, J. (2001), 'Enron: A Wake-Up Call', *Wall St. J.* (4 Dec.) p. A18.
Bratton, W.W. (2001), 'Berle and Means Reconsidered at the Century's Turn', 26 *J.Corp.L.* 737.
—— (2002a), 'Enron and the Dark Side of Shareholder Value', 76 *Tulane L. Rev.* 1275.
—— (2002b), 'Venture Capital on the Downside: Preferred Stock and Corporate Control', 100 *Mich. L. Rev.* 891.
Burkholder, S. (2002), 'Accounting: Outlook 2002', 34 *Sec. Reg. & L. Rep.*214.
Burns J. and Schroeder, M. (2002), 'Accounting Firms Ask SEC for Post-Enron Guide', *Wall St. J.* (7 Jan.) p. A16.
Cunningham, L.W. (2003), 'The Sarbanes-Oxley Yawn: Heavy Rhetoric, Light Reform (And It Just Might Work)', 35 *Conn. L. Rev.* 915.
Deutsch, C. and Abelson, R. (2001), 'Xerox Facing New Pressures Over Auditing', *N.Y. Times* (9 Feb.) p. C1.
Economist (2002), 'Leaders: The Lessons from Enron', *Economist* (9 Feb.) pp. 9–10.
Eichenwald, K. (2002), 'A Higher Standard for Corporate Advice', *N.Y. Times* (23 Dec.) p. A1.
Eisenberg, M.A. (1975), 'Legal Models of Management Structure in the Modern Corporation: Officers, Directors and Accountants', 63 *Cal. L. Rev.* 375.
Ernst & Young (2001), *Financial Reporting Developments; Accounting for Transfers and Servicing of Financial Assets and Extinguishments of Liabilities—FASB Statement 140* (May).
FASB (1975), *Statement of Financial Accounting Standards No. 5, Accounting for Contingencies* (March).
—— (1978), *Statement of Financial Accounting Concepts No. 1, Objective of Financial Reporting by Business Enterprises* (November).
—— (1980), *Statement of Financial Accounting Concepts No. 2, Qualitative Characteristics of Accounting Information*.
—— (1981), *Interpretation No. 34, Disclosure of Indirect Guarantees of Indebtedness of Others* (March).
—— (1982), *Statement No. 57, Related Party Disclosures* (March).
—— (1999a), *Preliminary Views on Major Issues Related to Reporting Financial Instruments and Certain Related Assets and Liabilities at Fair Value*.

—— (1999b), *Consolidated Financial Statements: Purpose and Policy* (proposed 23 February).

—— (2000), *Summary of Statement No. 140, Accounting for Transfers and Servicing of Financial Assets and Extinguishments of Liabilities* (September 2000).

—— (2001), *Statement of Financial Accounting Standards No. 141, Business Combinations* (June).

—— (2002a), *Principles-Based Approach to U.S. Standard Setting, No. 1125–001* (21 October).

—— (2002b), *Consolidation of Certain Special Purpose Entities—an Interpretation of ARB No. 51* (proposed 1 July).

—— (2002b), *Interpretation No. 45, Guarantor's Accounting Disclosure Requirements for Guarantees, Including Indirect Guarantees of Indebtedness of Others* (25 November).

Frost C.A. and Ramin, K.P. (1966), 'International Accounting Differences', 181 *J. Acct.* 62.

GAO (2002), The General Accounting Office Report to the Chairman, Committee on Banking, Housing, and Urban Affairs, U.S. Senate, *Financial Restatements: Trends, Market Impacts, Regulatory Responses, and Remaining Challenges* (Oct.) (GAO-03–138).

Herwitz D.R. and Barrett, M.J. (2002), *Accounting for Lawyers: Materials*, 3rd edn. (New York: Foundation).

Kahn, J. (2001), 'Accounting in Wonderland: Jeremy Kahn Goes Down the Rabbit Hole with G. E.'s Books', *Fortune* (19 March) 37.

Kaplow, L. (1992), 'Rules versus Standards: An Economic Analysis', 42 *Duke L.J.* 557.

Kennedy, D. (1976), 'Form and Substance in Private Law Adjudication', 89 *Harv. L. Rev.* 1685.

Levitt, A. (2000), 'Renewing the Covenant With Investors', Speech given at the New York University Center for Law and Business (10 May) (available at www.sec.gov/news/speech/spch (last visited 25 January 2004).

—— (2002), *Take On the Street: What Wall Street and Corporate America Don't Want You to Know, What You Can Do to Fight Back* (New York: Random House).

Liesman, S. (2002), 'Heard on the Street: Deciphering the Black Box', *Wall St. J.* (23 January).

Liesman, S. (2002), 'SEC Accounting Cop's Warning: Playing By Rules May Not Ward Off Fraud Issues', *Wall St. J.* (12 February) C1.

Maggs, G.E. (2000), 'Karl Llewellyn's Fading Imprint on the Jurisprudence of the Uniform Commercial Code', 71 *U. Colo. L. Rev.* 541.

Malloy, T.F. (2003), 'Regulation, Compliance, and the Firm', 76 *Temple Law Review* 451.

Morgenson, G. (2002), 'Worries of More Enrons to Come Give Stock Prices a Pounding', *N.Y. Times* (30 January) C1.

Nelson, M.W., Elliott, J.A., and Tarpley, R.L. (2000), 'Where Do Companies Attempt Earnings Management, and When Do Auditors Prevent It?' available at http://papers.ssrn.com/sol3/papers.cfm?abstract_id=248129 (last visited 2 August 2005).

Partnoy, F. (2003), 'A Revisionist View of Enron and the Sudden Death of "May"', 48 *Villanova Law Review* 1245.

Pitt, H.L. (2002), Testimony Concerning The Corporate and Auditing Accountability, Responsibility, and Transparence Act, Committee on Financial Services, House of Representatives p. 5. Available on the SEC website at <http: www.sec.gov/news/testimony/032002tshlp.htm> (last visited 2 August 2005).

Powers, W.C., *et al.* (2002), 'Report of Investigation by the Special Investigative Committee of the Board of Directors of Enron Corp.' available at 2002 WL 198018 p. 98.

Ragone D.J. (2000), 'Current Accounting Projects', 2000 Conference on SEC Developments (4 December).

Romero, S. (2001), 'Lucent's Books Said to Draw Attention of the SEC', *N.Y. Times* (10 February) C1.

Schipper, K. (2003), 'Principles-Based Accounting Standards', 17 *Accounting Horizons* 61.

Siegel, S. (1996), 'The Coming Revolution in Accounting: The Emergence of Fair Value as the Fundamental Principle of GAAP', 42 *Wayne L. Rev.* 1839.

Silverman R.E. and Brown, K. (2002), 'Five Companies: How They Get Their Numbers', *Wall St. J.* (23 January) C1, C16.

Simpson, G.R. (2002), 'Deals That Took Enron Under Had Many Supporters', *Wall St. J.* (10 April) A1.

Sunder, S. (2003), 'Rethinking the Structure of Accounting and Auditing', Yale ICF Working Paper No. 03–17 (29 May) (available at http://papers.ssrn.com/sol3/papers.cfm?abstract_id=413581) (last visited 26 January 2004).

Sunstein, C.R. (1995), 'Problems With Rules', 83 *Cal. L. Rev.* 953.

Tweedie, D. (2002), Testimony of Sir David Tweedie Before the Senate Committee on Banking, Housing and Urban Affairs (14 February).

9

The Oligopolistic Gatekeeper: The US Accounting Profession

JAMES D COX*

T HE GUARDIAN OF financial disclosure is the independent
accountant. Even before the Depression-era federal securities laws
mandated audited financial statements, the accounting profession
provided its important attest function to issuers who wished to signal
their greater trustworthiness by having their financial statements
certified as complying with generally-accepted accounting principles.
Upon their enactment, the federal securities laws made this formerly
isolated voluntary practice a requirement for public companies.[1] Thus,
the accountants became the most pervasive of all the gatekeepers that the
federal securities laws socialized into their mission of protecting
investors.[2]

This chapter explores the extent to which the highly-concentrated
structure of the accounting profession contributes to its failure to serve

* Brainerd Currie Professor of Law, Duke University. The author is grateful for the helpful
suggestions of Professors William Bratton, Deborah DeMott, Barak Richman, and Randall
Thomas and the participants of the Reflections on the Reform of Corporate Disclosure and
Accounting Rules Conference at Tilburg University April 2004. The author has benefitted
immensely by research assistance of Ms. Maria Hahan and Messrs. Christopher Fazekas
and Raegan Watchman.

[1] See Securities Act of 1933, 15 U.S.C. § 77aa(25)(26); § 13(a)(2) of the Securities Exchange
Act, 15 U.S.C. § 78m(a)(2).

[2] Gatekeeper responsibilities are imposed selectively in other provisions of the securities
laws. For example, underwriters and directors are impressed into service through their
obligations to undertake a reasonable investigation in connection with registered public
offerings. See Securities Act § 11(a)(2)(5) & (b)(3), 15 U.S.C. § 77k(a)(2)(5) and (b)(3).
Supervisors of brokers have a duty to supervise that imposes gatekeeper-like responsibilities
in appropriate settings. See Securities Exchange Act § 15(b)(4)(E), 15 U.S.C. § 78o (b)(4)(E).
And the control person liability provisions, § 15 of the Securities Act, 15 U.S.C. § 77o, and §
20(a) of the Exchange Act, 15 U.S.C. § 78t, can have this effect, particularly when read to
require the maintenance of compliance systems. See generally Cox *et al*. (2004: 748–50) for a
review of cases where the 'good faith' defense requirement mandates more than the absence
of knowledge.

the public interest by not being a diligent and independent gatekeeper of financial reporting. In Part I, data is presented that documents that the accounting industry is dominated by a few major firms so that it is correctly viewed as an oligopoly. The potential adverse effects of an oligopoly are described in Part II where we also review the conditions that enable firms within a highly-concentrated industry to misbehave as members of a cartel. As will be seen, industry concentration alone does not inevitably lead to adverse social welfare effects. Part III reviews the rising importance of consulting revenues to the dominant accounting firms and in Part IV the transformation of accounting firms into consulting firms is linked to the accountants being members of an oligopoly. Structure, not greed alone, is identified as an important cause of the accounting industry transforming itself from a profession to a business. The point developed in this chapter is that even though accountants compete aggressively with one another for audit clients, on closer examination we unravel just how the accounting firms pursue parallel conduct to maximize their collective wealth. Specifically, we find that during the past two decades a variety of forces drove the major accounting firms to place greater emphasis on their being providers of non-audit services to their audit clients and that the cartel-like structure allows them to pursue this course collectively.

Part IV also describes the negative social welfare that can arise when non-audit services are provided by auditors to their audit clients. It is this aspect of the auditors' business plan that the Sarbanes-Oxley Act of 2002 (the Act)[3] directs several of its key provisions that are examined in Part V. However, in Part VI we find some disturbing evidence that with regard to auditor behaviour; little has changed since the enactment of Sarbanes-Oxley so that the harmful effects of auditors vending non-audit services to their clients continues today at levels that pose the same threat to their independence. Part VII offers reforms that are necessary to assure that the industry competes on the basis of quality and not more harmful terrain. Part VIII concludes.

I. A FEW FISH IN A VERY LARGE POND

There can be little doubt that structurally the accounting industry is an oligopoly. Once we could aptly describe the US accounting industry by referring to the 'Big Eight.' Life, however, is never static. As a consequence of a flurry of mega-mergers between 1987–98—mergers that sometimes crossed international borders[4]—the Big Eight became the Big

---

[3] Sarbanes-Oxley Act of 2002, PL 107-204 (30 July 2002).

[4] For example, US-based Peat Marwick Mithchell, a member of the Big Eight, merged with a non-Big Eight firm, KMG Main Hurdman, an affiliate of European-based Klynveld Main Goerdeler, to form KPMG.

Five. Following the criminal conviction and consequent disappearance of Big Five member Arthur Andersen, we now can refer to the industry as the 'The Final Four.' Legitimate external forces drove the Big Eight to become participants in a wave of consolidations within their already heavily-concentrated industry. As clients became more international, their auditors needed to become more global.[5] With the rise of expensive data processing, there was the need for the accounting firms to achieve critical economies of scale.[6] Having more auditors married to an expensive infrastructure was a wise financial strategy especially if it also meant they would bring to the acquiring firm their clients as well.

By gaining auditors and clients, the surviving firm achieved important economies of scale that could support the expensive technology that became an integral part of the work of the industry. And, as audit clients became more specialized, global, and complex, there was the need on the part of the accounting firms to stay abreast with their audit clients, i.e., the auditing firm also had to acquire pockets of specialization, be global in its operations, and have an infrastructure that could address the complexities of their clients' businesses and systems. Finally, growth and consolidation were strategies to maintain market share of the surviving firms (GAO 2003a: 12–15).

In a masterpiece of understatement, a recent GAO study of the accounting industry observes (GAO 2003a: 16):

> [T]he large public company audit market is a tight oligopoly. ... In the large public company audit market, the Big 4 now audit over 97 percent of all public companies with sales over $250 million, and other firms face significant barriers to entry into the market. ... When comparing the top 25 firms on the basis of total revenues, partners, and staff resources, the Big 4 do not have any smaller-firm competitors ... [7]

Concentration within public accounting is evident from a variety of metrics. For example, the concentration for audit services within the industry is reflected by the fact that 2002 revenues of the fourth largest firm, KPMG, were eight times greater than those of the fifth largest firm, Grant Thornton and that KPMG had five times as many staff members as Grant Thornton (GAO 2003a: 17, table 1). Even more dramatic is that the

[5] Thomas, Schwab and Hansen (2001) describe the growth of accounting firms as being driven by the demands of their audit clients, and not by a quest to leverage their human capital; audit firm clients' are constantly increasing in size/complexity and becoming more international.

[6] Yardley *et al.* (1992: 163) speculate that economies of scale may be a influence in the market for very large audit clients.

[7] The high concentration is not limited to the United States. 90% of the companies listed in the Netherlands, and 80% of those listed in Japan are audit clients of a Big Four firm (GAO 2003a: 18).

total 2002 audit revenues of KPMG were 60 per cent greater than the total revenues of the next 21 largest firms (GAO 2003a).[8]

From another perspective, consider the Hirschmann-Herfindahl Index (HHI)—a metric commonly used by the US Department of Justice to assess the potentially anti-competitive effects of concentration within an industry. In 1998, the year of the last great merger within the industry—the combination of PriceWaterhouse with Coopers Lybrand—the HHI score for the accounting industry was more than 10 per cent above the level normally associated with a score that is likely to permit industry participants to maintain prices above competitive periods for significant periods of time (GAO 2003a: 19, Fig. 3). Following the demise of Arthur Andersen in 2002, the HHI increased to more than 40 per cent above this anti-competitive warning level (GAO 2003a).

Although it may seem improbable, the provision of audit services is even more concentrated than described above. Within certain industries, an individual accounting firm's expertise enables it to be a virtual monopolist because it enjoys the dominant body of expertise for audits within that industry. Stated differently, public companies seeking an auditor gravitate toward the audit firm they understand possesses industry-specific expertise. As a consequence, one or two accounting firms perform a substantial amount of the audits within certain key industry sectors. For example, 76.4 per cent of total assets of the petroleum and coal products industry were audited by Pricewaterhouse-Coopers, and nearly 60 per cent of the assets of non-depositary institutions were audited by KPMG. In 1997, before the demise of Arthur Andersen, 32.9 per cent and 31.6 per cent of total assets within the general building contractors industry were audited by Ernst & Young and Arthur Andersen, respectively; following the 2002 demise of Arthur Andersen, Ernst & Young's percentage rose to 60.7 per cent (GAO 2003a: 28–9, Fig. 7).[9]

The cause for such industry concentration cannot all be placed solely at the door of the auditors' clients. To be sure, large multinational firms can be expected to seek auditors of comparable geographical breadth and staffing relative to their audit competitors. But this should only explain a small amount of the forces causing accounting firms to be so highly concentrated in their provision of audit services. One can question skeptically what percentage of the 17,000 public companies and nearly 7000 mutual funds that file reports with the SEC for which each registrant must have financial statements certified by a public accountant are either

[8] In 2002 KPMG had total audit revenues of $2.016 billion and the next 21 firms combined audit revenues were $1.231 billion (*ibid.*).
[9] We also note a large number of industries in which two of the Big Four dominated in 2002 with the two firms in combination having a total market share in terms of assets audited in excess of 70% (GAO 2003a: App. IV, Figs. 13–14).

so global or so extensive that they require the services of a Big Four accounting firm. Big audit clients do not inherently call for their audits to be performed by members of an oligopoly.

II. A THEORETICAL FRAMEWORK FOR UNDERSTANDING AND HEALING THE ACCOUNTING INDUSTRY

Concentration within any industry is rife with the possibilities of collusion since collusion is more likely to be achieved, and successfully maintained, when a few members of an industry control the bulk of the goods produced than when production is dependent upon hundreds of producer firms. When an industry's production is dominated by a few firms, it is more likely that an agreement by three or four of them regarding price or production of a product will affect the products supply and its price since collectively they represent a dominant share of the market. Their actions in turn make it more likely that other producers will understand that their profits will increase by following the pricing or supply decisions of the colluding members. In this manner, the rising tide of prices lifts all industry-members boats. On the other hand, when there are numerous producers within an industry, agreement among enough of its participants to affect the market is very difficult to achieve. And, even if an agreement were reached, individual members are likely to defect from its terms thereby robbing the agreement of its intended effects. Moreover, an agreement among numerous industry members is far more likely to be detected by antitrust enforcers. Consequently, collusion is more likely to be successful within concentrated industries than those that are competitively structured. Industry concentration, therefore, always raises concerns that there will be either overt collusion or conscious parallel behaviour that yields the same effects as an agreement.

The adverse social welfare of collusive behaviour is well understood. Firms that are permitted to coordinate on price or production will see it is in their interest to do so. This strategy enables colluding firms to increase their collective profits at the expense of consumer welfare. Simply stated, an industry does best if its members act collectively to mimic the practices that would be engaged in by a monopolist. When an industry's market structure is that of an oligopoly, the power of an individual firm to increase its profits by changing the price of its product, or even by altering the quantity and quality of the goods or services it produces, depends on the actions of its competitors. Thus, pricing strategies within an oligopoly frequently reflect a good deal of interdependence among rivals within the industry.[10]

---

[10] See Areeda and Hovenkamp (2003: § 1429 at 207).

Despite the potential rewards of acting in parallel with industry members, the oligopolist faces the ongoing dilemma whether to act individually or collectively. Each firm has an incentive to obtain gains by undercutting its rivals but at the same time coordinated action by industry members holds the promise of monopoly-like rewards.[11] If the oligopolist decides to compete by deviating from a prevailing industry price or production level, the benefits of pursing such an individualistic course might prove fleeting and ultimately costly. By undercutting the price of others, the oligopolist seeks to increase its market share and/or its profits. But its success in doing so depends on the reaction of its rivals. Rivals who do not match the 'cheating' firm's lower price do so at their peril of ceding market share to the cheating rival. Rivals may, however, choose to match the pricing strategy of the cheating rival. If they do, then the revenues and profits of all industry members decline, so that the deviation from the earlier collective price results in benefits to consumers, not the oligopolists. In this case, cheating hurts not just the cheater, but its co-oligopolists. On the other hand, non-cheating rivals may decide that they all suffer if each meets the lower price of the cheater. They may conclude that the cheater will gain only a small amount of market share by its conduct (e.g., the cheating firm lacks the capacity to satiate much of the market's demand) so that their profits are likely to be larger by maintaining their present prices than if the rivals lowered their price to that of the cheating firm. The market share they concede to the cheater by not matching its strategy may not be so significant as to cause the noncheating firms to reduce the price of their product with the effect of lowering its overall profits by a greater amount than if it maintained its existing pricing strategy. The risks facing a firm that adheres to the earlier collusive price is endemic to a cartel. A firm can well see that holding to the earlier collusive practices is better for everyone.

Not all oligopolies misbehave by consciously parallel pricing or output decisions. In his now classic article, Professor George Stigler explains why not all oligopolies misbehave vis-a-vis consumer welfare (1964). His article isolates conditions that are necessary for a cartel to function effectively in ways similar to that of a monopoly: firms must be able to identify the terms of their coordination, they must be able to detect deviations, and once finding a deviation they must be able to punish those that deviate from the collusive strategy supported by the others.[12]

---

[11] This occurs even if greater production or sales lowers the product's price the defecting firm does not absorb the full cost of this lower price. See Hovenkamp (1994: § 4.1a at 143).

[12] Professor Hovenkamp (1994: § 4.1 at 141) adds to this list three other conditions that appear assumed by Stigler. Hovenkamp specifies (1) that the relevant cartelized product or service market must enjoy sufficiently high barriers to entry that prevent newcomers from undermining the cartel's pricing or production decisions; (2) that collectively the

Stigler's theory provides useful mileposts by which to gauge the behaviour of the accounting industry.

A non-critical view of the accounting industry indicates that the accounting industry has not behaved as an oligopoly by following socially harmful parallel conduct. Stated within Stigler's three factors there are reasons to conclude that none of these three conditions are present within the accounting industry. That is, the accounting firms do not misbehave as an oligopoly because they (1) lack a standardized commodity for which they can provide a coordinated price; (2) there is an inability to detect deviations from the agreed upon price; and (3) the industry lacks any means to punish cheating firms. First, historically, accounting firms have not been price gougers; indeed, their rates over the past two decades have not increased significantly. A leading study of auditor fees found that audit fees *declined* as a function of client assets (a comparison made to capture possible rising complexity and scope of the audit engagement) (Invancevich and Zardkoohi 2000).[13] Two, clients appear satisfied with the fees of their auditors, believing that whatever fee increases have occurred in the past decade have been the result of externalities such as increased regulation and litigation-based concerns.[14] Indeed, the complaint in the post-Enron era is that in the years leading up to the recent spate of accounting scandals audit clients too frequently retarded increases in audit fees sought by the auditors and which hindsight suggests would have been wise investments.[15] Only in post-Sarbanes-Oxley years have we seen significant increases in audit fees and

participating cartel members produce a sufficiently large share of the market so that non-member's production cannot undermine the decisions of the cartel (this condition can also be satisfied if something discourages the non-members from expanding their production); and (3) that they must be able to carry out their manipulation of production or price without detection by the government or other outsiders.

[13] Menon and Williams (2001) provide a sample of actual fees from 1989 through 1996, and show a decline of $3.4 to $2.8 million, adjusted for inflation.

[14] GAO (2003b: 10–12) states that 93% of 158 respondents reported an increase in fees, but only one-half believed consolidation within the industry was responsible.

[15] Estimates of the financial fraud uncovered in the peak years of 2001 and 2002 are difficult to calculate. The bubble market's collapse removed approximately $8.5 trillion in market value for publicly-traded securities (Kelly 2002). If one believed only 1% of the market decline was attributable to financial reporting problems, this would equal $85 Billion. This would appear quite conservative for what we witnessed in 2001–2 since the market losses during the preceding boom years—when there were fewer large financial collapses—are estimated to be about the same. McNamee *et al.* (2000) estimate losses attributable to accounting failures between 1993–2000 of at least $88 billion. All this resonates with an observation by a former SEC chairman (Hills 2002) who has served on many audit committees that audit committees too frequently saw as their task retarding any increase in audit fees rather than authorizing appropriate sums be paid to the auditors to assure a high quality audit.

[16] Salomon and Bryan-Low (2004) report that audit fees are estimated to rise by as much as 30% for 2004. A study of audit fees paid by 461 of the Fortune 500 firms found an average increase of 16% from 2002 to 2003 compared with an average increase of 22% for firms outside the Fortune 500 (Glass Lewis & Co. 2004). The greater percentage increase reported in 2004 as compared with 2003 increases reflects the effects of Sarbanes-Oxley's increased reporting requirements.

much of this can be attributed to additional compliance costs imposed by the Act as well as accounting firms responding to rising liability costs.[16]

A third consideration arises from the difficulty firms would face in reaching an agreement regarding the price to charge for their service or detecting a deviation from the agreed upon price. Information is a key feature of Stigler's (1964: 48) formula for an effective cartel since this is how deviations are detected. He predicts that 'collusion will always be more effective against buyers who report correctly and fully the prices tendered to them'. This condition of the model has implications for the accounting industry: the auditor's clients report in their annual filings with the SEC the sums paid to their auditors.[17] Such reporting arguably makes detection of cheating more likely and invites responses from competitors eager to meet the deviation by the cheating firm. However, antitrust theory informs us that, if the significant buyers of the vended product change their identity or otherwise the cost of the vended product or services is masked, collusion will be more difficult and cheating more prevalent (Stigler 1964: 48). This observation has relevance for the accounting industry; even though the client base of individual auditing firms is very stable (suggesting a lack of successful competition we would expect to find associated with the cartel-like behaviour), the services accountants provide to each client are tailored to that client's business and systems. Auditors do not in fact provide a uniform service but one that varies on a firm-by-firm basis. Since what they vend is not a commodity, their industry is rife with opportunities for a good deal of deviation with respect to pricing practices and even quantity and quality of services provided.[18] Stated differently, audit services are not a single commodity that lends itself to discrete market responses by an auditor's rivals. By not being commoditized, audit services are not amenable to tacit agreement as to its pricing, and departures from any understood price or quality would be difficult to detect. Thus, if harmful collusion is to occur, it must occur in some other area than the price and quality of the service provided since to be so focused is to premise the cartel's wealth on nondiscernible metrics.

[17] See Item 14 of SEC Form 10-K.

[18] Areeda and Hovencamp (2003: § 1429c at 209) describe oligopolists as more likely to compete via sales promotions or product variations which are not easily imitated and can sometimes be difficult for competitors to respond promptly to so that the deviating member reaps a strong first mover advantage. Similarly, any differences in preferences among buyers that give rise to differences in the product or service purchased 'complicates the process of observation, coordination, or retaliation' (Areeda and Hovencamp 2003: § 1429c at 211). It is difficult to determine to what extent the quality of services provided by an auditor varies across its audit clients. At the same time, it is equally problematic to suggest that a particular audit firm provides a higher quality of audit services than does its rivals. Eisenberg and Macey (2004) study earnings restatements and find that when factors are controlled for such variables as client size, time, and industry, there was no evidence of more frequent earnings restatements for companies audited by Arthur Andersen than by its rivals.

A final consideration is that there does not appears to be any effective means for the industry to discipline or otherwise punish a cheating member. Even though—until the passage of Sarbanes-Oxley—the industry maintained exclusive powers to discipline its members, there is no evidence that this power was ever used against a Big Eight or Big Five accounting firm. Moreover, the stability of their client base and steady growth in their revenues belies that members engaged in any meaningful sanctions of cheating rivals. After the passage of Sarbanes-Oxley, the chief role in disciplining accounting firms is lodged in the Public Company Accounting Oversight Board (PCAOB) as well as the SEC, each of which is autonomous from the industry.[19]

Consistent with the above is evidence that auditors have long been sensitive to price competition. After the American Institute of Certified Public Accountants removed its ban on bidding for audits in 1972, competition among major accounting firms has been 'intense and vicious.'[20] Moreover, this could explain the relative stability of the auditor's stable of clients, namely that auditors price their services to keep the client from defecting to a competitor. As we will see in Part III, there are possibly more ominous explanations for the auditors' ability to retain their respective clients for years and even decades. Price competition may well have contributed to the woeful poor performance of accountants to detect a host of financial frauds at the close of the last decade as well as the continuing oligopolistic structure of the industry. Absent price competition, monopoly-like profits garnered by the large accounting firms may well have either attracted new entrants or caused clients to seek lower-priced smaller accounting firms. But new entrants, and even existing smaller accounting firms, would confront serious barriers to entry, such as significant capital investment and reputational requirements, that must be overcome to serve large audit clients. Particularly important is evidence that a foremost consideration of firms opting to have their audits carried out by a Big Eight-Five-Four accounting firm is the reputational benefits they receive by signaling to investors their relatively higher quality by choosing a major auditing firm. That is, firms opt for a major accounting firm not so much because

[19] Sarbanes-Oxley Act § 104(a), 15 U.S.C. §§ 7214 & 7215 requires periodic inspections of registered auditing firms by the PCAOB and authorizing the agency to discipline violations of auditing standards.

[20] Zeff (2003a: 202) identifies the golden era of the accounting profession as 1940–60s and the introduction of competitive pricing, pursuant to pressure from the US Department of Justice, as a force leading auditors to be seen as members of an industry and not a profession. Professor Zeff observes, 'The heightened competitive climate in which the firms operated seemed to haunt partners' conduct of audit engagements' (Zeff 2003a: 203). For other evidence that price competition prevails within the industry and has a harmful effect on auditor independence, GAO (2003c: 41) finds that the removal of restrictions on advertising and direct solicitation of clients have had a more direct impact on auditor independence than consolidation within the industry.

of economies that are garnered with respect to their audits, but rather to signal their firm's higher quality to investors.[21] This too has significance for the accounting industry performing as monopolists: the relative size and reputation of auditors are intermingled so that in combination they pose significant barriers to entry.

As seen in Part I, the accounting industry's structure is unquestionably that of an oligopoly. Nevertheless, the foregoing discussion also reflects that the industry's members are intensely competitive in the pricing of audit services. Is this because, in Stigler's formulation, the industry lacks the ability to punish 'cheaters' because they lack the ability to coordinate on setting a price for their services, cannot detect deviations, or lack the ability to discipline deviating accounting firms? Insight into the failure of the major accounting firms to misbehave as oligopolists is provided by understanding the multiple roles that their provision of non-audit services to their audit clients plays in their overall business strategy as well as the strategic thinking of their audit clients. The next section examines this, and explores the charitable explanation for the rising importance of non-audit services: they are a means for accounting firms to diversify their services, leverage their client relationships, and deviate from oligopolistic pricing without being detected. That is, non-audit services can be understood as a form of non-price competition (Ginsburg 1993).

III. THE OLIGOPOLY SCRIPT: THE PROMINENCE OF NON-AUDIT SERVICES

Because the auditor's attest function is the heart of their engagement, the auditor's role is first and foremost that of a gatekeeper.[22] Other gatekeepers, such as underwriters and lawyers are also socialized into a gatekeeper function, but their role in this endeavor does not involve a

---

[21] Ireland and Lennox (2002) found that higher quality clients gravitate to Big Five accounting firms but incur higher fees in doing so than lower-quality clients; Peel and Roberts (2003) study of small UK audit clients found that they pay a premium when audited by Big Six accounting firms, which is consistent with their seeking benefits of signaling their higher quality over companies not audited; Chaney, Jeter and Lakshamanan (2004) show that private firms that are not publicly-held choose auditors by fees and do not otherwise discriminate between Big Five and non-Big Five firms.

[22] Apropos of the significance of any intertwining of the audit function with commercial relationships that jeopardize the independence of judgment of the auditor is the observation by Chief Justice Berger that the auditor's 'public watchdog's function demands that the accountant maintain total independence from the client at all times and requires complete fidelity to the public trust.' *United States v Arthur Young*, 465 U.S. 805, 818 (1984).

Gatekeepers have been closely examined by the commentators who generally attribute a prominent role to them, particularly the outside accountant. See generally Hamdani (2003); Coffee (2002); Partnoy (2001); Choi (1998); Jackson (1993); Kraakman (1986); and Gilson and Kraakman (1984: 613–21).

formal attestation.[23] Hence, only indirectly do they come to their role of being gatekeepers. It is a masterpiece of understatement, but no doubt diplomatic, to observe that the accounting profession has not earned rave reviews for its performance as gatekeepers in the aftermath of the recent financial and accounting scandals in which accountants either recklessly failed to detect their clients' false reporting or were their accomplices in their clients' fraud. This section links the accountants' failings to their metamorphoses from an auditing firm into consulting firms that provide audit services. The next section considers whether their metamorphosis can be further understood as being made possible by the highly-concentrated structure of the industry so that their recent evolution can be understood as their misbehaving as a cartel.

The prime suspect for the accounting profession's recent sorrowful performance as a gatekeeper against financial frauds is the rising importance of non-audit services in overall operations of the major accounting firms.[24] Non-audit service revenues now dominate the income statement of the large accounting firms. A 2002 study of 1224 large public companies by the Investor Responsibility Research Center found that in 2001 non-audit revenues garnered by the accountants exceeded $4 billion whereas their audit fees totaled $1.58 billion.[25] In

[23] Underwriters are among the select group of persons that are liable under § 11(a)(5) of the Securities Act if the registration statement for a public offering contains a material misrepresentation. See 15 U.S.C. § 77k(a)(5). See e.g., *In re WorldCom, Inc. Securities Litigation*, 2004 US Dist. Lexis 25155 (S.D.N.Y.). Lawyers find their role as gatekeepers now set forth in the SEC's attorney responsibility rules which impose a duty to report within the client organization when the attorney has a reason to believe a violation of the securities laws or fiduciary duty has occurred. See SEC (2004).

[24] There has long been regulatory action focused on shielding the auditor's independence from being compromised by the rewards and attractiveness of consulting revenues. See, e.g., SEC (1979): 'the growing importance of management advisory services to revenues, profits, and competitive position of accounting firms—are a cause for legitimate concern as to the impact of these activities on auditor independence, objectivity, and professionalism.' This release was later rescinded in the deregulatory wave of the Reagan Administration, although in Accounting Series Release 296 the SEC states it had not changed its views of the problem from that expressed in SEC (1979). Even before non-audit services became a dominant component in the accounting firms' business strategy, opinion was mixed whether the provision of non-audit services to audit clients compromised the accountant's independence. Schulte (1965) reports a survey of 383 managers of financial institutions showing that 55% believed the consulting function did not impair the accountant's independence. Indeed, when accounting firms were in the early stage of growing their consulting practices, positive support for marrying the auditor to its client's consulting needs was provided by the primary professional organ tasked with assuring the independence of auditors (Public Oversight Board 1979: l). Eight years later, an extensive survey by the AICPA's Public Oversight Board (1986) found over half the survey respondents believed certain business consulting practices, such as merger advice, valuation of assets, and providing actuarial services compromised the accountant's independence. However, a GAO study (1996: ch. 2) equivocated on whether consulting impaired the accountant's independence and instead called on the accounting profession to be attentive to the possibility that certain types of consulting could compromise the auditor's judgment. For a detailed review of studies of the impact of consulting on the accountant's independence, *see* Public Oversight Board (2000).

[25] See Morgenson (2002).

1976, audit fees constituted 70 per cent of accounting firm revenues; by 1998 audit fees had fallen to 31 per cent of the total. These changes occurred because non-audit revenues were increasing three times faster than revenues from audit services (Levitt 2000: 156; McNamee *et al.* 2000).[26]

As aptly put by then Big Eight member Deloitte Haskins & Sells' CEO, the

> ultimate goal … [is] to change Deloitte's self-image from that of a professional firm that happened to be in business (the traditional view among the giant CPA firms) to a business that happened to market Professional services.[27]

Indeed, by 1994, a blue-ribbon panel to study the accounting industry found that five of the top seven consulting firms in the United States and six of the top seven consulting firms worldwide were the then Big Six accounting firms.[28]

Accountants argue that the marriage of various consulting services to their audit function not only is efficient for their audit clients but also enables the accountants to discharge their audit function due to the heightened and more intense understanding of the client that comes through their consulting activities. This argument has a good deal of intuitive appeal but little empirical support. The one study of the link between the intensity of the audit (measured by the hours expended on the audit itself) and consulting found that billed audit hours increased as a function of the amount of consulting.[29] Thus, the provision of non-audit services does not appear to yield scale economies for the audit itself. Moreover, arguing that the provision of non-audit services enhances the audit raises a further question about the quality of audits carried out by accountants who do not enjoy a consulting relationship with their audit clients. Former SEC Chairman Arthur Levitt, in defending proposed limits on consulting by auditors before Congress, reported that

---

[26] Between 1990 and 1999, audit fees generated by the Big Five accounting firms for SEC registrants declined from 71% to 48% of total revenues while fees for tax work increased from 17% to 20% and consulting grew from 12% to 32% (Public Oversight Board 2000: 112). In absolute terms, the total 1999 revenues of the Big Five accounting firms derived from SEC registrants was $26.5 billion; of this amount, $9.5 billion was generated from auditing fees (Public Oversight Board 2000: 112). Public Accounting Report (2001) provides a breakdown of revenue sources for the Big Five accounting firms. One study found that non-audit revenues paid by 1224 companies to their auditors were 2.5 times higher than audit revenues. Morgenson (2002) discusses a 2001 study by Investor Responsibility Research Center that was repeated by IRRC in 2002 with similar results. The 2002 study found that 72% of total fees paid by 1245 SEC registrants were for non-audit services. Longstreth (2002) finds a 2.69:1 ratio of non-audit to audit fees.

[27] See Zeff (2003b).

[28] See Public Oversight Board (1994: 6).

[29] See Davis, Ricchiute and Trompeter (1993).

approximately 80 per cent of public reporting companies awarded no or very little consulting work to their auditors. He (2000: 6) observed,

> [w]e do not believe that anyone would argue that the audits those companies received were somehow inadequate because those companies did not receive non-audit services from their auditors'.

Of further note regarding Chairman Levitt's observation is that the significant revenues accountants derive from consulting arises from a distinct minority of their audit clients. Thus, non-audit services may well be a dominant component of the total revenues of Big Four accounting firms, but those revenues arise from a minority of their clients.

There are multiple reasons why the accounting firms placed such an emphasis on growing their non-audit services revenues. An unwitting accomplice in this effort was the efforts of many audit committees to gauge the committee's success by reducing the auditor's fees rather than, for example, enhancing the quality of the audit.[30] The pressure on audit fees also gave rise to a need for accounting firms to distinguish themselves from their competitors by offering a wider range of services.[31] Much of the revenue growth for non-audit services was based solely on client demand; clients, believing that their auditors knew the client's business better than anyone else, concluded that there would be economies by retaining the auditors for a range of consulting services rather than to select a provider that was unfamiliar with the client's business and supporting systems.[32] A further concern was the intense competition among accounting firms to recruit talent to the quiet life of the auditor. There was, of course, the quest to share the good life enjoyed by the well-compensated investment bankers and others with whom the accountants frequently interacted.[33]

Consider that the number of accounting majors declined 25 per cent between 1995 and 2000 matching a near similar decline in the number of individuals sitting for the national CPA exam.[34] To attract talented auditors, the accounting firms had to offer a broader professional profile than being solely an auditor.[35] This strategy also complemented the

[30] See Hills (2002).

[31] See Wyatt (2002).

[32] See Public Oversight Board (2000: 110–11); McNamee *et al.* (2000: 156).

[33] See Dugan (2002).

[34] Balhoff (2002) stated the number of accounting majors declined from 60,000 in 1995 to 45,000 in 2000; further, that in the decade 1991–2000 the total number of those taking the CPA exam had declined 33%. There is evidence that accounting has become more popular with undergraduates. Gullapalli (2004) reports an 11% increase in the number of accounting degrees awarded in 2003 over 2002; however, the number of accounting degrees awarded in 2003 were 10,000 less than the peak level of 60,000 in1994–95.

[35] See Copeland (2002): 'The best and the brightest seek positions that will allow them to develop their expertise, to learn, to work on cutting issues…'

reality that auditing work had by the 1990s become more complex and technical so that audit teams needed to include technical non-accounting experts who would have been underemployed absent consulting opportunities.[36] As a consequence, auditing firms found a significant portion of their staffs being made up of individuals who came from academic programs with less emphasis on professionalism and more on technical skills than historically prevailed in professional accounting programs.[37] Finally, the profit margins and growth opportunities were much greater with consulting than with auditing. Simply placed, profits could better be obtained through expanding their consulting operations than to expend efforts to rest audit clients from their competitors.

Therefore, various commercial forces that guided auditors and their clients to the joint position that their auditors should carry out consulting assignments for the client. From that point it was but a short step before these same forces spun a web that obscured the auditors from their primary professional undertakings. The popular media may rightly have characterized the role of auditing services with the national accounting firm's repertoire as a 'loss leader' whereby the provision of audit services enabled the accountants to get their foot in the door so that they could thereafter provide more lucrative consulting services.[38]

As seen earlier, audit fees when scaled to their client's size have declined in the last decade. But as also seen, audit hours actually increase with the level of non-audit services provided.[39] Thus, we might speculate what subtle trading occurred between the auditors and their clients that permit higher audit fees to accompany rising non-audit service revenues. Moreover, in view of the concentrated nature of the accounting industry joined by the importance to audit clients of their auditor having the stature of being a Big Four firm, there is cause to ponder why auditing could not be more lucrative than it has been. As seen earlier, the industry has long been dominated by a few national players so that conditions are rife with the potential for anti-competitive pricing of their audit services. However, the recent GAO (2003a: 25) study reports there is 'no evidence that price competition to date has been impaired' by the high concentration within the industry.

---

[36] See Public Oversight Board (2000: 112).

[37] See Wyatt (2002: 3).

[38] See Scheiber (2002). Consistent with the loss leader thesis is an Arthur Andersen internal memorandum imposing a cap on the firm's audit fees charged Waste Management Company because the client was viewed as a 'crown jewel' with respect to the level of non-audit revenues provided by Waste Management. See SEC (2001).

[39] See Davis, Ricciute and Trompeter (1993). For others finding no negative correlation between the level of audit fees and non-audit revenues, *see* Simunic (1980); Palmrose (1986). Evidence that no negative correlation exists between audit and non-audit revenues to the auditor's clients is inconsistent with the 'loss leader' thesis.

Moreover, the absence of anti-competitive pricing[40] for their audit services among the large public accounting firms is not driven by demand elasticity for the services they provide. There is no substitute for the service they offer; the law mandates that publicly-traded companies must be audited by an independent auditor. Hence, the 'loss leader' thesis gains some traction as their failure to act opportunistically when pricing the audit is consistent with the view they have, at least in until very recently, pursued a strategy to use the marketing power they enjoyed in one segment—the provision of audit services—to enter a more competitive and extremely lucrative consulting segment. Certainly the behaviour of the national accounting firms is consistent with the loss leader thesis. For example, Ernst & Young set targets for non-audit services that audit engagement partners were to meet with respect to each client; missing a target resulted in a 10 per cent salary reduction.[41] These developments had an obvious impact on the culture of the auditing firm. For example, firm leadership roles were more likely to be bestowed on those who were successful marketers rather than the most diligent and talented auditors (Wyatt 2002).[42] And, completing the snare into which the engagement auditor found herself, the auditors compensation was frequently linked directly to the overall revenues produced attributed to the audit client.[43]

Another more troubling explanation for the growth of non-audit services is that management easily saw this was a way to keep the outside auditor on a short leash. Management unhappy with the auditor's

[40] For a comprehensive study of the role fees played among 389 public firms that switched auditors between 1983–87, *see* Ettredge and Greenberg (1990: 208): average fee reduction of 23% in the first year after switching auditors with even a greater reduction (28%) when client selected auditor with perceived greater expertise within that industry as reflected by its dominant market share of audits within that industry. Of note is that when there has been greater government focus on whether auditors price their services competitively fees declined. See Maher, Tiessen, Colson and Broman (1992) for a review of audit fees during the 1977–81 period when the accounting industry was subject to Congressional, Department of Justice, and SEC scrutiny with respect to whether its was anti-competitive.

[41] See Dugan (2002). Brown and Dugan (2002) report that Arthur Andersen adopted a program in 1998 that called upon engagement partners to double revenues from their clients by cross selling non-audit services.

[42] Accordingly, technicians were eased out of management and became themselves consultants to the auditing staff who were increasingly being overseen not by the most talented auditors but those who could sell or possessed non-audit technical skills (Seidler 2002). For example, Arthur Andersen's engagement partner for Waste Management Company, a firm that would later be the focus of among the largest reporting violations to occur in the 1990s, was Robert Allgyer, a marketing director in Arthur Andersen's national office whose job it was to coordinate the firm's cross-selling efforts. See SEC (2001).

[43] Turner (2002) states that the magnitude of audit and consulting fees measured the profitability of the audit client and services of the engagement partner; Stewart (2002) characterizes the year evaluation of engagement partners to be focused on what 'kind of business you brought in.' There were even powerful incentives for engagement partners not to question former financial statements as the auditor's pay would be reduced when such a restatement occurred (Stewart 2002).

'second guessing' management's artful use of accounting principles can, of course, threaten to terminate the relationship. Under the current regulatory regime, this threat can easily be stared down by the auditor; to replace the accountant requires a prompt public disclosure on SEC Form 8-K,[44] raising eyebrows within the investment community, and likely inviting inquiry from the SEC. On the other hand, reducing or eliminating the amount of non-audit services provided by the auditor is not required to be disclosed on Form 8-K or anywhere else. Thus, the provision of significant levels of non-audit services by the auditors provides management with greater leverage over the auditor in the event of disagreements between management and the auditors. That is, managers who wish to conflict their auditor's judgment can more easily achieve this goal by increasing the revenues the auditor derives from the provision of non-audit services. Herein lies one of the major concerns underlying auditors providing non-audit services to their audit clients. A further bond between the auditor and their client is that audit clients hire a significant number of their auditor's partners and staff to become members of their senior management.[45] Thus, the auditor frequently finds herself staring across the desk into the piercing eyes of a former colleague, or even boss.

There is no solid empirical support that non-audit services in fact systematically compromise the quality of the outside accountant's audit.[46] One point to begin to explore whether such a connection exists is

[44] See Item 4 of Form 8-K. Form 8-K must be filed with the SEC within five days of a change (whether by dismissal or resignation) of auditors. The disclosures that must accompany notice of the change are extensive with respect to whether a dispute or disagreement between the issuer and its former auditor. See Item 304 or Regulation S-K, 17 C.F.R. § 229.304 (2004).

[45] See generally Securities Exchange Act Rel. No. 42994 (12 July 2000)(detailing these practices). Note in this regards that Sarbanes-Oxley adds § 10A(l), 15 U.S.C. § 78j-1(l) (Supp. 2003), to the Exchange Act barring auditors from certifying the financial statements of a reporting company if certain senior financial officers of the client if such officer had within one year carried out an audit of the reporting company for the auditing firm.

[46] It remains a matter of speculation whether the accountant's oversight of their audit clients' financial statements was diminished by the Supreme Court's holding in *Central Bank of Denver v First Interstate Bank of Denver*, 511 U.S. 164 (1994), that there was no aiding and abetting liability under the antifraud provision. Since accountants continue to be liable for misstatements and omissions in the financial statements they audit, *see Anixeter v Home-Stake Production Co.*, 77 F.3d 1215 (10th Cir. 1996), cf. *Wright v Ernst & Young LLP.*, 152 F.3d 169 (2d Cir. 1998), *cert. denied*, 525 U.S. 1104 (1999), it is difficult to conclude that *Central Bank* provides any more than perhaps a false sense of security to the auditor. Arguably, the most significant weakening of the legal environment for auditing occurred earlier when the Supreme Court held that scienter was required for there to be a violation of the antifraud provision. See *Ernst & Ernst v Hochfelder*, 425 U.S. 185 (1976). By eliminating the possibility of negligence as a basis for liability, one might conclude that *Ernst & Ernst* induces less caution on the part of the auditors. There are at least two weaknesses to this argument. First, there is no reasonable basis to conclude that negligence was ever the standard or even an acceptable standard before *Ernst & Ernst*. See Cox (1977). Secondly, scienter was and continues to be an acceptable standard of fault under the antifraud provision. See e.g., *Sanders v John Nuveen & Co.*, 554 F.2d 790, 793 (7th

with the odor emitted by the rise in earnings restatements. For the past decade, the period in which the auditors have been more than just auditors, financial markets have been treated with an ever increasing number of earnings restatements.[47] Even though restatements do not necessarily suggest fraud, they may nonetheless be seen as equivalent to fraudulent reporting *sans* scienter. Evidence of the link between the auditor's independence and the provision of audit services is mixed. An early study examining this connection points in the other direction. The Panel on Audit Effectiveness studied 126 audit engagements, identifying 37 (26 per cent) in which non-audit services were provided (Public Oversight Board 2000). The Panel concluded that in none of these cases did the provision of non-audit services compromise the quality of the audit; the Panel even opined that in one-fourth of the audits that were accompanied by non-audit services that the consulting work had a positive impact on the quality of the audit (Public Oversight Board 2000: 113).[48] The Panel report, however, did not probe the more subtle question of whether non-audit fees or even more generally the total fees received from the client compromised the auditor's judgment; the Panel's focus was instead on whether the act of providing *any* level of non-audit services impeded the audit function.[49]

That such a connection exists between the auditor's independence and consulting has a good deal of intuitive support. A more refined inquiry is whether the relative strength of any correlation between the auditor's financial ties with the client and compromises in the auditor's professional judgment is context dependent. This could well explain two strikingly dissimilar leading studies of whether non-audit services compromise the accountants' judgments. A 2002 study found no

Cir. 1977); *Kiernan v Homeland Inc.*, 611 F.2d 785, 788 (9th Cir. 1984). Thus, the auditor who becomes aware of a possible misrepresentation committed by management, but turns a blind eye to further investigating it would appear to have acted at least recklessly.

[47] In 1990, there were 33 earnings restatements. In five years, the number of restatements increased by 50% to 50 restatements. In 2000, there were 157 earnings restatements, more than triple the number five years earlier and five times the number at the beginning of the decade and in 2002 this number reached a record high of 330. See Huron Consulting Group (2003); Wu (2001). See generally GAO (2002). Earnings statements are accompanied by price adjustments in the security of the restating firm. One estimate places the loss in market value due to restatements made for the period 1998–2000 at $73 billion. See Moriarty and Livingston (2001). The GAO (2003d) estimated unadjusted market losses of $100 billion. Earnings restatements are symptomatic of the aggressive and opportunistic use of accounting principles. Opacity and lacunae in accounting metrics were shamelessly exploited by the firm's managers. Too frequently, it appears, the public accountants accorded their audit client the benefit of any ambiguity in accounting principles.

[48] Antel, Gordon, Narayanamoorthy and Zhou (2002) find no higher correlation between abnormal accruals and higher audit or non-audit fees, although other studies cited in this chapter have reached a contrary result; Frankel, Johnson and Nelson (2002) find the greater the non-audit services the more likely it is that analysts' forecasts will be met or exceeded and that there will be larger discretionary accruals.

[49] See Seidler (2002).

statistical correlation between non-audit service fees and the auditor providing a going concern qualification to its audit opinion (DeFond, Raghunandan and Subramanyam 2002).[50]

In contrast, another study published in 2002 finds that non-audit fees are positively associated with various indicia of earnings management by audited firms (Frankel, Johnson and Nelson 2002).[51] The latter study finds that the frequency of abnormal accruals increases as more non-audit services are provided by the firm's auditors. The conflicting results of the two studies need not lead to conflicting policy implications. Auditors may more easily succumb to management's manipulation of reported earnings when the firm is not financially distressed because the auditors view their own reputation and litigation exposure as not threatened in such context. On the other hand, when their client is financially distressed, the auditor's reputation and litigation exposure is increased so that it might be much less deferential to management judgments. Indeed, we should expect—absent self-serving concerns such as fear of litigation—that the auditor will accord a good deal of deference to the judgments and choices of their audit client. Well recognized cognitive forces no doubt compromise the auditor's independence. The most dominant force at play is that of self-interest. That is, individuals, even professionals, are not very good at acting impartially when their self-interest dictates otherwise.[52]

The GAO's study of the accounting profession found in its survey of clients, accountants, and academics mixed reports whether the consolidation that began within the industry in the late 1980s had made auditors less independent or otherwise adversely affect the quality of audits. For example, 60 per cent of the large public companies surveyed believed their auditors were more independent post- consolidation whereas 18 per cent believed their auditor's independence had become

[50] The study focused on 1158 firms that, during a 4 month period in 2001, were financially distressed (defined to mean the firm either had negative earnings or operating cash-flows) and within this group assessed whether a firm was less likely to obtain a going-concern qualification if their auditors in comparison to the ratio of non-audit to audit revenues. For a study finding no correlation between earnings restatements and the level of non-audit services provided by the accountants, Raghunandan, Read and Whisenant (2003) find that non-audit fees for 100 firms making earnings restatements not statistically different than larger sample that did not engage in restatements.

[51] The study finding that indicia of earnings management are exceeding forecasted earnings, and the magnitude of various discretionary accruals. Another study found such a correlation, but it was only statistically significant for non-Big Five auditors (Francis and Ke 2002).

[52] For a discussion of the social and psychological forces that can compromise the auditor's independence, *see* Moore, Tetlock, Tanlu and Bazerman (2005). Audit committees also may suffer behavioral limits when confronted with a reporting crisis, *see* Beecher-Monas (2003): cognitive dissonance makes it difficult for a committee to revisit its prior decisions and its risk preference may be magnified due to group polarization.

worse (2003a: 41).[53] There are abundant anecdotal reports of professional judgments being so compromised.[54] This indeed is an area where it would not be foolish to trust one's intuition. Doing so, however, has significant implications for considering the social welfare implications of auditors having collateral but dependent relationships with their audit clients (Wyatt 2002):

> [T]he loss of a client is a negative in one's career path. Since many decisions required of audit firm managers and partners are judgmental in nature, rather than clearly prescribed by extraneous forces, such judgments are, at the margin, sometimes influenced by perceptions of the attitudes of leaders of a given firm. If those perceptions by firm audit personnel are that the loss of a client is damaging to one's career path, the judgments made may be more in the direction of keeping the client than to achieving the fair presentation of financial statements.[55]

It is also possible to conclude it is myopic to focus so intently on the revenues associated with non-audit services. Audit failures predate the accounting industry's undertaking significant consulting activities (Pitt 2002). Indeed, a good deal of the auditor's independence is compromised by the sheer magnitude of the audit fees associated with a client, especially if they view these fees as a perpetuity (Breeden 2002).[56] With there being few instances historically of firms changing their auditors, the auditors can easily come to view the yearly audit revenues from a client as a perpetuity.[57] So seen, the value of a client relationship can easily be

---

[53] Of interest is the report of other possible impacts of other factors on audit quality. According to knowledgeable individuals, a variety of factors may have had a more direct impact on audit quality and auditor independence than consolidation. For example, they cited the removal of restrictions against advertising and direct solicitation of clients, the increased relative importance of management consulting services to accounting firms, legal reforms, changing auditing standards, and a lack of emphasis on the quality of the audit by clients and some capital market participants.

[54] For example, in the Enron/Andersen case, an Andersen e-mail reveals that members of the engagement team were concerned about Enron's financial statements, but that same e-mail also cautioned that future work for Enron 'could reach $100 million per year.' See Mayer (2002). McRoberts and Alexander (2002: 1) quote a former Andersen client who observed, '[T]he more consulting business we did with them, the more companies they would refer to me and the easier their audit partners would be in approving the deals'.

[55] Kaplan (2004: 366–68) details the pressures on the auditor to retain her client.

[56] See also Prentice (2000: 209) reviewing studies reflecting that auditors are more likely to accede to the client's reporting choice when the client is large.

[57] See e.g., GAO (2003b: 1): of 159 respondents to the GAO survey, 37 had switched accountants within 2 years due to the demise of Arthur Andersen, 3 switched accountants within 2 years for other reasons, 10 had switched within past 2–5 years and eighteen had switched within past 6–10 years. This means that the bulk of those surveyed had been with the same accounting firm for more than a decade. This changed in 2003, with slightly more than one-third of the Russell 3000 firms changing auditors (excluding changes caused by the demise of Arthur Andersen) (Krantz 2004). Michaels (2004) reports a study by Glass Lewis regarding 900 auditor changes in 2003.

determined by capitalizing the yearly audit fee at a low discount rate—low to reflect the small likelihood that the relationship will be terminated. This calculus yields a very high dollar value the engagement partner can place on preserving the relationship with the audit client.[58] It is that calculation that underlies the arguments advanced by those who favour the periodic rotation of auditors.

On the other hand, thoughts of strengthening the auditor's independence by mandating the periodic rotation of auditing firms must confront the realities of the marketplace, and more importantly the high concentration levels within the industry. The GAO (2003a: 26) study found that 88 per cent of those surveyed reported that if required to switch auditing firms periodically they would *not* consider a smaller (i.e., non-Big Four) firm.[59] This survey is supported by the practices followed by those firms who had been Arthur Andersen clients before its demise in 2002; 87 per cent of the former 1,085 former Arthur Andersen public company clients migrated to a Big Four firm (GAO 2003a: 107, Table 10).[60]

Finally, even those who support the belief there are social justifications for auditors to provide consulting services to their audit clients must address the awkward juxtaposition this poses since the same relationship, if carried out by a director, could prevent a director from being deemed independent as defined by applicable listing and SEC requirements. That is, an ongoing consulting relationship will prevent a director from being considered independent under both the NYSE and Nasdaq listing requirements,[61] but no such prohibition occurs for the accountant unless

---

[58] For example, the most recent audit fees Arthur Andersen received from Enron were $25 million. If viewed as a perpetuity and capitalized at 10%, the value of. the Arthur Andersen/Enron relationship to Arthur Andersen is $250 million.

[59] The study suggests that in light of likely serious costs and difficult to measure benefits of mandatory audit firm rotation the recommended course is to monitor closely the effects of Sarbanes-Oxley Act to determine if enhanced independence of auditors can be achieved through its provisions; GAO (2004) sets forth the questionnaires and summary of responses that were the basis for GAO (2003a).

[60] The number five firm, Grant Thornton, obtained over 30% of the former Arthur Andersen clients who did not engage a Big Four firm.

[61] Under NYSE Rule 303A.02, no director with a 'material relationship' with a listed company, either directly or as a partner, shareholder, or officer of an organization that has a relationship with the company, is deemed independent. Factors determining whether a 'material relationship' exists include consulting relationships. The board is to determine whether the relationship poses such a conflict; however, the NYSE provides that, among other factors, receipt during the prior three years of more than $100,000 per year in direct compensation from the listed company (other than director or committee fees) or being an executive officer of a company that receives payments which in any single fiscal year exceeds the greater of $1 million or 2% of such other company's consolidated gross income. The listing requirements for Nasdaq are slightly different as Nasdaq Rule 4200 reference point is. $60,000 in payments or being a partner, executive or controlling stockholder of an entity that received the greater of 5% of its consolidated gross revenues or $200,000. We could well find that a audit partner who garnered more than $100,000 (or $60,000 for a Nasdaq listed company) as a consequence of sharing in non-audit fees from the audit client would not meet the standard of independence applied to directors. Also, since it is the opinion of the audit firm and not the

it falls within one of the limited areas proscribed by Sarbanes-Oxley.[62] Both the auditor and the outside director serve crucial monitoring functions of management's stewardship. However, the auditor's task can be seen as the more demanding and important because the auditor is required to carry out a professional investigation discharged with reasonable care and to attest as to its findings. Just how can we demand of such a person a lower level of independence than we expect of the outside directors who depend on the auditor's services?

IV. PRACTICE MEETS THEORY

The evidence is clear that the Big Eight and later Big Five accounting firms collectively transformed themselves from audit firms to business consulting firms that also provided audit services. Their great competitive advantage over non-auditing consulting firms was that the accounting firms could bundle their audit function with their consulting services. By competing with pure consulting firms the accounting firms enjoyed operational efficiencies that flowed from their greater familiarity with their clients' problems and systems. Certainly there is every reason to believe there were operational synergies to be reaped by melding some of the staid audit functions with the early stages of a challenging consulting project. We might also speculate whether they enjoyed another advantage over the pure consulting rivals—the accountants could trade off the quality of their audits to obtain consulting revenues whereas their pure consulting rivals had nothing comparable to put on the bargaining table. As will be seen, the marriage of consulting to auditing poses distinct risks to the auditor's independence and, hence, the overall quality of the audit. To such risks we might question whether the market would not penalize firms whose auditor's independence was perceived as being seriously compromised by the provision of non-audit services. Financial theory supports the view that any such a disclosure risk (i.e.,

---

individual accountant, the focus arguably should be on the revenues of the audit firm and not the individual auditor. Under this approach, the audit firm's independence would be with reference to the $100,000 (or $60,000) figure. Former SEC Chairman Arthur Levitt (2000) also called for stricter standards for auditor independence: 'A public accountant acknowledges no master by the public. But when auditors engage in extensive services for an audit client truly unrelated to the audit, they must now also serve another master—management. In this role, the auditor who guards the integrity of the numbers, now both oversees and answers to management … [If auditing is a loss leader for valuable consulting] it is becoming more and more difficult to ascertain where one relationship ends and another begins'.

[62] Somewhat related is the notion that an investment by the auditor in its audit client or a direct 'business relationship' disqualifies the auditor, but providing non-audit services does not. See Longstreth (2002: 7): '[If the definition of] "business relationship" does not include audit services' one faces the absurdity of a rule that is absolute in banning financial and business relationships that are utterly inconsequential while appearing to allow any level of non-audit fees to be paid to the audit firm.'

weakened trustworthiness of a company's financial reports) will effectively raise the firm's cost of capital due to investors discounting the traded firm's security market price. Therefore, would not this be a market-based solution to possible abuses so that audit clients would find it in their interest to moderate or eliminate such a discount? Moreover, would not such a pricing dynamic cause some accounting firms to distinguish themselves from their rivals by taking the 'high road' of refusing to certify the financial statements of firms to whom they provided audit services?

Financial theory appears not to have guided the marketing department of any accounting firm. No accounting firms made any effort to enhance its relative reputation for independence and the quality of its audits by refusing to provide consulting services to its audit clients. Instead, each of the Big Eight and later Big Five and now Final Four firms aggressively pursued consulting services with their audit clients. None sought to step aside from the pack by assuring financial statement-users that its audit enjoyed greater independence than that of rivals because the auditor did not provide consulting services to its clients. Instead, all firms pursued the same parallel behaviour of leveraging their audit relationship to expand their profits through the rapid growth of consulting. There should be little doubt that each firm's pursuit of this parallel strategy was made possible by the industry's concentration.[63] In their joint pursuit of consulting, the dominant accounting firms behaved as a cartel and they were assisted in so behaving by the nature of auditing and the questionable goals of their audit clients. The contributions of each of these is examined below.

Auditing is not a service that can easily be commoditized. As seen earlier, the demands of each audit assignment invites discrete pricing decisions so that pre-agreed-to pricing by cartel members is not realistic and, correlatively, deviation from an agreed-upon price will be impossible to detect. But more importantly, external assessments by investors of the quality of a particular audit are equally impossible. The inability of financial statement users to determine the quality of an audit makes it highly problematic for market-based forces to either discipline or penalize firms obtaining poor audits. To be sure, the 'markets of lemons' argument is that the market will raise the cost of all firms by an

---

[63] Professors Macey and Sale (2003: 1177) provide a complementary view of the industry. Two important forces they identify as explaining why auditors in recent years have less concern for their professional reputation are the advent of the LLP form of their doing business and the SEC's commodification of 'independence.' These forces are not, however, independent of the industry's structure since a more competitive structure could be expected to introduce competition among auditors on the basis of their relative reputation and independence.

amount equal to the expected cost of weak audits averaged across all firms. Even this overstates the case for such market discounting. First, not until 2000 was there much disclosure regarding the amount any public firm paid its auditors for non-audit services. Before 2000, investors lacked information whether a specific publicly-traded company engaged its auditors as consultants. And, as will be examined below, today the disclosures that are now required are opaque. Secondly, there are other investor concerns that can be equally compelling bases for compromising the accountant's independence. An example of such a factor is the long-term relationship between auditors and their clients, and particularly the value of that relationship; as seen earlier, the Arthur Andersen/Enron relationship was not just a perpetuity, but a highly valuable perpetuity independent of the consulting fees that accompanied that relationship. Enron in this regard is no different than most public firms where changing accounting firms has long been seen as an infrequent event. Other compromising relationships appear in the degree former auditor firm staff members are now within the client's executive suite. Thirdly, the auditor assigned to the audit or the supervising attorney may wish to obtain a position with the audit client. The lure of a position with an audit client is well understood generally and has long been a potential perk of the sometimes nomadic and underpaid auditor. As a result, the audit personnel may be reluctant to raise with the audit client issues that will jeopardize her obtaining a future position with the client.

Fourthly, poor audits can arise for reasons other than a lack of independence. The quality of the auditors assigned to the engagement may be poor or their supervisors overworked or distracted. The latter is a real fear in light of the evidence, reviewed earlier, that audit fees have declined relative to the size and complexity of their audit clients. Thus, supervisors are responsible either for more audit clients or larger more involved audits than years earlier. Either event erodes the quality of the audit. Factors such as these confound the external assessment of the quality of an audit and the overall trustworthiness of a firm's financial statements so that markets are poor forces to discipline firms for retaining their auditors to provide consulting services. Thus, any market-based penalty that may be imposed because auditors perform auditing services for its client may at best be an obscured impact.

Quite independent of market-based incentives for firms to eliminate or moderate ties the auditors might have that compromise their independence is management's interest in obtaining a 'good' audit. This aspect of the professional issue poses a problem of definition. When we refer to a good audit from whose perspective is this assessment to be made? Management that has an interest in presenting a smoother earnings record, such as was sought by the management at Freddie

Mac,[64] would like an auditor that concurs in the host of accounting choices management makes in reporting the firm's financial performance and position. Similarly, a firm that wishes to report eye-popping double digit earnings growth, such as, Enron (and too many others that have now filled the headlines), will also think a 'good' audit is one with a minimum of second guessing of management's accounting decisions. As seen earlier, when the accountant has a relationship with the client that is seriously bounded with a valuable financial relationship, and especially when that relationship has a low reporting profile such that terminating that relationship is not a reportable event, the relationship necessarily poses a dire risk of impacting the degree of the auditor's independence. Unscrupulous managers, as well as managers who wish accounting decisions that place the best possible spin on the company's financial performance and position, each find a market for audit services that is not professionally independent. In a sense, this dynamic transformed audits from a service that was distinctly tailored to the needs of a client into a commodity. What was standardized was not the audit service, but the attestation that the audit provided. That is, evidence during the last two decades reflects that auditors did not raise their audit fees to assure reasonable staffing of audits. Instead, audit fees were secondary to the pursuit of non-audit revenues. One can only conclude that independence on the part of the auditor was not a valued commodity by either the auditor or its client; clean audit opinions were valued and that was what was sold to the clients.

Not all public companies have engaged in restatements or had their executives accused of cooking the firm's books. And, not all firms retained their auditors to provide consulting services or recruited their auditors to their managerial ranks. We can thus speculate that there might have been a market for a truly independent auditing firm if one wished to step forward by defining itself by what its rivals were not. But no accounting firm stepped forward to claim this niche market. Each of the big accounting firms followed the same course and with great reward to itself. One would have expected that in a competitively structured industry that one area of competition would be on the cornerstone of auditing, the appearance of independence from the client. That did not exist and suggests the strength of the cartel.

---

[64] In 2003, Freddie Mac announced a forthcoming restatement of approximately $4.5 billion. The restatement corrected accounting errors from the misapplication of reporting derivatives in 2001 and 2002. Management at Freddie Mac had structured financial transactions for the purpose of smoothing volatility in the firm's earnings. Through the misuse of Treasury securities—falsely characterizing them as derivatives and accounting for them as hedging transactions—Freddie Mac lowered its reported hedging costs. At the end of 2002, it held approximately $16 billion in Treasuries as debt hedges. Federal regulators later fined Freddie Mac $125 million for its accounting abuses. See generally, Dwyer and Miller (2003); Barta and McKinnon (2003).

V. THE REGULATORY RESPONSE: ARE WE ON THE RIGHT TRACK?

The procedures and practices to be followed by auditors of public companies have customarily been established by a body within the American Institute of Public Accounting (AICPA), the Public Oversight Board (POB). However, in May 2000, confidence in self-regulation was seriously shaken when the POB was thwarted in its effort to examine the impact on the auditor's independence vis-a-vis its client when the auditors were also providing to their clients substantial non-audit services, such as consulting, tax advice, or computer systems management. In response to this initiative, the AICPA cut off its funding to its POB.[65] Concern for the accounting profession's influence over both accounting principles and auditing standards prompted Congress to include in Sarbanes-Oxley authorization for the Public Company Accounting Oversight Board (PCAOB). Indeed, the formal name of the act includes 'Public Company Accounting Reform.'

Section 101 of Sarbanes-Oxley creates a five-person nonprofit corporation, the PCAOB, that will be led by five individuals who are appointed by the SEC (with the concurring approval of the Secretary of Treasury and Chairman of the Federal Reserve System).[66] Among the duties assigned to the PCAOB is overseeing the registration of public accounting firms (accounting firms cannot audit the financial statements of a reporting company unless the accounting firm is registered with the PCAOB), to establish or adopt rules regarding auditing procedures including auditor independence standards, and to conduct inspections, investigations and disciplinary proceedings. The PCAOB should enjoy greater independence than the predecessor POB because it is funded from a share of filing fees paid by public companies and registered accountants.[67] Incidentally, Congress was also concerned about the independence of the Financial Accounting Standards Board (FASB), the private sector's major authority for accounting principles (i.e., GAAP). Hence, Sarbanes-Oxley provides that a Self-Regulatory Organization (SRO) (here, read FASB) will no longer be considered an authoritative body with respect to GAAP unless, among other features, its funding

---

[65] The SEC practice section (SECPS) of the AICPA threatened to discontinue funding in May 2000. Following the receipt of its announcement, SEC Chairman Arthur Levitt stated (2000): 'This development is a significant setback to self regulation. Indeed, it raises serious questions as to the profession's commitment to self-regulation.' A storm of protest ensued and the AICPA reinstated funding for the POB. In doing so, the AICPA explained that it did not intend to cut funding for special reviews; it only intended to suspend work until an agreement between the SEC, the POB, and the SECPS was reached. See Tie (2000).

[66] See Sarbanes-Oxley Act, 15 U.S.C. § 7211(e) (4).

[67] See 15 U.S.C. § 7219.

comes solely from filing fees collected by the SEC.[68] The FASB hence has taken its cue and is funded by the fees of SEC registrants.

The PCAOB carries out annual reviews ('inspections') of audit work performed by accounting firms registered with it (an exception exists for once every three years for firms auditing 100 or fewer reporting companies). Copies of the report from each inspection is filed with the SEC as well as state accountancy boards. These reports provide the first basis in the history of the profession for collecting information relative to the quality, and hence deserved reputation, of the major accounting firms. As a self-regulatory organization, the PCAOB has the power to discipline its registrants and, hence, the power to carry out investigations for the purpose of possibly disciplining a registered accounting firm.[69] It may also refer a matter to the SEC for further investigation and enforcement action.[70] Section 107 provides the SEC with oversight responsibility for the PCAOB so that none of its rules become effective without the prior approval of the SEC, and the SEC may amend any existing PCAOB rule.[71]

In the hearings that preceded the enactment of Sarbanes-Oxley, several witnesses testified that the auditing process may be compromised because auditors view their responsibility as serving the company's management and not the full board of directors or, for that matter, the shareholders (US Senate 2002: 31). Auditors who have this perspective of their relationship pose two important concerns. Auditors who understand that their future retention depends on the same managers whose financial statements they are to review will behave accordingly. They cannot be expected to pose strong challenges to the accounting decisions made by management without knowing that by doing so they jeopardize their continuing relationship with the client. Also, auditors who view their professional relationship to be with the company's managers, and not its directors or stockholders, are more likely to view inquiries put to the auditors by the outside directors to be intrusive or simply irrelevant to their engagement.

Concerns related to the independence of the auditors from the company's managers are central to the Sarbanes-Oxley.[72] A key provision of the Act anchors the accountant's relationship in the audit committee

[68] See 15 U.S.C. § 7215 ((c)(4)(6).
[69] See also Public Oversight Board (2003).
[70] See 15 U.S.C. § 7215(b)(4)(B). The SEC's authority to discipline accountants who practice before it coexists with the PCAOB's disciplinary authority; indeed, the SEC's authority in this respect was affirmed in Sarbanes-Oxley. See Securities Exchange Act Section 4C, 15 U.S.C. § 78d-3, added by § 202 of Sarbanes-Oxley Act.
[71] [to come.]
[72] Notably, reform efforts have focused not on the substance of reporting obligations, but on strengthening the financial reporting culture to achieve better compliance with reporting standards. See generally Bratton (2003); Seligman (2002).

and not management.[73] The Act further buttresses its separation of the auditor from the managers by tightening the definition of independence for audit committee members from that embraced just a few years earlier by the Blue Ribbon Committee, mandating that audit committees maintain procedures to address complaints regarding the issuer's accounting, internal controls or other auditing related matters, and empowering audit committees to engage as necessary independent advisors at the issuer's expense.[74] Pursuant to authority set forth in a companion provision, the SEC has adopted criteria for a member of an audit committee to be considered a 'financial expert' and reporting companies are now required to disclose whether its audit committee includes a financial expert, and if not, the reasons for not having such a person on the committee.[75] The importance of financial expertise on the audit committee is supported by a comprehensive study of governance criteria linked to earnings restatements. The study found that mere independence of the board or the audit committee was unrelated to likelihood of a company engaging in an earnings restatement; however, the probability of an earnings restatement are significantly negatively correlated with the audit committee composed of those with an accounting or finance background (Agrawal and Chadha 2002).[76]

[73] See Sarbanes Oxley § 301 (amending § 10A of the Exchange Act, 15 U.S.C. 78f, mandating that the SEC direct that the exchanges and the NASD adopt rules that provide that the audit committee 'shall be directly responsible for the appointment, compensation, and oversight of the work' of the company's auditor). A few months before Sarbanes-Oxley was enacted, both the NYSE and Nasdaq tightened several of their governance requirements in areas that were later dealt with by Sarbanes-Oxley. For example, the proposed listing changes for both bodies require that audit committees must have the authority to retain and terminate the auditor. This requirement is, as seen above, now reflected in Sarbanes-Oxley.

For the view that anchoring the relationship in the audit committee may not be sufficient, see Cunningham (2004) who provides a thoughtful analysis of the benefits and burdens of auditors being retained by the reporting company's insurance carrier; Ronen (2002) provides a less refined model of the relationship recommended by Professor Cunningham.

Professor Bratton (2003: 482–84) argues the auditor's relationship should be developed from a positive law perspective and not narrowly on the shareholder primacy model so that the accountant's fidelity is to a system of fair, even conservative, reporting as contrasted with an agency model (anchored in the shareholders) where accounting choices are made to present a optimistic image of the firm's financial performance and position.

[74] See Sarbanes Oxley § 301, amending Exchange Act § 10 A(m), 15 U.S.C. § 78j–l(m) (barring any compensation to the audit committee member except director fees, whereas previously independence existed so long as the amount received did not exceed $60,000). The SEC does, however, have authority to grant exemptions as it deems appropriate (*ibid.*).

[75] See Section 407 (listing criteria for consideration); Item 401(h) of Reg. S-K, 17 C.F.R. § 229.401(h)(2006)(establishing a two-part test for financial expert); Item 309 of Reg. S-K, 17 C.F.R. § 229.309 (2006)(requiring disclosure of whether the audit committee includes a 'financial expert'). Investors appear to value financial expertise on the part of audit committee members. Davidson, Xie and Xu (2004) study 136 small public companies that announced appointments to audit committee found significant positive stock price reaction when the new members had financial expertise.

[76] The authors' data also show that the negative correlation is strengthened further if the audit committee includes the company's chief financial officer. They explain the puzzling

Importantly, the SEC's new rules, as well as the listing requirements of the NYSE and Nasdaq, impose a dialogue between the audit committee and the outside accountants for the purpose of eliciting any warning signs in the reporting system or management's disclosure policies and practices. The auditor is to report, among other factors, on material issues that have surfaced in its assessment of the firm's internal controls as well as any discussions it has had with management regarding the firm's internal controls. The auditors must also share with the audit committee written communications it has had with management regarding 'critical' accounting decisions with management as well as identifying 'critical' areas of the financial reports where an accounting estimate or principle change would affect the quality of the presentation.[77] The NYSE and Nasdaq listing requirements also mandate a discussion between management and the audit committee covering a range of topics, including a review of the quarterly and annual reports, earnings press releases, and earnings guidance given to analysts.[78]

Sarbanes-Oxley also restricts the revolving door through which the accountant's staff moved themselves into the managerial ranks of its audit clients. The pervasiveness of the steely eyes of the CFO looking into the glazed eyes of her former *protégé*, now auditor, is reflected in a study that found that among nearly 700 former Arthur Andersen clients one in five had at least one former employee of a major audit firm in the top executive ranks and, upon the demise of Arthur Andersen nearly one-half of the executives of firms formerly audited by Arthur Andersen who previously were themselves formerly in public accounting chose their former accounting firm to become their company's new auditor.[79] The Act, however, fell short of more sweeping steps to secure the accountant's independence. The Act does not bar all consulting for audit clients. Instead it forbids certain consulting to be engaged in and conditions other types of consulting on obtaining prior approval from the audit committee. Furthermore, the Act does not sunset the client-auditor relationship by requiring periodic rotation of audit firms.

---

result with respect to the CFO being a member of the audit committee as the CFO providing a convenient channel for the flow of pertinent information that enables the committee to be more effective. For further evidence of the positive effects of financial expertise on the audit committee, *see* Davidson, Xie and Xu, (2004).

[77] See Rule 2–07 of Reg. S-X, 17 C.F.R. § (210.207 (2006)).
[78] For example, the listing requirements of the NYSE call for the audit committee to 'discuss the company's earnings press releases, as well as financial information and earnings guidance provided to analysts and rating agencies.' NYSE Rule 303A.07(c)(iii)(C). See also Nasdaq Marketplace Rule 4350(d).
[79] See Countryman (2002).

VI. THE LIFE OF THE ACCOUNTANT: POST-SARBANES-OXLEY

So what has changed after the enactment of Sarbanes-Oxley Act of 2002? The most tangible measure of change is that audit fees have increased.[80] This is no doubt due to a variety of forces that include increased disclosure demands ushered in by Sarbanes-Oxley and SEC regulations (not all of which are compelled by the Act), greater litigation exposure on the part of accountants due to a post-Enron morality, and a need to replace reduced consulting revenues. As seen, post-Sarbanes-Oxley the accountants have a narrower field of consulting services they can provide their audit clients. Sarbanes-Oxley bars accountants from providing certain non-audit services to their clients and mandates pre-approval by the audit committee for those non-audit services not barred that are to be performed for the client. Nevertheless, reports confirm that auditors continue to earn from their audit clients significant consulting revenues. For example, the *Wall Street Journal's* tally for the thirty companies that make up the Dow Jones Industrial Average showed that in 2002 that 62 per cent of the revenues received by the auditors from their clients were for non-audit services (Bryan-Low 2003c).[81] The reported amount is down slightly from the year before figure of 75 per cent; however, it is unclear what portion of the decline can be attributed to a stagnant economy or, for that matter, an increase in charges for auditing. More recently, consulting fell slightly in 2003 from its year earlier level, but the 2003 decline could also reflect the effects of the first year effects of the SEC's more liberal definition of audit fees, examined later.[82] Investor concerns have caused some companies to terminate consulting projects with their auditors (Bryan-Low 2003b). One front where there is very little evidence that public companies are questing greater independence

---

[80] See Kimmel and Vasquez (2003) report an average increase of 27% in 2002 for audit fees among Standard and Poor's 500 companies; Glass Lewis & Co. (2004) report overall fees increased 16% from 2002 to 2003, based on information in the proxy statements of 2250 sample companies compared to assets of the sample firms increasing 10% and inflation increasing at 2.3%. It should be noted that audits in 2003 do not report one of the full effects of Sarbanes-Oxley: the heightened disclosures related to internal control evaluations that are mandated by § 404 of the act which do not become effective until 2004.

[81] It should be noted that three of the Final Four accounting firms have spun off their consulting operations. Only Deloitte Touche Tohmatsu has not, recently canceling its efforts to do so because of the inability to finance the spin-off of its consulting operations (Frank and Solomon 2003). The spinning-off of a firm's consultants does not mean that the auditing firm does no consulting. The spin-off involves a range of practice areas, but not all areas are spun-off. The most obvious practice area that continues within the auditing firm is the provision of tax advice.

[82] Plitch and Rapoport (2004) cite a study carried out by Investor Responsibility Research Center of 1652 companies that included most of the Fortune 500 firms that found that in 2003 non-audit fees represented 42% of total fees received by accountants from their audit clients. Weil (2004) reports data for 21 of the 30 companies making up the index, audit fees increased 18% whereas total payments to auditors declined 11%; nonetheless, 48.5% of total revenues paid accountants was due to non-audit services.

in their auditors is on their willingness to change auditing firms periodically. There is yet to appear evidence of a broad movement toward regular rotation of accounting firms. The relationship between auditor and client therefore continues to reflect a perpetuity so that the value of that relationship continues to pose its own challenge to the auditor's independence.

The subject of auditors providing consulting services to their clients is the most sensitive when the focus is tax services. Neither SEC nor PCAOB regulations prevent auditors from providing significant tax consulting services to their audit clients. The sensitivities of this consulting relationship arise on two fronts. First, tax consulting is a significant revenue source for accounting firms with much of that being derived from their audit clients. This consulting service matters a lot to accounting firms. Secondly, there is ample reason to believe that tax services pose a serious threat of compromising the auditor's independence.[83] Although broad SEC requirements warn that auditors are not independent when attesting on their own work,[84] this is a red light easily run by the accountants in the context of tax advice provided to their audit clients. The threat to their independence is particularly significant when accounting firms market 'off-the-rack' tax shelter products to their audit clients and subsequently attest that, among other items, the financial statements fairly present the client's tax expenses and liabilities. As a recent congressional study (US Senate 2003: 15–16) of the US tax shelter industry reported,

> KPMG's decision to market tax products to its own audit clients . . . created a conflict of interest. . . [because] the KPMG auditor reviewing the client's financial statements is required, as part of that review, to examine the client's tax return and its use of unusual tax strategies. In such situations, KPMG is, in effect, auditing its own work.

To what extent members of the audit committee have changed their behaviour in the post-Enron era, or in the shadow of the new requirements ushered in by Sarbanes-Oxley, remains to be seen. As seen

---

[83] Mr Michael Hamersley, a senior audit manager of KPMG LLP, testified before the US Senate Finance Committee that he was placed on administrative leave when he refused to 'sign off' on questionable tax transactions engineered by KPMG's tax consultants. See Bryan-Low (2003c). At that hearing, PCAOB Board Chair, William McDonough, testified that the PCAOB was examining whether the provision of tax services to audit clients compromised the accountant's independence and whether to restrict the tax services an auditor could provide clients (Bryan-Low 2003c).

[84] SEC (2000) identifies the following four overarching principles to guide determinations of whether an auditor is independent: has the client relationship (a) created a mutual or conflicting interest; (b) call for the accountant to audit its own work; (c) result in the accountant acting as a manager or employee of the client; or (d) place the accountant in an advocacy position for the client?

earlier, the relative percentage of the total revenues auditors garner from their audit clients from consulting has declined in the last few years. However, the decline may not be as great as it first appears. First, as discussed below, the disclosure requirements for non-audit fees became more relaxed in 2003 than they were in 2002, thereby permitting many former non-audit services to be now classified as audit or audit-related services. Secondly, the decline may be a change in scale and not a substantive change in how auditors view their relationship to the audit committee or the firm's shareholders. We might find some solace in the continuing increase in the number of earnings restatements: 2002 marked a record number of earnings restatements, with the number of restatements that year reaching 330, a 22 per cent increase over those for the preceding year[85] and only a slight decline to 323 for 2003, with a 28 per cent increase in 2004 to 414 reported restatements (Huron Consulting Group 2003: 2005).[86] The restatements may well portend both greater diligence on the part of the auditors as well as a stiffening of their resolve.[87] Each, of course, would be hopeful signs of an improved financial reporting culture.

Post-Enron, the metrics for financial reporting have been strengthened on many fronts. As is now well understood, Enron concealed significant liabilities by its deft and sometimes impermissible treatment of transactions carried out by special purpose entities (SPEs). To address these abuses, the Financial Accounting Standards Board in 2003 issued its interpretation No. 46 'Consolidation of Variable Interest Entities' (FIN 46). The short history of FIN 46 suggests that the reporting culture on this matter remains as disturbing as it was in Enron. One study of more than 500 large companies' financial reports found substantial evidence of non-compliance with the heightened disclosures called for by FIN 46 or a demonstrative lack of transparency in the reporting of their financial

---

[85] Surprisingly, the number of companies with over $1 billion in revenues nearly doubled over the number in 2001 (Huron Consulting Group 2003).

[86] Huron argues the rise in restatements for 2004 is likely due to the intense focus by reporting companies and their auditors on the registrant's internal controls as a result of complying with the new internal control reporting requirements mandated by § 404 of Sarbanes Oxley; Huron Consulting Group (2004: 4). Accounting restatements carry their own pain for investors. Palmrose, Richardson and Scholz (2004) study 403 restatements between 1995–9 and find an average negative return of 9% in the two days following the announcement with even greater reaction for restatements involving fraud. A GAO study (2002: 24–26) of 689 earnings restatements between 1 January 1997 and 26 March 2002 found an average three-day market decline following the announcement of 10% which translates to an average $139 million decline for each of the firms or $95.6 billion for all 689 firms.

[87] Professor Bratton (2003b: 487) provides the most acute description of the source of restatements: the restatements follow less from regulatory arbitrage than from strategic noncompliance—action under an interpretation of the law in conflict with the stated interpretation of the regulator.

relationship with their SPEs.[88] This should not surprise us since sitting CFOs continue to be under substantial pressure to meet analysts' expectations and report favorably on the firm's stewards, even if this masks the true financial position of the firm. The study's data complements the results of a recent survey of portfolio and fund managers. The survey asked the money managers to rate financial reporting by public companies. They gave financial reporting a weak C+ (AIMR 2003: 1). The survey also identified information about off-balance sheet assets and liabilities as their highest valued disclosure item (*ibid.*: 3). The survey appears to reflect the neglect that FIN 46 has suffered in the executive suites of CFOs.

One area showing no change is that of the politics of accounting and particularly the eagerness with which CEOs and CFOs are willing to exercise their considerable political muscle to shape their disclosure obligations. A key provision of Sarbanes-Oxley seeks to assure that the FASB is independent of the auditor's clients.[89] The Act therefore mandates that no standard-setter can be an authoritative source for accounting standards used in SEC filings unless its funding was derived from fees imposed by the SEC on its registrants.[90] This unquestionably is the most important development in the history of accounting standard-setting. The obvious hope of this provision is that the FASB's agenda or its pronouncements would no longer be influenced by its funding sources as had occurred in the past when the FASB received its funding from a trust that appointed its members to raise funding largely from the accounting profession. Earlier, these purse strings were held by the accounting firms and were the conduit through which their audit clients influenced the FASB's agenda as well as the content of audit standards. But influence from the regulated, certainly at the national level, can come from many levels. Thus, consider the on-going developments in the Congress.

The FASB has adopted a standard requiring the expensing of stock options.[91] Previously, the grant of a stock option is reported only in the footnotes of a firm's financial statements, where disclosure of the estimate value of the option to its recipient is disclosed. The option's value to its recipient is, on the other hand, a cost to the company since this reflects lost opportunity to the company to sell the option to a third party. The FASB has announced that it believes stock options should be reflected as a

[88] See Glass, Lewis & Co. (2003a)(finding that some companies are keeping the financial items for which they are responsible off their balance sheets via SPEs through liberal interpretation of FIN 46).
[89] See generally Cox (2003).
[90] See Sarbanes-Oxley Act 15 U.S.C. § 7218(b)(1)(iii).
[91] See FASB (2004): options issued by a company are to be reflected at their fair value on its financial statements.

charge, i.e., expense, on the company's financials statements. This essentially moves the estimated expense to a more prominent position; the estimates that are currently buried among the firm's financial statements under the standard proposed by the FASB will appear as an expense within the body of the firm's income statement thereby reducing the firm's reported net income for that fiscal period.[92] In adopting this new position, the FASB would be following the position recently taken by the International Accountings Standards Board which recently called for the expensing of stock options.[93]

Reflecting the view that an independent standard-setter is not in everyone's interest, a large group of executives (a significant portion being from the high tech industry)[94] have mobilized their financial muscle to secure passage—by nearly a three to one margin—in the US House of Representatives of HR 3574, 'The Stock Option Accounting Reform Act.' In broad overview, HR 3574 overrides any pronouncement that may be adopted by the FASB with respect to stock options that would require the expensing of stock options except with respect to the CEO and the next four most highly compensated executives. Thus, no expensing would be reported for options given to other employees (i.e., not the five most senior). Importantly, the magnitude of the amount to be reflected as an expense reduced by, among other provisions of the bill, by assuming no volatility in the stock's price. Moreover, small public companies need not expense their options and those that have recently become public enjoy a three-year grace period in reporting the costs of their executives' options. Independent of the social welfare of expensing or not expensing stock options, HR 3574, and more particularly the large congressional support it has gathered (including one of its sponsors, Congressman Oxley himself), raises an even larger issue: the significant compromise to the independence and authority of the FASB should HR 3574 be enacted appears beyond peradventure. The recent experience

---

[92] The issues that surround this debate are nicely summarized in a letter (Ciesielski 2004) recently directed to the sponsors of H.R. 3574, discussed later in the text: 'The issue of recognizing option compensation expense has been cloaked in many false garbs; options can't be valued properly, jobs will be lost to foreign countries, the stock market will fall if the expense is recognized. At the end of the day, it all comes down to executive compensation that's been shielded from investors' view. You manage what you measure: the stock compensation of the past decade has been not measured well, nor managed well (if at all, in some cases). Putting an expense figure into the income statement for stock compensation enables the markets to monitor the way shareholders' funds are being employed or wasted – not the sort of relevant information that managements would like to see shared freely. You can dress it up in all kinds of arguments about harm to various constituencies, but the bottom line is management resistance to any kind of effective governance by the markets when it comes to compensation.'

[93] See IASB (2004): the fair value of securities granted to employees must be reported as an expense reflecting the value of the securities.

[94] Incidentally, the industry group supporting HR 3574 is the same industry group who provide the momentum to pass the Private Securities Litigation Reform Act of 1995.

with HR 3574 reflects that Sarbanes-Oxley's call for independent funding of the financial reporting standard-setter has not removed the FASB from the political pressures that audit clients can bring to bear on the standard-setting process. To be sure, one positive feature of Sarbanes-Oxley is it has made those pressures more visible. Those exercising influence over financial reporting standards must now do so in a more open setting than heretofore. Nonetheless, the message is the same, namely that significant rents can be collected by politicians willing to support the reporting standards desired by their constituents. The advent of HR 3574, and particularly the executives that support it, is consistent with the fear that when it comes to financial reporting too many executives do not see independence as a desideratum.[95]

Sadly, it appears that Congress is not the lone rent seeker with respect to reporting issues post-Sarbanes-Oxley. The SEC appears also to be influenced by the desires of those it regulates. In January 2003, the SEC amended its disclosure requirements for registrants to disclose (either in the firm's proxy statement or its annual reporting form) the professional fees paid their independent accountants.[96] The 2003 amendments expanded the disclosure categories from three to four categories—(1) audit fees; (2) audit related fees; (3) tax fees; and (4) all other fees—and required disclosure for each of the two most recent fiscal years not just the most recent fiscal year as had been the requirement per its first regulatory foray into this area in 2000.[97] At first blush this appears to be very pro-regulatory since the provisions appear to call for more refined disclosure of the sources of fees paid to a company's auditor. However, several questionable features appear within the details of the 2003 amendments. First, the amendments expanded the definition of items included within 'audit fees,' so that the audit fee rubric thereafter will include all fees relevant to the accountant's discharging their responsibilities pursuant to 'generally accepted auditing standards.' This seems tame enough until one realizes that what is included is not just the fees that are 'billed ... for the audit' but also includes 'services that are normally provided by the accountant in connection with statutory or regulatory filings or engagements.'[98]

---

[95] Importantly for the position of this chapter, the Big Four accounting firms oppose the legislation and, thus, do not align themselves with many of their clients in opposing the changes the FASB proposes. See Nally *et al.* 2004.

[96] See SEC (2003).

[97] See 15 C.F.R. § 240.14a-101 Item 9 (2003).

[98] See SEC (2003: note 233): '[W]e are expanding the types of fees that should be included in this category to include fees for services that normally would be provided by the accountant in connection with statutory or regulatory filings or engagements. In addition to including fees for services necessary to perform an audit or review in accordance with GAAS, this category also may include services that generally only the independent accountant reasonably can provide, such as comfort letters, statutory audits, attest services, consents and assistance with and review of documents filed with the Commission.'

The breadth of this is appreciated when compared with the disclosure requirements that preceded the 2003 amendments; between 2000 and early 2003 the audit fee category included only:

> aggregate fees billed for professional services rendered for the audit of the registrant's annual financial statements ... and reviews of the financial statements included in the registrant's quarterly reports filed with the SEC.[99]

The 2003 amendments broadened the audit fee category to include comfort letters and consents and assistance with and reviews of documents filed with the SEC.[100]

Secondly, the 2003 amendment adds a new category, 'audit-related fees' that includes professional charges for professional assurances and related services provided by the auditor that traditionally have been carried out by the auditor such as employee benefit plan audits, due diligence related to acquisitions, accounting consultations, audits in connection with acquisitions, internal control reviews, attest services that are not required by statute or regulation, and consultation concerning financial accounting and reporting standards. Prior to the 2003 amendments these charges were set forth under the 'all other fees' rubric.[101] Thus, the 2003 amendments usher in two deregulatory changes for disclosing the relationship the auditor has with its client. First, it expands the 'audit fees' category to include services that are not specifically part of the audit and, secondly, it creates a mongrel category, 'audit-related fees': so that it significantly reduces the number of fees swept into the 'all-other-fees' category. In combination, these changes have provided an opening for important circumvention of Sarbanes-Oxley's pre-approval requirements for non-audit services. With respect to this fear, consider the reaction of a Big Four accounting firm following the 2003 amendments. Ernst & Young's manual instructs its audit clients that for items falling within either the audit or audit-related:

> a minimal level of consideration [by the client's audit committee] relating to pre-approval [is required] because they have not been thought to raise independence concerns'.

Ernst & Young further opines for its clients that audit-related services that 'generally improve audit quality and do not impair independence' and are,

---

[99] See 15 C.F.R. § 240.14a-10–101 (2002).
[100] See block quote above, note 98.
[101] See 15 C.F.R. § 240.14a-10–101 (2002).

by definition not the types of 'consulting services' that have given rise to concern about non-audit services in recent years.[102]

We might well question why there should be concern that some of professional fees will be labeled outside the all-other-fees category. Consider the implications of characterizing as 'audit-related fees' due diligence services performed by an auditor in connection with its acquisition of another company. For example, as a step toward approving its acquisition of another company, the client asks its auditor to carry out a due diligence review of the target firm. The auditor's review includes an evaluation of the worth of that firm's assets and the existence, quantity and quality of its earnings and cash flow. Post-acquisition, the same auditor might—in connection to its annual audit—discover that misjudgments or other errors were committed in its earlier due diligence investigation so that absent correction, the financial performance or position of the client will be materially misstated. The purpose of the pre-approval procedures for non-audit services is to allow the audit committee members to assess this risk independently. The purpose of highlighting the cost of these services in the firm's proxy statement or Form 10-K is both to reinforce the seriousness of the audit committee's pre-approval and to alert investors to risks of their auditors carrying out a task that might later pose a conflict of interest that adversely impacts the quality of the company's financial reports. By sweeping such due diligence reviews within the more neutral 'audit-related fees' without separately disclosing the function for which the fees were paid, as would be required for material items within the 'all-other-fees' category, the objectives of both pre-approval and disclosure are weakened.

It remains early in the life of Sarbanes-Oxley and today's reconstituted audit committees. Sarbanes-Oxley and the heightened listing requirements are unquestionably steps that have improved the financial reporting process by strengthening the independence of the auditor.[103] The evidence gathered in Part VI at least raises serious questions whether the reforms have gone far enough. The next section explores what more needs to be done.

---

[102] See Consumer Federation of America (2003).

[103] Unfortunately, little attention has been focused on whether strong social and psychological forces may prevent the audit committee from rising to the level of detached independence envisioned in today's reforms. For a review of many of these forces and skepticism that the audit committee will fulfill the reforms' objectives, see Beecher-Monas (2003).

VII. SOME STEPS TOWARD IMPROVING THE OLIGOPOLIST AS A GATEKEEPER

Part of the solution to improving the trustworthiness of financial reporting is reducing the avenues the accountant can pursue to cheat on the standards otherwise pursued by the accounting industry. Herein is the irony posed by the accounting profession as an oligopoly. In the more typical situation, competition within an oligopoly manifests itself by the cheater reducing its price or providing a superior service for the same price charged by its competitors. The evidence gathered in Part IV suggests that members of the accounting profession could not engage in product quality competition because of difficulties of their client's determining *ex ante* differences in the quality of services provided or because some members of the industry enjoyed an unerodable advantage in terms of expertise and reputation for carrying out audits within certain broad industry classifications. Their real competition was in the more competitive environment of consulting services where they faced each other as well as many non-accounting vendors of consulting services. Here the auditor enjoyed—and could well have exploited—a competitive edge that its consulting competitors could not rival: a pre-existing relationship with the client that afforded it an exploitable commercial advantage because its familiarity with the client's business and potential compromising of its independence in evaluating the quality of the client's financial reporting.

Because of the difficulty of assessing just how significant the information advantage the auditor enjoyed with respect to a consulting project offered by its client, or even the extent it could leverage compromises to its independence so as to reap consulting revenues, it was not possible for competing audit firms to engage in any behaviour except to mimic with their own clients the practices of their competitors. By doing so it did not behove any industry member to pursue a course different from the other big accounting firms and abstain from becoming a consultant to its audit clients.

There is reason to believe that auditing will now play a more important role in revenue growth of the accounting industry in the future. This is because many of the services once provided by the independent accountant are now proscribed by Sarbanes-Oxley, and all but one of the Big Four firms having divested certain features of their consulting services falling within these proscribed categories. The accountants still carry out a wide variety of services that swell their non-audit-related fees to levels greatly in excess of those falling within either the current 'audit' and 'audit-related' categories. Moreover, Sarbanes-Oxley has added a number of significant features to financial reporting so that audit responsibilities and their allied tasks have greatly expanded. With these rising costs and reduced flexibility to trade off audit quality for consulting, it is propitious to consider whether the cartel problem can be a virtue in the context of financial reporting.

Recall the dilemma each cartel member faces when it learns that a rival is cheating. A key feature to the cartel responding to a cheater is accurate information regarding deviance by a member of the oligopoly. Here we might consider whether the trustworthiness of financial reporting is advanced with more or less information respecting the cost of the audit provided by the auditor. Under the classic formulation, Auditor A who learns that its rival, Auditor B, is selling a product to a client for less than the going price can discipline Auditor B by, for example, matching the price or taking some disciplinary step. As seen earlier, this response is not likely in the case of audit services due to the lack of uniformity of the service offered, the competitive advantage of a pre-existing knowledge of the audit client, and expertise that appears imbedded within some accounting firms with respect to certain important industries.

The solution may be to impose discipline outside the cartel, namely market forces related to the pricing of the audit client's securities. Assuming that markets are sensitive to relationships that might compromise the accountant's independence, enhanced disclosure of those relationships likely will have positive social welfare implications. Comparing the cost of audits with the overall revenues garnered by the accountant from its audit client would better appraise investors and the audit committee of the risks non-audit service revenue poses to the independence of the attest function. This benefit itself should justify returning to the pre-2003 disclosure guidelines regarding disclosure of the composition of the auditor's income from its audit client.

A further weakening of the bond that non-audit services provide to management is to place the award, renewal, or discontinuation of material non-audit services to a reporting company's auditor on the same level as terminating its accountant. If the termination of the auditor as auditor and the termination or engagement of the auditor as consultant were each subject of being reported on Form 8-K it would remove some of the differential advantages non-audit services confers on managers vis-a-vis audit services in its bargaining with the accountants. Because of the additional friction this would pose to public companies, it may well open the consulting opportunities to other accounting firms. This could be the means for the issuer to gain confidence in another accounting firm so that changing accounting firms would be a less daunting task. This could also change the perspective of the company's current auditor so that it may cease viewing its relationship as a perpetuity so that it would have increased concern for its reputation and less for the relationship itself. Audit committees, as seen earlier, have sole responsibility for retention and renewal of the outside accountant. The audit committee is also charged with evaluating the inputs that produced the financial reports. Sarbanes-Oxley and the listing requirements of the NYSE and Nasdaq in combination seek to mandate a dialogue between the accountant and the committee's members for the purpose of assuring that the audit committee is fully engaged in carrying out this process. For example, the accountant is required to identify the critical accounting estimates and choices used in preparing the financial statements. A significant gap in the audit committee's engagement with the accountant is a standard by which they must measure their compliance with Sarbanes-Oxley and the firm's listing organization. Certainly, more should be required of the committee members than to receive a recitation of the critical accounting choices and estimates. By so limiting the obligations any hoped-for deliberations and conversation with the auditor are vacuous. For the CEO and CFO, the law now demands that they certify in reports filed with the SEC that the financial statements fairly present the firm's financial position and performance. This goes to the heart of financial reporting: the financial statements should reflect the economic realities and achievements of the firm.[104]

Given the temptations that some executives face, one might be cynical regarding the significance executive certifications will be in deterring rogue executives from cooking the books. This explains, in part, the prominent role cast for the audit committee by contemporary corporate governance requirements. A good audit committee will not be satisfied only with a recitation of just what were the critical accounting judgments and estimates. The 'why' and the 'effects' of those judgments will be examined by its members. Such inquiry should be a requirement for all audit committees of reporting companies who should be tasked to satisfy themselves that the choices and judgments made as identified by the auditor result in combination to a fair presentation of the firm's financial performance and position. With this requirement being added to the SEC's regulations, it provides the litmus for the committee members' understanding why they are to inquire as to the firm's critical accounting estimates and judgments. Moreover, it provides a more acute basis for the committee to assess the independence of the auditor. The PCAOB can complete the circle by requiring that part of the auditor's attest function be a separate report that explains why the *critical* accounting choices and estimates that have been made in preparing the financial statements 'fairly present' the company's financial performance and position.[105]

---

[104] The full significance of this is reflected in the classic case, *United States v Simon*, 425 F.2d 796 (2d Cir. 1969), which holds that mere compliance with generally accepted auditing standards and generally accepted accounting principles do not alone assure that the financial statements are not materially misleading.

[105] This idea was first advanced by Professor Elliot Weiss (2003: 512–14) and calls upon the auditor to (1) identify the critical accounting judgments; (2) describe the factors the auditor

Related to the auditor's independence is the role tax services provided by the auditor might have in compromising the accountant's independence. Recall that fees paid to the auditor for tax services are now separately reported. These fees are significant and continue to be a source of concern both because of their size as well as that they may relate to advice provided on transactions that are also the focus of the attest function.[106] The SEC has broadly proscribed auditors providing consulting services on transactions which auditors will later have to review in discharging a statutory audit. There continues to be concern that this standard is too general so that auditors may turn a blind eye to the possibility that their audit of a transaction is compromised by their earlier providing tax advice for that transaction.[107] While one response is a bar to accounting firms providing tax consulting to their audit clients, this may not be politically possible.[108]

An intermediate solution is to require the accountant to file a report as part of the registrant's proxy statement or annual report describing the five largest (in terms of revenues) tax consulting items provided the audit client and why its audit was not compromised by it having provided such advice. There would be a requirement that the audit committee acknowledge that it had received the report and had reviewed the report with the auditor. In combination, this would provide some useful oversight and caution to the accountant and its client in undertaking this side relationship.

It should be noted that none of the above suggested approaches will induce competitive responses from other members of the accounting industry. They rely upon strengthening the independent voices within the corporation, its audit committee, and facilitating market responses that can discipline issuers by raising their cost of capital. With the product of the accounting industry being a service tailored to the special systems and culture of the client, price competition and quality competition are less visible components. Moreover, the cartel problem may have the

considered in making its assessment of those accounting judgments; and (3) describe how the financial statements are sensitive to those judgments. Forty years ago, then Big Eight firm Arthur Andersen & Co. sought to decouple the fair presentation standard from the requirement that the financial statements be prepared in conformity with GAAP; this change would have permitted the firm to certify financial statements not prepared in accordance with GAAP when the auditor believed GAAP did not fairly present the firm's financial performance or position (Zeff 1992).

[106] Fees paid for tax work in 2003 by Fortune 500 firms represented 43% of audit fees (Glass Lewis & Co. 2003b).

[107] See e.g., Public Oversight Board (2004b): advising PCAOB of the need to develop rigorous standards addressing conflicts of interest that can be posed by tax services provided to audit clients.

[108] See Public Oversight Board (2004c): not preventing the auditor from carrying on substantial tax services for its clients with the major restriction being that it not promote to its clients questionable tax shelters or be rewarded by fees contingent on an outcome, such as favorable treatment by the IRS.

perverse effect of causing competitive responses that will lower the quality of the audit or, weaken auditor independence. If either of these were the competitive response then competition would be harmful. Nevertheless, disclosure of the presence or absence of questionable relationships and steps to assure independence of its audit staff may have favorable reputation effects for the practicing firm. To this end, enhanced disclosure can facilitate competition on this basis which would be a positive development. With truly independent and informed audit committees it might be possible for meaningful competition on the quality of services to occur. Certainly, a committee charged with responsibility for overseeing the quality of a firm's financial reporting would not be immune to competing presentations.

The above are but small steps that may well improve the overall quality of financial statements. Even more profound steps in improving the auditor's independence and the concomitant quality of financial reporting would occur if public companies were also required to rotate auditing firms periodically, for example every seven years, and by imposing an absolute bar to non-audit services. Opponents to mandatory rotation assert that this would visit unnecessarily high expenses on reporting companies.[109] A new audit team would face a steep learning curve that could only be surmounted by greater staffing and higher costs than would have been required if the audit were carried out by the auditing firm with a historical relationship with the client. This undoubtedly is true. But these concerns may well be overstated. In 2003 alone, approximately 900 companies engaged new auditors and did so as a matter of choice.[110] For the vast number of these changes, no reason was stated. With there being approximately 17,000 reporting companies, this reflects not less than 5 per cent of those companies changing auditors every year. A mandatory requirement of rotation every seventh year would call for this number to be tripled. We might ask whether such a requirement is such a significant change in scale. Although the number making changes slightly exceeds 5 per cent of all reporting companies, it suggests that a large number of firms can change auditors with no apparent harm to investors. It should be noted that if all firms were required to rotate auditors every ten years that the number of changes in any single year would be roughly double the number that occurred in 2003. Such rotation can be expected to lead to much less concentration within industries. The dominant position that individual Big Four firms

---

[109] GAO (2004) concludes that prudent course is to monitor and evaluate the effects of Sarbanes-Oxley and other reform efforts on the financial reporting process before incurring the costs and related uncertainties related to mandatory rotation of audit firms.

[110] See Glass, Lewis & Co. (2004). No reason was given for making the change of auditors for two-thirds of the companies. By mid-summer of 2004, the number of public companies changing auditors had already reached the level of 2003 (i.e., 900 companies) (Plitch and Wei 2004).

hold with respect to certain industries would be challenged by other firms realizing that a forced change in auditors provides each with the potential to obtain the business that historically belonged to another firm. This would cause rivals to raid each other's stable of audit partners with the desired experience so as to develop the necessary expertise and critical mass to be a credible competitor.

Removing non-audit revenues from the auditors income from their audit clients would have the salutary effect of forcing auditors to compete on price and quality of their audit services. Competition on quality will be possible by publicly available information that arises from the PCAOB's frequent inspection reports. Audit committees should become students of the results of PCAOB reports, certainly any that are focused on their auditor. Any disclosed systemic weaknesses in the quality of the firm's auditor is a clarion call for the audit committee to assure itself that those weaknesses do not recur with the audit being performed for it. If all accounting firms earn equally qualified or even weak reports, the audit committee's response is not to hide in the complacent bliss that one cannot do better. The correct response is to extract assurances from its auditor that those found weaknesses will not occur with its audit. These foci will introduce competition among accounting firms based on quality and quality assurances, a most healthy and long overdue development.

VIII. CONCLUSION

The recent financial and accounting scandals reflect that the accounting industry has performed badly. Not all of its problems are due to its oligopolistic structure. However, its oligopolistic structure facilitated consciously parallel action on the part of large accounting firms that caused each to pursue a strategy of transforming itself into a business that also provided auditing services. True reform of the industry requires sensitivity to how its concentration contributed to its ills. This chapter has set forth both an explanation of the cause and the cures for what ails this gatekeeper.

REFERENCES

Agrawal, A. and Chadha, S. (2002), 'Corporate Governance and Accounting Standards', Working Paper, available at http://papers.ua.edu/_aagrawal/papers.htm (last visited 19 August 2005).

AIMR (2003), *2003 AIMR Member Survey of Global Corporate Financial Reporting Quality*, available at http://www.cfainstitute.org/pressroom/pdf/financial_report_qlty.pdf (last visited 20 August 2005).

Antel, R., Gordon, E.A., Narayanamoorthy, G. and Zhou, L. (2002), 'The Joint Determinants of Audit Fees, Non-Audit Fees, and Abnormal Accruals', Yale ICF Working Paper No. 02–21, available at http://www.ssrn.com/abstract=318943 (last visited 20 August 2005).

Areeda, P.E. and Hovenkamp, H. (2003), *Antitrust Law: An Analysis of Antitrust Principles and Their Application* (Vol. 6, 2nd ed. New York; Aspen Law Publisher).

Balhoff, W.E. (2002), Prepared Statement of Wm. E. Balhoff before the Senate Banking, Housing and Urban Affairs Committee, 14 March.

Barta, P. and McKinnon, J.D. (2003), 'Freddie Regulator Seeks $100 Million in Settlement Deal', *Wall Street Journal*, 9 December, at A2.

Beecher-Monas, E. (2003), 'Corporate Governance in the Wake of Enron: An Examination of the Audit Committee Solution to Corporate Fraud', 55 *Administrative Law Review* 357.

Bratton, W.W. (2003a), 'Enron, Sarbanes-Oxley and Accounting: Rules Versus Principles *versus* Rents', 48 *Villanova Law Review* 1023.

—— (2003b), 'Shareholder Value and Auditor Independence', 53 *Duke Law Journal* 439.

Breeden, R.C. (2002), Prepared Statement of Richard C. Breeden, before the Senate Banking, Housing and Urban Affairs Committee, 12 February.

Brown, K. and Dugan, I.J. (2002), 'Sad Account: Andersen's Fall From Grace Is a Tale of Greed and Miscues', *Wall Street Journal*, June 7, 2002, at A1.

Bryan-Low, C. (2003a), 'Accounting Firms Earn More From Consulting', *Wall Street Journal*, 16 April, at C9.

—— (2003b), 'GM Will End Consulting Projects With Deloitte Touche Tohmatsu', *Wall Street Journal*, 7 April, at C7.

—— (2003c), 'Accounting Board To Look at Abuses In Tax Shelters', *Wall Street Journal*, 22 October, at A2.

Cassidy, J. (2002), 'The Greed Cycle', *New Yorker*, 23 September, at 64.

Chaney, P.K., Jeter, D.C. and Shivakumar, L. (2004), 'Self-Selection of Auditors and Audit Pricing in Private Firms', 79 *Accounting Review* 51–72.

Choi, S. (1998), 'Market Lessons for Gatekeepers', 92 *Northwestern University Law Review* 916.

Ciesielski, J. (2004), Letter of Mr. Jack Ciesielski to Representatives Richard H. Baker and Paul E. Kanjorski, U.S. House of Representatives, 1 March.

Coffee, J.C. (2002), 'Understanding Enron: Its About Gatekeepers Stupid', 57 *Business Lawyer* 1403.

Consumer Federation of America (2003), Letter of Consumer Federation of America, Consumers Union, U.S. Public Interest Research Group, Common Cause and Consumer@action to Mr. William Donaldson, Chairman of the SEC, 5 June.

Copeland, J.E. (2002), Prepared Statement of James E. Copeland before the Senate Banking, Housing and Urban Affairs Committee, 14 March.

Countryman, A. (2002), 'New Auditors, but Same Risk: Replacements for Andersen Tied to Clients', *Chicago Tribune*, 14 July, at C-1.

Cox, J.D. (1977), '*Ernst & Ernst v Hochfelder*: A Critique and Evaluation', 28 *Hastings Law Journal* 569.

—— (2003), 'Reforming The Culture of Financial Reporting: The PCAOB and the

Metrics for Accounting Measurements, 81 *Washington University Law Quarterly* 301.

Cox, J.D. *et al.* (2004), *Securities Regulations Cases and Materials* (4th ed. St Paul, Mn: Thomson:West).

Cunningham, L.A. (2004), 'Choosing Gatekeepers: The Financial Statement Insurance Alternative to Auditor Liability', 42 *University of California at Los Angeles Law Review* 413.

Davidson, W.N., Xie, B. and Xu, W. (2004), 'Market Reaction to Voluntary Announcements of Audit Committee Appointments: The Effects of Financial Expertise', 23 *J. Accounting and Public Policy* 279.

Davis, L.R., Ricciute, D.N. and Trompeter, G. (1993), 'Audit Effort, Audit Fees, and the Provision of Non-audit Services to Audit Clients', 68 *Accounting Review* 135.

DeFond, M.L., Raghunandan, K. and Subramanyam, K.R. (2002), 'Do Non-Audi Services Affect Auditor Independence? Evidence from Going-Concern Credit Opinions', 40 *Journal Accounting Research* 1247 (September 2002).

Dugan, I.J. (2002), 'Depreciated: Did You Hear the One About the Accountant? Its Not Very Funny', *Wall Street Journal*, 14 March, at A1.

Dwyer, P. and Miller, R. (2003), 'Freddie Mac Attack', *Business Week*, 7 July, at 34.

Eisenberg, T. and Macey, J.R. (2004), 'Was Arthur Andersen Different? An Empirical Examination of Major Accounting Firms' Audits of Large Clients', 1 *J. Corp. Empirical Leg. Stud.* 263. Also available at http://www.ssrn.com/abstract=468761 (last visited 20 August 2005).

Ettredge, M. and Greenberg, R. (1990), 'Determinants of Fee Cutting on Initial Audit Engagements', 28 *Journal of Accounting Research* 198.

FASB (2004), Statement No. 123(r), Share-Based Payment (16 Dec.).

Francis, J. and Ke, B. (2003), 'Disclosure of Fees Paid to Auditors and the Market Valuation of Earnings Surprises', available at http://www.ssrn.com/abstract=487463 (last visited 20 August 2005).

Frank, R. and Solomon, D. (2003), 'Deloitte Touche Cancels Plans to Split Off its Consulting Arm', 31 March, at C10.

Frankel, R.M., Johnson, M.F. and Nelson, K.K. (2002a), 'The Relation Between Auditors' Fees for Non-Audit Services and Earnings Quality', MIT Sloan Working Paper No. 4330-02.

—— (2002b), 'The Relation between Auditors' Fees for Non-audit Services and Earnings Management', 77 *Accounting Review* 71.

GAO (1996), *The Accounting Profession Major Issues: Progress and Concerns*, GAO/AIMD-96-98.

—— (2002), *Financial Statement Restatements: Trends, Market Impacts, Regulatory Responses, and Remaining Challenges*, GAO-03-138.

—— (2003a), *Public Accounting Firms Mandated Study on Consolidation and Competition*.

—— (2003b), *Government Accounting Office, Accounting Firm Consolidation. Selected Large Public Company Views on Audit Fees, Quality, Independence, and Choice*, Rept. No, GAO-03-1158.

—— (2003c), *Public Accounting Firms Mandated Study on Consolidation and Competition*, GAO-03–864, Report to the Senate Committee on Banking, Housing, and Urban Affairs and the House Committee on Financial Services.

—— (2003d), *Financial Statement Restatement Database*, GAO-03-395R.

—— (2003e), *Accounting Firm Consolidation Selected Large Public Company Views on Audit Fees, Quality, Independence, and Choice*, Rept. No. GAO-03-1158.

—— (2003f), *Public Accounting Firms, Required Study on the Potential Effects of Mandatory Audit Firm Rotation*, GAO-04-216.

—— (2004), *Mandatory Audit Firm Rotation Study, Study Questionnaires, Responses, and Summary Respondents' Comments*, GAO-04-217.

Gilson, R.J. and Kraakman, R.H. (1984), 'The Mechanisms of Market Efficiency', 70 *Virginia Law Review* 549.

Ginsburg, D.H. (1993), 'Nonprice Competition', 38 *Antitrust Bulletin* 83.

Glass, Lewis & Co. (2003a), *FIN No. 46—New Rule Not a Panacea* (11 November).

—— (2003b), *2003 Study of Audit Fees*, available at http://www.proxypaper.com.

—— (2004a), *Audit Fee Study*.

—— (2004b), *Auditor Turnover—What Invetors Should be Watching*.

Gullapalli, D. (2004), 'Crunch This! CPAs Become the New BMOCs', *Wall Streeet Journal*, 29 July, at C1.

Hamdani, A. (2003), 'Gatekeeper Liability', 77 *Southern California Law Review* 53.

Hills, R.M. (2002), Prepared Statement of Roderick M. Hills before the Senate Banking, Housing and Urban Affairs Committee, 12 February.

Hovenkamp, H. (1994), *Federal Antitrust Policy: The Law of Competition and Its Practice* (St Paul, Mn: West Group).

Huron Consulting Group (2003), *An Analysis of Restatement Matters: Rules, Errors, Ethics, For Five Years Ended December 31, 2002*.

—— (2004), *2003 Annual Review of Financial Reporting Matters*.

—— (2005), *2004 Annual Review of Financial Reporting Matters*.

IASB (2004), *International Reporting Standard No. 2* (20 February).

Invancevich, S. and Zardkoohi, A. (2000), 'An Exploratory Analysis of the 1989 Accounting Megamergers', 14 *Accounting Horizons* 155.

Ireland, J.C. and Lennox, C.S. (2002), 'The Large Audit Fee Premium: A Case of Selectivity Bias?', 17 *Journal of Accounting, Auditing & Finance* 73.

IRRC (2002), 'IRRC Finds Little Change in Potential Auditor Conflicts', 9 October, available at http://www.csrwire.com/article.cgi/1335.html (last visited 20 Aug. 2005).

Jackson, H.E. (1993), 'Reflections on Kaye, Scholer: Enlisting Lawyers to Improve the Regulation of Financial Institutions', 66 *Southern California Law Review* 1019.

Kaplan, R.L. (2004), 'The Mother of All Conflicts: Auditors and Their Clients', 29 *Journal of Corporation Law* 363.

Kelly, K. (2002), 'Industrials Near Worst Year Since '77: Nasdaq May See Third-Biggest Drop', *Wall Street Journal*, 31 December, at C1.

Kimmel, L and Vasquez, S. (2003), *The Increased Financial and Non-Financial Cost of Staying Public, Foley & Lardner, Attorneys at Law*.

Kraakman, R.H. (1986), 'Gakekeepers: The Anatomy of Third Party Enforcement Strategy', 2 *Journal of Law, Economics and Organization* 53.

Krantz, M. (2004), 'More Firms Part Ways with Auditors', *USA Today*, reported at http://www.usatoday.com/money/companies/2004–02–08-auditors_x.htm (last visited 19 Aug. 2005).

Levitt, A. (2000), Testimony of the Honorable Arthur Levitt, Chairman Securities and Exchange Commission before Subcommittee on Securities, US Senate Committee on Banking, Housing, and Urban Affairs, 28 September.

—— (2002), *Taking on the Street* (New York: Pantheon).

Longstreth, B. (2002), Prepared Statement of Bevis Longstreth, before the Senate Banking, Housing and Urban Affairs Committee, 6 March.

Macey, J. and Sale, H.A. (2003), 'Observations on the Role of Commodification, Independence, and Governance in the Accounting Industry', 48 *Villanova Law Review* 1167.

Maher, M.W., Tiessen, P., Colson, R. and Broman, A.J. (1992), 'Competition and Audit Fees', 67 *Accounting Review* 199.

Mayer, J. (2002), 'The Accountants' War', *New Yorker*, 22 April, at 64.

McNamee, M. *et al.* (2000), 'Accounting Wars', *Business Week*, 25 September 25, p. 157.

McRoberts, F. and Alexander, D. (2002), '1-Stop Tactic Casts Cloud on Andersen', *Chicago Tribune*, 4 March, at 1.

Menon, K. and Williams, D. (2001), 'Long Term Trends in Audit Fees', 20 *Auditing: A Journal of Practice and Theory*.

Michaels, A. (2004), 'Survey Reveals Changing Culture at Big Four Firms', *Financial Times*, 9 February.

Moore, D.A., Tetlock, P.E., Tanlu, L.D. and Bazerman, M.H. (2005), 'Conflicts of Interest and the Case of Auditor Independence: Moral Seduction and the Strategic Issue Cycling', Harvard Business School Working Paper No. 03115, available at http://www.ssrn.com/abstract=667363 (last visited 20 Aug. 2005).

Morgenson, G. (2002), 'Watchdog? LapDog? Why Have to Guess', *New York Times*, 17 February, at Sec. 3 page 1.

Moriarty, G.B. and Livingston, P.B. (2001), 'Quantitative Measures of the Quality of Financial Reporting', 17 *Financial Executive* (July).

Nally, D.M. (2004), Letter by Dennis M. Nally, Chairman and Senior Partner PricewaterhouseCooper LLP, Eugene O'Kelly, Chairman and Chief Executive Officer KPMG LLP, James H. Quigley, Chief Executive Officer Deloitte & Touche USA LLP, and James S. Turley, Global Chairman and Chief Executive Officer Ernst and Young to Congressmen Richard H. Baker and Paul E. Kanjorski, Subcommittee on Capital Markets, Insurance and Government Sponsored Enterprises, U.S. House of Representatives, 17 March.

Palmrose, Z.V. (1986), 'The Effect of Non-audit Services on the Pricing of Audit Services: Further Evidence', 24 *Journal of Accounting Research* 405.

Palmrose, Z.V., Richardson, V.J. and Scholz, S.W. (2004), 'Determinants of Market Reactions to Restatement Announcements', 37 *Journal of Accounting & Economics* 59.

Partnoy, F. (2001), 'Barbarians at the Gatekeepers? A Proposal for a Modified Strict Liability Regime', 79 *Washington University Law Quarterly* 491.

Peel, M.J. and Roberts, R. (2003), 'Audit Fee Determinants and Auditor Premiums: Evidence from the Micro-Firm Sub-Market', 33 *Accounting & Business Research* 207.

Pitt, H.L. (2002), Prepared Statement of Harvey L. Pitt, before the Senate Banking, Housing and Urban Affairs Committee, 21 March.

Plitch, P. and Rapoport, M. (2004), 'Non-audit Fees Fell Below Half of Auditor. Payment', *Wall Street Journal*, 8 July, at C3.

Plitch, P. and Wei, L. (2004), 'Auditor-Client Breakups Rise, While Disclosure Often Lags', The *Wall Street Journal* Online, 3 August, at C3.

Prentice, R.A. (2000), 'The Case of the Irrational Auditor: A Behavioral Insight into Securities Regulation', 95 *Northwestern University Law Review* 133.

Public Oversight Board of the AICPA (1986), *Public Perceptions of Management Advisory Services Performed by CPA Firms for Audit Clients.*

Public Oversight Board (1979), *Scope of Services by CPA Firms.*

—— (2000), *The Panel on Audit Effectiveness Report and Recommendations* (31 August).

—— (2001), *Public Accounting Report Special Supplement Annual Survey of National Accounting Firms—2001.*

—— (2003), *Rules on Investigations and Adjudications*, Release No. 2003–015.

—— (2004a), *The Advisory Panel on Auditor Independence, Strengthening the Professionalism of the Independent Auditor.*

—— (2004b), *Letter of Public Company Accounting Oversight Board Standing Advisory Group*, 27 August.

—— (2004c), *PCAOB Proposed Ethics and Independence Rules Concerning Independence, Tax Services, and Contingent Fees*, PCAOB Rel. No. 2004-015 (14 Dec.).

Raghunandan, K., Read, W.J. and Whisenant, S. (2003), 'Are Non-Audit Fees Associated with Restated Financial Statements? Initial Empirical Evidence', Working Paper, available at http://www.ssrn.com/abstract=394844 (last visited 20 Aug. 2005).

Ronen, J. (2002), 'Post-Enron Reform: Financial Statement Insurance and GAAP Revisited', 8 *Stanford Journal of Law and Business* 39.

Salomon, D. and Bryan-Low, C. (2004), 'Companies Complain About Cost of Corporate Governance Rules', *Wall Street Journal*, 10 February, at A-1.

Scheiber, N. (2002), 'Peer Revue: How Arthur Andersen Got Away With It', *The New Republic*, 28 January, at 19.

Schulte, A.A. (1965), 'Compatibility of Management Consulting and Auditing', 40 *Accounting Review* 587.

SEC (1979), 'Scope of Services by Independent Accountants', Accounting Series Release No. 264.

—— (2000a), 'Independent Consultant Finds Widespread Independence Violations at PricewaterhouseCoopers', (6 January 6) available at http://www.sec.gov/news/press/2000-4 (last visited 19 Aug. 2005).

—— (2000b), *Revision of the Commission's Auditor Independence Requirements*, Securities Act Rel. No. 7919.

—— (2001), 'Arthur Andersen LLP Agrees to Settlement', 19 June.

—— (2003), 'Final Rule: Strengthening the Commission's Requirements Regarding Auditor Independence', Sec.Act Rel. No. 8183 (28 January).

—— (2004), 'Standard of Professional Conduct for Attorneys Appearing and Practicining Before the Commission in the Representation of an Issuer', 17 C.F.R. § 205.2.

Seidler, L. (2002), Prepared Statement of Lee Seidler, before the Senate Banking, Housing and Urban Affairs Committee, 6 March.

Seligman, J. (2002), 'Conflicts of Interest in Corporate and Securities Law After Enron', 80 *Washington University Law Quarterly* 449.

Simunic, D.A. (1980), 'The Pricing of Audit Services: Theory and Evidence', 18 *Journal of Accounting Research* 161.

Stevens, M. (1991), *The Big Six: The Selling Out of America's Top Accounting Firms.*

Stewart, J.K. (2002), 'Incentives Feed Audit Woes', *Chicago Tribune*, 10 March, at Bus. Section 1.

Stigler, G.J. (1964), 'A Theory of Oligopoly', 72 *Journal of Political Economy* 44.

Thomas, R.S., Schwab, S.J. and Hansen, R.G. (2001), 'Megafirms', 80 *North Carolina Law Review* 115.

Tie, R. (2000), 'SEC Renews Push for More Oversight of Auditors', *Journal of Accounting*, (July), p.16.

US Senate (2002), Report of the Committee on Banking, Housing, and Urban Development on the Public Company Accounting Reform and Investor Protection Act of 2002.

—— (2003), U.S. Tax Shelter Industry: The Role of Accountants, Lawyers, and Financial Professionals, Four KPMG Case Studies: FLIP, OPIS, BLIPS, AND SC2, Report prepared by the Minority Staff of the Permanent Subcommittee on Investigation of U.S. Senate Permanent Subcommittee on Investigations, Committee on Governmental Affairs (2003).

Turner, L. (2002), Prepared Statement of Lynn Turner, before the Senate Banking, Housing and Urban Affairs Committee, 26 February.

Weil, J. (2004), 'Auditing Firms Get Back to What They Do Best', *Wall Street Journal*, 31 March, at C-3 .

Weil, J. and Schroeder, M. (2002), 'Heard on the Street, Waste Management Suit Brought By SEC Zings Andersen', *Wall Street Journal*, 27 March, at C1.

Weiss, E.J. (2003), 'Some Thoughts on an Agenda for the Public Company Accounting Oversight Board', 53 *Duke Law Journal* 491.

Wu, M. (2001), *Quantitative Measures of the Quality of Financial Reporting*, Financial Executive Institute.

Wyatt, A.R. (2002), Prepared Statement of Arthur R. Wyatt before the Senate Banking, Housing and Urban Affairs Committee, 27 February.

Yardley, J.A. *et al.* (1992), 'Supplier Behavior in the Audit Market', 11 *Journal of Accounting Literature* 151.

Zeff, S.A. (1992), 'Arthur Andersen & Co. and the Two-part Opinion in the Auditor's Report: 1946–1962', 8 *Contemporary Accounting Research* 443.

—— (2003a), 'How the US Accounting Profession Got Where It Is Today: Part I', 17 *Accounting Horizon* 189.

—— (2003b), 'How the US Accounting Profession Got Where It Is Today: Part II', 17 *Accounting Horizon* 267.

10

The Liability Risk for Outside Directors: A Cross-Border Analysis

BERNARD BLACK*, BRIAN CHEFFINS** AND
MICHAEL KLAUSNER***

I. INTRODUCTION

OUTSIDE DIRECTORS ARE a key component of most
prescriptions for good governance of public companies. In the
United States, outside directors play a central role in overseeing
external audits, hiring and firing chief executives, setting management
compensation, and responding to takeover proposals, among other
management decisions; the Sarbanes-Oxley Act of 2002 increases their
role. In Britain, since the early 1990s public companies have been subject
to a 'comply or explain' corporate governance code that offers extensive
guidance on the monitoring role that 'non-executive' directors are
supposed to play (Financial Reporting Council 2003: Combined Code,
Section 1A). A '*Kodex*' of best practice, added to German company law in
2002, contains numerous guidelines concerning the duty of the
supervisory board—comprised of outside directors—to monitor the
management board (Government Commission 2003: ch. 5). Similar trends
toward formalising the corporate governance role of outside directors are
evident in a wide variety of additional countries (*Economist* 2003).

This increasing reliance on outside directors as an integral element of
corporate governance raises a question regarding their incentives.
Outside directors rarely receive meaningful performance-oriented
remuneration (Black, Cheffins, and Klausner 2004: 46–47). So what gives
outside directors incentives to work hard, pay attention, and exercise

* University of Texas Law School and McCombs School of Business, University of Texas.
** Faculty of Law, Cambridge University.
*** Stanford Law School. This chapter was previously published in (2005) 11(2) European
Financial Management 153–171. The permission of Blackwell Publishing to republish is
gratefully acknowledged.

judgment independent of management? One answer, often left implicit, is that legal liability is an important factor in leading outside directors to do a good job.

Yet legal liability is problematic as a source of incentives. Fear of litigation may cause directors to shun risks that should be taken. Nervousness about lawsuits can also hamper the recruitment of qualified outside directors and induce some incumbent directors to resign (Korn/Ferry International 2003: 24).

Such concerns are not merely academic. At the same time as outside directors are being touted as a cure for corporate governance problems, one hears an increasingly loud chorus of concern over directors' liability risk. Most US outside directors believe that the scandal-driven enactment of the Sarbanes-Oxley Act and related corporate governance reforms have significantly increased the legal hazards they face (Corporate Board Member 2003: 5). Indeed, the conventional wisdom in the United States seems to be that 'being an outside director is often too risky' (Cox 2002). January 2005 settlements of suits brought under US securities law in which former outside directors of WorldCom and Enron agreed to pay a combined total of US$38 million out of their own pockets have amplified these concerns. Fears concerning potential liability are growing in other countries as well.

In this chapter, we examine the liability risk for outside directors in order to assess whether current fears are well founded. We study four representative common law countries (Australia, Canada, Britain, and the United States) and three representative civil law countries (France, Germany, and Japan).[1] In so doing, we distinguish between situations in which directors personally pay damages, fines, or legal expenses out of their own pockets (out-of-pocket liability) from situations in which all monetary amounts—legal expenses, payments to settle a case, an award of damages after a trial, or a fine—are paid by a director's company or by directors' and officers' (D&O) insurance (nominal liability).

Outside the United States, outside directors of public companies are rarely sued, so even the risk of nominal liability is small. For their US counterparts, suits are common so nominal liability is a significant risk. However, D&O insurance is almost universal and the law gives companies broad power to indemnify directors for directors' legal expenses, settlement payments, and for most types of cases, damage

---

[1] This chapter is a summary of two longer 'law' papers, Black, Cheffins, and Klausner (2004) and Black and Cheffins (2003). In these papers interested readers can find many more details and legal niceties, as well as the extensive citations that are customary in legal scholarship. We provide only highly selected citations here. The two papers were published with significant revisions as Black, Cheffins and Klausner (2006) and Cheffins and Black (2006). This chapter, other than some minor amendments to the footnotes and part III.f, has not been revised to reflect these revisions.

awards as well. To be sure, the Enron and WorldCom settlements, in which shareholders demanded out-of-pocket payments from the outside directors as a condition of settlement, raise concerns about whether these cases are exceptional or are harbingers of increased risk. Our best guess is that these cases are exceptions, and that in all seven countries, the risk of out-of-pocket liability will continue to be very small. If outside directors are apprehensive about ending up out of pocket, their fears are not yet justified by the facts.

In this chapter, we focus on the risk of liability for conduct not involving self-dealing and dishonesty. To be sure, the misappropriation of company assets and other self-serving conduct can expose outside directors to potential out-of-pocket liability. For instance, D&O insurance policies commonly exclude from coverage losses resulting from 'deliberate fraud' or the obtaining of 'illegal profits'. Outside directors, however, rarely have sufficient knowledge or influence to act in ways that would trigger this exclusion. Moreover, outside directors know they can protect themselves against liability for self-dealing by steering clear of transactions involving the company where they have a personal interest and other potentially self-serving arrangements. They have no such comfort, however, for their ordinary unconflicted activities, and it is this liability that concerns them most.

We believe that the 'functional convergence' across countries (Gilson 2001; Kraakman *et al.* 2004) that we find—for directors' out-of-pocket risk, though not their risk of nominal liability—is no accident. Instead, market forces and political dynamics that are common across national borders keep outside directors' liability risk low. Historically, when concerns about legal risk have become acute—for instance, because of an outlier case of out-of-pocket liability—there is often a reaction of some sort. Sometimes this has taken the form of expanded D&O coverage. In other instances there have been changes to the law that limit the circumstances in which directors are liable, cap the amount of damages payable, or expand a company's ability to indemnify its directors or buy D&O insurance. These market and political pressures return matters to the pre-existing equilibrium of very low out-of-pocket liability risk. These same dynamics give reason to expect that this equilibrium will be restored after future shocks, whatever their source may be.

Is this equilibrium good policy? A thorough analysis of this question lies beyond the scope of this chapter. We do, however, suggest reasons why a positive but tiny risk of out-of-pocket liability may be a sensible arrangement. We do so by reference to multiple goals, namely motivating outside directors to be diligent, discouraging them from avoiding risk in counter-productive ways, and encouraging good candidates to serve in the boardroom.

II. OUTSIDE DIRECTOR LIABILITY IN THE UNITED STATES

The received wisdom is that directors of public companies face greater legal risks in the United States than anywhere else. The United States thus constitutes the toughest test for our thesis that outside directors almost never make out-of-pocket payments, Enron and WorldCom notwithstanding. We therefore address the US situation first, and we do so in more detail than for the other countries we consider.

A. The Risk of Liability: in Theory

Directors of US public companies face an array of legal obligations. Under corporate law, directors owe duties to the company that can be divided into two broad categories: care and loyalty. Under US securities law, directors are liable if they fail to exercise 'due diligence' in verifying the information that a company provides to investors in connection with a public offering of securities, assuming that information turns out to be materially false or misleading (Securities Act of 1933: § 11). They are also liable for errors in corporate disclosures unrelated to the issuance of securities if they had knowledge of, or were reckless in failing to prevent, a materially false misstatement or omission (Securities Exchange Act of 1934, Rule 10 b-5).

Outside directors also face at least some risk of being sued under various other laws, with a recent prominent example being the Employee Retirement Income Security Act of 1974, or ERISA.[2] For example, Enron's outside directors recently settled for $85 million an ERISA suit brought by employees who had invested in an employee stock ownership plan. This amount was covered by Enron's ERISA insurance policy, but the Enron directors also paid $1.5 million out of pocket to settle a related ERISA suit brought by the US Department of Labor.

Various other features of the American legal system encourage litigation against outside directors. First, in contrast with the practice elsewhere, litigants pay their own legal expenses, win or lose.[3] This means a plaintiff bringing a marginal case does not have to worry about paying the defendant's legal costs in the event the claim is dismissed. The Private Securities Litigation Reform Act of 1995 (PSLRA) authorises judges to require plaintiffs' attorneys to pay the cost of defending a securities suit deemed to be frivolous, but judges have yet to invoke this provision.

---

[2] For a helpful summary of the possible sources of liability, see Knepper and Bailey (1998).
[3] Compare Coffee (1986: 674) with Andrews (2003: 1001).

Secondly, again in contrast with the practice elsewhere, the class-action suit and the 'derivative' suit (litigation brought by shareholders on behalf of the company) are well-established devices for solving the collective action problems that otherwise discourage shareholders from launching proceedings against directors. Under US civil procedure rules, class certification is routinely available for a suit brought by shareholders against directors, and almost all securities lawsuits are framed as class actions. Similarly, under derivative suit rules, any shareholder may bring proceedings against a director on behalf of the corporation for violating duties formally owed to 'the corporation'.

Thirdly, to a unique extent, the US legal system treats a plaintiff's attorney as an entrepreneur who seeks out legal violations and suitable clients rather than waiting passively for a prospective litigant to come to them (Coffee 1986). If a class-action suit is successful or settled out of court, the judge supervising proceedings will generally award legal fees out of the proceeds, with the amount being based on time expended or a percentage of the recovery to the class (Cole 1972: 260–61; Coffee 1986: 678–79). In a derivative suit, the corporation will pay the legal fees of the plaintiff's attorney so long as the settlement agreement recites that the suit has conferred a 'substantial benefit' on the corporation. The shareholders' lawyer routinely demands such a recitation as part of a settlement. Judges must approve settlements, but rarely object to the parties' characterisation.

B. The Small Risk of Actual Liability: Data

Again, a commonly repeated concern in the United States is that serving as an outside director is highly risky, largely due to the possibility of out-of-pocket liability. The level of concern, however, far outpaces reality. Admittedly, hundreds of lawsuits are filed against American public companies every year under corporate and securities law, and outside directors are often named as defendants. In many of these cases, in turn, at least some defendants make settlement payments to plaintiffs. This outcome, however, rarely translates into out-of-pocket liability for outside directors.

Consider first federal securities lawsuits, which are the largest source of risk. As Table 1 indicates, since 1990, roughly 3000 securities suits have been filed in US federal courts. We lack data on how many of these cases involved outside directors as defendants, but anecdotal evidence suggests that most did. Yet only four of these suits have gone to trial, none of which involved outside directors. The plaintiffs won in only one instance, and the defendants in this case were two officers (one of whom

Table 1: Securities Cases Against Directors, Tried to Verdict, 1990–2003

Type of Securities Law	Filed	Tried to Verdict			
		Against inside director only	Plaintiff Victories	Against outside director only	Plaintiff Victories
Federal	2930	2 (1 since PSLRA in 1995)	1 (0 since 1995)	0	0
State	< 49	0	0	1	0

was an inside director). The claims against the outside directors had been dismissed earlier in the proceedings.

Of the remaining securities lawsuits brought between 1990 and now, somewhat over half have settled, roughly 20 per cent have been dismissed, and the remainder are pending. There is no comprehensive source of information on the settlements, but after extensive inquiry, we know of only one instance prior to Enron and WorldCom: a 2002 settlement, where outside directors made out-of-pocket payments of $500,000 each.[4] There is also one ongoing case in which the corporation (Peregrine Systems) is insolvent and the D&O insurer is contesting coverage. The outside directors are currently paying their own legal expenses and may ultimately face out-of-pocket liability. It is unclear, however, whether the insurer will succeed in denying coverage.

Under other laws, whether corporate law, ERISA, or whatever, we know of only two cases where outside directors of a public company have ended up on the hook to pay damages out of their own pockets. One was the Enron ERISA settlement mentioned above. The other was the famous 1985 *Smith v Van Gorkom* case[5] under Delaware corporate law, where a court ruled that outside directors had failed to use sufficient care in approving a merger and ordered them to pay damages well in excess of the D&O coverage in place. Even here, the acquirer voluntarily paid the claims against the target's outside directors, so the directors did not pay damages in fact.

Table 2 summarises our US findings on out-of-pocket liability from 1968 to the present—including settlements and court rulings. Earlier research (Bishop 1968) finds a similar absence of instances of liability prior to that. We cannot rule out the possibility that we have missed a few

---

[4] Information about this settlement was provided to us in confidence, so we cannot state the company name or details that might let readers identify it.

[5] *Smith v van Gorkom*, 488 A.2d 858 (Del. 1985).

Table 2: Outside Director Actual Liability, 1968–2003

Type of Law	Number of Cases	
	Actually liable (not covered by indemnification or insurance)	Paid Damages
Corporate Law	1 (*Van Gorkom*, 1985)	0 (paid by acquirer)
Securities Law	0	0
Bankruptcy and Insolvency Law	0	0
Other (environmental, ERISA, tax, workplace safety, etc.)	0	

settlements in which outside directors paid personally. But if such cases exist, they are surely rare.[6]

C. The Small Risk of Actual Liability: Explanations

The rarity of actual liability derives from the interaction of multiple factors that are in play almost universally for US public companies. A full analysis is set out in Black, Cheffins, and Klausner (2004). We summarise that analysis here for the two most important classes of suits: class actions under federal securities law, and corporate law derivative suits. We begin the discussion by identifying procedural rules that screen out cases that fail to meet a threshold degree of gravity.

1. Procedural Hurdles

Suits brought under federal securities law will be dismissed unless the plaintiffs support their claim by pleading facts suggesting liability with sufficient particularity. Many claims brought against outside directors are dismissed on this basis. For derivative suits, corporate charter provisions, adopted by almost all public companies, eliminate director liability for all but the most egregious breaches of the duty of care (though not breaches that involve self-dealing or other intentional wrongdoing). Even without this liability shield, a judge will review board actions pursuant to the 'business judgment rule' and dismiss a derivative suit if

---

[6] The figures on trials and settlements provided here are only partial since the text was drafted before we had completed our investigation of the topic. For full results, see Black, Cheffins and Klausner (2006: 1062–74).

no conflict of interest was involved and the board followed a reasonable decision-making process.

2. Securities Law Cases

In securities cases, even if procedural hurdles are surmounted, directors remain well protected. Assume first a solvent company. The company invariably will be named as a defendant and, under all circumstances, will be liable whenever the directors would be. Thus, there is no additional recovery to be gained by suing the directors. It can nonetheless make strategic sense for plaintiffs' lawyers to name both inside and outside directors as additional defendants. Directors dislike the inconvenience and publicity associated with a trial and their discomfort will increase the company's willingness to settle.

At the same time, plaintiffs' counsel will understand that outside directors are not promising targets as sources for recovery. Not only are there no additional damages to be gained, but outside directors have defences to liability that are unavailable to the company itself. For example, for violations based on a misleading prospectus, the company is strictly liable but the directors will be exonerated if they prove they exercised 'due diligence' with respect to the disclosure. Moreover, proportional liability rules, based on relative culpability, make outside directors liable for only a fraction, perhaps a small fraction, of total damages. Since the outside directors' involvement in securities fraud typically involves only failures of oversight, as opposed to active misfeasance, their share of proportionate liability is likely to be low.

Again, nearly all securities fraud suits settle, and do so without an out-of-pocket payment from directors. The pressure to settle on these terms comes from all sides. For plaintiffs' lawyers, a trial and the probable appeal of a favourable judgment mean a long delay in recovery and uncertain success. The directors—both outside and inside—dislike the nuisance of being sued and will fear potential reputational harm from losing in court. If they are offered a settlement that will be fully covered by insurance or indemnification, they are highly likely to take it.

If plaintiffs and defendants agree to settle, D&O insurers will likely agree as well. For a variety of reasons, including reputational harm if an insurer forces a case to trial when the defendants want to settle, and legal rules that make it risky for an insurer to do so, insurers often lack the leverage to force a trial. None of the three securities trials since 1990 involved an insurer's refusal to settle, and we know of no such instance before then either. In the long run, insurers are not prejudiced by settling because they can estimate the likelihood and amount of securities fraud settlements and set premiums accordingly. Shareholders ultimately bear the cost of the insurance premiums, but thus far even institutional investors, who are vocal on other corporate governance issues, have not objected to the expensive insurance policies that provide outside directors with de facto insulation from out-of-pocket liability.

What would happen in the unlikely event that a securities suit against a public company's outside directors goes to trial and the directors are found liable? There would still be minimal risk of out-of-pocket liability if the company is solvent. The company will always be liable also, and will pay all damages directly. If, through some happenstance, directors were to pay anything, the company would indemnify the directors for both legal expenses and damages, under customary bylaws which make this indemnification mandatory.[7]

There is heightened risk of out-of-pocket liability when a company is insolvent, and hence can neither pay damages itself nor indemnify directors. However, directors will still have available a crucial second line of defence against out-of-pocket liability. Virtually all US public companies have D&O insurance, which will pay whatever the company cannot, up to policy limits. Moreover, there will be strong pressure for defendants, plaintiffs, and insurers to settle within the policy limits. Since the company cannot bail them out, the directors' incentives to strike a deal are obvious. The plaintiffs, meanwhile, face an odd dynamic. If they pursue a case through to trial, the directors will spend lavishly on their own defence, with the D&O policy covering their legal costs. If the plaintiffs win a judgment that exceeds the policy limits, an appeal is highly likely, with defence costs again being paid out of the policy. This prolonged litigation can shrink substantially the dollar amount—and even more sharply shrink the present value—of the principal 'deep pocket'—the D&O policy—from which the plaintiffs hope to collect.

Furthermore, if a securities fraud case goes to trial, the plaintiffs run the risk of proving too much. If they convince a jury that the directors knowingly participated in the wrongdoing, this could give the insurer grounds to deny coverage based on the standard policy exclusions for fraud and illegal profits. So, both plaintiffs and defendants will be keen to strike a deal within policy limits. The insurers will again probably agree.

To be sure, if a company is insolvent an outside director's liability risk will not be zero. Two factors affect this risk. First, some companies have D&O policies with unusually low limits (what counts as unusually low depends on company size, but $10 million is a plausible minimum for a small public company). If D&O limits are too low to offer much of a recovery, the plaintiffs' incentive to settle within those limits weakens. Moreover, the directors may well exhaust the policy based on their legal

---

[7] Under company bylaws, indemnification is typically mandatory, if permitted by company law. Company law, in turn, permits indemnification as long as the directors acted in 'good faith'. This restriction is not a significant concern in practice.

expenses alone. Also, D&O policies can sometimes have 'holes' that might let an insurer deny coverage. However, insurers face substantial legal and reputational pressure to use potential coverage holes to negotiate a reduced coverage amount rather than to seek to deny coverage entirely.

Ultimately, based on experience to date, outside directors of US public companies face a significant risk of out-of-pocket liability under federal securities laws only in two situations.[8] The first involves a 'perfect storm': the company is insolvent, there is significant evidence of outside director culpability, D&O insurance is inadequate (potential damages dramatically exceed available D&O coverage, the insurer has respectable grounds for denying coverage, or perhaps both), and one or preferably several outside directors have serious personal wealth.[9] This perfect storm description fits the one confidential settlement we know of involving out-of-pocket liability, discussed earlier. Still, in securities litigation, as in the movies, perfect storms are rare.

The new second possibility, illustrated by Enron and WorldCom, involves all of the perfect storm elements except a less than customary level of D&O cover, but adds a decision by the lead plaintiff in a securities suit to insist on out-of-pocket payments by the outside directors as a condition of settlement, in order to send a warning to directors of other companies. If the company is insolvent and potential damages (and thus the directors' risk of bankruptcy if they lose in court) are high enough, the directors may prefer to settle for a significant sum rather than risk a trial. Here, we can only speculate about the future, but our best guess is that the political and market forces that sustain an equilibrium of nonzero but low risk of out-of-pocket liability will ensure that Enron and WorldCom-type settlements remain rare.

3. Corporate Law Cases

Derivative suits under corporate law pose even less risk to outside directors' personal assets than securities law suits. Again, almost all US public companies have charter provisions that bar suits against directors based on a breach of the duty of care. A derivative suit thus needs to claim that the directors engaged in self-dealing or otherwise failed to act in 'good faith'. Some US courts have recently expanded the concept of

---

[8] In Black, Cheffins and Klausner (2006: 1109–10) we identify a third situation we label: 'Can't Afford to Win' where outside directors of insolvent companies can end up making personal payments. In this situation, due to a lack of D&O insurance or insufficient coverage, an outside director must pay his own legal expenses fo defend a suit. Under these circumstances, even a director facing a meritless lawsuit might go to make an out-of-pocket settlement rather than pay the additional legal bills required to defend the case further.

[9] The presence of just one rich outside director may not change the plaintiffs' calculus due to the securities law rule that caps liability based on proportionate fault.

bad faith to include extreme inattention to the company's affairs, in addition to self-dealing. But the ultimate prize sought by plaintiffs in suits against directors typically will be D&O insurance proceeds, and the insurer will be able to deny coverage for fraud and illegal profits. The result is a legal obstacle course: plaintiffs' counsel must typically allege that self-dealing occurred, so as to get around the charter provision, but then seek to settle in a way that keeps the D&O policy available. Going to trial and losing is not a desirable outcome. Neither, however, is going to trial and proving too strong a case! The settlement dynamics discussed earlier thus come into play: no party wants a trial, and a settlement funded by the insurer (in turn financed by premiums reflecting this risk) is the path of least resistance.

D. Forces Supporting the Current Equilibrium

The equilibrium consisting of frequent suits against directors yet very low out-of-pocket liability risk has been stable over time. Underlying the process has been a consistent pattern: as concerns about directors' legal risks have emerged, markets and lawmakers have responded so as to preserve the equilibrium. Examples of this legal and market response include the following:

— After a 1939 ruling by a New York court cast doubt on the power of companies to indemnify directors, Delaware and many other states amended their corporation statutes to ensure that companies had this power (Bishop 1966: 96–98).
— In the 1960s, in response to the emergence of securities suits, state corporate laws were amended to liberalise indemnification rules and specifically authorise companies to buy D&O insurance. Companies soon began to buy this previously rare type of insurance (*ibid.*: 96–103; Bishop 1968: 1081–86).
— In the mid-1980s the *Van Gorkom* decision, which nearly resulted in out-of-pocket liability for the defendant outside directors, led, in short order, to new statutory provisions that let companies adopt charter provisions eliminating liability for breaches of the duty of care, and to near-universal adoption of these provisions by public companies.
— A decade later, a surge in securities litigation prompted federal legislation (the Private Securities Litigation Reform Act of 1995) that reduced directors' exposure along several dimensions, including heightened pleading standards and proportionate liability rules.
— As gaps in D&O coverage open up from time to time, the standard contract forms quickly change to close the holes, usually before any outside directors have fallen through. For example, the 'perfect storm'

securities settlement described above occurred in part because of a new 'application fraud' defence to coverage that insurance companies raised. This coverage gap is now being addressed prospectively through changes in D&O insurance contracts.

These political and economic responses are not accidental. Lawyers acting on behalf of public companies and organisations representing business leaders (e.g., the Business Roundtable) have proved to be effective at lobbying for reforms designed to alleviate the fears that have arisen periodically concerning director liability. Moreover, managers of public companies have proved willing to spend large amounts of (their shareholders') money to obtain insurance policies protecting outside directors (along with themselves). There have been periodic fears of a litigation-driven 'insurance crisis' (Romano 1990) but insurers have in fact continued to service what has proved to be a lucrative market.

While there is strong momentum in favor of the containment of out-of-pocket liability, just as important there has been no significant countervailing pressure in either the political or the market arena. Institutional investors vocally support a variety of corporate governance reforms, but prior to the Enron and WorldCom settlements, expanding outside directors' out-of-pocket liability was not part of their agenda. Indeed, since they want companies to be able to recruit effective individuals to serve as outside directors, institutional investors have routinely voted to adopt charter provisions that shield directors from liability under corporate law for failing to exercise appropriate care, and have not objected to broad D&O coverage.

The current question is whether Enron and WorldCom are exceptional responses to exceptional frauds, or whether they signal a broader change in the views of public funds on the desirability of outside director liability (public funds were lead investors in both cases). Yet any large shift toward greater outside director liability would trigger fierce opposition from directors and from corporations concerned about their ability to recruit good directors. The historical success of directors and corporations in limiting out-of-pocket risk provides some reason to expect that Enron and WorldCom may turn out to be one-off exceptions.

Plaintiffs' attorneys, meanwhile, seeking new grounds to launch lawsuits, will predictably advocate rules that provide a high level of nominal liability. Forcing directors to pay their own damages and legal expenses, however, is not a priority. Indeed, plaintiffs' attorneys prefer generous insurance policies and indemnification practices since a company and its D&O insurer typically provide the deep pockets from which they are seeking to collect their fees. This, in turn, creates a 'package deal' that outside directors can tolerate. Some litigation risk is acceptable so long as someone else pays the legal expenses and settlement costs. In the United States, then, there is little tension between rampant litigation and trivial out-of-pocket liability risk.

III. OUTSIDE DIRECTOR LIABILITY OUTSIDE THE UNITED STATES

A. Scope of Our Research

Since outside directors in the United States face only a tiny chance of incurring out-of-pocket liability while operating in a singularly litigation-prone milieu, one would expect the risks to be no greater for outside directors in other countries. Verifying this intuition, however, is a challenging task. Discussions of director liability are usually limited to rules affecting directors in a single jurisdiction (Hopt 1992: 115), and often to a single type of law (such as company law).

We have therefore undertaken, in tandem with our research on the United States, a survey of outside director liability covering three representative common law countries (Australia, Britain, and Canada) and three civil law jurisdictions (France, Germany, and Japan) (Black and Cheffins 2003). The legal terrain, including the procedural obstacles to a suit against directors, the conduct for which outside directors can be found liable, and the sources of law that pose the greatest risk, varies substantially across borders. But for outside directors of public companies the bottom line ultimately is the same as in the United States: out-of-pocket liability is extremely rare.

For each country, we studied all sources of potential director liability, other than for self-dealing.[10] We also investigated the factors whose presence or absence could affect whether nominal liability will translate into out-of-pocket liability, and we sought to find any instances of out-of-pocket liability. Local experts offered assistance by reviewing drafts of our work for errors or omissions. We have also looked for other countries, besides those we directly studied, where out-of-pocket liability of outside directors might be common, but are not currently aware of any.

---

[10] We also did not take into account legislation authorising orders disqualifying individuals from serving in the boardroom, such as the Company Directors Disqualification Act 1986, (UK), ch. 46. A disqualification order may adversely impact the future income of the individuals affected. Nevertheless, it does not seem appropriate to treat disqualification as creating actual liability since a financial penalty is not an intrinsic aspect of the sanction.

B. Status of Outside Directors in the Sample Countries

It is helpful to begin by considering briefly the status of outside directors in our six sample countries. In Australia, Britain, and Canada public companies have a unitary board of directors on which executives join outside directors. All three countries have 'comply or explain' corporate governance guidelines designed to ensure that public companies have a sizeable contingent of independent outside directors.[11] Also, Australian, British, or Canadian companies that cross-list their shares in the United States on the New York Stock Exchange or NASDAQ are required by these markets' listing rules to have an audit committee composed entirely of independent directors.[12]

Under French company law, French public companies are established as SAs (*Sociétés anonymes*) and the inside directors (those serving under employment contracts) of a SA cannot exceed one-third of the total number of directors. In Germany, public companies operate as AGs (*Aktiengesellschaften*). The AG board structure is divided into a management component (*Vorstand*) and a supervisory component (*Aufsichtsrat*). Executives are precluded from serving on the supervisory board. In contrast, the boards of larger Japanese companies have traditionally been composed almost entirely of senior managers. Still, outside directors are becoming more popular in Japan, in large part because of a 2002 amendment to Japanese company law that expressly authorised companies to create board committees staffed by outside directors (Nikkei Report 2004).[13]

C. Director Liability: Sources and Layers of Protection

In our six sample countries, various laws provide a foundation for a suit by a private party against an outside director. Under legislation and case law directors in each country owe duties to their companies to act with care and skill, and investors have a cause of action against directors of a public company that has distributed false or misleading documentation in support of a public offering of shares. Moreover, in Australia, Britain, France, and Germany severe financial distress creates additional legal

---

[11] In Australia, see ASX (2003: Recommendation 2.1). In Canada, see TSX (2004: §§ 472–75. In Britain, see FRC (2003: Provision A.3.2).

[12] See New York Stock Exchange Rule 303 A.06; NASDAQ Rule 4350(d); Sarbanes-Oxley Act § 301 (requiring listed companies to have audit committees composed of independent directors).

[13] Japanese companies which cross-list their shares on US exchanges are not required to use independent directors on audit committees. Instead, the SEC has allowed the Japanese board of statutory auditors to function in lieu of an audit committee.

responsibilities for directors who fail to take appropriate steps to preserve assets for creditors.

In addition to civil liability, outside directors in each of the six sample countries can face criminal sanctions or related administrative penalties. Typically, companies' legislation will include numerous provisions under which directors can be fined for an infraction committed either personally or by their company. Various other legislative schemes, such as those dealing with employment issues, the environment, and consumer protection, also usually contain offences, punishable by fine or analogous financial penalty, that outside directors might commit.

In the six sample countries, neither indemnification nor D&O insurance provides protection as broad as that available in the United States. For indemnification, Canada's federal corporate statute is similar to US law. It authorises a corporation to reimburse a director who has acted in good faith for legal expenses and for amounts paid to conclude a settlement or to satisfy a judgment (Van Duzer 2003: 239-43). In Australia, the scope for indemnification is somewhat narrower, and in Britain it is narrower still since a UK company can reimburse a director only for legal expenses and can do so only if the director is successful at trial on the merits. French, German, and Japanese companies legislation does not explicitly allow companies to indemnify directors for adverse judgments, settlements or legal expenses, although at least some German commentators believe indemnification is permissible under certain circumstances (Fanto 1998: 83; Milhaupt 1996: 34; Baums 1996: 322).

The D&O insurance landscape offers somewhat happier news for directors. Australian, British, and Canadian law expressly authorises corporations to purchase D&O coverage. In France, Germany, and Japan, company law is silent, but D&O policies are widely offered by insurers and the consensus is that the purchase of such insurance is permissible (Baums 1996: 326; Fanto 1998: 83). D&O insurance has traditionally been much more popular in the United States than elsewhere, but, as will be discussed in Part III.G, D&O coverage in other countries is increasing.

D. Obstacles to Litigation

A key reason why indemnification and D&O insurance is less developed outside the United States is that suits against directors have been much less common (Fanto 1998: 83; Milhaupt 1996: 34). Both procedural hurdles and practical considerations discourage litigation. Two examples, arising under company law and securities law respectively, illustrate the point.

Derivative Suits under Company Law

Consider first a situation where outside directors of a financially viable public company have allegedly breached their duty to the company to act with due care. In all six of our sample countries, as well as the United States, the board of directors has the authority to manage the company and thus to decide whether the company will sue the directors. So long as relations between the potential defendants and the other directors are cordial, the board is unlikely to sue some of its own members (Baxter 1995: 538–39).[14]

In the United States, it is often feasible for shareholders to gain standing to conduct derivative suits against outside directors. Meanwhile, attorneys' fees, recoverable from the company if there is a settlement or the plaintiffs prevail in court, give entrepreneurial lawyers an incentive to commence suits on behalf of dispersed clients. In contrast, there is no direct equivalent to derivative litigation in France and Germany. Shareholders can request the appointment of a special representative who will sue in the company's name but this option is almost never invoked, in part because outside shareholders rarely own enough shares to meet prescribed minimum ownership thresholds.[15]

In Britain, shareholders can theoretically bring derivative suits but satisfying the standing requirements imposed by case law is very difficult, particularly when a widely-held company is involved. Obtaining standing to sue is more straightforward in Australia and Canada. Prospective plaintiffs are deterred, however, because, unlike in the United States, a losing party pays not only his own legal fees but must partially reimburse the winner's legal expenses. Moreover, lawyers have little incentive to take a lead role because neither country explicitly provides for the awarding of attorneys' fees.

Japan also has 'loser pays' civil procedure rules, and these likely deter derivative litigation to some degree. On the other hand, Japan's company law explicitly authorizes plaintiffs to recover attorneys' fees for successful derivative suits. After early 1990s reforms that cut filing costs dramatically, Japanese lawyers began to launch derivative suits with some frequency. To date shareholder victories and out-of-court settlements have been uncommon (West 2002). Nevertheless, the existence of

[14] Though the end result will likely be the same in Germany, deference cannot be assumed quite as readily. Under its two-tier board system the management board decides on suits against supervisory board members. Case law implies that the management board may breach a duty to the company if it fails to bring a suit when to do so would be in the company's interests.

[15] The text does not reflect changes made to the German law on derivative litigation in 2005. The amendments are unlikely to materially affect the sister supervisory board director's face (Cheffins and Black 2006: 1425–26).

reasonably frequent derivative suits suggests the importance of legal fee rules in Japan and likely elsewhere.

Securities Lawsuits

Consider now a securities lawsuit alleging misleading disclosure during a public offering of shares. As with derivative litigation, procedural rules do much to deter litigation against outside directors in the countries we are dealing with. A US-style securities class action is not feasible in France, Germany, or Japan since, as in most civil law countries, multi-party litigation is largely unknown (Hodges 2001: 4).

Australia, Britain, and certain provinces in Canada have each introduced reforms within the last decade to facilitate suits with numerous plaintiffs. The management of multi-party suits in these countries remains in flux (Hodges 2001: 4–7, 223–24, 235, 269–70, 288) so it is too early to know whether there will be a congenial setting for US-style securities class actions. Even if such litigation does become prevalent, however, there might well be few suits against outside directors.

One reason is that in each of the three countries a company that makes misleading disclosures is directly liable. This ensures that the plaintiffs will sue the company itself. Even if the plaintiffs also sue the directors, the company, if solvent, will most likely pay fully any damages granted to the plaintiffs under a settlement or judgment. Shareholders thus have little incentive to sue the outside directors in the first place.

To be sure, naming outside directors as defendants can increase pressure on the company to settle. But in all three countries, 'loser pays' rules governing legal costs strongly discourage suing outside directors. If a suit brought against outside directors is dismissed, then even if the plaintiffs are successful against other defendants, the outside directors can seek an order compelling the plaintiffs to reimburse their legal expenses. With the stakes raised in this way, leaving outside directors out of the picture will often be sensible, especially when defendants are available who are more culpable (e.g., the inside directors) and/or deeper-pocketed (e.g., auditors and other professional advisers).

A further factor discourages suits against outside directors, at least for now. In the United States, the prize sought by plaintiffs in suits against directors often is the D&O insurance proceeds. Since D&O insurance coverage is neither as prevalent nor as lucrative elsewhere, this potential 'deep pocket' is less attractive. Given this, and given the risks the 'loser pays' rule poses, only outside directors who are quite rich are attractive targets for civil suits. As will be discussed shortly, the equilibrium could shift toward more lawsuits, but even if this shift occurs, out-of-pocket liability will likely remain rare.

E. Public Enforcement

Even if private lawsuits pose little risk to directors outside the United States, public officials might step into the breach and seek sanctions against alleged wrongdoers. In each of the countries we analyzed, there are many statutory provisions under which directors can commit offences and be punished by way of a fine or similar financial penalty. Nevertheless, outside directors have little to fear in practice. To illustrate, in Britain, while there are numerous offences in companies legislation for which directors can theoretically be fined, the infractions prosecuted are rarely of the type an outside director is likely to commit. The experience with other key regulatory regimes, such as those dealing with environmental protection and workplace safety, is similar. Matters are much the same in Australia, Canada, France, Germany, and Japan. Indeed, in these countries, we are unaware of any successful prosecution of an outside director of a public company. If such cases exist, they were too low profile for us to uncover.

F. Exceptions

Despite the factors weighing against the likelihood of out-of-pocket liability, outside directors in our six sample countries are not fully insulated against legal risks. Instead, as we discuss in Black and Cheffins (2003), in each jurisdiction there have been isolated instances where outside directors have paid damages or a related financial penalty, or could have been in this position with a minor adjustment of the facts. We summarize three recent examples to illustrate that the risk of out-of-pocket liability is small but not absent.

1. Equitable Life

Former outside directors of Equitable Life, a venerable British insurer that suffered a deep financial crisis at the end of the 1990s, faced a serious risk of personal liability. The procedural factors that discourage derivative suits in the United Kingdom were not in play because there was a boardroom shake-up and the new board decided to sue fifteen former directors (including nine non-executives) alleging various failures of judgment. The defendant directors were insured, but damages claimed initially exceeded £1.8 billion, which dwarfed the £5 million policy limit (Bolger 2002; Tait 2004). Also, again exceptionally, there was a deep pocket amongst the non-executives, an outside director with a personal fortune of £320 million. In 2005 Equitable dropped its claim mid-trial and agreed to pay the legal expenses of the defendant directors, meaning that the outside directors did not incur any out-of-pocket liability.

2. Mannesmann

Following Vodafone Group PLC's controversial 2000 takeover of Mannesmann, a major German telecoms company, German prosecutors laid charges against two prominent members of Mannesmann's supervisory board (Josef Ackermann, chief executive of Deutsche Bank, and Klaus Zwickel, the head of a major German union), citing the supervisory board's decision to authorize $60 million in executive bonuses as a reward for a deal well done. The prosecution argued that the bonus payments breached a provision in Germany's criminal code making it an offence for those managing property on behalf of another (i.e., the Mannesmann directors) to fail to safeguard that property. After a high-profile trial, the judge dismissed the criminal charges, but the prosecutors launched a successful appeal. Moreover, the trial judge speculated in her judgment that the defendants had breached duties under German corporate law even if they had not committed a criminal infraction (Culp 2004).

3. Insolvent Trading in Australia

Under Australian companies legislation, if directors of an insolvent company permit a company to continue in business while having reasonable grounds for believing the company cannot pay its debts as they fell due, this constitutes improper 'insolvent trading.' The company's liquidator or the Australian Securities and Insurance Commission can then seek an order requiring the directors to compensate creditors for losses suffered. The law has rarely been invoked. However, the one instance of its use that we know of involving a public company (Water Wheel Holdings Ltd.) led to out-of-pocket liability for two outside directors. In a 2003 decision, the court ordered the two directors to pay collectively nearly A$2 million in compensation payments and fines. The outside director was subsequently declared bankrupt after failing to satisfy the judgment against him.

G. Political and Market Responses to Liability Risk

As Part II.D discussed, in the United States, when new sources of potential out-of-pocket liability emerge, these new risks typically prompt a response in the market for D&O insurance, the political arena, or both that returns the level of risk to a low level. In recent years, the same pattern has been emerging in other countries.

Though D&O insurance has traditionally been relatively uncommon outside the United States, apprehension about director liability has been fuelling its growth. In Germany and Japan D&O policies were largely unknown prior to the 1990s, but demand has grown steadily since then. The market has also been changing recently in Australia and Britain, with companies buying policies with higher coverage limits and with premiums rising. Likewise, in Canada the already small fraction of companies lacking D&O cover has been diminishing (Towers Perrin 2004: 21).

The expansion in D&O coverage ironically could serve as a catalyst for litigation against directors. As more companies take out D&O policies, and as coverage limits rise, it becomes increasingly likely that these policies will become potential deep pockets in civil suits. The risk-reward ratio associated with suing outside directors could then begin to shift in a pro-litigation direction. Nonetheless, the settlement incentives discussed in Part II.C would likely come into play, with all parties agreeing to settle claims against outside directors within policy limits. So, out-of-pocket liability risk should remain small.

Responses to director liability risk have also been evident on the political front. In Britain, the Equitable Life saga prompted successful lobbying for statutory changes giving directors greater financial protection in the event of a lawsuit (Cheffins and Black 2006: 1415). In Canada, amid concerns about 'liability chill' in the boardroom, the federal corporate statute was amended in 2001 to expand indemnification and insurance protection for directors and to strengthen directors' due diligence defences (TSX 1994: 33–37; Gray 2003: 11–12).

In Japan, two recent high-profile cases involving inside directors led to a change in the law. In 2000, a court found eleven executive directors of Daiwa Bank liable for $775 million in damages for failing to exercise due care (this amount was later reduced to $2 million). In 2001, allegedly inattentive Sumitomo Corp. executive directors agreed to pay half of their total retirement benefits ($3.58 million) to settle a derivative suit. Intense lobbying ensued, and in 2002, the legislature amended the Japanese Commercial Code to permit a company to amend its charter to limit lawsuit damages to amounts ranging from two years' annual salary for an outside director to six years' salary for inside directors.[16] With this cap in place, outside directors are unattractive targets for a suit, and will not have to pay substantial damages in the unlikely event they are sued, lose, and their company lacks D&O insurance.

---

[16] Companies which limit liability must reveal the total compensation paid to their board members, which otherwise is not required.

IV. CONCLUSION

This chapter has shown that, in a representative sample of economically advanced common law and civil law countries, outside directors of public companies rarely pay damages, financial penalties, or legal expenses out-of-pocket, absent self-dealing (which is itself rare for these directors). In any one country, this outcome reflects a complex interplay of different substantive laws, procedural rules, and the D&O insurance market, but the outcome is the same across countries. Moreover, a historical pattern emerges across these countries: whenever an event occurs that increases outside directors' risk of out-of-pocket liability, there is likely to be a market or political response that restores a low level of risk.

A full analysis of whether it is good policy for outside directors of public companies to be nearly immune from out-of-pocket liability is beyond the scope of this chapter. It is possible, however, to sketch out reasons why the outcome may be a sensible one. There are two main aspects to consider: what other forces might induce directors to pay attention and would greater out-of-pocket risk improve the quality of board decisions? With regard to the first question, even without much out-of-pocket liability risk, outside directors have various incentives to do a good job. To begin with, if a significant fraction of a director's personal wealth comes from owning company shares or options, the director has an incentive to be diligent, regardless of legal liability. Moreover, lawsuits, even without creating out-of-pocket liability, entangle directors in time-consuming and aggravating work. Desire to avoid these nuisance costs may promote greater vigilance.

Norms of good corporate governance and proper boardroom conduct are another potential force motivating director diligence. Lawyers can reinforce these norms when advising directors on the directors' duties. Furthermore, even without out-of-pocket liability, shareholder suits that publicize bad behavior, through court decisions and otherwise, help to create and disseminate boardroom norms (Rock 1997). Moreover, directors risk forfeiting their reputations as respected business figures if their company founders. The risk of harm to reputation strengthens in turn professional norms that encourage vigilance. The financial press reinforces both norms and reputational sanctions by publishing stories that expose board misconduct and highlight good behavior.

Turning to whether greater out-of-pocket liability risk would improve the quality of board decisions, there is reason to believe that a significant expansion of risk could lead to worse governance, rather than better. If out-of-pocket risk were significantly greater than today, many potential outside directors would decline to serve. Wealthy individuals would be particularly likely to say 'no.' This could adversely impact board quality.

Furthermore, those who did agree to serve would presumably demand higher compensation in return for bearing higher risk. But higher compensation could undermine independence. If board fees are a significant portion of a director's income, the director might hesitate to challenge other board members or management in a way that could threaten his position.

Out-of-pocket liability risk might also lead directors to act defensively in the boardroom and to decline to endorse sensible business gambles that shareholders would applaud, fearing bad outcomes. Moreover, board meetings might become longer and more frequent, as directors seek to increase the likelihood that their deliberations will pass muster in the event of a suit. Up to some unquantifiable point, careful deliberation and awareness of potential risks is beneficial. But if out-of-pocket liability were common, boards might spend too much time on the details of particular decisions, at the cost of having less time for less litigation-prone but nevertheless crucial long-term strategy issues. Paradoxically, then, significantly greater out-of-pocket liability risk could lead to less independence and worse governance.

Moreover, even if current arrangements are not optimal, it is doubtful that major changes in the level of out-of-pocket liability risk are either desirable or feasible. Both political and market dynamics create pressures that mute out-of-pocket liability. The US experience indicates that even if suits against outside directors are common, indemnification, D&O insurance, and settlement incentives largely negate out-of-pocket liability. Indemnification and D&O insurance could, in theory, be limited by law, but if such a change were made there would probably be few outside directors worth suing because people with substantial assets would decline to serve. Once again, out-of-pocket liability would be rare. Hence, we predict that, even in the post Enron and WorldCom world, outside directors will in all likelihood remain insulated from all but an occasional instance of out-of-pocket liability.

REFERENCES

Andrews, N. (2003), *English Civil Procedure: Fundamentals of the New Civil Justice System* (Oxford: Oxford University Press).

Aronson, B.E. (2003), 'Reconsidering the Importance of Law in Japanese Corporate Governance: evidence from the Daiwa Bank Shareholder Derivative Case', 36 *Cornell International Law Journal* 11.

ASX (2003), Australian Stock Exchange, Corporate Governance Council, Principles of Good Corporate Governance and Best Practice Recommendations (Sydney: Australian Stock Exchange). Available at http://www.asx.com.au/about/pdf/ASXRecommendations.pdf.

Baums, T. (1996), 'Personal Liabilities of Company Directors in German Law', 9 *International Corporate and Commercial Law Review* 318.

Baxter, C. (1995), 'Demystifying D&O Insurance', 15 *Oxford Journal of Legal Studies* 537.

Bishop, J. (1966), 'New Cure for an Old Ailment: Insurance Against Directors' and Officers' Liability', 22 *Business Lawyer* 92.

Bishop, J. (1968), 'Sitting Ducks and Decoy Ducks: New Trends in the Indemnification of Corporate Directors and Officers', 77 *Yale Law Journal* 1078.

Black, B. and Cheffins, B. (2003), 'Outside Director Liability Across Countries', Working Paper (Stanford Law School). Available at http://ssrn.com/abstract=438321.

Black, B., Cheffins, B., and Klausner, M. (2004), 'Outside Director Liability', Working Paper. Available at http://papers.ssrn.com/abstract=382422.

Black, B., Cheffins, B., and Klausner, M. (2006), 'Outside Director Liability', 58 *Stanford Law Review* 1055.

Bolger, A. (2002), 'Equitable Directors Insured for Only £5 M', *Financial Times*, 3 May, p. 6.

Cheffins, B.R. (1997), *Company Law: Theory, Structure and Operation* (Oxford: Oxford University Press).

Cheffins, B.R., and Black, B.S. (2006), 'Outside Director Liability Across Countries' 84 *Texas Law Review* 1385.

Coffee, J.C. (1986), 'Understanding The Plaintiff's Attorney: The Implications Of Economic Theory For Private Enforcement Of Law Through Class And Derivative Actions', 86 *Columbia Law Review* 669.

Cole, D.G. (1972), 'Counsel Fees in Stockholders' Derivative and Class Actions—Hornstein Revisited', 6 *University of Richmond Law Review* 259.

Corporate Board Member (2003), 'What Directors Think': Research Study 2003. Available at http://www.boardmember.com/network/WhatDirsThink2003.pdf.

Cox, J. (2002), 'Boards Find It Harder To Fill Hot Seats; Scandals, Legal Threats Make Many Decline Slot', *USA Today*, 31 July, p. A1.

Economist (2003), 'The Way We Govern Now', (US edition), 11 January pp. 59–61.

Fanto, J.A. (1998), 'The Role Of Corporate Law In French Corporate Governance', 31 *Cornell International Law Journal* 31.

FRC (2003), Financial Reporting Council, 'The Combined Code on Corporate Governance (UK)'. Available at http://www.frc.org.uk/about/combined.cfm.

Gilson, R.J. (2001), 'Globalizing Corporate Governance, Convergence Of Form Or Function', 49 *American Journal of Comparative Law* 329.

Government Commission (2003), 'German Corporate Governance Code'. Available in English at http://www.ecgi.org/codes/country_documents/germany/code_200305_en.pdf.

Gray, W.D. (2003), 'Corporations as Winners Uunder CBCA Reform', 39 *Canadian Business Law Journal* 4.

Hodges, C. (2001), *Multi-Party Actions* (Oxford: Oxford University Press).

Hopt, K.J. (1992), 'Directors' Duties to Shareholders, Employees, and other Creditors: A View from the Continent' in E. McKendrick (ed.), *Commercial Aspects of Trust and Fiduciary Obligations* (Oxford: Oxford University Press), pp. 115–32.

Kraakman, R. *et al.* (2004) *The Anatomy of Corporate Law: a Comparative and Functional Approach* (Oxford: Oxford University Press).

Knepper, W.A. and Bailey, D.A. (1998), *Liability of Corporate Officers and Directors* (6th ed.) (Charlottesville Va.: Lexis Law Publishing).

Korn/Ferry International (2003), Annual Board of Directors Study.

Milhaupt, C.J. (1996), 'A Relational Theory of Japanese Corporate Governance: Contract, Culture, and the Rule of Law', 37 *Harvard Journal of International Law* 3.

Nikkei Report (2004), '1 in 3 Listed Firms Hire Outside Directors: Nikkei Survey', Nikkei Report, 22 Aug., available on Westlaw, document 2004 WL 89300794.

Rock, E.B. (1997), 'Saints and Sinners: How Does Delaware Corporate Law Work?', 44 *UCLA Law Review* 1009.

Romano, R. (1990), 'Corporate Governance in the Aftermath of the Insurance Crisis', 39 *Emory Law Journal* 1155.

Tait, N. (2004), 'Equitable Cuts Claim for Damages by £1.5bn', *Financial Times*, 17 June p. 6.

TSX (2004), *Toronto Stock Exchange Company Manual*, (Toronto: Toronto Stock Exchange). at http://www.tse.com/en/productsAndServices/listings/tse/resources/resourceManual.html.

—— (1994), Toronto Stock Exchange Committee on Corporate Governance in Canada, Report: Where Were the Directors? Guidelines for Improved Corporate Governance in Canada (Toronto: Toronto Stock Exchange).

Towers Perrin (2004), 2003 Directors and Officers Liability Survey.

Van Duzer, J.A. (2003), *The Law of Partnerships and Corporations*, 2nd ed. (Toronto: Irwin Law).

West, M.D. (2002), 'Why Shareholders Sue: Evidence from Japan', 30 *Journal of Legal Studies* 351.

11

The Legal Control of Directors' Conflicts of Interest in the United Kingdom: Non-Executive Directors Following the Higgs Report

RICHARD C NOLAN*

E NGLISH COMPANY LAW sets strict standards of loyalty for directors; some would even say too strict.[1] Yet the enforcement of those obligations—whether prospectively through corporate governance structures or retrospectively through litigation—is one of the most intractable problems in the law. Enforcement of directors' duties through private civil litigation has proven problematic and unsatisfactory. Enforcement through public proceedings, such as criminal proceedings or, more recently, directors' disqualification proceedings, has become more prominent, but these methods of enforcement are still the subject of very mixed comment. In short, existing corporate governance structures apparently fail to control executive directors to the satisfaction of shareholders.

The recent Higgs Report (2003a) on Corporate Governance in the United Kingdom,[2] commissioned by the Department of Trade and Industry, does not adequately address these problems of enforcement. However, if suitably modified, the proposals in the Higgs Report could provide one useful basis—though not the only basis—for better legal

* Fellow of St. John's College and Senior Lecturer in Law, University of Cambridge; Barrister, Erskine Chambers, London. This chapter was previously published in (2005) 6 *Theoretical Inquiries in Law* 413–462. The permission of the editors of *Theoretical Inquiries in Law* to republish is gratefully acknowledged. The text is at it first appeared in 2005, and has not been updated since then.
  [1] The classic criticism of the severity of duties of loyalty in English law is Jones (1968).
  [2] The committee that produced the Report was led by Derek Higgs, deputy chairman of the British Land Company and a senior adviser to UBS Warburg.

control of directors' conflicts of interest in the listed (publicly-traded) companies to which the Report applies. In short, independent non-executive directors (outside directors) could and should be given the focused tasks of monitoring management in general and controlling executive directors' conflicts of interest in particular. The Higgs Report is wrong to suggest that non-executive directors, including independent non-executive directors, should continue to have a significant management function in addition to these other roles. Unsurprisingly, however, the new UK Combined Code on Corporate Governance, published on 27 July 2003, adopted the recommendations of the Higgs Report in this regard, as in most others (Financial Reporting Council 2003a).[3]

A clearer, less ambiguous role for independent non-executive directors would have several benefits. It would provide a plausible mechanism for the enforcement of duties that, in a widely-held company, cannot realistically be enforced by shareholders, save in rare cases. That need not encumber executive directors with inflexible, onerous terms of service, however. The control function of independent non-executive directors should include not merely power to enforce executive directors' duties, but also power to waive them after full and frank disclosure by the directors concerned. That would increase the efficiency of fiduciary duties as a mechanism for redressing the informational advantage enjoyed by managers of a firm in a situation where their duty and interest conflict. Strict duties, coupled with a realistic process for enforcing those duties, would act as a deterrent to disloyalty—as a 'stick.' An equally realistic process for seeking consent to a deviation from duty would act as a 'carrot': it would encourage managers to make disclosure in the hope of sanction for proposed action that would otherwise amount to a breach of their duties.

The suggested role for independent non-executive directors should also help to increase their effectiveness. It would free them from any conflicting pressures they might experience if they were managers of a company's business as well as monitors of the company's other directors. Furthermore, clear areas of responsibility, both for independent non-executive directors and for other directors, should reduce (if not eliminate) the occasions for conflict between those two groups of directors in any given company and allow management proper discretion to get on with running a successful business subject only to limited, and justifiable, intervention where management is at risk of deviating from its

---

[3] Hereinafter FRC (2003a) or 'New Combined Code'. The New Combined Code applies to listed companies with financial reporting years beginning on or after 1 Nov. 2003; see the Financial Reporting Council's press release: FRC (2003b). The press release also details the points (not relevant for the purposes of this chapter) at which the New Combined Code departs from the recommendations in the Higgs Report.

tasks. In turn, a clear role for independent non-executive directors should make it easier for shareholders to judge the performance of those directors.

This chapter begins its argument with a critical examination of two aspects of English law: the rules controlling directors' conflicts of interest and the mechanisms currently available for enforcement of those rules. The second aspect is every bit as important as the first: a proper appreciation of how directors' duties may be enforced is absolutely crucial for understanding corporate governance in the United Kingdom.

The chapter then considers the recommendations of the Higgs Report in the context of various earlier reports on corporate governance in the United Kingdom. While many aspects of those recommendations are useful, some are nevertheless seriously flawed. This chapter suggests that the Report is wrong to support the continued involvement of independent non-executive directors in the management of a company's business, partly because such involvement does not appear to improve the company's economic performance, but mainly because such a role will tend to undermine significantly the effectiveness of independent non-executive directors as monitors of management.

Next, the chapter turns to its positive proposals. Most importantly, it seeks to show why and how the existing, highly flexible structures of English company law can be used to give independent non-executive directors a strong, focused role monitoring executives and controlling those executives' conflicts of interest.[4] The frequently-expressed argument, that English law requires directors to be involved in the management of a company's business, is demonstrably wrong. So the present proposals most certainly need not involve the introduction of two-tier boards into English companies. Indeed, the structural rigidities that two-tier boards would introduce into English corporate law make them undesirable.

Of course, practical implementation of these suggestions requires a supply of suitable candidates to become independent non-executive directors; but limiting and focusing the tasks of such directors should make it easier to find the necessary candidates. This is because there should be more people properly suited to undertake a limited number of tasks than are suited to undertake both those and additional tasks. Professionals may well constitute one suitable and large group of people from which to draw independent non-executive directors, in addition to the businesspeople who currently serve as such.

It is unlikely, however, that markets alone will produce the suggested

---

[4] The Company Law Review, a thorough-going revision of corporate law in the United Kingdom, began in 1998 and has already generated a plethora of working papers and a White Paper (official UK government policy paper). The history and work of the review are at http://www.dti.gov.uk/cld/review.htm (last visited 2 Aug. 2005).

reforms, and certainly not within a politically realistic timescale. Consequently, this chapter goes on to advocate the use of a code of corporate governance to achieve these aims, created and enforced in the same way as the existing UK Combined Code on Corporate Governance (UKLA 2000) and its replacement, the New Combined Code (FRC 2003a). Such a code is needed to redress the inefficiencies of the normal contracting processes through which English corporate governance structures are formed. There is, however, no need for legislation to that end.

At this point, it is perhaps useful to describe briefly how codes of corporate governance are created and enforced in the United Kingdom, because they are complex, hybrid regulatory tools.[5] Such codes were, in the beginning, essentially private sector initiatives, responding to both private and public concerns, as well as to the risk of government intervention in outstanding questions of corporate governance. The codes grew out of the work of various different committees, later committees building on earlier work. Of particular interest for present purposes is the work of the Cadbury Committee (1992),[6] the Greenbury Committee (1995),[7] and the Hampel Committee (1998).[8] These committees were established by interested participants in the London financial markets, trade associations, and professional bodies; (*ibid.*: Foreword 1, 2; Cadbury 1992: note 7; Greenbury 1995: note 8, § 1.1) the committees consulted widely amongst interested parties, and they finally drew up codes or recommendations of best practice. In 2000, the work of these committees was consolidated into the original Combined Code. Later, the state became involved, but it did not usurp the private sector. So, while it was the Department of Trade and Industry that commissioned the Higgs Report, it was the Financial Reporting Council[9] that created the New Combined Code, after much consultation on the suggestions in the Higgs Report.[10]

Enforcement of the Combined Code and the New Combined Code was left to market regulators, first to a private body (the London Stock Exchange) and later, to a state agency (the United Kingdom Listing

---

[5] See generally, Ferran (2001: 384–85), discussing the Combined Code. The institutional structure relating to codes of corporate governance in the United Kingdom has changed slightly since that article was published.

[6] The chairman of the committee that wrote the report was Sir Adrian Cadbury, chairman of the Cadbury Group from 1965 to 1989 and a director of the Bank of England from 1970 to 1994.

[7] Sir Richard Greenbury is a former chairman and CEO of Marks & Spencer and, amongst other things, a director of Lloyds TSB, British Gas, ICI, and Zeneca.

[8] The Committee was chaired by Sir Ronnie Hampel, then the chairman of ICI.

[9] The Financial Reporting Council is a private organization funded by the United Kingdom accounting and legal professions, the financial community, commerce, and the government. See the information about the Financial Reporting Council at http://www.frc.org.uk/about.html (last visited 30 Sept. 2003).

[10] See the Financial Reporting Council's statements (FRC 2003c; 2003d).

Authority (UKLA).[11] These bodies (one followed by the other) set the Listing Rules with which a company listed—traded—on the London Stock Exchange must comply. One of the obligations of the Listing Rules is the obligation *either* to comply with the Code *or* to explain why not (so-called 'comply or explain').[12]. A company must agree (as a matter of contract) to abide by the Listing Rules in order to be traded on the Exchange.[13] Historically, this contract formed the basis for enforcement of the Listing Rules. Since 1984, however, first the London Stock Exchange and then UKLA have also had statutory powers to enforce the Listing Rules:[14] power to suspend or expel shares from trading,[15] power to publicize non-compliance (so called 'name and shame'),[16] power to fine a non-compliant company,[17] and power to fine a director of such a company.[18] Thus, the creation and enforcement of codes of corporate governance in the United Kingdom are complex mixtures of private and public action. There is, nevertheless, a clear trend of greater state involvement over time.

Finally, once the chapter has addressed the use of a code in implementing its suggestions, it briefly addresses some other possible techniques for limiting the agency costs faced by a company in respect of its executive directors: For example, the use of executive compensation packages and reliance on the market for corporate control. These techniques are not adequate substitutes in the United Kingdom at present for independent non-executive directors who monitor management, but neither are they ruled out by the proposals made in this chapter. Indeed, if some or all of those strategies proved more successful in future and came to command greater public confidence, they might supplant reliance on independent non-executive directors.

I. CONTROLLING DIRECTORS' CONFLICTS OF INTEREST IN ENGLISH COMPANY LAW THROUGH FIDUCIARY PRINCIPLES: LAW, THEORY, AND PRACTICE

Fiduciary obligations are still the central mechanism through which

---

[11] The Financial Services Authority, a government regulatory body with delegated, statutory powers, currently acts as the United Kingdom Listing Authority (hereinafter UKLA). The transfer of functions from the London Stock Exchange to UKLA was made by the Official Listing of Securities (Change of Competent Authority) Regulations 2000 (SI 2000/968).

[12] UK Listing Rules, r. 12.43.

[13] *Ibid.*, r. 1.1.

[14] See Financial Services and Markets Act 2000, §§ 77, 78, 91-94.

[15] UK Listing Rules, rr. 1.15, 1.19.

[16] *Ibid.*, r. 1.15.

[17] *Ibid.*, r. 1.8.

[18] *Ibid.*, r. 1.9.

English law controls directors' conflicts of interest. As will be seen, fiduciary obligations have been supplemented by statute, and by codes of conduct, but those obligations still have a vital, primary role in controlling directors' conflicts of interest. This central importance of fiduciary obligations emerges very clearly from even a glance at the law reports: breach of fiduciary duty remains the most common complaint against directors, whether litigated as a civil claim against the director(s) concerned or as the subject-matter of proceedings to disqualify a person from holding office as a director in the future.[19] A proper theoretical understanding of these obligations is therefore crucial if any stable corporate governance structures are to be built on them.[20] In recent years, the English courts, encouraged by developments in Australia,[21] have focused ever more carefully and closely on what is meant by fiduciary obligations—on just what is their function.[22] They have sought to refine and sharpen the usage of concepts that, historically, simply drew an analogy with principles of the law of trusts. Though it is still contested, the view clearly emerging from the leading cases can be summarized in two propositions. First, fiduciary obligations serve to secure due performance of a pre-existing, logically prior, undertaking where there is, or is likely to be, some temptation for the person performing that undertaking to subordinate it to his own interests or to other duties. Secondly, fiduciary obligations seek to achieve this goal by prohibiting certain conduct unless particular authorizations are obtained.[23] In company law, therefore, fiduciary obligations are principally concerned with prohibiting a director from taking action, without due authorization, where she has some interest or duty that conflicts, or might conflict, with her duty to manage the company properly for the benefit of its shareholders.

So, in English law, fiduciary obligations are not duties of good faith, in the sense that they do not mandate and require some higher quality of action or behavior from those subject to them. Fiduciary obligations invariably presuppose that a person has assumed some primary

---

[19] For an outline of such proceedings in the United Kingdom, see below, text accompanying note 77.

[20] The author is greatly indebted to Dr Matthew Conaglen, his former doctoral student at the University of Cambridge, for his work on, and immensely useful discussions of, fiduciary duties in England, Australia, and New Zealand.

[21] The leading Australian cases are *Breen v Williams* (1996) 186 CLR 71, and *Pilmer v Duke Group* (2001) 207 CLR 165.

[22] See especially *Bristol & West Building Society v Mothew* [1998] Ch 1.

[23] Fiduciary obligations prohibit action where there is a conflict of duty and interest, or a conflict of duty and duty. They do not per se mandate disclosure by the fiduciary to the principal: disclosure is not compliance with the duty but, rather, a prerequisite to release from it. See *Breen v Williams* noted by the author in Nolan (1997). See also Nolan and Prentice (2002).

undertaking to act,[24] and that undertaking almost invariably imports duties of diligence—care and skill.[25] The function of fiduciary obligations is to safeguard the undertaking, not to extend or expand it in any way: the undertaking (in the case of directors, a consensual undertaking) is prime, and it establishes the scope of the task(s) to be fulfilled by the person in question.[26] Consequently, fiduciary obligations are contractible[27]: they mould themselves to whatever undertaking they support[28] and can be modified explicitly or implicitly.[29] This has very significant consequences for corporate governance in England, which will be addressed shortly.

Understanding fiduciary obligations in English law as clearly contractible in positive law, and as amenable to contractarian theory and explanation, is only a part of explaining the current structure of those obligations. The fact that fiduciary obligations can be explained as implied bargain does not, of itself, explain the precise form of the obligations (the bargain) in English law. Various theoretical justifications for fiduciary obligations have been proffered in the literature[30]: for

[24] See *Bhullar v Bhullar* [2003] EWCA 424 Civ, [2003] 2 BCLC 241, for a recent leading case where the existence and extent of a director's duties of management were in question and were the single material determinant of whether that director had a conflict of interest in a transaction. In that case, the Court of Appeal explained the law, and justified its decision, by reference to the basic general principles about conflicts of interest and duty, rather than adopting and applying a specific doctrine about corporate opportunities.

[25] Directors are under increasingly strict duties of care and skill. The leading English authority is now *Re Barings plc (No. 5)* [1999] 1 BCLC 433, 486-89, approved, insofar as raised for its decision, by the Court of Appeal in [2000] 1 BCLC 523, 534-35.

[26] See, e.g., *Re Goldcorp Exch. Ltd*, [1995] 1 AC 74.

[27] See Cheffins (1991), as to whether such contractibility is desirable. Professor Cheffins reviews the relevant arguments and suggests that fiduciary duties should be contractible. The debate in North American jurisdictions about the extent to which directors' duties, particularly their fiduciary duties, should be contractible must be approached with some care in its application to the United Kingdom, however, because it is far from clear that the relevant law in the respective jurisdictions starts from the same premises about the very functions of fiduciary duties. The Australian High Court has articulated the extent to which the Australian (and UK) understanding of fiduciary duties is different from the North American, *see Breen v Williams* (1996) 186 CLR 71.

[28] See, e.g., *Kelly v Cooper* [1993] AC 205; *Clark Boyce v Mouat* [1994] 1 AC 428.

[29] In corporate law, this is most commonly achieved through the terms of a company's articles of association (constitution). Such stipulations even occur in the standard form articles: see regs 85 and following of Table A in the Companies (Tables A–F) Regs 1985 (SI 1985/805). This standard form of articles is colloquially (and hereinafter) simply called 'Table A.' Stipulations of this sort are generally effective in English law, notwithstanding § 310 of the Companies Act 1985, which attempts to limit contracting round directors' duties in response to failures in the contracting process. As to the genesis of the law currently re-enacted as § 310, see Greene *et al.* (1926: 46–47). For examples of defects in the process of contracting round directors' duties in a company's constitution, see below text accompanying n. 46. As to the current interpretation and application of § 310, See, e.g., *Movitex v Bulfield* [1988] BCLC 104, and, more generally, Rogerson (1997: 93).

[30] A relatively recent review of fiduciary obligations in English company law was undertaken for the English Law Commission by Cambridge University's Centre for Business Research. It formed the basis of §§ 3.19-3.31 of the Law Commission (1998). This consultation paper in turn formed the basis of further work by the Company Law Review.

example, fiduciary obligations have been rationalized as an attempt to counterbalance a principal's vulnerability to the improper exercise of power by her fiduciary[31]; or as a response to a principal's reasonable expectation of loyalty from her fiduciary[32]; or as a means to redress the informational advantage of a fiduciary over her principal in dealings that involve them both and to create an incentive structure in which the self-interest directs the fiduciary to act in the best interests of her principal.[33]

Each of these ideas explains some features of a fiduciary relationship, but they are hard pressed to explain the limited implication of fiduciary obligations in English law and to explain why fiduciary obligations in English law principally prohibit or proscribe certain conduct, unless duly authorized, rather than direct or prescribe particular action.[34] Why, for example, is a car mechanic not a fiduciary for his customer, forbidden by fiduciary duties from engaging in self-interested action, given the power of the mechanic to affect the customer's interests and given the informational imbalance between mechanic and customer, and so forth? From the perspective of English law, the answer seems to be that it is possible to control the car mechanic's action through specific, easily-contracted duties to perform a set task with a set measure of diligence. There is a bounded task around which parties can contract, not merely in theory, but in practice too: performance of the task can be assessed relatively easily, and consequently it is practicable *ex ante* to stipulate (or to have the law imply) specific constraints on the parties' conduct. In contrast, it is exceptionally difficult to stipulate specifically for the conduct to be undertaken by a trustee managing a trust fund or a by director managing a company, without abolishing managerial freedom: there are so many different circumstances that may arise in the course of conducting the undertaking and so many different, unobjectionable ways of performing the undertaking.[35]

Now, clearly, English law does not want the chilling effect on managers, particularly business managers, of strict duties of care and skill. English company law has for more than a century regarded such strict duties as inefficient and undesirable, tending to the inhibition of entrepreneurial business activity.[36] However, the rejection of strict,

---

[31] This idea has attracted considerable attention in Canada, see *Frame v Smith* [1987] 42 D.L.R. (4th) 81, 99. Note the varying reactions to the idea in *Lac Minerals Ltd v Int'l Corona Res. Ltd* [1989] 2 S.C.R. 574, and *Hodgkinson v Simms* [1994] 3 S.C.R. 377.

[32] See Finn (1989: 46).

[33] See generally Brudney (1985; 1997); Cooter and Freedman (1991); Campbell (1996).

[34] See above, text accompanying note 31.

[35] See Cooter and Freedman (1991).

[36] It should be remembered that the United Kingdom has no business judgment rule, but, instead, allows discretion and freedom of action to directors by setting a flexible (and relatively low) standard of diligence. The older cases display a particularly indulgent attitude

prescriptive duties to act, and to act with diligence, does not alone explain the proscriptive content of fiduciary obligations in English law. At first sight, it would appear that the law could have just as easily used broad, open-textured, open-ended prescriptive rules (for example, a duty to act in someone else's best interests) in order to control managers without unduly limiting their discretion. However, such rules would still be very uncertain in their application and therefore correspondingly likely to inhibit entrepreneurial activity. Consequently, English law has instead concluded that it is more efficient to imply duties that remove specified conduct from the realm of the permissible, because it would tend to jeopardize performance of the positive undertaking in question, rather than to impose duties which stipulate in very broad terms the way in which that undertaking should be performed. Proscribing particular conduct, where a fiduciary has an interest that conflicts (or may conflict) with some identified part of his undertaking, may not be a perfectly precise exercise, but it is at least clearer and more practicable than prescribing in necessarily vague terms the entire conduct of the undertaking.

The practical manifestations of this theoretical approach are the greater importance in English law of fiduciary obligations as a means by which to control directors, as opposed to duties of care and skill, and the corresponding importance of efficient means of enforcing fiduciary obligations, both *ex ante* and *ex post*. Unfortunately, the very contractibility of the obligations undermines their enforcement in company law. This problem has two aspects.

First, English law allows a company's constitution (which explicitly represents a bargain between the shareholders)[37] to modify directors' fiduciary obligations so that they can be waived *ex ante* by the company's board, usually provided the interested director takes no part in that decision and always provided that the decision is made bona fide in the best interests of the company—something that may be hard to disprove.[38] This all tends very materially to weaken *ex ante* control over directors' self-interested behavior. Directors who are together involved in the

to directors. See, e.g., *Re Denham & Co* (1884) 25 Ch. D. 752; *Re Cardiff Savings Bank* [1892] 2 Ch 100; *Re Brazilian Rubber Plantations* [1911] 1 Ch 425; *Re City Equitable Fire Insurance Co* [1925] Ch 407. More recently, the courts have expected greater diligence from directors, See, e.g., *Norman v Theodore Goddard* [1991] BCLC 1028; *Copp v D'Jan* [1994] 1 BCLC 561; *Re Barings plc (No. 5)* [1999] 1 BCLC 433 aff'd CA [2000] 1 BCLC 523. Consequently, cases about directors' incompetence are much rarer than those about their disloyalty; and the cases where directors have been held negligent far more often concern a failure of management *process* than poor business *performance*, as witness *Re Barings plc (No. 5)*.

[37] See Companies Act 1985, § 14; note also §§ 9 and 18 of the Act as regards changes to a company's constitution.

[38] See, e.g., Table A, above note 29, Regs 84–87, 94. The requirement of directors' bona fides is a general implication of law. See, e.g., *Re a Co* (No. 00370 of 1987) (1988) 4 BCC 506, 512.

management of a business are unlikely to constitute the best people to regulate each others' conflicts of duty and interest: considerations of collegiality and the incentives towards mutually supportive behavior at board meetings and elsewhere all make it unlikely that executive directors will adequately regulate each others' conflicts of duty and interest.[39]

Secondly, English law essentially allows a company's constitution to vest powers where it likes, unless mandatory rules provide otherwise.[40] In particular, the constitution may vest power in a company's board to institute proceedings *ex post* to redress a breach of directors' duties[41]; and virtually all company constitutions contain provisions to this effect.[42] For the reasons just given, executive directors are unlikely to be the best people to decide whether to sue one of their number or a former director. This tends very materially to weaken *ex post* control over directors' self-interested behavior. Occasionally, proceedings are brought against former directors when control of a company changes, following either a sale or the opening of insolvency proceedings.

Equally, there are occasions when the law will allow shareholders to bring proceedings against directors for the benefit of the company, but it is notoriously difficult to take advantage of those rare opportunities and often very risky to do so.[43] In fact, it is hardly surprising that the

---

[39] While considerations of collegiality may impede the regulation by executives of their peers' conflicts of duty and interest, those same executives may have the incentive of self-advancement to monitor their colleagues' underperformance. This may be suggested by Kaplan's work (1994a) on board turnover in Japan where boards tend to be dominated by insiders. Different considerations apply to German public companies, as to which, see Kaplan (1994b). German companies have a distinct supervisory board *(Aufsichtsrat)* to monitor the management board *(Vorstand)*. One possibly significant difference between the present situation—*ex ante* control of executives' conflicts of interest by their peers—and executives' monitoring of each others' performance is that when authorizing a conflicted transaction in advance, a director has the hope of similar indulgence from his colleagues in the future, whereas there are not such obvious incentives to overlook others' past incompetence in the same hope: people seem not to worry so much about the possibility of their own future failure.

[40] Note, by way of example, the provisions of Table A, above, note 29, Reg 70. See also *Automatic Self-Cleansing Filter Syndicate v Cuninghame* [1906] 2 Ch 34; *Quin & Axtens Ltd v Salmon* [1909] AC 442; *John Shaw & Sons (Salford) Ltd v Shaw* [1935] 2 KB 113. For examples of mandatory rules that limit this basic freedom, see below Part III.

[41] See, e.g., Table A, above note 29, Regulation 70; *Breckland Group Holdings Ltd v London & Suffolk Prop. Ltd* [1989] BCLC 100; *Mitchell & Hobbs (UK) Ltd v Mill* [1996] 2 BCLC 102.

[42] For the purposes of another article on voting rights in UK companies, Nolan (2003), the author undertook a survey of the constitutions of the FTSE 100 companies and of UK companies listed on the NYSE or NASDAQ. This survey confirms the assertion in the text: no company surveyed had a constitution with provisions different to those described in the text.

[43] Shareholder suits are still governed in the United Kingdom by the notoriously opaque rule in *Foss v Harbottle* (1843) 2 Hare 461, and the various exceptions to the rule. See generally *Prudential Assurance Co Ltd v Newman Industries Ltd* [1981] Ch 257 ; *Prudential Assurance Co Ltd v Newman Industries Ltd* [1982] Ch 204 ; Law Commission (1996b: § B). Just as important as those jurisdictional rules, however, are the rules about the costs of court proceedings. In

constitution of a listed company will contain provisions such as those just described, because the management of the company invariably proposes the terms of its constitution, to be simply adopted or rejected as a whole by shareholders. Consequently, shareholders generally accept the terms proposed by management: in the rhetoric of a shareholders' meeting they are easily justified as 'standard terms'; shareholders are often ignorant of the practical effect of terms that look unobjectionable on their face, and even those who have doubts are often unwilling to 'go nuclear' and reject the entire package proposed by management in a single resolution, so risking damage to the company by undermining or de-motivating its incumbent managers.[44]

The previous paragraphs demonstrate the central problem of English company law in controlling directors' conflicts of interest: fiduciary obligations are vitally important, but those fiduciary obligations are very difficult to enforce and are correspondingly rarely litigated.[45] The practical result of all this is to undermine radically the effectiveness of the law. In the absence of other control mechanisms, directors are left with significant scope for unchecked abuse of their positions.

Of course, there are other, non-legal factors that may restrict directors' behavior: reputational concerns, for example. The usefulness of these may be overstated, however. For example, executive directors in the United Kingdom have shown little sign of moderating their self-interested demands for remuneration in the face of considerable public and shareholder protest.[46] Indeed, even allowing that reputational controls have some useful effect, they alone have clearly not met investors' present dissatisfaction with directors' self-interested behavior, particularly in relation to directors' remuneration. It is no reply to question the utility of shareholders' wishes to control company managers. Shareholders may be unwise, or even irrational, in their

principle, a shareholder who brings a derivative action on behalf of a company will be responsible for his own costs; and contingency fees are very rare in English commercial litigation. The shareholder may pass those costs (or a fraction of them) on to a defendant who is found liable and is solvent, but correspondingly may have to bear the costs of a defendant who is not held liable. See Civil Procedure Rules 1998, Part 44.3. The shareholder can seek an indemnity from the company for any of these costs, but such indemnities are not often awarded. See Civil Procedure Rules 1998, Part 19.9(7).

[44] These are examples of failure in the process of contracting round directors' duties in a company's constitution. See above, note 29.

[45] Stapledon (1996: 13-14) notes that 'actions to enforce the duties of directors of quoted companies have been almost non-existent.' See also the position paper prepared by Cambridge University ESRC Centre for Business Research (2000: §§ 5.1 (particularly Table 4), 5.2).

[46] See the recent (2003) annual general meetings of, for example, Royal & Sun Alliance plc, Barclays plc, Reuters plc, Grenada plc, and the 'Shell' Transport and Trading Company, plc (Shell Oil). At its 2003 AGM, Tesco plc faced vocal shareholder resistance to its directors' remuneration report; it indicated that it would reconsider the contracts awarded to its directors.

judgment of directors, but their views are entitled to prevail unless their very role in the company is recast, so as to curtail the powers and liberties corporate law presently allows them.[47]

The problems outlined in this part of the chapter have, quite understandably, led policymakers to conclude that there should be some other mechanism(s) in English law for enforcing restraints on directors' self-interested behavior. However, before turning to the role of non-executive directors, it is useful to examine briefly other legal means of holding directors accountable in English law. They form a rather heavy-handed, incoherent, 'scatter-gun' selection of responses to the problems just described.

II. OTHER MECHANISMS FOR HOLDING DIRECTORS ACCOUNTABLE

The first response of UK legislators to the problems outlined in the previous part of this chapter has been to reserve power to shareholders by mandatory stipulation. Provisions of the companies legislation have limited the extent to which directors can be given the power in a company's constitution to validate self-interested behavior by one of their number. The number of such provisions has increased over the years.[48] Under Part X of the Companies Act, 1985, gratuitous payoffs to directors must be approved (§§ 312, 313); substantial property transactions between a company and its director (or someone connected to a director) must be prospectively authorized by shareholders (§§ 320–22); and loans by a company to its directors (or connected persons) are banned in most circumstances (§§ 330–42).

Under Part XA of the 1985 Act, substituted into the Act by the Political Parties, Elections and Referendums Act, 2000, political expenditure by companies must first be approved by shareholders. Under §§ 234B, 234C, and 241A of the 1985 Act, introduced on 1 August 2002, a report on directors' remuneration must be submitted to a vote by shareholders,

---

[47] The government has recently made it quite clear that the basic economic structure of the corporation in the United Kingdom is not to be changed: it will remain fundamental to English corporate law that a commercial company exists to create wealth for its shareholders, albeit in an 'enlightened' fashion. See DTI (2002: 9, 26). This paper set out the Government's response to the Company Law Review and endorsed the Review's conclusions as to the functions of company law, which were set out in Company Law Review Steering Group (CLRSG) (1999: ch. 5.1); CLRSG (2000a: ch. 3); and CLRSG (2000b: ch. 3.5). Consequently, this chapter takes it as axiomatic that the fundamental function of directors in a commercial company is to further the creation of wealth through the company for its shareholders. The aim of the paper is to consider some of the implications of the role conferred on such directors.

[48] See Law Commission (1998: App. C).

though the result of the vote is non-binding.[49] Regulators have also insisted on shareholders having power in relation to transactions where a director might have a conflict of duty and interest.

Under the Listing Rules issued by the United Kingdom Listing Authority, companies listed on the London Stock Exchange must normally obtain shareholder approval for 'related party transactions': That is, transactions between a company (or any of its subsidiaries) and a director or certain of his or her associates (UKLA 2000: §§ 11.4–11.8). This strategy of returning power to shareholders has its limitations, however, in a widely-held, listed company.[50]

First, any provision that requires the prospective consent of share-holders to a proposed transaction by a company will involve a general meeting of shareholders: the only present alternative—informally obtaining unanimous consent—is simply not a practical option in a listed company. Unless the transaction is sufficiently predictable that it can be scheduled for consideration at a company's annual general meeting (for example, approving directors' remuneration),[51] obtaining shareholders' consent will involve calling an extraordinary general meeting of the company, something that is slow, inconvenient, and expensive.[52] Furthermore, seeking shareholders' approval for a transaction that would otherwise be prohibited will necessarily involve full and frank disclosure of all material facts surrounding the proposal.[53] This can be inappropriate where it would risk disclosure to the world at large of commercially sensitive information.

Secondly, even where shareholder consent is required, but is not obtained, so that a civil remedy flows from that omission, the power to

---

[49] Before these provisions were introduced, Cheffins and Thomas (2001) predicted that shareholder voting would only operate as a check on executive pay when the pay deviates far from the norm. Their prediction appears to have been borne out in 2003, the first year in which companies had to put executive pay to a vote of shareholders. Only one such vote has been lost, in respect of a package that did deviate significantly from the norm: on 19 May 2003, shareholders in Glaxosmithkline plc, by a very narrow margin, rejected the company's remuneration report, principally because of the remuneration package of its CEO, Jean-Pierre Garnier, see GSK (2003a). The company's chairman, Sir Christopher Hogg, said 'Although Resolution 2 [on the remuneration report] is advisory, the Board takes this result very seriously' (GSK 2003b). In other shareholder votes on executive remuneration, major (institutional) shareholders have often abstained, to indicate concern about the remuneration, but they have not actually voted against it. See above, note 48.

[50] The evidence from the United States about shareholder proposals tends not to support the case for expanding shareholder powers in public companies; see Romano (2001); Black (1998); Karpoff *et al.* (1996).

[51] Generally, a company must in any event have an annual general meeting. Provisions that derogate from this general rule do not apply to listed public companies, see Companies Act 1985, §§ 366, 366A.

[52] Note, as regards 'corporate opportunities,' See, e.g., Deakin and Hughes (1999: § 5.2).

[53] See, e.g., *Imperial Mercantile Credit Association v Coleman* (1873) LR 6 HL 189, 201 ; *New Zealand Netherlands Society v Kuys* [1973] 1 WLR 1126. Note also the commentary on § 320 of the Companies Act 1985, in Arden *et al.* (1998).

bring proceedings is vested in the board, and consequently proceedings are unlikely to be brought.[54] Only one set of provisions—those in Part XA of the Companies Act, 1985 (political donations)—addresses this problem and allows a shareholder suit for breach of the prohibitions in that Part. However, even that does not resolve other, more serious problems. These are the problems of apathy and collective action.[55] Why should a particular shareholder in a company take action that will benefit all such shareholders, rather than just the one who took the action? Worse still, under English civil procedure, a shareholder litigant is at severe risk as to the costs of the litigation.[56] Unsurprisingly, these possibilities exert a severe chilling effect on contemplated litigation by shareholders. In short, there is very little reason or incentive for a particular shareholder to take action that has the aim and, if successful, the effect of procuring a remedy that, in legal terms, is awarded to the company and, in economic terms, inures for the benefit of all those with claims against the defined fund of assets known as the company's property. It is simply not worthwhile.

Another strategy adopted by English company law is to control directors' conflicts of interest through the criminal law.[57] The principal techniques used by the law are to criminalize conflicted conduct by a director[58] or to criminalize the director's failure to disclose the conflict.[59] It is highly questionable whether these criminal offences concerned with conflicted transactions by a director are in fact useful: they are virtually never prosecuted.[60] However, they are often defended on the grounds that they exert a severe chilling effect and thereby control directors' conflicts of interest.[61] It is argued that they do this principally through two mechanisms.[62] First, the threat of criminal sanctions is said directly to condition a director's behavior.

Secondly, it is suggested that the provisions give a lever to professional advisors who seek to ensure that directors do not fall into conflicts of interest: for example, a lawyer can point out the criminal sanctions

[54] See text at above note 49.
[55] See, e.g., Black (1990); Roe (1994). These works deal with the situation in the United States, but the situation in the United Kingdom is similar.
[56] See above, note 51.
[57] See generally, Daniels (1994–95), and the research note for the Company Law Review by Cambridge University ESRC Centre for Business Research (2000).
[58] For example, the Companies Act 1985, § 342, criminalizes certain loans made by a company to a director.
[59] For example, the Companies Act 1985, § 317, criminalizes a company director's failure to disclose his interest in a contract with the company.
[60] Law Commission (1998: § 10.3). See also DTI (2003a: § D).
[61] CLRSG (2000b: ch. 13); CLRSG (2002: ch. 15)
[62] See also Ferran (2001: 406–9), for a consideration of these arguments as well as others raised by the Company Law Review in favor of using criminal sanctions as a means to control directors.

attaching to certain conduct, tell the client to comply with the law, and refuse to be party to any illegal conduct.

It is very difficult to say whether these criminal sanctions are effective by virtue of the rather more oblique consequences suggested above. There is, however, one study in the United Kingdom that addresses professional advisors' reactions to criminal penalties for undisclosed, conflicted action by directors (Deakins and Hughes 1999: § 5.35). On the basis of 'background interviews with legal practitioners,' this study suggests that 'the possibility of criminal sanctions can concentrate the minds of directors,' because:

> [a]dvisers feel that without the threat of such sanctions, it would be more difficult for them to persuade certain directors to avoid certain transactions of dubious legality.

Consequently, the study concludes,

> We do not have any direct evidence of this use of the law, but frequent references by practitioners suggest that the threat of criminal liability may, through the medium of legal advice, have a significant influence on behavior in practice.

Suffice it to make three comments.

First, the author's experience in legal practise tends to suggest that those who are deterred by the criminal law, when it is manifestly not enforced, are those who also worry about, and are constrained by, civil liabilities and reputational concerns, while those who are not worried about such matters behave with cynical contempt for the criminal law—they simply calculate the likelihood of being held to account for a crime and conclude that it is not great in the present context.

Secondly, and much more importantly, it must be questionable for the law to rely on provisions the effectiveness of which is admitted to be anecdotal.[63] Thirdly, the control of dealing in securities by the criminal law (insider trading)[64] has been the subject of much criticism,[65] and Parliament has more recently enacted civil ('administrative') controls on transactions in securities.[66] There is, however, a new dimension to criminal sanctions, which may yet prove to be extremely important and render them very effective—perhaps too effective. This is the impact of

---

[63] Ferran (2001) also casts doubt on the continued heavy emphasis of criminal sanctions to control directors. That said, a policy consensus is likely to ensure that criminal sanctions will remain a feature of the English law of directors duties. See CLRSG (2002: § 15.4).

[64] See Criminal Justice Act 1993, Part V.

[65] See, e.g., Rider (1993). The number of prosecutions for insider trading each year in the United Kingdom is in low single figures. See DTI (2003a: 50).

[66] Financial Services and Markets Act 2000, Part VIII (the 'market abuse' regime).

the Proceeds of Crime Act 2002. The relevant portions of that Act (Parts 5 and 7) only came into force in December 2002 and February 2003. As they are so recent, they are not addressed in the existing scholarly literature on the efficacy of criminal sanctions in corporate law. This is a significant gap in the literature, which must certainly be filled.

The 2002 Act not only provides for the recovery of benefits made through criminal activity, but it can also implicate professional advisors. Under § 329 of the 2002 Act, a person who acquires, uses or has possession of 'criminal property' commits an offence, subject to applicable defenses. For these purposes, property is 'criminal property' if it constitutes a person's 'benefit' from criminal conduct, or it represents such a benefit, and the alleged offender knows or suspects that it constitutes or represents such a benefit. Section 329 could well catch fees earned by professionals who advise in connection with a transaction that involves commission of a criminal offence, given the width of the relevant definitions in § 340 of the Act. In addition, under § 328 of the 2002 Act, a person commits an offence, again, subject to relevant defenses, if he enters into, or becomes concerned in, an arrangement which he knows or suspects facilitates the acquisition, retention, use or control of 'criminal property' by or on behalf of another person. This too could catch professionals advising on corporate transactions that involve illegal action. A defence to both of these crimes is to make an 'authorised disclosure' of the facts to the relevant governmental authorities, under § 338 of the Act. In future, professional advisors may well have to make such a disclosure, and abstain from acting, in order to avoid committing a crime themselves.

Finally, under Part 5, Chapter 2 of the Act, any property which is obtained through unlawful conduct (and its proceeds) will be prima facie 'recoverable property', and so can be seized in civil recovery proceedings by the relevant governmental enforcement authority. All this may yet give real teeth to criminal sanctions in the context of corporate law.

The next, and much discussed, mechanism in English law for controlling directors' conflicts of interest is directors' disqualification proceedings.[67] Breach of fiduciary or statutory duty by a director is a ground, under § 6 of the Company Directors Disqualification Act 1986, for disqualifying that director. If a person acts as a director in breach of a disqualification order, she will be liable to criminal prosecution and will also be exposed to civil liability for the debts incurred by a company while she was wrongfully a director of it.[68] Public authorities—principally the Insolvency Service, an agency of the Department of Trade

[67] See generally Walters and Davis-White (2005).
[68] Company Directors Disqualification Act 1986, §§ 13, 15.

and Industry—enforce the disqualification regime, acting most commonly on the reports provided by liquidators of companies.[69]

There have been some very high-profile disqualification proceedings—directors of Barings Bank were disqualified for their managerial inadequacies in the 'Nick Leeson Scandal' that broke the Bank.[70] Nevertheless, the limitations of disqualification proceedings are readily apparent. Enforcement depends on public bodies, which tend to be underfunded. Furthermore, though the effect of proceedings in a particular case is salutary, discussions with practicing lawyers reveal that disqualification proceedings are taken in a small minority of possible cases.[71] More importantly still, the immediate effect of disqualification proceedings is inevitably after the event: Disqualification proceedings respond directly to the past wrongdoing or inadequacies of directors. The only prospective, normative effect of such proceedings is in the general culture they engender, something that is very difficult to measure. Given that there are considerably more directors' disqualification cases than prosecutions relating to directors' conflicts of interest,[72] it is very likely that disqualification proceedings have a much more significant normative impact than the threat of prosecution; but such indirect and nebulous effects are hardly a substitute for proper *ex ante* and *ex post* internal control mechanisms within a company.

The Department of Trade and Industry also has powers to investigate companies, principally contained in Part XIV of the Companies Act 1985, and especially § 447. These powers are used moderately (DTI 2003: 21), but generally only where there has been a fraud on creditors of a company or on the public at large (*ibid.*: 21–22). The provisions have little relevance to the control of directors' conflicts of duty and interest.

Finally, before turning to the Higgs Report itself, one more provision of

---

[69] See the guidance provided by the Insolvency Service at http://www.insolvency.gov.uk/information/guidanceleaflets/guide/chapter6.htm (last visited 30 Sept. 2003).

[70] *Re Barings plc (No. 5)* [1999] 1 BCLC 433; [2000] 1 BCLC 523 .

[71] Government statistics reveal that there are around 1800 disqualification orders made each year, see DTI (2003a: 49). This may seem like a large number—and it is by comparison with the number of criminal prosecutions for infractions of prohibitions on conflicts of duty and interest—but two points should be made. First, according to evidence from leading practitioners, it is but a small fraction of the cases for disqualification referred to the Department of Trade and Industry. Secondly, and more importantly, the number of disqualification orders is somewhat misleading, because they include not just court proceedings but also disqualifications by consent, see Company Directors Disqualification Act 1986 § 1A, though consent orders were made in substance by compromised court proceedings—the so-called 'Carecraft' procedure—before § 1A was introduced. So, 1275 of the 1777 disqualifications made in the year 2002–3 were made by consent: see DTI (2003a: 49). It must be admitted, however, that even disqualification by consent represents some effort at enforcement by the Insolvency Service.

[72] The point is made forcefully in the annual statistics prepared by the Department of Trade and Industry. For the most recent set of figures, see DTI (2003a: § D). Compare also text at note 69, above.

English company law deserves a brief mention, if only for the sake of completeness: § 459 of the Companies Act, 1985. Section 459 allows a shareholder to bring proceedings in her own name for redress of 'unfairly prejudicial conduct' of a company's affairs. The section has become extremely important in the context of small, 'quasi-partnership' companies, but it has little significance for large, listed companies. While a shareholder in a listed company can use § 459 to seek a remedy on behalf of the company of which she is a member,[73] and can thereby sidestep the procedural problems of a derivative action in the English courts,[74] § 459 does nothing about the lack of incentives for the shareholder to bring action on behalf of the company to remedy a wrong.[75] Furthermore, the courts will not give the shareholder such an incentive, by allowing him a personal remedy under the section. This is because the courts have restricted the meaning of 'unfairly prejudicial conduct' of a listed company's affairs to circumstances that involve the company's directors breaching their legal duties to the company,[76] and the courts appear unwilling to reward a shareholder with a personal remedy in respect of this sort of unfairly prejudicial conduct, even though they have jurisdiction to do so. Presumably, the reason for the courts' reluctance is that they are aware that an award of funds from a defaulting director to one particular shareholder could prejudice any chance of recovery by, or on behalf of, other shareholders whose interests were equally harmed.

Similarly, § 459 does nothing about the problems of funding shareholder litigation.[77] In short, § 459 has little relevance to listed companies. Given the various inadequacies of legal controls on the executive management of listed companies, it is hardly surprising that there has been great interest over the past fifteen years or so in the use of non-executive directors as a means by which executive directors can be held to account. Indeed, the evidence is that non-executive directors have already come to be the most significant mechanism for the control of executive directors' conflicts of duty and interest in listed companies (Deakin and Hughes 1999: § 5.1). Admittedly, such reliance may well suggest that other reforms of English corporate and procedural law are desirable. However, it is unlikely that there will be timely and effective reform of the relevant law. For example, while the current review of company law in the United Kingdom proposed a reformed derivative

[73] Companies Act 1985, § 461(2)(c).
[74] See above, note 51 and accompanying text.
[75] See text at note 65, above.
[76] See especially *Re Astec plc* [1998] 2 BCLC 556. Note also *Re Blue Arrow plc* [1987] BCLC 585; *Re Tottenham Hotspur plc* [1994] 1 BCLC 655.
[77] See above note 51 and text at note 65, above.

action,[78] the incentives to use a new, reformed derivative action will (apparently) remain unchanged, so that it will not likely be of significant utility. This reflects the deep policy ambivalence in the United Kingdom towards shareholders' engagement in corporate governance: shareholder activism is lauded and encouraged[79]; but the encouragement does not seem to go as far as shareholder litigation, which is seen as economically wasteful.[80] There is still less chance of increased public enforcement of directors' duties: Whatever the rhetoric, it is simply not a sufficient political priority to attract increased funding—and that may be no bad thing. In short, problems with other means of holding executive directors to account have turned the use of non-executive directors into the preferred method (at least for the time being) of improving corporate governance in UK listed companies. And given that such problems look set to continue (at least for the foreseeable future), change in the governance practices of UK listed companies will most likely come about in the short- to medium-term through the better use of non-executive directors.

III. MANAGERS AND MONITORS: THE DUAL ROLE OF NON-EXECUTIVE DIRECTORS

Non-executive directors rose to prominence in UK corporate governance following the report of the Cadbury Committee in December 1992. The Cadbury Report saw a wide role for non-executive directors: it stated that '[n]on-executive directors should bring an independent judgment to bear on issues of strategy, performance, resources, including key appointments, and standards of conduct' (Cadbury 1992: § 4.11). In particular, the Nomination Committee, a committee of the board that proposed directors for appointment, was to have a majority of non-executive directors (*ibid.*: § 4.30); and the audit committee was to be composed of non-executive directors (*ibid.*: § 4.35), a majority of whom ought to be 'independent' within the meaning of the Cadbury Report (*ibid.*: § 4.12).[81] These last two

---

[78] CLRSG (2000b: §§ 5.82–5.90); CLRSG (2002: §§ 7.46–7.51).

[79] See, e.g., Myners *et al.* (2001), which was endorsed by the UK government in the Chancellor of the Exchequer's Budget Speech of 7 Mar. 2001, available at http://www.hm-treasury.gov.uk/budget/budget_2001/bud_bud01_speech.cfm.

[80] A good example of the English courts' negative attitude is *Prudential Assurance Co Ltd v Newman Industries Ltd (No. 2)* [1982] Ch 204. This attitude has led one leading commentator, Professor Len Sealy, to comment bluntly that '[i]t has become far too easy for our [United Kingdom] judges to say to such a [shareholder] plaintiff: "Go away"' (1987: 1). For a comparison with the position in the United States, see DeMott (1999: 210).

[81] This means that apart from their directors' fees and shareholdings, they should be independent of management and free from any business or other relationship which could materially interfere with the exercise of their independent judgment. It is for the board to decide in particular cases whether this definition is met. Information about the relevant interests of directors should be disclosed in the directors' report.

important roles involve the monitoring of executive directors: non-executive directors could review the reappointment of executive directors, who are invariably elected to serve for a fixed period of time[82]; and they could monitor management of the company through their activities on the audit committee.

Nevertheless, the Cadbury Report envisaged a company's non-executive directors as more than just monitors of the company's other directors: the non-executives were to engage in managing the company through their input into the company's strategy. The subsequent report of the Greenbury Committee (1992) recommended that the board of a company, and particularly of a listed company, should create a remuneration committee, which would set executive directors' remuneration packages (*ibid*.: draft code § A1). This remuneration committee should be comprised exclusively of independent non-executive directors (*ibid*.: § A4). The board as a whole would continue to set non-executive directors' fees.

In January 1998, the Hampel Committee on Corporate Governance (1998: §§ 1.1, 3.8) reaffirmed the two roles of non-executive directors, monitoring and the formation of strategy. Indeed, the strategy role was emphasized above the monitoring role, something on which investors in the United Kingdom might usefully reflect:

> The importance of corporate governance lies in its contribution both to business prosperity and to accountability. In the United Kingdom the latter has preoccupied much public debate over the past few years. We would wish to see the balance corrected.
>
> ...
>
> Non-executive directors are normally appointed to the board primarily for their contribution to the development of the company's strategy. This is clearly right. We have found general acceptance that non-executive directors should have both a strategic and a monitoring function. In addition, and particularly in smaller companies, non-executive directors may contribute valuable expertise not otherwise available to management; or they may act as mentors to relatively inexperienced executives.

In June of that same year, the work of these various committees was consolidated into the Old Combined Code, which still forms an appendix to the United Kingdom Listing Rules and governs the behavior of companies, on a 'comply or explain basis,' so long as they seek to

---

[82] See Old Combined Code (UKLA 2000: Principle A.6); New Combined Code (FRC 2003a: Principle A.7).

maintain a listing on the London Stock Exchange.[83] The Old Combined Code broadly continued the previous arrangements for non-executive directors to act as a check on executive directors. So, non-executive directors were to comprise at least one-third of a board (UKLA 2000: § A.3.1).[84] A nomination committee still controlled recommendations for appointment to the board; and a majority of the committee's members were still to be non-executive directors (UKLA 2000: § A.5.1).[85] The audit committee was to continue to monitor management and was still to be composed of non-executive directors, and a majority were to be independent (UKLA 2000: § D.3.1).[86] A remuneration committee comprised of independent non-executive directors was to set executive directors' remuneration packages (UKLA 2000: §§ B.2.1, B.2.2).[87]

Yet, notwithstanding that the specifically identified tasks of independent non-executive directors are almost invariably concerned with controlling executive directors' conflicts of duty and interest, or else with monitoring executive management, the role of the non-executive director still apparently extends into managing a company's business. As the Old Combined Code (UKLA 2000: § A.1.5) put it,

> All directors should bring an independent judgement to bear on issues of strategy, performance, resources, including key appointments, and standards of conduct.[88]

Only the Law Commission, writing in September 1998, saw the role of non-executive directors as 'principally that of monitors rather than managers' (Law Commission 1998: § 3.46). It is, in itself, very interesting that government lawyers—law reformers—should have such different ideas from the businessmen (and their legal advisors) involved in writing the Cadbury, Greenbury, Hampel, and Higgs Reports. Much more recently still, the courts have drawn attention primarily to the monitoring function of non-executive directors:

> It is well known that the role of non-executive directors in corporate gover-nance has been the subject of some debate in recent years. ... It is plainly

---

[83] The Old Combined Code is superseded by the New Combined Code in relation to a listed company for the company's accounting years beginning on or after 1 Nov. 2003. See above, note 3.

[84] The New Combined Code requires at least one-half of the board to be comprised of independent non-executive directors, New Combined Code (FRC 2003a: A.3.2).

[85] Continued by New Combined Code (FRC 2003a: A.4.1), but specifically requiring the non-executive directors to be *independent*.

[86] Continued by New Combined Code (FRC 2003a: C.3.1), but again specifically requiring the non-executive directors to be *independent*.

[87] Continued by New Combined Code (FRC 2003a: B.2.1).

[88] The substance of that paragraph is continued by New Combined Code (FRC 2003a: Principle A.1 and Supporting Principles).

arguable, I think, that a company may reasonably at least look to non-executive directors for independence of judgment and supervision of the executive management.[89]

Clearly, the expectations of those businessmen and their advisors are not universally shared. Such a mismatch of expectations and understandings is fraught with the risk of disappointment and consequent strife. At the very least, therefore, what is needed is an open, prominent debate to establish the role of non-executive directors.

The Higgs Report has adhered to, indeed has re-emphasized, the dual management and monitoring role of non-executive directors in the United Kingdom.[90] It is worth setting out at some length what the Report (Higgs 2003a: §§ 6.1–6.3) has to say on the point:

> The role of the non-executive director is frequently described as having two principal components: monitoring executive activity, and contributing to the development of strategy. Both Cadbury and Hampel identified a tension between these two elements.
>
> Research commissioned for the Review drew a somewhat different conclusion. Based on forty in-depth interviews with directors, the research found that while there might be a tension, there was no essential contradiction between the monitoring and strategic aspects of the role of the non-executive director. Polarized conceptions of the role, the research noted, bear little relation to the actual conditions for non-executive effectiveness. An overemphasis on monitoring and control risks non-executive directors seeing themselves, and being seen, as an alien policing influence detached from the rest of the board. An overemphasis on strategy risks non-executive directors becoming too close to executive management, undermining shareholder confidence in the effectiveness of board governance.
>
> The research concludes that it is important to establish a spirit of partnership and mutual respect on the unitary board. This requires the non-executive director to build recognition by executives of their contribution in order to promote openness and trust. Only then can non-executive directors contribute effectively. The key to non-executive director effectiveness lies as much in behaviours and relationships as in structures and processes.

This chapter suggests that the Higgs Report is wrong to recommend continued, conflated management and monitoring roles for non-executive directors. The role of *independent* non-executive directors

---

[89] *Equitable Life v Bowley* [2003] EWHC 2263 at [41].
[90] See, e.g., Higgs (2003: § 4.2).

should be the audit of management in general, and in particular the control of managers' conflicts of interest, though a company should have the option of retaining other non-executive directors for other reasons, such as input into the company's business strategy. This suggestion has both positive and negative aspects. These are outlined below and are developed in more depth through the rest of the chapter.

On the positive side, properly focused, independent non-executive directors are well placed to monitor and control executive directors' conflicts of interest. Their continuous, if not day-to-day involvement in the governance of a company means that they do not face many of the difficulties, outlined earlier, that shareholders in a company encounter when trying to control its management. Also on the positive side, giving independent non-executive directors a more limited role, but more power within that role, would actually meet the concerns of executive directors who do not want to be constantly constrained when running the company's business. The executive directors would be allowed to get on with their economic function of managing the company for the shareholders' profit,[91] constrained by the independent non-executive directors only when there is a risk that they will deviate from that function, either because of conflicts of interest or because of negligence. In short, a clear, limited role for independent non-executive directors would preserve managerial freedom for executive directors: the role of independent non-executive directors can be so defined as to preserve executive management from undue interference.

On the negative side, it is suggested that giving a mixed set of functions to non-executive directors makes it less likely they will perform any of them well, particularly under pressure. The Higgs Report's confidence to the contrary is optimistic, to say the least. Furthermore, there is good evidence, addressed shortly, that nothing would be lost by removing the insistence that non-executive directors should participate in management, principally the formation of strategy.

The proposals put forward in this paper can be achieved within the current, very flexible structure of English company law, as will be demonstrated. Statements in the Higgs Report that suggest the contrary are, with respect, unsound as a matter of current English law. To give a clear monitoring role to independent non-executive directors would not mean adopting a German style two-tier board structure, something that, historically, has been anathema in the United Kingdom.[92] Present corporate structures, involving a unitary board, are quite flexible enough

---

[91] This has historically been the purpose of the managers of a commercial company. See above, note 55.

[92] See, for example, the response to consultation reported in CLRSG (2000a: § 2.17).

and are, for other reasons, preferable to the German system.[93] Indeed, for any suggestion to be practically and politically viable in the United Kingdom, it simply must involve a single board: neither business nor the government is willing to accept two-tier boards, as the Higgs Report itself very clearly recognized.[94] In addition, the suggested, more focused role for independent non-executive directors is practical—at the very least, as practical as the proposals of the Higgs Report.

A code will be necessary to ensure that change comes about, whether as proposed by the Higgs Report or as proposed by this chapter. A code will also be necessary to ensure that independent non-executive directors only serve for a limited period, so as to avoid the risk of long-serving independent non-executive directors becoming too close to management, thus impairing, or even subverting, their monitoring role. In fact, the Higgs Report itself makes suggestions to this end.[95] The provisions in such a code should be enforced in the same way as the Old and New Combined Codes: 'comply or explain.' This seems to have been effective so far, without being heavy-handed.[96]

IV. THE SUGGESTED CLEAR AND FOCUSED ROLES FOR NON-EXECUTIVE DIRECTORS

Independent non-executive directors could make a more useful contribution to the control of executive directors' conflicts of interest if monitoring and controlling management were explicitly made their central task. Non-executives are better placed than shareholders to discover other directors' conflicts of interest precisely because they are continuously involved in governing the company concerned, even if they do not run its business. For the same reason, they are better placed to exert control over such conflicts when required, and they do not face the same problems of collective action as shareholders. That is not to say they are a substitute for shareholder power, any more than a nation's constitutional separation of powers is a substitute for its democratic process. Indeed, there are good reasons not to place exclusive or even

---

[93] In short, if the law creates a single board structure for all companies, large and small, but allows sufficient flexibility in that structure, the law can avoid all the problems and complexities that arise from imposing different structures on different sizes of enterprise, problems that become very acute as an enterprise grows.

[94] See Higgs (2003: §§ 1.7, 4.2, 4.3, 14.1).

[95] The Higgs Report proposes that more than ten years' service as a director will raise an inference that the director has ceased to be 'independent,' *ibid.*: § 9.14, and suggested Code provision A.3.4. The New Combined Code (FRC 2003a: § A.3.1.), has reduced the period to nine years. It may be over-optimistic to expect a director's 'independence' to survive as long as nine years' service on a board.

[96] See CLRSG (2000a: § 3.129), and the empirical evidence cited there.

overly strong emphasis on non-executive directors, to the exclusion or marginalization of shareholders: non-executive directors must them-selves be chosen and held to account. There is no reason to expect an improvement in corporate governance if shareholders are expected to write a blank check to non-executive directors rather than executive directors: non-executive directors, if themselves unchecked, are unlikely over time to perform effectively.

There are, of course, practical issues entailed by this suggestion, but as will be seen, it should be possible to manage them adequately. Giving this more limited but more focused role to independent non-executive directors will make it possible to recruit such directors from a larger pool of people, including UK professionals, who are used to working for fees. Before addressing these practicalities at proper length, however, the proposal itself should be explored more fully.

The use of independent non-executive directors to control conflicts of interest within management would also allow the proper separation and performance of the two aspects of a conflicted transaction that have often been elided together. There has been for years a debate about the proper characterization of conflicted transactions: are they really management decisions, to be taken by management, or are they decisions about the enforcement of directors' fiduciary duties, to be taken by shareholders? This debate has often focused on the directors who want to take corporate opportunities or information, but it applies equally to questions of executive pay. The reality is that conflicted transactions raise both questions of management—whether the proposal is a good deal from the company's perspective—and questions of directors' fiduciary duties—whether it is prudent to waive a prohibition on directors' self-interested behavior, human nature being as it is.

The proposed use of independent non-executive directors to control directors' conflicts of interest would allow each aspect of a conflicted transaction to be given proper consideration. Executive directors would consider the merits of the transaction as they see it from the company's perspective, and if they think the transaction should be authorized, they would propose that, making the business case for it as is their job. The independent non-executive directors would then consider the risks of managerial disloyalty inherent in the transaction and confirm it only if they thought the business case for the proposal had been adequately established and outweighed the risks inherent in it. In this way, managerial discretion, limited by a flexible duty of competence, is reserved to those entrusted with management of the company; but the enforcement of the fiduciary duties, which buttress those duties of competence, is located elsewhere in independent arbiters. Admittedly, nothing will abolish the risk that, in a meeting, independent non-executive directors might be overly swayed by executives, though the risk could, if necessary, be mitigated by separate informal meetings of independent non-executive directors.[97] In any event, the risk is surely less than the risks of inappropriate collegial behavior when, as at present, executives vote on other executives' conflicts of interest.[98]

The strictness of directors' fiduciary duties in English law, coupled with a practical, workable gateway procedure for authorizing directors' conflicts of interest, should result in a balanced, effective mechanism for controlling those conflicts. Strict duties coupled with lax authorization procedures are useless: hence the criticisms of the current situation in many companies where the board (other than the director concerned) can authorize a director lawfully to engage in a conflicted transaction. Strict duties with onerous authorization procedures, such as a requirement of shareholder consent, either involve costly compliance with those authorization procedures[99] or else invite attempts to avoid the duty by asserting that there is no conflicted behavior.[100] Neither consequence is desirable. By contrast, strict duties, coupled with an effective and practical authorization procedure, would encourage managers to disclose fully any potential conflicts of interest and seek the requisite consent to act, notwithstanding the conflict. The consequences of a breach of fiduciary obligation, weighed against the practical possibility of obtaining binding consent to an act that would otherwise amount to a breach of duty, would give directors incentives either to comply with their fiduciary obligations or to seek permission to engage in a conflicted transaction, rather than to avoid those obligations. In short, this would increase the efficiency of fiduciary duties as a mechanism for redressing the informational advantage enjoyed by managers of a firm in a situation where their duty and interest conflict [101] and thereby reduce the risk that the managers will deviate from their set tasks.[102]

So far, the focus has been on the role of a company's independent non-executive directors as gatekeepers, authorizing conflicted transactions (or not). There is no reason, however, why their role should be limited to control *ex ante*. It would be quite possible to vest in them the power to enforce directors' duties *ex post*, by giving them the power to cause the company to bring proceedings against directors who have breached their duties. This would mitigate the problems in English law of

[97] The New Combined Code (FRC 2003a: § A.1.3), already adverts to this possibility.
[98] See above, note 41 and accompanying text.
[99] The evidence as regards listed companies is that shareholder authorization is rarely sought, precisely because it is expensive, see Deakin and Hughes (1999: § 5.2).
[100] The author has on various occasions encountered this line of reasoning in professional practice. Overly strict duties may also have undesirable second-order effects, such as directors' premature resignation from office or potential directors' reluctance to serve on a board; See, e.g., Daniels (1994-95); Chapman (1995-96).
[101] See Law Commission (1998: §§ 3.30-3.31).
[102] See above, Part II of this chapter.

enforcing directors' duties, problems noted earlier, without thereby opening the company to a plethora of shareholder actions.[103]

Another advantage of the suggestions made in this chapter is that giving a more closely-defined role to independent non-executive directors would have the corresponding effect of liberating management in its proper sphere of activity. The independent non-executive directors would be powerful within their competence, but their power would only interfere with managers in precisely those circumstances where it is too risky to leave management unconstrained. This division of powers would have several beneficial consequences.

First, it should help to alleviate the concern that the reforms proposed in the Higgs Report will undermine the collegiality and effectiveness of a single managerial board, because it will pit executive directors against non-executive directors, creating tension and hostility.[104] Indeed, there is a risk of this problem precisely because the role envisaged for non-executive directors by the Higgs Report is so wide and could easily trespass on the proper territory of executive management. Clearly defined, separate, but complementary roles for different directors are much less likely to result in 'turf wars' between directors. Of course, there will inevitably be occasions of tension between executive and independent non-executive directors, when each group wants a different result in respect of a transaction that concerns them both: those tensions are inherent in a control mechanism. Nevertheless, a properly-defined and distinct role for each group would at least reduce the number of occasions for such conflict, and its likelihood: while executive directors of a company might properly be concerned by the threat of a 'perpetual rolling audit' of their activities, the control of their conflicts of interest, and possibly also a periodic review of executive directors' performance, should not alarm an executive director who is, by definition, an accountable agent and not a free actor.[105]

Indeed, an agent's resistance to proposals for duly-limited monitoring and control should be a source of concern, not a reason to abandon the proposals. Secondly, distinct roles for executive and independent non-executive directors should make it easier for companies to find and retain effective directors. It is inherently more likely that a company will find an individual who has one set of skills—be they entrepreneurial

---

[103] Compare the practice of using litigation committees in the United States.

[104] See also Higgs (2003: § 6.2).

[105] Following the recommendations of the Higgs Report (2003a: §§ 11.19-11.24), the idea of performance reviews of the board, of board committees, and of individual directors has been incorporated into the New Combined Code (FRC 2003a: § A.6). The possible drawback to entrusting a performance review to independent non-executive directors (rather than just a review of executive directors' conflicts of duty and interest) is the risk that independent non-executive directors will trespass onto the proper domain of management, though that need not necessarily occur.

skills, managerial skills, or monitoring skills—than an individual who has all of them. The mixed role for non-executive directors proposed by the Higgs Report will require non-executive directors to have a very wide set of skills if they are to perform their tasks adequately. By contrast, more focused roles require narrower—but more readily available—sets of skills. So, if the suggestions made in this chapter were adopted, companies would be more easily able to meet another goal of the Higgs Report, namely, the recruitment of non-executive directors from a wider range of backgrounds (2003a: ch. 10).[106] This would, in turn, have another beneficial effect: if independent non-executive directors are recruited from a wider range of backgrounds, they will likely be more effective, because they will correspondingly be less likely still to form a

> closed cadre of directors who sit on each others' boards and enjoy a common culture on matters such as [executive] contracts—a culture not shared by anyone else (*Times* 2003).[107]

Separating the roles of executive and independent non-executive directors should improve corporate governance, but failing to do so is not merely an opportunity cost: A confused role for non-executive directors carries within it inherent risks to good governance. If non-executive directors are to function effectively as part of the management of a company's business, they have to get on with their co-directors: some degree of collegiality is necessary for a board to function. If that it so, it is hard to see how non-executive directors are especially well-placed to resist the temptation of trading their managerial goals against their audit functions: they may well not monitor and control other directors as closely as they could because they wish to secure cooperation from those directors in another business context.[108] This may go some way to explain why non-executive directors so far do not appear to have been very successful in controlling levels of executive pay.[109] None of this is to say that non-executive directors as proposed by the Higgs Report will never

---

[106] See also below, Part VII.

[107] The same point was made more bluntly the very next day: '[B]ecause many chief executives sit on each other's remuneration committees, there is a suspicion of mutual back-scratching' Haskins (2003).

[108] Franks *et al.* (2001: §§ 5.1.2, 5.3.2) argue that the present difficulties faced by UK (rather than US) non-executive directors in holding other directors to account in fact encourages non-executives to focus on their role as business advisors, rather than monitors of management. The proposals in this chapter would address such problems.

[109] The evidence from the United States generally suggests that independent non-executive directors currently tend not to limit executive remuneration. See Core *et al.* (1999); Yermack (1997); Boyd (1994). Drawing non-executive directors from a wider range of backgrounds might well help to improve their performance in this connection: there might be less cultural collusion amongst directors in setting remuneration packages.

be effective in controlling directors' conflicts of interest. It is, rather, to say that there are significant risks in vesting too many functions in a non-executive director.

In summary, while the various roles of the Higgs non-executive director can be complementary, they are not necessarily so[110]; and problems will tax the weak points in any strategy, not its strengths. Furthermore, in a time of significantly-reduced public confidence in corporate governance, there is ever more force in the argument that conflicts must not only be controlled but must be seen to be controlled.[111]

There are other reasons why the Higgs Report envisages a managerial role for non-executive directors: it started from the premise that:

> [n]on-executive directors play a central role in UK corporate governance. The Company Law Review noted 'a growing body of evidence from the United States suggesting that companies with a strong contingent of non-executives produce superior performance' ... From the point of view of UK productivity performance, progressive strengthening of the quality and role of non-executives is strongly desirable.

In fact, the proposals made in this chapter can accommodate these points, if they are correct; but there is good evidence that they are not.

First, there is no reason why a company should not be free to recruit talent in the shape of non-executive directors, who will add value to the company's business, as well as having *independent* non-executive directors to control conflicts of interest. The suggestions in this paper about independent non-executive directors do not preclude the recruitment of other directors (including non-executive directors) for other purposes, though limits on the size of a functional board will constrain such recruitment.[112]

Secondly, it is in fact highly questionable that non-executives directors per se add value to a company's business. A majority of studies do not indicate any relationship between board composition and the firm's performance, as variously defined (Hermalin and Weisbach 1988; Mehran 1995).[113] Several other studies suggest that increasing the representation of independent non-executive directors on the board is actually associated with weaker performance (Yermack 1996; Barnhart and

---

[110] But see Higgs (2003: § 1.12).

[111] Popular opinion is moving alarmingly against the directors of listed companies, *see* Blitz (2003). Politicians have been known to react to popular opinion.

[112] See Higgs (2003: §§ 4.9-4.10); FRC (2003a: Part A.3, Supporting Principles).

[113] Stapledon and Lawrence's Australian study (1999) suggests analogous conclusions. Baysinger and Butler report (1985) that independent non-executive directors may be associated with higher performance, but with an unusually and dubiously long time-lag of ten years.

Rosenstein 1998; Bhagat and Black 1999; 2002).[114] Interestingly, one area in which boards dominated by independent non-executive directors have performed better is in relation to the risk of fraud in financial reporting: the risk of fraudulent accounts seems to diminish (Dechow *et al.* 1996; Beasley 1996).

Furthermore, UK firms with independent boards seem to adopt fewer income-increasing accounting techniques (Peasnell *et al.* 1998), though evidence from the United States is equivocal (Wright 1996). Finally, the findings cited in the Higgs Report are open to a rather more cynical interpretation. There is every reason of self-interest to expect that executive directors will not be delighted at the prospect of greater control. While such a response is in part perfectly legitimate (it has long been recognized that management cannot effectively manage if there is constant interference in its management activities), the need for managerial freedom does not justify a failure to control conflicts of interest. What it does justify is a properly-defined and limited monitoring of such conflicts that does not elide into the inhibition of management.

V. ARE THE SUGGESTED STRUCTURES TECHNICALLY VIABLE?

What is suggested by the Higgs Report is a code, not legislation (2003a: 3). Indeed, at present, there is little evidence of any enthusiasm in the United Kingdom for widespread legislative intervention in the control of directors' conflicts of interest,[115] though that may change if politicians perceive codes to have failed.[116] The question therefore arises: Can the suggestions made in this paper be realized within the present structures of English company law? This is an important question. If they cannot, the suggestions will certainly lie as marginal comment for years yet. There are two aspects to this question.

First, is English company law sufficiently flexible to encompass the allocation of powers suggested by this chapter? The answer is a resounding 'yes.' English company law explicitly proceeds on the basis that the allocation of powers within a company is fundamentally

[114] Klein (1998) finds that the composition of the audit, compensation, and nomination committees (where independent non-executive directors are supposed to be most important) has little impact on performance; however, *insider* representation on investment committees is associated with better performance.

[115] The Department of Trade and Industry currently plans to codify existing directors' duties in statute (see DTI (2002: Pt. II(3))), but that is not a matter that affects the present issues.

[116] In the United Kingdom, the levels and terms of executive pay constitute the one area of continuing, significant public concern about directors' conflicts of duty and interest, notwithstanding the various codes of corporate governance. See above, notes 48, 51, 128 and accompanying text. Consequently, the government is exploring further action to meet such concern. See DTI (2003b).

contractible[117]: formal power vests where those who create the company's constitution choose to put it, save only as mandatory law provides otherwise.[118] No mandatory rule of law precludes the allocation of powers suggested in this chapter; consequently, such allocation could be accomplished by means of appropriate terms in a company's constitution. Alternatively, a company's board could delegate its management powers to the company's executive directors and its monitoring powers (including the control of directors' conflicts of interest, so far as these are presently a matter for the board) to independent non-executive directors, leaving the entire board to review these arrangements periodically.[119] Indeed, a company can already choose to create an ad hoc committee of independent directors to determine the fate of a proposed conflicted transaction; and the author (as counsel) has in fact encountered this practice.

There is another problem, however. Does English law demand a certain, irreducible, minimum degree of activity from directors—involvement in the business of their company—which they could not satisfy if the suggestions made in this chapter were adopted? The Higgs Report (2003: § 4.4) asserts as follows:

> In the UK, the general legal duties owed to the company by executive and non-executive directors are the same. All directors are required to act in the best interests of the company. Each has a role in ensuring the probity of the business and contributing to sustainable wealth creation by the company as a whole.

This is an ambiguous statement. Under English law, all the directors of a company must involve themselves in the management of the company's *affairs*; but it is simply not true that the law requires all directors of a company to be involved in the management (as opposed to review) of the company's *business*. Recent case law in the United Kingdom on directors' duties makes this plain. There is, therefore, no legal bar to adoption of the suggestions put forward by this chapter.

---

[117] Companies Act 1985, §§ 9, 14, 18. There is no evidence that this will change when corporate law in the United Kingdom is reformed and re-enacted as anticipated by DTI (2002). Chapter 1, sub-chapter IV, of the Delaware General Corporation Law is similarly permissive, very largely allowing corporators to allocate power as they think fit, but contrast the rather more proscriptive approach of the ALI's Principles of Corporate Governance: Analysis and Recommendations § 3.02 (Functions and Powers of the Board of Directors)(1994).

[118] See note 48, above and accompanying text.

[119] Indeed, at present a listed company's Audit Committee, Nomination Committee, and Remuneration Committee, being committees of its board, derive their powers from the board by delegation under the company's articles. (All companies' articles permit delegation by the company's board to committees, See, e.g., Table A, note 29, above, Reg 72. This is confirmed by a survey undertaken by the author in another context, see Nolan (2003)).

Nevertheless, given the importance of the point at issue, it is well worth examining the cases carefully, if briefly. In *Re Westmid Packing Services Ltd*,[120] a directors' disqualification case, Lord Woolf M.R. made various important points about a director's duties when delivering the judgment of the Court of Appeal. These can be summarized as follows. First, the collective responsibility of the board of directors of a company of fundamental importance to corporate governance under English company law. Secondly, that *collective* responsibility is based on the *individual* responsibility of each director to keep himself informed of the company's affairs. Thirdly, a proper degree of delegation is permissible, but not total abdication of responsibility. Fourthly, a director must not permit himself to be dominated by a co-director. None of this is at all inconsistent with the suggestions made in this chapter. Non-executive directors may be used to oversee and control directors' conflicts of interest, and they must certainly review and monitor the conduct of the company's business and the rest of its affairs; but non-executive directors do not have to be business managers. So too in *Re Lendhurst Leasing Ltd*,[121] another directors' disqualification case, Hart J accepted that,

> [e]ach individual director owes duties to the company to inform himself about its affairs and to join with his co-directors in supervising and controlling them,

adopting Lord Woolf's approach in *Westmid*.[122] Hart J certainly does not assert that directors are obliged to be business managers: monitors, reviewers, and ultimately controllers, yes; business managers, not necessarily.

The leading English authority on directors' duties of diligence—what they must do for a company, rather than what they must refrain from doing—is now *Re Barings plc (No. 5)*.[123] This is another directors' disqualification case, one that arose out of the spectacular collapse of Barings Bank in 1995. It, too, is consistent with the suggestions made in this chapter. The judge, Jonathan Parker J, started from first principles:

> Directors have, both collectively and individually, a continuing duty to acquire and maintain a sufficient knowledge and understanding of the company's business to enable them properly to discharge their duties as directors.[124]

---

[120] [1998] 2 All ER 124.
[121] [1999] 1 BCLC 286.
[122] [1998] 2 All ER 124, 130.
[123] [1999] 1 BCLC 433, 486–89. The ruling of Jonathan Parker J was upheld by the Court of Appeal, which endorsed those aspects of his judgment it was invited to review, at [2000] 1 BCLC 523, 534–35.
[124] [1999] 1 BCLC 433, 489A.

Consequently,

> Each individual director owes duties to the company to inform himself about its affairs and to join with his co-directors in supervising and controlling them. ... This does not mean, of course, that directors cannot delegate. Subject to the articles of association of the company, a board of directors may delegate specific tasks and functions. Indeed, some degree of delegation is almost always essential if the company's business is to be carried on efficiently: to that extent there is a clear public interest in delegation by those charged with the responsibility for the management of a business.[125]

So directors can delegate specific tasks and functions (how else could a company be run?), but *overall responsibility* is not delegable. Even where there has been delegation and even though the delegate may appear trustworthy and competent, each director still owes the company a duty to take reasonable steps to monitor and control what is going on. The extent of this duty will depend on the facts of each case. Finally, Jonathan Parker adopted and approved the following statement of a director's duty of care and skill set out in the Australian case of *Daniels v Anderson*.[126]

> A person who accepts the office of director of a particular company undertakes the responsibility of ensuring that he or she understands the nature of the duty a director is called upon to perform. That duty will vary according to the size and business of the particular company and the experience or skills that the director held himself or herself out to have in support of appointment to the office. None of this is novel. It turns upon the natural expectations and reliance placed by shareholders on the experience and skill of a particular director. ... The duty includes that of acting collectively to manage the company.[127]

The application of these general standards will depend on the facts of the case, but factors such as the business of the company, the size of the company, the organization of the company, the role assigned to or assumed by the director, and the experience and skills the director has or has held himself out as having will all be relevant in filling out the standard. As well as directors' general duties, which would not stand in the way of the suggestions made in this chapter, there are circumstances where all the directors of a company must act in relation to a proposed transaction.[128] However, these are very often circumstances where a

---

[125] [1999] 1 BCLC 433, 485–86.
[126] [1995] 16 ACSR 607.
[127] *Ibid.* at 668, adopted in [1999] 1 BCLC 433, 488.
[128] One important example is that the all directors of the intended target of a takeover offer must give their views (not necessarily the same views) on the offer: United Kingdom Takeover Code, Rule 25, supplemented by Rule 19.2.

decision involves both commercial aspects, where input from the company's executive directors is vital, and the opportunity for the executive directors to further their own interests at the expense of the company's shareholders, where independent non-executive directors should target their input. In other words, these circumstances require participation by all directors precisely where this chapter would suggest it, and they do not, therefore, constitute a reason for rejecting the proposals in this chapter on the grounds of impracticability. Indeed, circumstances where all directors must act in relation to a transaction are relatively very uncommon and, as such, should not dictate the form of basic corporate structures: If need be, independent non-executive directors could, exceptionally, participate in a management decision if the law demanded it, without undermining the benefits that would flow from focusing their attention on monitoring executive directors. Corporate law has never been a matter of complete ideological purity.

In summary, the Higgs Report is correct to point out that '[i]n the unitary board structure, executive and non-executive directors share *responsibility* for both the direction and control of the company' (2003: § 4.2) [emphasis added]; but that certainly does not imply, as the Higgs Reportt (2003: § 6.6) suggests, that:

> [t]he role of the non-executive director is therefore both to support executives in their leadership of the business and to monitor and supervise their conduct.[129]

There is a clear distinction to be drawn between responsibility for a company and a role-setting strategy for a company: the one, which is required by law, does not necessarily entail the other. Unfortunately, the Higgs Report blurs this important legal and practical distinction. It is, in other words, quite possible to give effect to the suggestions in this chapter without modification of the English law of directors' duties. Indeed, legislation to alter directors' duties, and formally to partition the roles and responsibilities of various types of director, would introduce quite undesirable structural rigidities into English law: a particular pattern of governance introduced by legislation may very well not exactly suit all companies within the scope of the relevant statute.[130] A code such as that proposed by the Higgs Report, based on principles of 'comply or explain,' leaves the flexibility to cope with the non-standard case. That is not to say the 'comply or explain' is perfect: there is still the risk that investors will not read and give due consideration to the explanations of those who do

---

[129] See also suggested Code Provision A.1.4 in Annex A to the Report, *ibid.*, implemented in substance by FRC (2003a: § A.1).

[130] For a consideration of the relative merits and suitability of the various techniques of regulating companies, see Ferran (2001).

not comply and that this will therefore encourage a 'box-ticking,' mechanistic approach to compliance.[131] Nevertheless, imperfect as it may be, 'comply or explain' at least allows the possibility of flexibility: it does not lock practice into a particular path in anything like the same firm way as mandatory statute law. This flexibility also allows the principles of a code to be drafted in comprehensible, relatively broad language: a code does not need to draw extremely sharp distinctions or to stipulate for every contingency. Consequently, as investors can readily understand such a code, it gives them comfort and confidence. By contrast, traditional, mandatory statute law is implemented in a much stricter fashion and must be drafted tightly with that in mind. None of this prevents a code having statutory force, however: indeed, both the Old and New Combined Codes already have the backing of statute.[132]

Finally, codes allow satisfactorily for the evolution of corporate structures in response to market practices and concerns: if some term of a code is proven to be inappropriate or inadequate, it can be changed without great difficulty. This has been demonstrated in the development of codes from the Cadbury Report to the New Combined Code.[133] By contrast, statute law changes but slowly, at least at present.[134] This distinction might become less important, however, if new institutional arrangements allowed for swifter development and revision of the statute law that governs companies.[135]

VI. ARE THE SUGGESTED STRUCTURES PRACTICAL?

The proposals made in this chapter are, therefore, technically viable. The next question is whether they are practical. In particular, there are three significant questions: who will be these independent non-executive directors, how will they be appointed, and what will motivate them to undertake their tasks?

---

[131] One frequently repeated criticism is that 'comply or explain in practice means comply or else face the same tedious questions every time, until it's not worth the hassle' (*Daily Telegraph* 2003). This criticism is rejected by the Higgs Report (2003: § 1.19). Indeed, if investors keep on asking the same question until there is compliance, that could be taken as evidence that the Code is being implemented efficiently, just as much as evidence that the terms of the Code are inappropriate.

[132] See note 21, above and accompanying text.

[133] See text accompanying note 6, above.

[134] The current Company Law Review process in the United Kingdom is regarded as the most fundamental review of the country's corporate law since 1862. See the speech delivered at Cambridge University of the minister responsible for corporate law reform in the United Kingdom, the Rt. Hon. Patricia Hewitt (2002). Even the review process is itself now progressing more slowly than originally anticipated; see the government's announcement in Press Release, U.K. Government, New Companies Legislation (10 July 2003), available at http://www.dti.gov.uk/companiesbill/index.htm.

[135] See generally Ferran (2001).

The first question is by far the easiest. The Higgs Report itself addressed this question, recommending that more care be given to the selection of non-executive directors and that they be drawn from a wider pool of talent (Higgs 2003: § 10.15–10.343). The pool could easily extend to include professionals who, while they may not be used to running a business, are nevertheless highly alert to conflicts of interest and used to judging and controlling them, Arthur Andersen notwithstanding (Higgs 2003: § 10.29); and there are plenty of suitably-qualified professionals in London (and the United Kingdom at large) who could act as independent non-executive directors.[136] Indeed, the suggestions made in this chapter, that independent non-executive directors should have a focused role, controlling directors' conflicts of interest, should actually make it easier to find the necessary talent. It is inherently more likely that a company will find an individual who has monitoring skills than an individual who has entrepreneurial skills, managerial skills, *and* monitoring skills.[137]

What, then, of the mechanisms for appointing non-executive directors? The Higgs Report is right to ensure independence in the process of appointing non-executive directors, recommending that:

> [a]ll listed companies should have a nomination committee which should lead the process for board appointments and make recommendations to the board. ... The nomination committee should consist of a majority of independent non-executive directors (2003: § 10.9).[138]

The board, acting on the recommendations of the nomination committee, would then ensure that, in due course, names of non-executive directors were put to a vote of shareholders.

Setting the necessary incentives so that independent non-executive directors are likely to perform their monitoring task efficiently is a much more difficult matter. The Higgs Report essentially envisages fees for non-executive directors, rather than any more sophisticated form of remuneration,[139]

---

[136] London, for example, has a huge professional service sector, one of the largest in the world; see the empirical evidence at http://www.cityoflondon.gov.uk/business_city/research_statistics/pdf/lonny/chapter6london.pdf (last visited 30 Sept. 2003).

[137] See text at note 131, above.

[138] The further recommendation, that the nomination committee 'may include the chairman of the board, but should be chaired by an independent non-executive director,' was not adopted, following fierce criticism from company chairmen. Illustrative criticism is reported in the Business Opinion section of *The Times*, Cole (2003). Confirmation that the recommendation was deliberately not adopted as part of the New Combined Code is at http://www.frc.org.uk/publications/publication419.html (last visited 30 Sept. 2003).

[139] See generally Higgs (2003: §§ 12.20–12.30). A similar position has been taken in Australia, see ASX (2003: Principle 9.3).

recommending that non-executive directors' fees should be more clearly built up from an annual fee, meeting attendance fees (to include board committee meetings) and an additional fee for the chairmanship of committees (typically a multiple of the attendance fee) or role as senior independent director. The level of remuneration for non-executive directors should be a matter for the chairman and the executive directors of the board.

In addition, companies should expect to pay additional, reasonable expenses in addition to the director's fee to cover related costs incurred by their non-executive directors (such as travel and administrative costs). Any significant support of this kind should be agreed in advance (Higgs 2003: §§12.24–12.25).

In addition, the Report recommends that non-executive directors be permitted to take shares in the company concerned, in lieu of a cash fee, but that non-executive directors should not hold options over the company's shares. Fees are hardly novel; but they are an appropriate mechanism for remunerating someone whose function is not primarily entrepreneurial.[140]

If an independent non-executive director is put in office to undertake certain specific, limited tasks, his role is much more like that of a professional advisor than an entrepreneur. Professionals in the United Kingdom are used to working for fees, and this has not stopped London from becoming one of the world's leading centers for professional services. Indeed, the use of professionals as non-executive directors has another benefit: they can be both motivated and controlled by the effect of good or bad performance in a given task on their respective professional reputations. Indeed, reputation, for a professional in a highly competitive market like London, is vital to economic survival.

By contrast, the recommendations of the Higgs Report, which envisage some sort of management role for non-executive directors, will surely

---

[140] It has been suggested that investors should both seek to appoint and meet the fees of non-executive directors who look after investors' interests, possibly individually, possibly collectively. See Gilson and Kraakman (1991). For the moment, there is no prospect of investors, particularly institutional investors, shouldering that burden directly in the United Kingdom. Even if there were, such remuneration would have to be structured very carefully to avoid the risk of non-executive directors being captured by the large, institutional investors who would meet all, or a very substantial portion of, their fees. Quite aside from any unwillingness to meet the costs of non-executive directors, there are at least two reasons in the United Kingdom why institutional investors might not want to appoint and meet the costs of non-executive directors. First, there is a risk that they could become shadow directors under the Companies Act 1985, though this risk could be adequately managed. Secondly, and more importantly, they could easily come into possession of unpublished price-sensitive information relating to a company through a director whom they had appointed to its board, with the consequence that they would be debarred *pro tempore* from trading in its securities under one or both of the insider trading regime (see Part V of the Criminal Justice Act 1993, imposing criminal sanctions) and the market abuse regime (see Part VIII of the Financial Services and Markets Act 2000, imposing administrative penalties).

face greater problems in setting the correct incentives for non-executive directors to act (at least in part) as entrepreneurial management. Why should non-executive directors who act in an entrepreneurial capacity be willing to accept rewards so very different in quality, and not just quantity, from those of executive directors? In short, there is no getting away from the problems of incentives, but the suggestions made in this chapter, to create a clear, focused role for independent non-executive directors, ameliorate the problem, if not resolving it entirely. By contrast, the recommendations of the Higgs Report regarding the remuneration of non-executive directors run directly into problems generated by the mixed role for those directors that the Report so advocates.

Aside from these problems, there is still one aspect of the recommendations in the Higgs Report that is truly worrying. This is the suggestion that executive directors should set the pay of non-executive directors. There are real risks in creating a situation where those who are controlled by non-executive directors in turn, through remuneration, control those very non-executives. (There is a clear analogy to be drawn with the position of auditors who, in substance, if not in form, were appointed by management to check on management[141]; and it need hardly be said where such a system can lead.) Instead, the non-executive directors themselves could propose their fees, subject to approval by shareholders. Though shareholder approval is a cumbersome process, this item of business, being recurrent and predictable, could easily be undertaken at an annual general meeting.[142]

VII. IMPLEMENTATION—DO WE NEED A CODE?

This chapter has already expressed a preference for a code, rather than legislation, as the means through which its suggestions might be implemented.[143] Yet is has so far assumed that there is a need for some degree of regulation to ensure the use, and proper use, of independent non-executive directors as it suggests. The actual justification for such

---

[141] See Companies Act 1985, Part XI, ch. V: auditors are appointed by a shareholders' resolution (other than auditors appointed to fill temporarily a casual vacancy); but directors propose the resolution to the shareholders. The New Combined Code (FRC 2003: § C.3.2), seeks to mitigate this risk by prescribing that a company's Audit Committee should recommend the appointment of the company's auditors and review their retainer, following the recommendations of Smith *et al.* (2003). See also Higgs (2003: §§ 13.4–13.7). In Singapore it is now proposed to require by law (not just by a code) that a listed company have an audit committee, comprising a majority of independent non-executive directors, and to give the committee power to nominate the company's auditors. See Companies (Amendment No. 2) Act 2003 (Sing.), available at http://www.mof.gov.sg/cor/doc/DraftCosBill 2003-PublicCons.doc.

[142] See text at n 61, above.

[143] See text at n 130, above.

intervention in companies lies in the processes through which their corporate governance structures are created.

The distribution of competences within an English company is achieved essentially by two mechanisms: the terms of the company's constitution, which are adopted by shareholders and operate as a binding agreement between them,[144] and delegation of functions pursuant to the constitution.[145] Both of these raise problems for shareholders, however.

The formation of the company's constitution is not an efficient process from the perspective of shareholders in a widely-held company. Though in legal form, shareholders contract for what they want in a company, the reality is that the company's directors employ lawyers to draft the constitution (and subsequent amendments to, or replacements of, it) in terms that reflect what the directors want, tempered by their good faith to shareholders and, in some cases, by their appreciation of what the shareholders will accept. Given recent resistance to the Higgs Report from many boardrooms,[146] it is very unlikely that proposals to implement the Report, still less any more radical suggestions, would come from the boards of many leading companies. Some degree of compulsion, however gentle, is clearly needed to redress inefficiencies in the process of contracting for corporate constitutions. Directors who are well intentioned may choose to implement proposals without compulsion; but those who wish to resist proposals emanating from shareholders, or from those who campaign for the investor interest in companies, are well placed to do so. For reasons mentioned earlier,[147] a code (enforced on the basis of 'comply or explain') has much to recommend it as the appropriate means of enforcement in the present context.

The other mechanism through which powers are distributed within a company is delegation by those with power—normally the board—in accordance with the company's constitution. This mechanism of distributing power within a company is also problematic from the perspective of shareholders who wish to ensure good corporate governance. Such delegation is an executive act; and as such, it is very difficult indeed for shareholders to direct or control it. Again, some degree of compulsion is necessary to redress an imbalance of power. Indeed, that is what has happened so far: both the Old Combined Code and the New Combined Code ordain that certain powers of a listed company's board should be delegated to, for example, the company's

---

[144] See Companies Act 1985, §§ 9, 14, 18.
[145] See, e.g., Regs 71 and 72 of Table A, above note 29, terms that are adopted in substance, if not in exact form, by all companies, as confirmed by the author's survey detailed in Nolan (2003).
[146] See, e.g., Cole (2003).
[147] See note 121, above and accompanying text.

Audit Committee, its Nomination Committee, and its Remuneration Committee.[148]

VIII. THE INTERACTION OF SUGGESTIONS MADE IN THIS CHAPTER AND OTHER APPROACHES TO THE CONTROL OF CONFLICTS OF INTEREST

The suggestions made in this chapter crucially involve the use of independent non-executive directors. There are, however, other significant approaches to managing directors' potential conflicts of interest. For the present, at least, these other approaches would not form an adequate substitute for independent non-executive directors, properly utilized. Nevertheless, they could be tested in companies that do make appropriate use of independent non-executive directors, to establish whether they would constitute a useful adjunct to independent non-executive directors or even, in due course, a substitute for them. The main means of controlling or constraining directors' conflicts of interest that are of relevance here are compensation packages for directors who seek to align their interests with those of shareholders, the market for corporate control, and the use of 'invested directors' as self-interested guardians of the company's interests. Each has its problems. In reality, executive compensation packages are the product of one-sided bargaining arrangements that favor management,[149] and public faith in such arrangements is low.[150] The disciplinary effect on managers of the market for corporate control is equivocal.[151] Any attempt to align managers' and owners' interests by ensuring that a company's directors are also shareholders in it faces difficulties when applied to widely-held, listed companies. Admittedly, a private equity house that holds a large stake in a firm may nominate directors of the firm whose personal interests are closely aligned to the firm's interests.[152] Nevertheless, the director of a listed company will very rarely hold a significant stake in the company, and when faced with a conflict of interest and duty, the benefit to that director from self-interested action may well exceed the return she will see as an investor in the firm if duty were done.

---

[148] See notes 85–87, above and accompanying text.
[149] See especially Bebchuk *et al.* (2002).
[150] See note 107, above and accompanying text.
[151] See Franks *et al.* (2001).
[152] There has recently been a strong call in the United Kingdom for institutional investors to take a greater role in the oversight of companies. See Myners (2001) and the subsequent trenchant comment of the author of that report, Paul Myners (2003), Travers Smith Braithwaite Lecture, delivered at University of Cambridge's Centre for Corporate and Commercial Law, 7 May 2003.

Crucially, however, these problems are not the real issue for present purposes.[153] The point is, rather, that investors—particularly institutional investors—at present require independent non-executive directors to safeguard shareholders' interests: investors do not seem presently to have enough confidence in other means of managing directors' conflicts of interest. That is not to say that these other means of controlling directors' conflicts of interest are irrelevant or unsuitable: the use of independent non-executive directors does not preclude a market for corporate control, nor properly-structured executive compensation packages, nor other directors with different motivations, such as investor-directors. Indeed, proper use of independent non-executive directors can maintain—or even increase—confidence whilst other methods of controlling directors' conflicts of interest gather support, or not. If, in due course, independent non-executive directors are no longer needed, so be it: it is hardly news that solutions to the problems of corporate governance are context- and time-specific.

CONCLUSIONS

To date, non-executive directors appear to have a mixed record as monitors: they generally appear to be a useful mechanism for securing honest financial reporting, but they have not done much, if anything, to control levels of executive pay. However, contrary to the assertions of the Higgs Report, they do not appear to add much, if anything, to a company's economic performance. So long as the role of non-executive directors remains mixed and unfocused, there is no reason to believe this will change. Even if more and better people are recruited to be non-executive directors, as envisioned by the Higgs Report, a confusion of roles will still make it difficult for them to be effective. The Higgs Report represents a lost opportunity to revise and clarify what non-executive directors are expected to do.

The central concern of this chapter is to devise the best strategy for the use of independent non-executive directors in the governance of English companies. Independent non-executive directors should act essentially as monitors within a company, controlling whatever possible conflicts of duty and interest the company's executive directors may have and monitoring the company's performance and systems. Any other non-executive directors of a company should be free to play whatever role—in business development or otherwise—that the company sees fit.

---

[153] See, for example, the policies of activist fund-managers such as Morley and Hermes, available, respectively, at http://www.morleyfm.com/cgov.pdf and www.hermes.co.uk/corporate-governance/PDFs/International_Governance_Principles.pdf (both last visited 30 Sept. 2003).

Such a focused role for independent non-executive directors is quite feasible and, it is suggested, useful as part of a strategy to control directors' conflicts of interest.

The basic flexible structures of English company law are well suited to accommodate the proposals made in this chapter. Indeed, it is to be hoped that the Company Law Review retains the basic flexibility of UK corporate structures, precisely because it is so useful in accommodating the very different circumstances and objectives of different enterprises, though the technical detail of those structures might usefully be clarified. Other aspects of the law, such as that relating to shareholder actions, might very usefully be reformed, however.

Codes of corporate governance (whether backed by statutory powers or not) are an appropriate mechanism through which the reforms suggested in this chapter can be achieved. Codes are much preferable to 'traditional' forms of legislation: codes can respond to events and experience much more easily than such legislation, maintaining their objectives and thereby retaining their legitimacy, while evolving their techniques of implementation. The Higgs Report has much to commend it, but its treatment of non-executive directors is flawed. Nevertheless, the Report's recommendations have largely been implemented, with only relatively few amendments, none of which addresses the concerns of this chapter. If, in the coming years, it transpires that the concerns raised in this chapter are well founded, the Financial Reporting Council and the UKLA should act swiftly to amend the New Combined Code. Otherwise, the chances are that political pressure will build for legislative intervention, whatever the economic drawbacks of such action: politicians, who control Parliament, do not respond solely to the dictates of long-term economic rationality.

REFERENCES

ALI (1994), *ALI's Principles of Corporate Governance: Analysis and Recommendations.*

Arden, M.H. *et al.* eds. (1998), *Buckley on the Companies Acts* (15th ed.).

ASX (2003), Australian Stock Exchange, Corporate Governance Council, Principles of Good Corporate Governance and Best Practice Recommendations, available at http://www.shareholder.com/shared/dynamicdoc/ASX/364/ASXRecommendations.pdf.

Barnhart, S.W. and Rosenstein, S. (1998), 'Board Composition, Managerial Ownership and Firm Performance: An Empirical Analysis', 33 *Financial Review* 1.

Baysinger, B.D. and Butler, H.N. (1985), 'Corporate Governance and the Board of Directors: Performance Effects of Changes in Board Composition', 1 *Journal of Law, Economics and Organization* 101.

Beasley, M.S. (1996), 'An Empirical Analysis of the Relation Between the Board of Director Composition and Financial Statement Fraud', 71 *Accounting Review* 443.

Bebchuk, L.A. *et al.* (2002), Managerial Power and Rent Extraction in the Design of Executive Compensation, 69 *University of Chicago Law Review* 69.

Bhagat, S. and Black, B.S. (1999), 'The Uncertain Relationship Between Board Composition and Firm Performance', 54 *Business Lawyer* 921.

—— (2002), 'The Non-Correlation between Board Independence and Long-term Firm Performance', 27 *Journal of Corporation Law* 231.

Black, B.S. (1990), 'Shareholder Passivity Reexamined', 89 *Michigan Law Review* 520.

— (1998), 'Shareholder Activism and Corporate Governance in the United States', in 3 *The New Palgrave Dictionary of Economics and the Law* 459 (Peter Newman ed.) (New York: Palgrave).

Blitz, R. (2003), 'UK Survey Shows Wide Distrust of Directors', *Financial Times*, 30 June 2003, at 1.

Boyd, B.K. (1994), 'Board Control and CEO Compensation', 15 *Strategic Management Journal* 335.

Brudney, V. (1985), 'Corporate Governance, Agency Costs, and the Rhetoric of Contract', 85 *V* 1403.

—— (1997), 'Contract and Fiduciary Duty in Corporate Law', 38 *Boston College Law Review* 595.

Cadbury, A. *et al.* (1992), Report on the Financial Aspects of Corporate Governance available at http://www.ecgi.org/codes/country_documents/uk/cadbury.pdf.

Cambridge University ESRC Centre for Business Research (2000), Economic Effects of Criminal and Civil Sanctions in the Context of Company Law, *at* http://www.dti.gov.uk/cld/deakin_z.pdf.

Campbell, R.B. (1996), 'A Positive Analysis of the Common Law of Corporate Fiduciary Duties', 84 *Kentucky Law Journal* 455.

Chancellor of the Exchequer's Budget Speech of 7 March 2001, available at http://www.hm-treasury.gov.uk/budget/budget_2001/bud_bud01_speech.cfm.

Chapman, B. (1995–96), 'Corporate Stakeholders, Choice Procedures and Committees', 26 *Canadian Business Law Journal* 211.

Cheffins, B.R. (1991), Law, Economics and Morality: Contracting Out of Corporate Law Duties, 19 *Canadian Business Law Journal* 28.

Cheffins B.R. and Thomas, R.S. (2001), Should Shareholders Have a Greater Say over Executive Pay? Learning from the US Experience, 1 *Journal of Corporate Law Studies* 277.

Cole, R. (2003), 'Welcome Response to Higgs Critics', *The Times*, May 10, 2003, at 51.

CLRSG (Company Law Review Steering Group) (1999), *Modern Company Law for a Competitive Economy: The Strategic Framework* (London: DTI).

—— (Company Law Review Steering Group) (2000a), *Modern Company Law for a Competitive Economy: Developing the Framework* (London: DTI).

—— (Company Law Review Steering Group) (2000b), *Modern Company Law for a Competitive Economy: Completing the Structure* (London: DTI).

—— (Company Law Review Steering Group) (2002), *Modern Company Law for a Competitive Economy: Final Report* (London: DTI).

Cooter, R. and Freedman, B.J. (1991), 'The Fiduciary Relationship: Its Economic Character and Legal Consequences', 66 *New York University Law Review* 1045.

Core, J.E. et al. (1999), 'Corporate Governance, CEO Compensation, and Firm Performance', 51 *Journal of Financial Economics* 143.

Daily Telegraph (2003), 'Where Higgs Would Be Truly on the Money', 15 May.

Daniels, R.J. (1994–95), 'Must Boards Go Overboard? An Economic Analysis of the Effects of Burgeoning Statutory Liability on the Role of Directors in Corporate Governance', 24 *Canadian Business Law Journal* 229.

Deakin, S. and Hughes, A. (1999), Directors' Duties: Empirical Findings—Report to the Law Commissions, available at, http://www.lawcom.gov.uk/files/study.pdf.

Dechow, P.M. *et al.* (1996), 'Causes and Consequences of Earnings Manipulation: An Analysis of Firms Subject to Enforcement Actions by the SEC', 13 *Contemporary Accounting Research* 1.

DeMott, D.A. (1999), 'The Figure in the Landscape: A Comparative Sketch of Directors' Self-Interested Transactions', 3 *Company Fin. & Insolvency L. Rev.* 190.

DTI (2002), *Modernising Company Law* (London: DTI).

—— (2003a), Department of Trade & Industry, Companies in 2002–2003, available at http://www.dti.gov.uk/cld/dtiannualreport.pdf.

—— (2003b), Department of Trade & Industry, Rewards for Failure: Directors' Remuneration—Contracts, Performance and Severance, available at http://www.dti.gov.uk/cld/4864rewards.pdf.

Ferran, E.V. (2001), 'Corporate Law, Codes and Social Norms—Finding the Right Regulatory Combination and Institutional Structure', 1 *Journal of Corporate Law Studies* 381.

Finn, P.D. (1989), 'The Fiduciary Principle', in *Equity, Fiduciaries and Trusts* 1, 46 (Timothy G. Youdan ed.) (Toronto: The Law Book Company).

Franks, J. *et al.* (2001), Who Disciplines Management in Poorly Performing Companies? (Centre for Economic Policy Research Discussion Paper 2949) available at http://www.cepr.org/pubs/new-dps/dplist.asp?dpno=2949.

FRC (2003a), Financial Reporting Council, Combined Code on Corporate Governance, available at http://www.frc.org.uk/documents/pdf/combinedcodefinal.pdf.

—— (2003b), press release at http://www.frc.org.uk/publications/publication419.html (last visited 2 August 2005).

—— (2003c), Financial Reporting Council's statements at http://www.frc.org.uk/publications/publication415.html (last visited 2 August 2005).

—— (2003d), Statement and http://www.frc.org.uk/summary.html (last visited 2 August 2005).

Gilson, R.J. and Kraakman, R. (1991), 'Reinventing the Outside Director: An Agenda for Institutional Investors', 43 *Stanford Law Review* 863.

Greenbury, R. *et al.* (1995), Directors' Remuneration: Report of a Study Group chaired by Sir Richard Greenbury available at http://www.ecgi.org/codes/country_documents/uk/greenbury.pdf.

Greene *et al.* (1926), The Report of the Company Law Amendment Committee 1925–26, §§ 46–47 available at http://www.takeovers.gov.au/Content/ Resources/CASES/CompanyLawAmendment.asp.

GSX (2003a), Glaxosmithkline plc AGM Poll Results, 19 May, available at http://www.gsk.com/financial/AGM_Poll_Results_2003.pdf.

—— (2003b), Glaxosmithkline plc Press Release, 19 May, available at http://www.gsk.com/media/pressreleases.htm.

Hampel, R. *et al.* (1998), Report of the Hampel Committee available at http://www.ecgi.org/codes/ country_documents/uk/hampel_index.htm.

Haskins, C. (2003), 'Investors Need Help to Tackle Corporate Greed', *Financial Times*, 21 May.

Hermalin, B.E. and Weisbach, M.S. (1988), 'The Determinants of Board Composition', 19 *Rand Journal of Economics* 589.

Hewitt, P. (2002), Secretary of State for Trade and Industry, Keynote Speech to the Cambridge Faculty of Law (5 July), available at http://www.law.cam.ac.uk/ cccl/Keynote_speech.pdf.

Higgs, D. *et al.* (2003), *Review of the Role and Effectiveness of Non-Executive Directors* (London: DTI).

Jones, G.H. (1968), 'Unjust Enrichment and the Fiduciary's Duty of Loyalty', 84 *Law Quarterly Review* 472.

Kaplan, S.N. (1994a), 'Top Executive Rewards and Firm Performance: A Comparison of Japan and the US', 102 *Journal of Political Economy* 510.

—— (1994b), 'Top Executives, Turnover and Firm Performance in Germany', 10 *Journal of Law, Economics and Organization* 142.

Karpoff, J.M. *et al.* (1996), 'Corporate Governance and Shareholder Initiatives: Empirical Evidence', 42 *Journal of Financial Economics* 365.

Klein, A. (1998), 'Firm Performance and Board Committee Structure', 41 *Journal of Law, Economics and Organization* 275.

Law Commission (1996), Consultation paper. Shareholder Remedies, available at, http://www.lawcom.gov.uk/files/cp152.pdf.

—— (1998), Consultation paper Company Directors: Regulating Conflicts of Interests and Formulating a Statement of Duties, available at http:// www.lawcom.gov.uk/files/cp153.pdf.

Mehran, H. (1995), 'Executive Compensation Structure, Ownership and Firm Performance', 38 *Journal of Financial Economics* 163.

Myners, P. (2003), Travers Smith Braithwaite Lecture, delivered at University of Cambridge's Centre for Corporate and Commercial Law, 7 May, available at http://law.cam.ac.uk/cccl/Paul_Myners_Speech.doc.

Myners, P. *et al.* (2001), *Institutional Investment in the UK: A Review* (London: HM Treasury).

Nolan, R.C. (1997), 'A Fiduciary Duty to Disclose?', 113 *Law Quarterly Review* 220.

—— (2003), Indirect Investors: A Greater Say in the Company?, 3 *Journal of Corporate Law Studies. 73.*

Nolan, R.C. and Prentice, D.D. (2002), 'The Issue of Shares—Compensating the Company For Loss', 118 *Law Quarterly Review* 180.

Peasnell, K.V. *et al.* (1998), Outside Directors, Board Effectiveness and Earnings Management (Working Paper), available at http://papers.ssrn.com/ paper.taf?abstract_id=125348.

Rider, B.A.K. (1993), *Insider Crime: The New Law* (Bristol: Jordans).

Roe, M.J. (1994), *Strong Managers, Weak Owners: The Political Roots of American Corporate Finance* (Princeton: Princeton University Press).

Rogerson, P.J. (1997), 'Modification and Exclusion of Directors' Duties', in *The Realm of Company Law* 93 (Barry A.K. Rider ed.) (The Hague: Kluwer Law International).

Romano, R. (2001), 'Less Is More: Making Institutional Investor Activism a Valuable Mechanism of Corporate Governance', 18 *Yale Journal of Regulation* 174.

Sealy, L.S. (1987), 'Problems of Standing, Pleading and Proof in Corporate Litigation', in *Company Law in Change* 1, 1 (Ben G. Pettet ed.) (London: Butterworths).

Smith, R. *et al.* (2003), Audit Committees: Combined Code Guidance, available at http://www.ecgi.org/codes/country_documents/UK/ac_report.pdf.

Stapledon, G. (1996), *Institutional Shareholders and Corporate Governance* (Oxford: Oxford University Press).

Stapledon, G. and Lawrence, J.J. (1999), 'Do Independent Directors Add Value?' (Working Paper, Univ. of Melbourne) (on file with author).

The Times (2003), 'Blame the Board for GSK Fiasco', *The Times*, 20 May, at 23.

The UK Listing Authority, Combined Code on Corporate Governance (2000) an Appendix to the United Kingdom Listing Rules.

UK Government (2003), Press Release: New Companies Legislation (10 July), available at http://www.dti.gov.uk/companiesbill/index.htm.

Walters, A. and Davis-White, M. (2005), *Directors' Disqualification & Bankruptcy Restrictions* (London: Sweet and Maxwell).

Wright, D.W. (1996), Evidence on the Relation between Corporate Governance Characteristics and the Quality of Financial Reporting (Working Paper), available at http://papers.ssrn.com/sol3/papers.cfm?abstract_id=10138.

Yermack, D. (1996), 'Good Timing: CEO Stock Option Awards and Company News Announcements', 40 *Journal of Financial Economics* 185.

—— (1997), 'Good Timing: CEO Stock Option Awards and Company News Announcements', 52 *Journal of Finance* 449.

Part IV
Reforming EU Company Law and Securities Regulation

12

Enron and Corporate Governance Reform in the UK and the European Community

PAUL DAVIES[*]

W HY WERE THERE European responses? The collapse of Enron and of a number of other companies[1] in the United States over the period between late 2001 and the middle of 2002 has had a striking impact on the process of corporate law reform. That these events should have had an impact in the United States itself, notably in the shape of the enactment of the Sarbanes-Oxley Act of 2002[2] and the reforms of the rules of the New York Stock Exchange and the NASDAQ, is not surprising, though the speed of the reaction and its location at the federal level rather than with the states, which have traditionally carried the main burden of corporate law legislation, are notable aspects of the US reforms (Chandler and Strine 2003).[3] However, the reach of Enron in terms of its impetus to corporate law reform has extended beyond the borders of the United States, and this chapter explores the European impact, notably in the United Kingdom and at the level of the European Community.

A visitor to the company law website of the Department of Trade and Industry (DTI),[4] the department of the British government with responsibility for the state of domestic company law, would in early 2005 see 'Post-Enron initiatives' listed in red as one of nine main areas with

---

[*] Cassel Professor of Commercial Law at the London School of Economics.

[1] Notably WorldCom, Global Crossing, Tyco. Unfairly, but inevitably, the name 'Enron' has become a shorthand to refer to all these US corporate collapses and will be so used, where the context requires, in this chapter.

[2] Public Company Accounting Reform and Investor Protection Act of 2002, 15 U.S.C. § 7201 *et seq.*

[3] It is no accident that the authors of this article are respectively Chancellor and Vice-Chancellor of the Delaware Court of Chancery.

[4] The DTI website is located at, http://www.dti.gov.uk/cld/ (last visited 2 Aug. 2005).

which the department is and has recently been concerned and two further areas[5] are either wholly or mainly concerned with this topic. These initiatives produced a number of significant reports dealing with the regulation of audits and auditors, audit committees and the role of non-executive directors,[6] and, just as significant, the inquiries which led to the reports were put in train by the Secretary of State at the Department (Patricia Hewitt) in February 2002, i.e., very soon after the Enron collapse and well before the full extent of the problems in the United States had become clear.

The British reaction was by no means an isolated one. An equally speedy and wide-ranging response can be seen on the part of the European Commission. As early as April 2002, in the Commission's note for the informal Ecofin Council meeting held in Oviedo and entitled 'A first EU Response to Enron related policy issues' (European Commission 2002a), one finds not only auditors and auditing, but also board structure and composition, executive remuneration, reporting by financial analysts and the operation of credit-rating agencies identified as matters of concern. This note and the Council's decision on it led, amongst many other things, to an expansion of the remit of the High Level Group of company law experts so as to embrace additional corporate governance issues, including the role of non-executive directors and supervisory boards, management remuneration and the responsibility of management for financial statements. The report of that Group (High Level Group 2002) dealt with these matters as, in turn, did the Commission's response to the High Level Group's report in its company law Communication of 2003 (European Commission 2003a). However, the Commission's response to Enron was by no means channelled wholly through the High Level Group. As we shall see, an equally, if not more, important part of the Commission's response lay in the area of accounting and auditing, where the Commission was already active on its own part. Its post-Enron reflections in that area were encapsulated in its Communication on the statutory audit (European Commission 2003b), published at the same time as the company law Communication.

Responses to Enron from Member States other than the United Kingdom can also be found.[7] Should we be surprised at the speed and scope of the response in Europe? In one respect it is certainly surprising. Although an immensely newsworthy scandal, the collapse of Enron had

---

[5] 'Review of Non-executive Directors', which is intimately linked to the initiatives specifically labelled as 'Post-Enron', and the 'Companies (Audit, Investigations, and Community Enterprise) Act 2004', one of the main purposes of that Act being to make the legal changes necessary to implement the recommendations resulting from the 'Post-Enron' initiatives.

[6] For an initial analysis see Davies (2004: 185).

[7] For example, in France Loi n° 2003-706 du 1er août 2003 du sécurité financière, Journal officiel de la République française du 2 août 2003, p. 13220.

relatively little economic impact outside the United States. The European assets of Enron (and the other US companies) passed into new hands with very little economic disruption. If one thinks of job losses, slimming down by continuing US corporations, such as the car-makers Ford and GM, has had a much bigger impact over the past two years on jobs in Europe than the collapse of Enron.[8] Nor, at the time that these early British and Community initiatives were launched had there occurred any European equivalents to Enron. It seems to have been the case that fear on the part of governments of other countries that similar events could occur in their jurisdictions was sufficient to drive law reform.

It is an indication of the interconnectedness of the world economy and, more precisely, of the commonality of approaches to corporate governance across the developed world that Enron produced impetuses for law reform even in jurisdictions where the collapses caused no economic damage. Some people in Europe, of course, took the view that Enron-type scandals were a unique feature of the US system of corporate governance. However, the initial reaction that 'it could not happen here' did not long survive examination—a wise analysis in the light of subsequent European collapses such as that of Parmalat in Italy. What needs to be emphasized, however, is that even before Parmalat and Ahold, the process of reform in reaction to Enron had been set in train at both Community and Member State level. Thus, if Enron confirms the old adage that there is nothing like a good scandal to produce company law reform, it is novel, perhaps unique, in being a foreign scandal producing law reform in Europe.

I. THE NATURE OF THE EUROPEAN RESPONSES

However, it is worth pausing for a moment to analyze the nature of the reforms which have eventuated in Europe in the wake of Enron. At the opposite end of the spectrum from those who took the view that 'Enron could not happen here' were those who analyzed Enron as challenging existing corporate law rules in a fundamental way, in particular the modern emphasis on shareholder value. This was as difficult an analysis to sustain as the one which propounded the view that there was no need for a European response to Enron. The shareholders of Enron—unless connected with the management of the company or lucky enough to bail out before disaster struck—were surely one of the victims of that collapse. They lost their investment in the company which meant, for those shareholders who were also ordinary employees of the company, that in addition their pensions disappeared with their jobs. Fortunately, the more

---

[8] See, for example, BBC (2004).

extreme reactions in Europe to the Enron debacle did not find their way into legislation. For example, some way-out proposals emerged from the partially inaccurate perception that the creation of subsidiaries had been central to the financial obfuscation which the US companies had engaged in. Some therefore suggested going back on the principle which was at the heart of the Gladstonian reforms of the 1840s, i.e., the entitlement of private parties to create a company by going through a simple bureaucratic procedure. Thus, it was said, either state approval for the creation of new companies should be reintroduced or, at least, a waiting period of six months between creation and commencement of business should be introduced (Hopt, this volume, ch. 13). This is a bit like saying that because pens can be used to commit forgeries, all potential users of pens should be required to obtain state permission to own and use one.

In fact, the striking feature of the post-Enron reforms in Europe is that they do not break the mould of the traditional legal strategies used to regulate problems in the area of corporate governance, but simply modernize and extend those legal strategies so as to deal with new factual circumstances. To that extent, the post-Enron wave of reforms has been less significant than some would have wished. In order to understand why traditional legal strategies have been deployed post-Enron it is necessary to identify the generally accepted analysis of the governance failures in the United States and subsequent European scandals. This analysis is based around conflicts of interest. To take the Enron case itself, the management of the company had a self-interest in presenting the company's financial position in a more attractive light than the facts warranted, especially in view of the important role which stock options played in the make-up of their remuneration package; the auditors had an interest in not investigating the company's accounting arrangements too closely or disagreeing too vigorously with management's proposed accounting treatments of the company's transactions, in order to preserve their much more valuable non-audit work with the company; and the non-executive directors had an interest in a quiet life and not rocking the boat (Davies 2004: 186).[9]

However, these are examples of the standard agency problems, the regulation of which lies at the heart of company law and always has done so since modern company law emerged in the middle of the 19th century. Therefore, company law has developed tried and tested techniques for addressing these problems and it is perhaps not surprising that the legislative response to Enron has consisted in a further strengthening of

[9] There were also conflicts of interest at the level of the analysts (putting out more favorable buy recommendations that the facts warranted) and the investment banks (which participated in, sometimes even proposed, the sophisticated transactions whose proper treatment for accounting purposes was later controversial), but these conflicts are not dealt with in this chapter.

those techniques. Legislative reform has focussed, therefore, on matters such as strengthening the position of non-executive directors, further regulation of the independence of auditors and of supervision of auditors and greater controls over directors' remuneration packages. None of these was an area of non-regulation before the recent reforms and none became an area where entirely novel regulatory elements were introduced post-Enron; but they are all areas where a significant ratcheting up of the applicable rules has taken place.

II. PUTTING NEW ITEMS ON THE REFORM AGENDA

However, 'ratcheting up' should not be dismissed as a trivial type of law reform. In fact, Enron seems to have had three main impacts on the process of company law reform in Europe. First, and undoubtedly the most significant, Enron put onto European reform agendas proposals for which previously there was not sufficient support, even though minority elements within Europe were attempting to promote such changes. Both British and Community examples can be given. Between 1998 and 2001 in the United Kingdom, i.e., ending pre-Enron, there was a comprehensive government-inspired but independent review of British company law, imaginatively entitled the Company Law Review.[10] It is clear from one of the many Consultation Documents put out by the Steering Group that both the Steering Group itself and those it consulted were conscious of the threats to auditor independence arising from the increasing importance to accounting firms of the supply of non-audit work to audit clients and were doubtful about the adequacy of the existing rules to remove or sufficiently reduce those threats.[11] However, the Steering Group made only very limited proposals to deal with the issue, because, as it was doing its work, the government was separately doing a deal with the accountancy professions largely to perpetuate professional control of auditing. The Steering Group thus concluded, in the civil service language of these reports, that in the circumstances it would be 'not helpful' for it to go further (Company Law Review 2000: paras 5.137–38). Post-Enron, however, in the United Kingdom and throughout the EU, professional self-regulation has given or is about to give way to independent regulation of the audit, in terms of auditing standards, the

---

[10] The author should disclose that he was a member of its Steering Group.

[11] 'There is a question therefore, given the centrality of the auditors' independence as a check and balance in the system, whether the existing statutory requirement for auditor independence combined with a self-regulatory system of rules and discipline is adequate. There is , moreover, a danger after a long period of economic recovery and market buoyancy that the risks of abuse of this conflict are currently being under estimated.' (Company Law Review 2000a: para 5.136).

monitoring of audit quality, disciplinary action against failing auditors and ethical guidance for auditors; and the rules on auditor independence have been substantially strengthened. Thus, in the United Kingdom the 2004 Act[12] makes the necessary changes to implement the British reforms as adopted post-Enron. Moreover, whilst the 2004 Act has put on the statute book the necessary legal changes to accommodate the regulatory reforms of auditing, the earlier but more wide-ranging proposals of the Company Law Review proceed at a much more leisurely pace through the policy-making procedures of the Department and are unlikely to reach the statute book before 2006.[13]

A somewhat similar story can be told at Community level. In 1998 the Commission issued its Communication the statutory audit (European Commission 1998). In the section dealing with the action it proposed to take on the basis of the Communication the Commission was extremely cautious. Subsidiarity and proportionality were referred to; new or amended legislation 'is not necessarily envisaged'; only in response to the urgings of the European Parliament did the Commission confirm that it would not hesitate to propose legislation where necessary. Indeed, the document contained no proposals for legislation, but rather the Commission's aims were to be pursued with and through the Member States and the professional bodies. Post-Enron, however, the Commission was able to move, first in 2002, to a Commission Recommendation on the independence of the statutory auditor (European Commission 2002b) and then in early 2004 to a proposal for a Community Directive[14] on the duties of auditors, their independence and ethical standards, external quality assurance and public oversight of the audit (European Commission 2004a). Thus, even if the British government had not acted of its own motion, the rules on the independence and supervision of auditors would be about to change in any event as a result of Community legislation.[15] Moreover, in a further proposed Directive of October 2004, to amend the existing Fourth and Seventh Directives, the Commission aimed to deal,

---

[12] Above n 5. See in particular its Part I. The overall reform proposals are contained in the Final Report of the Co-ordinating Group on Audit and Accounting Issues (CGAAI 2004), but since many of these reforms are to be implemented by standard setters, gathered together under the auspices of the Financial Reporting Council, the 2004 Act is as much concerned with conferring powers on the relevant bodies as creating regulatory structures or making substantive rules. The precise role for legislation is discussed in DTI (2003a).

[13] See now DTI (2005), Company Law Reform Bill 2005.

[14] Recital 15 of the Commission Recommendation (European Commission 2002b) had suggested that the Commission would not review the operation of the, admittedly narrower, Recommendation until three years after its adoption.

[15] In consequence, the UK government took a reasonably relaxed view of the Commission's proposals, except in the few areas where they both departed from the recent domestic reforms and cut across some issue which the government regarded as a matter of principle. An example was the proposal's requirement for an audit committee and its specification of the duties of the committee, which matters are dealt with in the UK on a 'comply or explain' basis under the Combined Code. See DTI (2004).

inter alia, with a matter thought to be at the heart of Enron, namely, off-balance sheet transactions (European Commission 2004b).

A somewhat similar but less dramatic story can be told in relation to the additional items placed on the agenda of the High Level Group as a result of Enron.[16] The result of these additions was to expand the Community's interest in corporate governance issues. However, since the Group in general took a sceptical view of the benefits to be gained from giving a strong role to the Community in the area of corporate governance,[17] some of these particular additional corporate governance items fell subject to the same approach. Thus, in relation to both non-executive/supervisory board directors and management remuneration the Group recommended Community action only in the form of non-binding Commission Recommendations (High Level Group 2002: 61, 67).[18] However, in relation to management responsibility for financial statements, the Group accepted (High Level Group 2002: 68) that this was an area where the Community already had legislative standing through the Fourth and Seventh Directives on accounts, and so this matter was dealt with in the proposed Directive to amend those Directives (European Commission 2004b). The tension between pure corporate governance matters, where previously the Community has not legislated and where the Group was unwilling to recommend general legislative powers, and matters of accounts and audit, where the Community has exercised legislative powers since the late 1970s, is neatly illustrated by the Commission's provisions on companies' audit committees. The Group recommended that these be dealt with as part of the Commission's non-binding Recommendation on non-executive directors (High Level Group 2002: 71), and indeed such a provision appears in the Commission's Recommendation (European Commission 2005: section II). However, audit committees and their functions were proposed to be mandated by the Directive on the statutory audit, and this was, as we have seen, one of few provisions of that proposal to which the British government voiced serious objection.[19]

---

[16] See p. 416 above.

[17] In particular, it rejected the notion of a Community Corporate Governance Code: High Level Group (2002: 72).

[18] These Recommendations have now eventuated as the Commission Recommendation on the role of non-executive or supervisory directors and on committees of the (supervisory) board (European Commission 2005) and the Commission Recommendation on fostering an appropriate regime for the remuneration of directors of listed companies (European Commission 2004c).

[19] Above n 15. The British government states in its Consultation Document that 'it is neither appropriate nor desirable for the proposed Directive to deal with audit committees and related corporate governance matters.' (DTI 2004: para 12.9).

III. ACCELERATION AND RE-CHARACTERIZATION

A second impact of Enron, falling short of putting items on the European legislative agenda which were not previously there, was the giving of an extra impetus to items already proposed. Thus, the Commission made use of its Note for the Ecofin Council (European Commission 2002a) to stress the importance in the new post-Enron context of the adoption of its already proposed Regulation requiring the use of international accounting standards,[20] of its proposed Recommendation on auditor independence (European Commission 2002b), and of the proposed Directive on market abuse.[21] From here it is only a short step to a third 'effect' of Enron on European reform, which is the presentation of items recently enacted as presciently aimed at solving a problem whose significance was subsequently underlined by Enron. Thus, the reforms made to the British Companies Act in the middle of 2002,[22] to require greater disclosure of the policy behind directors' remuneration arrangements and a shareholder advisory vote on the directors' remuneration report, can be seen as part of a response to the perverse incentives generated by directors' share option schemes, one of central conflicts of interest identified in Enron. In fact, however, these reforms were driven by long-running domestic concerns about 'fat cat' pay but their appropriateness as part of the solution to the post-Enron issues cannot be denied.

The rest of this chapter is devoted to trying to make some assessment of the significance of the reforms whose implementation has been aided, in one or other of the ways identified above, by Enron. As far as core company law is concerned, the three main conflicts of interest that were identified as contributing to the scandals which occurred were those involving the executive directors/management of the company, its non-executive directors, and its auditors. We will look at each in turn, beginning with the executive directors, whose relevant conflict of interest was perceived largely to be one arising out of the process by which their remuneration was set.

[20] Ultimately adopted as Reg (EC) No 1606/2002 of the European Parliament and of the Council of 19 July 2002 on the application of international accounting standards, [2002] OJ L243/1.
[21] Later adopted as Dir 2003/6/EC on insider dealing and market manipulation (OJ L96/16, 12.4.2003).
[22] By SI 2002 No 1986, introducing new ss 234B–234C and new Sched 7A into the Companies Act 1985.

IV. DIRECTORS' REMUNERATION

In my view the path to wisdom in relation to remuneration begins with acceptance of the proposition that allowing executive directors to play a substantial role in the setting of their own remuneration puts them in a very unusual and privileged position and generates a very high-powered conflict of interest situation. Money constitutes a very important part—though of course not the whole—of what people expect to get out of work; and a large income stream and periodic large capital gains generated by share option schemes or in other ways give those in receipt of them a freedom of action and a level of security which is denied to those who do not have access to them. So, to allow any group who receive remuneration in exchange for work to decide on what that remuneration should be is likely to produce high levels of opportunism, or worse, on the part of the remuneration-setters—unless of course, as may be the case in a partnership or small company, the employers and the workers are largely the same people, so that no real transfer of resources is involved and the only substantial issue is one of creditor protection.

So much was clear to the company law judges of the Victorian era, who refused to give the board sole authority to decide remuneration issues by application of the general principle that the company was entitled to the unbiased advice of all its directors.[23] If that was not available, because one or more of them was involved in the transaction, any resulting contract would be voidable and sums paid to the directors would be recoverable by the company, unless the contract had been approved by the company, meaning in this context, not approval by the non-conflicted members of the board, but the shareholders in general meeting. In this way the shareholders were given a veto right over directors' remuneration.

Even today, one still finds that rule in the model set of articles with regard to the setting of directors' fees,[24] but it did not survive very long in relation to the setting of directors' remuneration as executives. By use of the semi-fiction that the articles constitute an agreement between the shareholders for the time being and the company it became doctrinally possible to shift decision-making on this issue back to the conflicted board of directors, by appropriate provisions in the articles. The articles constituted, it was argued, the expression of the shareholders' consent to the decision on remuneration being taken by conflicted agents, and the

---

[23] *Imperial Mercantile Credit Association v Coleman* (1871) LR 6 Ch App 558.
[24] Thus Art 82 of Table A: 'The directors shall be entitled to such remuneration as the company may by ordinary resolution determine ...'

courts accepted the argument.[25] That is the position one finds today in all large companies.[26]

No doubt there were some good practical reasons, in terms of speed of decision-making, for giving this task to the board; otherwise, the hiring process for executive talent would be subject to an increased level of uncertainty. However, we should not be surprised at the potential for manipulation of payments systems which is created by such an arrangement whereby directors can have a substantial influence over their own remuneration. That remark applies as much to the design of so-called performance-related remuneration schemes as much as it does to the setting of basic remuneration—in fact, perhaps it applies even more strongly to performance-related pay whose structure is inevitably more complex than basic salary and which provides correspondingly greater opportunities for distortion, notably in the setting of the performance criteria by which the payments are assessed.[27]

One question which might thus be asked is: how far have the 2002 amendments to the Companies Act moved us back towards acceptance of the Victorian position that remuneration decisions should involve the shareholders in a meaningful way?

V. WEAK SHAREHOLDER INVOLVEMENT

It is suggested that there is a strong and a weak way of involving shareholders in decisions over directors' remuneration. The weak way is simply to require the company to disclose to the shareholders information about remuneration decisions taken by the board and to leave the shareholders to react adversely, if they wish to do so. Formally, the remuneration decision remains with the board, but it is capable of being overturned by subsequent shareholder action. To have any chance of success, such a strategy requires a sophisticated set of rules about disclosure of directors' remuneration to the shareholders and a legal regime which makes it easy for shareholders to exercise their governance rights in the light of the disclosures. Of course, it is arguable that social factors alone, such as shareholder outrage (as it has been termed)

[25] *Costa Rica Railway Co. Ltd v Forward* [1901] 1 Ch 746; see Gower and Davies (2003: 394-5). The development was a general one about conflicted transactions between a company and its directors and was not confined to remuneration decisions. The underlying equitable law rule and its stringent remedies revive if remuneration is awarded without shareholder sanction and otherwise than in accordance with the provisions of the articles: *Guinness plc v Saunders* [1990] 2 AC 663.
[26] As reflected in Arts 84 and 85 of Table A. Art 94 prohibits the interested director from voting, but companies sometimes disapply even that provision and, in any event, the voting restriction does nothing to prevent 'mutual back-scratching'.
[27] For an overarching critique, see Bebchuk and Fried (2004).

(Bebchuk and Fried 2004: 64–66) at excessive remuneration decisions, will be effective whether or not shareholders are able to respond legally to the disclosures, but effective governance rights for shareholders give that outrage a sharper edge.

This weak form of decision rights for shareholders was a well-established pre-Enron strategy, at least in the common-law world. Thus, the Listing Rules of the London Stock Exchange required highly detailed and, importantly, individualised disclosure of executive directors' remuneration.[28] In the United Kingdom there are also rules making it relatively easy for shareholders to convene meetings and to dismiss directors.[29] By contrast, in continental Europe individualised disclosure is still resisted in many states (for example, Germany)[30] and removal of directors before the end of their period of office is often not possible, except for cause.[31] The European Commission's Action Plan (European Commission 2003a) proposed individualised disclosure but only via a non-binding Community Recommendation (European Commission 2004c).

VI. STRONG SHAREHOLDER INVOLVEMENT

The stronger version of the decision-rights strategy gives the shareholders an input into the remuneration decision itself, normally by way of a veto right over a decision previously taken by the board. The veto rights strategy is one the British legislature has deployed in relation to particular remuneration decisions for some time, in particular in end-game situations, in order to control directors' termination payments.[32] In end-game cases the departing director no longer has the

---

[28] Listing Rule 9.8.8, implementing the recommendations of the Greenbury Committee. After the amendments to the Companies Act in 2002 the purely disclosure aspects of the Listing Rules may be downgraded.

[29] CA 1985, ss 303 and 368.

[30] *Financial Times* (2004a), reporting a call by the eminent German corporate lawyer, Professor Theodor Baums, for mandatory individual disclosure of directors' remuneration details on an individualised basis.

[31] Again for Germany see AktG art 84(3)—removal of member of the management board by the supervisory board only for cause—though cause includes a vote of no-confidence in the shareholders' meeting unless passed 'for manifestly arbitrary reasons'.

[32] CA 1985, ss 312–16 and 319. None of these sections, however, effectively deals with contractual entitlements to termination payments (of the type exemplified in *Taupo Totara Timber Co v Rowe* [1978] AC 537, where the director's service contract provided that he could resign within 12 months of a takeover and receive a lump-sum payment of five times his annual salary.) Nor does the Combined Code deal explicitly with them. Contrast § 200F of the Australian Corporations Act 2001, as amended in 2004, which requires shareholder approval for termination payments in excess of the generous level of one year's pay for each year of service up to a maximum of seven, though the limit applies apparently to the value of all termination payments taken together, i.e. gratuitous, by way of damages for breach and contractual.

prospect of a continuing relationship with the company to restrain his financial demands and the other directors may be tempted to make large pay-offs in order to not to expose divisions in the ranks, not least of all to the shareholders. The risk here is of the so-called 'rewards for failure', a topic which has much occupied the British government in recent years (DTI 2003b).[33]

Well established also are the Listing Rules requirements for shareholder approval of share option schemes,[34] a rule originally introduced by way of extension of the principle that share issues by the company should be subject to shareholder approval, in order to prevent dilution of the shareholders' cash flow or voting rights.[35] In other words, the rationale for this rule was not based originally in the need to subject directors' remuneration decisions to shareholder approval. Thus, the Listing Rule requirement of shareholder approval does not apply to annual bonus awards, which, together with the basic salary, stock options or other long-term incentive plans and pension provisions form the fourth element in the make-up of the typical remuneration package of the directors of large companies.

Thus, particular elements of the remuneration of directors have long been subject to shareholder approval. What is interesting about the amendments made to the Companies Act in 2002 is that they cautiously extend shareholder voting to the whole of the remuneration package, at least in the case of 'quoted' companies.[36] At the same time the quality of the information disclosure to shareholders has been improved. No longer is it necessary just to reveal information about what individuals receive. The board's policy on the remuneration front must be explained,[37] i.e., the board must attempt to provide a justification of the remuneration position rather than just simply reveal the facts and leave it to the shareholders to ask probing questions. In particular, the board must reveal its policy on whether performance conditions are used for share option schemes and other long-term incentive plans; on its choice of performance conditions, if such were used; and how those conditions

---

[33] It seems likely, however, that this initiative will not lead to further legislation but rather, at least for the time being, to reliance of self-regulation, notably in the shape of a recent Joint Statement by the Association of British Insurers and the National Association of Pension Funds (ABI/NAPF, 2004). See also Ministerial Statement, Trade and Industry, Hansard, 25 January 2005 (Commons).

[34] Listing Rule 9.4.1. The obligation now extends to approval of most long-term incentive schemes as well.

[35] The current debate over the expensing of share options for reporting purposes continues the dilution discussion in a new form.

[36] A quoted company is one incorporated under the Companies Acts whose equity share capital is officially listed in any EEA state or on the NYSE or NASDAQ: s 262(1).

[37] Sched 7A, para 3.

were applied in practice.[38] It is clear that one of the British government's main reasons for moving to a statutory requirement for a remuneration report was that, under the Listing Rules, where the matter was previously regulated, there was insufficient disclosure of the board's remuneration policies, which one may take as a coded reference to inadequate justification for that remuneration.[39]

The vote on the remuneration report, however, is only advisory. No director's contractual entitlement to remuneration is affected by an adverse vote.[40] The purpose of the advisory vote, one may say, is to make it easier for the shareholders to express an opinion on the information disclosed to them by reducing their collective action problems. The shareholders do not need to convene a meeting or secure the placing of an item on the agenda of a meeting in order to be able to express an opinion on directors' remuneration: they must be given an opportunity to vote at the shareholders' meeting at which the annual accounts are considered. The vote, if you like, can help to crystallise the investors' dissatisfaction and provide a symbol of the dissatisfaction which it is difficult for the board simply to ignore.

What can we expect from such advisory votes? It is not likely that shareholders will be interested in lowering the levels of directors' remuneration just for the sake of it, so that those who look at this issue from the point of view of distributive fairness are likely to be disappointed. However, shareholders are likely to be interested in making stronger links between directors' remuneration and the performance of the company. Certainly where large sums of money are at issue and where the pay/performance link appears to be negative, one can expect adverse shareholder reaction to be expressed through the advisory vote. This seems to be the British experience to date, notably in the celebrated cases of *GSK* (the only case where a remuneration vote was lost) and *Sainsbury* (where the board withdrew a large section of its report in the face of shareholder opposition).

Research carried out for the DTI by Deloittes (2004) supports this analysis.[41] This found that after the introduction of the Regulations a number of specific changes occurred in companies' remuneration practices which strengthened the pay/performance link. These were: the 'almost complete' reduction in directors' notice periods to one year; the removal in new plans of automatic vesting of share options (irrespective of performance conditions being met) upon a change of control; the

---

[38] None of these requirements apply, however, to annual bonus awards.

[39] DTI (2001: para 2.12) pointed to inadequate disclosure of policy under the Listing Rules (as opposed to remuneration packages where there was 'an acceptable level of transparency') as a major reason for moving the rules on disclosure into the Companies Act 1985.

[40] § 241A(8)—unless, of course, the director and the company contract for this to be the case.

[41] The research was confined to the FTSE 350 companies.

removal from new plans of provisions for re-basing performance conditions if it becomes clear that the original conditions are unlikely to be met; and the introduction of graded performance conditions so that the full award is dependent upon more stringent performance conditions being met. Overall, there was much greater *ex ante* consultation by companies with major shareholders and a greater willingness to alter remuneration policies. However, the Report also identified areas where further progress could be made in linking pay with performance and suggested ways of developing the Regulations or industry guidance so as to promote this outcome. These included disclosure, at least on an historical basis, of the performance conditions for annual bonuses and greater clarity on what the Regulations required by way of the disclosure of the company's policy on performance conditions in general.

Are these significant achievements in public policy terms? There are two reasons for thinking that they are. First, they help restore the link between work and pay. Pay can be a motivator of effort, but only if pay is reward for work and not something that is received whether work is done or not. Secondly, in so far as the growth of executive pay in relation to the rewards of other sections of the community results from sudden, abnormal leaps in pay levels in particular cases which then become part of the norm, shareholder advisory votes may in fact do something to slow the rate of growth of executive pay—though there is no firm data to this effect currently available. Overall, large actual remuneration rewards in the face of poor corporate performance are likely to be more difficult to push through under the new regime, whether those payments occur on severance or not. Companies are likely to become more sensitive to the question of whether they are crossing this particular line and to consult in advance with their major shareholders when they think they may be.

This still leaves the question whether we should go back to the 19th century and move from an advisory vote to a veto vote for the shareholders. Should the director's contractual entitlement to remuneration be dependent upon shareholder approval? At the hiring stage, the costs to the company and therefore to the shareholders are likely to be high, because there may be competition for the best executive talent on a global scale and a country which insists on shareholder approval will therefore put its companies at a competitive disadvantage in the hiring process. Boards should thus be left free to hire in line with their remuneration policy, subject to subsequent reporting to the shareholders and a shareholders' advisory vote. It is less clear, however, that companies need such flexibility in relation to subsequent remuneration decisions. One could envisage a rule in which subsequent remuneration changes would come into force as soon as decided on by the board, but they would be subject a condition subsequent of share-holder approval. If that approval was not forthcoming, remuneration would revert to the previous level (or some other higher level agreed by the shareholders) but none of the increase actually paid would be repayable. This would sharpen the incentive on boards to formulate remuneration decisions in such a way as to win approval and promote the process of engagement with institutional shareholders in this area, which seems to be the best available, if not perfect, mechanism for preventing conflicts of interest over remuneration decisions becoming uncontrollable, which in the recent past they have often appeared to be.

VII. AUDITOR INDEPENDENCE

Although the underlying problem in Enron can be argued to have been the perverse incentives generated by the management's remuneration package, more attention focussed, both in the United States and in Europe, on the failure of Enron's auditors to reveal that the company's accounts did not reflect the economic reality of the situation in which the company found itself. In the United Kingdom a substantial reform effort was devoted to this topic, via the Co-ordinating Group on Audit and Accounting Issues, established jointly by the DTI and the Treasury, which looked generally at the regulation of auditors and auditing, whilst the Financial Reporting Council appointed a group chaired by Sir Robert Smith to report on the role of audit committees of the board (FRC 2003, 'Smith Report'). The Companies (Audit, Investigation, and Community Enterprise) Act 2004 put in place the legal changes necessary to effect the reforms recommended in the Final Report of the Co-ordinating Group (CGAAI, 2003), whilst the Smith Report's recommendations were implemented via a revised version of the Combined Code on Corporate Governance produced in July 2003. At Community level the Commission produced in March 2004 a proposal (European Commission 2004a) for a Directive to replace and considerably expand the existing Eighth Directive, which covered much of the same ground as the British initiatives. It is not proposed to analyze those aspects of the reform proposals which relate to the regulation in general of the accounting and auditing profession, but instead to concentrate on their approach to the specific issue of auditors' conflicts of interest. Nor is it proposed, for reasons of space, to consider auditors' liability for negligent audits. Although it is strongly arguable that such liability potentially constrains the willingness of auditors to give in to the temptation to conduct lax audits, extension of auditors' liability for negligence was part of neither the Co-ordinating Group's Report nor that of Mr Smith. On the contrary, under pressure from the accounting profession, the debate over liability has focussed subsequently on the relaxation of the constraints which currently limit the freedom of auditors to agree with the audit client company restrictions on the auditor's liability for negligence.[42]

A. The Nature of Auditors' Conflicts of Interest

The issue of the independence of auditors is hardly new. A threat to auditor independence is inherent in the fact that the auditor is paid the audit fee by the client whose financial statements the auditor is employed to verify. Although the audit is mandatory (for all but small companies), it is not mandatory for the client to engage any particular auditor and so it is potentially possible for audit firms to compete for engagements on the basis of their laxity in scrutinising the accounts. This risk is clearly accentuated where, as in Enron, the company is in a position to offer to the auditor additional non-audit work, the revenues to the accounting firm from which may be considerably greater than that provided by the audit itself.

Up until Enron, it was often argued that a non-legal constraint in the form of reputational considerations was extremely powerful in constraining auditors from giving way to temptation and that, accordingly, legal constraints played an essentially supplementary role. The argument here was that the analysis of competition on the basis of laxity misunderstood the incentives to which auditors are subject, because it was essentially a single-period analysis. Let us suppose that an audit firm obtains an engagement on the basis that it has indicated to the management of the company that it will not scrutinise the make-up of the accounts rigorously, thus permitting the management to present the financial position of the company in a more favorable way than the facts warrant. Let us assume also, as is realistic, that sooner or later, the truth of the company's financial position emerges as does the auditors' role in the earlier misstatements. At this point the audit firm suffers a reputational loss. This will cause problems for the firm, above all in relation to managements who have no desire to mislead others about the true state of the company's finances and who will therefore not want to use audit firms whom shareholders, the investing public or creditors do not fully trust. However, it will also reduce the firm's attractiveness to managements who do wish to mislead, because for such managements an essential ingredient of their strategy is that the auditors should be regarded as trustworthy by others. In short, reputational loss for an audit firm destroys its business model.[43] Therefore, for an audit firm selling

---

[42] Companies Act 1985, s 310. For the latest government thinking see DTI (2005: para 3.5).

[43] The collapse of Andersens as a global practice in the wake of the conviction of some of its Texas partners for criminal activities associated with the Enron scandal is a dramatic illustration of the reputational risks that firms run.

one's reputation to management would seem to be viable only as an end-game strategy and, even then, presumably only where the firm thinks it can make more money be ruining its reputation than by retaining it and selling the goodwill of the business to other participants in the market for the supply of audit services. Of course, in auditing, as in any other profession, there will be some firms or, more likely, individuals within firms who, for one reason or another, prefer short-term gain to maximising their income stream over a longer period of time, and for them professional and legal regulation are necessary controls, but the thrust of the above argument is that conniving with management is not a systemic risk of the auditing process.

Enron cast considerable doubt on this comforting argument. As Professor Coffee (2003) has argued, the equilibrium posited by the above argument seems to have been threatened by changes both on the supply and the demand side in the 1990s. On the one hand, the possible gains to auditors from conduct falling below professional standards increased as a result of the explosion in the value of non-audit work which accounting firms did for their clients; on the other, the reputational costs of slackness appeared in the 1990s to go down. The pursuit by audit firms of non-audit work substantially increased the potential benefits to be obtained from conniving with management over the preparation of the company's financial statements. In the United States the big accounting firms moved the proportion of their total income earned from consulting from 12 per cent to 50 per cent over the last quarter of the 20th century (Ebke 2004: 522–23).[44] Of course, not all this consulting income was derived from audit clients, but there is no doubt that being the company's auditor places the firm in an ideal position to sell non-audit services to the audit client, and some firms offered cash bonuses to their staff to sell non-audit services to audit clients. In particular, information technology, taxation and legal services all proved major areas of expansion (*ibid.*). In the United Kingdom recent figures show that the Big Four earned from their audit clients between one and a half and two and a half times as much fee income from the supply of non-audit services as from audit services (OFT 2004: Fig. 5).[45]

These developments by themselves might have been enough to increase significantly the proportion of firms—or, more likely, individuals within firms—choosing short-term gain over the preservation of reputational capital. However, there is evidence that in the 1990s the harm done to reputation through lax auditing fell because, in an exuberant market, investors and creditors attached much less value to the

---

[44] By 2000 audit fees constituted less than one third of the income of the major accounting firms.

[45] Overall, the Big Four earned from the FTSE 100 companies some £234m in audit fees and £454m in non-audit fees in 2003 (OFT 2004: Fig 4).

numbers appearing in the company's accounts and therefore to the certification of those numbers by the auditors (Coffee 2003: 36).[46] Thus, by the beginning of the new millennium, there was much less reason to be confident that the incentive structure for accounting firms would ensure the previously level of adherence to professional standards. However, it should be noted that the demand-side aspect of this analysis probably has corrected itself. It is difficult to believe that appetite for paying large sums of money for the securities of companies whose accounts reveal that they have not yet made any profits and are unlikely to do so for some years has survived the collapse of the dot.com bubble. Perhaps for this reason, the focus of reform has been on the supply-side, i.e., on regulation of the auditors' conflicts of interest rather than the gullibility of investors.

VIII. LEGAL STRATEGIES

How radical have the reforms, implemented or likely to be implemented, turned out to be? In particular, have they broken new ground in the deployment of legal strategies for the control of the auditors' conflicts of interest or is it the case, as with directors' remuneration, that the reform has remained within the established parameters? The most obvious radical strategy to deal with the conflict identified above would be to prohibit auditors from providing non-audit services to audit clients, contemporaneously with the audit services and within a certain period before or after supplying audit services. This strategy is open to the criticism that many non-audit services can be provided more cheaply by the auditors than anyone else because of the understanding of the business obtained through the audit. Thus, prohibiting the supply of non-audit services by the auditor will increase the costs of those services to companies and so the question becomes whether those additional costs are outweighed by the reduction of the costs arising out of the conflict created by the supply of the non-audit services. Since no ultimately convincing data seems to be available on that issue, it is perhaps not surprising that most legislatures have refrained from implementing this strategy, though the Commission proposes to study whether such a rule should be introduced (DTI 2001: para 6.3).

Failing a complete prohibition, a partial prohibition could be considered. This is the approach of the Sarbanes-Oxley legislation, which prohibits to auditors the provision of eight types of non-audit service.[47] European law-making in this area has always preferred principles to

---

[46] See also the quotation from the CLR, above n 11.

[47] Plus any other service determined by the Public Company Accounting Oversight Board to be impermissible: § 10A of the Securities Exchange Act 1934, as amended.

rules and so the Commission's Recommendation of 2002 on auditor independence proposed as a general principle that auditors providing non-audit services should neither take any decision nor take part in any decision-making on behalf of the client or its management while providing a non-audit service (European Commission 2002b: Art. 7). This approach was presumably intended to leave auditors free to provide a rather wide range of non-audit services, but the re-casting of the principle in the draft Directive (European Commission 2004a) created some doubt on that interpretation. Having reiterated the management decisions point, the draft went on to require Member States to ensure that the auditor shall not have a business relationship with the client, 'including the provision of additional services', which 'might compromise' the auditor's independence. On a strong interpretation of this Article, the provision of all but insignificant non-audit services would have to be prohibited since they 'might' compromise independence.[48] The adopted version of the directive retreated from this strong approach by prohibiting only relationships which 'an objective, reasonable and informed third party' would conclude compromised the auditor's independence.[49]

A. Disclosure of Information

Beyond that, the legal strategies deployed to regulate auditors' conflicts of interest arising out of the provision of non-audit services become the familiar ones of disclosure of information; removing the appointment/removal decision vis-a-vis the auditor from the management of the company; and the specification of bright-line rules to deal with limited situations regarded as ones of high risk. Disclosure is tackled both from the perspective of the company and from the perspective of the auditor. The 2004 Act (section 7) replaced the existing section 390B of the Companies Act 1985, which already empowered the making of regulations for the annual disclosure of the aggregate amounts paid to the auditors for non-audit services, with a new section 390B which places the disclosure on a disaggregated basis, according to the nature of the service provided. Article 38 of the Directive requires firms which carry out audits of public interest entities[50] to produce an annual transparency report,

---

[48] Draft text of the Directive as approved by the Parliament and the Council on 11 October 2005, Art. 22(1a).

[49] The British government thought this an 'unintended and adverse consequence' of the draft (DTI 2004).

[50] This will include all companies with securities traded on a regulated market, banks and other financial institutions and insurance companies: Directive Art 2(11) (draft text).

which has to list, among other things, 'financial information showing the importance of the audit firm such as the total turnover divided into fees from the statutory audit …and fees charged for other assurance services, tax advisory services and other non-audit services.' This is a somewhat awkwardly-worded provision. Presumably it is not the importance of the audit firm which has to be shown but the importance to the audit firm of different classes of income. However that may be, the Co-ordinating Group in the United Kingdom had recommended a similar principle, albeit one to be implemented on a voluntary basis, at least initially (CGAAI 2004).

B. Decision Rights

The principle of taking decisions over the appointment and removal of auditors and fixing their remuneration away from management and vesting it in the shareholders is already well established in the Companies Act 1985.[51] It is doubtful whether these rules do much to combat the conflict of interest under consideration here. For the reasons given above, it is unlikely that those conflicts would drive management to seek the appointment of auditors who had a reputation for complaisance. The mere fact that the formal appointment is made by the shareholders is unlikely to constitute a significant control, for to outward appearances there will be no basis for the shareholders to question the board's nomination. Further, the 'bribe' of substantial remuneration for non-audit services does not depend in any way upon a threat by the management to remove the auditors or to pay them large sums by way of audit fee. In fact, the attraction to dissembling management of the non-audit route to influence over the auditor lies precisely in the fact that this strategy does not require management to take any formal action which might need to be explained to the shareholders. Thus, if after appointment a 'corrupt' relationship develops between management and auditor, this will not be readily visible to the shareholders—indeed, it is important to both management and auditor that it should not be—so that it will not influence shareholders' decisions on removal or re-appointment, at least until it is too late to matter.[52]

---

[51] §§ 385, 391, and 390A—there are modifications to deal with private companies which have dispensed with the laying of accounts before the general meeting.

[52] Moreover, in the absence of a good reason to change, it is entirely rational for the shareholders to stay with the existing auditors. It is well established that the first audit conducted by new auditors are likely to be unchallenging because the auditor is still learning the business. See further below on auditor rotation.

Nevertheless, Article 35 of the Directive mandates what is probably the practice in most Member States of shareholder appointment, but Article 36 deals with removal by stating that auditors 'may only be dismissed where there are proper grounds, divergence of opinions on accounting treatment or audit procedures shall not be a proper ground for dismissal.' This is probably a sensible rule—though again not much directed at the conflict arising out of the provision of non-audit work—if the removal decision lies in the hands of the management. If, however, as under the British Act, removal as well as appointment lie in the hands of the shareholders, it seems a positively counter-productive rule. Shareholders would no longer be able to remove the auditor on suspicion that there is something inappropriate in the auditor's relationship with the management but would seem to have to be able to prove their suspicion.[53]

Overall, increasing the shareholders' decision rights in relation to the appointment or removal of auditors does not seem a strategy well directed at addressing the conflicts of interest arising out of the provision of non-audit work to the auditors. What is needed is a closer continuing scrutiny by a body independent of management of the development of the auditor/management relationship after the shareholders have exercised their rights of appointment, a task which the shareholders themselves, who meet only episodically, are not well placed to undertake. Thus, the main thrust of the reforms within the company to tackle auditor/management conflicts of interest has been via a further strengthening of the role of the audit committee of the board of listed companies, as recommended by the Smith Committee (FRC 2003), endorsed by the Co-ordinating Group (CGAAI 2004: para 1.54 *et seq.*), given effect to in the United Kingdom by the revised Combined Code in July 2003; and now required at EU level for public interest entities by Article 39 of the Directive. Focussing monitoring of the management/auditor relationship in a small and expert board committee, meeting relatively frequently, stands a much better chance of success than expecting the large and possibly inexpert body of shareholders, meeting only infrequently, to play an important role of this type. The Combined Code spells out the audit committee's monitoring role in considerable detail.[54] That role is by no means confined to the

---

[53] In relation to auditors who do resist management's blandishments a useful reform would be a requirement on auditors who are ceasing to hold office (whether by resignation or by not seeking re-election) to report in all cases to the shareholders on the circumstances connected with this event, i.e., a strengthening of the current s 394 of the CA 1985 which requires such a statement only where the auditor 'considers' that circumstances exist which ought to be brought to the shareholders' attention. See Audit Quality Forum (2005). This proposal also goes beyond Art 36(2) of the Draft Directive.

[54] Combined Code, provision C.3.2.

auditor/management relationship, but in that crucial area it requires the committee to monitor the auditor's independence, objectivity and effectiveness and to develop and implement a policy on the provision of non-audit services to the company by the auditor. Since the Committee is also to 'monitor the integrity of the financial statements of the company' and to review 'significant financial reporting judgements' contained in the company's financial statements, the auditors will also have to deal with the audit committee, and not just the management, on all important matters relating to the compilation of the company's annual accounts.

As with all schemes for using non-executive directors to control the self-interest of the executives, one must wonder whether they will be up to the task. The Combined Code says that the audit committee (of three persons or two in smaller listed companies) should consist entirely of independent non-executive directors of whom at least one must have 'recent and relevant financial experience.'[55] The Directive is less prescriptive in one sense, not specifying the minimum number of members and requiring only one of them to be an independent NED (who must also have 'competence in accounting and/or auditing'). The Directive is more prescriptive in another, since its rules are mandatory, whilst those of the Combined Code operate on a 'comply or explain' basis.[56] However, it is difficult to believe that listed[57] companies will find it easy to explain to their shareholders non-compliance with the audit committee provisions of the Combined Code and so the matter may not be very important in practice. Nevertheless, if the Combined Code and the Directive take some steps to promote independence (of management) and expertise on the audit committee, the question still remains whether the members of that committee have sufficient incentives to do a good job. The tone of the Smith report, when describing potential problems between committee and management, was notably adversarial: The committee might have to 'pit its judgement ... perhaps on technically complex issues' against both senior management and auditors and for that reason its members would need to be 'tough, knowledgeable and independent-minded' (FRC 2003: 22–24). The lack of appropriate incentives is perhaps showing itself in a reported reluctance of people holding top positions in companies to take on the role of chair of the audit committee in other companies, on the one hand (*Financial Times* 2005),

---

[55] C.3.1, worryingly suggesting that the other two may not have such knowledge.

[56] Listing Rule 9.8.6.

[57] Art 39 applies to all companies with securities traded on a regulated market (above n 50) and so is potentially much more wide-ranging than the Combined Code which applies only to listed companies. However, in the UK much of force of this extension has been removed by the decision of AIM to cease to be a regulated market. Article 39 permits small and medium-sized 'public interest entities' to have the audit committee's functions discharged by the board as a whole.

and decisions by companies to raise the pay of non-executive directors in general and audit committee chairs in particular.[58]

C. Bright-line Rules

An alternative strategy for addressing the lack of visibility to the shareholders and the outside world in general of any lack of rigor in the relationship between the auditors and the management is the deployment of bright-line rules which do not require the exercise of discretion on the part of any person. Such rules are simple to apply, but may involve costs arising from the fact that they catch both situations where intervention is required and those where, in fact, it is not, because the rule is not capable of distinguishing between the two situations. As we have seen, uncertainty about the balance of costs and benefits has so far prevented adoption at either EU or UK level of the simple rule that auditors should not be permitted to provide non-audit services to non-audit clients. Less stringent bright-line rules have proved acceptable, however. Thus, rules have been introduced, or proposed, requiring the rotation of the lead audit personnel after the relationship with the management has lasted for a certain period of time. The thought is that the risk of too 'cosy' a relationship between management and auditors increases with the length of that relationship and that at some point a change in the personnel involved on the audit side should be imposed, without proof that the quality of the relationship has in fact deteriorated.

Article 40(2) of the Directive requires Member States to impose rotation of the 'key' audit partner after seven years in the case of public interest entities. In the United Kingdom the Auditing Practices Board of the Financial Reporting Council has already moved to five-year rotation of audit engagement partner (from the previous seven-year rule) under pressure from the Co-ordinating Committee.[59] However, neither in the United Kingdom nor in the rest of the EU[60] has mandatory rotation of the audit firm proved a popular rule.[61] The argument against it is that it involves a complete loss of the expertise built up by the existing audit

[58] GSK is reported to pay £30,000 per annum to its NEDs, an extra £20,000 those NEDs who chair its remuneration and appointment committees; and an extra £30,000 to the chair of the audit committee (*Financial Times* 2004b).

[59] CGAAI (2004: paras 1.20–1.22). See the Auditing Practices Board, Ethical Standard 3, 2004. For a 'key' audit partner who is not the engagement or independent partner the Standard requires rotation every seven years, a position the proposed Directive would appear to change.

[60] Of the EU of the 15 only Spain and Italy have imposed it. Spain later abandoned the rule and Italy imposes it (on a nine-year rotation) only on small number of large companies: CGAAI (2004: 26).

[61] Nor does Sarbanes-Oxley require it: § 10A of the Securities Exchange Act, as amended, imposes a five-year rotation rule for the lead audit partner.

team, leaving the new team to begin from scratch, with the likely consequence that the first audit from the new team will be both more costly and less searching than the previous year's audit.[62] In other words, a continuing relationship between client and auditor generates the risk of cosy relationship developing but also the strong likelihood that valuable expertise will be acquired by the audit team. This argument convinced the Co-ordinating Group that mandatory rotation of the firm should not be imposed (CGAAI 2004: paras 1.23–1.30), and the Directive will not prompt a re-think.[63]

IX. NON-EXECUTIVE DIRECTORS

The third problematic area identified by analyzers of the Enron scandal concerned the failure of the non-executive directors to discover what the management was doing—a failure put down in part to their self-interest in having a quiet life and not standing up to management, who were not likely to take their interventions kindly, but also to structural weaknesses in the position of the non-executives on the board which limited what it was feasible to expect them to do. Thus, it was not surprising that, in parallel with the Smith inquiry, established by the FRC (2003), into the role of the audit committee of the board, the DTI itself established a general investigation by Mr Higgs (2003) into the functioning of non-executive directors. Both inquiries reported on the same day and both were carried forward, eventually, into a single set of revisions to the Combined Code.

Despite the fact that the joint reforms are generally referred to as the 'Higgs reforms' it is arguable that those made in relation to the audit committee and discussed above were more significant than the reforms proposed in the role of the non-executive directors elsewhere.[64] If the Smith reforms were more evolutionary than revolutionary, the reforms proposed by Higgs can be regarded as purely incremental in character. They built on the foundations laid by the Cadbury Committee (1992) a decade earlier, a report to which Mr Higgs gave the accolade: 'the

[62] Alternatively, this result might be avoided by the audit team (minus presumably the lead partner) moving to the new audit firm, a consequence which would totally undermine the initial objectives of the rule.

[63] A further important specific rule to be found in the proposed Directive is the prohibition in Art 40(d) that the key audit partner may not take up a 'key' management position in the audit client (where that is a public interest entity) within two years of ceasing to be the audit partner—an extension of s 27 of the CA 1989 which applies only to contemporaneous appointments, but one already recommended by the Co-ordinating Group (CGAAI 2004: para 1.61) and adopted by the professions in respect of listed companies.

[64] The remuneration committee acquired extra significance as a result of the reforms discussed above, but they resulted from legislation, not the Higgs proposals.

fundamentals of corporate governance in the United Kingdom are sound, thanks to Sir Adrian Cadbury' (*ibid.*: 3). Consequently, although there was much to welcome in the Higgs Report, its main recommendations were limited: the proportion of non-executive directors on the board should be raised from one-third (of whom under the old Code only the majority had to be independent) to one-half (all independent); and the desirability of not having the roles of CEO and chair of the board held by the same person was stated in more prescriptive language than previously.[65]

A similar pattern can be seen at Community level. The Community proposals on audit committees, as we have seen, have been embodied in a Directive, whilst the Community developments on non-executive directors have taken the form of a non-binding Recommendation (European Commission 2005). Of course, the Commission was better placed to proceed with 'hard' law in relation to the audit committee, because audit was already accepted as an area for regulation by Directive (albeit within a narrow compass), whilst Member States for many years had fiercely resisted Commission attempts to regulate the board structure of national companies. Nevertheless, it is probably true to say that at both national and Community level the perception was that management and auditors were more to blame for the Enron scandal than the non-executive directors.[66] At any rate, the impact of Enron was not enough to overcome the traditional opposition of the Member States to Community regulation of issues of board structure.

Despite the limited nature of the reforms proposed by Mr Higgs, the reaction of the management of British companies was initially one of fierce resistance. Even though Higgs proposed no changes in the comply-and-explain system via the Listing Rules nor, in relation to the substantive content of the Code, was it proposed to introduce new elements but simply to strengthen the existing elements, nevertheless opposition from management circles was especially strong, and not just on the grounds that this was the straw which breaks the camel's back. The main ground for management's opposition, in my view, was the parallel changes which government had been promoting, independently of Enron, in the role of institutional shareholders as holders of governance rights within companies. Since non-observance of the Code carries sanctions for companies only to the extent that shareholders respond adversely to explanations of non-compliance, a more active shareholder body has the potential to impart to what seem relatively straightforward developments in the Code a qualitatively different character.

---

[65] For a more detailed discussion of the Higgs proposals and their implementation in the UK. See, e.g., Nolan (this volume, ch 11).

[66] Sarbanes-Oxley did not deal with board structure either—traditionally a matter for state law also in the US—but there were some changes in the rules of the NYSE.

However, is the level of shareholder activism, which management so fears, a realistic prospect in the United Kingdom? Despite the potential for greater shareholder activism in portfolio companies which institutional shareholding has created, there is general agreement that the levels of such activism have been, and still are, sub-optimal. By sub-optimal in this context is meant that less intervention in the affairs of portfolio companies occurs than would be the case if the institutions, individually or collectively, were single-mindedly committed to the maximization of the value of their portfolios. Both Black and Coffee (1994), and Stapledon (1996), found levels of intervention to be sub-optimal, despite increasing absolute levels of intervention. Partly, such sub-optimal behavior is due to competition among the fund managers acting on behalf of institutional shareholders and the consequent temptation for any one manager to free-ride on the efforts of others when it comes to forming a coalition to exercise corporate governance rights. The recent Company Law Review identified conflicts of interest as an important additional contributor to sub-optimality, again especially at the fund-management level (Company Law Review 2000b: paras 5.2–5.12; Company Law Review 2001: paras 6.19–6.40). Financial conglomerates which provide investment management services to institutions are reluctant to be active shareholders in portfolio companies if this would jeopardize their corporate finance links with the management of those companies.

The government's interest in changing that situation was revealed most clearly with the appointment of Paul Myners (2001: 147–51) to carry out a review of institutional investment, whose report was received in 2001, i.e. before Higgs was appointed. This report accused institutional shareholders of failing to discharge their obligations to those on whose behalf they held the shares by failing to exercise their voting power at meetings of the company and more generally by failing to exercise their governance rights so as to influence the management of portfolio companies. The government proposed legislation, partly derived from US model of the ERISA,[67] to require greater activism. For the time being, however, the institutional shareholders seem to have staved off that threat by adopting a voluntary code which commits them to monitoring the performance of portfolio companies, including compliance with the Combined Code; intervening where necessary, up to and including seeking to change the board; and reporting the results of their activities to their clients (Institutional Shareholders' Committee 2002). However, that the pressure is still on the institutions is shown by the recent Treasury review of the Myners principles in operation (HM Treasury 2004: esp. 27–29).

[67] Employee Retirement Income Security Act 1974 (29 USC § 1001 *et seq.*).

The prospect of more active institutional scrutiny of areas where companies are were not in compliance with the Combined Code was enough to generate on the part of management of large British companies a spirited opposition to Higgs' proposals, when they were first announced. In particular, management feared that institutions would not take seriously companies' explanations of their reasons for not complying with areas of the new Code, so that the Code would become based de facto on compliance, rather than comply or explain. However, the government holds the whip hand: the threat of legislation. Once the government made it clear it supported the Higgs proposals, management had little choice but to accept them, for fear of the government deciding to take the Combined Code system out of the Listing Rules and placing it in the Companies Act, just as it had done with the regulation of directors' remuneration.[68] Thus, in the end the Financial Reporting Council, the body responsible for the Combined Code, accepted the Higgs proposals with essentially cosmetic changes, and they came into effect in the second half of 2003.[69]

The recent post-Enron reform of the Combined Code demonstrates two interesting features of the mechanisms which make an important source of regulation. First, despite its non-legislative status, reform of the Code is driven by the threat of legislation or, more precisely, by the desire on the part of those affected by it to avoid direct legislation for fear, presumably, that legislation would be even less palatable than the Code. Secondly, the day-to-day sanction behind the Code is provided not simply by the requirement, which is legally sanctioned,[70] to disclose and justify areas of non-compliance, with possible reputational costs where the justification is thought to be inadequate. Rather, the ultimate sanction appears to be the fear of adverse investor reaction to disclosure of non-compliance, expressed either through the market for the company's shares or, more likely, through the exercise by shareholders of their governance rights in a way which is adverse to the interests of the incumbent management.

X. CONCLUSIONS

'Enron' opened up the path to some important corporate governance

---

[68] See above, text to n 28.

[69] The current version of the Combined Code is available at: http://www.frc.org.uk/about/combined.cfm.

[70] Listing Rule 12.43A requires the company to state annually the extent of its compliance with the Combined Code and to explain areas of non-compliance, and breach of a Listing Rule attracts the sanctions laid down in FSMA 2000, notably in s 91 which permits the FSA to impose penalties on the issuer and/or its directors for contravention of the Listing Rules.

reforms in Europe which previously had not been accessible. Legislating in reaction to the latest scandal has its dangers, of course, not least the danger of over-reaction, of legislating before a robust and dispassionate analysis has been established of the lessons to be learned from that scandal. On the other hand, in democracies a public scandal makes available for reformers that most precious of legal commodities, legislative time. For corporate law, not otherwise likely to be given a high political ranking, the scandal, by breaking down the stranglehold which interest groups are often able to lay upon the process of reform, may provide an important opportunity to make changes which the prior consensus had prevented (and which it is beyond the competence of the courts to achieve). Neither in the United Kingdom nor at the level of the Community can it be said that the temptation of over-reaction has been much in evidence. Well before the events in the United States unfolded, respected voices were criticizing the European and domestic rules on auditors', managers' and non-executive directors' conflicts of interest, and the reforms proposed or enacted in the United Kingdom and at Community level have generally eschewed the options which were likely to do more harm than good. In this respect, the fact that Enron pointed clearly to the dangers of the governance systems of large companies, as then configured, but did not inflict in Europe the scale of direct harms to the investors and employees which were suffered in the United States, seems to have provided the correct blend of stimulation without panic which the political process, domestic and European, needed to produce valid results.

REFERENCES

ABI/NAPF (2004), Joint Statement by the Association of British Insurers and the National Association of Pension Funds, 'Best Practice on Executive Contracts and Severance', December 2004.

Audit Quality Forum (2005), *Auditor Resignation Statements*, February 2005.

BBC (2004), News, World Edition, 'GM cuts 10,000 jobs in Germany' 9 December 2004: http://news.bbc.co.uk/2/hi/business/4083159.stm.

Bebchuk, L. and Fried J. (2004), *Pay Without Performance: The Unfulfilled Promise of Executive Compensation* (Cambridge, MA: Harvard University Press).

Black, B.S. and Coffee, J.C. (1994), 'Hail Britannia?: Institutional Investor Behavior Under Limited Regulation' 92 *Michigan Law Review* 1997.

CGAAI (2003), Final Report of the Co-ordinating Group on Audit and Accounting Issues, URN 03/567, 29 January 2003.

Chandler, W.B. and Strine, L.E. (2003), 'The New Federalism of the American Corporate Governance System: Preliminary Reflections of Two Residents of One Small State' 152 *University of Pennsylvania Law Review* 953.

Coffee, J.C. (2003), 'Gatekeeper Failure and Reform: The Challenge of Fashioning Relevant Reforms', Columbia Law School Center for Law and Economic Studies, Working Paper No. 237, September 2003.

Company Law Review (2000a), *Developing the Framework*, URN 00/656 (London: DTI).

—— (2000b), *Completing the Structure*, URN 00/1335 (London: DTI).

—— (2001), *Final Report*, Vol 1, URN 01/942 (London: DTI).

Davies, P. (2004), 'Post-Enron Developments in the United Kingdom' in Ferrarini *et al.* (eds), *Reforming Company and Takeover Law in Europe* (Oxford: Oxford University Press), 185.

Deloitte (2004), Report on the impact of the Directors' Remuneration Report Regulations, November 2004.

DTI (2001), Directors' Remuneration: A Consultative Document, URN 01/1400 (London: DTI).

—— (2003a), Review of the Regulatory Regime for the Accountancy Profession, URN 03/589 (London: DTI).

—— (2003b), 'Rewards for Failure': Directors' Remuneration—Contracts, Performance and Severance, URN 03/652 (London: DTI).

—— (2004), Proposal by the European Commission for a Directive on the Statutory Audit of Annual and Consolidated Accounts: Consultation Document, URN 04/1382 (London: DTI).

—— (2005), Company Law Reform, Cm 6456 (London: TSO).

Ebke, W. (2004), 'Corporate Governance and Auditor Independence' in Ferrarini *et al* (eds), *Reforming Company and Takeover Law in Europe* (Oxford: Oxford University Press).

European Commission (1998), Communication from the Commission, *The Statutory Audit in the European Union: the Way Forward* (OJ C143/12, 8.5.1998).

—— (2002a), *A First EU Response to Enron Related Policy Issues*, note prepared for Ecofin Council meeting in Oviedo: http://europa.eu.int/comm/internal_market/company/docs/enron/ecofin_2004_04_enron_en.pdf.

—— (2002b), Commission Recommendation on the Statutory Auditors' Independence in the EU: A Set of Fundamental Principles (OJ L191/22, 19.7.2002).

—— (2003a), Communication from the Commission to the Council and the European Parliament, *Modernising Company Law and Enhancing Corporate Governance in the European Union—A Plan to Move Forward*, COM(2003) 284 final, 21.5.2003.

—— (2003b), Communication from the Commission to the Council and the European Parliament, Reinforcing the statutory audit in the EU, COM(2003) 286 final (OJ C 236/2, 2.10.2003).

—— (2004a), Proposal for a Directive on statutory audit of annual accounts and consolidated accounts, COM(2004) 177 final, Brussels, 16.3.2004.

—— (2004b), Proposal for a Directive amending Council Directives 78/660/EEC concerning the annual accounts of certain types of companies and consolidated accounts: http://europa.eu.int/comm/internal_market/accounting/docs/board/prop-dir_en.pdf

—— (2004c), Commission Recommendation on fostering an appropriate regime for the remuneration of directors of listed companies (OJ L 385/55, 29.12.2004).

—— (2005), Commission Recommendation on the role of non-executive or supervisory directors and on committees of the (supervisory) board (OJ L52/51, 25.02.2005).

Financial Times (2004a), 'Berlin "should reveal top pay"', 20 September 2004.

—— (2004b), 5 October 2004.

—— (2005), 'UK chiefs reluctant to take on audit role', 31 January 2005.

FRC (2003), Financial Reporting Council, Audit Committees: Combined Code Guidance. A report and proposed guidance by an FRC-appointed group chaired by Sir Robert Smith.

Gower, L.C.B. and Davies, P.L. (2003), *Principles of Modern Company Law*, 7th ed (London: Sweet & Maxwell).

Higgs, D. (2003), *Review of the role and effectiveness of non-executive directors* (London: DTI).

High Level Group (2002), A Modern Regulatory Framework for Company Law in Europe, Brussels, 4 November 2002: http://europa.eu.int/comm/internal_market/en/company/company/modern/consult/report_en.pdf.

HM Treasury (2004), Myners principles for institutional investment decision-making, December 2004.

Institutional Shareholders' Committee (2002), The Responsibilities of Institutional Investors and Agents—Statement of Principles.

Myners, P. (2001), 'Institutional Investment in the UK: A Review', (London: HM Treasury).

OFT (2004), An assessment of the implications for competition of a cap on auditors' liability, July 2004 (OFT 741).

Stapledon, G. (1996), *Institutional Shareholders and Corporate Governance* (Oxford: Oxford University Press).

13

Modern Company and Capital Market Problems: Improving European Corporate Governance After Enron

KLAUS J HOPT[*]

[*] Professor and Director, Max Planck Institute for Comparative and International Private Law, Hamburg. This article was originally presented as the inaugural lecture of the Anton Philips Chair at Tilburg University on 6 September 2002. At that time, the Enron tragedy had happened hardly a year before and the Sarbanes-Oxley Act was just six weeks old. But not only this: the lecture was given before the publication of the Second Report of the High Level Group of Company Law Experts (A Modern Regulatory Framework for Company Law in Europe, Brussels, 4 November 2002). In this context, some the views expressed here were my own which were reflected later in the Group's Report; others deviated from the views of my fellow members in the Group or went further into areas not covered by the Report. For the publication in the *Journal of Corporate Law Studies*, the events and publications up to the spring of 2003 were taken into consideration. It is against this background that this article should be read. When the editors asked me to have the article reprinted in this book, it was clear that an actual updating was out of the question, since company and capital market law in Europe have developed rapidly in the meantime, as did the post-Enron law and legal literature in the United States and indeed all over Europe. It would have meant writing a completely new article, as I actually did and published at OUP in 2005 (Hopt, 2005; see also Hopt and Voigt 2005). On the other hand, leaving the article just as it was did not seem to be satisfactory either. So I chose a middle way, well aware of the delicacy of such an endeavour. Apart from a few instances, I made only minor changes in the text, in such a way that the reader could still see where, in hindsight, my assessments proved to be correct or else where law and politics in Europe moved in a different direction. But time and again I have referred in the footnotes to developments which have happened since and seem to me crucial for understanding where European Union company and capital market law is moving and why it is doing so. An earlier version of this chapter was published in (2003) 3 *Journal of Corporate Law Studies* 221–268.

I. ENRON AND COMPANY AND CAPITAL MARKET LAW IN EUROPE: THE NEED FOR IMPROVING CORPORATE GOVERNANCE

A. Financial Scandals and Legislation: The Case of Enron

IF ONE STUDIES the history of investor protection by company and capital market law since the Middle Ages,[1] the two prominent factors in shaping this history seem to be economic needs on the one side, and financial collapses and scandals on the other. Legislators seem to respond more to the latter events, the so-called bubbles. Instead of acting, they react and then very often overreact—a historical observation that supports modern public choice theory's doubts as to the rationality of regulation. Early prominent examples are the notorious South Sea Bubble in England, which led to the Bubble Act in 1720, and John Law's financial operations in Paris in the same year. Modern securities regulation—in particular the 1933 and 1934 US American blueprint, as well as the rules relating to auditors, bank and insurance company supervision, insider dealing, market manipulation, and prospectus liability—all trace their origins back to such events.

For the United States, it is beyond doubt that Enron[2] and its followers will go down in the history of American company and capital market law. Some observers have gone so far as to state that Enron will stand out as a marking point in the chronology of regulation: the time before and after Enron. The Sarbanes-Oxley Act passed in July 2002 is intended '(t)o protect investors by improving the accuracy and reliability of corporate disclosures made pursuant to the securities laws....' It contains far-reaching rules on accounting oversight, auditor independence, corporate responsibility, enhanced financial disclosure, analyst conflict of interest, and corporate and criminal fraud accountability. Some of these rules, such as the mandatory division between audit and non-audit services, have been debated for years and, for good or bad, simply would not have been passed without Enron. With others, especially the penal parts of the law and the rules on barring persons from serving as officers or directors, the legislators have once more resorted to the dubious panaceas of drastic criminal sanctions and quick professional

---

[1] See the survey and sources in Lehmann (1895); Hopt 1975: 15–50; 1980: 128–68; Merkt (2001); Davies (2003: 18–44); Frentrop (2003); Gepken-Jager *et al.* (2005).

[2] See Senate Committee on Governmental Affairs, The Role of the Board of Directors in Enron's Collapse, 107th Congress, 2nd Session, Report 107–70, 8 July 2002. In the meantime there has been a host of very different legal, economic, and political explanations and reactions to Enron and the ensuing Sarbanes-Oxley Act, among them Bratton (2002); Coffee (2002; 2004; this volume, ch 6); Brown (2005); Romano (2005); Davies (this volume, ch 12); Deaking and Konzelmann (this volume, ch 4).

disbarments, without giving enough credit to the mixed experiences with the prosecution of white-collar crimes and possibly even to the basic rights of freedom of profession.[3]

B. Consequences for European Company and Capital Market Law?

What follows from this for Europe? Enron and, in its aftermath, President Bush's ten-point program that led to the Sarbanes-Oxley Act, have been discussed widely all over Europe. Two irreconcilable patterns have emerged in this discussion. For many politicians as well as auditors and other professionals, Enron, WorldCom, and all the others are just an American phenomenon without direct relevance for Europe. According to them, Enron is a problem that is specific to US GAAP and so could not have occurred under the present EU or international accounting standards. Further, on this view, if there is an impact on Europe, it is in the improved chances of having the IAS/IFRS adopted universally and—what an illusion![4]—even in the United States in the form of a compromise between US GAAP and IAS. On the other side of the discussion, populist politicians who have a feel for public fears denounced 'greedy directors and crony auditors' and cried out for drastic reforms in Europe as well. Some proposals elaborated for the European Commission did run straight against the modern principles of facilitating the creation and running of companies and business and of deregulation and flexibilization of company and capital market law: proposals such as introducing outright state approval for newly formed companies or a waiting period of six months before a company can be created have been floated—as though every company were a potential vehicle for conspiracy against investors, tax fraud, money laundering, and even terrorism. Fortunately enough, these proposals were shelved very quickly.

As always, the truth lies somewhere between these extremes. Though there are major differences between the United States and 'The Control of Corporate Europe' (Barca and Becht 2001), Enron, WorldCom, and their

---

[3] This assessment from September 2002 reflects a widely shared feeling in Europe by 2006 which pertains not only to the Sarbanes-Oxley Act and its aftermath, but even more so to well-meaning but too bureaucratic legislative reform activities in Europe since 2003. *Cf.* for example from a Swiss perspective Zuberbühler (2004).

[4] The chances of a rapprochement have improved in the meantime, but I still do not believe in a full reciprocal recognition, as welcome as that would be. This makes the transatlantic corporate governance dialogue in the field even more crucial, both between the American and European supervisory bodies (see Hellwig 2005) as well as more broadly between practitioners and academics in the field; *cf.* The Transatlantic Corporate Governance Dialogue as started by the American Law Institute and the European Corporate Governance Institute (New York Conference on 27 September 2005).

associates are by no means just an American balance-sheet scandal; they can and should teach Europe a lesson (certainly at the latest after the fall of Parmalat (Ferrarini and Guidici this volume, ch 5) on how to act in a timely fashion—not just through reaction, perhaps even overreaction—but by well-thought-out company and capital market law reforms concerning corporate governance. There seems to be a consensus as to the need for reform in these fields, both in the Member States and at the EU level. What remains controversial is the concrete reform package, and there are a panoply of reform proposals indeed, in both fields and all over Europe.

Many Member States such as France, Germany, Italy, and others have already reformed or are about to reform their company laws and their capital market regulation.[5] The most prominent is Great Britain's upcoming centennial company law reform.[6] This is not just a reaction to certain scandals, but was prepared in such a broad, deep, and open reform discussion process that it can serve as an example for company and capital market law-making in other Member States as well.

As to Europe, the European Commission mandated the High Level Group of Company Law Experts (hereafter the Expert Group) with helping to set afloat again the 13th Directive on public takeovers and, more broadly, to come up with a vision on where the priorities of a European company law should be. In a direct reaction to Enron, the European Council's meeting on 21 and 22 June 2002 in Seville extended the mandate of the group to include:

> issues related to best practices in corporate governance and auditing, in particular concerning the role of non-executive directors and supervisory boards, management remuneration, management responsibility for financial information, and auditing practices.[7]

The Expert Group delivered its takeover report on 10 January 2002[8] and after extensive consultation[9] came up with its second report on 4 November 2002.[10] In its Action Plan of 21 May 2003, the European

[5] France: Nouvelles Régulations Economiques of 2001; Germany: KonTraG of 1998, Transparenz- und Publizitätsgesetz of 2002; Italy: Testo unico of 1998 and the reform proposals of the Mirone Commission and the Vietti Commission; see Hopt and Leyens (2004); High Level Group (2005).

[6] See DTI (2002), the Higgs Report (2003) and most recently Davies (this volume, ch 12).

[7] Presidency Conclusions, Seville European Council, 21 and 22 June 2002, SN 200/02, p. 15.

[8] High Level Group (2002a). Much—though not all—of what the High Level Group recommended in its first report was taken up by the European Commission in its draft of the 13th Directive of 2 October 2002, but the ultimate text of the 13th Directive as of 21 April 2004 deviated considerably from it by allowing options, see below Part IV.C.

[9] A summary of the comments submitted can be found in Annex 3 of the European Commission High Level Expert Group (2002b) p. 136 *et seq.*

[10] High Level Group (2002b).

Commission (2003) went along with many of the recommendations of the Expert Group.[11]

Identifying the key elements of, and most desirable reforms for, corporate governance is difficult enough, but the challenge reaches further: the fact that a rule may be good or even necessary for good corporate governance is not yet an answer to the question of whether such a rule is appropriate on the European level. This distinction is admittedly a fine one, and it has been neglected in most oral contributions to the group hearings as well as in many written comments in response to the consultative document. The group was well aware of the acute debate between the race-to-the-bottom and the race-to-the-top advocates[12] and has been carefully weighing whether rules at the European level are needed or rules in the Member States suffice. It has, for example, come to the conclusion that it is not recommendable to have one single European corporate governance code issued by the European Commission, but considers that it is better to have various national corporate governance codes that are embedded in the national corporate law and securities regulation and compete with each other.[13] This does not impede efforts of the European Commission to coordinate Member States' efforts on a non-binding basis.[14] Similarly, it has refrained from recommending a more far-reaching harmonization of core company law, for example of the duties of care of the board members or of substantive board member liability rules.[15] Instead it has singled out key areas and core rules that may seem better suited than national rules to protect investors and markets across the Member States by maintaining or raising confidence in the proper functioning of the internal market.[16] It has done so following the example of the Forum Europaeum Corporate Group Law (2000), of which I also was a member, that has rejected the idea of a 9th Directive on company groups, but has come forward instead with a number of more nuanced recommendations on European and/or national rules for specific problems created by groups in the internal market (See also Schneider 2005). Even if European rules seemed recommendable, the Expert Group preferred disclosure as a regulatory

---

[11] A comprehensive international discussion can be found in Ferrarini, Hopt, Winter, and Wymeersch (2004). See also Hopt (2005).

[12] See, for example, Romano (1993; 2002). At least for Europe, a more cautious position as to the workable competition of rules and regulators is rightly taken, for example, by Grundmann (2001) and by Merkt (1995). But see most recently Armour (this volume, ch 14) and Hertig and McCahery (this volume, ch 15) as well as McCahery et al (2002).

[13] High Level Group (2002b: ch. III.6).

[14] High Level Group (2002b: ch. III.6). The European Commission has convened a European Corporate Governance Forum to coordinate corporate governance efforts of Member States through a non-legislative Commission initiative.

[15] High Level Group (2002b: ch. III.4).

[16] As to the confidence argument, see Moloney (2003).

instrument to substantive rules, as described in more detail in Part III.A. Last but not least, even if European initiatives are recommended, it is open to further thought what kind of instrument is best suited—i.e., regulation, directive, recommendation, or further study by the European Commission—and what kind of priority should be given to the various initiatives. In its Action Plan, the European Commission has done exactly this and has specified the legal forms and priorities it intends to give to the various instruments proposed by the Expert Group (European Commission 2003).[17]

The host of reform problems faced in the various Member States makes rigorous selection unavoidable. Selection means focusing on what is essential and leaving aside everything else, as interesting or original as it may be. Therefore, the thesis for this inaugural lecture will be that *the lesson of Enron and the key to European company and capital market law reform* should be *the improvement of European corporate governance*. As to company law or, as some say, to internal corporate governance, in my view the focus is clearly on the board. There is a need to ensure that we have efficient, loyal, and competent boards (Part II). Of course, institutional and other rules aimed at instituting such boards are not sufficient without appropriate control mechanisms, in particular independent auditing (Part III). Corporate governance cannot succeed through company law alone, but needs capital market law rules as well. This is by no means a truism in all countries: in some, an older generation of company lawyers feels threatened by the wave of functional, market-driven, Anglo-Saxon securities regulation. Again, securities regulation or capital market law is a vast area, and so is capital market law reform. The focus of this article will be on information and intermediation problems where there is the key to investor protection and better corporate governance (Part IV). The main distinction will be between primary markets, secondary markets, and the market for corporate control. For primary market regulation, the ongoing discussion on European framework rules for prospectus liability will be picked up as an exemplary reform problem. In the secondary markets, the most urgent need of investor and investor protection is the need for loyal and competent intermediaries. As to the market for corporate control, the 13th Directive and the golden share judgments of the European Court of Justice are most relevant. The chapter will be concluded by Part V, which consists of a summary in the form of sixteen theses.

---

[17] On European company law, see Grundmann (2004).

II. IMPROVING CORPORATE GOVERNANCE BY COMPANY LAW: EUROPEAN RULES FOR EFFICIENT, LOYAL, AND COMPETENT BOARDS

A. Shareholder Decision-Making and the Role of the Board

The shareholders of a public company delegate the management and the control over the officers of the company to the board. This creates the well-known principal-agent problem between the shareholders and the board, and is the reason why the focus of internal corporate governance is on the board (Kraakman *et al.* 2004, 11 et s., 34 *et seq.*). This does not preclude corporate governance reform needs as to shareholder decision-making.[18] Such reforms are intricate for two obvious reasons: the average shareholder/investor is known for his rational apathy, and institutional investors tend to continue to follow the 'Wall Street rule', i.e., to move out of their investment rather than to monitor within the company. Though there are instances of internal monitoring activity by institutional investors,[19] primarily in the United States but also in Europe, and these activities should be fostered (Myners 2001: 89; Davies 2003b; see also Gerke *et al.*, Garrido and Rojo, and Garrido in Hopt and Wymeersch 2003: 357, 427 and 449),[20] the basic pattern seems to remain unchanged.[21]

Still, shareholder participation in the general assembly and voting should be facilitated as far as possible. It is at odds with corporate governance that in many listed companies, a majority of shareholders do not attend and are not represented by proxies at the general meetings. Modern technology allows much quicker and better shareholder information, communication, and decision-making. This is particularly true in the international context, where the shares are typically not held

---

[18] The European Commission plans to mandate a study of the consequences of an approach aimed at achieving full shareholder democracy (one share / one vote), at least for listed companies. See European Commission (2003). The concept of equality of shareholders (De Cordt 2004) and its application on the voting rights is highly controversial, politically as well as theoretically. Multiple voting rights are common in a number of Member States, in particular in Scandinavia and France. The economic argument is that the variations in voting rights are priced at the market. Nevertheless, Commissioner McCreevy has affirmed his intention to go ahead in late 2005.

[19] For the US *cf.* Romano (2001); she tries to explain why empirical studies suggest that corporate governance activism has an insignificant effect on targeted firms' performance. As to EC regulation, see Welch (2002) and the proposals of the High Level Group (2002b: ch. III.3.3). See also the contributions in Baums, Buxbaum, and Hopt (1994).

[20] The European Commission plans to require enhanced disclosure for institutional investors of their investment and voting policies through a directive. See European Commission (2003).

[21] Apart from this, the idea of agents watching agents has its shortcomings, in particular where institutional agents watching firm agents have conflicts of interest with other shareholders. See Woidtke (2002).

directly but via one or more domestic or foreign intermediaries. In many Member States, voting by company proxies has been permitted and modern technology has entered both the meeting rooms and the company laws.[22]

Facilitating participation and electronic voting is one thing. But *forcing* shareholders—even institutional shareholders—to make use of these modern facilities or even to vote at all, as is occasionally prescribed to institutional investors, is quite another thing. Such a rule could have the practical effect that the institutional votes would routinely be cast in favor of management, as we can observe in the proxy voting practice of German banks.[23] This would strengthen the board rather than enhancing control over it, apart from extremely bad situations where red lights are already flashing (and bank credits are in danger).

Despite these practical limitations, shareholder decision-making remains a basic principle of corporate governance. It is the shareholders who are the ultimate risk-bearers in the company. The creditors and particularly the employees of the company and other stakeholders have their own means to protect themselves; if not, they are to be protected by rules other than general company law rules, such as 'piercing the corporate veil,'[24] tort law, and insolvency law.[25] Labour co-determination in the board, at least in its far-reaching parity or quasi-parity German form, is a problematic exception.[26]

The apportionment of decision-making between the shareholders and the board is a classical question addressed by all company laws (Kraakman *et al.* 2004). Fundamental decisions and significant transactions, such as alterations of the company charter, mergers, and other reorganizations, are for the shareholders. Many other decisions, even far-reaching ones, are fully delegated to the board because of the advantage of a centralized management. It is true that the line between what is to be decided by the board and what should remain for the shareholders is difficult to draw and is drawn rather differently in national company laws. It suffices to mention the German judge-made

[22] The European Commission intends to set up an integrated legal framework to facilitate efficient shareholder communication and decision-making (participation in meetings, exercise of voting rights, cross-border voting) through a draft directive of January 2006.

[23] See Köndgen (1994). A comparative law survey on the proxy systems in Germany, the UK, Spain, France, and Italy can be found in Becker (2002). On the German financial system, see Krahnen and Schmidt (2005).

[24] In Anglo-American corporate law this is seen as a general company law doctrine, while in German and other continental European laws this is considered to be part of general civil law, which applies to all kinds of legal personalities.

[25] High Level Group (2002a).; See also the nuanced view of Davies (2002a: 266 *et seq.*). See generally Hansmann (1996).

[26] See below II.D.

Holzmüller doctrine,[27] a godsend donation to company lawyers and company law professors because it is difficult to know in advance when a transaction is substantial enough to need the authorization of the general assembly. Nevertheless, in some critical fields, especially if the personal interests of the board are affected, corporate governance may be improved by devolving the decision to the shareholders.

Examples of two good candidates for shareholder decision-making—at least in listed companies—are the frustration of public takeover bids by the directors of the target company and payments to the directors, the latter at least as far as the framework for such payments is concerned. In these cases, the advantages of centralized management are outweighed by the conflict of interest of the board members. In its first report the Expert Group has recommended this solution for the frustration of public takeover bids, thereby following the British approach. In its second report the Expert Group considered whether European company law should also give the shareholders a role in fixing the principles and limits of board remuneration.[28] Both the European anti-frustration rule, as controversial as it is in Germany and some other countries and ultimately also under the 13th Directive of 2004, and shareholder decision-making on the principles and limits of board remuneration, seem beneficial for the European internal market: the first because of the impacts of takeovers as to synergies and disciplining management,[29] and the second because of the need to maintain public confidence in remuneration and decision- making on remuneration.[30]

B. Efficiency: Board Structure and Organization, in Particular the One-Tier/Two-Tier Board Debate and Board Committees

In public companies, centralized management by the board is the rule. It serves shareholders best, provided that the board is efficient, loyal, and competent (Kraakman *et al.* 2004; Böckli 2004: § 13). In most Member States, it is felt that not all of these three desiderata are generally fulfilled, and reform is under discussion. Efficient board structure and organization comes first, because even fully loyal and competent board members cannot fulfill their function without an adequate structural and organizational framework. As to board structure, there is an extensive and ongoing academic discussion about the pros and cons of the one-tier

---

[27] *Holzmüller* case, German Federal Bundesgerichtshof, *Entscheidungen des Bundesgerichtshofes in Zivilsachen (BGHZ)* (Köln Berlin, Heymanns 1982) 83, 122. Most recently the court has limited the Holzmüller doctrine.
[28] High Level Group (2002a: 27 *et seq*); High Level Group (2002b: ch. III.4.2).
[29] See below IV.C.
[30] See below II.C.

and the two-tier board system. Marcus Lutter (2000) and Paul Davies (2000) shed light on the superiority or inferiority of the German two-tier system in relation to the British one-tier system.[31] Of course, both are aware that, in practice, especially in listed companies, there is considerable convergence between both systems. But Paul Davies (2000: 455) concludes that:

> (t)he German supervisory board continues to be a rather ineffective monitor, whereas the U.K. board has not only taken on the monitoring task formally but is better placed to discharge it effectively in practice.

I tend to agree with Paul Davies, though, like him, I think less effective monitoring might be outweighed by gains in networking, and which finally benefits shareholders the most is an empirical question (Davies 2000: 453) that is hard to answer in a methodologically correct way.

As a consequence, board structure is a candidate for corporate governance reform.[32] Yet it is certainly not for European corporate governance law to make either one of the two systems mandatory, as was tried many years ago by the early draft 5th Directive. This is even more true since practitioners on both sides of the Channel—how surprisingly!—overwhelmingly believe that their own system is clearly the better one.[33]

But it would be worthwhile to introduce another European rule, namely that which requires the Member States to give companies the choice between the different systems.[34] France was the first to offer such a choice. Italy is following suit, and is even offering three models to choose from. Also on the European level, the statute of the European company has for the first time set an unexpected precedent for such a libertarian rule, though of course this is still confined to the European Company *(Societas Europaea)*.[35] The French experience was that whilst the vast majority of companies stuck to their traditional one-tier model, a significant number of listed and multinational companies preferred a structural division between management and control.[36] A European rule

---

[31] See also Maassen (2000). See also the Higgs Report (2003).

[32] In Germany a joint symposium of the two leading commercial and company law reviews, *ZHR* and *ZGR*, has dealt with this topic; see Hommelhoff *et al.* (2002).

[33] See Hampel (1998); Theisen (1998: 260).

[34] Hopt (1997a: 14); High Level Group (2002b: ch. III.4.1.a). As to France and Italy, see Hopt and Leyens (2004). The European Commission plans to give all listed companies a choice, through a directive, between the two types (monistic/dualistic) of board structures. See European Commission (2003).

[35] Council Regulation of 8 October 2001, OJ L 294/1, 10.11.2001, Art. 39 *et seq.* on the two-tier system, Art. 43 *et seq.* on the one-tier system.

[36] Only 4% of all public companies, but 20% of the companies making up the CAC 40-index (for example, Axa, Pinaut-Printemps-Redoute, PSA, Vivendi Universal and Aventis); see Cozian, Viandier, and Deboissy (2005: no.611); Le Cannu (2000); Guyon (2002).

requiring Member States to pass the choice between the two systems on to the companies themselves would allow the shareholders to tailor their board structure in conformity with their particular company size and market needs. It is true that German mandatory labour co-determination does not fit in easily with such a choice, but this is a particular German problem and will probably prevent the creation of any German one-tier board European companies.

Board structure extends to the questions of the composition of the members of the board. Here the labour co-determination issue comes in once more. It is well known that this issue has upheld progress in European company law harmonization for decades and has led to an uneasy compromise in the regulation of the European Company which may very well be a blueprint for dealing with this issue in future directives, quite to the detriment of German companies (Lutter 2003: 87; Hopt 1994; Pistor 1999). German-style labour co-determination also led to significant problems under the Sarbanes-Oxley Act (Krause 2003). It is telling that in the Netherlands, the traditional system of co-optation of the board under parity rights of the shareholders and labour (which anyhow never affected large multinational companies) is giving way to a more clear-cut one-third representation of labour in the board, while since 2002 in France there has been a mandatory representation of one or two representatives of employee shareholders if they hold at least three per cent of the stock. This is independent of the option for companies to appoint employees of the company as directors, at a rate of up to one-third of the total directors in office. It remains to be seen whether Germany will follow the international lead (Baums and Ulmer 2004) which has been advocated strongly by business and academia (Ulmer 2002a). Yet the chances for this under the new coalition government are slim.

In the Member States, there is also a certain tendency toward more separation between management and board. But again, this is either optional—as under the new regime in France, where the president director general no longer automatically combines the functions of Chief Executive Officer and Chairman/ President of the board—or it has been left to the codes or listing requirements, as in the UK under the Combined Code. This indicates that such a rule is no candidate for European harmonization. Quite another reform question is the role of non-executive directors, which will be treated separately in Part II.D.

As to board size and board organization, much has been improved during recent years by board reform in various Member States, though again in Germany, the matter of board size—typically twenty (!) in large co-determined companies—has proved to be a taboo for reform because of labour co-determination and the German trade unions. The German

Corporate Governance Commission, while coming up with hundreds of reform proposals, many of which are small and technical (though reasonable), has not even touched this problem, and it has been criticized for this.[37] Many of the possible improvements of board organization— such as committee structure, frequency, preparation and carrying- out of the meetings, and the role of the chairman—are not for the legislator at all but should be left either to the listing requirements of the stock exchanges or to the companies themselves. Even less should they be part of a European corporate governance rule.

A different answer may, however, be given to the question of whether European law should make audit committees mandatory. In the United Kingdom and in other countries with a one-tier board, audit committees are common. In large German companies audit committees are frequent, but overall they are much less common than in other Member States.[38] This is in part due to the two-tier system, and in part because the tasks of the audit committee are fulfilled by other committees such as the presidential committee or the finance committee. The 2002 German Corporate Governance Code recommended the establishment of such a committee by listed companies under the comply-or-explain system. In view of the two-tier board system, the German Code does not contain independence rules beyond the suggestion that the chairman of the auditing committee should not be a former member of the management board. This contrasts with the British Combined Code, according to which all or the majority of the members of the auditing committee (as well as of the remuneration and appointment committees) should be independent directors. In the United States, the American SEC already caused the stock exchanges in 1999 to require listed companies to have audit committees with special tasks and independent member requirements. In reaction to Enron, the Sarbanes-Oxley Act of 2002 further tightened the rules on public company audit committees, in particular as to their independence and responsibility.

In the light of Enron and the general confidence crisis that may also affect the internal market, there is a case for a European rule requiring listed companies to have audit committees that are responsible for the appointment (or at least the preparation of it), compensation, and oversight of the work of the auditors of the company with at least a

---

[37] Hopt (2002a). The recent decision of the Allianz Corporation to transform its legal form from a German corporation into a European corporation in early 2006 will have the highly welcome side effect of reducing the size of the board from 20 to 12. Labour co-determination at parity must be maintained for political reasons, but due to the future representation of foreign workers in the board, the influence of German trade unions will drop considerably.

[38] As to the board committees in Germany, see Hopt and Roth (2005: section 107 comments 228–450).

majority of independent members.[39] While the details are many and not easy to decide and should be left to the stock exchanges or listing authorities to decide, the question of independence is, of course, crucial and highly controversial.[40]

C. Loyalty, in Particular Payments to Directors

One suggestion, first made several years ago, is that the duty of loyalty of directors—in contrast to their duty of care—might be a good candidate for European harmonization (Tunc 1991: 211 *et seq.*). The argument brought forward is that virtually all company laws contain the duty of loyalty in one way or another, and that loyalty is an absolutely essential requirement for board members, as indeed for all agents. Yet this suggestion raises doubts for a number of reasons. On closer inspection, the extent to which the duty of loyalty is developed in the various Member States is very different. In general, it can be said that in the United States and the United Kingdom, the duty of loyalty and more generally the critical appreciation of conflicts-of-interest situations are highly marked, while in Germany, France, and some other civil law countries, this is much less so.[41]

Furthermore, while the principle of loyalty is generally agreed upon, the case situations of conflict of interest are manifold[42] and their treatment may be highly difficult and controversial indeed, in particular in groups of companies as well as in takeover situations.[43] It is true that the UK company law reform shows that the basic principle of how to treat transactions involving conflicts of interest can very well be codified.[44] But the details are still best handled by case law.

Finally, it would be odd to have a European company law rule dealing with the duty of loyalty while leaving aside the duty of care and other general principles by which directors are bound,[45] though in the vast majority of cases they are practically more relevant even if there is a business judgment rule.[46]

---

[39] The new European auditing directive, which is expected to be finally adopted in 2006, will require companies of public interest to have such an audit committee. While this would be mandatory, there is the recommendation of the Commission of 15 February 2005, according to which listed companies should have three key committees, namely for nomination, remuneration, and audit.

[40] See more detail in the context of independent directors below II.D.

[41] See Hopt (1996a: 917, 921 *et seq.*); Kraakman *et al.* (2004: 101 *et seq.*, 128 *et seq.*).

[42] Hopt (1985); Enriques (2000); Hopt and Roth (2005: § 100 comments 131–98).

[43] See Hopt (2002b) and more generally Hopt (2004).

[44] Schedule 2 para 5 of the British draft Companies Bill (DTI 2002).

[45] See Schedule 2 paras 1 *et seq.* of the British draft Companies Bill (DTI 2002).

[46] As to the hidden differences between the US and the German business judgment rules, see Hopt (1996a: 919 *et seq.*). In Germany the business judgment rule has been codified in 2005 in section 93 of the Stock Corporation Act.

These arguments do not hold for the payment of directors (Bebchuk and Fried 2004; Bebchuk, Fried and Walker 2002). There is no need to mention the many scandals that have come up in many of our countries and have been denounced at length in the financial press. For Germany, the 30 million Euros that the remuneration committee of the supervisory board of Mannesmann granted to the outgoing chairman of the management board, Klaus Esser, after the takeover by Vodafone was cleared continues to stir up public concern and envy. Because there is no way for single shareholders to attack this payment via a derivative action under present German company law, the case has been denounced to the public prosecutor, a criminal proceeding was started against the remuneration committee members for embezzlement of company assets, and after the 21 December 2005 decision of the Bundesgerichtshof which reversed the acquittal a final conviction has become rather probable. Although it has been observed with some justification that German society—in stark contrast to American society and much more than many other European societies—is an envy society, it is obvious that stock options and other forms of management remuneration open the door for exorbitant payments, which are of concern to the general public and threaten to make the whole system untrustworthy. This is of concern to the European internal market, too, since such payments tend to undermine the confidence of the shareholders and their willingness to invest in domestic and foreign companies. In conformity with its extended mandate, the Expert Group recommended European rules on management remuneration for listed companies,[47] and in the meantime the European Commission has come out with its recommendation of 14 December 2004. Three types of European rules may be particularly relevant: disclosure, shareholder decision-making, and accounting for share-based remuneration (on these proposed rules, see Hopt 2005,133–37; see also generally Ferrarini and Moloney 2004; as to accounting, Crook 2004)

D. Loyalty, Competence, and Non-executive Directors

As we have already seen, it is hard to find appropriate rules that define and solve the problem of board loyalty, particularly in cases of conflicts of interest. One way out may be to have persons on the board who are not subject—or are less subject—to such conflicts, i.e., independent non-executive directors. Indeed, in the last decades, in particular in the United States and in Great Britain but also in other countries, there has been a marked movement toward having non-executive directors on the board

---

[47] High Level Group (2002b: ch.III.4.2).

and especially on its key committees, though the initial enthusiasm for outside directors has been somewhat dampened, since no clear correlation has yet been found between having independent directors and firm welfare.

This tendency toward independent non-executive directors is less marked in countries with a two-tier board system such as Germany, because this system as such provides for mutual exclusivity of membership of the two boards. In Germany, therefore, some argue that the supervisory board members are per se outside or non-executive directors. Of course, this is only true insofar as there is a mandatory separation between the management board and the supervisory or control board, which both have to be comprised of different persons. But this neither precludes, as often happens, the movement of a former chairman of the management board into the supervisory board after retirement—typically assuming the role of chairman—nor does it touch upon the question of financial relations between the supervisory board members and the company. It is telling that the German Corporate Governance Code recommends only very cursorily that at any time the board must also comprise members who are sufficiently independent, and that no more than two former members of the management board should be members of the supervisory board.[48] As to the auditing committee, it contains the statement that the chairman of the auditing committee should not be a former member of the management board, but this statement is only a suggestion, not a recommendation for which the comply-or-explain rule would be valid.[49]

Attempts to formulate a European mandatory rule on non-executive directors are faced with two major difficulties: ensuring competence and ensuring independence.[50] The first difficulty is the trade-off between loyalty and competence. While non-executive directors do not face the same conflicts of interest as executive directors, they may be less familiar with the company's affairs and, depending on who is ineligible and who remains as a candidate, less competent than executive directors. This is already the case for many supervisory board members, particularly under labour co-determination. It may become even more so for non-executive directors if strict independence requirements are set up, although the problem is less pronounced in a one-tier board system, where non-executive directors are members of the same board and so

---

[48] German Corporate Governance Code 5.4.1, 5.4.2. For details, see Hopt and Roth (2005: § 100 comments 184 *et seq.*).

[49] German Corporate Governance Code 5.3.2.

[50] The European Commission has shied away from a mandatory rule by means of a directive and instead adopted a recommendation as of 15 February 2005. See also High Level Group (2002b: ch. III.4.1). On the recommendation, see Hopt (2005: 133 *et seq.*).

have better access to information. Therefore, ensuring competence becomes a real problem.

The tradition of directors' ex post liability does not help—certainly not under the traditional[51] English subjective standard of care, nor even under the objective Continental standard—if one takes into consideration the business judgment rule and, apart from this rule, the reticence of judges to interfere with the directors' business decision in liability suits.[52]

One possibility would be a rule requiring all directors to be competent or 'fit and proper,', similar to the regulation for bank and insurance company directors, but leaving the responsibility for checking competence with those who nominate the directors because of the lack of an authority corresponding to the banking or insurance supervisory agencies. Specifying what competence involves—for example, being able to read balance sheets or demonstrating 'financial literacy'—could help, but it may unduly restrict companies' choice of directors. Not all board members need to have financial expertise. Others might bring valuable experience, and others yet may simply have a talent for the business and for monitoring its conduct. Moreover, different businesses may benefit from different directors. The German Corporate Governance Code recommends that at any time, the supervisory board should comprise members who have the knowledge, skills, and experience necessary for fulfilling its tasks.[53] It seems that the commission which drafted the Code was not aware of how awkward this formula was, or that it may just have made allowances for labour co-determination: what it actually says is that it is enough if one or two members have the said faculties, while all the others do not need to have the knowledge, skills, and experience necessary to fulfil the board's tasks. What are they paid for then?

A way out of this dilemma may again be disclosure, that is, a rule requiring the company to disclose why each non-executive director is considered competent or fit and proper for his office, and to require the authority competent for listing on the stock exchange.

A better solution might be to require competence, but to give the listing authorities or stock exchanges the mandate to concretise this and to ask for training, including continuous professional education as in other professions. In addition to this, as mentioned before, the non- executive directors should have access to appropriate outside professional advice

---

[51] Over the past 10 years the standard has become somewhat more objective and there are now reform plans to change to an objective standard.

[52] See the figures for Germany in Hopt (1999: § 93 comment 16 *et seq.*), and in more detail in Ihlas (1997). As to the relationship between the business judgment rule and directors' liability, see M. Roth (2001).

[53] German Corporate Governance Code 5.4.1.

and to internal information from the company, as the British Combined Code requires.[54]

An even greater difficulty is independence. The concepts of what 'independence' is meant by and who or how many of the directors should be independent in the sense of the relevant rule differ widely. In the United Kingdom, for example, the Combined Code requires that at least one-third of the board as a whole should be non-executive directors, most of whom should be independent. Independent is defined as 'independent of management and free from any business or other relationship with the company which could materially interfere with the exercise of their independent judgment.'[55] Non-executive directors should be the only members, or a majority of the members, of the audit, remuneration and appointment committees. These requirements of the Combined Code strike a convincing balance between the necessity of having at least a majority of disinterested members in the three key committees, particularly in the audit committee, while leaving the necessary flexibility concerning the board as a whole.

Yet as a European rule for all Member States, this creates considerable difficulties for countries with labour co-determination, in particular for Germany.[56] In large companies there is a delicate ten to ten (in coal and steel industry ten to one to ten) balance in the board between capital and labour. If the independence requirement of the Combined Code were applied solely to the ten shareholders' representatives, this would weaken the shareholders' voice in the supervisory board even further. If the independence requirement is also applied to the labour side, as in the Netherlands, this would be even worse for the shareholders because the consequence would be weakening the voice of the employees, who know the company best and have a keen interest in its prosperity, for the sake of their own jobs and salaries. Instead, even more labour union representatives would move in, with interests that do not necessarily coincide with those of the particular company. Of course, it could be said—and is said by many in Germany (Ulmer 2002a: 271)[57]—that the actual regime of

---

[54] Combined Code, para A.1.3; Davies (2000: 440 *et seq.*).

[55] Combined Code, para A.3.2; Davies (2000). Compare also the Sec. 301 of the Sarbanes-Oxley Act with the new Sec. 10A(m)(3) of the Securities Exchange Act of 1934 defining independence for each member of the audit committee: 'may not ... (i) accept any consulting, advisory, or other compensatory fee from the issuer; or (ii) be an affiliated person of the issuer or any subsidiary thereof.'

[56] See the heated discussion in Germany on the Sarbanes-Oxley Act's independence requirements, which might be irreconcilable with German labour co-determination; *cf.* Institut der Wirtschaftsprüfer/Wirtschaftsprüferkammer (2002: 594). The former German Minister of Justice even protested that the American Act is being applied extraterritorially. This has been rightly refuted. For details, see Lanfermann and Maul (2002).

[57] But see also Davies (2002a: 274).

paritary labour co-determination in Germany is dated anyway, or at least needs to be overhauled. But this is not for the European Union to decide.

It might, therefore, be better to content oneself with a broader European principle[58] according to which, first, the board as a monitoring body should be independent of management and, Secondly, in the audit, remuneration, and appointment committees there should be at least a majority of members also independent from the company, in the sense of the Combined Code. Again, disclosure could help, i.e., a rule requiring the company to disclose which members it considers to be independent. In addition, these members should also file a personal declaration that they are (and continue to be) independent.

European rules for an efficient, loyal, and competent board as discussed so far may enhance corporate governance. But they need to be backed up by control and enforcement. Law in action is needed, not just law in the books. The experience with rules relating to the board, including liability rules, teaches that more than one control mechanism is needed, i.e., control from inside and from outside the company. In the next part, therefore, I shall briefly discuss three such mechanisms: control by the market via disclosure, control by the shareholders via better investigation and liability suit rules, and especially control by appropriate auditors.

III. CONTROLLING THE BOARD FROM INSIDE AND OUTSIDE: MARKETS, SHAREHOLDERS, AND AUDITORS

A. Control by the Market: The Case for Disclosure

Disclosure to the shareholders and to the market has long been a key mechanism in company and capital market law. The forerunners in company law were the Gladstonian reforms of 1844 and 1845. One hundred years later the US securities regulation of 1933 and 1934 gave the world a blueprint for the use of disclosure in securities regulation. Brandeis' dictum that the sun was the best disinfectant already had an early precedent in 1837 from the famous Prussian reformer Hansemann (1837: §109 at 104; Davies 2003a: 590 *et seq.*), who said:

> Among the means by which the management of a large company limited by shares can be kept law-abiding and efficient, is to be counted that it must be exposed to a certain degree to the public. This is the most effective control.

---

[58] See now in the same sense the recommendation of the European Commission of 15 February 2005.

Disclosure is also a powerful tool for improving corporate governance in Europe.[59] First and foremost, this type of regulation is most compatible with a market economy because it interferes least with freedom and competition of enterprises in the market. This is particularly relevant when, as seen before, there is considerable uncertainty and difference of opinion as to what the correct rules for European corporate governance. Under such circumstances, disclosure allows for greater flexibility, and in a way, can function as an experimental tool before the imposition of substantive legal provisions. Disclosure also avoids the well-known petrifying effect of European substantive law (Buxbaum and Hopt 1988: 241 *et seq.*).

It is true that there is considerable theoretical controversy as to the effectiveness of disclosure in efficient capital markets. Yet in reality, capital markets may not be that efficient; otherwise, Enron could hardly have happened the way it did. There is no need to go into the various forms of the efficient capital market theories here and to argue why the 'strong form' may be less than convincing. It suffices to record that modern theory justifies mandatory disclosure by its function of facilitating and enhancing corporate governance. According to this theory, corporate governance—not investor protection—provides the most persuasive justification for imposing on issuers the obligation to provide ongoing disclosure (via shareholder voting, shareholders enforcing management's fiduciary duties and capital allocation) (Fox 1999; Hopt 2001: 260).[60]

Some examples of how to promote corporate governance by disclosure have already been mentioned. If one accepts that shareholders of listed companies should have a say in the frustration of public takeover bids by the directors of the target company and in the principles and limits of payments to the directors, it is obvious that they need full disclosure in order to be able to make an informed decision of their own.[61] Disclosure may also be a useful tool for dealing with the problem of competence and independence of board members.[62]

The Expert Group has recommended that listed companies be required to disclose fully their capital and control structures, in particular possible defensive structures established in the company, in order to enable the market to react with discounts and a higher cost of capital.[63] The Expert

---

[59] The European Commission plans enhanced corporate governance disclosure requirements and increased disclosure of group structure and relations, both financial and non-financial, through directives amending existing legislation. See European Commission (2003). As to disclosure in securities regulation, see below IV.A.

[60] See more generally the comparative and interdisciplinary study by Fleischer (2001).

[61] See above II.A.

[62] See above II.D.

[63] High Level Group (2002a: 25 *et seq.*); see also SWX (2002: 18 *et seq.*) and Hofstetter (2002: 29 *et seq.*).

Group has gone further and recommended that listed companies should
be required to describe briefly the key elements of their governance
structure and practices, whether they arise from mandatory law, default
provisions, articles of association, or whether they are based on particular
codes.[64] In the answers to the questionnaire, there was overwhelming
consent for using disclosure to improve corporate governance. Examples
of what could be disclosed in this context include the following: major
shareholders of the company; shareholders rights, especially minority
rights; appropriate information about the board and the auditors, in
particular as to their independence and remuneration; the risk
management system within the company, etc. Disclosure should not be
restricted simply to financial information, but should be extended to
qualitative disclosure. A checklist of what to disclose should be
developed, and presentation in one comprehensive statement could be
required in order to help shareholders compare and evaluate companies
throughout the internal market based on their corporate governance
system.

Of course, non-disclosure and, even more, false disclosure must have
consequences for the directors.[65] The Sarbanes-Oxley Act provides for
drastic sanctions, both criminal and civil. As mentioned before, there are
considerable doubts about the sections on criminal accountability. The
most stringent civil sanction is forfeiture of certain bonuses and profits
under section 304. Forfeiture is mandatory if the issuer is required to
prepare an accounting restatement due to the material noncompliance of
the issuer, as a result of the misconduct, with any financial reporting
requirement under the securities laws. If this is the case, the CEO and the
CFO of the issuer shall reimburse the issuer for the amount of any bonus
or other incentive-based or equity-based compensation received from the
issuer during the last 12 months, and for any profits realized from the sale
of securities of the issuer during that 12-month period. In my view, this
rule as it is presently phrased is far too strict in its automatism and rigour
and might not stand up to constitutional scrutiny in certain Member
States of the EU. But it is true that it provides a powerful sanction
that could also be considered as a European rule if there is not an
automatic forfeiture, and if the individual contribution of the director
to the non-disclosure and false disclosure can duly be taken into
consideration.

[64] High Level Group (2002b: ch. III.2). The key items to be included in the annual corporate
governance statement are listed un *ibid.*, 46 *et seq.*
[65] The European Commission plans confirmation of collective responsibility of board
members for key non-financial statements through a directive amending existing legislation.
See European Commission (2003).

B. Control by the Shareholders: Investigation and Liability

Control by mere disclosure may not be enough. Not only may disclosure not be observed, but the facts may be so complicated that they just cannot be grasped and understood easily by the shareholders and by the market. This is particularly the case for international groups with complicated structures.[66] The case of the BCCI insolvency, which led to the so-called 'BCCI Directive' of the European Union of 29 June 1995, on better supervision of banks, insurance companies, and investment firms,[67] gives an excellent example of how difficult it is for markets—as well as for supervisory agencies—to evaluate the dangers inherent in complicated international group structures. Under European bank supervisory law, the need to organise enterprises and group structures of the said enterprises in a way that complete, consolidated supervision remains possible has been clearly articulated.[68] Such requirements do not exist for all companies apart from banking, insurance business, and investment services. But it is clear that the shareholders of companies other than the latter may have to cope with similar difficulties as the supervisory agencies in the said special enterprise sectors. This is truer still when there is a suspicion that the management of the company or of its parent company has behaved incorrectly.

For such cases, the special investigation procedure is a means of shareholder protection that is provided for in many Member States, such as Germany (since 1897), France (*expert de gestion* since 1966), the United Kingdom, the Netherlands, Belgium, Denmark, and others outside the EU such as Switzerland (Forum Europaeum Corporate Group Law 2000: 207 *et seq.*) The core provisions are rather similar, but the details vary considerably. There are also clear differences as to the actual frequency of such special investigation procedures in the various states. In some they are quite rare, as in Germany and Switzerland, while in others they are more frequent; in some, such as the Netherlands (Germoth and Meinema 2000), the experience is definitely positive. Yet in most, even when there are only a few cases, there tends to be agreement that this is an instrument of considerable protective importance that performs a preventative function in the hands of minority shareholders. Usually the special investigation may be ordered by the general meeting or by a court on the application of a minority of shareholders of ten or five per cent, or even of one single shareholder alone. The investigation as such is

---

[66] The European Commission plans increased disclosure of group structure and relations, both financial and non-financial, through a directive amending existing legislation. See European Commission (2003) and later draft instruments.

[67] Directive of 29 June 1995, OJ L 168/7, 18.7.1995.

[68] Preamble 58 of the Consolidated Bank Supervision Directive of 20 March 2000, OJ L 126/1, 26.5.2000.

conducted by the court or an administrative body or by a professional under its supervision. Recently, the president of the German Federal Agency for Financial Services Supervision, which has no authority to supervise the auditors, has suggested that the agency be empowered to institute a special investigation if the balance sheet of a listed company is seriously flawed. A special investigation of the company organs was also envisaged for the European company in the draft statutes of 1970 and 1975. In the later—watered-down—versions, this rule was omitted. The Forum Europaeum Corporate Group Law (2000: 216 *et seq.*) has already suggested that there should be a European rule on this, albeit only a framework rule that would leave it to the Member States to fit the special investigation into their particular procedural laws. The Expert Group came forward with a similar proposal in its questionnaire and received much support for it in the answers it received. Indeed, as one British observer (Davies 1997: 701) remarked, the special investigation seems 'to be the most effective method yet devised to detect corporate misconduct and to bring to book the perpetrators of it'.[69] In a single market the special investigation seems to be indispensable, not only for companies active across borders, but for reasons of fair competition for all others as well. The European Commission agrees to this.[70]

A successful special investigation can serve as a basis for a court claim, and indeed in some countries the two sets of proceedings are closely linked. This leads to the issue of the liability of directors. All Member States have rules on directors' liability. Yet these rules vary enormously from one State to another, both in the company acts, and even more in their practical application. Relevant as general directors' liability rules may be for corporate governance, there is little chance of successfully harmonizing these rules, or even simply the core of them. Under the aspect of better corporate governance, such harmonization may not even be desirable because, as mentioned before, the business judgment rule that was developed in an exemplary way in the United States has already become, or is becoming, part of the company law of many Member States. It serves as a safe harbour for the business behaviour of directors, provided certain requirements concerning information and other issues are fulfilled. Therefore, harmonizing these rules may lead to less rather than more liability of directors (this should not be understood as a critique of the business judgment rule, which is vital for entrepreneurial behaviour and therefore serves the interests of the shareholders themselves).

[69] See High Level Group (2002b: ch. III.3.4).

[70] The European Commission plans to enhance the responsibilities of board members by a special investigation right through a directive or a directive amending existing legislation. See European Commission (2003). More specifically, the draft Auditing Directive includes a framework rule on special investigations and sanctions concerning insufficient audits.

This reserve in implementation does not, however, extend to certain rules creating a special liability for directors, namely the United Kingdom's 'wrongful trading' and the French and Belgian *action en comblement du passif*. Under these and similar concepts, the directors of a company may be held liable for parts of or all the outstanding debts of the insolvent company if they have not checked in time whether there are enough chances to keep the ailing company afloat. Once again, the details of the Member States' laws vary considerably. In some countries, the rule applies not only to the independent company, but, via the concept of the '*de facto*' or 'shadow' director of the subsidiary, also to the parent company in a group. Again, the Forum Europaeum Group Law (2000: 246) has made proposals for harmonization. The Expert Group shares this view[71] and the European Commission agrees.[72] The beauty of the rule consists in the fact that the law does not interfere with the ongoing business decisions of the directors. The business judgment rule remains fully intact. Yet the directors act at their own risk if they continue to do business for a company in crisis. If they foresee that the company will not be able to pay its debts, they must either try to rescue the company or put it into liquidation. Otherwise they may be held liable. Having a European framework rule on wrongful trading could be a considerable improvement for the functioning of companies and groups of companies.[73]

The action for wrongful trading or the *action en comblement du passif* would be brought by the official receiver in the bankruptcy proceeding. The problem of shareholder passivity or of shareholders not having the standing to sue does not exist in the case of this specific directors' liability suit. This is quite different for other cases of directors' liability. As stated above, the actual frequency of liability suits in the Member States varies considerably, sometimes despite the fact that the relevant company law provisions are the same or rather similar. The reason for this is differences in the standing of individual or minority shareholders and other

[71] High Level Group (2002b: ch. III.4.4, ch. IV.4).

[72] The European Commission plans to enhance the responsibilities of board members by a wrongful trading rule through a directive or a directive amending existing legislation. See European Commission (2003).

[73] See the reasons and citations given in *ibid.* It is true that there are few wrongful trading cases in the UK, and some observers doubt whether this would be a good candidate for export, for example Wood in a conference of the *Zeitschrift für Unternehmens- und Gesellschaftsrecht (ZGR)* on 13 January 2006 in Kronberg. Yet Wood and other City practitioners agree that liability for wrongful trading is indeed a major deterrent in practice once the survival of a company becomes doubtful. Apart from this, a European rule would not necessarily have to adopt the UK wrongful trading rule as it stands, but could shape it in a way to give it more teeth. *Cf.* Fleischer (2004: 393 et seq). On the other side, a European framework rule allowing the implementation of a group's policy might be helpful; see High Level Group (2002b: ch. V.3). The European Commission agrees and plans a framework rule for groups, allowing the adoption at subsidiary level of a coordinated group policy. See European Commission (2003).

procedural law rules. Of course, this is even truer in comparison to US law, the homestead of the derivative action and the class action. Therefore, it is hardly surprising that in civil law countries as well, including Sweden and most recently Germany, there has been research on whether the US and Canadian experiences could also be useful on this side of the ocean.[74]

As mentioned before, the fact that a rule is relevant for better corporate governance is not enough to recommend a European rule. Furthermore, we have said that European harmonization of directors' liability is not—or at least not yet—advisable. But things may be different for a procedural framework rule. It is true that liability is not a panacea, but it is one important building block of corporate governance. Liability may be less relevant for violations of the duty of care due to the business judgment rule, but it is certainly most relevant for violations of the duty of loyalty. As to such violations, including, as seen above, exorbitant payments to directors, there must be an effective means of control and sanctioning. The instrument of wrongful-trading liability may not be of much help in this respect because not all violations of directors' duties, in particular of the duty of loyalty, are bound to end up in the insolvency of the company (though in a number of the American cases which stood at the outset of this lecture this was ultimately the case). Nevertheless, the confidence of investors and creditors is most disturbed by such violations.

This might be a reason for recommending European framework rules on directors' disqualification[75] and on facilitating the bringing of an action for holding directors (and auditors) liable. The details of such a rule should be left to the Member States. They may approach the problem quite differently, be it through a derivative action of each shareholder or a small majority of shareholders, opening the possibility for bundling shareholder actions, introducing a kind of company and capital market class action,[76] or, last but not least, by giving the courts or a supervisory office the right to disqualify a person from serving as a director of companies (across the EU)[77] and to initiate restitution proceedings against a director (Fleischer 2002: F 115 *et seq.*).

---

[74] See the Hamburg Max Planck Institute study commissioned by the German Ministry of Justice: Basedow, Hopt, Kötz, and Baetge (1998). See also the comments by Koch (2001) and Stadler (2002). In August 2005 Germany introduced a statute allowing the bundling of capital market law actions insofar as the same issues are at stake.

[75] The European Commission plans to enhance the responsibilities of board members by a rule on directors' disqualification through a directive or a directive amending existing legislation. See European Commission (2003). *Cf.* Fleischer (2004: 408 *et seq.*); on the mixed British experience with disqualification, see also Ferran (2004b: 427 *et seq.*).

[76] See Hopt and Baetge in Basedow *et al.* (1998: 47 *et seq.*).

[77] Because of the constitutional problems, further review by the European Commission is needed; see High Level Group (2002b: ch. III 4.5).

C. Control by the Auditors: The Conflict-of-Interest Problem

The third and most prominent control mechanism is control by the auditors. There is no need here to reiterate the central role of the auditors for checking on companies' accounting and reporting, nor to describe their functions under company law. Important parts of this have already been harmonized by the 4th, 7th, and 8th Directives of 1978, 1983, and 1984. Since the mid-1990s, the European Commission has been preparing further action. In 1996, the 'Green Book' on the role, position, and liability of the statutory auditor within the European Union was published. In 1998, the European Commission made a communication concerning its future plans on auditing. On 16 May 2002, the lengthy Commission recommendation on the basic principles of auditors' independence in the European Union was passed. In the light of Enron, it is common opinion that all this is not sufficient. In many countries, dramatic failures and financial scandals have appeared without previous notice by the auditors. In some instances, only months before auditors had still given their certification of the financial statements of the company without any limitation. The watchdogs have just not barked. As a consequence, public confidence in accurate and impartial auditing has fallen dramatically. The auditing profession in the United States as well as in the European countries is well aware of this so-called expectation gap, which seems to be the most serious crisis in the profession since the international economic crisis in the 1930s. There is a consensus that legislators must react—not only those of the Member States, but also those of the European Union. The American Sarbanes-Oxley Act has come forward first with far-reaching reforms concerning auditing standards, quality control standards, rules of incompatibility between auditing and non-auditing services, audit partner rotation, conflicts of interest, and a study on mandatory rotation of registered public accounting firms.[78] Many of these reform proposals, including harsher auditors' liability and possibly also third-party liability, are discussed in many Member States as well as in the European Union (Kalss 2002). In the context of prospectus liability, which will be covered in Part IV.A, auditors' liability is also under discussion (Fleischer 2002: F 66).[79] This is not the place to deal with the role, tasks, and professional duties of the auditing profession in general. Only four reform measures that are possible candidates for a European rule shall be picked up and briefly treated:

[78] Sarbanes-Oxley Act Secs. 103, 201 *et seq.*

[79] The draft auditing directive which is expected to replace the 8th Directive in 2006 contains a provision requiring the Member States to have effective, reasonable, and deterrent sanctions for auditing failures, though it leaves it to the Member States to have civil, criminal, or administrative law rules on this.

appointment and remuneration of the company auditors by the auditing committee; the requirement of admission of auditors of listed companies by the financial supervisory authority; incompatibility between auditing and non-auditing services; and mandatory rotation like, for example, in Italy and in the future in Austria.

The first reform measure has already been mentioned above in the context of the auditing committee. While, for example, in Germany the auditors for the financial statements are chosen by the shareholders, it should be the task of the audit committee, not of the board, actually to appoint the auditors of the company and, more important, to decide on their remuneration.[80] This is clear for the one-tier board system because only the auditing committee is to consist fully or in its majority of independent members. In the two-tier board system, the nomination and the remuneration of the auditors is usually up to the supervisory board as a whole, though this task may be delegated to the auditing committee if such a committee exists. Such delegation is also recommended by the German Corporate Governance Code.[81] In view of the critical independence question mentioned above, the European rule on the auditing committee and the independence requirement for it should also reserve the decisions on the appointment and the remuneration of the auditors of the company to the auditing committee.

Furthermore, in the case of listed companies, the auditors should be required to be admitted by the financial supervisory authority. In a sense, the auditors of a listed company perform a financial service with clear relevance for the investors and the capital market. The admission and continuous control by the financial supervisory authority is just the logical consequence. Introducing such a European rule would have the additional advantage of mutual assistance and international supervision by the Member State agencies. This would clearly benefit the internal market.

Incompatibility between auditing and non-auditing services has long been a highly controversial issue. In the United States, the question is now decided by the Sarbanes-Oxley Act, and there is a good chance that it will be decided the same way in some European countries. Yet it may still be premature to recommend a mandatory European rule on auditor incompatibility. In several Member States there are still committee inquiries going on as to whether the advantages of such an incompatibility as to independence outweigh the disadvantages for the profession. This should also be done at the European level if such a rule is

---

[80] As to auditing practices and the tasks of the audit committee, see High Level Group (2002b: ch. III.5).
[81] German Corporate Governance Code 5.3.2.

considered. It is well known that auditing is financially much less rewarding than certain non-auditing services. If separation becomes mandatory, the question on how to secure adequate auditor remuneration becomes urgent. Already, 'low- balling,' i.e., the ousting of a competitor by considerable remuneration cuts, and even auditing activities without cost-covering is occurring as more than an exception. A determination should also be made of what consequences mandatory separation has on the market for the different services and on possible economic concentration. In the end, it may very well be that the better arguments are for separation, especially because the leading auditing firms active in the United States as well already had or have no alternative to separation now. But this needs to be prepared with caution and decided upon in full knowledge of all relevant facts and consequences.

Finally, another far-reaching reform measure is mandatory rotation of the audit partner, as well as of the audit firm. Again, the pros and cons of such a mandatory rule must first be established before it can be recommended. The benefit of mandatory rotation for more independence of the auditor from the company may be outweighed by the disadvantage of a loss of information and intimate knowledge of the company affairs as a consequence of the rotation. This could be particularly relevant if a company is already ailing. According to statements from the profession, in complicated cases and group structures, the new auditing firm may need a year before it becomes fully acquainted with the internal affairs and pitfalls of the company.[82]

D. *Quis Custodiet Custodes?*

Trust in the auditors is not enough. The perennial question continues to arise: who is watching the guardians? This is a highly complicated issue that cannot be treated here. In the international discussion, three models[83] stand out: peer review and supervision by the self-regulatory bodies of the profession itself; external quality control and supervision by a supervisory body (wholly or predominantly) consisting of professionals other than auditors and independent from the auditing profession; and supervision by a state supervisory agency, either the financial services supervisory agency or a specialized state body under the supervision of the former. It is certainly not the task of the European Community to decide this question. Different traditions in the various Member States

---

[82] *Cf.* also Arruñada and Paz-Ares (1997).

[83] Apart from the particular French system of the 'double commissariat,' i.e., of having a full double-check by two auditors. This is a rather far-reaching and costly system. But the French stick to it; see Rapport Bouton (2002: 18).

and path dependencies must be respected.[84] A single rule for all Member States is neither appropriate nor in sight.

IV. IMPROVING CORPORATE GOVERNANCE BY CAPITAL MARKET LAW: INFORMATION AND INTERMEDIATION PROBLEMS

A. Primary Markets: Toward European Framework Rules for Prospectus Liability

Corporate governance is not just a matter for company law, but also for capital market law, namely, securities regulation. Control of the board by the market via disclosure has already been touched on in the discussion above concerning mandatory disclosure of corporate capital and control structures.[85] But shareholders are protected by markets more generally: indirectly by competitive product markets; and much more directly by the capital markets, both primary and secondary as well as the market for corporate control. If a company needs fresh equity finance, its investors may hesitate to provide additional equity if the board is known for not paying enough attention to shareholders' interests, a reaction which will be anticipated by the board. The law may contribute to this corporate governance function of the primary market for securities of the company. The two key problems the law has to cope with are information and intermediation. Intermediation problems, in particular the conflicts-of-interest problems of various intermediaries, are more prominent in the secondary market and will be treated there,[86] though they are present also insofar as the issuer and the underwriters as distinguished from the actual investors are concerned. As to information, primary market law may help to alleviate the information asymmetry between the different sides of the market. On the European level, this is what the prospectus directive tries to achieve.

This is not the place to go into more detail on the well-known controversies about the reform of the Prospectus Directive which was finalized in November 2003.[87] These controversies concern, among others, the issuers concerned (exceptions for small and medium enterprises), the form and content of the prospectus (choice between one or two prospectus documents, information to be disclosed, continuous disclosure, etc.), and the prospectus regime of the supervisory authority of the state of origin or of the place where the securities are issued and a

---

[84] See Hopt (2002c: 183 *et seq.*). See also Esty and Gerardin (2001).
[85] Above Part III.A.
[86] See below Part IV.B.
[87] Prospectus Directive of 4 November 2003, OJ L 345/64 31.12.2003 fin.

possible choice of the issuer as to this supervision (Moloney 2002; Ferran 2004). As mentioned before, controversies also exist more fundamentally in economic theory as to whether mandatory prospectus disclosure is really necessary.[88] The arguments for prospectus disclosure are in essence the same as for disclosure in general: the lack of fully developed capital markets in the European internal market; the limited role of institutional investors who might have the market power to bargain for economically efficient market conditions, which then are available also to the investors in general; the historical experience of securities fraud, in particular with issuance and at the primary markets; and, more generally, the nature of information about the issue and the issuer as a public good.[89]

If one considers that a European prospectus is of key relevance for the internal market as a European passport for issuers and an essential means for shareholders to get the information they need to make their investment decision and thereby promote corporate governance, it is of course essential that the European prospectus be true and fair. A prospectus requirement goes hand-in-hand with prospectus control and prospectus liability. Among many regulatory problems concerning the primary market and its function for corporate governance, prospectus liability merits some remarks because it is new for European law.

The former Stock Exchange Prospectus Directive of 1980[90] did not contain a rule on prospectus liability; instead, it considered this to be a matter for the Member States. So did the Directive of 1989 on the requirements for the drawing-up, scrutiny, and distribution of the prospectus to be published when transferable securities are offered to the public.[91] This is due to the traditional view that—apart from antitrust law, for example—the sanctions and the enforcement of European directives are not under the competence of the European Community. This is strange, of course, since substantive rules and sanctions and enforcement are a system of corresponding tubes, with the best European rules serving little purpose if they remain only as 'law in the books'. In European capital market law, this issue was finally addressed when insider dealing was regulated. The Insider Dealing Directive of 1989 contains a compromise in Article 13: 'Each Member State shall determine the penalties to be applied for infringement of the measures taken pursuant to this Directive. The penalties shall be sufficient to promote compliance with those measures.[92] The 2001 draft of the Prospectus Directive contented itself with a similar provision in Article 23.

---

[88] Above III.A.
[89] See Fleischer (2002a: F 41 *et seq.*) with further references.
[90] Stock Exchange Prospectus Directive of 17 March 1980, OJ L 100/1, 17.4.1980.
[91] Sales Prospectus Directive of 17 April 1989, OJ L 124/8, 5.5.1989.
[92] Insider Dealing Directive of 13 November 1989, OJ L 334/30, 18.11.1989.

Yet for prospectuses, the traditional means of sanctioning and enforcing compliance with the prospectus requirements is prospectus liability. This is so in practically all countries that have a capital market law, though the details vary considerably. The classic example is given once more by section 11 of the US Securities Act 1933. The British Financial Services and Markets Act 2000 contains a modern prospectus liability rule according to which those responsible for the prospectus are liable unless they 'reasonably believed (having made such enquiries, if any, as were reasonable) that the statement was true and not misleading.'[93] In other Member States, particularly France, Italy, and Spain, prospectus liability is part of the general tort law that is applied to untrue and incomplete prospectuses by the courts (Hopt and Voigt 2005). In Germany, matters are complicated by a dual development. Stock exchange prospectus liability is regulated in detail by legislation, as is prospectus liability in investment law. But despite patent abuses in the capital markets, German legislators failed to extend these statutory rules to non-listed securities and other investments. In this situation, the German courts intervened in response to the needs of the investing public and developed a general civil law prospectus liability (Assmann 1997; Hopt 2000; Ehricke in Hopt and Voigt 2005: 187). Although this was very helpful and, indeed, necessary, it has led to a complicated dualism of liability under which various forms of investment are treated differently without cause.

If harmonization of the prospectus requirement is considered necessary for the internal market in order to have a general European passport for issuers of securities, such harmonized rules need to be enforced appropriately so as to have their intended effect. General admonitions to Member States to provide for adequate enforcement are simply not enough. It is true that the European Commission could take steps to force Member States to comply with such a general rule, and the European Court of Justice could possibly be asked to examine whether a national law is sufficient to promote compliance. But all this is long, complicated, and not very effective. Accordingly, the quest for a European prospectus liability rule has been brought forward in the past (Grundmann and Selbherr 1996; Fleischer 2002: F 75). But it was not until 2002 after a detailed comparative law study[94] that the German

[93] See Financial Services and Markets Act 2000, 2000 Chapter c.8, Sec. 90 (1), (2), Schedule 10: statements believed to be true.
[94] The Hamburg Max Planck Institute for Private Law in Hamburg undertook a comparative study for the German Ministry of Finance on the law of all Member States and on an appropriate European framework rule. First results were available in November 2002; a more detailed publication has recently appeared (Hopt and Voigt 2005).

government officially took the position in Brussels that the Prospectus Directive should contain a general prospectus liability rule.

The Directive of 4 November 2003 followed these proposals and contains such a rule in Article 6. Para 1 states the principle:

> Member States shall ensure that responsibility for the information given in a prospectus attaches at least to the issuer or its administrative, management or supervisory bodies, the offeror, the person asking for the admission to trading on a regulated market or the guarantor, as the case may be.

These persons must be clearly identified in the prospectus together with a declaration that, to the best of their knowledge, the information is in accordance with the facts and there are no relevant omissions. Paragraph 2 says: 'Member States shall ensure that their laws, regulation and administrative provisions on civil liability apply to those persons responsible for the information given in a prospectus.' It adds that 'no civil liability shall attach to any person solely on the basis of the summary, including any translation thereof, unless it is misleading, inaccurate, or inconsistent when read together with the other parts of the prospectus.'

In my view, this marks real progress, though there are many theoretical and practical problems as to what such a European framework rule should contain and what problems the Member States face when transforming the rule into their national civil law. While the acute problem of harmonization of prospectus liability, i.e., primary market liability, has been tackled by the Prospectus Directive, another even more complicated problem not touched upon in the directive is whether primary and secondary market liabilities can remain totally separated as is traditionally the case, or whether a general rule in liability for information given to the financial market, whether primary or secondary, would be preferable, be it on the national level or even as a framework rule on the European level as well (Hopt and Voigt 2005).

B. Secondary Markets: The Need for Loyal and Competent Intermediaries (Issuers and their Directors, Broker-Dealers and Investment Advisers, Analysts, and Rating Agencies)

As to secondary markets, economic developments and regulatory challenges may be even more conspicuous than those at the primary markets. It suffices to mention such far-reaching processes as institutionalisation, disintermediation, technological change, segmentation, and demutualization (Merkt 2002b: G41 *et seq.*; Ferrarini 1999; 2002). As always, competition is a primary factor in this.[95] The reform problems resulting from these developments for secondary market regulation reform have been discussed broadly in many Member States and are under discussion for European law as well in the context of the Financial Services Action Plan and its aftermaths (European Commission 2005). The fundamental revision of the Investment Services Directive (now MiFID) which was finalized in 2004[96] is among them (Moloney 2002; Ferran 2004). Again, information and intermediation are also the two key problems the law faces for the secondary markets, though the need for loyal and competent intermediaries is more prominent here. This shall be my focus, leaving aside all the rest. For corporate governance of rules, the impact of ensuring loyal and competent intermediation has been best illustrated by the realisation, post-Enron, that deficiencies in corporate governance will be covered up, and even amplified, if the intermediaries in the secondary markets—such as broker dealers, investment advisers, analysts, and rating agencies—do not live up to the expectations set for them by the markets and the general public. The role of auditors has already been dealt with.[97] To improve European corporate governance after Enron, one must also look at these intermediaries (or gatekeepers) (Kraakman1986; Grundmann and Kerber 2001; Fleischer 2002: F 34 *et seq.*; for the US, see Choi 2004) and possible reform measures for keeping them loyal and competent. Keeping them loyal may be more difficult than keeping them competent, since the market may be more apt to reveal and penalize incompetence than disloyalty, which almost always tends to be hidden. Again, rules on the disclosure of conflicts of interests or, going further, on minimizing them to the extent that is economically feasible, may be the answer. As to disclosure, it should be mentioned that the need for gatekeeper rules is controversial in economic theory: the argument is that market forces and the need for maintaining a reputation at the market are sufficient and stronger constraints than legal rules.[98] The arguments for regulation are similar to those in support of disclosure discussed above.[99]

In a sense, issuers and their directors also have an intermediation function on the secondary markets. The prospectus they issue is not only relevant for the first placement, but also influences later dealings on the secondary market, so long as the prospectus remains valid and

---

[95] See Hopt, Rudolph, and Baum (1997: 222 *et seq.*, 361 *et seq.*, 375 *et seq.*); Merkt (2002b: G 58, 114).
[96] Directive on Markets in Financial Instruments (MiFID) of 21 April 2004, OJ L 145/1.
[97] See above Part III.C.
[98] As to market defects of gatekeeping (certifiers) and the need to rethink legal intervention, see Choi (1998; 2004).
[99] Above Parts III.A, IV.A.

continuous disclosure requirements are in place. While this has been dealt with in the treatment of prospectus liability, the modern discussion goes further and asks the question whether there should not be a more general responsibility borne by the issuer and its directors for public statements—whether orally or in written form, either before or after the issuance of securities—if the investing public is misled (Fleischer 2002: F 62 *et seq.*, F 101 *et seq.*; Hopt and Voigt 2005). In the context of instant disclosure statements, as required by the Prospectus Directive and most relevant for preventing insider dealing, the liability question has become acute particularly in the German reform discussion. The relevance of such liability rules for the board and for corporate governance is obvious. One of the many controversial issues is whether such duties and liabilities should be imposed on the issuer, or on the directors personally, or on both. Imposing them on the issuer usually gives the shareholders a more solvent debtor, but it amounts to having all existing shareholders carry the burden. Imposing them on the directors may tend to have a positive influence on their remaining loyal and attempting to be competent.

Of course, the key intermediaries between the company and its shareholders and holders of other securities of the company are the brokers and dealers and the investment advisers. There is a large body of rules on the duties and liabilities of this class of intermediaries, both in the Member States as well as on the European level.[100] The duties listed by the Market in Financial Instruments Directive for investment firms are basically appropriate. It is true that the directive contains rules on duties and their control by supervisory bodies, but leaves aside civil liability.[101] This has led to difficult questions concerning the relationship and mutual influence of administrative duties under the Directive and the national transformation acts and civil law duties and liabilities as developed by the courts.[102] Yet on the whole, this may not be a key concern for improving European corporate governance. The existing rules may not be fully satisfactory, but they do cover a good part of the ground. Furthermore, there is typically a contractual or precontractual relationship between these intermediaries and the investor client which gives rise to civil law duties and liabilities in favor of the investor.

Much more pressing and indeed keenly relevant for corporate governance are appropriate analysts and rating agencies, both of which

---

[100] In the 2003 version of this article, certain shortcomings of the Investment Services Directive were criticised. In the meantime, the Directive was modernized. Investment advice is no longer a mere non-core service, but is considered as investment service (Annex I Section A (5) of the MiFID). Therefore, independent investment firms are now covered by the Directive.

[101] There is only a rather general obligation on the Member States to monitor compliance with the rules of the regulated market and with other legal obligations (Art. 43 of the MiFID).

[102] See (for the Investment Directive) Bliesener (1998).

belong to the core institutions that support strong securities markets.[103] In most Member States there is no fully fledged body of law concerning these intermediary professions. Enron has taught the lesson that analysts are very often in a position that gives rise to serious conflicts of interest. They are employees of banks and other investment firms or independent contract partners without a direct contractual relationship with the investors. They can be on the 'selling' side as employees of investment banks, or on the 'buying' side as employees of investment companies or insurance companies. In both cases, they need to maintain a good relationship with the companies on which they report in order to get the relevant information, and as employees they must avoid endangering the interests of their employers. Herd behaviour may add to these dangers. Rules designed to ensure that analysts are both competent and loyal are indispensable. Fair presentation of the information they produce or disseminate and disclosure of their interests or indication of conflicts of interest are of key importance, as Article 6 (5) of the draft Market Abuse Directive rightly requires.[104] Yet this may not go far enough. More concrete rules on analysts' professional duties, and in particular on conflicts of interest, may be necessary, be it by stock exchange rules or professional codes of conduct. One part of such rules might be a provision against the analyst trading in securities that he analyses, at least for a certain period. The Market for Financial Instruments Directive of 2004 now includes investment research and financial analysis and other forms of general recommendation relating to transactions in financial instruments at least as an ancillary service,[105] thereby making certain rules of conduct also applicable to analysts. Imposing civil liability on analysts is more difficult, since they are not in a special contractual or precontractual relationship with the investor (Kalss 2001: 655; Fleischer 2002a: F131 *et seq.*).

Rating agencies are not covered at all by European law or by the law of most Member States (Kübler 1997; Peters 2001; Fleischer 2002: F 132 *et seq.*). In the United States, rating agencies can be recognized by the SEC as nationally recognized statistical-rating organizations. Switzerland has followed this example. There is much controversy over whether the regulation of rating agencies is economically sound, yet more recently the arguments in support of regulation have been growing stronger, in particular after the experiences with Enron. Nevertheless, the problems of the regulation of rating agencies are complex. They concern minimum requirements for their recognition, their possible liability toward

[103] See Black (2001: 812; 2000: 1590); Fleischer (2002a: F 131).
[104] See also Commission Directive of 22 December 2003 as regards the fair presentation of investment recommendations and the disclosure of conflicts of interest, OJ L 339/73 24.12.2003.
[105] See Annex I Section B (5) of the MiFID.

investors, and the optional or even mandatory use of ratings in the context of adequate capital requirements of investment firms, eligibility rules, and disclosure of ratings in prospectuses and investment advice. The discussion on whether and—if so—how to regulate is still in its initial stages, both in terms of economic theory and legal policy. Therefore, it would be premature to ask for European regulation. What could be recommended, however, is that the European Commission study the question of regulation.[106]

C. The Market for Corporate Control (The Role of Takeovers in the Internal Market, Mandatory Bids, Golden Shares, and the European Court of Justice)

The relevance of the market for corporate control for improving European corporate governance is even more direct and obvious than the relevance of the primary and secondary markets. Public takeover bids challenge the target's board and its performance and give the shareholders an exit option, especially if there is a provision for a mandatory bid to be made by the offeror if a certain control threshold—usually 30 per cent or more—is reached. Traditional research has underlined the disciplinary function of takeover bids, especially—but not exclusively—of hostile bids. It is true that more recent empirical literature has cast doubts on this function because both badly managed and well-managed companies with a bright future have been seen to be targets of public takeover bids (Franks and Mayer 1996; Franks, Mayer, and Renneboog 2001). One of the best examples of the latter was the—finally successful—takeover bid by Vodafone made to Mannesmann shareholders in 2001. In such cases, takeovers are more motivated by synergistic motives, though experience indicates that the expected synergies (or those that are said to be expected) are ultimately not attained in the majority of cases. One of the standard international treatises on corporate finance counts merger waves as one of the ten unsolved riddles of finance (Brealey and Myers 2000: 1015 *et seq.*). If economists have not solved it and cannot present convincing answers that are agreed upon in essence by the profession, lawyers and legislators must not pretend to be able to give *the* answer; instead, they must give *an* answer as best they can. In this sense it may be assumed that the threat of takeovers may have as much effect as actual takeovers on boards and that the takeover threat, though not inducing the board to maximize shareholder utility, may at least put a floor under board performance (Davies 2002a: 212). This is also the basis for the

---

[106] Most recently in January 2006, Commissioner McCreevey declared that the Commission will not undertake regulation.

recommendations of the Expert Group, which maintains that the availability of a mechanism for takeover bids is basically beneficial.

> Takeovers are a means to create wealth by exploiting synergies and to discipline the management of listed companies with dispersed ownership, which in the long term is in the best interest of all stakeholders, and society at large.... This is not to say that takeover bids are always beneficial for all (or indeed) any of the parties involved.[107]

This is not the place to go into the many problems of takeover regulation, to compare the various systems of the Member States, to question whether European rules are necessary for the internal market (of which I am convinced), or to analyse the 13th Directive of 21 April 2004 which is a typical political compromise.[108] Instead, I shall briefly take up two issues that even after the enactment of the 13th Directive are still controversial. I consider them to be crucial for a European takeover regulation, along with possible benefits resulting from it for improving corporate governance. These issues are the mandatory bid as provided for in Article 5 of the directive, and the possible role of the European Court of Justice in setting limits to defences against takeovers.

The mandatory bid rule, which is modelled on the example of the British Takeover Code, has gradually crept into nearly all modern European takeover legislation. Differences do exist, especially as to the level of ownership which must be reached before the bidder will be subject to the mandatory bid requirement, and as to the price which the bidder must then offer. But the basic assumption is that such a rule is useful both economically and for the shareholders.

Yet the wisdom of the mandatory bid rule is by no means undisputed. Economists tell us that the rule is costly and may prevent beneficial takeovers from taking place (Burkart and Panunzi, and Enriques in Ferrarini *et al.* 2004: 737 and 767; more generally McCahery *et al.* 2004). Comparative law teaches that the United States, apart from some states such as Pennsylvania and Maine, fares well without such a rule, though in practice it seems that in most cases bidders end up making a bid to all shareholders. Takeover lawyers know that such a rule is based on rather broad principles, such as equal treatment and sharing the control premium (under the corporate asset doctrine), and that it tends to lead to inconsistencies (Skog 1995; Wymeersch 1992; Davies 2002b: 20 *et seq.*; Hansen in Wahlgren 2003: 173).

In Paul Davies' and my view (Davies and Hopt in Kraakman 2004: 178 *et seq.*), a good rationale for a mandatory bid is the fact that such a rule

---

[107] High Level Group (2002a: 2).

[108] OJ 2004 L 142/12 30.4.2004. See Hopt (2002d); Dauner-Lieb and Lamandini (2003); Lehne and Haak (2003).

gives an early exit option to shareholders who fear they will end up with a majority shareholder having control and possibly exercising it to their detriment in the future. The second rationale put forward for the rule, i.e., that it protects shareholders who are not close to the market and who might not react in time to the opportunity afforded by the raid seems less convincing to me. The early exit option rationale anticipates that there is a strong likelihood of majority/minority conflicts after the acquisition of control. Experience shows that in many—though of course not all—cases, this turns out to be true. This is certainly the experience with the German law of groups, under which many cases of minority oppression become apparent and are brought before the courts. This may be different in other countries without a law of groups. But then the relative absence of publicly known cases of abuse of control may very well stem from the fact that there are no effective legal means of protection, and the shareholders realize this and do not go to court.

As to Germany, one remembers the stiff opposition of German industry and the German government to any kind of mandatory bid rule, with the argument that German law of groups already takes care of this. This position was never really convincing because the protective devices of the German law of groups are *ex post*, once control is reached, and lead to long judicial controversies, some of which can take more than ten years and are of uncertain outcome. It is interesting to see that Sweden was also originally against a mandatory bid rule, as evidenced by a long and impressive plea by Rolf Skog (1995), the secretary to the Swedish Company Law Committee, working within the Ministry of Justice. But in a well-known about-face, Sweden changed its position and introduced a mandatory bid rule itself. Some say that this was because leading industrialists reconsidered their own position and, for future takeover bids by foreign bidders, concluded that such a rule might benefit themselves after all.

The second issue on which I shall make some very brief comments is the difficult question of the possible role of the European Court of Justice in setting limits to defences against takeovers. The Commission and many observers, including the Expert Group, had feared that the court might follow the Advocate General in the Golden Share decisions,[109] and they were greatly relieved that it did not. There is no need to describe in more detail what the court decided (Grundmann and Möslein 2001–2002). In a nutshell, it is the following:

---

[109] European Court of Justice, Judgments of 4 June 2002, Case C-367/98, C-483/99 and C-503/99, *Commission of the European Community v Portugal/Commission v French Republic/Commission v Belgium*; see *Europäische Zeitschrift für Wirtschaftsrecht (EuZW)* 2002, 429, 433, 437. In the meantime there have been more decisions; for an example, see Judgment of 13 May 2003, Cases C-98/01 and C- 463/00, *Commission v UK/Commission v Spain*.

The national rules in question constitute, *per se*, exceptions to the principle of free movement of capital and, consequently, to the principle of freedom of establishment, and can be justified, according to the Court, only if the objective pursued falls within the ambit of a general or strategic interest and the measures prescribed are based on precise criteria which are known in advance, are open to review by the courts and cannot be attained by less restrictive measures.[110]

This holding of the European Court of Justice is based on the same premises as those articulated by the Expert Group in its first report on takeover defences in January 2002.[111]

The most interesting question is the outcome of future cases, especially the German Volkswagen Act case. This act is a special law for the privatised Volkswagen company. It dates from 21 July 1960, and was revised on 31 July 1970. The Federal Republic and the State of Lower Saxony are to be protected by this act in a threefold way:

1. Section 2 provides for a voting cap, which under the 1970 Reform Act limits the votes of a single shareholder to 20 per cent. The transfer of shares of the company that would circumvent this prohibition is not only forbidden, but the shares so transferred may not be claimed back.
2. Under section 3, votes may not be exercised by a proxy in his own name. Powers of attorney must be in writing, and banks and other professionals who exercise proxies need specific instructions by the shareholders in order to vote. Representatives must disclose fully whom they represent, and nobody may exercise the votes in the general assembly for more than 20 per cent of the votes.
3. Finally, according to section 4, the Federal Republic of Germany and the State of Lower Saxony may each send two representatives to the supervisory board of the Volkswagen company, as long as they hold shares of the company (regardless of the amount of such shareholdings). For resolutions concerning the establishment and transfer of manufacturing plants, the supervisory board needs a majority of two-thirds instead of a simple majority. All resolutions of the general assembly, which—as in cases of changing the constitution of the company—are normally to be taken by a quorum of three-quarters of the capital present at the vote, need to be taken by a quorum of four-fifths.

As to the compatibility of the Volkswagen Act with the golden share cases of the European Court of Justice, predictions are very hard to make for the following reasons. The Volkswagen Act does not contain limits for the participation of non-nationals like the Portuguese golden shares, nor does it provide for an *ex ante* permission of the state as in France, and, indeed,

[110] European Court of Justice, Press release of 4 June 2002.
[111] High Level Group (2002a: 34).

not even for an *ex post* permission of the transfer of shares as in the Belgian case. Instead, there is a voting cap provision that applies not only to the state, but to all shareholders alike. It is true that in the 53 motives of the German Act of 1998, which deleted the former voting cap permission of the Stock Corporation Act, it is expressly stated that voting caps and double or multiple voting rights restrict the capital markets because takeovers are frustrated and therefore 'takeover fantasy' is lacking.[112] But treating voting caps and even multiple voting rights as exceptions to the principle of free movement of capital and, consequently, to the principle of freedom of establishment goes a full step further than the present golden share judgments. The same is true, though to a lesser degree, for the right to nominate a certain number of directors which is quite common in statutory practice.

Yet once this step is made—a decision that would require a lot of courage—the chances of the Volkswagen Act passing the second test—i.e., that the objective pursued falls within the ambit of a general or strategic interest—would be slim.[113] It is hardly conceivable that it might be proved that there is a convincing general or strategic interest in preventing any shareholder from getting control of the company. After all, the car industry is an industry like many others, not a strategic one such as armament, defence, or energy. It has been speculated that the interest of reserving the share to the general public, i.e., the structure of the shareholdings, would be protected under the property clause of Article 295 of the EC Treaty. But this would hardly be compatible with the holding of the golden share cases, in particular since the act at the same time secures a considerable role for the state as a major shareholder. Even less valid is the argument that the Volkswagen company has symbolic value in Germany. This relatively clear legal consequence under the second test might lead the court to check even more carefully whether voting caps—or indeed the other rules in the Act, taken separately, such as the right of the state to deputize representatives into the supervisory board regardless of the amount of shareholding—really suffice to cause a collision of the Act with freedom of establishment.

On the other hand, while mere rules on voting caps and so on might not be sufficient to be considered exceptions to the principle of freedom of establishment, this might be different for the Act as a whole.[114] Taken together, the combination of rules in the Volkswagen Act singles out this specific privatised company with the clear aim of making a takeover practically impossible, while maintaining, for the state, the right to

---

[112] German Stock Corporation Reform Act (KonTraG), Motives to the Draft, BT- Drucksache 13/9712, p. 20.
[113] See also Bayer (2002: 2291); Ruge (2002: 424); Krause (2002).
[114] See Hopt (1997b: 415 *et seq.*).

intervene by combining voting caps and other restrictive rules on voting and quorums with the rights of the Federal Republic and Lower Saxony to deputize four representatives to the supervisory board regardless of the number of shares these two public entities hold. Indeed, as experience shows, mere voting caps have in many cases proven insufficient to prevent takeovers completely. This may be different, or at least the legislators expect it to be different, with the full range of preventive rules as laid down in the Volkswagen Act. But it is exactly this that may bring the Volkswagen Act in Germany under the ban of golden shares as in France. Maintaining the full influence of the national public sector on a privatised company without further ado and court control may be sufficient to qualify the Act as an exception to the principle of freedom of establishment under the Treaty. And again, if this were accepted, the second test could still hardly be passed.

In 2003, when this article was first written, I concluded that is was hard to predict the further destiny of the 13th Directive. If it ultimately had failed to be enacted—which would be to the great detriment not only of the European takeover market, but also of European corporate governance—the only hope would have rested in the European Court of Justice to once more act as a motor of European integration, as far as a court can act. Now after the enactment of the 13th Directive, as short-winded and 'softly-softly' as it is, the need for the European Court to step in for the sake of the European takeover market is less acute. Furthermore, the situation at the Volkswagen Corporation has changed with the acquisition of a major share block by Porsche, Lower Saxony now being only the second largest blockholder. The threat of Volkswagen being taken over has vanished. Yet the question of state statutes blocking takeovers remains acute, and the decision of the Court could still be a landmark.

V. SUMMARY AND THESES[115]

A. Enron and Company and Capital Market Law in Europe: The Need for Improving Corporate Governance

1. Enron, WorldCom, and associates are by no means *just* an American balance sheet scandal. Rather, they can and should teach Europe a lesson on how to act in a timely manner—instead of just reacting like the US American Sarbanes-Oxley Act or even overreacting—by well-thought- out company and capital market law reforms.

---

[115] These theses were presented to the Tilburg lecture audience on 6 September 2002. They have not been changed, and I still stand fully behind each of them now in 2006.

2. One of the key concerns of European company and capital market law reform should be *improving European corporate governance*. For company law, the focus is clearly on the board. But corporate governance cannot function with company law alone; it needs the capital markets and capital market rules as well or, as some say, external corporate governance. The High Level Group of Company Law Experts is challenged to propose a coherent European reform package for corporate governance that makes allowance for both internal and external corporate governance rules and mechanisms.

B. Improving Corporate Governance by Company Law: European Rules for Efficient, Loyal, and Competent Boards

3. In some critical fields, especially if the interests of the board are affected, corporate governance may be improved if the shareholders are to make decisions. Two good *candidates for shareholder decision-making*, at least in listed companies, are the frustration of public takeover bids by the directors of the target company and the remuneration of directors by stock options. Apart from this, the participation of the shareholders in the general assembly and their voting should be facilitated as far as possible. Modern technology allows much quicker and better shareholder information, communication, and decision-making.

4. Regarding board structure, there is an extensive and ongoing academic discussion on the pros and cons of the *one-tier and* the *two-tier board system*. Whether the less effective monitoring of the two-tier board might be outweighed by gains in networking, and what ultimately benefits shareholders more, is an empirical question. While it is certainly not for European corporate governance law to make either one of the two systems mandatory, it would be worthwhile discussing a rule requiring the Member States to *give companies the choice* between the different systems, as was introduced recently for the European company.

5. Board size and board organization is up to the Member States, including the combination or separation of the functions of chief executive officer and president of the board. So is labour co-determination. But in light of Enron and the general crisis of confidence that may also affect the internal market, there is a case for a European rule *requiring listed companies to have audit committees* that are responsible for the appointment, compensation, and supervision of the work of the auditors of the company and are composed *of at least a majority of independent members*.

6. *Exorbitant payments* to the directors threaten to make the whole system

unreliable. This is of concern to the European internal market, too, since such payments tend to undermine the confidence of the shareholders and their willingness to invest in companies across the internal market. Shareholder decision-making on the principles and limits of board, full disclosure (also of the individual remuneration), and mandatory accounting of stock options under revised international accounting standards might be useful European rules. Non-executive directors should be remunerated appropriately, but neither directly nor indirectly in stock options, though holding shares of the company should remain possible.

7. Control needs *competent as well as independent controllers*. While the necessary board member competence varies from company to company, a European rule requiring the company to disclose which members it considers to be competent and for what reasons could be useful. As to independence, there is a case for requiring the board as a monitoring body to be independent of management (non-executive directors or supervisory board), and for the audit, remuneration, and appointment committees to have at least a majority of members that are also independent of the company.

C. Controlling the Board from Inside and Outside: Markets, Shareholders, and Auditors

8. Notwithstanding theoretical controversies as to the effectiveness of disclosure in efficient capital markets, *disclosure* is a *powerful tool for improving corporate governance in Europe*. It interferes least with freedom and competition of enterprises in the market and also avoids the well-known petrifying effect of European substantive law. Candidates for disclosure are—among others—the corporate governance regime of the company, including takeover defences, board remuneration, and competence and independence of the board. Non-disclosure and, even more so, false disclosure must have immediate consequences for the directors. Forfeiture of certain bonuses and profits will have most impact, but it cannot be automatic.

9. Control by the shareholders could be enhanced by better investigation and more serious liability. *Special investigation* seems to be the most effective method yet devised to detect corporate misconduct and to prepare liability suits. A European rule on *wrongful trading* that makes use of the British and the French and Belgian experience (*action en comblement du passif*) could improve the functioning of companies and groups of companies considerably. This might also be true for a European procedural framework rule on *facilitating the bringing of an action against directors (and auditors)*. The details, such as derivative

actions, bundling of claims, class actions, or specific rights and duties of the courts, would be left to the Member States.

10. *Control by the auditors* is the most common and prominent control mechanism. It should be the task of the auditing committee rather than the board to appoint the auditors of the company and to decide on their remuneration. Auditors of listed companies should need to be admitted by the financial supervisory authority. Incompatibility between auditing and non-auditing services has many pros and cons. The same is true for mandatory rotation not only of the audit partner, but of the audit firm as well. On both issues, recommending a mandatory European rule would be premature, but the European Commission should keep an eye on the needs for mandatory rules and the experiences with them. The international market for auditing services and the impact of the US American Sarbanes-Oxley Act may press leading firms to go this way even without such a European rule.

11. *Quis custodiet custodes?* As important as this question is, it is unsuitable for a uniform European rule. The traditions and path dependencies in the various Member States, in particular regarding self-regulation and state supervision, are too different. As to auditing listed companies, it may be wise to give a role to the financial supervisory body, whether state or self-regulatory.

D. Improving Corporate Governance by Capital Market Law: Information and Intermediation Problems

12. Shareholders are protected more generally by markets: indirectly by competitive product markets, and much more directly by the capital markets, both primary and secondary as well as the market for corporate control. For *primary markets*, the reform of the Prospectus Directive is under way. A European framework rule on *prospectus liability* (as contained in Article 6 of the European prospectus directive of 4 November 2003) is useful.

13. Regarding the *secondary markets*, a key problem is the need for loyal and competent intermediaries. Various reform measures are under discussion, both at the European and at the Member State level. They concern issuers and their directors, broker-dealers and investment advisers, and analysts as well as rating agencies.

14. As to the *market for corporate control*, public takeover bids may be motivated in many cases by synergistic motives, but the threat of them is also a challenge to the board of the target and its performance. Appropriate framework rules for this specific market (see now the 13th Directive of 21 April 2004) are definitely needed and may be an important contribution to corporate governance in the internal market.

15. The *mandatory bid rule* is common in Europe but not in the United States, and it is controversial in economic theory. The rule may best be justified on the basis that it gives an early exit option to the shareholders who fear to end up with a majority shareholder having control or exercising it to their detriment in the future. As such, the rule is necessary even in countries with a full-fledged corporate group law such as Germany.
16. The recent judgments of the European Court of Justice concerning *golden shares* are landmark cases for freedom of establishment and the internal market. It remains to be seen whether the court will go further in this direction. A test case could be the German Volkswagen Act case. If the 13th Directive ultimately had failed to be enacted—which would have been to the great detriment not only of the European takeover market, but also of European corporate governance—the only hope would have rested in the European Court of Justice to once more act as a motor of European integration, as far as a court can act as such.

REFERENCES

Arruñada, B. and Paz-Ares, C. (1997), Mandatory Rotation of Company Auditors: A Critical Examination, 17 *International Review of Law and Economics* 31.

Assmann, H.-D. (1997), 'Entwicklungslinien und Entwicklungsperspektiven der Prospekthaftung,' in H.-D. Assmann *et al.* (eds.), *Wirtschafts- und Medienrecht in der offenen Demokratie, Freundesgabe für F. Kübler* (Heidelberg: C. F. Müller), 317.

Barca, F. and Becht, M. (2001), *The Control of Corporate Europe* (Oxford: Oxford University Press).

Basedow, J., Hopt, K.J., Kötz, H. and Baetge, D. (eds.) (1998), *Die Bündelung gleichgerichteter Interessen im Prozess—Verbandsklage und Gruppenklage* (Tübingen: Mohr Siebeck).

Baums T. (ed.) (2001), *Bericht der Regierungskommission Corporate Governance* (Cologne: Otto Schmidt).

Baums, T., Buxbaum, R.M. and Hopt, K.J. (eds.) (1994), *Institutional Investors and Corporate Governance* (Berlin/New York: de Gruyter).

Baums, T. and Ulmer, P. (eds) (2004), *Unternehmens-Mitbestimmung der Arbeit-nehmer im Recht der EU-Mitgliedstaaten* (Heidelberg: Recht und Wirtschaft).

Bayer, W. (2002), 'Zulässige und unzulässige Einschränkungen der europäischen Grundfreiheiten im Gesellschaftsrecht,' *Betriebs-Berater (BB)* 2002, 2289.

Bebchuk, L. and Fried, J. (2004), *Pay without Performance, The Unfulfilled Promise of Executive Compensation* (Cambridge, Mass. and London: Harvard University Press).

Bebchuk, L.A., Fried, J.M. and Walker, D.I. (2002), 'Managerial Power and Rent Extraction in the Design of Executive Compensation,' 69 *University of Chicago Law Review* 751.

Becker, B.C. (2002), *Die institutionelle Stimmrechtsvertretung der Aktionäre in Europa* (Frankfurt *et al.*: Lang).

Black, B.S. (2000), 'The Core Institutions that Support Strong Securities Markets,' 55 *Business Lawyer* 1565.

—— (2001), 'The Legal and Institutional Preconditions for Strong Securities Markets,' 48 *University of California at Los Angeles Law Review* 781.

Bliesener, D. H. (1998), Aufsichtsrechtliche Verhaltenspflichten beim Wertpapierhandel (Berlin, New York: de Gruyter).

Böckli, P. (2004), Schweizer Aktienrecht, 3d edn (Zurich: Schulthess).

Bratton, W.W. (2002), 'Enron and the Dark Side of Shareholder Value,' 76 *Tulane Law Review* 1275.

Brealey, R.A. and Myers, S.C. (2000), *Principles of Corporate Finance* (Boston *et al.*: McGraw-Hill, Inc., 6th edn).

Brown, G. M. (2005), 'Changing Models in Corporate Governance—Implications of the US Sarbanes-Oxley Act,' in K. J. Hopt, E. Wymeersch, H. Kanda and H. Baum (eds), *Corporate Governance in Context* (Oxford: Oxford University Press), 143.

Buxbaum, R.M. and Hopt, K.J. (1988), *Legal Harmonization and the Business Enterprise* (Berlin, New York: de Gruyter).

Cheffins, B.R. and Thomas, R.S. (2001), 'Should Shareholders have a Greater Say over Executive Pay? Learning from the US Experience,' *Journal of Corporate Law Studies* Dec., 277.

Choi, S. (1998), 'Market Lessons for Gatekeepers,' 92 *Northwestern University Law Review* 916.

Choi, S. J. (2004), 'A Framework for the Regulation of Securities Market Intermediaries', *Berkeley Business Law Journal* 45.

Coffee, J.C. (2002), 'Understanding Enron: It's About Gatekeepers, Stupid,' 57 *Business Lawyer* 1403.

—— (2004), 'Gatekeeper Failure and Reform: The Challenge of Fashioning Relevant Reforms,' in G. Ferrarini, K.J. Hopt, J. Winter and Wymeersch, E. (eds.), *Reforming Company and Takeover Law in Europe* (Oxford: Oxford University Press), 455.

Cozian, M., Viandier, A. and Deboissy, F. (2005), *Droit des sociétés*, 18e éd. (Paris: Litec).

Crook, K. (2004), 'Accounting for Share-based Remuneration,' in G. Ferrarini, K.J. Hopt, J. Winter and Wymeersch, E. (eds.), *Reforming Company and 62 Takeover Law in Europe* (Oxford: Oxford University Press), 347.

Dauner-Lieb, B. and Lamandini, M. (2003), 'Der neue Kommissionsvorschlag einer Übernahmerichtlinie und das Europäische Parlament,' *Der Konzern* 3/2003, 168.

Davies, P. (2000), 'Board Structure in the UK and Germany: Convergence or Continuing Divergence?' *International and Comparative Corporate Law Journal* 2 (2000) 423, 435; German version in *Zeitschrift für Unternehmens- und Gesellschaftsrecht (ZGR)* 2001, 224.

—— (2002a), *Introduction to Company Law* (Oxford: Oxford University Press).

—— (2002b), 'The Notion of Equality in European Takeover Regulation,' in J. Payne (ed.), *Takeovers in English and German Law* (Oxford: Hart Publishing), 9.

—— (2003a), *Gower and Davies' Principles of Modern Company Law* (London: Sweet & Maxwell, 7th edn).

—— (2003b), 'Shareholder Value, Company Law, and Securities Markets Law: A

British View,' in K.J. Hopt and E. Wymeersch (eds.), *Capital Markets and Company Law* (Oxford: Oxford University Press), 261.

Davies, P. and Hopt, K.J. (2004), 'Control Transactions,' in R. Kraakman, *et al.*, *The Anatomy of Corporate Law, A Comparative and Functional Approach* (Oxford: Oxford University Press), ch. 7.

De Cordt, Y. (2004), *L'égalité entre actionnaires* (Brussels: Bruylant).

DTI (2002), *Modernising Company Law* (London: DTI), Cm 5553-I, II.

Enriques, L. (2000), 'The Law on Company Directors' Self-Dealing: A Comparative Analysis,' 2 *International and Comparative Corporate Law Journal* 297.

Esty, D. and Gerardin, D. (eds.) (2001), *Regulatory Competition and Economic Integration—Comparative Perspectives* (Oxford: Oxford University Press).

European Commission (2002), Proposal for a Directive of the European Parliament and the Council on Takeover Bids, Brussels, 2 October 2002, COM (2002) 534 final.

—— (2003), Modernising Company Law and Enhancing Corporate Governance in the European Union—A Plan to Move Forward, Brussels, 21 May 2003, COM (2003) 284 final.

—— (2005), Green Paper on Financial Services Policy (2005–2010), COM(2005) 177.

European Commission High Level Group of Company Law Experts, see High Level Group

Ferran, E. (2004a), *Building an EU Securities Market* (Cambridge: Cambridge University Press).

—— (2004b), 'The Role of the Shareholder in Internal Corporate Governance...,' in Ferrarini *et al.* (eds.), *Reforming Company and Takeover Law in Europe* (Oxford: Oxford University Press), 417.

Ferrarini, G. (1999), 'The European Regulation of Stock Exchanges: New Perspectives,' 36 *Common Market Law Review* 569 .

Ferrarini, G. (2002), 'Securities regulation and the rise of pan-European securities markets: An overview,' in G. Ferrarini, K. J. Hopt and E. Wymeersch (eds.), *Capital Markets in the Age of the Euro* (The Hague: Kluwer Law International), 241.

Ferrarini, G. and Moloney, N. (2004), Executive Remuneration and Corporate Governance in the EU: Convergence, Divergence, and Reform Perspectives, in Ferrarini *et al.*, *Reforming Company and Takeover Law in Europe* (Oxford: Oxford University Press), 267.

Ferrarini, G., Hopt, K.J., Winter, J. and Wymeersch, E. (eds.) (2004), *Reforming Company and Takeover Law in Europe* (Oxford: Oxford University Press).

Fleischer, H. (2001), *Informationsasymmetrie im Vertragsrecht* (Munich: Beck).

—— (2002), *Gutachten F zum 64. Deutschen Juristentag, Berlin* (Munich, Beck).

—— (2004), 'The Responsibility of the Management and Its Enforcement,' in Ferrarini *et al.*, *Reforming Company and Takeover Law in Europe* (Oxford: Oxford University Press), 373.

Forum Europaeum Corporate Group Law (2002), 'Corporate Group Law for Europe,' *European Business Organization Law Review (EBOR)* I (2002) 165.

Fox, M.B. (1999), 'Required Disclosure and Corporate Governance,' (1999) 62 *Law and Contemporary Problems* 113.

Franks, J. and Mayer, C. (1996), 'Hostile takeovers and the correction of managerial failure,' 40 *Journal of Financial Economics* 163.

Franks, J., Mayer, C. and Renneboog, L. (2001), 'Who Disciplines Management in Poorly Performing Companies?' 10 *Journal of Financial Intermediation* 209.

Frentrop, P. (2003), *A History of Corporate Governance 1602–2002* (Brussels: Deminor).

Gepken-Jager, E., Van Solinge, G. and Timmerman, L. (eds.) (2005), *VOC 1602–2002, 400 Years of Company Law* (Deventer: Kluwer)

German Corporate Governance Commission (2001), see T. Baums (ed.) (2001).

Gernoth, J. and Meinema, M. (2000), 'Niederländisches Enqueterecht: Vorbild für das deutsche Sonderprüfungsrecht?', *Recht der interrnationalen Wirtschaft (RIW)* 2000, 844.

Grundmann, S. (2001), 'Wettbewerb der Regelgeber im Europäischen Gesellschaftsrecht—jedes Marktsegment hat seine Struktur,' *Zeitschrift für Unternehmens- und Gesellschaftsrecht (ZGR)* 2001, 783.

—— (2004), *Europäisches Gesellschafsrecht* (Heidelberg: C.F. Müller).

Grundmann, S. and Kerber, W. (2001), 'Information Intermediaries and Party Autonomy—The Example of Securities and Insurance Markets,' in S. Grundmann *et al.*, *Party Autonomy and the Role of Information in the Internal Market* (Berlin/New York: de Gruyter).

Grundmann, S. and Möslein, F. (2001–2002), 'Golden Shares—State Control in Privatised Companies: Comparative Law, European Law and Policy Aspects,' *Revue européenne de Droit bancaire & financier/European banking & financial law journal (EUREDIA)* 2001–02/4, 623–676.

Grundmann, S. and Selbherr, B. (1996), 'Börsenprospekthaftung in der Reform,' *Zeitschrift für Wirtschafts- und Bankrecht (WM)* 1996, 985.

Guyon, Y. (2002), 'Éloge funèbre de la société à directoire en droit français,' in *Liber amicorum Lucien Simont* (Brussels: Bruylant), 733.

Hampel (1998), The Hampel Report (Committee on Corporate Governance, Final Report, London, January 1998).

Hansemann, D. (1837), *Die Eisenbahnen und deren Aktionäre in ihrem Verhältniß zum Staat* (Leipzig, Halle: Vollckmar).

Hansmann, H. (1996), *The Ownership of Enterprise* (Cambridge: Belknap Press).

Hellwig, H.-J. (2005), 'The Transatlantic Financial Markets Regulatory Dialogue,' in K.J. Hopt, E. Wymeersch, H. Kanda and H. Baum (eds.), *Corporate Governance in Context* (Oxford: Oxford University Press), 363.

Higgs, D. (2003), *Review of the role and effectiveness of non-executive directors* (DTI London)

High Level Group of Company Law Experts (2002a), *Report on Issues Related to Takeover Bids* (Brussels: European Commission), also in G. Ferrarini, K. J. Hopt, J. Winter and E. Wymeeersch (eds.) (2004), *Reforming Company and Takeover Law in Europe* (Oxford: Oxford University Press), Annex 2, 825–924.

—— (2002b), *A Modern Regulatory Framework for Company Law in Europe* (Brussels: European Commission), also in G. Ferrarini, K. J. Hopt, J. Winter and E. Wymeeersch (eds.) (2004), *Reforming Company and Takeover Law in Europe* (Oxford: Oxford University Press), Annex 3, 925–1086.

—— (2005), 'European Corporate Governance in company law and codes,' *Rivista delle società* 2005, 534–587.

Hofstetter, K. (2002), *Corporate Governance in Switzerland, Final Report of the Panel of Experts on Corporate Governance* (Zurich: economiesuisse).

Hommelhoff, P. *et al.* (eds.) (2002), *Corporate Governance* (Heidelberg: Recht und Wirtschaft).

Hommelhoff, P., Hopt, K.J. and von Werder, A. (eds.) (2003) *Handbuch Corporate Governance* (Cologne and Stuttgart: Otto Schmidt and Schäffer-Poeschel).

Hopt, K.J. (1975), *Der Kapitalanlegerschutz im Recht der Banken* (Munich, Beck, 1975).

—— (1980), 'Ideelle und wirtschaftliche Grundlagen der Aktien-, Bank- und Börsenrechtsentwicklung im 19. Jahrhundert,' in H. Coing and W. Wilhelm (eds.), *Wissenschaft und Kodifikation des Privatrechts im 19. Jahrhundert, vol. V, Geld und Banken* (Frankfurt: Klostermann), 128.

—— (1985), 'Self-Dealing and Use of Corporate Opportunity and Information: Regulating Directors' Conflict of Interest,' in K. J. Hopt and G. Teubner (eds.), *Corporate Governance and Directors' Liabilities* (Berlin/New York: de Gruyter), 285.

—— (1994), 'Labor Representation on Corporate Boards: Impacts and Problems for Corporate Governance and Economic Integration in Europe,' 14 *International Review of Law and Economics* 203.

—— (1996), 'Die Haftung von Vorstand und Aufsichtsrat,' in *Festschrift für Ernst-Joachim Mestmäcker: Zum siebzigsten Geburtstag* (Baden- Baden: Nomos), 909.

—— (1997a), 'The German Two-Tier Board (Aufsichtsrat), A German View on Corporate Governance,' in K. J. Hopt and E. Wymeersch (eds.), *Comparative Corporate Governance—Essays and Materials* (Berlin/ New York: de Gruyter), 3.

—— (1997b), 'Europäisches und deutsches Übernahmerecht,' *Zeitschrift für das gesamte Handelsrecht und Wirtschafsrecht (ZHR)* 161 (1997) 368.

——. (1999), 'Comments to Section 93 of the German Stock Corporation Act (liability of the managing board),' in K. J. Hopt and H. Wiedemann (eds.), *Großkommentar Aktiengesetz* 4th edn, 11th issue (Berlin/New York: de Gruyter).

—— (2000), 'Kapitalmarktrecht (mit Prospekthaftung) in der Rechtsprechung des Bundesgerichtshofes,' in A. Heldrich and K. J. Hopt (eds.), *50 Jahre Bundesgerichtshof, Festgabe aus der Wissenschaft*, vol. II (Munich: Beck), 497.

—— (2001), 'Disclosure Rules as Primary Tool for Fostering Party Autonomy—Observations from a Functional and Comparative Legal Perspective,' in S. Grundmann *et al.* (eds.), *Party Autonomy and the Role of Information in the Internal Market* (Berlin/New York: de Gruyter), 246.

—— (2002a), 'Unternehmensführung, Unternehmenskontrolle, Modernisierung des Aktienrechts—Zum Bericht der Regierungskommission Corporate Governance –,' in P. Hommelhoff *et al.*, *Corporate Governance* (Heidelberg: Recht und Wirtschaft).

——. (2002b), 'Takeovers, Secrecy and Conflicts of Interest: Problems for Boards and Banks,' in J. Payne (ed.), *Takeovers in English and German Law* (Oxford: Hart Publishing), 33.

—— (2002c), 'Common Principles of Corporate Governance in Europe?' in J. A. McCahery, P. Moerland, T. Raaijmakers and L. Renneboog (eds.), *Corporate*

Governance Regimes, Convergence and Diversity (Oxford: Oxford University Press), 175.

———. (2002d), Takeover regulation in Europe—the battle for the 13th directive on takeovers, (2002) 15 *Australian Journal of Corporate Law* 1.

—— (2003), 'Corporate Governance in Germany,' in K. J. Hopt/E. Wymeersch (eds), Capital Markets and Company Law (Oxford: Oxford University Press), 289.

—— (2004), 'Trusteeship and Conflicts of Interest in Corporate, Banking and Agency Law: Toward Common Legal Principles for Intermediaries in the Modern Service-Oriented Society,' in G. Ferrarini, K. J. Hopt, J. Winter and E. Wymeersch (eds.), *Reforming Company and Takeover Law in Europe* (Oxford: Oxford University Press), 51.

—— (2005), 'European Company Law and Corporate Governance: Where Does the Action Plan of the European Commission Lead?' in K.J. Hopt, E. Wymeersch, H. Kanda and H. Baum (eds.), *Corporate Governance in Context* (Oxford: Oxford University Press), 119.

Hopt, K.J. and Leyens, P. (2004), 'Board Models in Europe—Recent Developments of Internal Corporate Governance Structures in Germany, the United Kingdom, France and Italy', (2004) *European Company and Financial Law Review* 135.

Hopt, K.J. and Roth, M. (2005), 'Comments to Sections 95–116 of the German Stock Corporation Act (the board),' in K. J. Hopt and H. Wiedemann (eds.) *Großkommentar zum Aktiengesetz*, 4th edn, 24th issue (Berlin: de Gruyter), 1450 p.

Hopt, K.J., Rudolph, B. and Baum, H. (eds.) (1997), *Börsenreform—Eine ökonomische, rechtsvergleichende und rechtspolitische Untersuchung*—(Stuttgart: Schäffer Poeschel).

Hopt, K.J. and Voigt, H.-C. (eds.) (2005), *Prospekt- und Kapitalmarktinformationshaftung* (Tübingen: Mohr Siebeck).

Hopt, K.J., Wymeersch E., Kanda H. and Baum, H. (eds.) (2005), *Corporate Governance in Context—Corporations, States, and Markets in Europe, Japan, and the US* (Oxford: Oxford University Press).

Ihlas, H. (1997), *Organhaftung und Haftpflichtversicherung* (Berlin: Duncker & Humblot).

Institut der Wirtschaftsprüfer/Wirtschaftsprüferkammer, 'Stellungnahme 17 September 2002 (Sarbanes-Oxley-Act),' *Fachnachrichten des Instituts der Wirtschaftsprüfer (IDW-FN)* 2002, 593.

Kalss, S. (2001), 'Die rechtliche Grundlage kapitalmarktbezogener Haftungsansprüche,' *Österreichisches Bankarchiv (ÖBA)* 2001, 641.

—— (2002), 'Die Haftung des Abschlußprüfers gegenüber Gläubigern, Gesellschaftern und Anlegern,' *Österreichisches Bankarchiv (ÖBA)* 2002, 187.

Koch, H. (2001), *Zeitschrift für Zivilprozeßrecht (ZZP)* 114 (2001) 235.

Köndgen, J. (1994), 'Duties of Banks in Voting Their Clients' Stock,' in Baums, T., Buxbaum, R.M. and Hopt, K.J. (eds.), *Institutional Investors and Corporate Governance* (Berlin, New York: de Gruyter), 531.

Kraakman, R.H. (1986), 'Gatekeepers: The Anatomy of a Third-Party Enforcement Strategy,' 2 *Journal of Law, Economics, and Organization* 53.

Kraakman, R., Davies, P., Hansmann, H., Hertig, G., Hopt, K. J., Kanda, H. and

Rock, E.B. (2004), *The Anatomy of Corporate Law, A Comparative and Functional Approach* (Oxford: Oxford University Press).

Krahnen, J.P. and Schmidt, R.H. (eds.) (2004), *The German Financial System* (Oxford: Oxford University Press).

Krause, H. (2002), 'Von 'goldenen Aktien,' dem VW-Gesetz und der Übernahmerichtlinie,' *Neue Juristische Wochenschrift (NJW)* 2002, 2747.

Krause, R. (2003), 'Sarbanes-Oxley Act und deutsche Mitbestimmung,' *Zeitschrift für Wirtschafts- und Bankrecht (WM)* 2003, 762.

Kübler, F. (1997), 'Rechtsfragen des Rating,' in W. Hadding, K. J. Hopt and H. Schimansky (eds.), *Bankrechtstag 1996* (Berlin, New York: de Gruyter).

Lanfermann, G. and Maul, S. (2002), 'Auswirkungen des Sarbanes-Oxley Acts in Deutschland,' *Der Betrieb (DB)* 2002, 1725.

Le Cannu, P. (2000), 'Pour une évolution du droit des sociétés anonymes avec directoire et conseil de surveillance,' *Bulletin Joly* 2000, 483.

Lehmann, K. (1895), *Die geschichtliche Entwicklung des Aktienrechts bis zum Code de Commerce* (Berlin: Heymanns).

Lehne, K.-H. and Haak, A.M. (2003), 'Das Ringen um die Übernahmerichtlinie aus der Sicht des Europäischen Parlaments,' *Der Konzern* 3/2003, 163.

Lutter, M. (2003), 'Les expériences européennes de cogestion. L' expérience allemande,' in K. J. Hopt, M. Menjucq and E. Wymeersch (eds.), *La Société Européenne, Organisation juridique et fiscale, intérêts, perspectives* (Paris: Dalloz), 81.

Lutter, M. *et al.* (2002), 'Stellungnahme der Group of German Experts on Corporate Law zum Konsultationspapier der High Level Group of Experts on Corporate Law', *Zeitschrift für Wirtschaftsrecht (ZIP)* 2002, 1310.

Maassen, G.F. (2000), *An International Comparison of Corporate Governance Models, A Study on the Formal Independence and Convergence of One-Tier and Two-Tier Corporate Boards of Directors in the United States of America, the United Kingdom and the Netherlands* (Amsterdam: Spencer Stuart).

McCahery, J.A.. *et al.* (eds.) (2002), *Corporate Governance Regimes, Convergence and Diversity* (Oxford: Oxford University Press).

McCahery, J.A., Renneboog, L., Ritter, P. and Haller S. (2004), 'The Economics of the Proposed European Takeover Directive,' in G. Ferrarini *et al.*, *Reforming Company and Takeover Law in Europe* (Oxford: Oxford University Press), 575.

Merkt, H. (1999), 'Das Europäische Gesellschaftsrecht und die Idee des 'Wettbewerbs der Gesetzgeber,' *Rabels Zeitschrift für ausländisches und internationales Privatrecht (RabelsZ)* 59 (1995) 545.

—— (2001), *Beiträge zur Börsen- und Unternehmensgeschichte* (Frankfurt: Lang).

—— (2002), *Gutachten G zum 64. Deutschen Juristentag Berlin 2002* (Munich: Beck), G 41.

Moloney, N. (2002), *EC Securities Regulation* (Oxford: Oxford University Press).

—— (2003), New frontiers in EC capital markets law: From market construction to market regulation, 40 *Common Market Law Review* 809.

Myners, P. (2001), *Institutional Investment in the UK: A Review* (London: HM Treasury).

Perakis, E. (ed.) (2004), *Rights of Minority Shareholders* (Brussels: Bruylant).

Peters, A.C. (2001), *Die Haftung und die Regulierung von Rating-Agenturen* (Baden-Baden: Nomos).

Pistor, K. (1999), 'Codetermination: A Sociopolitical Model with Governance Externalities,' in M. Blair/M. J. Roe (eds.), *Employees and Corporate Governance* (Washington: Brookings Institution Press), 113.

Rapport Bouton (2002), *Pour un meilleur gouvernement des entreprises cotées* (Paris).

Romano, R. (1993), *The Genius of American Corporate Law* (Washington D.C.: American Enterprise Institute Press).

—— (2001), 'Less is More: Making Institutional Investor Activism a Valuable Mechanism of Corporate Governance,' 18 *Yale Journal on Regulation* 174.

—— (2002), *The Advantage of Competitive Federalism for Securities Regulation* (Washington D.C.: American Enterprise Institute Press).

—— (2005), 'The Sarbanes-Oxley Act and the Making of Quack Corporate Governance,' 114 *Yale Law Journal* 1521–1611.

Roth, M. (2001), *Unternehmerisches Ermessen und Haftung des Vorstands* (Munich: Beck).

Ruge, R. (2002), 'Goldene Aktien und EG-Recht,' *Europäische Zeitschrift für Wirtschaftsrecht (EuZW)* 2002, 421.

Schäfer, A. (2003), 'Expérience de la cogestion en Allemagne,' in K. J. Hopt/M. Menjucq/E. Wymeersch (eds.), *La Société Européenne, Organisation juridique et fiscale, intérêts, perspectives* (Paris: Dalloz), 87.

Schneider, U. H. (2005), 'Konzern—Corporate Governance,' in R. Waldburger *et al.* (eds.), Wirtschaftsrecht zu Beginn des 21. Jahrhunderts, Festschrift für Peter Nobel zum 60. Geburtstag (Bern: Staempfli), 337.

Schwarz, G.C. and Holland, B. (2002), 'Enron, WorldCom... und die Corporate-Governance-Diskussion,' *Zeitschrift für Wirtschaftsrecht (ZIP)* 2002, 1661.

Seibt, C.H. (2002) 'Deutscher Corporate Governance Kodex und Entsprechens-Erklärung (§ 161 AktG-E),' *Die Aktiengesellschaft (AG)* 2002, 249.

Senate Committee on Governmental Affairs (2002), The Role of the Board of Directors in Enron's Collapse, 107th Congress, 2d Session, Report 107- 70, 8 July 2002.

Skog, R. (1995), *Does Sweden Need a Mandatory Bid Rule? A Critical Analysis* (Stockholm: Juristförlaget).

Stadler, A. (2002), *Rabels Zeitschrift für ausländisches und internationales Privatrecht (RabelsZ)* 66, 171.

SWX (2002), Directive on Information Relating to Corporate Governance, reprinted in Swiss Business Federation (ed), *Swiss Code of Best Practice for Corporate Governance*, (Zurich: economiesuisse).

Theisen, M.R. (1998), 'Empirical Evidence and Economic Comments on Board Structure in Germany,' in K. J. Hopt *et al.* (eds.), Comparative Corporate Governance (Oxford: Oxford University Press), 259.

Tunc, A. (1991), Corporate Law, in Buxbaum, R.M., Hertig, G., Hirsch, A. and Hopt, K.J. (eds.), *European Business Law, Legal and Economic Analyses on Integration and Harmonization* (Berlin/New York: de Gruyter), 199.

Ulmer, P. (2002a), 'Paritätische Arbeitnehmermitbestimmung im Aufsichtsrat von Großunternehmen—noch zeitgemäß?' *Zeitschrift für das gesamte Handelsrecht und Wirtschaftsrecht (ZHR)* 166, 271.

—— (2002b), 'Der Deutsche Corporate Governance Kodex—ein neues

Regulierungsinstrument für börsennotierte Aktiengesellschaften,' *ZHR* 166, 150.

Wahlgren, P. (ed.) (2003), *Scandinavian Studies in Law Vol. 45 Company Law* (Stockholm: Stockholm University).

Welch, J. (2002), 'The Sophisticated Investor and the ISD,' in G. Ferrarini, K. J. Hopt and E. Wymeersch (eds.), *Capital Markets in the Age of the Euro—Cross-Border Transactions, Listed Companies and Regulation* (The Hague *et al.*: Kluwer Law International), 101.

Woidtke, T. (2002), 'Agents watching agents?: Evidence from pension fund ownership and firm value,' 63 *Journal of Financial Economics* 99.

Wymeersch, E. (1992), 'The Mandatory Bid: A Critical View,' in K. J. Hopt and E. Wymeersch (eds.), *European Takeovers—Law and Practice* (London: Butterworths).

Wymeersch, E. (2002), 'Editorial: Will 2002 Be a Historical Turning Point in the Development of Company Law?' 4 *International and Comparative Corporate Law Journal* iii.

Zuberbühler, D. (2004), Finanzmarktregulierung und kein Ende? in A. Héritier Lachat and L. Hirsch (eds.) *De lege ferenda, Études pour le professeur Alain Hirsch* (Geneva: Slatkine).

14

Who Should Make Corporate Law? EC Legislation versus Regulatory Competition

JOHN ARMOUR*

I. INTRODUCTION

T HE BEGINNING OF the twenty-first century has brought with it an extraordinary set of stimuli for company law reform in the EU. A series of well-publicized recent scandals on both sides of the Atlantic have shaken faith in existing company law frameworks. Contemporaneously, in the wake of the European Court of Justice's (ECJ) decisions in the *Centros* line of cases,[1] EU Member States are, for the first time, seemingly on the threshold of regulatory competition over the content of company law. The result has been protracted debates about the optimal 'model' for company law, informing an un-precedented volume of reform activity, both at EU and Member State level. A logically prior question concerns the allocation of jurisdiction to *make* the relevant reforms across the vertical, or 'federal', dimension—as

* Faculty of Law and Centre for Business Research, University of Cambridge. This chapter is based on the text of a *Current Legal Problems* lecture given on 25 Nov. 2004. I thank Brian Cheffins, Simon Deakin, Luca Enriques, Eilís Ferran, Martin Gelter, Joe McCahery, Barry O'Brien and especially Angus Johnston for helpful discussions and comments on earlier drafts and members of the audience at the lecture for their thoughtful questions. This chapter was previously published in (2005) 48 *Current Legal Problems* 369–414. The permission of Oxford University Press to republish is gratefully acknowledged.
[1] Case C-212/97 *Centros Ltd v Erhvervs-og Selskabssyrelsen* [1999] ECR I-1459, [2000] Ch 446; Case C-208/00 *Überseering BV v Nordic Construction Company Baumanagement GmbH (NCC)* [2002] ECR I-9919; Case C-167/01 *Kamel van Koophandel en Fabrieken voor Amsterdam v Inspire Art Ltd* [2003] ECR I-10155.

between the EU and Member States.[2] This question is the subject of the current chapter.

The analysis begins from the starting point that, given diversity amongst firms and national systems of corporate governance, a federal legislator cannot be sure which, if any, regulatory measures will be optimal. The chapter's basic argument is that regulatory competition between Member States' company laws is likely to be a better way to stimulate the development of appropriate legal rules than is the European legislative process.

Whilst the theoretical possibilities for regulatory competition are now fairly well understood, a number of commentators have argued either it is unlikely to be a significant force in Europe, or that if it is, it may be of the pathological, 'race to the bottom,' variety.[3] My basic argument is that regulatory competition is likely to be both a significant and a beneficial mechanism for the development of European company law. A recurring theme will be that national diversity implies that the process will operate differently from the way it has done in the United States: whilst there will be regulatory competition, no Member State will come to dominate as Delaware has done.

This argument will be developed in three stages. First, I will suggest that the EU is rapidly moving towards a framework within which companies will be both willing and able to locate their registered offices so as to secure a company law that is favorable to their requirements. For 'start-up' enterprises, this follows in the wake of recent landmark ECJ cases, and is motivated by entrepreneurs' desire to avoid barriers to entry created by capital maintenance rules. Moreover, it seems likely that EC legislation will soon also permit established companies to change their registered offices. For these firms, arbitrage will plausibly be motivated by a desire to ensure an appropriate 'fit' between ownership structure and the applicable governance regime. Most specifically, continental European companies which wish to shift from concentrated to dispersed ownership may find reincorporation in the United Kingdom to be an attractive option.

Secondly, I will argue that some Member States, and in particular the United Kingdom, will have incentives to engage in regulatory *competition* to attract companies, or to prevent them from being attracted elsewhere. For the United Kingdom, this will not be driven by tax revenues, as is the motivation for Delaware, but rather by professional services firms facing an increasingly competitive global environment. Other Member States are

---

[2] There is a second dimension, which may be termed the horizontal, or domestic, aspect. This concerns the selection of the appropriate body, within a given jurisdiction, for formulating the rules that govern the operation of corporate enterprise: namely, legislators, judges, regulators or private parties.

[3] See, e.g., Enriques (2004a); Gelter (2005); Kieninger (2005); Tröger (2005).

likely to respond with 'defensive' competition, either by removing inefficient rules or by further developing the complementarities of their systems. In the case of 'start-up' companies, recent and proposed legislative changes to European capital maintenance regimes provide evidence that this is already taking place.

My third claim is that the European regulatory competition will not result in a destructive 'race to the bottom'. In particular, proposed EU legislation governing the *process* by which established companies will be able to change their registered offices will give affected constituencies the ability to influence the outcome, so that arbitrage will be motivated by a desire to increase total value rather than the private interests of one group. The only way Member States will succeed in attracting such companies will be through providing company laws which enhance firm value. National legislators will therefore have incentives to engage in mutual learning: generally (sub)optimal rules will come to be (discarded) adopted; at the same time, particular national specializations will tend to be enhanced.

Finally, I will extend the argument, rather more tentatively, to the case of corporate insolvency law. The better view is that Member States will not be able to preserve restrictive creditor protection rules from scrutiny under EC free movement law merely by recharacterizing them as insolvency law, rather than company law. Moreover, I will suggest that the framework of the European Insolvency Regulation could permit a degree of regulatory competition to take place over aspects of corporate insolvency law—in particular, the nature of any 'corporate rescue' proceedings that may be available. It is sensible to consider their selection as part and parcel of the company law arbitrage, because there may be complementarities between the two.

The rest of the chapter is structured as follows. Part II sets the scene for the analysis by considering the scope of 'company law', the rationale for EU company law legislation, and the mechanisms of regulatory competition. Part III contains the basic argument and Part IV is the extension to corporate insolvency. Part V concludes with the suggestion that regulatory competition is likely to be superior than EC legislation for all aspects of company law on which there is no EU-wide consensus as to the appropriate regulatory choices.

II. SETTING THE SCENE

A. What is 'Company Law', and What Does it Do?

In order to make sense of the issues, it is necessary to begin with a working definition of 'company law'. From a traditional domestic perspective, this may be thought to be obvious: namely that which is found in the companies legislation. Yet from a European perspective, this traditional answer is unsatisfactory, because the scope of 'company law' is understood differently in different jurisdictions.[4] It is therefore helpful to begin with a framework that is neutral across jurisdictions. For this purpose, a functionalist approach is useful.

A functionalist account of a particular set of legal rules or legal institutions focuses on the purposes served for society by the institution in question. Company law's role is to regulate and facilitate the operation of business firms. Thus, a functionalist explanation of the subject seeks to explain how the rules in question do this. A leading functionalist account of corporate law views the subject as doing two basic things (Kraakman *et al.* 2004: 1–31): establishing the structure of the corporate form (and in particular, property rules which partition corporate assets from the assets of individuals associated with the company),[5] and seeking to prevent opportunism within voluntary relationships between participants. All company laws view 'participants' as including shareholders and directors; most include, to some extent, creditors, and some—the German system, for example—also include employees.[6]

Thus company law establishes a fund of corporate property, and provides a set of rules to govern the voluntary arrangements between the individuals associated with the business. A contentious question at the level of domestic corporate law is whether the rules governing the 'terms' of these relationships—that is, the rules that seek to minimize opportunistic conduct—are adequate. The debate typically turns on whether such rules should be mandatory in their content, or whether 'default' terms will suffice, and in either case, what the preferred content of the rule should be.[7] In relation to each of the axes along which the law has an impact—shareholder-creditor, director-shareholder, shareholder-employee, and so on, it is possible to find a welter of academic and political opinion in either direction.[8] Moreover, it seems highly plausible

---

[4] On differences in the scope of company law in other jurisdictions, see Kraakman *et al.* (2004: 15–17). The proper scope of the subject has been extensively debated at the domestic level in the course of the UK's recent Company Law Review. See, e.g., Company Law Review Steering Group (CLSRG 1999: 33–55; 2001: 41). See also DTI (2005a: 10).

[5] See also Hansmann and Kraakman (2000); Armour and Whincop (2005).

[6] See generally Kraakman *et al.* (2004: 61–67). On employees, see Gospel and Pendleton (2004).

[7] See generally, Easterbrook and Fischel (1991); Cheffins (1997: 126–262).

[8] For an impressionistic introduction, see (i) on manager-shareholder conflicts, Gompers *et al.* (2001) arguing that weaker shareholder rights imply reduced performance; cf. Larcker *et al.* (2004) describe corporate governance indicators as poor explanators of performance; (ii) on shareholder-creditor conflicts, La Porta *et al.* (1997) describe the relationship between debt finance and creditor protection as ambiguous; Kraakman *et al.* (2004: 77–96) argue that there are different systems of creditor protection; and (iii) on employee-shareholder conflicts, Frick and Lehmann (2004: 133–34) find the evidence on codetermination inconclusive.

that for any given regulatory issue, there may be no single 'best' approach for all European systems. Company law's regulatory choices are complementary to other aspects of a corporate governance system and of the regulation of the economy more generally—including tax, labor, competition and pension regulation and corporate ownership structure. The diversity of national corporate governance regimes,[9] coupled with such complementarities, implies that different legal rules are likely to be best for different systems.[10] For the purposes of this chapter, we need not engage in seeking answers for these debates, but may simply ensure that we keep their existence in mind by adopting, as an heuristic device, a perspective of 'regulatory agnosticism': that is, we can be sure of the desirability of neither rule nor content in any given case.

B. European Company Law

The European Community was established with the goal, inter alia, of forming a genuinely common market between Member States. This entailed the removal of barriers to trade and competition, and of other less direct distortions.[11] The variety of different national solutions to the questions of company law formed the original impetus for the European company law programme (Edwards 1999: 3–5). In particular, there was concern that different national law structures might encourage harmful regulatory arbitrage, whereby companies were given incentives to relocate their operations or legal personality in other jurisdictions, not for sound economic reasons, but simply to avoid complying with domestic rules of company law. The plethora of different national law rules leads to a further distorting effect: namely, the increased transaction costs incurred by companies and their advisors when doing cross-border deals involving aspects of company law (for example, corporate finance or inward investment). The solution was to press for 'harmonization' of national laws so as to minimize these costs.

The early years of the European project saw a consensus that the solution to these distorting effects of differences in national company law systems was to be found in the 'federal' (that is, EC-level) prescription of company law rules, which would ensure mutual compatibility.[12] This technique was employed in the early company law harmonization efforts, such as the First and Second Company Law Directives on safeguards for

---

[9] See Fioretos (2001); Carlin and Mayer (2002: 334–36).

[10] See Schmidt and Spindler (2004); Amable (2003: 54–66).

[11] See Preamble and Arts. 2, 3 EC; Barnard (2004: 6) cites Comité Intergouvernemental Créé par la Conférence de Messina, Rapport des Chefs de Délégation aux Ministres des Affaires Etrangères, Brussels, 21 April 1956 (the Spaak Report) Mae 120 f/56, 14.

[12] See Ficker (1973: 66).

third parties and share capital respectively.[13] As the European project has evolved, political consensus has become harder to find, with the result that progress has only been possible in the company law legislative programme by first focusing on specific areas.[14] From the early 1990s onwards, a range of less intensive techniques started to be employed, such as so-called 'framework' measures, which specify only general principles and leave Member States to specify the details at a later date. These less prescriptive measures have the manifest benefit of permitting greater adherence to the principle of subsidiarity, as well as being more politically feasible. The most interesting recent developments include the provision of a 'menu' of federal rules (as with the Takeover Directive),[15] and the 'comitology' process of devolution of legislative competence to a committee of experts in relation to securities regulation.[16] A third, and even less prescriptive form of approximation, is what has been termed 'procedural' harmonization (Deakin 2001: 209–13). This involves rules which, rather than seek to impose substantive solutions on Member States, aim instead to govern or influence the *process* by which legislation is passed.

In the wake of a series of high-profile corporate collapses, the European Commission (2003) announced in the summer of 2003 an 'Action Plan' for company law reform in Europe. Much of the programme consists of measures for updating earlier EC legislation, but it contains a limited number of proposals for further substantive harmonization. Most interesting for present purposes is the Commission's explicit recognition of the importance of national diversity, and the championing as part of the reform programme of measures which will allow companies to increase their jurisdictional mobility. These measures, which will stimulate regulatory competition, can be understood as a form of procedural harmonization—that is, regulation intended to influence indirectly the way in which Member States legislate by establishing an orderly framework within which regulatory competition can take place.

C. Regulatory Competition

As a third 'building block' for the argument that follows, we shall now consider what is meant by 'regulatory competition'. This may seem an obvious point, but it is one that is frequently misunderstood, or at least is

---

[13] First Council Directive 68/151/EEC [1968] OJ L65/8; Second Council Directive 77/91/EEC [1977] OJ L26/1.

[14] See Wouters (2000: 268–76); Grundmann (2004); McCahery and Vermeulen (2005: 10–18).

[15] Directive 2004/25/EC [2004] OJ L142/12. See Hertig and McCahery (this volume, ch. 15).

[16] See Ferran (this volume, ch. 16).

used in different senses in different contexts. A brief scene-setting exercise may therefore be helpful.

Regulatory *competition* implies that national legislatures compete to attract firms to operate subject to their laws.[17] The preconditions for this occurring are as follows. First, firms must engage in regulatory *arbitrage*: that is, they select the law that governs their activities in a way that will minimize their costs of operation. In turn, this implies that firms are permitted to do so, and that the costs of switching jurisdictions are less than the savings thereby achieved. Secondly, even if such arbitrage occurs, for regulatory competition to follow, individual jurisdictions must have something to gain (lose) by firms (not) conducting business subject to their laws. If both conditions are met, then jurisdictions will seek to enact laws designed to encourage firms to 'use' their regulations, as opposed to those in other jurisdictions. The key point is that the law reform process will come to be driven, at least in part, by the preferences of firms that are subject to the regulation in question.

Applied to company law, regulatory competition can operate with respect to the law governing a company's internal affairs, the so-called *lex societatis*, where firms are able to select this freely as between different jurisdictions. The US experience in this regard forms a well-known example.[18] It is worth considering in a little detail the institutional foundations of this case study. First, arbitrage. Federal conflicts rules rely on a 'place of incorporation' connecting factor in relation to the 'internal affairs' of a corporation, whereby a US corporation's governance arrangements will be subject to the law of the state where it was formed. Moreover, almost all US states permit corporations (i) to reincorporate 'inwards' from another jurisdiction and (ii) to reincorporate 'outwards' in favor of another jurisdiction. These rules combine to permit a corporate entity to reincorporate in State B and have the laws of that state govern its internal affairs, even though the entirety of its business is physically located in State A, and its only connection with State B is incorporation there. It is not costly for firms to reincorporate, and a significant number of firms have chosen to do so, almost all in favor of the same jurisdiction: Delaware.[19]

Secondly, competition. Delaware is a small state, which derives a significant proportion of its tax revenues from charges levied on the grant of corporate charters (Cary 1974: 664; Romano 1973: 15–16).[20] It does not

---

[17] See generally, Esty and Gerardin (2001); Murphy (2004). The classic model of regulatory competition responding to arbitrage by regulated parties is due to Tiebout (1956).

[18] See generally, Romano (1993); Drury (2005).

[19] See, e.g., Romano (1985: 244) states the 82 per cent of reincorporating firms chose Delaware; Alva (1990: 887) states that over 40 per cent of NYSE listed firms and over 50 per cent of Fortune 500 firms incorporated in Delaware.

[20] *cf.* Kahan and Kamar (2002: 687–94).

prohibit companies from switching out of Delaware once they have chosen to establish their registered office, should Delaware law cease to be attractive. Moreover, there is no viable alternative source of revenue to replace the charter dollars. Romano argues that the state's willingness to render itself vulnerable to the loss of this revenue, should it cease to satisfy its corporate 'customers' is part of its initial attractiveness. This is thus a 'hostage' given to them in order to signal Delaware's willingness to engage in continuous reform to its corporate law so as to reflect the preferences of firms that have incorporated there (Romano 1993: 38). In addition, the Delaware bar are said to enjoy substantial revenues from the work they do in relation to firms incorporated in that state. As a well-organized and influential lobby-group, their concerns are thought to be taken seriously by the Delaware legislature (Macey and Miller 1987: 472; Romano 1993: 28–31; Daines 2002).[21]

The process of regulatory competition is viewed with suspicion by some, who label it pejoratively as a 'race for the bottom.'[22] Indeed, the desire to avoid such an outcome was one of the original rationales for the European company law harmonization project (Edwards 1999: 3). It is easy to show why this might be the case if it is assumed first that a particular variety of regulation is unequivocally in the public interest and, secondly, that compliance imposes a net private cost on regulated firms. If regulatory arbitrage occurs along the margin of minimization of private costs by regulated firms, then regulatory competition will undermine the ability of such regulations to further the public interest.

However, both assumptions are unrealistic when applied to company law. First, 'regulatory agnosticism' implies that we cannot be sure about the relationship between regulatory provisions and the public interest.[23] Secondly, regulations which further the public interest will not necessarily impose net private costs on firms. In particular, regulations that seek to correct a market failure may, if they work effectively, result in a net *benefit* to firms that comply. This will be felt through the price mechanism of the market in question. For example, measures designed to ameliorate the costs of information asymmetries between shareholders and managers ('agency costs') may result in firms being able to lower their costs of corporate finance (Winter 1977; Romano 1985; Easterbrook and Fischel 1991: 212–27). Where regulation seeks to correct market failure, and if the federal legislature has no privileged knowledge as to the 'best' type of regulation, then regulatory competition can act as a 'race to the top.' Under these assumptions, the 'market' for the regulatory

[21] *cf.* Kahan and Kamar (2002: 694–700).

[22] The phrase was first coined in relation to corporate law by Bill Cary (1974: 666), lamenting the 'Delaware effect' in the US.

[23] See above, text to nn. 8–10.

provisions can act, in the fashion celebrated by Hayek, to stimulate innovation and to aggregate the information available to firms about regulatory effectiveness.[24] Similarly, if diversity of systems means that there *is* no global 'best' regulatory choice, but rather simply locally-optimal solutions, then a 'market' for regulatory provisions may result in greater specialization, if states perceive the best way to attract incorporations as being to capitalize on complementarities.[25] Again, innovation and mutual learning may be expected. Under these preconditions, then, regulatory competition can promote the beneficial development of national company laws where a federal legislator is faced with regulatory agnosticism.

The crucial precondition for beneficial regulatory competition is that the price mechanism operate as a binding constraint on firms' choices. An extended and ultimately inconclusive debate on this point has taken place in relation to the case of Delaware. Critics of the US system point to the fact that reincorporation decisions are typically taken by a simple majority shareholder vote, responding to an agenda which will have been put forward by the board of directors.[26] Therefore, they suggest that there may be a tendency for companies to tend to select corporate laws that favor managers, for example through permitting the use of defensive tactics following hostile takeover bids.

The empirical literature has, however, not given strong support to the critics' claims. A number of studies have reported that reincorporation in Delaware appears to have a positive impact on a firm's stock price, suggesting that the move is viewed by the market as value-increasing.[27] Others have sought to examine factors which determine a decision to reincorporate in Delaware, as opposed to remaining in the initial 'home state'. Some found that firms are more likely to remain in their home state where this has adopted an anti-takeover statute, implying inefficient decisions (Subramanian 2002; Bebchuk and Cohen 2003). Yet others have found weak evidence that firms *avoid* states with antitakeover statutes (Daines 2002: 1596–97; Kahan 2004), and choose to incorporate in jurisdictions with more flexible corporate laws and better-quality judiciary (Kahan 2004). However, it is unnecessary for present purposes to form a firm view on the merits of US regulatory competition. This is because, as we shall see, the process will operate differently in the EU, such that the concerns of the US critics are unlikely to be replicated.[28]

---

[24] See Deakin (2001: 216–17); Romano (2005).

[25] See Choi (2002: 1705–6); Heine and Kerber (2002).

[26] See, e.g., Bebchuk (1992).

[27] See, e.g., Daines (2001). Earlier studies are reviewed by Romano (1993: 16–24). However, see also Subramanian (2004) arguing that any beneficial effect on firm value of Delaware reincorporation has diminished over time.

[28] See below, text to n. 89ff.

III. THE BASIC ARGUMENT

Following from these ideas, I shall now argue that as a general matter, regulatory competition in European company law can be both feasible and desirable.

A. To What Extent Does EU Law Permit Companies to Migrate?

Until recently, it was thought that the legal obstacles to regulatory arbitrage over company law within the EU were profound.[29] First, the conflicts of law rules of the vast majority of Member States made use of the so-called 'real seat' theory in determining the existence and proper law of a company. In contrast to the 'incorporation theory' used in the United States, this applies the law of the place where the company has its main place of business or 'real seat.' When combined with rules on the recognition of the existence of corporate persons, it effectively prevented regulatory competition from taking place at all. For example, if a company incorporated in Member State A (which applied the incorporation theory) then carried on business in Member State B (which applied the real seat theory), the courts of Member State B would reason that the company's proper law would be that of Member State B, and consequently, because it was not incorporated under that law, it was not validly formed at all.

However, matters have changed dramatically following the ECJ decisions in *Centros, Überseering* and *Inspire Art*.[30] These cases relate to company law arbitrage at the point of *formation*. Each of the decisions concerned the treatment by Member State B of companies incorporated in Member State A, but having their 'real seat' in Member State B. The ECJ considered that the application of the real seat theory so as to deny recognition of the existence of the company in Member State B because it was not validly incorporated amounted to an interference with the company's freedom of establishment. Essentially, the court ruled that as a matter of EC law, a company, once validly formed under the laws of *any* Member State, becomes a 'person' and is consequently entitled to exercise the Treaty Freedoms.[31] Moreover, the mere fact that the company was incorporated in Member State A solely to avoid laws which would otherwise apply, were it incorporated in Member State B, does not

---

[29] See, e.g., Cheffins (1997: 426–31).
[30] Above, n. 1.
[31] A voluminous literature has grown up on the legal consequences of the *Centros* line of cases. See, e.g., Wymeersch (2000; 2003a); Micheler (2000); Baelz and Baldwin (2002); Siems (2002); Bachner (2003); Kersting and Schindler (2003); Roth (2003); Lowry (2004); Rammeloo (2004); Zimmer (2004); Ebke (2005).

constitute an 'abuse' of that freedom. The consequence is that any laws of Member State B which tend to make the exercise of that freedom less attractive to companies incorporated in Member State A will therefore be struck down unless they satisfy the four-stage criteria set out in *Gebhard*[32]: that is, they are (i) applied in a non-discriminatory manner; (ii) are justified by imperative requirements of the public interest; (iii) secure the attainment of their objective; and (iv) are not disproportionate in their effect.

As the dust gradually settles from the ECJ's recent crusade in this area, it is coming to be appreciated that analyses of regulatory competition in European company law must consider the question in relation to two quite different contexts.[33] The first, heralded by the recent ECJ case law, is that of entrepreneurial 'start-up' companies, over which the competition will be for *formations*. The second context is that of established firms. Notwithstanding the developments in relation to 'start-up' companies, there remain a number of legal obstacles to *reincorporation* by established companies from Member State A to Member State B. First, and most obviously, the laws of many Member States (including the United Kingdom) do not permit such corporate 'emigration'.[34] The ECJ's ruling in *Daily Mail*,[35] as affirmed in *Überseering* and *Inspire Art*, seems to establish that this does not interfere with companies' freedom of establishment, for the court has held that companies are 'creatures' of the national law under which they are formed and can exercise Treaty freedoms only consistently therewith. Secondly, many Member States impose 'exit taxes' on companies which seek to relocate either their registered or head office (again, as evidenced by the rule challenged in *Daily Mail*), which act as a financial disincentive to so doing.

However, it is my view that these legal obstacles to change of primary establishment by existing companies are unlikely to persist. At the national level, some Member States—such as the United Kingdom—are proposing to change their company laws so as to permit free juris-dictional (e)migration.[36] At the European level, a limited power to reincorporate in another jurisdiction has already been introduced by the Regulation implementing the European Public Company, or *Societas Europaea* (SE).[37] SEs may be formed under the laws of any Member State by transformation from an existing public company, or through the merger of two or more such companies. Moreover, once established, an

---

[32] Case C-55/94 *Gebhard v Colsiglio dell'Ordine degli Avvocati e Procuratori di Milano* [1995] ECR I-4165.

[33] See Tröger (2005); Gelter (2005); Kieninger (2005: 762–65).

[34] On the UK, see Smart (1998: 348–49).

[35] Case 81/87 *The Queen v H.M. Treasury and Commissioners of Inland Revenue, ex parte Daily Mail and General Trust plc* [1988] ECR 5483.

[36] See DTI (2005a: 48–49).

[37] EC Council Regulation 2157/2001 [2001] OJ L294/1.

SE may subsequently change its jurisdiction of registered office.[38] More pertinently, the proposed Tenth Directive on Cross-Border Mergers (European Commission 2003a),[39] and/or the draft Fourteenth Directive on Transfer of Registered Office,[40] are likely to introduce mechanisms by which a transfer of registered office may be achieved without necessitating a transfer of head office.

Turning to exit taxes, it seems most likely that, once companies are granted freedom to relocate by European legislation (thereby bypassing *Daily Mail*), such fiscal rules will come to be viewed as unlawful restrictions on the freedom of establishment which companies would otherwise be able to exercise: a sort of corporate equivalent of the recent *de Lastreyie du Saillant* ruling which outlawed exit taxes levied by French law upon a natural person.[41] In a similar vein, the Merger Tax Directive outlaws tax impediments to cross-border mergers.[42]

Table 1 summarizes the current and anticipated position. Not only is it legally possible for 'start-up' companies to engage in company law arbitrage on formation, but it seems likely that it will also soon be possible for established companies to do so through reincorporation.[43]

B. Even if Regulatory Arbitrage is Legally Possible, Will Firms Wish to Take Advantage?

For it to be legally *possible* for regulatory arbitrage to occur is, of course, only the starting point. If firms are actually to exercise this option, the

---

[38] *Ibid.*, Art. 8. However, the extent to which this may be used as a mechanism of regulatory arbitrage is limited by the requirement that the head office—that is, the 'seat'—must always be in the same jurisdiction as the registered office: Art. 7. Enriques (2004: 79-84) argues that SE statute may itself facilitate regulatory competition' cf. McCahery and Vermeulen (2005: 18-22).

[39] The Tenth Directive received approval from the European Council on 25 November 2004. See European Commission (2004a).

[40] See European Commission (1997; 2004b).

[41] Case C-9/02 *Hughes de Lastreyie du Saillant v Ministère de l'Économie, des Finances et de l'Industrie* [2004] 3 CMLR 39. This will be applicable because the Tenth and Fourteenth Directives will give companies, for the first time, a power based in European legislation to change their registered offices. Daily Mail will be distinguishable because its major premise, that a company is a creature of the law of the Member State in which it was formed, is valid only insofar as the scope of the company's powers are not determined by European law.

[42] Council Directive 90/434/EEC [1990] OJ L225/1. It is unclear whether the Merger Tax Directive applies to the formation of a SE by merger: see Enriques (2004a: 1261–62). However, an overwhelming majority of the respondents to the Commission's consultation as respects transfer of seat were in favor of the express application of the Merger Tax Directive: see European Commission (2004c: question 14).

[43] The discussion in the text does not consider the effect on the legal potential for regulatory arbitrage of double taxation treaties and other similar instruments of international law. This is because these principally impact upon attempts to transfer assets, and the discussion in the text is concerned solely with arbitrage through transfer of registered office.

Table 1: Current and Anticipated Legal Framework for Company Law Arbitrage

Formation: 'start-up' companies		Reincorporation: established companies	
Barriers	Removal	Barriers	Removal
Real seat theory	*Centros* etc: national laws must permit *immigration*	*Daily Mail*: no need for national law to permit *emigration*	10th, 14th Directives will shortly permit emigration
Unnecessary and disproportionate measures failing *Gebhard* test	Case-by-case challenge	Exit taxes commonly levied	Likely to fail *Gebhard* test; prohibited by Merger Tax Directive; will probably also be prohibited by 14th Directive

benefits to them from doing so must exceed the costs. A number of scholars doubt whether this will be the case, at least on any significant scale. First, it is argued that there may be little legal benefit to be had from 'jurisdiction-shopping'. The existing harmonization initiatives have reduced the differences between Member States' company laws, at least compared with those that existed between states' corporate laws in the United States in the late nineteenth and early twentieth century, when Delaware developed its dominant position.[44] Moreover, litigation by minority shareholders being much rarer in Europe than in the United States (Enriques 2004a: 1262), the expected benefits from switching to a more 'favorable' company law regime may be small.

A second factor concerns the nature of share ownership patterns. Unlike their Anglo-American counterparts, public companies in continental Europe typically have concentrated share ownership, with control being exercised by a single large blockholder or a coalition of blocks.[45] This alters the nature of the corporate law 'product' in which that such firms would be interested (Romano 1993: 136–38). Rather than being concerned with protecting dispersed shareholders against the risk of managerial misbehavior, shareholders in a blockholder system are more interested in the extent to which a majority is able to exert control.[46] If, as is likely, corporate laws and ownership patterns have co-evolved over time in European jurisdictions, there are likely to be strong complementarities between the two (Bebchuk and Roe 1999). Thus, it is argued, there will be little to be gained by a firm reincorporating under a

[44] See Cheffins (1997: 433); Enriques (2004a: 1269); Kieninger (2005: 769).
[45] See La Porta *et al.* (1999: 491–98); Barca and Becht (2001); Roe (2003).
[46] See Kraakman *et al.* (2004: 22, 53–54, 60–61).

different corporate law that will be likely to be maladapted to its particular governance requirements (Gelter 2005).

Thirdly, some argue that problems over litigation will act as a brake on regulatory arbitrage (Dammann 2004: 492–502; Kirchner *et al.* 2004: 23–35). A company whose centre of business is located in Member State B but which has reincorporated in Member State A would then have to decide where disputes should be litigated. To do so in Member State A would, it is thought, be undesirable in many cases, because of the need to retain different lawyers, to follow a different procedural system, and to consider issues in a different language (Kirchner *et al.* 2004). On the other hand, litigation in Member State B would have the obvious drawback of having judges in Member State B decide questions on the laws of Member State A, with accompanying problems of linguistic and conceptual translation. To be sure, jurisdiction or arbitration agreements could be used to structure matters in most cases so that the problem is minimized, but on issues relating to the validity of the corporate constitution and the acts of its organs, the exclusive jurisdiction rule of Article 22(2) of the Judgments Regulation[47] would mandate that litigation take place in Member State A (Dammann 2004: 495). Thus the problems could not be avoided entirely.

A fourth and closely-related difficulty with regulatory arbitrage is thought to be the difficulties involved in getting appropriate legal advice both in relation to the possibility of making the change and in structuring affairs subsequently (Dammann 2004: 503–7; Enriques 2004: 1264).[48] The languages of possible states of reincorporation are likely to be different from that spoken by the company's management. Moreover, any suggestion regarding change is likely to encounter hostility from incumbent legal advisors. What lawyer would propose reincorporation in a different jurisdiction, if this will result in legal work being transferred to another advisor? If the company's existing legal team are unable to advise, it will be necessary to retain another law firm, which is likely to be based in the state of reincorporation, to advise instead. This may entail considerable risk, if the company does not have a good knowledge of the reputations of law firms in the new jurisdiction.

I shall suggest that the arguments of the pessimists are unconvincing, and particularly so if it is posited that the United Kingdom might be the jurisdiction of choice for reincorporation. Once more, it is helpful to

---

[47] EC Council Regulation 44/2001 [2001] OJ L12/1. Art 22(2) grants exclusive jurisdiction to the courts of the Member State where the company has its 'seat'. For jurisdictions using the incorporation theory, the 'seat' will be interpreted as meaning the place of incorporation. This rule is mandatory, and may not be ousted by a jurisdiction clause: *ibid.*: Art. 23(5).

[48] These arguments are based on evidence from the US that the a company's legal advisors are often key players in its decision (not) to reincorporate: see Romano (1985: 274); Daines (2002: 1580–81).

divide the discussion into the separate cases of arbitrage by formation and by reincorporation. As far as formation is concerned, the driver of regulatory arbitrage by entrepreneurs is clearly the restrictive capital adequacy and maintenance requirements of many continental jurisdictions. As the Second Company Law Directive does not apply to private companies, there is considerable scope for variety between Member States' laws, and the United Kingdom undoubtedly has a more permissive regime than most continental European jurisdictions. Thus, for an entrepreneur wishing to form a company without complying with expensive minimum capital requirements, the United Kingdom is clearly likely to be the jurisdiction of choice.

To be sure, such a selection will entail increased legal risk owing to the need to litigate some issues in the United Kingdom, as opposed to local courts, and the need to obtain UK legal advice. There are reasons for thinking, however, that these costs are unlikely to act as a significant brake. First, there is likely to be little risk of litigation over the company's internal affairs in the United Kingdom if it is owned only by a small group of shareholders, who might bind themselves with a shareholder agreement for good measure. External affairs could be directed towards the jurisdiction of choice through jurisdiction clauses as part of the company's standard terms. As far as legal advice is concerned, it would appear that there is a market opportunity for lawyers serving the needs of such entrepreneurs to start to offer their services. An entrepreneur is unlikely to consult a lawyer frequently, and so the idea of 'incumbent lawyer resistance' is not particularly compelling. The indications are that specialist 'formation agents' are already targeting their services at continental European entrepreneurs in an attempt to win this business.[49] Further evidence comes from the recent dramatic increase in the number of companies located in continental Europe incorporating in the United Kingdom. To exemplify this, Figure 1 reports numbers of 'German' companies incorporating in the United Kingdom.

These were identified by searching data from Companies House (2005) for companies with largely German-language names,[50] but ending with the word 'Limited.'[51] To be sure, the data are only

---

[49] A typical example of many such agents found by a Google search is Coddan CPM UK, which offers, via the internet, same-day incorporation of a UK private company for a fee of £42. The website has versions, explaining arbitrage opportunities, in Spanish and German. See www.ukincorp.co.uk.

[50] The relevant companies were identified by searching for names including the following terms: '*AG*', '*GmbH*', '*Gesellschaft*', '*und*', '*mit*' and '*handel*'. This methodology follows Kirchner *et al.* (2004: 6–7), but by searching on a wider range of German words, a larger number of companies were identified. The results were checked manually to ensure that the names were in German.

[51] The suffix 'Limited' excludes firms incorporated in Germany but registered in the UK as an 'overseas company.'

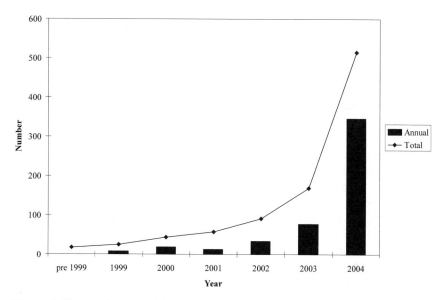

Figure 1: 'German' companies incorporating in UK

impressionistic[52]; moreover, they represent only a tiny fraction of the total number of companies incorporated in the United Kingdom.[53] What is significant about the figures is the way in which the rate of such incorporations surged after the *Überseering* and *Inspire Art* decisions in 2002 and 2003 respectively.

Turning to larger companies, the discussion necessarily becomes more speculative. However, if a typical listed company is taken as the paradigm, there are still good reasons for thinking that the United Kingdom may be an attractive reincorporation choice to many, notwithstanding the foregoing objections. First, despite the early harmonization efforts, many feel that the United Kingdom's company law still has a substantially more flexible character than the company laws of many other European jurisdictions.[54] To be sure, the difference is nowhere near as significant as the regulation gradient between Delaware and its competitors in the early twentieth century. Yet it is not simply the content of corporate law that makes reincorporation attractive. Commentators in the United States have argued that a significant part of Delaware's advantage comes from the way in which adjudication is conducted. This

---

[52] The data may be both under- and over-inclusive. On the one hand, the search methodology does not capture all German-language names. On the other hand, the data do not tell us whether these companies in fact carry on any business in the UK.

[53] There were over two million companies registered in the UK in 2003–4: DTI (2004: 33).

[54] See, e.g., CLSRG (1999: 96–98); Dammann (2004: 525).

includes the quality, expertise and 'business-friendliness' of its judiciary.[55] Thus it is notable that Delaware is the only state in the United States to have a specialist court for the trial of corporate matters (Kahan and Kamar 2002: 708–15), and Kahan's recent empirical study of incorporation decisions (Kahan 2004) suggests that judicial quality is at least as important to firms choosing where to incorporate as the relative flexibility of key provisions in the corporate code. Other related factors are the existence of a rich body of precedents accumulated over many years of judicial law-making, which enhance the certainty of legal rules, and the availability of high-quality legal advice through Delaware's specialist corporate law bar (Romano 1993: 41).[56]

Throughout Europe, the United Kingdom is perhaps uniquely positioned to capitalize on these procedural aspects of corporate law choice (Cheffins 1997: 442–43). Similarly to Delaware, the United Kingdom has a specialist court list devoted solely to corporate matters.[57] This is presided over by judges who have spent many years in practice specializing in corporate matters, in contrast to the practice in many other Member States of appointing judges direct from law school (Shapiro 1981: 150; Cappelletti 1989: 220).[58] In terms of certainty, it appears that English judges place even greater weight on precedents than their American counterparts.[59] This combination of legal flexibility and certainty permits UK companies to structure their affairs as they wish and with a low risk of legal challenge.

However, for European companies considering reincorporating, these factors may be less salient than for their US counterparts, owing to the relatively low litigation rates in Europe.[60] Yet to focus on 'hard law' alone would be to miss entirely the juiciest part of the 'carrot' that will attract such firms. This is because much of what is important about the English approach to regulating the control of listed companies is not found in the companies legislation at all, but in the body of 'soft law' rules and codes that apply to companies listed on the London Stock Exchange. The most important of these are the UK Listing Rules and the City Code on Takeovers and Mergers. These deal with a range of matters that might equally well be regulated by company law,[61] including rules regarding

---

[55] See Romano (1993: 39–40); Kahan (2004).

[56] *cf.* Kamar (1998).

[57] See Brooke (2004: paras. 1–143, 2G-14).

[58] However, it should be noted that many civilian jurisdictions provide for judicial specialization in corporate/commercial matters.

[59] See Atiyah and Summers (1987: 118–27); Posner (1996: 84–92).

[60] See above, text following n. 44.

[61] See UK Listing Rules, rr. 10.5, 10.37 (significant transactions requiring shareholder approval); ch. 11 (related party transactions requiring shareholder approval); rr. 4.16–21 (pre-emption rights); ch. 15 (share repurchases); and ch. 12 and Model Code (directors' share dealings).

substantive corporate governance (UKLA 2003), and most obviously, takeovers (Takeover Panel 2002).[62]

As compared with 'true' company law, these self-regulatory rules offer two key advantages in terms of functionality. First, they are capable of being continuously updated in response to developments in the market, and secondly, they are promulgated and enforced by persons with relevant business and market expertise. Both the Listing Rules and the City Code originated as self-regulatory rules.[63] They owe their content and mode of enforcement largely to the preferences of UK institutional investors, who hold in excess of 60 per cent of the shares listed on the London Stock Exchange.[64] These institutions have sufficiently large interests to make it worthwhile to become involved both in setting up self-regulatory structures and lobbying government to avoid further encroachment of legislation.[65] The regulatory structures which have emerged are those which these institutions consider serve their interests, as is most obviously the case with the Combined Code on Corporate Governance and the City Code on Takeovers. These codes are regularly updated by reviews which respond rapidly to changes in the way in which the market operates,[66] and invariably take into account the wishes of institutional investors.

It seems that the self-regulatory aspect of the UK system is in practice far more significant for companies than the content and enforcement of company law itself. To illustrate: during the year 2002–3, the Takeover Panel were involved in advising on 305 transactions raising issues in relation to the Takeover Code, of which 108 resulted in published takeover or merger proposals (Takeover Panel 2003: 14). Yet in the same period, there were only four cases decided in UK courts raising issues of company law involving listed companies.[67] This is not, however, to say

[62] A regularly updated version of the City Code can be viewed at www.thetakeoverpanel. org.uk.

[63] The Listing Rules are now, of course, promulgated and enforced by the Financial Services Authority. The implementation of the Takeover Directive will see a statutory basis put in place for the Takeover Panel's jurisdiction, but will not, it seems, result in significant changes to the Panel's composition or mode of operating: see DTI (2005b: 11–24).

[64] Becht and Mayer state that the level is 62 per cent (2001: 26).

[65] See Black and Coffee (1994: 2034–41); Stapledon (1996: 55–153); Cheffins (1997: 364–421); Davies (2003a: 279–87); Armour and Skeel (2005).

[66] Thus, the 'Combined Code' of corporate governance has been revised three times since its first incarnation as the 'Cadbury Code' in 1992 (following the Greenbury Report in 1995, the Hampel Report in 1998 and the Higgs Report in 2003). Similarly, the Code Committee of the Takeover Panel meets four times annually to review the workings of the City Code and propose revisions: see Takeover Panel (2004: 10–12).

[67] *Criterion Properties plc v Stratford UK Properties LLC* [2002] EWCA Civ 1883, [2003] 2 BCLC 129 (validity of corporate transaction); *Chaston v SWP Group plc* [2002] EWCA Civ 1999, [2003] 1 BCLC 675 (financial assistance); *PNC Telecom plc v Thomas* [2002] EWHC 2848 (Ch), [2004] 1 BCLC 88 (whether notice of EGM served by fax valid); *Re Marconi plc* [2003] All ER (D) 362 (scheme of arrangement). These were identified using LEXIS. A further 12 cases involved issues of insolvency law relating to companies that had formerly been listed.

that company law is irrelevant. Rather, it is a feature of the United Kingdom's *system of company law* that it permits such activities as takeovers to be regulated by the Code and enforced by the Panel as opposed to by the company law and the judiciary respectively.

The implications of this picture for our discussion are as follows. For a company with dispersed equity ownership, or which wishes to move towards it, the UK system provides an extremely attractive set of solutions to the managerial agency problem: hostile takeovers, shareholder control of related party and significant transactions, and pre-emption rights protection. This is combined with a system of company law that is relatively flexible, and is enforced by a highly specialist judiciary. At present it is possible for a company to opt into the Listing Rules by applying to join the UK Official List regardless of where its registered office or seat is located.[68] In contrast, it is not currently possible for a company that is not 'resident' in the United Kingdom—a test equivalent to the 'real seat'—to be subject to the Takeover Panel's jurisdiction. With the implementation of the Takeover Directive, however, this will change. The Takeover Panel will shortly take jurisdiction over offers in respect of any company with its real seat within the EU that is listed in the United Kingdom and which has a registered office in the United Kingdom.[69]

Such a system is, to be sure, most unlikely to be attractive to a continental company subject to stable control by a large blockholder.[70] Such a blockholder is likely to enjoy significant 'private benefits of control'.[71] Compliance with the UK Listing Rules would lessen their ability to enjoy these, through the one-share one-vote rules that outlaw complex and opaque ownership structures, and the restrictions on related party transactions. Moreover, the body of rules directed towards minimizing managerial agency costs would be irrelevant for such a company, where the large blockholder will already be well placed to keep management under careful scrutiny.

However, if such a blockholder wished to 'unwind' their holding, reincorporation in the United Kingdom would, by contrast, seem a much more attractive option to consider. This is because there is likely to be limited liquidity in any market for large blocks of shares.[72] Much greater liquidity could be obtained by breaking up the block and selling the shares to many small dispersed shareholders. To do so in a blockholder system would not, however, raise the maximum possible revenue. This is because, in a system which permits private benefits of control to be

---

[68] Listing Rules, r. 3.2.
[69] See Takeover Panel (2005: 5–6).
[70] See Bebchuk (1999).
[71] For evidence relating to continental Europe, see Gugler (2001).
[72] See Becht (1999).

extracted, a dispersed ownership structure is unstable—that is, there are gains to be made by acquiring a controlling block and extracting the private benefits (Bebchuk 1999). Shares generally would then trade at a discount in anticipation of the unfavorable possibility of being in the minority when control had been taken by a blockholder.[73]

Thus the argument is that controlling shareholders in continental European companies that wish to liquidate (or diversify) their holdings could do so most effectively through listing and reincorporating in the United Kingdom.[74] The extent to which such blockholdings will unwind is, of course, contentious. Nevertheless, there are strong reasons for thinking that significant numbers of blockholders in continental Europe will wish to make this transition. The value of the rents which a blockholder may extract are declining owing to European integration's enhancement of product market competition[75]; at the same time, reductions in capital gains taxes have eliminated a former penalty to divestment of blockholdings (Frick and Lehmann 2004: 123). Consistently with these suggestions, the early evidence suggests that even within the strongly blockholder system of Germany, there has been a reduction in ownership concentration over the past ten years.[76]

The preceding discussion does of course beg the question of whether blockholders wishing to avail themselves of opportunities for regulatory arbitrage will be able to obtain appropriate legal advice. Indeed, the idea of 'lawyer resistance' is one of the most heavily-pressed reasons for thinking that regulatory competition will not occur. However, it overlooks the transformation that has recently been effected in the European market for legal services. Large London-based law firms have aggressively expanded by merging with, or taking over, their continental counterparts.[77] Whilst the so-called 'magic circle' of London law firms have maintained offices in locations around the world for many years, these had until recently been little more than symbolic outposts. However, since the late 1990s, several of them have changed strategy in favor of practising 'local law.' As a result, they are now truly multi-jurisdictional in their orientation (International Financial Services London 1999; 2003; 2005). Table 2 shows the dramatic increase in the number of 'overseas' fee-earners in these firms over the period 1999–2005. This expansion in geographic scope has been mirrored by a similarly dramatic encroachment of their brand names upon continental European

---

[73] See Bebchuk and Roe (1999: 142–53).

[74] Another plausible scenario is that a private equity firm would purchase the blockholder's stake, and then having restructured the firm, seek to take the company public again in a way that would increase the value of the share price. See Timmons (2005).

[75] See Roe (2001).

[76] See Wojcik (2003); Thomsen (2004: 306–12).

[77] Linklaters, for example, merged in Germany, Belgium and Sweden (*The Lawyer* 2004).

Table 2: The International Transformation of Large 'London' Law Firms

Name	% fee-earners outside UK		
	1999	2003	2005
Clifford Chance	41	63	62
Freshfields Bruckhaus Deringer	50	61	66
Linklaters	n/a	52	55
Allen & Overy	35	48	53
Lovells	23	55	57

Source: International Financial Services London, City Business Series: Legal Services, 1999–2005.

markets for legal services. For example, nearly all of the 'top ten' German firms in 2004 were organizations that had either merged with, or formed a 'strategic alliance' with, a London firm.[78]

This transformation has been driven by globalization and consolidation in the financial services sector, with law firms growing in size as they seek to capture economies of scale associated with increased deal size (Thomas, *et al.* 2001; Hodgart 2001: 194–202).[79] The process of globalization has brought with it increasingly direct competition with American law firms, which are able to draw upon work from deals generated by an economy approximately seven times the size of that of the United Kingdom. It seems a natural response for UK firms to seek to integrate the European market for legal services.[80] Thus these former 'London' firms are now pan-European, multi-jurisdictional and multi-language in their operations, and ideally placed to mediate between European jurisdictions.[81] Against this background, jurisdictional arbitrage is an obvious service offering.[82] If a particular system of corporate law does offer cost advantages for large corporate clients (be they procedural or substantive), then these firms may be expected to offer this aggressively to their clients. The 'lawyer hostility' problem is greatly

[78] See JUVE (2004).
[79] On the historical background in London, see Lee (1992).
[80] However, the US firms are also competing aggressively throughout Europe: See, e.g., Griffiths (2004).
[81] See Wymeersch (2003b: 286–87).
[82] Hence the marketing of English law to clients can credibly be seen as a means of saving the client money as opposed to maximizing fee income ('rents') for the lawyers.

reduced where the incumbent and the new advisor are both within the same firm.[83]

To recapitulate: regulatory arbitrage is already occurring at the level of 'start-up' incorporations. Moreover, there are good reasons for thinking that once reincorporation becomes legally possible for large companies, continental firms that wish to shift from blockholder to dispersed ownership may wish to engage in regulatory arbitrage in favor of the United Kingdom, the system which offers the best-adapted legal and regulatory environment for this ownership pattern. In so doing, they will be able to obtain advice from international law firms.

C. Will Member States have Incentives to Compete to Attract (Re)incorporations?

Regulatory arbitrage is a necessary but not sufficient condition for regulatory competition. True regulatory competition requires that lawmakers respond to the threat or opportunity posed by firms' arbitrage activities so as to retain or attract incorporations. Once again, a number of scholars have voiced the opinion that such regulatory competition will not emerge to any significant extent within Europe. In other words, the necessary preconditions for the *supply* of corporate law in response to companies' preferences will not exist (Romano 1993: 133–34; Enriques 2004a: 1266–73; Dammann 2004: 520–21; Gelter 2005; Tröger 2005). Unlike the position in the United States, EU Member States are unable to derive significant amounts of revenue from 'charter taxes' levied on companies because these are prohibited by EU law, save in the Member State where the company has its real seat.[84] Moreover, it is thought that there is little prospect that the relevant Directive will be repealed, because business interest groups are likely to lobby against such change (Hertig 2004: 370).

There seems little doubt that the particular conditions which originally gave rise to Delaware's ascendancy at the turn of the twentieth century will not be replicated in Europe. Yet simply because no European state will have the same incentives as Delaware does not mean that regulatory competition cannot emerge. Once again, it is helpful to segment the analysis into law reforms that will make a jurisdiction attractive to

---

[83] To be sure, there may be an inter-branch agency problem within such a firm. That is, lawyers in the branch in Member State B will naturally be loath to recommend to their local clients that they reincorporate in Member State A and thereby transfer their account to a different branch. This effect will be pitted against the firm's need to survive as a whole, which will depend upon successfully implementing its strategy. Lawyers in Member State B may therefore find their remuneration being structured so as to overcome such opposition, or being encouraged to retool in the law of Member State A. Future generations of lawyers in Member State B may indeed seek to qualify or learn the law of Member State A instead: Delaware's is the substantive corporate law taught at top law schools throughout the US.

incorporations, and those which will be relevant for larger, established companies. It appears that continental legislatures have already become concerned at the prospect of large-scale evasion of their legal capital requirements through incorporations in the United Kingdom. Some, such as France and Spain, have already relaxed their capital maintenance regimes;[85] others, such as Germany, are considering ways to respond (Rammeloo 2004: 409). The UK government, which has already acknowledged its desire to ensure English company law is internationally 'competitive,'[86] has recently announced further deregulation of legal capital requirements in relation to private companies, including outright abolition on the prohibition on the giving of financial assistance by such a company for the acquisition of its own shares (DTI 2005a: 41–43). These sorts of changes are by definition, regulatory competition.

To be sure, once—as seems highly likely to happen—legal capital rules are relaxed for private companies by other Member States, it seems unlikely that the United Kingdom's emergent 'competitive advantage' in this field will remain. With this obstacle removed at home, entrepreneurs will no longer have a compelling reason to incur the transaction costs of incorporating abroad. This will be more a case of 'defensive' regulatory competition than the 'active' version exhibited by Delaware, but it will be regulatory competition nevertheless.

Let us now consider the same issue in relation to the law relating to listed companies. I have suggested that the United Kingdom is likely to be the jurisdiction of choice for firms wishing to reincorporate so as to optimize their company law regime to a dispersed ownership structure. There are two reasons for thinking that the United Kingdom will have powerful incentives to adjust its company law environment so as to attract them, notwithstanding the lack of franchise taxes.

The first factor is the importance of legal services revenues to the UK economy. Having so much at stake, the United Kingdom-oriented pan-European law firms constitute a powerful interest group in lobbying for or against legal change that is likely to affect the competitiveness of English law (Cheffins 1997: 437–38). The power of legal professionals' ability to drive regulatory competition has recently been demonstrated by Sitkoff and Schanzenbach's study (2005) of the dramatic evolution of tax-haven trust structures in the United States, a practice which, given the function of these vehicles, is clearly not motivated by tax revenues derived by the states which are 'competing.'

---

[84] Council Directive 69/335/EEC [1969] OJ L249/25 (prohibiting the levying of taxes or above-cost charges for the formation or registration of a company except in the case of prescribed 'capital duties' levied in the country where the company has its centre of management: Arts. 2(1), 10).

[85] See Simon (2004); Kieninger (2005: 768).

[86] See CLSRG (2001: xi, 6); DTI (2005a: 9).

In this regard, it is worth pointing out that the United Kingdom's legal profession is also much better placed to spur regulatory competition than is Delaware's. Kahan and Kamar (2002: 694–98) have argued that Delaware lawyers, as an interest group, are not a significant motor for regulatory competition. On their analysis, the marginal revenues to lawyers practising in Delaware from legal business related to out-of-state incorporations attracted to Delaware are insignificant. Yet the revenues of lawyers practising in Delaware are likely to be a small fraction of the total economic value derived from Delaware law by US legal practitioners. Most of the legal advice to listed firms incorporated in Delaware is not provided by lawyers practising in Delaware, but in large cities such as New York.[87] In contrast, a much larger proportion of the legal services revenues generated by UK company law would be captured by the United Kingdom. This is because London, the financial centre where many of the legal service providers are based, is geographically within the United Kingdom. As voters, taxpayers and experts, London lawyers may therefore be expected to be an influential interest group in the development of UK company law.[88]

The second reason for thinking that the UK company law environment will be highly responsive is closely related. It centres on the 'soft' or 'private' nature of crucial regulation such as the Takeover Code. Private legislatures are able to capture a much greater proportion of the economic benefits of marginal revenues generated by 'users' of their laws than do public legislatures (Hadfield and Talley 2004). A public legislature is required to use tax revenues to provide public services, and so faces a steeply-declining marginal utility curve from extra tax income. A private legislature, on the other hand, is effectively providing a service as a business and so derives a much greater marginal utility than its public counterpart from additional revenues generated by 'users'. It can therefore be expected to be much more responsive to the preferences of those who make use of it. This, coupled with the potential size of the professional services revenues, makes it likely that the United Kingdom has incentive enough to compete for reincorporations of listed companies.

[87] Whilst leading New York M&A firms such as Cravath, Swaine & Moore; Davis, Polk & Wardwell; Simpson, Thacher & Bartlett; Sullivan & Cromwell; and Wachtell, Lipton, Rosen & Katz do not have offices in Delaware, their practices encompass high-profile M&A transactions and associated litigation under Delaware law (source: law firm websites, consulted 1 May 2005).

[88] The Company Law Committees of the Law Society and the City of London Law Society are well-organized and powerful lobby groups that are in a position to offer effective arguments in favor (against) a change that will enhance (decrease) the attractiveness of English law to their clients. See, e.g., responses to the DTI's White Paper (2002).

D. Will Safeguards be in Place to Ensure a 'Race to the Top' Rather Than 'to the Bottom'?

My prediction is that, following the likely liberalization of rules regarding transfer of registered office, there is real potential for a market in European company law to develop, and a significant possibility that the United Kingdom will be the favored state of immigration for many continental listed companies. This in turn raises the question of whether this will be desirable. In other words, will the 'race' be to the bottom or to the top?

Once again, my suggestions will be sanguine. It is apposite to begin with the theoretical critique of regulatory competition in US state corporate law. Bebchuk and others argue that because shareholders have insufficient control over the reincorporation decision, choices are likely to be made in favor of jurisdictions that entrench managers, as opposed to maximizing the value of firms. Under most corporate codes in the United States, a decision to reincorporate may be made by a simple majority of the general meeting, following a proposal put by the board. Bebchuk's claim is that, in an environment of dispersed share ownership, a simple majority is too low a threshold to overcome the owner-manager agency problem (Bebchuk 1992: 1459–61, 1470–75). Thus managements' proposals for reincorporation will tend to be biased towards jurisdictions with pro-manager provisions—especially laws that facilitate defences to hostile takeovers (as does Delaware).

Put more generally, the potential problem is this: laws that embody restrictions which will maximize value in the face of agency costs are unlikely to be adopted where the choice of law is itself pervaded by the same agency problem. Indeed, it is possible that such agency problems could be present not just along the manager-shareholder axis, but also along shareholder-shareholder, shareholder-creditor and the shareholder-employee axes. The solution in each case is to ensure that procedural safeguards are in place so that the group who stand to be potentially disadvantaged by a change in corporate law will have been able to exercise genuine voice in the process. Thus Bebchuk argues that the perceived problem in the dynamics of US reincorporation could be solved by a federal rule that increases shareholder involvement in decisions about reincorporation, thus making it considerably more likely that the choice will benefit shareholders by enhancing the firm's overall value, as opposed simply to transferring wealth from shareholders to managers (Bebchuk and Farrell 2001: 152–53, 161–63; Bebchuk 2005: 868–69). In the EU context, this sort of federal rule, which seeks to influence the *process* by which state law develops, as opposed to the *substance* of the rules themselves, has been termed by Deakin 'procedural harmonisation' (Deakin 2001: 209–13). Put most generally, this refers to rules intended to direct regulatory competition towards 'the top' rather than 'the bottom'.[89]

It seems highly likely that in the EU context, the opening of the road to regulatory competition in corporate law will be accompanied by the implementation of procedural safeguards to protect affected constituencies from proposed changes driven by opportunistic motives. Once again, it is helpful to distinguish the contexts of 'formation choice'— already permitted under EU law—and 'midstream reincorporation', which it has been argued will soon be generally facilitated by the proposed Cross-Border Mergers and Transfer of Registered Office Directives. Put at its most general, the difference is this: on formation, all parties are able to bargain for appropriate protection. Midstream changes, however, can be passed without unanimous consent of the affected parties, and so offer the possibility of opportunistic dilution of agreed protections.[90] For policy purposes, the analysis of a company's choice of governing law is no different from the way in which any other aspect of a company's constitution might be selected.

Consider, first, competition over 'formation choice.' Here, every shareholder, creditor and employee has the opportunity to bargain with the new enterprise, and either to secure for herself terms that are satisfactory, or to decline to become involved. Provided adequate notice is given, then in principle any selected law should be value-maximizing. To be sure, there may be problems of information asymmetry, or inequality of bargaining power. To the extent that such problems exist, they can be ameliorated either by substantively harmonized provisions, as has been the case with employment law rules and securities regulation, or by Member State national laws that are capable of satisfying the *Gebhard* criteria: that is, they are both 'effective and proportionate' at achieving the goal of ameliorating the market failure in question.

Now consider 'midstream changes'. The concern here is encapsulated by the following hypothetical: protections for a particular constituency (say, codetermination rights for the employees) are embodied in the company law of Member State B. Such provisions may be economically justified—for example, in relation to firms where employees are asked to make significant investments in firm-specific human capital. Entitlements to influence the firm's governance may reassure the employees that the firm will not renege on any implicit promises to share supracompetitive

---

[89] It should be noted that Bebchuk's pessimistic assessment is vigorously disputed by others in the US: See, e.g., Romano (1993). For present purposes, it is unnecessary to take a view on the merits of the US debate. The discussion in the text is simply concerned to show that European regulatory competition will not result in a 'race to the bottom': this is done most effectively by demonstrating that the concerns of the US pessimists will not be replicated in Europe.

[90] Bebchuk argues for restrictions on post-formation alterations of corporate constitution, owing to greater shareholder information costs (Bebchuk 1999).

profits with the employees *ex post* in return for the latter's *ex ante* investments.[91] Regardless of whether this reasoning justifies mandatory (as opposed to default) protection for employees,[92] any such protection will be rendered entirely worthless if the firm has the option to renege on its commitments *ex post* simply by reincorporating in a jurisdiction where codetermination is not recognized.

This problem, in relation to employees, has long been a roadblock to negotiation of the Tenth and Fourteenth Directives. However, the solution agreed in respect of the *Societas Europaea* will probably form a blueprint for the final versions of the other two proposals.[93] For employees, the principal protection is given through the provision for structured bargaining on formation of an SE.[94] This requires the management of pre-SE entities to engage in precursory negotiations with a body of employee representatives, with a view to agreeing employee participation rights in relation to the new entity.[95] If no agreement is reached after six months,[96] then as a default, a set of employee information/consultation and/or participation rights is put in place, the content of which is determined by the most employee-favorable of the regime(s) applying to the pre-SE entity or entities from which the European public company is formed.[97] The effect is to encourage an agreement that is no less favorable to the employees than their entitlements under the pre-SE entities (Davies 2003b: 84–90; Deakin 2001: 212–13). Of course, if the employees can be persuaded to agree, then it is possible to abandon, or at least modify, the existing participation rights.[98] Thus the negotiation structure permits the parties to abandon participation rights if it is efficient to do so—that is, the benefits of such change exceed the costs to the employees, who will need to be

---

[91] See, e.g., Blair (1995); Kelly and Parkinson (1998); Njoya (2004).

[92] Mandatory rules of a 'one size fits all' character are inappropriate where there exist a substantial number of firms for which the relevant rule is inappropriate. The extent to which firms rely upon firm-specific human capital is an empirical question, but it seems likely that in any system there will be many firms for which this rationale for employee-friendly governance rules is not present.

[93] Provisions of the SE regulation and Directive in relation to employees, is incorporated in European Commission (2003a: Art. 14); See also: European Commission (2004b)

[94] See generally, Davies (2003b).

[95] Council Directive 2001/86/EC [2001] OJ L294/22, Arts. 3–5. See also Edwards (2003: 459–62).

[96] The parties may consensually extend the negotiating period to one year: Directive 2001/86/EC, Art. 5(2).

[97] *Ibid.*: Art. 7 and Annex.

[98] See Teichmann (2003: 319–21). An exception is where the SE is created by transformation of an existing public company, in which case the new entity must provide at least as much participation for employees as they enjoyed beforehand (Directive 2001/86/EC, Art. 4(4)). However it would be simple enough to evade this requirement by creating an SE by merger into a shell company: see Enriques (2004b: 5).

compensated in order to induce them to agree.[99] The SE legislation, albeit complex, therefore provides a sound blueprint for the protection of employee interests.[100]

Moreover, it is quite plausible that, with such procedural protection in place, a certain amount of *specialization* might occur in national corporate law structures. Thus, it has been argued that German codetermination structures provide a means of offering employees a 'credible commitment' that their investments in firm-specific human capital will be protected. Firms for which such commitments are valuable will have no incentive to renege upon them by reincorporating in jurisdictions such as the United Kingdom, which do not have codetermination rules. But the process rule model of the SE legislation would permit firms for which such codetermination is inappropriate to opt out by reincorporating, provided that the value realized in so doing is greater than the cost imposed on the employees.[101] By so protecting the interests of employees in any firm that seeks to switch 'out' of codetermination, the SE's structured bargaining mechanisms will ensure that this cannot be used as a tactic to undermine the credibility of such commitments.[102]

Similar safeguards can be put in place to protect shareholders from opportunistic transfer of governing laws by management. Again, the SE legislation provides an instructive model. Under the SE regulation, at least a supermajority (two-thirds) shareholder vote is required in order to transfer the registered office[103] or to form an SE by merger.[104]A similar rule would apply under the proposed Fourteenth Directive (European Commission 1997: Art. 6). Under the proposed Cross-Border Mergers Directive, the 'general meeting' must approve the terms of any proposed merger, but the contours of the process which followed will be left to the national laws of the Member States governing the companies concerned.[105]

---

[99] On the use of bargaining levers to protect employee interests, See generally, Armour and Deakin (2003: 448–62, 458–60).

[100] See Edbury (2004).

[101] Above, text to nn. 98–99.

[102] Indeed, there is no legal reason why firms which are unable to offer such commitments under their governing law but would like to do so could not switch to German company law.

[103] Regulation 2157/2001, Arts. 8(6), 59(1). Two-thirds is a mandatory floor, which may be raised if the relevant national law requires a higher majority.

[104] *Ibid.*: Art. 17(2) (incorporating by reference the approval procedure prescribed by the Third Council Directive, 78/885/EEC [1978] OJ L295/36). See Edwards (2003: 452–54). It is unnecessary to consider the other three methods of forming an SE, namely holding or subsidiary SEs and transformation of an existing public company, as these cannot bring about a change of registered office without subsequent invocation of the Art. 8 procedure.

[105] Proposal for Tenth Directive, above, n. 40, Art. 6 ('the general meeting' shall approve proposed mergers); See also Art. 2 (provisions of national law shall govern the decision-making process relating to the merger, save as otherwise provided in the Directive).

As regards creditors, the SE Regulations, and the proposals for the Tenth and Fourteenth Directives, will leave the question of any safeguards prior to transfer of registered office to the national laws of the company concerned.[106] However, the treatment of creditors is complicated by the fact that many countries choose to protect them through corporate insolvency law, and so the discussion of the desirability of regulatory competition in relation to this constituency is postponed until the next part, where the question is tackled directly in relation to insolvency law.

To summarize, this part has suggested that (i) regulatory competition is already occurring in relation to 'start-up' companies; (ii) the existing legal obstacles to regulatory competition in relation to company law for public companies are likely to be removed in the next few years; (iii) the United Kingdom is likely to be the jurisdiction of choice for many such companies, although there will also be new possibilities for jurisdictional specialization in particular 'models' of company law; and (iv) procedural harmonization at the EU level (summarized in Table 3) will ensure that the 'race' is not to the bottom.

Table 3: Procedural Protection for Constituencies in Company Law Arbitrage

	Formation	Reincorporation
Shareholders	—Initial bargain with firm	—Supermajority vote requirement
Employees	—'Effective and proportionate' restrictions under national law (if any)	—'Acquired rights' carried over or waiver agreed by employees

IV. EXTENDING THE ARGUMENT: INSOLVENCY LAW AND CREDITOR PROTECTION

In the final part, the analysis turns to the extent to which regulatory competition may and should be permitted to operate in relation to Member State laws designed to protect creditors. The issue is considered separately because in many jurisdictions, the protection of corporate creditors is understood to be a matter of corporate insolvency law. This body of law is often treated separately from company law, typically being understood either as a procedural matter or as part of commercial law. This impression of partition is reinforced by the fact that jurisdiction and

---

[106] Regulation 2157/2001, Art. 8(7); European Commission (2004b), Art. 2; European Commission (1997), Art. 8.

choice of law in European insolvency proceedings is governed by *sui generis* legislation, the European Insolvency Regulation (EIR).[107] Significantly for present purposes, the EIR is widely thought to be based upon connecting factors that bear more in common with the 'real seat' theory than the incorporation theory.

Two salient questions arise. First, can it be argued that corporate insolvency law constitutes an entirely separate regime from company law, such that the principles established in the recent ECJ corporate freedom of establishment cases do not apply to it? If so, then this might have the effect of stopping the nascent regulatory competition for 'start-up' formations dead in its tracks: in place of company law creditor protection rules that impede freedom of establishment, Member States could simply substitute identical rules located in their corporate insolvency law.

I will argue that no such presumptive partition can be supported. This is in keeping with the functional approach to the scope of company law which formed the first 'building block' for our analysis.[108] Corporate insolvency law supplies rules which govern companies experiencing financial distress, and so it is appropriate to consider it as being within the scope of a functional account of 'company law'.[109] In particular, there may be complementarities between insolvency law and other aspects of a country's corporate governance regime,[110] which implies that if it is desirable to permit companies to select a company law regime so as to achieve a better 'fit' with their corporate governance requirements, it is likely also to be desirable for them to be able to select the associated corporate insolvency law. This in turn leads on to the second question: to what extent might it be possible for regulatory arbitrage—and thence competition—to take place in relation to rules of insolvency law? In this regard, it will be suggested—contrary to the popular perception—that the EIR's scheme could indeed permit a significant and valuable degree of regulatory competition.

A. Is Insolvency Law a Constraint on Company Law Arbitrage?

To prepare the way for the discussion that follows, it is first necessary to give an overview of the EIR's operation. The Regulation establishes

---

[107] EC Council Regulation 1346/2000 [2000] OJ L160/1. Jurisdiction over insolvency proceedings was specifically excluded from the Brussels Convention (now consolidated as EC Council Regulation 44/2001 [2001] OJ L12/1: see Art. 1(2)(b)).

[108] Above, text to nn. 4–6.

[109] A point which has been emphasized by David Skeel (1994; 2004: 1550–62). See also Armour and Whincop (2005: 25).

[110] See Skeel (1998); Armour *et al.* (2002).

uniform rules for jurisdiction and choice of law in relation to international insolvencies occurring within the EU, and provides for their automatic recognition by the courts of other Member States.[111] Choice of law largely follows the allocation of jurisdiction, so that the *lex concursus* (law of the jurisdiction where insolvency proceedings are opened) will govern most of the effects of the proceedings, both procedural and substantive.[112] Thus the rules concerning the allocation of jurisdiction are fundamental.

The EIR's jurisdiction-allocation scheme has two tracks. The first provides that 'main' proceedings shall be opened in the jurisdiction in which the debtor's 'centre of main interests' (COMI) is located.[113] Main proceedings are to have universal effect throughout the EU, except and insofar as a territorial 'carve-out' created by the second track is utilized. This provides that 'secondary' proceedings may be opened in any Member State (other than that of the COMI) in which the debtor has an 'establishment.'[114] Any such secondary proceedings are limited in their effect to the territory of the Member State in which they are opened and must be conducted in cooperation with the main proceedings.[115] Main proceedings may encompass either liquidation (that is, the sale of the debtor's assets and distribution of proceeds amongst creditors) or 'corporate rescue' (that is, a 'crisis governance' procedure seeking to preserve the company or its business from failure) proceedings. In contrast, secondary proceedings may only involve liquidation of local assets.[116] Table 4 summarizes the key features of the foregoing discussion.

We shall now consider whether the EIR's jurisdiction allocation scheme conforms to the 'real seat' or the incorporation theory. Given the centrality of the concept of the debtor's COMI to the scheme's operation, it is most unfortunate that its definition is shrouded in ambiguity, reflecting an ugly drafting compromise between Member States' preferences as between these two theories.[117] Thus, the Preamble to the

---

[111] See generally, Fletcher (1999); Moss *et al.* (2002); Ferber (2004); Omar (2004).

[112] Regulation 1346/2000, Preamble para. 23, Art. 4(2). To this principle there are a number of 'carve outs', including the effects of insolvency on: (i) rights *in rem*, reservation of title claims, contracts relating to immoveables and rights of third-party purchasers of such assets (each governed by the *lex situs*: Arts. 5, 7, 8 and 14); (ii) rights of set-off (governed by the law applicable to the insolvent debtor's claim: Art. 6); (iii) contracts of employment (governed by the proper law of the contract: Art. 10) and (iv) rights subject to registration (governed by the law of the place of the register: Art. 11).

[113] *Ibid.*: Art. 3(1).

[114] *Ibid.*: Art. 3(2).

[115] *Ibid.*: Arts. 16, 17, 27.

[116] Compare *ibid.*: Annex A (proceedings which may be opened in COMI, including corporate rescue procedures) with Annex B (secondary proceedings, including only liquidation procedures). Both Annexes have recently been amended by EC Regulation 603/2005 [2005] OJ L100/1.

[117] See Fletcher (1999: 260–62); Omar (2004: 97–99).

Table 4: Summary of the EIR's Scheme

	Main proceedings	Secondary proceedings
Scope	Universal (EU-wide)	Territorial
Type of procedure	Rescue or liquidation	Liquidation only
Jurisdiction allocation	COMI	Place(s) of establish-ment(s)

EIR provides that the COMI shall 'correspond to the place where the debtor conducts the administration of his interests on a regular basis and is therefore ascertainable by third parties.'[118] On the other hand, Article 3(1) raises a presumption in the case of corporate debtors that the COMI is the place of the registered office. The uncertainty concerns the degree of strength that should be accorded to this presumption. Member States' jurisprudence—even in the United Kingdom—has to date tended to treat the presumption as easily rebutted by factual evidence concerning where the debtor conducted business.[119] Thus, as currently interpreted in national case law,[120] the notion of COMI conforms more to the real seat than the incorporation theory. Moreover, it is clear that even if a corporate debtor's COMI were not in the jurisdiction of its 'real seat,' the debtor would nevertheless certainly have an 'establishment' there, so that secondary proceedings could be opened.

It follows that if a company is incorporated in Member State A, but carries on all its business in Member State B, then creditors who lend to it in Member State B can be assured that the insolvency law of Member State B will apply, at the very least to assets situated in that jurisdiction. This leads some commentators to suggest that corporate insolvency law should be treated as falling outside the scope of the regulatory competition recently ushered in by the ECJ.[121] If this view, which we might term the 'partition theory', were correct, it would follow that Member States wishing to preserve restrictive creditor protection rules should simply transfer them from 'company' to 'insolvency' sections of their civil codes. The only limit to such recycling would be a casuistic determination whether the rules in question were properly characterized

---

[118] Regulation 1346/2000, Preamble para. 13.

[119] See *Re Daisytek-ISA Ltd* [2004] BPIR 30 at [16]–[17] ('where the debtor enters into the majority of his financing arrangements'); See also R*e BRAC Rent-A-CarInternational, Inc.* [2003] EWHC (Ch) 128, [2003] 1 WLR 1421 at [4]–[5]. For a thorough survey of other Member States' jurisprudence, see Ferber (2004: 31–74).

[120] This understanding is questioned below, text to nn. 129–131.

[121] See, e.g., Kersting and Schindler (2003: 1290); Koller (2004: 341–43); Ferber (2004: 86–111); Rammeloo (2004: 403–6); Zimmer (2004: 1137–38).

as 'company law' or 'insolvency law.'[122] The unappealing implications of this analysis may be seen by considering its application to the issues in *Inspire Art*. As will be recalled, that case concerned the application of the Dutch WFBV or 'law applicable to formally foreign companies', under which companies operating in the Netherlands but with only a nominal connection to their jurisdiction of incorporation were required to comply with minimum capital requirements consistent with those imposed upon companies incorporated domestically. Were the partition theory valid, then it could plausibly be argued that the WFBV's impact could be preserved by enacting an 'insolvency version' of the statute.[123] That is, to legislate that should a company that failed the relevant capitalization requirements enter insolvency proceedings, the liquidator should have an action to make the directors liable to contribute the 'missing capital' for the benefit of the company's creditors.[124]

The better view is that the impact of *Inspire Art* cannot be constrained in the way suggested by the partition theory.[125] The EIR does not purport to govern the content of insolvency laws, merely the connecting factor for choice of jurisdiction and choice of law. The ECJ's judgment in *Inspire Art* is framed not in terms of connecting factors in company law, but of legal provisions that impede corporate freedom of establishment. Why should this apply any differently to rules formally characterized as 'corporate insolvency law' than to rules of 'company law'? The correct question, after *Inspire Art*, is not whether a rule is properly taxonomized as 'company' or 'insolvency,' but rather whether its effect is to impede the exercise of corporate freedom of establishment, subject of course to the exception for provisions which satisfy the four-stage *Gebhard* test.[126]

Whether a rule that is characterized as part of the host state's 'insolvency law' would fail this test will depend upon the impact that (non) compliance would have on the shareholders and/or directors of a foreign company that wishes to establish its business in that state. In

---

[122] There is some relevant ECJ jurisprudence, albeit directed to the sibling question of the scope of the exclusion from the Brussels Convention for 'insolvency proceedings' (above, n. 107). In *Gourdain v Nadler* (Case C-133/78, [1979] I ECR 733), the ECJ held that the French *action en comblement du passif* (loosely: failure by directors to take steps to initiate insolvency proceedings sufficiently quickly) was properly characterized as part of insolvency proceedings, on the ground that the action was open only to the liquidator, and that the proceeds went to enlarge the assets available to the creditors.

[123] As the Dutch legislature appear to have attempted: see Rammeloo (2004: 407–8) and Lowry (2004: 343 n. 32).

[124] It would be at least arguable that such a provision could be brought within the ECJ's characterization of 'insolvency proceedings' in *Gourdain v Nadler*: see above, n. 122.

[125] A point also made by Kieninger (2005: 752–54).

[126] This can also be seen by considering the tax cases: in *de Lastreyie du Saillant* (above, n. 41), the court ruled that tax laws impeding individuals' freedom of establishment would be struck down; the reason for not so ruling in *Daily Mail* (above, n. 35) was on the basis of the court's peculiar conception of the 'status' of a company as governed by the provisions of its state of incorporation: see above, text to nn. 34–35.

terms of the ECJ's freedom of establishment jurisprudence, a rule that has such an effect which is more than 'indirect and uncertain' will fail this test.[127] It is the nature of insolvency proceedings that they only take place if the debtor is unable to pay their debts. Assuming that the company is solvent at the point it wishes to establish itself in the host state, most rules which operate in insolvency would be likely to be no more than 'indirect and uncertain' in their impact on the company's establishment decision, because of the small probability that they would ever apply.[128] Yet there are situations where the impact might be more direct. The most obvious would be where the insolvency code imposes retrospective liability for actions (not) taken during the period of the company's existence which go beyond the obligations imposed by the home state company law during solvency and are excessive compared to the requirements of the debtor's home state. It seems that re-enacting the WFBV as 'insolvency law' would be precisely such a situation. It is not difficult to see that in such a case, shareholders and directors of companies such as Inpsire Art Ltd would be deterred from establishing their company in the host state because of the risk that, had they failed to capitalize it in accordance with the WFBV, they would face concomitant liability to contribute to its assets in insolvency. They could only safely avoid such potential liability by incurring a significant cost at the time of (re)establishment. In contrast, insolvency liabilities for (in)actions immediately preceding entry to insolvency proceedings—such as, for example, for wrongful trading— would be unlikely to have a direct and certain impact, because they would only be incurred in relation to (in)actions during the 'twilight period,' which would be no more than a distant possibility at the time of (re)establishment.

B. Could Regulatory Arbitrage in Corporate Insolvency Law be Possible?

The foregoing discussion suggests that insolvency law is capable of imposing only an indirect constraint on arbitrage (and hence competition) for company law. We now turn to the second question: that is, whether regulatory competition in relation to corporate insolvency law itself would be feasible within the EU. Given the EIR's scheme, the answer will turn upon the proper interpretation of the notion of COMI. If this were tightly bound to a company's registered office, then a company

---

[127] See, e.g., Case C-19/92 *Kraus v Land Baden-Württemerg* [1993] ECR I-1663; Case C-190/98 *Graf v Filzmoser Mashinenbau GmbH* [2000] ECR I-493; Joined Cases C-51/96 and C-191/97 *Deliège v Ligue Francophone de Judo et Disciplines Associées ASBL* [2000] ECR I-2549.

[128] This point is hinted at by Tröger (2005).

which was registered in Member State A but which had its real seat in Member State B would thereby be able to engage in some arbitrage over corporate insolvency law as well as company law. However, the EIR's two-track scheme imposes an outer boundary on the extent to which such arbitrage would be possible. This is because, even if the company's COMI is in Member State A, the corporate insolvency law of Member State B will still be available for secondary proceedings conducted in that jurisdiction. The choice of COMI will therefore matter primarily for (i) the availability, and nature, of any corporate rescue proceedings (because the secondary proceedings under Member State B will be limited to liquidation); and (ii) the insolvency law rules applicable in third countries.

It is not implausible, notwithstanding the prevailing view in the national case law, that a corporate debtor's COMI could be interpreted as tightly bound to its registered office. As the concept is a creature of EC legislation, it will bear an autonomous meaning in European law. The ECJ has been called to rule upon the application of COMI in the pending case of *Bondi*.[129] There are good reasons for suggesting that the court should treat the presumption created by Article 3(1), that a corporate debtor's COMI shall ordinarily be the state of its registered office, as a strong one. According to the Virgos-Schmidt Report, the unofficial interpretive guide to the Regulation, insolvency is a foreseeable risk to creditors, and therefore that it is important that the jurisdiction in insolvency be one which they are able to predict easily (Virgos-Schmidt 2002: para. 75). A priori, it is hard to see how a test based on where business is in fact conducted renders creditors of international businesses more certain as to where insolvency proceedings will be conducted than a rule based on state of incorporation. This point is strengthened when it is borne in mind that local creditors will in any event be protected by the possibility of territorial secondary proceedings in any jurisdiction where business is carried on. Where a debtor conducts substantial business activities in more than one jurisdiction, the registered office will often be easier to determine than where the majority of the debtor's financial arrangements were conducted. What is worse, a purely geographic connecting factor is subject to change simply by the physical movement of the debtor, with the possibility that a transfer may be effected to a 'debtor-friendly' jurisdiction on the eve of insolvency.[130]

In contrast, tying COMI to the place of registered office would be

---

[129] Case C-341/04 *Bondi v Bank of America NA*; application for urgent decision under the accelerated procedure refused, 15 September 2004.

[130] See *Skjevesland v Geveran Trading Co Ltd* [2003] BPIR 924 at [4]; *Shierson v Vlieland-Boddy* [2004] EWHC 2752 (Ch), [2004] All ER (D) 420 at [13]–[23], esp. at [21]: '[T]he creditors are always at risk of such a change [of COMI], and they cannot safely make any assumptions as to the insolvency law which will apply in due course.' (per Mann J).

readily ascertainable by creditors even where business is conducted in more than one state. Moreover, because the registered office is a legal rather than a geographic matter, corporate debtors could be prevented from 'switching COMI' to the detriment of their creditors through the simple expedient of a rule banning changes of registered office in contemplation of insolvency.[131] Most fundamentally, even in cases where such particular problems do not arise, equating COMI with registered office would promote certainty amongst creditors at least as well as the geographic location-of-business test in a day and age when all that is required to determine the relevant information is an internet search.

C. Would Regulatory Arbitrage in Corporate Insolvency Law be Desirable?

Were COMI interpreted in accordance with these suggestions, it would then become possible for companies to select the law which would govern any main insolvency proceedings in the same way as they can (or in the case of established companies, soon will be able to) do in respect of their company laws. It might be objected that having the law of Member State A (the home state) govern insolvency proceedings is impractical when the debtor's assets and business are located in Member State B (the host state). Yet it should be recalled that secondary proceedings could be opened in the host state. Rather, the only significant question which would be determined in this case by the COMI would be the availability, and nature of, any corporate rescue proceedings.

More fundamentally, it might be feared that permitting arbitrage over choice of insolvency law will lead to a 'race to the bottom', with companies incorporating in jurisdictions with weak insolvency laws so as to be able to benefit shareholders at the expense of creditors. To understand this, it is helpful to segment creditors into 'adjusting' and 'nonadjusting' categories.[132] The objection focuses upon the perceived plight of nonadjusting creditors—that is, those parties who extend 'credit' involuntarily (the paradigm case being tort victims), or in such small amounts that the transaction costs of becoming informed and adjusting their positions outweigh the benefits of doing so. The argument would assert that many Member States' insolvency regimes contain mechanisms

---

[131] Such a rule would, on this chapter's analysis, be a good candidate for EU legislation as a 'procedural harmonization' provision.

[132] The terminology is derived from Bebchuk and Fried (1996). The possibility that the presence of nonadjusting might distort firms' investment incentives so as to exploit them was first noted in Scott (1979).

designed to protect such creditors,[133] and that permitting companies to engage in regulatory arbitrage would allow them to undermine this protection.[134] Were this possible, shareholders would be able to benefit themselves at the expense of such creditors by selecting an insolvency law that would offer minimal protection. If this were unchecked, then it would clearly be an example of a 'race to the bottom.'

Yet such an outcome would not eventuate. First, under the EIR's scheme, insolvency priority rules designed to protect nonadjusting creditors would in any event be available to them through territorial proceedings in the jurisdiction in which they claim. Thus, they will be made no worse off by permitting regulatory arbitrage over corporate rescue proceedings. Secondly, vulnerable creditors can be protected more effectively and precisely by mechanisms other than the re-ordering of priorities in insolvency.[135] If such regulatory requirements constituted prima facie restrictions on freedom of establishment, there seems little doubt that carefully-targeted provisions would satisfy the requirements of the *Gebhard* formula to be justified in the overriding public interest.

Thus, the limited regulatory arbitrage which the EIR could permit over insolvency law would not impose costs on non-adjusting creditors. Not only would it not *harm* these groups, but it would also bring significant benefits. To understand these, it is necessary to consider the way in which sophisticated—'adjusting'—creditors might be expected to respond to such arbitrage (Guzman 2000: 2180–81). The could be expected to adjust the terms of their credit transaction to reflect the effect of a debtor's choice of COMI. Where this is harmful to such creditors, the debtor will incur a higher cost of credit, or find it difficult to raise credit at all. Where the regime leaves gaps, such creditors may be expected to contract for protection in the form of loan covenants, security interests, and the like. If the costs of such contracting are high, then the debtor will have an incentive to select an insolvency regime which creditors would prefer. Member States wishing to attract, or not to deter, companies would respond by providing insolvency codes that offer the appropriate protection: regulatory competition resulting in a 'race to the top,' rather than to the bottom.

As we have seen, the choice of COMI will matter, from creditors' point

---

[133] For example, the 'prescribed part' of floating charge assets which must be set aside for unsecured creditors in UK corporate insolvencies following the Enterprise Act 2002: see Insolvency Act 1986, s 176A.

[134] See, e.g., LoPucki (1999: 720–23).

[135] For tort victims and environmental claims, mandatory insurance or statutory guarantee requirements for those engaging in hazardous activities provide clearly-targeted incentives. For unsophisticated voluntary creditors, such as consumers, employees and trade creditors, credit insurance can be provided—either through statutory mandate or by market providers—by sophisticated creditors who then price the risk into their transactions with the debtor.

of view, principally in regard to corporate rescue proceedings. There are reasons for thinking that this area is one in which the operation of regulatory competition would be particularly fruitful.[136] The extent to which a legal regime should seek to foster 'rescue' of troubled companies, and the way in which control of the distressed company should be organized therein, are highly contentious matters. A vocal group of US scholars has argued that debtors should be permitted to design their own insolvency regimes by contract with their creditors, as opposed to being able to participate only in mandatory state-sanctioned insolvency procedures.[137] Permitting regulatory competition over insolvency laws would be an approximation to this result, with the added benefit that each regime on the 'menu' from which debtors could select would come with a ready-made body of case law interpreting and applying it, enabling the market to assess the likely consequences with confidence. Moreover, to the extent that corporate rescue regimes complement other aspects of a corporate governance system, permitting firms to opt into these as well as the other parts of the regime will further promote special-ization if this is indeed the direction taken by European regulatory competition. Thus, corporate rescue procedures seem a prime candidate for a stance of regulatory agnosticism at the EU level, and for the forces of regulatory competition to be harnessed so as to permit a learning process as to the most appropriate legal regime.

To recapitulate: permitting regulatory arbitrage over corporate insolvency law to the extent which it could take place within the EIR framework would be a desirable step. The structure of the EIR means that it would principally affect the availability, and form of, any corporate rescue proceedings. This is a matter which adjusting creditors can be expected to take into account in pricing the firm's cost of credit, thereby forcing firms to internalize the impact of insolvency on creditors in their arbitrage decisions.[138] The position of nonadjusting creditors would be protected through territorial measures which are either given effect to in secondary proceedings, or which are necessary and proportionate in their impact—thus satisfying the *Gebhard* test. The EIR's jurisdictional-allocation scheme, if COMI is interpreted in accordance with the argument of this chapter, would thus act as a form of procedural harmonization in corporate insolvency law, so as to guide the process of the development of insolvency laws towards *beneficial* regulatory

---

[136] See Skeel (1994: 517–23).

[137] See, e.g., Rasmussen (1992); Schwartz (1997). The argument is extended to the context of international insolvencies in Rasmussen (1997).

[138] This would be the case both for formation and reincorporation choices, as adjusting creditors could easily include loan covenants specifying that reincorporation without their consent would constitute an event of default.

competition. The availability of secondary proceedings truncates the possibilities for a 'race to the bottom', leaving only opportunities for a 'race to the top' over corporate rescue proceedings.[139] Member States' regulatory responses could be expected to follow a pattern of mutual learning, permitting a beneficial evolution and the ultimate adoption of the most appropriate corporate rescue regimes.

V. CONCLUSION

The question this chapter set out to address was whether European corporate law would in future best be made by 'federal' legislation or regulatory competition between Member States. As EC legislation carries with it well-known problems, the answer to the question depends on an assessment of the prospects for European regulatory competition in the field. If regulatory competition would be pathological, then EC legislation might be justified as a 'lesser evil'. Therefore, although 'crystal ball gazing' is a risky activity, I have sought—perhaps recklessly—to offer a view of the likely future development of European regulatory competition.

My conclusions on regulatory competition are largely sanguine. It seems plausible that regulatory competition will come to be a motor for the development of Member States' company laws and corporate governance systems. Arbitrage by 'start-up' firms is already legally possible, and this is starting to lead to responsive changes throughout Europe in laws applicable to private companies. For established companies, arbitrage will in all likelihood soon be facilitated by European legislation, in the form of the Tenth and Fourteenth Company Law Directives. This will not be attractive to all companies, because difference in ownership structure complement differences in national governance systems. However, it seems plausible that the United Kingdom, with a governance system adapted to dispersed ownership, will be an attractive destination for companies whose owners wish to exit blockholdings and shift to dispersed ownership. This process will be facilitated by the newly pan-European law firms. Hence the United Kingdom's professional services sector has a powerful incentive to ensure that the governance regime—most especially, the self-regulatory aspects—is kept attractive to firms thinking about moving there. Other Member States, faced with this

---

[139] The structure is designed to protect local creditors, but not to permit them to stymie rescue proceedings. Thus, the insolvency practitioner conducting main proceedings is empowered to stay secondary proceedings so as to effect a rescue, provided that adequate protection is offered for the interests of creditors in the secondary proceedings: Regulation 1346/2000, Art. 33.

apparent challenge, are likely to respond by 'defensive' regulatory competition. Precisely how this will develop is unclear, but it seems plausible that a likely strategy would be to enhance further those aspects of their systems which will complement firms with concentrated ownership. This would yield a process of path-dependent specialization, rather than convergence.

Underpinning this process will be EC legislation governing how established firms will be able to make their reincorporation decisions. This 'procedural' regulation will ensure that affected constituencies are parties to the decision-making process, and so transfers of jurisdiction motivated by a desire to expropriate them will not succeed. This will remove the prospect of a detrimental 'race to the bottom.'

Some Member States may seek to recharacterize creditor protection rules as part of their corporate insolvency codes, but the better view is that this will not insulate them from the possibility of being held to constitute unlawful impediments to corporate freedom of establishment. Indeed, perhaps my most radical suggestion is that the framework of the European Insolvency Regulation could actually permit a certain amount of arbitrage—and thence competition—over corporate rescue proceedings. As the relevant rules may complement other aspects of corporate law, it seems desirable that they should be subject to a similar process of development.

A positive assessment of regulatory competition makes the drawbacks of harmonized EC legislation all the more stark. Harmonized legislation runs two risks which are avoided by a process of benign regulatory competition. First, such legislation tends to encourage Member States to converge their laws on a central model, which may be inappropriate where one 'size' does not 'fit' all. Decentralized solutions can permit Member States to continue patterns of diversity, whilst regulatory arbitrage allows individual firms for which the national model is inappropriate to opt out. Secondly, harmonization presupposes that the European legislator is able to specify the 'best' regulatory solution to any given problem. In an area such as company law, where the configuration of the optimal rules is hotly debated, regulatory competition can promote innovation and mutual learning between national legislatures.

In conclusion, then, the answer to our starting question is that the future of European company lawmaking would better be left with Member States than take the form of European legislation, save for areas in which a uniform consensus has emerged regarding the appropriate regulatory choice. This does not seem inconsistent with the thinking behind the European Commission's recent Company Law Action Plan, which recognizes the benefits of national diversity and proposes EC legislation only in certain limited areas. It is to be hoped that time will be permitted to demonstrate the soundness of this approach.

REFERENCES

Alva, C. (1990), 'Delaware and the Market for Corporate Charters: History and Agency', 15 *Delaware Journal of Corporate Law* 885.

Amable, B. (2003), *The Diversity of Modern Capitalism* (Oxford: OUP).

Armour, J. and Deakin, S. (2003), 'Insolvency and Employment Protection: The Mixed Effects of the Acquired Rights Directive' 22 *International Review of Law and Economics* 443.

Armour, J. and Skeel, D.A. (2005), 'Who Makes the Rules for Hostile Takeovers, and Why?' Working Paper, University of Cambridge/University of Pennsylvania Law School.

Armour, J. and Whincop, M.J. (2005), 'The Proprietary Foundations of Corporate Law', ESRC Centre for Business Research Working Paper 299.

Armour, J. *et al.* (2002), 'Corporate Ownership Structure and the Evolution of Corporate Bankruptcy Law: Lessons from the UK' 55 *Vanderbilt Law Review* 1699.

Atiyah, P.S. and Summers, R.S. (1987), *Form and Substance in Anglo-American Law* (Oxford: Clarendon Press).

Bachner, T. (2003), 'Freedom of Establishment for Companies: A Great Leap Forward', 62 *Cambridge Law Journal* 47.

Baelz, K. and Baldwin, T. (2002), 'The End of the Real Seat Theory (*Sitztheorie*): the European Court of Justice Decision in *Überseering* of 5 November 2002 and its Impact on German and European Company Law', 3(12) *German Law Journal*.

Barca, F. and Becht, M. (eds) (2001), *The Control of Corporate Europe* (Oxford: OUP).

Barnard, C. (2004), The Substantive Law of the EU: The Four Freedoms (Oxford: OUP).

Bebchuk, L.A. (1989), 'Limiting Contractual Freedom in Corporate Law: The Desirable Constraints on Charter Amendments' 102 *Harvard Law Review* 1820.

——(1992), 'Federalism and the Corporation: The Desirable Limits on State Competition in Corporate Law', 105 *Harvard Law Review* 1435.

—— (1999), 'A Rent-Protection Theory of Corporate Ownership and Control' NBER Working Paper No 7203.

—— (2005), 'The Case for Increasing Shareholder Power' 118 *Harvard Law Review* 833.

Bebchuk, L.A. and Cohen, A. (2003), 'Firms' Decisions Where to Incorporate', 46 *Journal of Law and Economics* 383.

Bebchuk, L.A. and Farrell, A. (2001), 'A New Approach to Takeover Law and Regulatory Competition' 87 *Virginia Law Review* 111.

Bebchuk, L.A. and Fried, J.M. (1996), 'The Uneasy Case for the Priority of Secured Claims in Bankruptcy' 105 *Yale Law Journal* 857.

Bebchuk, L.A. and Roe, M.J. (1999), 'A Theory of Path Dependence in Corporate Ownership and Governance', 52 *Stanford Law Review* 127.

Becht, M. (1999), 'European Corporate Governance: Trading off Liquidity Against Control' 43 *European Economic Review* 1071.

Becht, M. and Mayer, C. (2001), 'Introduction' in Barca, F. and Becht, M. (eds), *The Control of Corporate Europe* (Oxford: OUP), 1.

Black, B.S. and Coffee, J.C. (1994), 'Hail Britannia? Institutional Investor Behavior Under Limited Regulation', 92 *Michigan Law Review* 1997.

Blair, M.M. (1995), Ownership and Control: Rethinking Corporate Governance for the Twenty-First Century (Washington, DC: Brookings Institution).

Brooke, Rt Hon Lord Justice (ed) (2004), *Civil Procedure, Vol 2* (London: Sweet and Maxwell).

Cappelletti, M. (1989), *The Judicial Process in Comparative Perspective* (Oxford: Clarendon Press).

Carlin, W. and Mayer, C. (2002), 'How do Financial Systems Affect Economic Performance?' in J.A. McCahery *et al.* (eds), *Corporate Governance Regimes: Convergence and Diversity* (Oxford: OUP), 325.

Cary, W.L. (1974), 'Federalism and Corporate Law: Reflections on Delaware', 88 *Yale Law Journal* 663.

Cheffins, B.R. (1997), *Company Law: Theory, Structure and Operation* (Oxford: OUP).

Choi, S. (2002), 'Law, Finance and Path Dependence: Developing Strong Securities Markets', 80 *Texas Law Review* 1657.

CLSRG (1999), Company Law Review Steering Group, *The Strategic Framework*, URN 99/654 (London: DTI).

—— (2001), Company Law Review Steering Group, *Final Report, Vol I*, URN 01/942 (London: DTI).

Comité Intergouvernemental Créé par la Conférence de Messina, *Rapport des Chefs de Délégation aux Ministres des Affaires Etrangères*, Brussels, 21 April 1956 (the 'Spaak Report') Mae 120 f/56, 14).

Companies House (2005), *DVD-ROM Directory* (April 2005 edn).

Daines, R. (2001), 'Does Delaware Law Improve Firm Value?', 62 *Journal of Financial Economics* 525.

—— (2002), 'The Incorporation Choices of IPO Firms', 77 *New York University Law Review* 1559.

Dammann, J.C. (2004), 'Freedom of Choice in European Company Law', 29 *Yale Journal of International Law* 477.

Davies, P.L. (2003a), 'Shareholder Value, Company Law, and Securities Markets Law: A British View' in K. Hopt and E. Wymeersch (eds), *Capital Markets and Company Law* (Oxford: OUP), 261.

—— (2003b), 'Workers on the Board of the European Company?' 32 *Industrial Law Journal* 75.

Deakin, S. (2001), 'Regulatory Competition Versus Harmonization in European Company Law' in D. Esty and D. Gerardin (eds), *Regulatory Competition and Economic Integration* (Oxford: OUP), 190.

Drury, R. (2005), 'A European Look at the American Experience of the Delaware Syndrome', 5 *Journal of Corporate Law Studies* 1.

DTI (2002), White Paper, *Modernising Company Law* (Cm 5553), available online at http://www.dti.gov.uk/cld/modern/index.htm.

—— (2004), *Companies in 2003–4* (London: TSO).

—— (2005a), *Company Law Reform*, Cm 6456 (London: TSO).

—— (2005b), Implementation of the European Directive on Takeover Bids URN 05/511 (TSO: London).

Easterbrook, F.H. and Fischel, D.R. (1991), *The Economic Structure of Corporate Law* (Cambridge, MA: Harvard University Press).

Ebke, W.F. (2005), 'The European Conflict-of-Corporate-Laws Revolution: Überseering, Inspire Art and Beyond', (2005) *European Business Law Review* 9.

Edbury, M. (2004), 'The European Company Statute: A Practical Working Model for the Future of European Company Law Making?' 15 *European Business Law Review* 1283.

Edwards, V. (1999), *EC Company Law* (Oxford: OUP).

—— (2003), 'The European Company—Essential Tool or Eviscerated Dream?' 40 *CML Rev* 443.

Enriques, L. (2004a), 'EC Company Law and the Fears of a European Delaware', 15 *European Business Law Review* 1259.

—— (2004b), 'Silence is Golden: The European Company Statute as a Catalyst for Company Law Arbitrage', 4 *Journal of Corporate Law Studies* 77.

Esty, D. and Gerardin, D. (eds) (2001), *Regulatory Competition and Economic Integration* (Oxford: OUP).

European Commission (1997), 'Proposal for a Fourteenth European Parliament and Council Directive on the Transfer of the Registered Office of a Company from one Member State to another with a Change of Applicable Law', doc no XV/D2/6002/97-EN REV.2.

—— (2003a), 'Proposal for a Directive of the European Parliament and of the Council on Cross-Border Mergers of Companies with Share Capital' COM (2003) 703 final, 18.11.2003

—— (2003b), Modernising Company Law and Enhancing Corporate Governance in the European Union—A Plan to Move Forward COM (2003) 284 final, Brussels 21.5.2003.

—— (2004a), 'Commission welcomes Council agreement on making cross-border mergers easier' Press Release IP/04/1405, 25.11.2004).

—— (2004b), 'Company Law: Commission Consults on the Cross-Border Transfer of Companies' Registered Offices', IP/04/270, 26.02.2004.

—— (2004c), 'Public consultation on the outline of the planned proposal for a European Parliament and Council directive on the cross-border transfer of the registered office of a company'.

Ferber, M.M. (2004), *European Insolvency Regulation* (Osterspai: Ditmar Weis).

Ferran, E. (2004), *Building an EU Securities Market* (Cambridge: CUP).

Ficker, H.C. (1973), 'The EEC Directives on Company Law Harmonization' in C.M. Schmitthoff (ed), *The Harmonization of European Company Law* (London: UNCCL), 66.

Fioretos, O. (2001), 'Varieties of Capitalism in the European Community' in P.A. Hall and D. Soskice (eds), *Varieties of Capitalism* (Oxford: OUP), 213.

Fletcher, I.F. (1999), *Insolvency in Private International Law* (Oxford: Clarendon Press).

Frick, B. and Lehmann, E. (2004), 'Corporate Governance in Germany: Ownership, Codetermination and Firm Performance in a Stakeholder Economy' in Gospel and Pendleton (eds), *Corporate Governance and Labour Management* (Oxford: OUP).

Gelter, M. (2005), 'The Structure of Regulatory Competition in European Corporate Law', 5 *Journal of Corporate Law Studies* 1.

Gompers, P.A. *et al.* (2001), 'Corporate Governance and Equity Prices', NBER Working Paper No 8449.

Gospel H. and Pendleton, A. (2004), 'Corporate Governance and Labour

Management—An International Comparison' in Gospel and Pendleton (eds), *Corporate Governance and Labour Management* (Oxford: OUP).

Griffiths, C. (2004), 'The UK firms are thinking global, but the savvier US practices are starting to act local', *The Lawyer Global 100*.

Grundmann, S. (2004), 'The Structure of European Company Law: From Crisis to Boom', 5 *European Business Organization Law Review* 601.

Gugler, K. (2001), 'Beneficial Block-Holders versus Entrenchment and Rent Extraction?' in K. Gugler (ed), *Corporate Governance and Economic Performance* (Oxford: OUP), 26.

Guzman, A.T. (2000), 'International Bankruptcy: In Defence of Universalism' 98 *Michigan Law Review* 2177.

Hadfield, G. and Talley, E. (2004), 'On Public Versus Private Provision of Corporate Law', USC Law and Economics Working Paper No 04–18, USC CLEO Research Paper No C04-13.

Hansmann, H. and Kraakman, R. (2000), 'The Essential Role of Organisational Law', 110 *Yale LJ* 387.

Heine, K. and Kerber, W. (2002), 'European Corporate Laws, Regulatory Competition and Path Dependence', 13 *European Journal of Law and Economics* 47.

Hertig, G. (2004), 'Efficient Fostering of EU Regulatory Competition', SZW/RSDA 5 *Kurzbeiträge*.

Hodgart, A. (2001), 'Globalization and the Future of International Law Firms—The Perspective of a Management Consultant' in J. Drolshammer and M. Pfeifer (eds), *The Internationalisation of the Practice of Law* (London: Kluwer Law International), 173.

International Financial Services London (1999), *City Business Series: Legal Services* (London: IFSL).

—— (2003), *City Business Series: Legal Services* (London: IFSL).

—— (2005), *City Business Series: Legal Services* (London: IFSL).

JUVE (2004), JUVE Handbook of German Commercial Law Firms 2004, 'Ranking National Review', available at http://www.juve.de/html/ha.html (last visited 10 Aug. 2005).

Kahan, M. (2004), 'The Demand for Corporate Law: Statutory Flexibility, Judicial Quality, or Takeover Protection', NYU Law and Economics Working Paper No 04–015.

Kahan, M. and Kamar, E. (2002), 'The Myth of State Competition in Corporate Law', 55 *Stanford Law Review* 679.

Kamar, E. (1998), 'A Regulatory Competition Theory of Indeterminacy in Corporate Law', 98 *Columbia Law Review* 1908.

Kelly, G. and Parkinson, J. (1998), 'The Conceptual Foundations of the Company: A Pluralist Approach', *Company, Financial and Insolvency Law Review* 174.

Kersting, C. and Schindler, C.P. (2003), 'The ECJ's *Inspire Art* Decision of 30 September 2003 and its Effects on Practice', 4 *German Law Journal* 1277.

Kieninger, E.-M. (2005), 'The Legal Framework of Regulatory Competition Based on Company Mobility: EU and US Compared', 6 *German Law Journal* 740.

Kirchner, C. *et al.* (2004), 'Regulatory Competition in EU Corporate Law after *Inspire Art*: Unbundling Delaware's Product for Europe', Working Paper, Humboldt University, Berlin and University of Illinois.

Koller, T. (2004), 'The English Limited Company—Ready to Invade Germany' 15 *International Company and Commercial Law Review* 334.

Kraakman, R. *et al.* (2004), *The Anatomy of Corporate Law* (Oxford: OUP).

La Porta, R. *et al.* (1997), 'Legal Determinants of External Finance' 52 *Journal of Finance* 1131.

La Porta, R. *et al.* (1999), 'Corporate Ownership Around the World', (1999) 44 *Journal of Finance* 471.

Larcker, D.F. *et al.* (2004), 'How Important is Corporate Governance?' Wharton School Working Paper.

Lee, R.G. (1992), 'From Profession to Business: The Rise and Rise of the City Law Firm' in P.A. Thomas (ed), *Tomorrow's Lawyers* (Oxford: Blackwell), 31.

LoPucki, L. (1999), 'Cooperation in International Bankruptcy: A Post-Universalist Approach' 84 *Cornell Law Review* 696.

Lowry, J. (2004), 'Eliminating Obstacles to Freedom of Establishment: The Competitive Edge of UK Company Law', 63 *Cambridge Law Journal* 331.

Macey, J. and Miller, G.P. (1987), 'Toward an Interest-Group Theory of Delaware Corporate Law', 65 *Texas Law Review* 469.

McCahery, J.A. and Hertig, G. (2003), 'Company and Takeover Law Reforms in Europe: Misguided Harmonization Efforts or Regulatory Competition?' 4 *European Business Organization Law Review* 179.

McCahery, J.A. and Vermeulen, E.P.M. (2005), 'Does the European Company Prevent the "Delaware-effect"?' 11 *European Law Journal* 785.

Micheler, E. (2000), 'The Impact of the *Centros* Case on Europe's Company Law', 21 *Company Lawyer* 179.

Moss, G. et al. (2002), *The EC Regulation on Insolvency Proceedings* (Oxford: OUP).

Murphy, D.D. (2004), *The Structure of Regulatory Competition* (Oxford: OUP).

Njoya, W. (2004), 'Employee Ownership and Efficiency: An Evolutionary Perspective' 33 *Industrial Law Journal* 211.

Omar, P. (2004), *European Insolvency Law* (Aldershot: Ashgate).

Posner, R. (1996), *Law and Legal Theory in England and America* (Oxford: OUP).

Rammeloo, S. (2004), 'At Long Last: Freedom of Establishment for Legal Persons in Europe Accomplished',11 *Maastricht Journal of European Law* 379.

Rasmussen, R.K. (1992), 'Debtor's Choice: A Menu Approach to Corporate Bankruptcy', 71 *Texas Law Review* 51.

—— (1997), 'A New Approach to Transnational Insolvencies' 19 *Michigan Journal of International Law* 1.

Roe, M.J. (2001), 'The Shareholder Wealth Maximization Norm and Industrial Organization' 149 *University of Pennsylvania Law Review* 2063.

—— (2003), Political Determinants of Corporate Governance (Oxford: OUP).

Romano, R. (1985), 'Law as Product: Some Pieces of the Incorporation Puzzle', 1 *Journal of Law, Economics and Organization* 225.

—— (1993), *The Genius of American Corporate Law* (Washington, DC: AEI Press).

—— (2005), 'The States as Laboratory: Legal Innovation and State Competition for Corporate Charters', ECGI Law Working Paper No 34/2005.

Roth, W.-H. (2003), 'From *Centros* to *Überseering*: Free Movement of Companies, Private International Law, and Community Law', 52 *International and Comparative Law Quarterly* 177.

Schmidt, R.H. and Spindler, G. (2004), 'Path Dependence and Complementarity in

Corporate Governance' in J.N. Gordon and M.J. Roe (eds), *Convergence and Persistence in Corporate Governance* (Cambridge: CUP), 114.

Schwartz, A. (1997), 'Contracting About Bankruptcy', 13 *Journal of Law, Economics and Organization* 127.

Scott, J.H. (1979), 'Bankruptcy, Secured Debt and Optimal Capital Structure' 32 *Journal of FInance* 1.

Shapiro, M. (1981), *Courts: A Comparative and Political Analysis* (Chicago: University of Chicago Press).

Siems, M. (2002), 'Convergence, Competition, *Centros* and Conflicts of Law: European Company Law in the 21st Century', 27 *EL Rev* 47.

Simon, J. (2004), 'A Comparative Approach to Capital Maintenance: France' 15 *EL Rev* 1037.

Sitkoff, R. and Schanzenbach, M.M. (2005), 'Jurisdictional Competition for Trust Funds: An Empirical Analysis of Perpetuities and Taxes', Northwestern Law & Econ Research Paper No 05–07.

Skeel, D.A. (1994), 'Rethinking the Line Between Corporate Law and Corporate Bankruptcy' 72 *Texas Law Review* 471.

Skeel, D.A. (1998), 'An Evolutionary Theory of Corporate Law and Corporate Bankruptcy' 51 *Vanderbilt Law Review* 1325.

—— (2004), Corporate Anatomy Lessons' 113 *Yale Law Journal* 1519.

Smart, P. (1998), *Cross-Border Insolvency*, 2nd ed. (London: Butterworths).

Stapledon, G.P. (1996), *Institutional Shareholders and Corporate Governance* (Oxford: Clarendon Press).

Subramanian, G. (2002), 'The Influence of Antitakeover Statutes on Incorporation Choice: Evidence on the "Race" Debate and Antitakeover Overreaching', 150 *University of Pennsylvania Law Review* 1795.

—— (2004), 'The Disappearing Delaware Effect', 20 *Journal of Law, Economics and Organization* 32.

Takeover Panel (2002), City Code on Takeovers and Mergers and the Rules Governing Substantial Acquisitions of Shares, 7th ed. (Bowne International: London) plus updates.

—— (2003), Report on the Year Ended 31 March 2003.

—— (2004), Report on the Year Ended 31 March 2004.

—— (2005), Explanatory Paper: Implementation of the European Directive on Takeover Bids (20 January 2005).

Teichmann, C. (2003), 'The European Company—A Challenge to Academics, Legislatures and Practitioners' 4 *German Law Journal* 309.

The Lawyer (2004), The Lawyer UK 100.

Thomas, R.S. *et al.* (2001), 'Megafirms', 80 *North Carolina Law Review* 115.

Thomsen, S. (2004), 'Convergence of Corporate Governance during the Stock Market Bubble: Towards Anglo-American or European Standards?' in A. Grandori (ed), *Corporate Governance and Firm Organization* (Oxford: OUP), 297.

Tiebout, C. (1956), 'A Pure Theory of Local Expenditures', 64 *Journal of Political Economy* 416.

Timmons, H. (2005), 'Private Equity Investors are Reshaping the Landscape of European Business', *New York Times*, 5 May, C12.

Tröger, T.H. (2005), 'Choice of Jurisdiction in European Corporate Law: Perspectives of European Corporate Governance', 6 *European Business Organization Law Review* 3.

UKLA (2003), *The Combined Code on Corporate Governance*, available at www.fsa.gov.uk/pubs/ukla/lr_comcode2003.pdf.

Virgos, M. and Schmit, E. (2002), Report on the Convention on Insolvency Proceedings, reprinted in Moss, G. et al., *The EC Regulation on Insolvency Proceedings* (Oxford: OUP).

Winter, R.K. (1997), 'State Law, Shareholder Protection, and the Theory of the Corporation', 6 *Journal of Legal Studies* 251.

Wojcik, D. (2003), 'Change in the German Model of Corporate Governance: Evidence from Blockholdings 1997–2001' 35 *Environment and Planning A* 1431.

Wouters, J. (2000), 'European Company Law: *Quo Vadis?*', 37 *CML Rev* 257.

Wymeersch, E. (2000), '*Centros*: A Landmark Decision in European Company Law' in T. Baums *et al* (eds), *Corporations, Capital Markets and Business in the Law* (London: Kluwer Law International), 629.

Wymeersch, E. (2003a), 'The Transfer of the Company's Seat in European Company Law', ECGI Law Working Paper No 08/2003.

Wymeersch, E. (2003b), 'Company Law in Turmoil and the Way to "Global Company Practice"' 3 *Journal of Corporate Law Studies* 283.

Zimmer, D. (2004), Note on *Inspire Art*, 41 *CML Rev* 1127.

15

Company and Takeover Law Reforms in Europe: Misguided Harmonization Efforts or Regulatory Competition?

GÉRARD HERTIG* AND JOSEPH A McCAHERY**

T HE IMPORTANT ROLE played by investor protection in the world economy is now widely accepted. In particular, it is generally recognized that corporate governance institutions play an essential role in limiting the agency problems that result from conflicting interests, in particular between managers and shareholders or among shareholders.

Recent empirical studies in the United States and Europe provide evidence of a correlation between corporate governance and the share price.[1] In light of this comparative research, lawmakers, who are under pressure to undertake reforms following corporate scandals across jurisdictions (see the Ahold, Enron, Global Crossing, Mannesmann, Swiss Life, Vivendi, and WorldCom affairs), have begun to diagnose weaknesses in their existing legal regimes and propose new arrangements. In a sense, the recent corporate governance failures have provided the ideal circumstances under which lawmakers can focus on identifying the institutions and practices that may ameliorate the defects in corporate performance. Yet, one should refrain from jumping to the conclusion that government policymakers are likely to solve agency

* Professor of Law and Economics, EidgenössischeTechnische Hochschule Zürich.
** Professor of Corporate Governance, University of Amsterdam—Center for Law and Economics and Professor of International Business Law, Tilburg University Faculty of Law. We thank Bruno Frey, Jeffrey Gordon, Andrew Guzman, Reinier Kraakman, Amir Licht, Katharina Pistor, Peer Ritter, as well as participants in the *A Modern Regulatory Framework for Company and Takeover Law in Europe Conference* (Syracuse, May 2003), and the *Tenth Comparative Law and Economics Forum* (Berkeley, June 2003) for their comments on earlier drafts. This chapter was previously published in 4 *European Business Organization Law Review* 179–211. The permission of the Asser Press to republish is gratefully acknowledged.

[1] See e.g., Mueller and Yurtoglu (2000); La Porta *et al.* (1997).

problems through a new round of policy commitments and legal provisions designed to address governance deficits. Even if government regulators agreed on the need for reform, there would still exist a problem that surfaces in all comparative corporate governance debates: namely, which packages of reforms offer optimal results for a given national system?

Indeed, whilst lawyers and economists applaud good corporate governance, the concept has many different meanings. The traditional legal approach to shareholder protection, which favors mandatory provisions driven by fairness and equality considerations, significantly differs from 'hardcore' law and economics approaches, which consider that only contractible default rules can increase investor welfare. Likewise, 'captured' policymakers focus on protecting their constituency, viz. controlling shareholders or top managers, whereas their more independent colleagues have so far arranged to introduce codes of best practices designed to foster socially-responsible conduct on the part of directors and executive officers.

Unfortunately, an apparent weakness of this polarized situation is that it can lead to the conclusion that the aim of corporate governance, and more generally corporate law and securities issuer regulation, is to maximize a single value. By contrast, recent research on the relation between economic development, shareholder and financial market structure, political and cultural components on the one hand, and corporate and securities laws on the other hand, provides the basis for a strong challenge of the 'one-size-fits-all' model. To be sure, it is generally accepted that, for example, it is important for directors and executive officers to be responsive to the interests of shareholders rather than merely pursue their own financial and ego concerns. One cannot, however, ignore the existence of regulatory tradeoffs or that jurisdictions are not homogeneous. For example, increasing managerial responsiveness to the interests of shareholders as a class may be detrimental to minority shareholder and other stakeholder interests. Similarly, underlying legal, economic and social structures vary from one national system to the other or even from region to region.

The implications for EU corporate law reform are clear: there is no simple model for corporate regulators to use when designing reforms. While current efforts to modernize European Union (EU) company law and to create a takeover regime are influenced by shareholder value maximization considerations, one must not forget that there are political barriers to transplanting the Anglo-Saxon approach in continental Europe. Given the important differences between corporate governance systems in Europe, the appropriate regulatory approach is to provide firms with the freedom to select the regulatory environment that suits their needs. We argue that an institutional environment that gives firms the opportunity to match rules to complement their firm characteristics and stages of development can offer significant costs advantages. Analyzing the EU's reform packages on corporate governance shows that the current proposals are too static and incomplete in their formulation and do not provide legal substitutes that may be essential for introducing incentives and promoting competition. Our analysis also highlights why the 2002 proposal for a Takeover Directive created, on balance, significant problems for continental European corporate governance systems because it proposed the so-called 'breakthrough' rule that would, in effect, have altered the structures of ownership and concentration of voting rights of firms. One nearly immediate consequence of this rule would have been the reduction of the substantial differences between ownership structures and takeover defenses based on EU company law. We conclude that the tensions that result from the EU's reform packages on company law and corporate governance are apt to give rise to few tangible governance benefits.

This chapter proceeds as follows. Part I will examine the recent trends in regulatory arbitrage and competition in Europe.[2] The analysis demonstrates that a competitive environment for reincorporations has yet to materialize. We show the even if incentives to compete are present, state competition may be subject to structural barriers that inhibit the evolution of rules. Although we conclude that the real seat doctrine will continue to restrict firm mobility despite recent European Court of Justice (ECJ) case law, we explain that Member States have started to show interest in supplying new business statutes. Their motives are threefold: (1) to improve the environment of small and medium-size businesses by actively attempting to attract investment or business; (2) to promote the competitiveness of indigenous industries by adopting the most favorable business form: (3) to respond to competitive threats posed by offshore jurisdictions. We argue that should the future bring a swell in the number of firms migrating to the most favorable jurisdictions, as envisaged by the ECJ in *Centros* and *Überseering, Inspire Art*,[3] the pressure from interest groups on states to adopt responsive legislation can be expected to significantly increase.

---

[2] Regulatory arbitrage refers to firms' choice of the legal regime that best suits their preferences, whereas regulatory competition refers to regulators' attempt to attract or not to loose firms due to a more favorable legal environment. See Woolcock (1996). Strong national preferences or path dependence may result in regulatory arbitrage in the absence of regulatory competition. See Heine and Heiner (2000).

[3] Case C-212/97 *Centros Ltd. v Erhvervs-og Selskabsstyrelsen* [1999] ECR I-1459, [1999] 2 CMLR 551; Case C-208/00 *Überseering BV v NCC Nordic Construction Company Baumangement GmbH (NCC)*, [2002] ECR I-9919; and Case C-167/01 *Kamer can Koophandel en Fabrieken voor Amsterdam v Inspire Art Ltd (NL)* [2003] ECR I. These judgments are available at http://europa.eu.int/cj/en/content/auris/index.htm

Contemplated EU corporate law reforms are analyzed in Part II. The dominant view among corporate law scholars has been that the EU's approach to harmonization has the advantages of encouraging simplicity and lowering administrative costs for firms. However, supporters of the EU harmonization program have made no attempts to show empirically that the implementation of company law directives has resulted in the desired effects. In contrast, we argue that uniform rules often lead to higher costs for different types of firms and that this approach to legal change is cumbersome and not sufficient to regulate externality problems. Recently, the European Commission has adopted an action plan that should address the remaining gaps in the harmonization process and strengthen the Commission's role as a driving force in corporate law reform. Though we support the Commission's desire to introduce arrangements that are more flexible and fill in the gaps of EU corporate law, we are skeptical about the merits of this action plan and whether it will lead to extensive changes in corporate law practice. More importantly, those planed changes that could make a difference are more likely to favor bureaucratic intervention than to facilitate transactions. In our view, this approach is unfortunate, as more enabling or market-oriented litigation mechanisms might contribute to the freedom of choice while encouraging regulatory innovation.

Part III discusses the long winding efforts of the EU to adopt a new takeover law regime. EU experts defended the introduction of two legal principles (viz. board neutrality and the breakthrough rule) to create a level playing field for EU takeovers and provide the basis for the transition to a dispersed ownership structure. It is doubtful, however, that the level playing field concept is not a suitable approach for takeover regulation. It is also doubtful that board neutrality and the breakthrough rule will, given that virtually all Member States have opted out of both provisions, have any significant effect economically. Yet, this does not mean that the Takeover Directive will not have much influence in creating economic benefits by promoting the development of an integrated market for corporate control. The adoption of the mandatory bid, and the squeeze out and sell out rights will contribute to a better performing cross-border takeover market. Part III turns from considering select provisions of the Takeover Directive to analyzing a choice-enhancing proposal that would allow firms to opt into the proposed EU regime or elect to be governed by state law. We advocate a EU takeover regime that would offer firms the choice to be governed by the proposed EU takeover code or State law alternatives, which could stimulate the competitive pressures between states and lead to better takeover rules. Part IV concludes.

I. REFLECTIONS ON REGULATORY ARBITRAGE AND COMPETITION

Two central trends are clearly beginning to emerge regarding state competition. First, the evidence suggests that, while regulatory competition remains close to nonexistent within the EU, the appearance of new judgments from the ECJ supports the inference that regulatory arbitrage is an imminent possibility. Secondly, the threat of state competition, which is less attractive to weakly-responsive states, such as France and Germany, can provide a new impetus for EU harmonization. We begin our examination of regulatory competition by discussing, in Part I.A, how the European Court of Justice has signaled its willingness to move in the direction to allow states to compete for reincorporations. Part I.B will then assess the need for harmonizing corporate law in the EU.

A. An Emerging Path

One of the most important debates in European company law is whether a 'market for corporate law' will ultimately emerge within the European Union, and if so, whether it will be based on a Delaware-like model in which companies can freely select their country of incorporation.[4] This is, of course, a politically-charged question and therefore a somewhat undifferentiated debate. In particular, commentators often fail to distinguish between corporate finance, company formation and restructuring issues.[5] Conversely, competition between states in the United States is generally assumed to be very active, whereas recent research shows that reality is subtler.[6] However, there is evidence that domicile choices by US corporations can affect their value and/or provide significant benefits for their managers and controlling shareholders.[7] The absence in Europe of anything resembling American charter competition must therefore mean that there are substantive regulatory barriers to jurisdictional competition.[8]

To start, EU company law can be viewed largely as an incomplete and rather ineffective set of provisions.[9] The reasons: Member States have

---

[4] See, e.g., Ebke (2000: 625–28) (explaining that competitive lawmaking has become a dominant theme in European company law); Cheffins (1997: 421–51) (explaining the potential role of the market for incorporations for deepening European economic integration).

[5] See Grundmann (2002).

[6] See e.g. Kahan and Kamar (2002); Bebchuk and Hamdani (2002).

[7] See Bebchuk, Cohen, and Ferrell (2002); Daines (2001).

[8] See Deakin (2001: 205).

[9] See, e.g., Hopt (2002: 175) (arguing that the EC has done little to enact measures that regulate the relations between shareholders and managers or with minority investors rights); Coffee (1999: 651) (contrasting federal systems that permit a market for incorporation with the different market and institutional environment of jurisdictions that are not committed to a reincorporation regime).

been repeatedly unable to agree on important substantive issues, the pro-decentralization presumption resulting from the EU subsidiary principle, and lack of implementation of EU Directives by Member States.[10]

This has allowed for continuing diversity in Member State corporate law.[11] At the same time, the rather strong divergence about the 'optimal' corporate regime has had the effect of sustaining significant opposition to regulatory arbitrage and competition. Nevertheless, US commentators, in particular, have argued that change is imminent. Cross-border acquisitions by firms that have cheaper access to external capital, because of higher investor protection levels, should bring corporate governance amendments.[12] The replacement of banks by institutional shareholders, as the main corporate governance actor, should have a similar effect.[13] In other words, transformations occurring in the market place will result in increased convergence of rules (Gilson 2001).

In contrast, many European scholars are not as optimistic about the prospects for market-induced reform, given the existence of a strong coalition of interest groups and other path-dependent forces.[14] In particular, the repeated failures to pass a Directive on Takeovers shows the power of those who benefit from the status quo to block transformational measures.[15]

Of course, institutional barriers at the EU level are not the sole or even main reason for past regulatory and judicial conservatism.[16] Under the *siège réel* (real seat) doctrine, which is followed by the majority of EU Member States, a corporation must be incorporated in the Member State where it has its central administration. As a result, opting into another Member State's corporate law is often unattractive because of significant tax implications, especially for corporations that have used conservative accounting to build up hidden reserves. This barrier to regulatory arbitrage and competition is compounded by employee-participation structures, German co-determination being the best known but not the only example. Indeed, by reducing the ability of legislators to respond to managerial or shareholder preferences, employee participation favors regulatory conservatism.[17] Judicial conservatism, for its part, has at least as much to do with Member States' reluctance to facilitate or merely permit shareholder litigation than result from EU law deficiencies.

[10] See Wouters (2000: 275).
[11] See, e.g., Berglöf (1997: 93).
[12] See Shleifer (2000: 135).
[13] See, e.g., Gordon (1998).
[14] See McCahery and Vermeulen (2001: 863).
[15] See also Roe (2001) (providing a theoretical explanation).
[16] See also McCahery and Vermeulen (2001: 863–64).
[17] See Wymeersch (1998).

It would be wrong, however, to underestimate the tension created by market changes. ECJ case law is a good indicator, given the court's record in providing early warnings regarding forthcoming legal reform. As a matter of fact, the ECJ's recent decisions in *Centros, Überseering* and *Inspire Art* is likely to eventually undermine the real seat doctrine and set the stage for effective regulatory arbitrage and competition among Member States.[18] To be sure, commentators may still take refuge behind a phalanx of obscure and convoluted statements in the ECJ case law in order to defend the real seat doctrine.[19] We, on the other hand, expect the ECJ to continue along the doctrinal path it developed in *Centros*. In this respect, it is worth pointing to the *Überseering* case, which involves a Dutch close corporation that had moved its headquarters to Germany. The ECJ ruled that such a corporation could not be denied the capacity to bring legal action before the courts of the Member State in which it has its central administration on the ground that its home/foreign corporate law regime does not satisfy host/domestic corporate law requirements.

As a consequence of *Centros, Überseering* and *Inspire Art*, start-up firms should be able to incorporate under the corporate law regime they deem most favorable among the regimes offered by the various Member States. Established firms should be able to take advantage of the newly-available European Company Statute to similar effect.[20]

In this context, the United Kingdom could become the leading jurisdiction for European incorporations.[21] Indeed, UK legislators have moved fast to develop a menu of new corporate forms that caters to the needs of entrepreneurs, while its courts are respected and productive—characteristics that have significantly contributed to Delaware's US dominance.[22] Admittedly, charter revenue may not be sufficient to prompt UK legislators to engage into sustained regulatory competition.[23] On the other hand, additional incorporations will mean increased revenue for UK accountants and lawyers—which is one of the main reason why Delaware legislators keep their corporate law in tune with market demands. It is true that UK accountants and lawyers are still

---

[18] Case C-212/97 *Centros Ltd. v Erhvervs-og Selskabsstyrelsen* [1999] ECR I-1459, [1999] 2 CMLR 551; Case C-208/00 *Überseering BV v NCC Nordic Construction Company Baumangement 1987 GmbH* (NCC), [2002] ECR I-9919; and Case C-167/01 *Kanner can Koophandel en Fabrieken voor Amsterdam v Inspire Art Ltd (NL)* [2003] ECR I. Compare Case 81/1987 *Regina v H.M. Treasury and Comm'rs of Inland Revenue, ex parte Daily Mail and General Trust Plc* [1988] ECR 5483.

[19] See Halbhuber (2001: 1409).

[20] See Enriques (2003). Note that *Centros* does not seem to facilitate cross-border restructurings of existing corporations. See Behrens (2002).

[21] See also McCahery and Vermeulen (2001: 864–65).

[22] See, e.g., Black (1990: 590); Romano (1985).

[23] See Cheffins (1997: 435) (explaining that the UK, unlike Delaware, does not impose a franchise tax or an annual fee on incorporated firms and does not charge fees for amendments to the corporate constitution).

rather passive when it comes to making corporate law responsive to the demands of the market place, especially compared to their Delaware counterparts. However, UK lawyers and accountants will adjust fast as soon as it will become clear that regulatory competition magnifies both the benefits of attracting new business and the risks of losing existing clients—especially in an environment that is less mature than the US regulatory market.[24]

The likeliness of this scenario is reinforced by early reactions to recent UK company law reforms. Major jurisdictions, such as France and Germany, are reacting with uncharacteristic speed to adopt legislation aiming at minimizing firm migrations to the United Kingdom.[25] Smaller jurisdictions, such as Ireland and Luxembourg, may join the fray and decide to act entrepreneurial themselves, tempted by what they could see as a chance to get additional chartering revenue.[26]

B. Harmonization and the Regulatory Competition Debate in the EU

The question, then, is whether corporate law regulation should be left to Member States rather than undertaken at the EU level. Those favoring centralization believe it is necessary to eliminate barriers to trade, as well as distortions of competition (Inman and Rubenfeld 1997). Moreover, it allows for the internalization of significant spillovers. Proponents of legal federalism, on the other hand, rely on the economic theory of jurisdictional competition to support devolutionary initiatives.[27] They claim that regulatory competition shapes a wide range of regulatory outcomes at Member State and local levels because menus of regulation figure prominently in the location decision of firms and factors of production. Such regulatory outcomes tend to correspond to citizen/firm preferences, since only public goods and regulatory restrictions for which citizens are willing to pay will survive (Weingast 1995). Two conditions, however, must be satisfied: (1) lower level regulation must not generate significant externalities; and (2) borders must be open for the free movement of capital and labor.

Debates within the EU aimed at reconciling both positions are strongly affected by the importation of the regulatory competition concept and its races to the top and to the bottom stories. According to the race to the top story, uniform rules carried the risk of regulatory capture (by managers

---

[24] Compare Bebchuk and Cohen (2003) (US firms display a substantial 'home state bias' in favor of incorporating in the state in which they are located).

[25] For France, see Conac (2002): for Germany, Baums (2003); See also Bachmann (2001: 365).

[26] Note that double taxation treaties and other tax issues may reduce the charter benefits of regulatory competition. See Cheffins (1997: 435); ECJ *Ponente Carni Spa* [1993] ECR 1947.

[27] See e.g., Romano (1991: 1–40; 2001).

or controlling shareholders), while competitive diversity would lead to regulation tailored to the need of local preferences, deter opportunism, and encourage regulatory innovation. According to the race to the bottom story, in absence of effective harmonization, national level lawmaking would involve complexity, uncertainty, and undesirable competitive deregulation.

By linking together mutual recognition of corporate law systems, subsidiarity (viz. lawmaking is restricted to the Member State level unless credible circumstances support harmonization) and minimum requirements, EU lawmakers have created a legal structure that supplies a degree of useful tension between regulatory competition and harmonization. In particular, EU lawmakers have recognized that, while mutual recognition is necessary for the operation of a well-functioning market for legal rules, asymmetric information could undermine the willingness of actors to participate in the market (Tjiong 2002: 83). To shed light on this problem, let us examine a concrete example. We assume that a Member States is unable to reject corporations organized under another Member State's law to avoid more restrictive domestic requirements. In these circumstances, we can expect difficulties to arise when it is complicated and costly for investors and creditors to evaluate the quality of the non-domestic corporate law system.

Taken alone, mutual recognition could also make it easier for managers to reincorporate in a Member State that has an anti-takeover regime that suits their interests rather than those of shareholders. Furthermore, following the eastward expansion of the EU in 2004, new Member States will come under increased pressure to make changes in their company law rules in order to compete for inward investment. This is likely to have a direct effect on the level of minority shareholder and non-trade creditor protection (Berkowitz, Pistor, and Richard 2003; Black, Kraakman, and Tarassova 2000). In addition, some new Member States are likely to adopt inefficient business forms in order to attract firms that will operate outside their jurisdiction, thus internalizing charter and other benefits while externalizing costs.

In other words, mutual recognition presupposes that Member States remain empowered to restrain foreign business forms that do not offer minimum protection to investors, creditors and other stakeholders. This, in turn, means that 'minimum requirements' must be defined centrally for regulatory competition to be significant. Indeed, as we know from past and current EU experiences, diversity resulting from decentralized definitions should permit ample room for Member States to limit regulatory competition to trivial levels.

The task of defining 'minimum requirements' can theoretically be left to the EU judiciary, but such a procedure is rather slow and piecemeal. In practice, minimum requirements are rather designed by the EU legislative, where regulatory capture generally leads to the adoption of over-inclusive mandatory rules that excessively limit regulatory arbitrage and competition.

With respect to corporate law, this means that EU harmonization has tended to favor the interests of managers and stakeholders such as controlling shareholders and lenders. On the other hand, regulatory capture has not reached Delaware levels. As already mentioned, centralized rule-making has remained incomplete and conservative, interest groups and other path dependent forces having made it difficult to depart from the status quo.

However, recent corporate governance scandals involving publicly-traded firms, the generally recognized need to improve the integration of the EU's capital markets, and increasingly pro-mutual recognition ECJ case law have given a new impetus to EU regulatory efforts. Hence, the European Commission has recently undertaken further harmonization of corporate and takeovers law. We discuss these harmonization attempts in Part II and III and analyze whether they are needed to facilitate transactions or enable regulatory competition.

II. THE PROPOSED EU COMPANY LAW REFORMS

Part I examined the prospects for state competition in corporate law in the EU. In this part, we assess the proposals of a group of experts that were commissioned by the EU to review its corporate law Directives and make recommendations for reform. Their report, published in November 2002, recommends simplifying existing rules, the elimination of barriers to cross-border transactions and better freedom of choice between alternative forms of organization, but does not make any fundamental proposals.[28]

While this outcome may reflect a consensus that no further harmonization is necessary to allow for regulatory arbitrage or prevent regulatory undercutting, it is more probable that a conjunction of vested interests continues to favor the status quo. Interest groups opposed to regulatory competition or market integration had no reason to push for significant reforms. Interest groups favorable to freedom of choice also had few incentives to undertake concerted action to influence the reform agenda. Indeed, experience shows that harmonization efforts often result in costly compromises that raise rather than decrease barriers to cross-border activity.

[28] See *Report of the High Level Group of Company Law Experts on a Modern Regulatory Framework for Company Law in Europe* (Nov. 2002, available at europa.eu.int).

That said, the report makes various specific recommendations that are of interest for a transaction facilitation and regulatory competition analysis. First, a permanent structure should be established to provide the European Commission with independent advice on future regulatory initiatives, whereas Member States should establish enforcement agencies to sanction unfit directors. Secondly, it is proposed to further harmonize disclosure, board structure, director liability and capital requirements.

The European Commission has adopted most of the experts' recommendations in its recently published action plan.[29] In addition, the reinforcement of EU provisions on statutory audit is debated by EU law makers.[30] We believe, however, that most of the considered changes would prove ineffective. More unfortunately, those considered changes that could prove effective are, with one exception, likely to favor bureaucratic intervention whereas some market-oriented mechanisms have been expressly rejected.

A. Ineffectiveness

The proposed reforms are likely to prove ineffective for two, somewhat related, reasons: the EU is not a principal regulatory player, and its proposals are unlikely to make a difference.

The EU plays second fiddle to more global or powerful bodies when it comes to disclosure requirements for listed firms. For example, EU influence in the accounting area is at best indirect, due to the central role of played by the Financial Accounting Standard Board (FASB) and the International Accounting Standard Board (IASB).[31] Similarly, firms and Member States alike are more concerned by national securities regulators' practices than by to-be-implemented EU requirements. In other words, as long as there is no European SEC, EU activism in the corporate disclosure area is likely to prove largely irrelevant.[32]

Moreover, even if one assumes that the EU can play a disclosure role, the proposed rules are unlikely to provide previously unknown information to the controlling shareholders that dominate both listed and non-listed EU firms (Barca and Becht 2002; La Porta, Lopez-de-Silanes, and Shleifer 1999). A far as minority shareholders are concerned, any improvement in their situation presupposes that they can credibly

---

[29] Action Plan on Modernizing Company Law and Enhancing Corporate Law in the EU (May 2003, available at europa.eu.int).
[30] Communication from the Commission, Reinforcing the Statutory Audit in the EU (May 2003, available at europa.eu.int).
[31] See Reg. (EC) No. 1606/2002 on the application of international accounting standards [2002] OJ L243/1.
[32] See Hertig and Lee (2003).

threaten to request a special investigation. This does not seem realistic, considering the 5 per cent threshold to be met by shareholders of listed firms and the limited benefits of transparency requirements for shareholders of non-listed firms.[33]

Board structure and liability proposals are also unlikely to make a difference. For example, requiring that firms must have a choice between one-tier and two-tier boards is of limited value, given that one-tier companies can imitate two-tier decision-making by using committees.[34] Similarly, forcing companies to explain why individual non-executive directors are qualified to serve on the board in their particular role is a requirement that is past its prime. Or, to take another example, harmonizing the definition of 'shadow' directors and requiring Member States to adopt wrongful trading provisions will have little or no impact unless these requirements are coupled with an enforcement mechanism— a topic that we will discuss below. Moreover, assuming again that EU law could make a difference, for example when it comes to the setting-up of audit committees or director independence and remuneration, they mostly duplicate requirements that already exist at the Member State level.

Capital formation and maintenance proposals could prove less ineffective, but most are of rather marginal importance. For example, the proposals to eliminate expert valuation requirements would only make a difference if they were generally applicable and not merely limited to some contributions in kind. Similarly, extending creditors' rights to require security for all restructuring transactions is unlikely to be useful for those creditors that are not already secured.

B. Fostering Bureaucracy

In their report, the experts commissioned by the EU recognize that cross-border corporate mobility and restructuring must be facilitated. However, they generally favor increased uniformity over facilitating regulatory arbitrage and competition to achieve such a result.

Such bias is relatively harmless as long as it merely affects the fine-tuning of what constitutes minimum requirements. On the other hand, it could have very damaging consequences if it translates into excessive regulatory intervention. In our opinion, the chances of such an outcome are very real.

Admittedly, reinforcing auditor monitoring by replacing self-regulatory regimes through state supervisory is a move that is both likely

---

[33] For a more optimistic view, see e.g. Hopt (this volume, ch. 13).
[34] See Hansmann and Kraakman (2004a).

to improve investor confidence and prevent auditor liability to become prohibitive in the wake of the Enron and similar accounting scandals.[35]

However, the prospects are much less positive in other areas. First, proposing to set-up a permanent body to provide advice on future EU regulatory initiatives favors state intervention as the members of such a body are likely to be rewarded for regulatory activism. Secondly, the report's underlying philosophy is that listed firms should be subject to a certain level of uniform and compulsory detailed rules, i.e. their autonomy must be much more restricted than for closed corporations. It may well be that the availability of a rather rigid European company form may prove beneficial, as long as firms remain free to choose among a rather broad range of alternative corporate forms.[36] Nevertheless, current proposals seem both to foster unnecessary changes and reduce the alternatives available to listed firms.

For example, it is proposed that director nomination and remuneration must be decided exclusively by non-executive directors who are in the majority independent as defined by EU law. Such a rule cannot be considered essential for preventing 'race to the bottom' problems. Moreover, to the extent it is not drafted in very broad terms and thus ineffective, it is unlikely to take into account EU diversity. The same objections apply to proposal that squeeze-out and sellout rights should be given to shareholders that have acquired, at the minimum, 90 per cent, or, at the maximum, 95 per cent of the capital of listed firms. Or, to take another example, given the limited scope of EU capital maintenance requirements (they do not apply to closed corporations) and the debatable persuasiveness of their critics,[37] it is far from clear why the EU should undertake reforms in this area.

Thirdly, it is proposed to impose director's disqualification at the EU level. UK practice shows that the disqualification sanction may deter violations of the wrongful trading rule and other fiduciary duties. Nevertheless, as made clear by early UK experiences and a comparison with France, an effective disqualification mechanism presupposes the existence of a well-funded enforcement agency.[38] It is difficult to understand why the existence of such agency is a minimum requirement for regulatory competition to be acceptable. Moreover, assuming that the

---

[35] Reputation and litigation issues are related, given that the former is eroded by the latter. Conversely, introducing state supervision should enhance auditor reputation as well as induce legislators and courts to keep the liability risk within reasonable limits. See also Coffee (2001).

[36] See Hansmann and Kraakman (2004b); Bebchuk and Ferrell (2001).

[37] See Mühlbert and Birke (2002); Enriques and Macey (2001). In particular, we are not persuaded that limitations regarding the acquisition of own shares or financial assistance by the company in case of third-party acquisition of its shares are as damaging as alleged.

[38] See also Hertig and Kanda (2004).

EU must reduce barriers to enforcement, it certainly would be preferable to use more market-oriented mechanisms.

Indeed, it is quite obvious that litigation by minority shareholder is rare in Europe, which in turn permits managers and controlling shareholders to pay significantly less attention to corporate law requirements than their US counterparts.[39] Given that listed firms in continental Europe still have quite concentrated shareholder structures, there is a good case for facilitating shareholder access to justice.[40]

A combination of four market-oriented measures may prove sufficient EU contribution to reducing barriers to enforcement. First, shareholders should be recognized standing to sue, regardless of the number of shares they own and the direct or indirect nature of the alleged damage to their interests. Secondly, Member States should be required to allocate shareholder litigation to specialized courts, building upon either the Delaware Chancery, the French *Tribunal de commerce* or the German *Handlesgericht* models. Thirdly, the legality of contingent fees (which are already a common, albeit often concealed, practice throughout Europe) should be introduced. Such a reform would likely serve to reduce the incentive gap between European and US shareholder litigation. Fourthly, cross-border litigation, including cross-mass litigation and temporary injunctions should be facilitated—for example, by making it easier for attorneys to represent multiple clients, by facilitating discovery or by eliminating remaining obstacles to intra-EU recognition of judgments.

The obvious advantage of such measures is to force managers and controlling shareholders better to take into account the interests of minority shareholders due to the increase in the litigation threat. To be sure, facilitating litigation is also potentially costly and therefore safeguards against abusive litigation may be needed. It may also prove necessary to adopt transition or grandfathering provisions to reduce negative midstream effects for established firms. We believe, however, that the adoption of mitigating mechanisms can wait until experience has been gathered with new enforcement mechanisms.

In particular, expressed fears about abusive enforcement are more likely to reflect a status quo bias rather than frivolous litigation concerns. Moreover, EU minimum requirements are low enough to make it unattractive for Member States from engaging in races to attract frivolous litigation. Conversely, EU minimum requirements are high enough to prevent Member States from engaging in welfare-reducing races to protect managers and controlling shareholders against minority shareholder activism—including those planning a takeover bid. In other words, the facilitation of minority shareholder litigation seems unlikely

---

[39] See Enriques (2004).
[40] See Hertig (2001).

to have immediate negative effects regarding enforcement levels or investor and stakeholder expectations regarding established firms.

Unfortunately, the introduction of litigation-friendly procedures does not constitute a part of the reform agenda. For example, collective action mechanisms are summarily dismissed by the experts' report, whereas improvements in shareholder standing to sue are not even discussed. This reluctance to consider private litigation mechanisms is not only regrettable because it reflects a bureaucratic rather than market-oriented approach to corporate law. In the context of enlargement, the failure to adopt strong court-centered reforms increases the risk that Member States will enforce corporate law according to a protectionist or otherwise political agenda. The approach is also an obstacle to the competitiveness of the legal profession across Europe, as the fostering of private litigation would make it profitable for European law firms to modernize and compete with US law firms within and outside the EU. In turn, this may even reduce the US litigation risk of European firms if the threat of EU litigation brings them to improve their legal risk management systems.

Our point here is that the proposed EU corporate law reforms are likely to be either ineffective or unnecessary to ameliorate market failures. In addition, they bring the risk of excessive state intervention (supervision of auditors excepted) while ignoring the much needed private action mechanisms. Our own view is that an alternative approach, that addresses corporate law reform in terms of supporting the introduction of non-statutory mechanisms in key areas of company regulation while strengthening the incentives for the enforcement of director's duties, would lead to a fundamental change in the pattern of EU company law.

III. THE TAKEOVER DIRECTIVE

Part II questioned whether the EU's approach to creating a modern regulatory framework for corporate law in Europe is likely to facilitate competitive law making across the EU. In this part, we discuss the regulatory impact of the European Commission's efforts to devise a set of 'level playing field' regulations for takeover bids. The 2 October 2002 draft Takeover Bids Directive is largely inspired by proposals made by a group of experts (the High Level Group).[41] Like the earlier draft 13th Directive, the October 2002 proposal met resistance from Germany and other Member States on several substantive issues.[42]   As with general

---

[41] See *Report of the High Level Group of Company Law Experts on Issues Related to Takeover Bids* (January 2002, available at europa.eu.int).
[42] See EUR. PARL. DOC. (COM(2002) 534 –C5-0481/2002 –2002/0240(COD)) (2002)

company law, the central regulatory problem is determining the optimal balance between harmonization and diversity. One benefit of the proposal was the provision of simple common rules (e.g. board neutrality) that avoid some of the costs of having complex and differing national regimes. On the other hand, it is far from clear that Member States with different laws and traditions would have been better served by some of the harmonization proposals.[43]

Ultimately, the proposal to include multiple voting rights as prohibited defensive measures undermined support for the commission's proposal is a sensible compromise allowing companies to opt out of defensive measures and Member States to relax prohibitions on defensive actions without Shareholder approval where a bidder emerged from a country where poison pills are permitted was approved 27 November 2003. The resulting Takeover Directive aims at setting minimum requirements for corporate conduct and transparency in the takeover context.

More specifically, the Takeover Directive provides for: (1) strict board neutrality on the part of the target board; (2) a mandatory bid rule that ensures that an offeror cannot obtain a controlling stake without making a controlling bid; (3) breakthrough rules which stipulate that, during the period of acceptance of a bid, any restrictions on the transfer of securities contained in the articles of association and contractual arrangements (but not in national legislation) are not enforceable against the offeror; (4) disclosure rules according to which the offeror must announce his intention to make an offer and make public an offer document containing at least a minimum of information; (5) 'squeeze-out' and 'sell-out' rules that would have to be implemented at a fair price; and (6) an opt out provision that allows Member States to exempt companies from applying the board neutrality and break-through provisions.

It is worthwhile emphasizing that a key issue in the debate on the Takeover Directive concerned whether the 'level playing field' concept is necessary for the regulation of hostile takeovers in Europe. To the High Level Group, rules aiming at balancing regulatory advantages are a pre-requisite to the emergence of an integrated market for corporate control. The Commission believed that in passing the Takeover Directive it would create a level playing field in takeovers, reducing further reliance on coercive measures and other protective devices.

More fundamentally, however, the question over the Takeover Directive is whether concentrated control should be significantly reduced in Europe (Gordon 2003). The desirability of a dispersed ownership system is unlikely to be persuasive to blockholder systems, particularly in the absence of evidence of the comparative advantage of the two systems

---

[43] See *ibid.* at 14 (proposed Amendment 16 of Art. 5(1), which provides for a uniform definition of the mandatory bid threshold trigger).

(Bratton and McCahery 1999: 230). On the other hand, shareholder structures tend to become less concentrated and there is a growing awareness of the need to protect shareholders against the related increase in managerial opportunism, as well as the necessity generally to protect minority shareholders against controlling shareholder opportunism.

While we welcome legislation that aimed at keeping managerial discretion and controlling shareholders' private benefits within acceptable limits, we are skeptical, however, of the promised advantages of the level playing field concept. The objective should be to adopt as few EU mandatory rules as possible and to limit further EU intervention to improving companies' freedom to choose the regulatory environment in which they wish to operate. The Takeover Directive struck a balance between the level playing field concept and the freedom to choose. The question is whether the evidence will show whether the balance struck was a reasonable one.

Below we begin our examination by discussing the market for corporate control (A). We then look at the proposed board neutrality rule (B). Next, we examine the draft mandatory bid rules, in particular the Directive's equitable price provision (C), and the breakthrough rule (D).[44] Finally, we review the level playing field concept (E) and take into account the opt out provisions included in Article 12 (F).

A. The Market for Corporate Control

Concentrated ownership structure makes the successful conclusion of hostile takeovers difficult, if not impossible, in continental Europe. However, many commentators have shown that other factors may decrease the probability of hostile acquisitions. For example, when the target company has widely dispersed ownership, no individual shareholder affects the success of the tender offer (free-rider problem), which may prevent bidders from recovering the costs of their bid (e.g., information and search costs) (Grossman and Hart 1980).

Various schemes can overcome the free-rider problem (Bebchuk 1994; Burkart, Gromb, and Panunzi 1988). Allowing the bidder to freeze out remaining shareholders at a price below the target's full value after the completion of the takeover may ensure that free riders will tender at a price where the bidder achieves a profit (Yarrow 1985). Similarly, permitting the bidder to acquire an initial toehold in the target company will allow the bidder to retain some of the public benefits of the eventual takeover gains (Shleifer and Vishny 1986).

The free-rider problem, however, does not arise if there are sufficient

---

[44] See EUR. PARL. DOC., above, n. 47 (proposed Amendments 28 and 29 of Art. 11).

private benefits of control left in the firm for the new majority shareholder to finance its bid. Also, there is no free-rider problem when shareholders are uncertain about the success of the proposed bid. Even if the bid price is below the stand-alone value of the target firm, dispersed shareholders may be under pressure to tender because they expect other shareholders to tender (Bebchuk 1985).

The above argumentation shows that, in order to increase the flow of takeover bids, it is necessary that minority shareholders neither participate in the full value of the firm nor be induced to tender for a bid that leaves them worse off than before the bid. Whether or not increasing takeover flows is efficient is the subject of debate. Some argue that takeovers create value improvements by exploiting buyer and seller synergies. Others point to the higher number of value-decreasing bids and the high costs associated with takeovers that are primarily motivated by managerial compensation and the expropriation of the target firm's stakeholders.

Given the trend towards less concentrated ownership across Europe and the increasing awareness of the need to protect minority shareholders against controlling shareholder opportunism, EU policymakers must attempt to balance a trade-off. On the one hand, they should promote policies that make takeovers less costly and thus produce more bids; on the other hand, they have to insure for shareholder protection and equal treatment (Berglöf and Burkart 2003).

B. Board Neutrality

Consequently, a recurrent theme in EU takeover policy discussions concerns the balance that policymakers must strike between protecting shareholders from the effects of managerial opportunism (represented in the form of pre- and post-bid defenses) by adopting a board neutrality rule and deferring to the judgment of management.

In the main, the debate in corporate legal theory over takeovers falls into two broad schools of thought. The board defense approach holds that shareholders are unable, due to limited experience, collective action and coordination problems, to make informed choices in the takeover context. Hence, boards should be permitted to erect defenses on the grounds that they are better placed to protect the interests of shareholders.

In contrast, the shareholder choice perspective holds that boards are self-interested in their response to takeover bids and consequently should not be permitted to create defenses (Bebchuk, this volume, ch. 13). Not only does board discretion reduce welfare by limiting the disciplinary effect of takeovers, but it also reduces shareholder value by attracting only friendly deals, allowing managers to extract a disproportionate share of rents produced by such transactions. While there is no doubt that shareholders are disadvantaged in ordinary day-to-day business decisions, proponents conclude that shareholders are best positioned to take the ultimate decision in a takeover bid.

Dissatisfaction with the shareholder choice approach has led recently to the emergence of a hybrid view which holds that undistorted shareholder choice may be insufficient to remove most of the barriers to takeovers (Kahan and Rock 2003; Kihlstrom and Wachter 2003). In particular, it is argued that managers can simply entrench themselves further by employing pre-bid defenses embedded in a firm's contractual arrangements (Arlen and Talley 2003).

Against this background, the issue with the EU regulation of takeover bids becomes the extent to which its board neutrality rule is required. It has been argued that the policy choice between board neutrality and board discretion depends on the relative efficiency of capital markets (Wachter 2003). If there are sufficiently large externalities in the takeover context, board intervention can be justified. The main trade-off entails bad managers entrenching themselves by rejecting value-enhancing tender offers against good managers seek to maximize shareholder value by rejecting value-reducing tender offers. While there are good arguments that support both sides of the trade-off, empirical evidence is not available.[45]

It is therefore useful to take into account the role of board neutrality provisions in a key Member State, Germany. The 2002 Takeover Act is consistent with the general 'duty of neutrality' that prohibits the management from taking any unilateral action to frustrate the hostile takeover offer. However, shareholders can authorize target management to implement defense mechanisms such as: i) issuance of new shares, ii) buy-back of shares (generally limited to 10 per cent) and iii) sale of key assets and other major transactions.[46] Moreover, the 'duty of neutrality' does not apply to acts that would also have been performed in the ordinary course of performance, such as looking out for a competing offer and acts approved by the supervisory board of the target company.[47]

Whether and to what extent the German Act constrains management remains unclear. On the one hand, the range of actions that target management may undertake on its own is quite limited and the use of defense mechanisms that require shareholder ratification must be approved by 75 per cent of voting shares, which in fact is a considerable impediment to overcome. In addition, actions that directly alter the

---

[45] See Kahan and Rock (2003).
[46] See §§ 71, 186 *Aktiengesetz* (Stock Corporation Act).
[47] See § 33 *Wertpapiererwerbs- und Übernahmegesetz* (Securities Acquisition and Takeover Act), translated in Stohlmeier (2002).

shareholder structure may be subject to shareholder approval.[48] Moreover, the target's management and supervisory boards must not breach their fiduciary duty to loyalty and care.

On the other hand, there is no apparent agreement in the literature regarding the scope of shareholder authorization requirements.[49] In addition, it is argued that supervisory board approval can be used to override shareholder decisions (Seivt and Heiser 2002). Moreover, the managerial fiduciary duties are defined with respect to the interests of shareholders, employees and the interests of society as a whole, which leaves room for considerable discretion (Hirte 2002: 643).[50]

The German situation shows why it might be preferable for reasons of transparency to have a single, simple EU rule on board neutrality. To the extent it does not affect the allocation of decision-making power in the general course of the company's business, the strict board neutrality rule currently proposed by the EU is justified. However, the provisions under Article 12 that allow Member States to opt out of the rule will make a few companies vulnerable to takeovers as few jurisdictions have incentives to implement the board neutrality rule.

C. The Mandatory Bid Rule

Article 5 of the draft Takeover Bids Directive is designed to trigger a full mandatory bid when the bidder acquires a percentage of voting rights that confers on him the control of the target. Member States should determine both the percentage of voting rights conferring control and the method of its calculation.[51] Member States should also adopt rules on information.[52]

Perhaps the best rationale in favor of the mandatory bid rule is that it provides an exit mechanism for shareholders who do not tender in connection with a takeover bid. It also decreases market uncertainty, which enables the bidder and shareholders to capitalize on the cost of the bid and on the cost of exit respectively. On the other hand, if the bidder must obtain control from a blockholder, the mandatory bid rule is likely to prevent the incumbent blockholder from getting compensation for the loss of enjoyment of the private benefits of control. The implication, of course, is that a mandatory bid rule should avoid value-decreasing

---

[48] See the *Holzmüller* doctrine, *Entscheidungen des Bundesgerichtshofes in Zivilsachen* BGHZ 83 (1982), 122.
[49] See Krause (2002); Schneider (2002).
[50] Hirte quoting the justification for the law given by the German government.
[51] See Art. 5(1), 5(3) Takeover Directive.
[52] See Art. 6(3) Takeover Directive.

takeovers but may preclude some value-increasing takeovers—for example, when private benefits are necessary for the controlling shareholder to engage into monitoring management in the interest of all shareholders.

The notion of the 'equitable exit price' is the key in the proposed mandatory bid context. The Takeover Directive adopts the highest-price rule recommended by its experts (whereas Member States can grant exemptions under certain circumstances). Minority shareholders must be offered the highest price paid for the shares of the relevant class in a period between six to twelve months prior to the bid in market and over-the-counter transactions.[53]

In this context, imposing a mandatory bid rule at the EU level but leaving the definition of the trigger threshold to Member States is a sensible approach: some protection of minority shareholders is guaranteed, while room remains for differences among Member States. On the other hand, mandating the highest price as the 'equitable exit price' prevents regulatory competition to minimize the costs in terms of precluded value-enhancing takeovers. Arguably, regulatory competition may not be strong if national equitable price rules are complicated, but there are better ways than mandating the highest-price rule to take care of this issue.

There could have been better ways to achieve a similar result, such as for the EU to adopt an 'equitable exit price' rule that equates a prescribed percentage discount on previous block trades. Another, possibly cumulative, option would have been to prescribe offering the stock market price in a specified period prior to the bid. For example, the voluntary German Takeover Code in place before 2002 specified the highest stock market price in the three months prior to the bid as the 'equitable exit price'. In other words, the stock market price rule is seen as guaranteeing all shareholders the stand-alone value of the firm.

D. The Breakthrough Rule

The High Level Group of Experts appointed by the European Commission proposed a novel idea called the breakthrough rule. The rule was designed to eliminate a wide variety of pre-bid defenses that are viewed as significant impediments to the emergence of a well-functioning cross-border takeover market.

The major breakthrough rule endorsed the view that a bidder should

---

[53] See Recommendation II.2 of the High Level Group Report, above, n. 48; Art. 5(5) Draft Takeover Bids Directive. Compare Art. 32(4) Swiss Stock Exchange Law (the exit price cannot be less than 75% of the highest price paid by the bidder in the past 12 months).

be permitted, upon the acquisition of 75 per cent of cash flow rights (or any relevant threshold not higher than 75 per cent set forth by the Member States), to convene a general meeting of shareholders at short notice and impose one-share one-vote. Thus, any mechanisms or structures that deviate from the principles of shareholder decision-making and proportionality between risk-bearing and control will be 'broken through'.

So, for example, upon reaching the required threshold, the bidder will be permitted to: (1) amend the articles of association and other constitutional documents; (2) remove any pre-bid takeover defenses approved by shareholders; (3) remove voting caps and differential voting rights; (4) remove provisions denying voting rights; (5) remove voting rights on non-risk-bearing capital; (6) appoint, suspend, and dismiss the board members other than those appointed by third parties; (7) determine the composition of the board; (8) remove any staggered and/or fixed period provisions; and (9) override special control rights attached to golden shares.

The defensive device that is receiving most attention in the political debate is the multiple voting right share structure. For this reason, the breakthrough rule will be analyzed in the light of such a structure.

The designers of the breakthrough rule understood clearly that no single form of corporate charter is optimal. In the context of takeovers, however, it was assumed that one type of corporate charter arrangement is preferred, namely a one-share-one-vote structure. In this regard, increasing takeover incidence has become a goal in itself that will eventually determine the contents of a firm's corporate charter (Berglöf and Burkhart 2002). Proponents of the breakthrough rule argued that a dual class stock regime lowers the probability of a takeover and reduces, in turn, the incentives of managers to undertake value-maximizing projects for the benefit of the firm's residual investors. In contrast, supporters of dual class stock argue that dual class shares produce a number of desirable effects including: (1) protection against shareholder opportunism and misjudgments due to lack of information; (2) protection against predatory bid tactics; (3) reduction of agency problems; and (4) compensation for greater firm specific risk. A rigorous analytical framework of (non)optimality conditions of the one-share–one-vote rule in takeover context was introduced by pioneering works of Grossman and Hart (1988), and Harris and Raviv (1988). Though the proposed settings differ in some respects, the authors' general conclusion is that distribution of voting rights affects the value of the firm and, under qualifying conditions (almost always), the one-share–one-vote rule is not value maximizing.

The consequences of dual class shares are well documented in the United States (Coates 2001). A number of empirical studies point out that anti-takeover provisions merely influence the takeover probability and the premium of the target firm (Hannes 2002). Most empirical studies, moreover, have found that takeover defenses have little or no impact on bid outcomes (Brickley, Coles, and Terry 1994). This is consistent with practicing lawyers' positions about takeover defenses not doing much harm and mattering only at the margins.[54]

Finally, even if one would look at the whole picture, not merely takeover events, various studies show that the company value consequences of dual class structures is ambiguous (Grullon, Kanatas, and Weston 2005; Morck, Shleifer, and Vishny 1998).

Unlike in the United States, there are few empirical studies in Europe that analyze the wealth effects of pre-bid defenses by shareholders. A recent study investigates the performance of Danish firms that adopted dual class shares for the period between 1995 and 1999 (Rose 2002). It shows that unprotected firms do not outperform firms protected by dual class stock. One offered explanation: other corporate governance mechanisms, including blockholder monitoring, appear to limit managerial opportunism.

Based on the above, the efficiency implications of dual class stock, and thus of break through rules, are inconclusive. More importantly, many scholars, such as Berglöf and Burkart (2002), argued convincingly that the breakthrough rule is inconsistent with the mandatory bid rule.

The main effect of the breakthrough rule would be to transform a bid for a company with a concentrated ownership structure into a dispersed bid. If the incumbent controlling shareholders have access to sufficient funds to launch a counter bid, the bidder will in turn be forced to bid at least as much as the incumbent shareholder. The maximum bid of the incumbent shareholder will include the sum total of his private benefits and the stock market valuation of the target firm. But, if the incumbent is financially constrained, the bidder will not offer more than the public value of the target firm after the completion of the takeover.

As a result, the bidder's dominant strategy will be to use the breakthrough rule as a means of acquiring control, even if the incumbent management is in principle willing to enter into negotiations. In legal terms, the breakthrough rule leads to the acquisition of control not by passing a threshold on voting share holdings but by effecting a change in a corporate charter. It is, however, unclear whether such a control transfer would trigger a mandatory bid. If a mandatory bid is not triggered, the problems associated with two-tier takeover bids would be reintroduced.

At the same time, under the assumption that an incumbent shareholder is not willing to tender, the breakthrough rule does not open

---

[54] See Bebchuk, Coates, and Subramian (2002) (analyzing empirical evidence on effect of takeover defenses).

up the possibility of effecting a squeeze out to the new controlling shareholder. Another important implication of the breakthrough rule is that it could alter ownership structures and concentration of voting rights. For example, some predict that breakthrough rule might induce firms—particularly new firms—to substitute a dual-class structure with a pyramiding structure.[55] Such a step may in turn give rise, among other things, to problems related to monitoring, managerial incentives, and liquidity.

As a consequence of these arguments and concerns that imposing specific breakthrough rules would not only result in inconsistency and uncertainty, but have little positive effect on the creation of a competitive market for corporate control, the EU adopted a compromise that makes the breakthrough rule optional.

E. Reevaluating the Level Playing Field Concept

Supporters of the on-going reforms point out that, even if EU reforms do not contribute to the emergence of a competitive regulatory environment, harmonization is, nevertheless, necessary to assure a level playing field.

For example, it has been argued that EU takeover law should not permit a French company to acquire a German company if the differences between French and German law gives a French bidder a systematic advantage. Correspondingly, the EU experts have argued that the breakthrough rule and board neutrality are necessary to create a level playing field for takeover bids. Similarly, some members of the European Parliament endorsed a reciprocity claim also made by the EU experts, according to which Member States should be permitted to block bids from a third country to prevent distortion in competition due to differences in legal rules—especially between US and EU firms, which was incorporated in Article 12 of the Takeover Directive.

Nevertheless, it is far from clear that reciprocity is ultimately the basis upon which the European Union has to make its policy choices. Interestingly, supporters of the level playing field have made little attempt to justify their policy reform efforts on economic grounds.[56] Our analysis questions whether it can be taken for granted that the differences in national regulatory policies should be regarded as the basis for a reciprocity process. To the extent that jurisdictions have divergent regulatory policies, the sources of the differences may be due to a range of

---

[55] But *cf.* Gordon (2003) (arguing that pyramids are not a low-cost substitute for firms going public).

[56] See Gilson (1992: 192, n. 95) (arguing that 'in the absence of an economic justification for hostile takeovers, the reciprocity claim seems much more of a political justification for harmonization').

factors (i.e., preferences, endowments, technologies, etc.). Substantive legal differences alone may not reflect significant economic differences in the competitive advantage between states. In sum, because there is little empirical evidence that differing national preferences and regulatory policies have any effect on trade patterns, we argue that legislators should not be distracted by arguments based on equal treatment.

F. Opt-Outs and an Opting-In Menu

As noted above, the uncertainty about the passage of the Takeover Bids Directive led the Member States to agree to the compromise proposed by the Italian Presidency in November 2003. Stimulated by the Portuguese delegation, and later taken up by the Italian Presidency, the compromise included a menu of simple provisions allowing companies the choice of applying the rules on defensive measures.

The compromise was designed to enable companies to choose the takeover regime they prefer. Two broad policy issues derive from such approach: (1) which provisions should be mandatory and which should be enabling; and (2) which rules should govern takeover contests of firms with different corporate charters.

In our view, the balance struck by the compromise makes sense as takeover rules should be unbundled. Board neutrality and mandatory bid rules are a different matter than selecting voting arrangements, mandatory bid thresholds or exit prices for minority shareholders. On the one hand, the board neutrality and mandatory bid rules should be allowed to vary across the EU. On the other hand, we believe that the Directive should have included a menu of simple and transparent opt-in provisions—the incorporation regime remaining applicable otherwise.

Taking this point further, the second step would have been to design a set of opt-in provisions regarding share classes, mandatory bid thresholds and exit prices for minority shareholders. For instance, the Directive might have offered opt-in provisions for three types of shares, each having different voting and dividend rights. What matters, of course, is simplicity and transparency. If one or more of the X, Y, Z share classes were to be adopted, the incorporation regime would not remain applicable and the opt-in as well as its consequences should be made transparent for investors.

Similarly, the Directive could have provided a menu of opt-in provisions regarding mandatory bid threshold (e.g. 33 per cent or 50 per cent) and exit prices for minority shareholders (e.g. average stock market price in the six month preceding the bid or highest stock market price in the three months preceding the bid). Here again, the incorporation regime would remain not remain applicable and the opt-in as well as its consequences should be made transparent for investors

In our view, the third step would have been to decide whether decisions to opt in should be left with management or shareholders—and if it is shareholders, what share class would be admitted to vote. We would recommend leaving the opt-in decision with shareholders, with participation of all holders of voting rights.

The fourth and final step on this logic would have to do with the applicable law for takeover contests between firms with different regimes. It is submitted that companies that have opted for EU rules are bound to them whether they become a bidder or a target. The opt-in approach offered here presumes shareholder choice and stock market pricing of a variety of corporate governance arrangements. It follows that lawmakers should drop the demand for reciprocity in the sense that the same rules must apply for every party in a takeover contest.

Since an EU menu would coexist with national codes, it could be expected that stock markets would react to firms' decision the opt-in, which could result in regulatory competition and the introduction of lower cost forms of regulation at the Member State level. Conversely, if such a menu failed to satisfy market demand, firms may still stick with their incorporation regime or opt out of the EU regime back into Member State law.

IV. CONCLUSION

In this chapter, we have sought to assess the prospects for competitive lawmaking in the EU. Under the present conditions, we have shown that a competitive environment for regulatory arbitrage and regulatory competition is beginning to develop. In reviewing the recent history of EU company law reform, we argued, moreover, that the introduction of further harmonization of disclosure regulation is unlikely to create significant advantages for investors.

We also put forward the claim that proposed board and liability reforms will be ineffective and that institutional and enforcement proposals will increase state intervention rather than facilitate cross-border activity. Instead, we propose to reduce barriers to enforcement by adopting four market-oriented measures: granting standing to sue to all shareholders, requiring the setting-up of specialized courts, stating the legality of contingent fees and facilitating cross-border litigation—for example, by making it easier for attorneys to represent multiple clients, by facilitating discovery or by eliminating remaining obstacles to intra-EU recognition of judgments.

We assessed, furthermore, the recent efforts to create a takeover regime. We have shown that a minimized harmonized regime would enhance transparency and shareholder protection. First, we argued that the board neutrality rule should apply to takeover bid situations, not least because of shareholding structures tending to become less concentrated in continental Europe. Secondly, we suggested that the mandatory bid rule is a sound device to prevent expropriation from shareholders. It also limits the two-tier bid, which reduces the pressure to tender problem.

We have also demonstrated that there are good reasons to reject the breakthrough rule and the level playing field approach. In particular, there is no question that the break through rule violates the principle of shareholder decision-making upon which the board neutrality rule is based and therefore the compromise allowing firms to opt out makes sense.

Finally, in contrast to the approach taken by the EU's Takeover Directive, we suggest that a default approach would have been more efficient in that it allows firms to select legal arrangements that meet their needs. We argue that the default approach gives Member States incentives to adopt the proposed Takeover Bids Directive. Furthermore, we show that offering firms the choice to opt out of the EU takeover regime and opt in to state law could lead to some competition between suppliers of rules and encourage innovation in corporate law. This promising alternative, we argue, would have led to the selection of better takeover law rules and contributed better to the development of an active cross-border takeover market in the EU.

REFERENCES

Arlen, J. and Talley, E. (2003), 'Unregulable Defenses and the Perils of Shareholder Choice', 152 *University of Pennsylvania Law Review* 577.

Bachmann, G. (2001), 'Grundtendenzen der Reform geschlossener Gesellschaften in Europa, Dargestellt am Beispiel des britischen Reformprozesses und der Europäischen Privatgesellschaft', 30 *Zeitschrift Für Unternehmens—Und Gesellschaftsrecht* 351.

Barca, F. and Becht, M. (eds) (2002), *The Control of Corporate Europe* (Oxford: Oxford University Press).

Baums, T. (2003), 'Company Law Reform in Germany', 3 *Journal of Corporate Law Studies* 181.

Bebchuk, L.A. (1985), 'Toward Undistorted Choice and Equal Treatment in Takeovers', 98 *Harvard Law Review* 1695.

—— (1994), 'Efficient and Inefficient Sales of Corporate Control', 109 *Quarterly Journal of Economics* 957.

—— (2003), 'The Case for Empowering Shareholders' (Working Paper).

Bebchuk, L.A. and Cohen, A. (2003), 'Firms' Decision Where to Incorporate', 46 *Journal of Law and Economics* 383.

Bebchuk, L.A. and Ferrell, A. (2001), 'Federal Intervention to Enhance Shareholder Choice', 87 *Virginia Law Review* 111.

Bebchuk, L.A. and Hamdani, A. (2002), 'Vigorous Race or Leisurely Walk: Reconsidering the Competition over Corporate Charters', 112 *Yale Law Journal* 553.

Bebchuk, L., Coates, J.C. and Subramian, G. (2002), 'The Powerful Antitakeover Force of Staggered Boards: Theory, Evidence, and Policy', 54 *Stanford Law Review* 887.

Bebchuk, L.A., Cohen, A. and Ferrell, A. (2002), 'Does the Evidence Favor State Competition in Corporate Law?', 90 *California Law Review* 1775.

Behrens, P. (2002), *Centros* and the Proper Law of Companies, in Ferrarini, G., Hopt, K.J., and Wymeersch (eds) *Capital Markets in the Age of The Euro* (The Hague: Kluwer Law International).

Berglöf, E. (1997), 'Reforming Corporate Governance: Redirecting the European Agenda', in *European Economy: A European Forum.*

Berglöf, E. and Burkart, M. (2003), 'European Takeover Regulation, 36 *Economic Policy* 171.

Berkowitz, D., Pistor, K. and Richard, J.-F. (2003), 'The Transplant Effect', 51 *American Journal of Comparative Law* 163.

Black, B.S. (1990), 'Is Corporate Law Trivial?—A Political and Economic Analysis', 84 *Northwestern University Law Review* 542.

Black, B.S., Kraakman, R. and Tarassova, A. (2000), 'Russian Privatization and Corporate Governance: What Went Wrong?', 52 *Stanford Law Review* 1731.

Bratton, W.W. and McCahery, J.A. (1999), 'Comparative Corporate Governance and the Theory of the Firm: The Case Against Global Cross-Reference', 38 *Columbia Journal of Transnational Law* 213.

Brickley, J.A., Coles, J.L. and Terry, R. L. (1994), 'Outside Directors and the Adoption of Poison Pills', 35 *Journal of Financial Economics* 371.

Burkart, M., Gromb, D. and Panunzi, F. (1998), 'Why Higher Takeover Premia Protect Minority Shareholders', 106 *Journal of Political Economy* 172.

Cheffins, B. (1997), *Company Law: Theory, Structure and Operation* (Oxford: Oxford University Press).

Coates, J.C. (2001), 'Explaining Variations in Takeover Defenses: Blame the Lawyers', 89 *California Law Review* 1301.

Coffee, J.C. (1999), 'The Future as History: The Prospects for Global Convergence in Corporate Governance and Its Implications', 93 *Northwestern University Law Review* 641.

—— (2001), 'The Acquiescent Gatekeeper: Reputational Intermediaries, Auditor Independence and the Governance of Accounting' (Columbia Law and Economics Working Paper) available at http://papers.ssrn.com/sol3/papers.cfm?abstract_id=270944 (last visited 15 January 2005).

Conac, P-H. (2002), *La Regulation Des Marches Boursiers Par La Cob Et La Sec.*

Daines, R. (2001), 'Does Delaware Law Improve Firm Value?', 62 *Journal of Financial Economics* 525.

Deakin, S. (2001), 'Regulatory Competition versus Harmonization in European Company Law' in Esty, D. and Geradin, D. (eds), in *Regulatory Competition and Economic Integration* (Oxford: Oxford University Press).

Ebke, W.F. (2000), '*Centros*—Some Realities and Some Mysteries', 48 *American Journal of Comparative Law* 623.

Enriques, L. (2003), 'Silence is Golden: The European Company Statute as a catalyst for Company Law Arbitrage' (ECGI Law Working Paper) available at http://papers.ssrn.com/sol3/papers.cfm?abstract_id=384801 (last visited 15 January 2005).

Enriques, L. and Macey, J. (2001), 'Creditors Versus Capital Formation: The Case Against the European Legal Capital Rules', 86 *Cornell Law Review* 1165.

Federal Supreme Court (1982), Entscheidungen des Bundesgerichtshofes in Zivilsachen BGHZ 83, 122 (25 February).

Gilson, R.J. (1992), 'The Political Economy of Takeovers: Thoughts on Harmonizing the European Corporate Governance Environment', 61 *Fordham Law Review* 161.

—— (2001), 'Globalizing Corporate Governance: Convergence of Form or Function', 49 *American Journal of Comparative Law* 329.

Gordon, J.N. (1998), 'Deutsche Telekom, German Corporate Governance, and the Transition Costs of Capitalism', 1998 *Columbia Business Law Review* 185.

—— (2003), 'An International Relations Perspective on the Convergence of Corporate Governance: German Shareholder Capitalism and the European Union, 1990–2000', in Gordon, J.N. and Roe, M.J. (eds), *Convergence and Persistence in Corporate Governance* (Cambridge: Cambridge University Press).

Grossman, S.J. and Hart, O. (1980), 'Takeover Bids, the Free-Rider Problem, and the Theory of the Corporation', 11 *Bell Journal of Economics* 42.

—— (1988) , 'One Share-One Vote and the Market for Corporate Control', 20 *Journal of Financial Economics* 175.

Grullon, G., Karatas, G., and Weston, J. (2005), 'Managerial Incentives and Capital Structure', (Working Paper, Rice University, Graduate School of Management).

Grundmann, S. (2002), 'Regulatory Competition in European Company Law—Some Different Genius?' in Ferrarini *et al.* (eds) *Capital Markets in the Age of The Euro* (The Hague: Kluwer Law International).

Halbhuber, H. (2001), 'National Doctrinal Structures and European Company Law', 38 *Common Market Law Review* 1385.

Hannes, S. (2002), 'The Hidden Virtues of Antitakeover Defenses' (Harvard Law & Economics Discussion Paper No. 354), available at http://www.ssrn.com/abstract=304389 (last visited 2 August 2005).

Hansmann, H. and Kraakman, R. (2004a), 'Agency Problems and Legal Strategies, in Kraakman, R. *et al.* (eds), *The Anatomy of Corporate Law* (Oxford: Oxford University Press).

Hansmann, H. and Kraakman, R. (2004b), 'The Basic Governance Structure', in Kraakman, R. *et al.* (eds), *The Anatomy of Corporate Law* (Oxford: Oxford University Press).

Harris, M. and Raviv, A. (1988), 'Corporate Governance: Voting Rights and Majority Rules', 20 *Journal of Financial Economics* 203.

Heine, K. and Heiner, W. (2000), 'European Corporate Laws, Regulatory

Competition and Path Dependence', 13 *European Journal of Law and Economics* 257.

Hertig, G. (2001), 'Regulatory Competition for EU Financial Services', in Esty, D. and Geradin, D. (eds) *European Company Law, in Regulatory Competition And Economic Integration* (Oxford: Oxford University Press).

Hertig, G. and Kanda, H. (2004), 'Creditor Protection', in Kraakman, R. *et al.* (eds), *The Anatomy of Corporate Law* (Oxford: Oxford University Press).

Hertig, G. and Lee, R. (2003), 'Four Predictions about the Future of EU Securities Regulation', 3 *Journal of Corporate Law Studies* 359.

Hirte, H. (2002), 'Verteidigung gegen Übernahmeangebote und Rechtsschutz des Aktionärs gegen die Verteidigung', 31 *Zeitschrift Für Unternehmens—Und Gesellschaftsrecht* 623.

Hopt, K.J. (2001), 'Common Principles of Corporate Governance in Europe', in McCahery, J.A. *et al.* (eds) *Convergence And Diversity In Corporate Governance Regimes And Capital Markets* (Oxford: Oxford University Press).

Inman, R.B. and Rubinfeld, D.L. (1997), 'Rethinking Federalism', 11 *Journal of Economic Perspectives* 43.

Kahan, M. and Kamar, E. (2002), 'The Myth of State Competition in Corporate Law', 55 *Stanford Law Review* 679.

Kahan, M. and Rock, E. (2003), 'Corporate Constitutionalism: Antitakeover Charter Provisions as Pre-Commitment', 152 *University of Pennsylvania Law Review* 473.

Kihlstrom, R.E. and Wachter, M.L. (2003), 'Managing Market Anomalies versus Maximizing Corporate Value', 152 *University of Pennsylvania Law Review* 523.

Krause, H. (2002), 'Die Abwehr feindlicher Übernahmeangebote auf der Grundlage von Ermächtigungsbeschlüssen der Hauptversammlung', 57 *Betriebs-Berater* 1053.

La Porta, R. *et al.* (1997), 'Legal Determinants of External Finance'. 52 *Journal of Finance* 1131.

La Porta, R., Lopez-de-Silanes, F. and Shleifer, A. (1999), 'Corporate Ownership around the World', 54 *Journal of Finance* 471.

McCahery, J.A., and Vermeulen, E.P.M. (2001), 'The Evolution of Closely Held Business Forms in Europe', 26 *Journal of Corporation Law* 855.

Morck, R., Shleifer, A. and Vishny, R. (1988), 'Managerial Ownership and Market Valuation: An Empirical Analysis', 29 *Journal of Financial Economics* 293.

Mueller, D.C. and Yurtoglu, B.B. (2000), 'Country Legal Environments and Corporate Investment Performance', 1 *German Economic Review* 187.

Mühlbert, P.O. and Birke, M. (2002), 'Legal Capital: Is there a Case Against the European Legal Capital Rules?', 3 *European Business Organization Law Review* 695.

Roe, M.J. (2001), 'Rents and their Corporate Law Consequences 53 *Stanford Law Review* 1463.

Romano, R. (1985), 'The State Competition Debate in Corporate Law', 1 *Journal of Law, Economics and Organization* 225.

—— (1991), *The Genius of American Corporate Law* (Washington, D.C.: American Enterprise Institute Press).

—— (2001), 'The Need for Competition in International Securities Regulation', 2 *Theoretical Inquiries In Law* 1.

Rose, C. (2002), 'Corporate Financial Performance and the Use of Takeover Defenses', 13 *European Journal of Law and Economics* 91.

Schneider, U.H. (2002), 'Die Zielgesellschaft nach Abgabe eines Übernahme—oder Pflichtangebots', 47 *Aktiengesellschaft* 125.

Seivt, C.H. and Heiser, K.J. (2002), 'Die neue Vorschlag einer EU-Übernahmerichtlinie und das deutsche Übernahmerecht', 2002 *Zeitschrift für Wirtschaftsrecht* 2193.

Shleifer, A. (2000), 'Comments on Hellwig, On the Economics and Politics of Corporate Finance and Corporate Control', in Vives, X (ed.) *Corporate Governance, Theoretical And Empirical Perspectives* (Cambridge: Cambridge University Press).

Shleifer, A. and Vishny, R.W. (1986), 'Large Shareholders and Corporate Control', 94 *Journal of Political Economy* 461.

Stohlmeier, T. (2002), *German Public Takeover Law* (New York: Aspen Publishing).

Tjiong, H. (2002), 'Breaking the Spell of Regulatory Competition: Reframing the Problem of Regulatory Exit', 66 *Rabelsz* 66.

Wachter, M.L. (2003), 'Takeover Defenses when Financial Markets are (only) Relatively Efficient', 151 *University of Pennsylvania Law Review* 787.

Weingast, B. (1995), 'The Economic Role of Political Institutions: Market Preserving Federalism and Economic Development', 1 *Journal of Law, Economics and Organization* 1.

Woolcock, S. (1996), 'Competition among Rules in the Single European Market', in Bratton, W.W. *et al.* (eds) *International Regulatory Competition and Coordination* (Oxford: Oxford University Press).

Wouters, J. (2000), 'European Company Law: *Quo Vadis?*', 37 *Common Market Law Review* 257.

Wymeersch, E. (1998), 'A Status Report on Corporate Governance Rules and Practices in Some Continental European States', in Hopt, K.J. *et al.* (eds) *Comparative Corporate Governance: The State of the Art and Emerging Research* (Oxford: Oxford University Press).

Yarrow, G. (1985), 'Shareholder Protection, Compulsory Acquisition, and the Takeover Process', 34 *Journal of Industrial Economics* 3.

16

The Regulatory Process for Securities Law-Making in the EU

EILÍS FERRAN[*]

I. INTRODUCTION

THIS CHAPTER IS concerned with the making of EU regulation for the single securities market. Since our understanding of the ways in which laws may foster the development of strong securities markets is still in its infancy, it is not possible to claim that the bureaucrats and politicians involved in the regulatory process are on a sure path that has been legitimized by scientific proof as being exactly what needs to be done by way of refinements to the legal system in order to promote the development of a securities market.[1]

The lack of definitive guidance on how law matters to the development of securities markets suggests that there could be dangerous uncertainty in the regulatory process, involving strong risks of counter-productive policy decisions about the necessary rules, potential for exploitation by agenda-controlling bureaucrats intent on empire-building or by powerful interest groups that have influence over them, and vulnerability to political distortions. The quality of the regulatory process influences how much weight we should attach to these concerns. If there are effective safeguards built into the process that minimize the chances of policy mistakes and curb opportunities for bureaucratic excess or political or private distortions, the fact that we do not have a clear starting point, in the form of a comprehensive blueprint of all the laws that are conducive to securities market growth, becomes a much less troubling concern than it might be otherwise.

---

[*] Faculty of Law, Cambridge University. This chapter was previously published as Chapter 3 of E. Ferran, *Building An EU Securities Market* (Cambridge University Press, 2004). The permission of Cambridge University Press to republish is gratefully acknowledged.
[1] See Ferran (2004: ch 2).

Formulating policy in the EU is a complex and multi-faceted undertaking. These complexities, combined with wide variations in policy processes across the vast range of EU activity, make it hard to reduce policy-making down to a few key features (Wallace 2000a). What is sometimes said of EU policy-making is what it is not: the product of a rational model of decision-making (Nugent 1999: 385). Although the discussion here is selective, focusing on securities law, the regulatory process in this field is vulnerable to the difficulties that beset EU policy-making in general. These general concerns include[2]:

— difficulties in securing agreement because of the large number and diverse interests of the participating parties;
— persistent path-dependent differences between countries that can impede efforts at coordination;
— tactical manoeuvring between the parties that can slow up the processes and erode the clarity and coherence that may have existed in initiatives when they were first proposed;
— political compromises that can result in 'package deals' whereby seemingly unconnected matters become linked to each other as Member States trade off their competing interests;
— the division of policy-making responsibilities between the internal institutions (in particular as between the European Commission, European Parliament and Council of the European Union) that can lead to disagreements and conflicts; and
— the openness of the processes to lobbyists that can result in regulation tainted by self-interest.

Yet somehow (some have suggested 'muddling through' as a good description) (Richardson 2001a), EU policy-making has managed to transcend these difficulties and has evolved sophisticated policy capabilities that are beyond those of other transnational organizations (Wallace 2000b). The EU has provided a forum for consensus-building out of which have come remarkable regulatory achievements, particularly in the development of a single market. For example, the 1992 internal market program contained some 300 legislative proposals to remove barriers and open up European markets (Thatcher 2001). Rather than being harmful, the involvement of many public and private actors, including significant support from big business, in the development of the single market program has often helped to define appropriate policy responses and to take them forward (Young and Wallace 2000).

[2] On EU policy-making generally, see Wallace and Wallace (2000); Nugent (2001).

The technical mechanisms by which policy decisions are converted into law are also complex (Dashwood 2001: 232),[3] involving complicated voting requirements and what has been described as a 'maze of intricate legislative procedures' (de Búrca 1999). Law-making in the EU involves elements of diplomacy (Harlow 2002: 31–32), and the behind-the-scenes political bargaining between Member States that this inevitably entails results in some lack of transparency in the legislative processes.

This chapter examines the strengths and weaknesses of the EU regulatory process relating to securities laws and assesses the likely effectiveness of efforts that have been made to insulate the process from some of the difficulties that can arise. Part II outlines the emergence of the new process (which is generally known as the 'Lamfalussy process') and identifies its key features. Part III evaluates elements of the Lamfalussy process and the interaction of the various bodies and groups that are involved in it. Part IV notes that the improvements that can be gained through the Lamfalussy process are subject to a powerful limitation because that process is not designed to override national protectionism or other deep-rooted influences that may lead Member States to oppose proposed new EU laws. Part V considers the more radical option than that represented by the Lamfalussy process: namely, the establishment of an EU-wide securities regulatory agency which has rule-making and supervisory powers. It suggests that the adoption of the regulatory agency model could create more problems than it solves and that it would be a premature step given securities market conditions across the EU. Section F draws the conclusion that, though not perfect, the Lamfalussy process is a step in the right direction. For the immediate future, the course of action that commends itself therefore is to concentrate on refining and upgrading the Lamfalussy process so as to enable it to work more efficiently and effectively rather than to pursue more radical and risky alternatives.

II. RECENT REFINEMENT OF THE REGULATORY PROCESS—THE LAMFALUSSY MODEL

A. The Path towards Reform of the Regulatory Process

In July 2000 the Council (in its Economic and Finance ministers formation) appointed a Committee of 'Wise Men' under the chairmanship of

---

[3] Dashwood (2001: 232): 'A high price is paid, in the coin of democratic accountability, for the increasing complexity of a process of making EU law that is unintelligible except to Brussels professionals.'

Baron Alexandre Lamfalussy to conduct a broad examination of the mechanisms for regulating and supervising EU securities markets.[4] The Lamfalussy Committee published an initial report in November 2000 and a final report in February 2001 (Lamfalussy Committee 2000, 2001).[5]

The Lamfalussy Committee's Reports were very critical of the established regulatory process, finding it to be too slow, too rigid, complex and ill-adapted to the pace of global financial market change. The Committee suggested a new approach involving a four level structure: Level 1 (in essence primary legislation decided upon by the Council and Parliament in accordance with established law-making procedures); Level 2 (implementing measures, or more detailed rules, decided upon by the Commission acting in accordance with EU comitology procedures that had been developed in other fields but not previously used in securities law-making); Level 3 (a drive towards consistent implementation and transposition of legislation at Member State level); and Level 4 (greater emphasis on monitoring and enforcement). An overview of the Lamfalussy process follows as Table 16.1. Detailed aspects of the structure outlined in this table are considered throughout this chapter. The Lamfalussy Committee's view of the inadequacies of the existing regulatory process and its suggestions for change were speedily endorsed at the highest political levels, by the Council[6] and the Heads of EU States or Governments at their Summit Meeting in Stockholm in March 2001 (Stockholm European Council 2001). Then, with equal rapidity, the European Commission moved in June 2001 to give effect to the new approach recommended by the Lamfalussy Committee.[7]

Is there an explanation for such speed, remarkable because the EU is not usually noted for its swift reactions in institutional reform? In simple terms, the likely answer is that the Committee, under the chairmanship of 'a veteran of Brussels bureaucracy',[8] had done its homework well and was therefore able to make proposals that were

---

[4] The establishment of this Committee to look at radical options for the development of the single securities market was the brainchild of Laurent Fabius, the French finance minister: See *Economist* (2001a).

[5] The final report (Lamfalussy Committee 2001) is referred to in this chapter as the *Lamfalussy Report* and the earlier one (Lamfalussy Committee 2000) is referred to as the *Lamfalussy Initial Report*.

[6] See Council of Economics and Finance Ministers (2001) and Stockholm European Council (2001).

[7] Commission Dec (2001/528/EC) establishing the European Securities Committee [2001] OJ L191/45 (ESC Decision) and Commission Dec (2001/527/EC) Establishing the Committee of European Securities Regulators [2001] OJ L191/43 (CESR Decision).

[8] Baron Lamfalussy was the one-time general manager of the Bank for International Settlements, and president of the European Monetary Institute, the forerunner of the European Central Bank: See *Economist* (2002a).

Table 16.1: Level 1: framework principles

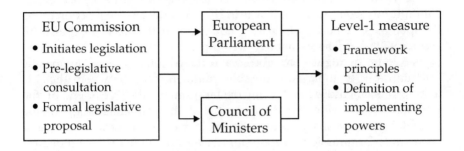

- Level-1 measures designed as framework legal acts
- Adopted by conventional co-decision procedure
- Fasttrack: institutions are encouraged to work towards adoption of level-1 measure after first reading in EP
- Level-1 measure contains definition of Commision's powers in enacting level-2 measures
- After adoption by EP and Council, level-1 measures have to be transposed into national law by EU member states and applied in regulatory and supervisory practice

informed by a good understanding of what would be politically feasible. Key groundwork to ensure a favorable political reception by Member States for proposals designed to speed up the legislative process for a single financial market had been done at the highly-ambitious 'dotcom' Lisbon Summit Meeting in June 2000 (Gillingham 2003: 328–29): in Lisbon, European leaders had set themselves the target of becoming the most competitive and dynamic knowledge-based economy in the world by 2010, with improvement of existing processes identified as being key to implementation of this strategic goal (Lisbon European Council 2000). The European Heads called specifically for steps to ensure adoption by 2005 of the legislative measures set out in the European Commission's Financial Services Action Plan (FSAP). For the European Commission, the Lamfalussy Committee's identification of problems with the law-making process was more of an endorsement of its own long-held view than a new insight: there had been calls from the Commission stretching back many years for a more streamlined, flexible and faster legislative approach.[9]

The Member States, Council and Commission's rapid support for the Lamfulussy recommendations was in sharp contrast to the reaction of the European Parliament, which did not endorse the new process until February 2002. [10] The Parliament was concerned about potential dilution of its role in the regulatory process and the resultant loss of democratic safeguards.[11] It took considerable manoeuvring between the EU institutions, including a formal declaration by the President of the Commission assuring the Parliament that the implementation of the Lamfalussy proposals would mean no loss of democratic control and expressing Commission support for Treaty amendments to rationalize general EU comitology procedures so as to reflect properly Parliament's co-legislative role (an issue that goes far beyond securities law),[12] to overcome the considerable inter-institutional tensions.[13] Even then, parliamentary support was guarded and provisional (McKee 2003). In particular it insisted upon the use of 'sunset' clauses whereby any implementing powers afforded to the Commission would come to an end after four years.[14] The establishment of a more permanent settlement in place of this transitional arrangement is bound up with the wider debate on Treaty reform and an EU constitution.

---

[9] See, e.g. European Commission (1998). See further Moloney (2002: 854–56).

[10] European Parliament Resolution on the Implementation of Financial Services Legislation (2001/2247(INI) P5_TA(2002)0035).

[11] The *Lamfalussy Report*, ch II acknowledges the European Parliament's concerns about potential dilution of its role. Moloney (2002: 864–65) elaborates further.

[12] 'Comitology' is the process whereby technical, implementing rules are adopted by the European Commission. It usually requires proposals to be channelled through a comitology committee in accordance with procedures laid down in Council Dec 99/468/EC Laying Down the Procedures for the Exercise of Implementing Powers Conferred by the Commission [1999] OJ L184/23 (Comitology Decision). Article 202 of the EC Treaty provides the Treaty base for the Council to empower the Commission to exercise implementing powers. The Council can impose certain requirements on the exercise of such powers and it can reserve the right to exercise them directly in specific and exceptional cases. The special rights enjoyed by the Council in this respect sit very uneasily with the status of the Council and Parliament as co-legislators because Parliament's rights under comitology procedures are confined to being kept informed and being able to require the Commission to reconsider proposals if Parliament considers them to exceed the scope of implementing powers. Comitology procedures have attracted considerable academic attention because of concerns about lack of transparency and accountability: See Harlow (2002: 67–71); Craig (1999); de Búrca (1999). Parliamentary suspicion of comitology is explored further in Bradley (1997). Generally on the Commission's commitment to reform of comitology: see European Commission (2001a).

[13] The text of this declaration (Prodi Declaration) is available via http://www.europarl. eu.int/comparl/econ/lamfalussy_process/ep_position/prodi_declaration.pdf (last visited 20 August 2005).

[14] European Parliament Resolution above n 10.

B. Co-operation between the Commission, Council and European Parliament in the Lamfalussy Process

The uneasy settlement between the Commission, Council and Parliament on securities law-making under the Lamfalussy process has two main strands. The first relates to ensuring effective co-operation between the three institutions through disclosure and consultation. Stipulations on openness and consultation range from high-level expressions of support for the need to involve all of the institutions throughout the regulatory process from its earliest stages,[15] through to specific statements about procedural matters such as entitlements to attend meetings and internet publication of documentation.[16] As part of the delicate negotiations to secure parliamentary support for the new process, the Commission has given the Parliament a formal promise of transparency in the regulatory process and specific undertakings to allow it time to comment on and examine measures that are subject to comitology procedures.[17] These specific stipulations reinforce general EU arrangements for transparency and dialogue that are intended to facilitate inter-institutional co-operation in the operation of comitology.[18]

C. Formal Allocation of Regulatory Responsibilities as between the Commission, Council and European Parliament under the Lamfalussy Process

The second strand concerns the formal allocation of legislative powers: that is, 'who does what?' On this, the European Commission's position as the initiator of new regulation is formally unchanged. On the actual making of new laws, there is a major change in the distinction that is now drawn between framework principles (Level 1) and implementing measures (Level 2). The significance of the split is that only Level 1 principles go through the full legislative process of co-decision by Council and Parliament.[19] Level 2 measures are adopted by the Commission in accordance with comitology procedures. Decisions about

---

[15] e.g., Stokholm European Council (2001: para 2).

[16] e.g., European Parliament Resolution above n 10 at para 5.

[17] The European Parliament has three months to comment on any proposed implementing measure that is formally submitted to the European Securities Committee and a further month for deliberations after the ESC has given its view.

[18] Considered generally in Joerges and Vos (1999).

[19] There is more than one EU legislative procedure but the text concentrates on the co-decision procedure, in which the Council and European Parliament are co-lawmakers, because most securities laws are made in this way: Moloney (2002: 845–47).

where to draw the line between Level 1 and Level 2 are thus potentially very significant, particularly for the Parliament because it is on a lesser footing to the Council in matters dealt with via comitology. It is for the Commission to make suggestions on where the split should lie but the final decision is for the Council and Parliament 'on a case-by-case basis and in a clear and transparent way' (Stokholm European Council 2001: para 3). Similarly, whilst the Commission must suggest the scope of the Level 2 implementing powers that should be permitted to it, the nature and extent of Level 2 implementing measures are ultimately for the Council and Parliament to determine.[20]

The Market Abuse Directive[21] was the first FSAP measure in which the Lamfalussy law-making process was employed and it can be used to illustrate its operation as regards timing and the way in which the Parliament and Council seek to retain control over the Level 2 process via the drafting of the Level 1 measure. In outline the Level 1 chronology of this Directive was as shown in Table 16.2. [22]

Had the institutions agreed on the text at an earlier stage, the process could have been truncated. The *Lamfalussy Report* supported the idea in principle of 'fast tracking' Level 1 securities legislation, whereby measures would be adopted after a single reading in the European Parliament (Lamfalussy Committee 2001: 21). Initial reactions on this point were somewhat sceptical of the likelihood of widespread use of this facility save for uncontroversial or essentially procedural proposals.[23] These concerns may have been assuaged to some extent by experience with the Transparency Directive where, despite being a substantive measure with various controversial features, it was passed in Spring 2004 with a single reading in the European Parliament.[24] However, the circumstances were a little unusual in this case because the looming enlargement of the EU on 1 May 2004 and forthcoming elections to the

[20] See the ESC Decision and the CESR Decision above n 7.

[21] Dir 2003/6/EC of the European Parliament and of the Council of 28 January 2003 on insider dealing and market manipulation (market abuse) [2003] OJ L96/16.

[22] A more detailed tabular account of the Level 1 process is provided in Inter-Institutional Monitoring Group for Securities Markets (IIMG 2003a: Fig. 3).

[23] Reg (EC) No 1606/2002 of the European Parliament and of the Council of 19 July 2002 on the application of international accounting standards, [2002] OJ L243/1 (agreed after one reading) falls into this category because it established the procedural framework mechanism for the adoption of the standards, leaving the much more controversial issues arising in relation to actual adoption for a later stage. From Commission proposal (February 2001) to adoption (July 2002) this measure took 17 months. Concerns about potentially limited use of the fast track facility are expressed in IIMG (2003a: 26–27).

[24] Dir 2004/109/EC on the harmonization of transparency requirements in relation to information about issuers whose securities are admitted to trading on a regulated market and amending Dir 2001/34/EC, [2004] OJ L390/38.

Table 16.2

May 2001	Commission presents its proposal for a Directive.
14 March 2002	European Parliament completes its First Reading and inserts amendments.
7 May 2002	Council achieves political agreement on Common Position.
19 July 2002	Council formally adopts Common Position.
24 October 2002	European Parliament gives proposal its Second Reading and inserts further amendments.
3 December 2002	Council agrees on the text approved by European Parliament at Second Reading.
28 January 2003	Market Abuse Directive formally adopted by Parliament and Council.
12 April 2003	Directive comes into force on publication in *Official Journal*; Member States given 18 months in which to implement Directive in their national laws.

European Parliament in June 2004 created an environment in which there was particular pressure on all parties to come to agreement quickly.

Another, as yet untested, mechanism for making Level 1 securities laws effective more quickly is to pass them in the form of a Regulation rather than a Directive. Under EU law a Regulation takes effect directly in Member States on the date specified in it whereas a Directive's effectiveness is ordinarily dependent on its transposition into the national laws of Member States and Member States are given a grace period in which to make the necessary changes. The *Lamfalussy Report* called for more use to be made of Regulations, rather than Directives, in order to speed up the legislative process (Lamfalussy Committee 2001: 26). The establishment of the mechanism for the adoption of International Accounting Standards was effected by means of a Regulation but all of the Level 1 FSAP laws proposed or adopted in accordance with the Lamfalussy process have been in the form of Directives. The choice between a Directive or a Regulation has been more of a real issue at Level 2 where both have been used. Although a Regulation, once adopted, can take effect in Member States more quickly than a Directive, a counter-balancing consideration is that the process of adopting a Regulation may be slower than for a Directive because the inherent lack of flexibility in a Regulation may well complicate the process of securing Member States' agreement on issues that are politically contentious.

The use of Regulations raises some concerns with regard to the subsidiarity principle because, according to a protocol on the application of the principles of subsidiarity and proportionality that is annexed to the EC Treaty, forms of legislation that leave the Member States the greatest room for manoeuvre are to be preferred to more restrictive forms of action.[25] This protocol implies that there has to be a particularly good reason to opt for Regulations rather than Directives and that pace of implementation alone may not suffice. In areas where Regulations have been used in Level 2 securities laws the European Commission has made the case by emphasizing 'legal certainty' and 'legal clarity' as justification for choosing this form of legal instrument.[26] Such justification relies less on the feature that Regulations can take effect more quickly than Directives than on the fact that direct application without transposition cuts down the scope for variation to creep in via differences in drafting at national level.

With regard to exerting control over the Commission in its exercise of Level 2 implementing powers, the Market Abuse Directive empowers the Commission to adopt implementing measures concerning the 'technical modalities' of various aspects of the Directive[27] but it expressly provides that implementing measures must not modify the essential elements of the Directive.[28] Additionally, the Directive specifies certain procedures[29] and the general principles that the Commission should respect in exercising implementing powers. The general principles are:[30]

— the need to ensure confidence in financial markets among investors by promoting high standards of transparency in financial markets;
— the need to provide investors with a wide range of competing investments and a level of disclosure and protection tailored to their circumstances;
— the need to ensure that independent regulatory authorities enforce the rules consistently, especially as regards the fight against economic crime;
— the need for high levels of transparency and consultation with all market participants and with the European Parliament and the Council;
— the need to encourage innovation in financial markets if they are to be dynamic and efficient;

---

[25] Protocol 30, para 6.
[26] e.g., DG Internal Market Services (2003: 4).
[27] Art 10.
[28] Recital 42 and Art 17.2.
[29] Recital 7 (general comitology procedures) and Recital 9 (three-month period for Parliamentary scrutiny of draft implementing measures).
[30] Recital 43.

— the need to ensure market integrity by close and reactive monitoring of financial innovation;
— the importance of reducing the cost of, and increasing access to, capital;
— the balance of costs and benefits to market participants on a long-term basis (including small and medium-sized businesses and small investors) in any implementing measures;
— the need to foster the international competitiveness of EU financial markets without prejudice to a much-needed extension of international co-operation;
— the need to achieve a level playing field for all market participants by establishing EU-wide regulations every time it is appropriate;
— the need to respect differences in national markets where these do not unduly impinge on the coherence of the single market; and
— the need to ensure coherence with other Community legislation in this area, as imbalances in information and a lack of transparency may jeopardize the operation of the markets and above all harm consumers and small investors.

Giving effect to the compromise deal between the Parliament and other EU institutions on the operation of the Lamfalussy process,[31] the Directive contains a sunset clause providing for the delegation of implementing powers to the Commission to come to an end after four years, although with the possibility of renewal.[32]

The approach adopted in the Market Abuse Directive for controlling Level 2 aspects of the securities law-making process—clear warnings that the Commission must act within the parameters and procedures set by the Level 1 measure, deadlines for stages in the Level 2 law-making process, recognition of the Parliament's entitlements under the political deal between itself and the other EU institutions, specification of principles within which the Commission must exercise its powers and a time-limit on the powers conferred on the Commission—has been followed and refined in subsequent securities law Directives to the point where it has now become largely standard form.[33]

---

[31] European Parliament Resolution above n 10; Prodi Declaration above n 13.
[32] Market Abuse Directive above n 21 at Art 17.4.
[33] e.g., Dir 2003/71/EC of the European Parliament and of the Council of 4 November 2003 on the prospectus to be published when securities are offered to the public or admitted to trading and amending Dir 2001/34/EC, [2003] OJ L345/64 ('Prospectus Directive'), Recital 40 and Art 24 (compatibility with essential elements of the Level 1 measure and with certain procedures), Recital 41 (guiding principles), Recital 42 (three-month time period for Parliamentary scrutiny of draft implementing measures) and Art 24 (sunset clause). This model is also followed in the Transparency Directive which includes provisions on: Recital 22 (deadlines), Recital 24 (procedures), Recital 25 (three-month time period for Parliamentary scrutiny of draft implementing measures), Recital 26 and Art 23 (compatibility with essential

The *Lamfalussy Report* endorsed calls for guiding principles covering all financial services legislation (Lamfalussy Commitee 2001: 12, 22). The idea of a clear set of principles against which particular pieces of legislation can be benchmarked has also been endorsed more recently by an independent group of securities market experts which was established by the European Commission to take stock of the FSAP (Securities Expert Group 2004: 9–10).[34] Yet it is open to question whether such a long and diffuse list of general principles, as appears in the Market Abuse and later Directives, serves much beyond a symbolic purpose. The overall scope is so broad that it is hard to envisage situations in which the Commission would struggle to justify its proposals by reference to one or more of the principles. There is no order of priority as between the various principles, a gap which leaves scope for them to be played off against each other. Furthermore, given the weak standards of judicial review applied by the European Court of Justice in areas of complex socio-economic policy choices, there is little chance of these principles forming the basis for a successful legal challenge of the Commission's decisions.

In addition to the controls over Level 2 that the Council and Parliament can impose in the empowering Level 1 measure, there are also further institutional controls over the Level 2 process. Under the EC Treaty, the Council can amend or block comitology decisions and take implementing decisions itself (the 'call back' power).[35] The Parliament does not have an equivalent Treaty power, a difference that is rooted in the history of the EU but which is now anomalous because it fails properly to reflect the Parliament's status as a co-legislator with the Council.[36] However, under

---

elements of the Level 1 measure and with certain procedures), Recital 26a (guiding principles), and Art 23 (sunset clause). The standard form recitals have also found their way into Dir 2004/39/EC of the European Parliament and of the Council of 21 April 2004 on markets in financial instruments amending Council Dirs 85/611/EEC and 93/6/EEC and Dir 2000/12/EC of the European Parliament and of the Council and repealing Council Dir 93/22/ EEC, [2004] OJ L145/1 (Financial Instruments Markets Directive, also known as the revised Investment Services Directive or ISD2) and Directive 2002/87/EC of the European Parliament and of the Council of 16 December 2002 on the supplementary supervision of credit institutions, insurance undertakings and investment firms in a financial conglomerate and amending Council Dirs 73/239/EEC, 79/267/EEC, 92/49/EEC, 92/96/EEC, 93/6/EEC and 93/22/EEC, and Dirs 98/78/EC and 2000/12/EC of the European Parliament and of the Council, [2003] OJ L35/1 ('Financial Conglomerates Directive'): See Reinhardt (2004: 11).

[34] This report is available via http://www.europa.eu.int/comm/internal_market/en/finances/actionplan/docs/stocktaking/fasap-stocktaking-report-securities_en.pdf (last visited 20 August 2005).
[35] EC Treaty, Art 202.
[36] Historically the European Parliament's involvement in the legislative process was slim but over the years, via various Treaty changes, it has acquired various co-legislative powers with the Council. Shackleton (2002: 95–117) describes the evolution of the Parliament's legislative powers.

comitology procedures the Parliament can require the Commission to reconsider a proposal if it considers that it would exceed the scope of the implementing powers. Additionally, under the compromise deal that was entered into to secure the backing of the European Parliament for the Lamfalussy process, there is a specific undertaking from the Commission to 'take the utmost account of the Parliament's position if it considers that the Commission has exceeded its implementing powers.'[37]

Although this is not a formal veto, it seems unlikely that the Commission and Council would seek to force through a measure in the face of opposition from the Parliament, not least because to do so would surely seriously undermine the chances of securing parliamentary support for the continuance of the Lamfalussy process on a more permanent basis.

Yet, having noted that in practice the Parliament's position may not be as weak as constitutional formalities might suggest, it is undeniable that the Council is in a stronger position. As well as the formal differences in their Treaty powers, Council control over the Level 2 process is reinforced by a provision in the resolution of the Council endorsing the Lamfalussy process in which it was noted that the Commission had committed itself to 'avoid going against predominant views which might emerge within the Council, as to the appropriateness of such measures' (Stokholm European Council 2001: para 5). Council control is also evident in the composition of the regulatory committee which assists the Commission in the adoption of Level 2 measures because this closely reflects the composition of the Council itself.

D. The Establishment of New Committees to Assist the Regulatory Process

1. Existing Committees and Bodies that Contribute to Securities Law-making

There is quite an array of EU committees and other bodies involved in the development of EU securities regulation. Some committees are part of the Council infrastructure, others the Parliament, whilst some are Treaty-based, self-standing organizations. Some of the most significant are as follows. The Council's assessment of strategic policy concerns is informed by the Financial Services Committee (previously called the Financial Services Policy Group). The FSC, established in 1998, comprises personal representatives of the ECOFIN Council Ministers. It assisted the

---

[37] Prodi Declaration above n 13.

European Commission in drawing up the FSAP and continues to meet periodically with the Commission for fairly high-level discussions on issues of concern to Member States' finance ministries.[38] Since it focuses more on strategic policy issues than on the nitty-gritty of legislative proposals, the FSC is likely to play an important role in shaping the post-FSAP agenda, for the period from 2005 onwards.

When Commission legislative proposals reach the Council, in accordance with general EU procedures they go through the Committee of Permanent Representatives (COREPER) before they are considered at ministerial level (Arnull, Dashwood, Ross and Wyatt 2000: 26–27). Coreper is pivotal to EU decision-making because it is at or below this 'engine room' level that much of the work is done to strike compromises between divergent national interests and to reach solutions (Lewis 2002). The Council's sectoral Economic and Financial Committee, which was established in 1999 (Nugent 1999: 151), has begun to exert a powerful influence in financial matters[39] but Coreper remains responsible for the development of legislation in this field.[40]

Within the European Parliament, the Standing Committee on Economic and Monetary Affairs (ECON or EMAC) has responsibility for financial services and does much of its detailed work in this area.[41] This Committee has worked hard to assert its claim for full involvement in the securities regulatory process and has secured specific undertakings from the European Commission with regard to transparency and to mechanisms for formal and informal dialogue between the two bodies (Bolkestein 2001). The European Parliament's Legal Committee also plays a significant role.

A self-standing Treaty organization with a role to play is the European Economic and Social Committee. This Committee was established by Treaty in 1957 as a separate EU institution.[42] It comprises representatives of socio-economic interests divided broadly into three groups: employers, workers and other public interests such as consumer groups. The

[38] Brief notes of the meetings are available via http://www.europa.eu.int/comm/internal_market/en/finances/actionplan/fspg14_en.htm(last visited 20 August 2005).

[39] The EFC is charged with keeping economic and financial conditions under review. As an illustration of its developing significance, it was an EFC report on financial regulation, supervision and stability in October 2002 that was the catalyst for the extension of the Lamfalussy process into banking and insurance: Economic and Financial Committee (2002a). See also Economic and Financial Committee (2002b), which sets out a series of steps for policy-makers to take in order to deliver the full benefits of financial integration.

[40] The relationship between COREPER and the EFC has been described as 'somewhat delicate': Arnull et al. (2000: 26).

[41] The powers and responsibilities of this Committee are contained in the Rules of Procedure of the European Parliament and are available via http://www2.europarl.eu.int/omk/.

[42] Generally on the European Economic and Social Committee, see Nugent (1999).

Committee's opinion must be sought on financial services legislative proposals. However, its ability to influence such proposals is weak because its opinions, which are often sought at quite a late stage in proceedings and under severe time-constraints, carry no binding force.

The European Central Bank, another independent Treaty organization,[43] tends to exert a more powerful role. The ECB has a Treaty entitlement to be consulted on any proposed Community act within its field of competence.[44] Proposed new securities laws fall into this category because they are measures to ensure the integrity of the Community's financial markets and to enhance investor confidence and financial stability.[45] The ECB's opinions cover the general effects of the proposed legislation, the impact on the ECB and national central banks, and any other points that the ECB chooses to raise.

As a result of the *Lamfalussy Report*, two new important committees have come onto the securities regulatory scene. These committees play a key part in the development of Level 2 legislation, but their role is not confined to this dimension.

2. New Committees under the Lamfalussy Process (1): European Securities Committee

The first such body is the European Securities Committee (ESC) established in June 2001 by a decision of the European Commission.[46] The ESC plays a twofold role, acting in both advisory and regulatory capacities. In its advisory capacity the ESC advises the Commission on policy issues and draft legislation relating to securities markets. In this respect the ESC has assumed the functions of the High Level Securities Supervisors Committee, which was established by the Commission on an informal basis in 1985.

The ESC also functions as a regulatory committee under comitology procedures. In essence this means that it has the right to deliver an opinion on draft Level 2 implementing measures before they can be adopted by the Commission.[47] If the Commission proposes measures that are not in accordance with the ESC's opinion or the ESC does not deliver an opinion, this stalls the process: the matter must go back to the Council, and the European Parliament must be informed.

The voting structure of the ESC is that a simple majority is required to

[43] On its establishment, see Weatherill and Beaumont (2000: 767–69).
[44] EC Treaty, Art 105.4.
[45] The ECB's competence to give a view is stated in these terms in relevant opinions: See, e.g., European Central Bank (2001, para 2; 2003, para 2).
[46] ESC Decision above n 7.
[47] Comitology Decision above n 12.

approve a proposal from the Commission.[48] If ESC approval is not forthcoming, the Council can block the measure by a qualified majority vote. The requirement for a blocking, as opposed to a supporting, vote at Council level dilutes the Council's control over the Level 2 process to some extent because so long as the Commission's proposal is supported by a qualified minority the measure will pass.

The ESC is comprised of a representative from each of the Member States under the chairmanship of a representative from the European Commission. Serving members of the ESC are usually senior officials from Member States' finance ministries. Full meetings of the Committee take place at roughly monthly intervals and a summary record of the proceedings at the meetings is made public.[49] In full meetings each member can be accompanied by only one expert (European Securities Committee 2003a). As from May 2003 representatives from the 10 countries that were to join the EU on 1 May 2004 began attending ESC meetings as observers (European Securities Committee 2003b). Meetings and missions costs are met out of EU allocations.[50]

3. New Committees under the Lamfalussy Process (2): Committee of European Securities Regulators

The second new body is the Committee of European Securities Regulators (CESR), again formally established by the Commission in June 2001.[51] CESR, which comprises representatives from national regulators (in practice the heads of the national securities regulator) of Member States plus Norway and Iceland, is responsible for advising the European Commission on the detailed implementing rules needed to give effect to framework securities laws. The countries that acceded to the EU on 1 May 2004 began to participate in CESR discussions as from 2003 (CESR 2003). As a 'technical' adviser with regard to Level 2 measures, in public CESR can eschew any function with regard to political decision-making (van Leeuwen 2002). Yet given the regulatory expertise of its members, it seems reasonable to assume that it plays a significant behind-the-scenes role in setting the pace for regulatory decision-making.

CESR traces its origins back to the Forum of European Securities Commissions, which was established on an informal basis in 1997. FESCO was an independent body operating outside the remit of the formal EU institutions. Although still independent of the EU

---

[48] For differing views on the implications of these voting entitlements, See Hertig and Lee (2003: 365) and McKee (2003).

[49] These Summary Records are available via http://europa.eu.int/comm/internal_market/en/finances/mobil/esc_en.htm (last visited 20 August 2005).

[50] ESC Decision above n 7.

[51] CESR Decision above n 7.

institutions,[52] CESR has been brought inside the EU tent to the extent that it is accountable to the European Commission through the mechanism of an annual report.

In its Charter CESR has also committed itself to submitting this report to the European Parliament and the Council, to reporting periodically to the Parliament, and to maintaining strong links with the ESC.[53] CESR's role in providing technical advice to the European Commission on Level 2 implementing measures has been the primary focus of early attention because of the pressure of the FSAP deadlines but it is worth noting other CESR functions because these give an indication of just how influential this currently fledgling (McKee 2003) body could eventually become. In the *Lamfalussy Report*, enhanced co-operation and networking amongst EU regulators to ensure consistent and equivalent transposition of Level 1 and Level 2 legislation were identified as necessary complementary aspects of the process, or, in Lamfalussy terms, its 'Level 3' (Lamfalussy Committee 2001: 37). CESR provides a forum that is conducive to the development of common EU-wide policies, practices and philosophies amongst regulatory authorities and to the establishment of an effective operational network to enhance day-to-day consistent supervision and enforcement (McKee 2003). As part of its Level 3 role, CESR performs a standard-setting function, i.e., it can issue standards, rules and guidance that are not binding EU rules but which, in a manner akin to the 'enforceability' of other forms of international 'soft law', are underpinned by loose commitments from CESR members to give effect to them in their national regulatory systems.[54] CESR also plays a peer review role, monitoring regulatory practices within the single market.[55]

It is envisaged that over time CESR's role in relation to peer review and peer pressure could bring about significant convergence in securities regulatory practices across Europe (IIMG 2003a: para 1.5).[56] CESR is also charged with keeping an eye on global developments in securities regulation and considering their impact on the regulation of the single market for financial services.[57] Despite this extensive range of functions, CESR's practical capabilities are limited by its rather modest resources.

[52] 'CESR is an independent Committee of European Securities Regulators', proclaims the opening sentence of its 2003 *Annual Report*: CESR (2004a).

[53] CESR Charter, Art 6, available via http://www.cesr-eu.org (last visited 20 August 2005). CESR's *Annual Reports* are also available at the website.

[54] CESR Charter, Art 4. For example, the British regulatory regime for alternative trading systems is now based on CESR (2002): Financial Services Authority (2003: paras. 1.3–1.9). The FSA notes that most CESR members are believed to have given effect to the CESR Standards (2003: 2.15–2.16).

[55] CESR Charter, Art 4.

[56] Scott (2002: 68) sees the emergence of CESR as the body responsible for implementation and application of EU securities law as 'displacing' the Commission from this role. However, as discussed later in this chapter, it is rather early to form any clear view on this.

[57] ESR Charter, Art 4.5.

CESR is funded entirely by its members (Alexander 2002). Its budget for 2003 was just EUROS2 million. The full-time and seconded staff working for its secretariat by the end of 2003 numbered only around 15 people (CESR 2003). In practice this means that much of CESR's work is effectively subsidized by its members through in-house devotion of resources at national level.

Full meetings of CESR take place around four times a year (CESR 2004a: Table 2).[58] Most of the detailed work is done by Expert Groups that are established to deal with specific issues and then disbanded.[59] CESR has two permanent sub-groups, CESR-Fin, which deals with accounting issues, and CESR-Pol, which deals with surveillance and enforcement concerns. In its Level 2 role, CESR makes decisions by qualified majority voting.[60] At Level 3 CESR makes decisions by consensus.[61]

E. The Mechanics of Level 2 Legislation

The Market Abuse Directive can be used to illustrate the operation of Level 2 of the process.[62] The chronology of the first Level 2 measures adopted under this Directive (these were also the first such measures adopted under the Lamfalussy process) was as shown in Table 16.3.

F. Role of the Private Sector and a New Emphasis on Transparency and Consultation

In its Communication announcing the FSAP, the Commission acknowledged past failings rooted in a piecemeal and reactive approach to new regulatory needs (2002c). It suggested that its strategic approach and also its selection of the best technical solutions could be improved, not only by closer co-operation with the Council and Parliament, but also by better dialogue with EU interest groups including market participants and consumers (*ibid.*). As with much else in the FSAP, this was more of a reiteration of a long-held view than a radical new initiative.[63] A strong commitment to openness in the securities regulatory process is consistent with the Commission's current thinking on its general approach to

---

[58] A minimum of four meetings per year is required by the CESR Charter, Art 5.
[59] CESR (2004a) provides details of the way in which the work of Expert Groups is structured, their arrangements for consultation, the frequency of their meetings and so forth.
[60] CESR Charter, Art 5.
[61] *Ibid.*
[62] IIMG (2003a: Fig. 4) provides a more detailed tabular account of the Level 2 process.
[63] It had, for example, been foreshadowed in European Commission (1998).

Table 16.3

December 2001	European Commission begins work on draft mandate to CESR.
March 2002	European Commission provisionally[a] requests CESR to provide technical advice on:
	— definitions of key terms ('inside information', 'market manipulation', 'financial instrument');
	— technical methods and procedures for appropriate public disclosure of inside information and for fair presentation of research and other relevant information; and
	— technical conditions under which share buyback programs and stabilisation should be allowed.
December 2002	After extensive consultation, CESR delivers technical advice to Commission.
March 2003	Commission publishes three working documents outlining its thinking on:
	— A Level 2 Directive defining key terms and dealing with information disclosure;
	— A Level 2 Directive on presentation of investment recommendations; and
	— A Level 2 Regulation on share buybacks and stabilization.
	These working documents were not formal Commission draft proposals but were issued so as to give the Parliament and other interested participants an opportunity to comment before the Commission began drawing up its formal proposals at the end of April 2003.
July 2003	Formal Commission drafts of two Level 2 Directives and one Level 2 Regulation published.
September 2003	First revised drafts of Directives and Regulation.
October 2003	Second revised drafts of Directives and Regulation.
29 October 2003	Final versions of Directives and Regulation agreed by the ESC.
22 December 2003	Directives and Regulation published in the *Official Journal*.[b]

[a]This request anticipated the adoption of the Level 1 Directive and its provisional status was necessary so as not to compromise the principle that it is for the Council and Parliament to define the split between Levels 1 and 2.

[b]Commission Dir 2003/124/EC of 22 December 2003 implementing Dir 2003/6/EC as regards the definition and public disclosure of inside information and the definition of market manipulation [2003] OJ L339/70; Commission Dir 2003/125/EC of 22 December 2003 implementing Dir 2003/6/EC as regards the fair presentation of investment recommendations and the disclosure of conflicts of interest [2003] OJ L339/73; Commission Reg (EC) No 2273/2003 of 22 December 2003 implementing Dir 2003/6/EC as regards exemptions for buy-back programs and stabilization of financial instruments [2003] OJ L336/33.

governance (2001a: para. 3.1; 2002c: para 1.1).[64] It is publicly committed to achieving a pervasive 'reinforced culture of consultation and dialogue' across its range of activities (*ibid.*). The need to involve the private sector more effectively in the regulatory process is something on which all of the main EU institutions were able quickly to agree. The Lamfalussy Committee took a positive view of the role of the private sector in providing constructive input in the regulatory process, strongly recommending its early and institutionalized involvement (Lamfalussy Committee 2001: 48). In its Stockholm Resolution, the Council invited the Commission to make use of early, broad and systematic consultations with all interested parties in the securities area, in particular by strengthening its dialogue with consumers and market practitioners. The European Parliament also stressed the need for private sector involvement in the regulatory process and called specifically for the establishment of a market participants' advisory committee.[65]

The Lamfalussy Committee gave specific content to its call for early involvement of the private sector in a recommendation that the Commission should consult with market participants and end-users 'in an open, transparent and systematic way' before it drew up any proposal for new Level 1 legislation, as well as iterative consultation throughout the legislative process. This call came too late for some of the measures in the FSAP because work on these had advanced beyond the policy formation stage by the time the Lamfalussy Committee reported. Pre-legislative consultation was, however, possible in respect of measures considered in the later stages of the FSAP, such as the Transparency Directive and the Financial Instruments Markets Directive (ISD2).

To facilitate dialogue with the private sector, the European Parliament's Economic and Monetary Affairs Committee has established its own advisory panel of experts (Advisory Panel of Financial Services Experts (APFSE)). This panel is composed of six market practitioners and four university professors. Its reports are only made available to the Committee (IIMG 2003b: 23). An emphasis on consultation has been passed down through the legislative process. In the decision establishing CESR, the Commission stipulated that it should 'consult extensively and at an early stage with market participants, consumers and end-users in an open and transparent manner',[66] and made provision for the establishment of working groups.[67]

CESR responded with commitments in its Charter to openness, engagement in meaningful consultation and to the establishment of working consultative groups to facilitate dialogue with the private

---

[64] See further Wincott (2001).
[65] European Parliament Resolution above n 10.
[66] CESR Charter, Art 5.
[67] *Ibid.*, Art 4.

sector.[68] CESR also published its own public statement on consultation practices (2001).[69] CESR's consultative processes have three key elements (Inel 2003a). Responding to the European Parliament's request for a standing advisory committee, CESR set up a Market Participants Consultative Panel in July 2002 to act as a 'sounding board' on CESR's work program, major financial market evolutions and other matters.[70] Alongside this panel, as the second element in the process CESR establishes ad hoc groups to provide specialist market expertise on particular areas. The third element is open public consultation.

III. ASSESSING THE LAMFALUSSY PROCESS

The previous section identified the main bodies involved in the securities regulatory process in the EU and sketched out their functions, responsibilities and interaction. This section evaluates elements of the process. This evaluation is subject to a number of preliminary considerations. First, the process heralded by the work of the Lamfalussy Committee is still relatively new and this inevitably limits what can credibly be said about it. It could be that a much more nimble and responsive regulatory system will emerge from the decision to devolve rule-making powers to the Commission and that CESR, supported by the private sector, will significantly assist the Commission in producing better-quality legislation. However, the short period during which the process has operated means that it would be premature to attempt any sort of definitive assessment.[71] Secondly, it is important to bear in mind that there could be distortions in the process flowing from the fact that, as all the participants know, the design of the regulatory machine is unstable because of concerns about the European Parliament's ability to control the Commission's exercise of rule-making powers under the Lamfalussy process. A new settlement between the Commission, Council and Parliament as to their respective roles in the regulatory process could well change institutional patterns of behavior and attitudes in ways that are hard to anticipate. This means that any currently discernible trends and practices may need to be viewed as transitional rather than as settled.

The third preliminary point is to note the broad contextual background against which issues concerning the EU's approach to the regulation of

[68] CESR Charter, Art 5.
[69] CESR (2004a: 9–10) provides an overview of CESR's views on the aims of consultation and on the processes that it adopts
[70] CESR (2004a: 11–13) outlines the role of the panel, its composition and its activities to date.
[71] This was also the view taken in IIMG, *First Interim Report*, introduction. In its *Second Interim Report*, p 8 the IIMG went a little further with its 'interim' conclusion that the Lamfalussy process was proving to be a better device for securities market legislation than previous practice.

securities markets arise. Tensions between the Commission, Council and Parliament in the area of securities regulation are but a small part of much larger concerns about how the EU institutions operate and the new pressures on the institutional framework resulting from enlargement to a 25-member Union. Reform of the institutional system is firmly on the EU agenda.[72] Although this chapter is focused on the interaction of the institutions in a relatively narrow, specialized field rather than bigger picture questions, such as the EU's democratic accountability and legitimacy and the general implications of enlargement, it is recognized that answers to the big questions that may emerge from wide-ranging deliberations on the constitutional future of the EU and the governance of EU institutions could have significant implications for the securities law-making process.

Fourthly, what follows is a selective assessment of key issues arising in relation to recent developments in the EU securities law-making process rather than an exhaustive evaluation. This approach is appropriate given the potentially transient nature of some aspects of the new process.[73]

A. Expansion of the Commission's Role: Empire-building or Advancing towards a New Model of Collaborative Governance?

As the initiator of securities regulatory proposals the Commission has always been in a very strong position. The Lamfalussy reforms appear to reinforce its dominant position by giving it new powers to write detailed regulatory rules.

Some observers of the Commission characterize it as a 'policy entrepreneur', by which is meant that it selects the policies that promote its own interests, presents these in ways that restrict the choices available to Member States and continually presses and negotiates until it gets its way (Hix 1999: 235–37). However, others point to various limitations on the Commission's entrepreneurial role including the pervasive problem of lack of capacity (Wallace 2000a: 15). Overall the Commission has a very small staff compared to the enormous range of policy areas for which it has responsibility. The problems of understaffing and overstretched

---

[72] The program of internal reform of the European Commission under the Prodi Presidency is outlined in Nugent (2002: 156–62). Inter-institutional issues are addressed in the Constitution for Europe. IIMG, *Second Interim Report*, pp 15–16 discusses the overhaul of the EU's comitology infrastructure by a draft version of the EU Constitution and assesses its potential application to Level 2 securities laws.

[73] For example, the system of 'parallel working'—where CESR works on its advice regarding Level 2 implementing measures on the basis of provisional mandates at the same time as the Level 1 measures are proceeding through the co-decision process—may not be necessary once the burden of meeting deadlines that were adopted before the Lamfalussy process became effective is lifted: Barclays Bank (2003).

resources are serious in financial services (of which securities is just one part), with the Commission having only around 100 people working in the area (*Economist* 2001a).[74] This suggests that simply coping with the demands that are put upon it is likely to be more of a priority for the Commission than pursuit of an empire-building agenda in which it positively seeks out and promotes ideas to build up its own power and influence. Seen in this light, the expansion of the Commission's role under Lamfalussy is not triumphal, institutional self-aggrandizement. Rather it is a functional response to the need for a more streamlined regulatory process, and whatever new benefits flow to the Commission as a result of it are probably counterbalanced by plenty of additional burdens.

If there had been fears from market participants and others about the concentration of power in the European Commission, these would presumably have surfaced in response in the *Lamfalussy Report*. In fact, the *Lamfalussy Report* received a favorable reception from industry participants and from regulatory organizations (*Economist* 2001b), as well as from the Council of Ministers and Heads of State or Government. Although the European Parliament had concerns, these related more to current weaknesses in the Parliament's constitutional powers to scrutinize the Commission's work rather than the basic principle that the Commission should play an expanded role in securities regulation.

Since its establishment, the operation of the Lamfalussy process has been kept under review by the Inter-Institutional Monitoring Group (IIMG) set up by the Commission, Council and European Parliament. The IIMG's reports have identified certain causes for concern about the Lamfalussy process but regulatory excess by the Commission has not featured prominently amongst them. Occasional references to the prospect of 'a flood of bureaucratic standards' aside (Federation of German Industries 2003), the overall tone of responses to the IIMG's reports has tended to be supportive of the Commission's role but with an emphasis on the need for fine-tuning of certain aspects, particularly with regard to consultation.[75]

There are calls for an increase in the Commission's resources to work on financial markets matters in the May 2004 report from a group of securities market experts that was established to take stock of the FSAP (Securities Expert Group 2004: 8). Had the members of this group harbored serious concerns about an over-powerful Commission they had

---

[74] IIMG (2003b: 16–17) highlights concerns about deficiencies in the Commission's resources.

[75] Responses to the IIMG's reports are available at http://europa.eu.int/comm/internal_market/en/finances/mobil/lamfalussy-comments_en.htm (last visited 2005).

a powerful platform from which to express them; the absence of comments to such effect in their report is therefore significant.

If the Commission's capacity is overstretched, this raises other potential concerns: the real center of power could be elsewhere and the Commission could be at risk of being captured by interest groups pressing the case for legislation designed to protect their private interests.[76] Post-Lamfalussy, CESR is the obvious candidate for the role of power behind the throne but it is too early to say which is the dominant partner in the relationship between it and the Commission (Norman 2002a). Signs thus far suggest that although the Commission draws heavily on CESR's work, it is prepared to depart from CESR's advice and does not simply rubber-stamp its recommendations.

The unfolding relationship between the Commission and CESR can be illustrated by looking at the process for the development of Level 2 implementing measures. As indicated in Table 3.1, the Commission starts the Level 2 process by issuing a formal request to CESR for technical advice. After consultation with market participants, CESR delivers its advice to the Commission. The Commission responds to this with the publication of a 'working document' containing a draft of the proposed implementing measures. After a further round of consultations, the Commission publishes its formal draft proposed legal text for consideration by the ESC and European Parliament. Once the approval of the ESC and European Parliament has been obtained, the Commission adopts the final version of the implementing measures.

Experience thus far indicates that the Commission will disagree with CESR on points of substance in proposed Level 2 measures where it considers it appropriate to do so.[77] The Commission is also prepared to make detailed, technical changes to drafting.[78] The Commission's propensity to redraft CESR's advice has raised concerns. Level 2 measures operate at a technical level and, so, seemingly minor differences in wording could well have significant practical implications.[79] For the

---

[76] On regulatory capture, see Stigler (1971).

[77] e.g., European Commission (2003a) which indicates the Commission's changes of substance in the implementing measure for the Prospectus Dir above n 33. The Commission did not issue an explanatory memorandum of this sort on the early implementing measures for the Market Abuse Dir above n 21 (where it did disagree with the substance of some of CESR's advice, particularly as regards the position of rating agencies). The change of approach in relation to the Prospectus Dir above n 33 has been welcomed as a helpful innovation: see Securities Expert Group (2004: 14).

[78] Inel (2003b) looks generally at the Commission's proposals and how they compare to the CESR advice.

[79] This point is made in various responses to Commission working documents outlining Level 2 rules in draft form—see, e.g., the response by the International Primary Market Association, 22 April 2003. Public responses to Commission working documents are available via http://europa.eu.int/comm/internal_market/en/finances/mobil/market-abuse_en.htm (last visited 20 August 2005).

Commission to rely more heavily on the form of CESR's advice would be a way of speeding up the Level 2 process that could reduce the risks of last-minute mistakes creeping in unnoticed because of subtle drafting changes.[80] It could also avoid duplicative consultation and/or disillusionment by those consulted by CESR as to the usefulness of participation in that exercise. On the other hand, inter-institutional sensitivities and concerns about democratic accountability make it particularly important to ensure that the process of writing implementing measures is a genuine exercise involving the Commission, with input from the Council via the ESC and from the Parliament, and not merely a rubber-stamp. There are issues, too, about the location of the appropriate expertise and capacity—CESR's very limited resources and the Commission's long experience in writing rules that are suitable for pan-European application are compelling factors in favor of looking to it to draft the legal text. So long as it is plain to participants in CESR's consultations that CESR's advice is just that, they should have no legitimate grounds for disillusionment when they see the text of the advice redrafted by the Commission. Industry concerns about the possibility of late drafting changes resulting in unintended changes of substance can be (and, to an extent, have been) (Inel 2003b: 11–12) alleviated through the provision of a late round of public consultations on the Commission's working documents.

There is admittedly something rather cumbersome about a model in which CESR provides carefully worded and heavily consulted-upon advice and then the Commission, assisted by further rounds of consultations, redrafts it in the form of legal text. In principle the system would be far smoother if the departures from CESR's text were limited to areas where there are policy issues that CESR is unable to resolve or where the Commission feels absolutely compelled to depart from the CESR view. It seems likely that, as the system beds down, some streamlining will be possible whilst still respecting the formal allocation of responsibilities as between the various bodies—for example the gap between the form of CESR's advice and what is suitable for adoption as legal text could narrow[81]—and there is certainly scope for improvement in the management of related consultation exercises, as discussed later in this chapter. It is possible to see evidence of a degree of refinement of the

---

[80] In its response to the IIMG (2003a), the French Association of Investment Firms calls for CESR to be given formal responsibility for the form and content of Level 2 measures under the oversight of the Commission. This response is available via http://forum.europa.eu.int/Public/irc/markt/markt_consulttions/library?l=/financial_services/lapplication_lamfalus sy&vm=detailed&sb=Title (last visited 9 January 2006). Inel (2003b: 11) notes generally that 'rare' critics have pointed out that the process would be speedier if CESR produced legal drafts.

[81] IIMG (2003b: 28) recommends that 'CESR formulates technical advice as concretely and clearly as possible—thus contributing to the drafting of Level 2 implementing measures.'

process already taking place in the Commission's provisional request to CESR for technical advice on implementing measures for the Financial Instruments Markets Directive (ISD2). The Commission included a new passage in its mandate letter (European Commission 2003b) to the effect that the technical advice given by CESR to the Commission would not take the form of a legal text but that CESR should follow a 'structured approach', by which it meant that CESR should

> provide the Commission with an 'articulated' text in a language which is easily understandable and respects current legal terminology used in the field of financial securities law.

However, care needs to be taken not to allow law-making power to shift too far in CESR's direction because this could undermine positive features of the model that has emerged in which this power is shared between the Commission, the ESC, the European Parliament and CESR. Recent theoretical analysis of regulation in complex fields such as financial services emphasizes the fragmentation of regulatory resources as between state and private actors (Scott 2001; Black 2001; 2002).

The existence of informational asymmetries as between regulated firms and specialist securities regulators and, in turn, as between specialist regulators and government legislators is an obvious example of such fragmentation. Decentralized analysis of regulation has implications for its institutional design because it suggests that designers should pay careful attention to how they can best capitalize on fragmented resources and draw them all into the regulatory process (Scott 2001: 347). One good design strategy would be explicitly to recognize that regulation is the product of interaction between numerous actors and to build networks accordingly.[82] It is possible to regard the collaborative arrangements between the Commission, ESC, European Parliament and CESR as an attempt to do this. The arrangement can be characterized as one that seeks to establish interdependence between the various bodies, with each of them providing their own internal checks and balances on the others' activities thereby giving rise to an accountability-enhancing system of multiple control.[83] On the one hand, the burden of turning technical advice into legal text can be viewed as a helpful discipline that forces the Commission, ESC and European Parliament to scrutinize CESR's work very closely. If CESR had the qualitatively different role of providing draft legal text for endorsement by the Commission, ESC and European Parliament, arguably the limits of CESR's role would be more blurred

---

[82] Comitology has been described 'as a network of European and national actors within which the Commission acts as co-ordinator': See Joerges (1999: 318).

[83] Majone (1996: 300) concludes that multiple control systems, in which no one controls but the system is 'under control' provide a solution to the problem of regulatory legitimacy.

and the discipline would be de facto relaxed. This could leave more scope for CESR to engage in surreptitious illegitimate policy-making in the guise of draft rules, and could result in the production of rules that reflect the narrow preoccupations of one group (regulators) rather than broader economic considerations. On the other hand, a consensus on technical needs that is established by CESR in close consultation with market experts should act as a discipline on the Commission and the ESC, since departures from it are likely to attract attention from the European Parliament and other parties (McKee 2003).

B. Consultation and Transparency by the Commission and CESR: the Development and Management of Dialogic Webs[84]

The operation of the new consultative processes prompts a number of lines of inquiry. Two important questions are whether their use is making a positive difference to the quality of EU securities law and whether they are enhancing the overall legitimacy and accountability of the regulatory system. Adopting Francis Snyder's (1999) definitions, 'legitimacy' is used here to mean 'the belief that a specific institution is widely recognized or at least accepted as being the appropriate institution to exercise specific powers', and 'accountability' means that

> the institution is, or is deemed to be, more or less responsive, directly or indirectly, to the people who are affected by its decisions.

A subsidiary question, which can be considered alongside the quality assessment, is whether the mechanics are working well or are in need of fine-tuning.

C. Consultation and Transparency as Quality-enhancing Devices

Quality is hard to measure and causal links between elements of a process and the outcomes of that process are hard to pinpoint authoritatively. Nonetheless, there are some indications that changes in the Level 1 pre-legislative consultation process are producing beneficial results with regard to the quality of legislation. The Commission's first drafts of the Market Abuse Directive and the Prospectus Directive, published in May 2001, did not have the benefit of open pre-legislative

---

[84] Braithwaite and Drahos (2000: 550–63) explore the ideas of 'webs of dialogue' and 'webs of reward and coercion'. They identify a strongly positive role for dialogic webs as mechanisms for, amongst a range of matters, defining problematic issues and motivating agreement and compliance.

consultation, a move that the Commission sought to justify on grounds of urgency and by reference to 'extensive' (but non-specific) informal consultations it had carried out with Member State Governments, regulators and supervisors, industry and other interested parties (European Commission 2001b: 5; 2001c: 2). This proved to be a serious misjudgment.

As the *Economist* noted, the drafts were greeted with 'howls of protest from practitioners, and even from some national regulators' that the proposals were 'half-baked' (2001a). For example, it was claimed that the first version of the Prospectus Directive, reputedly drafted by a Commission official with no experience of wholesale capital markets, threatened to dismantle parts of the European international capital market (Guerrera and Norman 2002). It took a concerted lobbying effort by groups such as the European Banking Federation,[85] British Bankers Association and International Primary Market Association,[86] and pressure from Members of the European Parliament (Dombey and Skorecki 2003) to secure amendments designed to preserve most of the flexibility on which the success of that market had been built. The Commission's initial proposal to revise the Investment Services Directive (2002b)[87] got a warmer reception, with the difference in quality being widely attributed to the fact that the Commission had gone through two rounds of open consultations before publishing the first draft of the revised Directive (Reinhardt 2004: 13).[88] However, the journey from proposal to new legislation (Financial Instruments Market Directive or ISD2) provides a telling illustration of the limits of pre-legislative open consultation as a mechanism for improving the quality of draft legislation because the text of the draft that was finally published by the Commission departed in certain key respects from the tenor of the ideas consulted upon. One of the most controversial provisions in the draft (on pre-trade transparency) had not been exposed to pre-legislative open consultation (Reinhardt 2004: 15). A consequence of the late insertion of this provision by the Commission was that diluting its potentially damaging impact unavoidably became a major preoccupation during the legislative process (Villiers 2003).

---

[85] The Financial Markets Adviser for the EBF (Burçak Inel) received an award from the Compliance Monitor for her lobbying campaign on the Prospectus Dir above n 33, which was considered to have contributed to a key improvement of the original draft, as noted in: See Inel (2004).

[86] Links to IPMA's work on the Prospectus Dir are available via http://www.ipma.org.uk/cu_index.asp.

[87] The market reception to this proposal is noted in *Economist* (2001a).

[88] The main elements of the Commission's approach to pre-legislative consultation are available via http://www.europa.eu.int/comm/ internal_market/en/finances/mobil/isd/index.htm (last visited 20 August 2005).

The proposal went through these rather secretive changes prior to its publication essentially for reasons connected with national protectionism by certain Member States.[89] The key point at issue in the dispute over pre-trade transparency was whether banks and investment firms should be permitted on a Euro-wide basis to 'internalize' client orders to buy and sell equities rather than putting them through regulated markets. The established position, sanctioned by the old ISD, left it to Member States to choose whether to permit internalization: some, such as the United Kingdom, did but others, including France and Italy, maintained a requirement for the concentration of orders on exchanges. The dispute essentially focused on the conditions governing internalization, with States that wanted to protect a favorable position for formal exchanges arguing for restrictions and limitations on internalization that, argued the United Kingdom, threatened to destroy the ability of banks and investment houses to compete effectively with exchanges. The eventual outcome in the final version of the Financial Instruments Markets Directive (ISD2)[90] requires pre-trade transparency (i.e. publication of firm quotes in shares) and, to this extent, it represents a victory for the opponents of internalization; however, this disclosure obligation only applies under certain conditions,[91] and the limitations on its scope go some way towards meeting the concerns of the banks and investment houses (Skorecki and Buck 2004). It is too early to say whether this will prove to be a workable and satisfactory compromise but what does emerge clearly from the experience is a simple political reality: open and early consultation by the Commission can improve the quality of legislative proposals but it is likely to be insufficiently robust to insulate the legislative process from political distortions.

In theory there is less likelihood of the benefits of consultation on Level 2 measures being undermined by political machinations between Member States because issues touching upon national sensitivities should have been resolved at Level 1. Early signs are that Member States are making some use of the ESC to amend proposed Level 2 measures in their own interests (Inel 2003b: 17) but the extent to which this has happened has not been so great as to derail or disrupt seriously the legislative program.

---

[89] *Financial Times* (2002) outlines the chain of events: last-minute lobbying from French and Italian stock exchanges prompted the Commission President, Romano Prodi, to intervene personally to have the pre-trade transparency requirement inserted into the text.

[90] Art 27.

[91] It applies to firms that are 'systematic internalizers' in shares admitted to trading on a regulated market and for which there is a liquid market. However, it only applies to systematic internalizers when dealing for sizes up to standard market size.

D. Consultation and Transparency Processes: the Functioning of the Machinery

Experience relating to the development of Level 2 measures has thrown up some difficulties with the mechanical aspects of the consultative processes. Foremost amongst these has been the pressure of short consultation deadlines set by CESR in respect of its draft advice.[92] To an extent, this problem is linked to the superimposition of the Lamfalussy process onto a pre-existing legislative agenda, the FSAP, in which the timetable was already fixed. The problem should therefore recede as the Lamfalussy process becomes embedded in the securities law-making machinery since this should mean that in future the need to structure the legislative timetable so as to allow sufficient time for proper consultation will be clear from the outset.

Teething trouble in the way that CESR approached the task of consulting market participants was always likely. In its early days CESR made itself a target for criticism by issuing poorly constructed, excessively detailed consultation papers that were insufficiently attuned to established market practices (Revell 2003). This undermined the credibility of claims that the new approach was more in touch with the markets. CESR was also criticized for not talking to the right people, with the absence of any representative from the country with the largest capital market in the world outside the United States (i.e. the United Kingdom) on CESR's Consultative Working Group for the Prospectus Directive used to illustrate the point (*ibid.*). Examples such as this could be taken to suggest that CESR is vulnerable to distortions because consider-ations other than the location of the appropriate expertise may influence choices about the composition of the committees and working groups that do the bulk of its work. Yet, as time has gone on, criticism of CESR's consultative practices has begun to die down, and there are no current indications of major disquiet.[93]

---

[92] IIMG (2003b: 26) notes widespread agreement among market participants on inadequate time for responses on Level 2 issues. A response to the IIMG by the European Savings Banks Group provides a valuable commentary on experience with CESR consultation practices and the impracticability of the deadlines that applied in relation to implementing measures for the Market Abuse Dir and Prospectus Dir. The response is available via http://www.europa.eu.int/comm/internal_market/en/finances/mobil/docs/lamfalussy/2003–07-comments-esbg_en.pdf (last visited 20 August 2005).

[93] IIMG (2003b: 21–29) provides an extensive review of the practical operation of consultation mechanisms under the Lamfalussy Process.

E. Consultation and Transparency as Mechanisms for Improving Accountability and Legitimacy

In a world where regulatory capabilities are fragmented and knowledge is unevenly distributed between different actors, the development of dialogic webs between epistemic communities is both essential and inevitable.[94] Legitimacy and accountability considerations make it important to pay attention to the institutional management of such dialogue. Commission and CESR officials might, arguably, be able to inform themselves quite well on the appropriate regulatory response to issues through private, informal conversations with selected market experts. However, this type of behind-the-scenes consultation could well create the impression of bias towards certain groups on the inside track of the regulatory process. An organized process of public consultation mitigates this concern. Furthermore, widespread involvement in the process of rule-formulation through open consultation should reinforce the propensity towards compliance, on the basis that public respect for the legitimacy of rules is likely to be increased where those affected by them feel that they have had a say in their development. The opportunities to enhance the legitimacy of regulation through public participation and due processes do not stop at the point where policy is decided upon and rules are made. It is inevitable that those who are sufficiently engaged in a process to respond to consultation papers and to engage in dialogue will often have a particular underlying interest that they want to project. This means that rather than helpfully illuminating the appropriate way forward, consultation exercises may instead produce a heap of contradictory advice from lobbyists, each of whom is motivated more by a desire to promote particular business and/or national interests than a detached concern for the development of good regulation (Baldwin and Cave 1999: 157). What matters, then, is how this mass of information is distilled and evaluated (Slaughter 2003: 1057–58). At the evaluation stage, a requirement for the recipient of the information to give reasons for its choices can therefore perform an important legitimacy and accountability-enhancing function. Feedback can be a powerful discipline because a requirement to explain fully and openly what has been done with expert input should limit the scope for perverse choices (i.e. where the selector favors the expert advice that is most consistent with its own preconceptions) or poor choices (e.g., where the selector

---

[94] Haas (1992: 3) defines 'epistemic communities' as networks 'of professionals with recognized expertise and competence in a particular domain and an authoritative claim to policy-relevant knowledge within that domain or issue-area.'

goes along with a proposal simply because a numerical majority of the respondents are in favor of it).[95]

Overall the signs are fairly positive for the legitimacy and accountability-enhancing effects of the improvements in consultation and transparency under the Lamfalussy process. The weakest spot is lack of transparency when regulatory decisions depart from the clear results of consultation. Here CESR has led the way at Level 2 by issuing feedback statements explaining how it has arrived at Level 2 advice proffered to the Commission, although there is some suggestion that the quality of such feedback could be improved.[96] The Commission attracted criticism for not providing similar feedback on its decision to depart from CESR advice on implementing measures for the Market Abuse Directive[97]; but its feedback statement on implementing measures for the Prospectus Directive indicates that this gap is closing (2003a). It is at Level 1 where substantial problems still remain. Unexplained departures from consultation results, as occurred with the Financial Instruments Markets Directive (ISD2), are unhelpful,[98] as too are assertions from the Commission that legislative proposals remain broadly intact despite significant and controversial changes made by the Parliament and/or Council during the legislative process, as again occurred in relation to that Directive.[99] No doubt the Commission's language in such situations is finely judged so as not to exacerbate inter-institutional tensions but the impression it creates can be quite misleading.

[95] Majone (1996: 292): 'The simplest and most effective way of improving transparency and accountability is to require regulators to give reasons for their decisions.'

[96] This point is made in several of the responses to the IIMG (2003a). The responses are available via http://www.europa.eu.int/comm/internal_market/en/finances/mobil/lamfalussy-comments_en.htm (last visited 20 August 2005).

[97] Possibly this was a short-term problem caused by deadline pressures rather than a deliberate policy decision by the Commission not to provide feedback: See Inel (2003b: 12).

[98] Criticism of the last-minute changes to the draft proposal that were done at the political level just prior to its publication are voiced in particular in the following two responses to the IIMG *First Interim Repor*t: Federation of European Securities Exchanges, Futures & Options Association, International Swaps and Derivatives Association, International Primary Market Association, International Securities Market Association, London Investment Banking Association, Swedish Securities Dealers Association and European Banking Federation, *Joint Response to the Inter-Institutional Monitoring Group First Interim Report* (June 2003), available via http://www.europa.eu.int/comm/internal_market/en/finances/mobil/docs/lamfalussy/2003-07-comments-bdb_en.pdf (last visited 20 August 2005); British Bankers Association (2003).

[99] e.g., European Commission (2003c).

F. Consultation and Transparency: Can There be too Much of a Good Thing?

Thus far this section has concentrated on the potential for consultation and transparency to deliver the entwined benefits of better-quality regulation produced by a process that is widely regarded as being legitimate and safeguarded by appropriate mechanisms of accountability. However, to leave the discussion at this point would risk giving an unbalanced picture. Large-scale public consultation takes time and its management is likely to absorb potentially scarce personnel and other resources. The provision of post-consultation feedback presents the same dilemma: although legitimacy and accountability-enhancing, it also puts an additional burden on strained resources. Further, excessive use of consultation risks generating 'consultation fatigue' which could impair its effectiveness as an evidence-gathering technique. Worse still, it could arouse suspicion that the over-use is a deliberate ploy designed to cloak proposals in a shroud of consultation-based legitimacy when in fact no one has had the time and resources to consider them properly. As the Lamfalussy process moves from infancy into a more mature stage, one key issue will be how well the Commission and CESR deal with the challenges of reconciling these competing considerations.[100]

The trick will be to find a balance that satisfies legitimacy and accountability concerns without compromising the system's ability to deliver procedural and substantive efficiencies in the form of good regulation produced cost-effectively and in a timely fashion. To pull this off, a range of consultation and feedback strategies is needed; deciding which ones are appropriate to which circumstances will be an exercise requiring sensitive and expert judgment.

G. Boundaries between Levels of Regulation within the Lamfalussy Process

1. Level 1 and Level 2

Level 1 legislation should contain only framework principles, described by the *Lamfalussy Report* in these terms (Lamfalussy Committee 2001: 22–23):

> The framework principles are the core political principles, the essential elements of each proposal. They reflect the key political choices to be taken by the European Parliament and the Council of Ministers on the basis of a pro-

---

[100] Recognition of the need for balanced use of consultation has started to emerge: IIMG (2003b: 28).

posal by the European Commission. They determine the political direction and orientation, the fundamentals of each decision.

'Essential elements' is not a precise legal concept in EU jurisprudence.[101] Where the line between Level 1 and Level 2 is drawn will thus reflect political choices made on a case-by-case basis rather than being the outcome of the application of a predetermined system of legal classification (IIMG 2003a: 27). Some unevenness and inconsistency is therefore inevitable, and is already apparent: some quite detailed provisions appear in Level 1 legislation because the main EU institutions did not want to cede direct control over the issue in question (IIMG 2003b: 13–14). This feature undermines the overall coherence of Level 1 legislation. Over time it could result in the emergence of a very muddled regulatory structure that is inexplicable except to those who can still recall the stale political battles of the past that dictated the allocation of each regulatory matter to a particular legislative Level.

Although this feature of the Lamfalussy process is not ideal, realistically it does seem to be the only practically feasible way of reconciling the various tensions arising in relation to EU legislative functions. The most optimistic prognosis is that a pro-Level 2 momentum will develop from experience in using the procedures. One of the factors on which this potential development is obviously dependent is a satisfactory resolution of the European Parliament's general concerns in relation to comitology.

2. Level 2 and Level 3—a New 'Boundaries' Issue that Could Become Increasingly Significant

As Table 16.1 indicates, Level 3 of the Lamfalussy process embraces a range of activities, some of which have more to do with supervisory functions than with regulation in its narrow, rule-making sense.[102] Nonetheless, it is important to note that there is a regulatory component at Level 3 in the form of non-binding rules, standards, and guidelines agreed by CESR members. Although there is already some Level 3 activity,[103] the potential importance of Level 3 regulation was not fully

---

[101] Avgerinos (2002: 282): 'the delegation of powers under Community law and the distinction between essential rules and implementing measures like so many things, is more a political problem than a point of law.'

[102] CESR has said that Level 3 covers three areas: co-ordinated implementation; regulatory convergence (which is the aspect considered in the text); and supervisory convergence: CESR (2004b: 5).

[103] IIMG (2003b: 31–32), noting various CESR initiatives, including the development of recommendations/standards on clearing and settlement by a CESR–ESCB Working Group. CESR has also produced common standards on Investor Protection and on Alternative Trading Systems and is working on standards connected to the Market Abuse Dir above n 21 and the Prospectus Dir above n 33: see Reinhardt (2004: 26).

appreciated while the pressure was on to complete the FSAP agenda because that tended to focus attention on Level 1 and Level 2 laws. As the distorting effect of the FSAP disappears, the regulatory convergence possibilities at Level 3 will move more into the foreground.[104]

There are in principle two broad areas in which there is room for the operation of Level 3 regulation: first, to add further detail to matters that are covered by binding Level 1 and Level 2 law; and secondly, to address issues that are not explicitly covered in binding EU law and for which formal Community legislative competence, as determined by the EC Treaty, may not even exist. If Level 3 CESR-driven regulation were to move into areas where Community legislative competence is lacking, this would be a further example of the 'competence creep' through the use of non-binding standards ('soft law') that is evident across EU governance as a whole (Scott and Trubek 2002: 7). In areas where there is scope for Level 1 and Level 2 law, the potential for Level 3 intervention necessarily depends on whatever decisions have been made at the higher levels by the various EU institutions. In practice this is likely to include CESR because its regulatory expertise should give it a strong voice in policy deliberations notwithstanding that its formal status is that of technical adviser. Clear criteria for drawing the line between Level 2 and Level 3 have yet to be established (IIMG 2003b: 33–34). One suggestion is that issues might be relegated down to Level 3 where it is impossible to secure political agreement at Level 1 or Level 2 (*ibid.*). However, whilst it is possible to envisage occasional circumstances where it might be useful for Level 3 regulation to perform this default role, it could be dangerous to treat this as its main function because that might encourage disagreement designed cynically to manipulate the Lamfalussy process so as to insulate established, divergent local practices from mandatory change. Level 3 regulation would be better seen as a positive policy choice that can avoid the rigidity of Level 1 and Level 2 law but with the potential to bring about a helpful degree of regulatory convergence more quickly than could be expected to emerge from a process of regulatory competition between Member States.

I have previously argued for a mixed strategy for securities market regulation, which embraces both harmonized law and regulatory competition (Ferran 2004). Advocating a positive role for non-binding standards and best practices agreed by national regulatory bodies is consistent with this argument because it is a further option that adds to the mix and which may be appropriate in some circumstances.[105] CESR has quickly developed a positive reputation for fostering co-operation

[104] That attention is turning in this direction is evident from CESR (2004b).

[105] Securities Expert Group (2004: 11) advocates non-binding solutions, including CESR standards, as potentially offering faster and more flexible responses to market developments, thus allowing more room for innovation.

and constructive dialogue between European regulators amongst themselves and also between regulators and the European financial services industry (Guerrera and Norman 2002). Based on current trends, CESR thus looks well positioned to become a force for regulatory convergence across Europe through the mechanism of Level 3 standards and guidance. This prospect is not entirely problem-free, however, because CESR could develop into a strong European regulatory 'club' whose members are tempted to engage in rent-seeking behavior resulting in excessive regulatory intervention across Europe. This prospect implies a need for robust accountability mechanisms to rein in any tendencies towards bureaucratic excess within CESR.

H. CESR's Relations with the Commission and with Interest Groups: Legitimacy and Accountability Concerns

Evaluating CESR's role presents a particularly tricky challenge because of the relatively short period for which it has been in operation and the limited amount of evidence about how it works that is publicly available. Early indications from the process of developing Level 2 implementing measures do not suggest that CESR has yet moved into a dominant role vis-a-vis the Commission, and its ability to do so in the future is likely to be somewhat constrained by its modest resources. Yet the potential for CESR to dominate the Commission (another overstretched, resource-constrained institution) in the regulatory process is clearly present because CESR can draw upon its superior understanding of regulatory issues based on its members' day-to-day experience of grappling with the operation of financial markets (Norman 2002a).

One specific suggestion that has been made is that CESR, in its Level 3 role, may displace the Commission as the key body for monitoring uniformity in the implementation of regulation across the EU (Scott 2002: 68). However, thus far, CESR has been at pains to emphasize that it is the Commission which is the 'Guardian of the Treaty' and that its role is to *complement* the Commission in ensuring that Member States meet their obligations to give effect to EU securities laws (CESR 2004b: 6–7). It will take time and experience to see whether words and deeds coincide. A natural assumption is that Commission officials would want to keep CESR in check so as to resist encroachments on their own power and prestige but it is possible to envisage a scenario in which the forces pushing for a shift in the balance of power towards CESR become practically irresistible. In that event the Commission could be at risk of capture by CESR because ambitious Commission officials could well decide that it is within CESR that the best opportunities for career progression will be found.[106] However, no doubt many varied personal preferences and interests underlie the career aspirations of Commission officials and it would seem unwise over-readily to assume that they would be attracted to (or necessarily have the requisite skills for) a career within a more narrowly defined regulatory organization.

However things progress, there can be no doubt that CESR is a powerful body, and that its influence is likely to increase over time. It is therefore necessary to pay close attention to its accountability and legitimacy. It is doubtful whether the present system of control, which rests on commitments to openness and consultation, and requirements to report periodically to the EU institutions, will prove adequate in the longer term, particularly with regard to CESR's potentially highly significant Level 3 functions. Level 3 activity could take CESR into areas that technically fall outside Community competence thus giving rise to some quite tricky questions about the standing of EU institutions to review them. At worst, this could be characterized as a structure that is deliberately designed so as to evade accountability via EU organs (Harlow 2002: 76). CESR members are, to be sure, accountable within their national regulatory systems but the mechanisms that operate at that level could be focused more on domestic issues than on agencies' supranational activities; and such mechanisms are also subject to all of the vagaries that may affect different accountability structures within the Member States. There is a risk that the effectiveness of national accountability mechanisms could be threatened by agencies' involvement in CESR—for example, where an agency participates in a CESR decision to develop a controversial new regulatory standard but then clings to the moral high ground of needing to be a 'good European partner' to justify imposing that standard in the face of strong, national opposition.

National protectionism leading to dispute and division between CESR members would act as a practical brake on the development of its power, particularly at Level 3 where consensus is required. However, that would be an unhealthy type of control. CESR's role in eroding the national biases and preoccupations of regulatory agencies should therefore be welcomed and encouraged as part of an overall system that accommodates some commonality and some diversity. Whatever problems of concentration of power that this process could engender should be addressed directly.

Fears about CESR developing into a body with immense, inadequately controlled powers over the operation of European securities markets lead into concerns about the powers behind CESR itself. It is only to be

---

[106] Majone (2002a: 329–30; 2002b) puts forwards this type of argument generally, not specifically in relation to securities regulation.

expected that, as CESR's power and influence grows, it will attract increasing attention from lobbyists. There is a long-standing tradition of interest group involvement in EU processes.[107] This can take a variety of forms embracing both indirect lobbying via national governments and direct lobbying of EU institutions. Firms may lobby individually or in coalitions. A standard pattern is that the intensity of Euro-orientated lobbying increases broadly in tandem with the growth of EU policy responsibilities in any area.

The European Commission has a reputation for being particularly open to lobbyists, a phenomenon that is associated with the twin pressures of the large and often highly complex range of issues with which it must deal and its thin internal resources. This has both advantages, in terms of enabling the Commission to make better-informed, evidence-based decisions about appropriate regulatory responses, and drawbacks, in terms of the Commission's susceptibility to the views of the best-organized, most well-resourced interest groups. CESR's position is not dissimilar to that of the Commission—it is a relatively new bureaucracy that must engage in dialogue with market participants if it is to have any real hope of working out sensible solutions to highly complex questions arising in relation to securities markets. By sharing the regulatory burden with market participants in this way it can reduce the pressure on its own tiny resources. At the same time, however, there is an ever-present risk that CESR will cross the line between drawing upon expert input constructively and being in thrall to it.

Overall, there are insufficient empirical data publicly available to assess authoritatively the role that interest groups have played in influencing the development of EU securities regulation (Hertig 2001: 218). Anecdotally, however, there are various indications that the establishment of CESR and the Lamfalussy process more generally have (unsurprisingly) triggered a growth in euro-lobbying (Guerrera and Norman 2002). The multinational firms that, for obvious reasons, were ahead of the game in lobbying for securities market opening measures are increasingly being joined by financial trade associations and other industry groups that historically concentrated their lobbying efforts at the domestic level. Looking, for example, at the responses to the IIMG's interim reviews of the Lamfalussy process, these reveal the formation of powerful coalitions that are likely to be well equipped to mobilize for desired regulatory outcomes.[108] The opening of offices by national bodies

---

[107] A general review of the literature is provided by Mazey and Richardson (2001: 217–37).

[108] See joint submissions from groups including the Federation of European Securities Exchanges, Futures & Options Association, International Swaps & Derivatives Association, International Primary Market Association, International Securities Market Association, London Investment Banking Association, Swedish Securities Dealers Association and European Banking Federation. Responses to the IIMG Reports are available via

in European regulatory centers is a further physical sign of the growing awareness of the importance of developing and maintaining good connections with European policy-makers. The Secretary-General of the Federation of European Stock Exchanges (Arlman 2004) has drawn attention to this trend:

> The FSAP has dramatically and definitively shifted the centre of legislation for the internal market in financial products to Brussels. By way of illustration, even the City Corporation of London is now opening an office in the European capital.

Some groups have lagged behind others in developing EU-orientated lobbying capabilities. There is some evidence that issuers, insurance companies and asset managers feel that their interests have been under-represented (IIMG 2003b: 29). However, the group that is most conspicuous by its absence is retail investors. The IIMG has noted the lack of responses to its work from investor groups and consumers (*ibid.*). Retail investor groups traditionally lag behind industry groups in engagement in lobbying on European issues.

There are various possible explanations for this imbalance. Some are rooted in general considerations that tend to put retail consumers and public interest groups at a disadvantage to business groups in lobbying efforts, such as diffusion of interests, poorer organizational capabilities and thinner resources. Securities market conditions, in particular the continuing fragmentation of retail investment in Europe along national lines, may also play a part because these may mean that retail investors have not yet felt the full implications of the Europeanization of regulatory power. The experience with the FSAP suggests that EU policy-makers (which will increasingly include CESR) need to develop a better understanding of retail investor issues if they are to make successful policy choices in this area. Although broadly wholesale market-orientated (a justifiable bias taking the view that regulatory strategy should be against intervention in areas where there is a strong likelihood of poorly-informed decisions because of deficiencies in information-gathering mechanisms), the FSAP has taken the EU regulatory program further into retail investor territory than ever before, particularly in the Financial Instruments Markets Directive (ISD2) which contains a raft of measures intended to ensure investor protection.[109] The treatment of

http://www.europa.eu.int/comm/internal_market/en/finances/mobil/lamfalussy-comm ents_en.htm (last visited 20 August 2005).

[109] Moloney (2004) considers the increasing reliance on promotion of investor confidence as the rationale for securities regulation within the EU. Moloney (*ibid.*: 12) identifies revision of the ISD as signalling a shift in emphasis in regulatory policy towards prioritizing the protection of investors.

'execution only' dealings in the original version of this Directive, as proposed by the Commission, provided an example of shaky judgment on how best to deliver effective and efficient investor protection in the interests of retail investors. Had the Commission's original draft been adopted, its impact could have been very damaging to retail investors because, by imposing costly obligations on firms to gauge the suitability of investments for clients, it potentially jeopardized the continued viability of low-cost, execution-only securities trading business.[110]

Under the Lamfalussy model, it is CESR that will be expected to provide technical advice on the appropriate regulatory response to retail investor issues. For example, CESR is likely to have to get to grips with many retail investor-related issues in its work on implementing measures for the Financial Instruments Markets Directive (ISD2). As yet, however, CESR does not appear to have engaged significantly in dialogue with retail investor groups. As Moloney (2004: 42) has noted, its Market Participants Group, which is a core element of its Level 2 consultation mechanism, is dominated by wholesale market interests.

Admittedly CESR members should be in touch with retail investor concerns through their domestic activities[111] but this may not be sufficient to ensure that such concerns receive due attention at the EU level. Furthermore, this sort of indirect representation of retail investor concerns at EU level arguably fails from a legitimacy perspective. Failure to seek out direct input from diffused and poorly organized groups, such as retail investors are likely to be, could undermine regulatory legitimacy and create at least a perception of industry capture. The Commission has recognized that there is a gap in the input that is offered to it by lobbyists:

> The Commission already receives much valuable input into its policy initiatives from the financial services industry but recognises the need for a closer dialogue with users of retail financial services.

To close this gap it has established 'FIN-USE', which is a forum of 12 financial services experts, who will formulate policy recommendations to the Commission on EU financial services initiatives, with particular focus on problems encountered by users (retail consumers and small and medium-sized businesses). It is too early to assess the usefulness of this group but it does represent a positive attempt to give a formal voice within the system to interests whose views might not otherwise be heard. There is a case for CESR to consider a similar initiative to bring (and to be

---

[110] The issue was addressed by means of amendments to the text inserted by the European Parliament and Council.

[111] IIMG (2003b: 29) notes that it has been suggested that national regulators take particular responsibility for retail investor issues.

seen to bring) retail investor issues more directly into the mainstream of its activities.

I. The Role of the European Securities Committee (ESC)

It has been said of the ESC that it is simply the Council 'writ small' and a prediction that has been drawn from this is that political disputes will slow up and impair Level 2 of the Lamfalussy process in just the same way as they can impede the progress of legislation that passes through the full (or, in Lamfalussy terms, Level 1) EU legislative channels (Hertig and Lee 2003). Although it is not quite formally correct to see the ESC as a mini-Council because it operates on the basis of a different voting structure (McKee 2003), it is undeniable that the ESC could be a venue for time-consuming arguments rooted in national protectionism and for messy compromises. How much weight should be attached to the fact that the Commission could ultimately push through a measure that is not supported by the ESC so long as it has the qualified minority support of the Council is questionable given that to do so would surely provoke major inter-institutional tensions and a likely backlash in the form of opposition by the Council to any further use of the Lamfalussy process (Hertig and Lee 2003: 365–66) Moreover, the existence of the 'Aerosol' clause[112] to describe the Commission's commitment to 'avoid going against predominant views which might emerge within the Council'—though replete with uncertainty (IIMG 2003a: 39),[113] suggests that measures to which there is substantial opposition should not even reach the point of being put to the vote in any event. However, even though the mechanism might never be tested in practice, it is possible that the mere existence of favorable voting requirements at Council level could strengthen the hand of Commission officials in discussions with the ESC members and thus affect the dynamics of their meetings.

Whilst the potential for the ESC to undermine the realization of a smooth-running legislative machinery clearly exists, in its favor stands the, admittedly small, body of evidence of how it has actually operated. To date, there is no indication that work on implementing measures has been significantly slowed up by political manoeuvring,[114] nor that the

---

[112] This is obscure EU terminology, derived from the first use of this method of blocking the adoption of implementing rules in the 1970s in relation to EU legislation on chlorofluorocarbon emissions from spray cans: IIMG (2003a: fn 17).

[113] Reinhardt (2004: 9) interprets this to mean that a simple majority in Council or even possibly the opposition of one or two larger Member States would require the Commission to review its position.

[114] Experience thus far does not bear out the suggestion that the existence of Level 2 could delay rather than speed up the legislative process: See Avgerinos (2003a). Arguments on the superiority of the single regulator model are developed further in Avgerinos (2003b).

quality of such measures has been seriously compromised by late insertions into legislative texts to protect national interests. To be sure, the ESC's constructive stance could be a temporary phenomenon flowing from goodwill towards the new system and a shared willingness to give it a fair chance. It could though be a sign of a more permanent positive development in the evolution of an efficient EU securities regulatory process. A key feature of the Lamfalussy process is that politically sensitive issues are meant to be separated off from technical concerns but in practice a watertight distinction will be hard to maintain. The ESC provides a mechanism for the resolution of minor political skirmishes without invoking the full panoply of Level 1 and it has at least the potential to operate more flexibly and quickly than might be possible within the formalities of the Council.[115]

Although most of the focus of attention on the ESC has been with regard to its potentially malign influence on the regulatory process, it is also worthwhile to consider its potential for good.[116] In principle it is possible to envisage the ESC making a positive contribution to the development of high-quality legislation by acting as a route through which the expertise and experience of national finance ministries in the drafting of technical securities legislation can be fed directly into the process. However, it is unclear yet whether the ESC will wish to develop significantly its technical contribution. Thus far its role appears to have been largely confined to acting as a political mechanism to secure a measure of Member State control over the Level 2 regulatory process.

J. The Role of the European Parliament

In its handling of FSAP Level 1 measures the European Parliament has developed a strong reputation for correcting market-insensitive aspects of legislative proposals (*Economist* 2002b). Amongst its significant contributions were amendments to the Prospectus Directive that alleviated the regulatory burden on smaller companies and preserved flexibility within international bond markets. Most of the success was attributed to the individual MEPs who acted as rapporteurs in respect of specific measures and, as such, steered the legislative proposals through

It is impossible to be sure whether the Dirs passed under the Lamfalussy process would have proceeded more or less slowly had that process not been available but the history of EC securities regulation (noted in the *Lamfalussy Report*, p 14) strongly suggests that progress would have been much slower.

[115] This prediction is consistent with evidence of the usually consensual nature of the work done by regulatory committees across the range of EU activities: See Dehousse (1999).

[116] Hertig and Lee (2003: 366) present a caricature of the ESC's role as being 'either futile or useless'.

the Economic and Monetary Affairs Committee of the Parliament and through voting by the Parliament in plenary session.[117]

Like the other EU institutions the European Parliament can usually draw from a deep pool of expert advice proffered to it by lobbyists (Mazey and Richardson 2001: 229–30). Although the work of the Economic and Monetary Committee's Advisory Panel of Financial Services Experts (APFSE) is not in the public domain, some of the Parliament's success in contributing helpful amendments to draft legislation has been attributed to its access to the advice of market experts (Reinhardt 2004: 15). This Committee has also made some effort to include retail investor representatives directly in discussions.[118]

The European Parliament is not immune to making decisions that are distorted by protectionist national considerations. The starkest recent example of this in the securities field was provided by the July 2001 tied (and therefore unsuccessful) European Parliament vote on the proposed Takeover Directive. Almost all German MEPs voted against the measure, which was opposed by a coalition of conservative German business interests and by trade union federations (Dumbey 2001). However, overall the European Parliament has made a positive contribution to the development of recent securities laws. This assessment casts its concerns about the inter-institutional implications of the Lamfalussy process into a favorable light. EU securities law passed before the European Parliament acquired significant legislative powers (i.e. the bulk of the pre-FSAP legislative framework) was hardly a beacon of success. Although it is impossible to make firm predictions on how FSAP measures will fare in the longer term, broadly speaking parliamentary interventions do seem to have anticipated and addressed at least some of the potential problems that might well have been encountered had measures been adopted in their original form. This suggests that it is important to ensure that the Parliament's role is not emasculated through excessive or inadequately-controlled reliance upon comitology processes.

IV. THE LIMITATIONS OF PROCESSES

There is no doubt that over the last 25 years the locus of decision-making power for the regulation of securities markets in Europe has shifted significantly in favor of the EU. This trend intensified with the FSAP.

---

[117] e.g., Trefgarne (2002: 39) commends the work of Christopher Huhne MEP as rapporteur to the Prospectus Dir above n 33.

[118] e.g., Public Hearing on Revision of Investment Services Dir, 18 February 2003, which included a presentation from ProShare, a UK private shareholder representative organization. Details and papers available via http://www.europarl.eu.int/hearings/20030218/econ/hay.pdf (last visited 20 August 2005).

Whereas some of the early initiatives were fairly modest in their reach, a much broader regime has begun to emerge. The old system, characterized by harmonization only to the extent needed to establish a sufficient level of trust in each other's standards to enable mutual recognition to operate (minimum harmonization), is giving way to a more aggressive approach in which the power of Member States to impose their own additional requirements over and above the harmonized core is being limited.

The new approach also moves significantly beyond regulation in the strict sense of rule-writing with the establishment of the CESR infrastructure for closer co-operation and co-ordination between national supervisory bodies and with a new focus on ensuring consistency in supervision and enforcement across the EU via CESR and also the European Commission. The rather technocratic nature of older EU securities laws may well have been a factor explaining why they came into being and were not blocked by coalitions of Member States intent on preserving their own national interests. Furthermore, with supervision and enforcement responsibilities remaining firmly rooted in fragmented national systems, there was scope for Member States to go along with the adoption of new EU laws whilst quietly leaving room for themselves to apply them in ways best suited to meeting perceived national interests. (*Economist* 2001a) And, in any case, Member States could usually postpone the day when they needed to think about the practical, operational impact of new EU laws because such laws usually only took effect after they had been implemented into national laws, a process over which Member States could drag their feet.[119]

The current significant expansion in the scope and depth of the EU securities regulatory regime, the upgraded efforts by the European Commission to pursue countries that fail on timely implementation (*Economist* 2004), and the development of peer review processes via CESR, combine to shatter the argument that the Europeanization of securities market regulation is attributable simply to the fact that it is all too technically rarefied and remote for anyone to care enough about it to engage in serious blocking efforts.[120] Yet the dreary character of early measures could have been crucial in that their adoption helped establish the principle that regulation of securities markets was something that could appropriately be done at the European level, and thus provided a platform for the incremental development of more ambitious forms of

---

[119] As of 1997, it was estimated that Germany had failed to implement more than one in nine Dirs: *Economist* (1997). By 2003, France and Italy were topping the table for foot-dragging: See *Economist* (2004).

[120] Though as late as 2002 the British Prime Minister was quoted in the press as having described a European Summit Meeting on which financial services regulatory reform featured prominently on the agenda as being mainly concerned with 'nerdy' issues of interest only to 'anoraks': Brewer (2002).

regulatory intervention. It is easy to see that Member States will be willing to support EU regulatory intervention where the advantages of collective action are judged to outweigh any disadvantages involved in pooling sovereignty. But this begs the question: what are the possible advantages offered by a collective approach that might encourage states to engage in intergovernmental bargaining? In addressing this question, it needs to be kept in mind that a well-known feature of EU policy development is that Member States can often agree on the need for a European approach whilst at the same time having quite different perceptions of its potential advantages.[121]

Self-interest in capturing the projected macroeconomic benefits associated with the establishment of a truly integrated financial market will lead states to give broad support to proposals that can be credibly associated with the realization of that goal. Officially the European 'line' tends to be that such benefits will apply across Europe as a whole and that, by coming together internally, the overall ability of Europe to compete with the United States, Japan, and China will be enhanced. Reading between the lines, however, it is often possible to find a different story in which British and German agreement on the benefits of a single financial market masks an underlying fierce competition between them on whether its center of power is to be London or Frankfurt, whilst France waits in the wings as the 'ideal' compromise choice for the location of the business of regulating the pan-European financial industry (*Economist* 2002b).

The application of the auditor oversight provisions of the Sarbanes-Oxley Act[122] to foreign auditors of US listed firms provided an opportunity to test the theory that the collective weight of Member States, acting through the European Commission, would be a more effective counter-balance to US power in the operation of securities markets than the efforts of Member States acting individually. The 'extra-territoriality' of Sarbanes-Oxley provoked a furious transatlantic row, including loosely-veiled threats of reciprocation, such as the possibility of an EU Directive on the consolidated supervision of financial conglomerates being applied so as to put an additional regulatory burden on US firms (*Economist* 2002a). A compromise on auditor oversight, brokered by the European Commission in negotiations with the US regulatory agencies (Dombey and Sevastopulo 2003), eventually emerged, whereby there will be certain changes to EU laws on auditors and reciprocal registration

---

[121] Tsoukalis (2001: 164–65, 176) discusses how France's fear about its ability to compete with Germany drove France's support for monetary union whilst for Germany the motivations were more to do with embedding the economy and state within a wider European framework.

[122] Formally the Public Company Accounting Reform and Investor Protection Act of 2002.

requirements will apply.[123] Although it is impossible to say whether Member States, acting individually, could have made their own deals with the US authorities, the fact that EU finance ministers made specific requests (European Commission 2003e) to the Commission for it to act as their voice suggests that some advantages in a collective approach were recognized on the European side. According to some reports, the US Public Company Accounting Oversight Board (PCAOB) did not want to do bilateral deals with individual Member States (*Forbes* 2003), and the EU's strength as a trading bloc was identified as a reason why the PCAOB paid particular attention to its concerns (Dombey 2004). Yet it is open to question who really will benefit most from the EU's collective approach on this matter. The US authorities presumably welcomed the convenience of dealing with a single EU 'voice', though it appears that they will continue to deal individually with certain EU Member States too (*ibid.*).[124] Arguably it is the European Commission that is worst off because it now faces the hard task of conducting delicate political negotiations to secure Council and European Parliament support for changes to EU laws on auditing that could appear to amount to caving in to US demands for a Sarbanes-Oxley mimicking auditor oversight regime within the EU (Ferran 2004: ch 6).

Externality considerations are also influential as a reason for Member States to support collective action at EU level. Countries that already have sophisticated securities laws have an incentive to support the extension of high standards across the EU to avoid being dragged down by association with poorer-quality regulatory regimes elsewhere in the EU. Equally, states with less-developed regimes may welcome European intervention because it relieves them of the burden of having to invest in national law reform exercises to upgrade their rules to more acceptable international standards.

The prospect of having 'its' high standards adopted across Europe carries with it the related benefit for a country that its firms may gain a competitive advantage through their established familiarity with the rules and their avoidance of significant adaptation costs (Heritier 1996). This motivation can be described as a form of 'regulatory imperialism' (Macey 2003). It can also be seen as a defensive action designed to reduce

[123] The outline of this compromise solution was announced during a visit to Brussels in March 2004 by William McDonough, chairman of the PCAOB: See Dombey (2004).

[124] Dombey reports that until the EU system is up and running (estimated to be four years after it has been through the EU legislative process (which in itself could be time-consuming), the PCAOB will step up collaboration with individual jurisdictions such as the UK, France, and Germany. Under PCAOB (2004), there is a 'sliding scale' regulatory procedure for non-US auditors, which is intended to be less stringent in those countries where audit control is closest to the US.

incentives for firms to relocate to other European countries with laxer regulatory regimes (Baldwin and Cave 1999: 173–75).

Another motivation that sometimes underpins international (including EU) consensus-formation is that this can be designed indirectly to break down entrenched national opposition: an unpopular measure can acquire an enhanced legitimacy through having been agreed at international level or, where it is part of a package, it may be possible to present it as a trade-off that was pragmatically necessary in order to secure other benefits (Slaughter 2003: 1054). Support for European regulatory expansion in relation to securities markets can also be seen as a response to globalization. Securities markets facilitate the international flow of capital unimpeded by national borders but they also present challenges that national regulatory regimes struggle to meet on their own. The challenges are multidirectional. From a public interest perspective, we can envisage states coming together in order to devise regulation that enables legitimate international business and investment to take place cost-effectively and, at the same time, limits the opportunities for international financial fraud and market manipulation. From a public choice viewpoint, however, regulatory co-ordination by states can look rather more like 'cartelization' so as to prevent national regimes becoming powerless in the face of the opportunities for regulatory arbitrage that globalized markets make available to firms (Macey 2003). The pooling of sovereignty to deal with the opportunities and risks presented by globalization is a regulatory technique that is not exclusive to Europe (Stiglitz 2002: 222–24)[125] but the institutional structure and legal system of the EU enable it to operate in a particularly developed form (Hertig 2001: 229).

The fundamental freedoms enshrined in the EC Treaty provide a further, if somewhat attenuated, incentive for Member States to engage with the harmonization program (Andenas 1998). Simply by becoming a Member State of the EU, a country is, in effect, pre-committing itself to support the integration process (Majone 2002a: 324). Under ECJ jurisprudence, protectionist Member State legislation is liable to be struck down if it impedes the efforts of firms to rely on Treaty freedoms to carry on cross-border financial services business (Moloney 2002: 311–35; O'Keefe and Carey 2002). Harmonized legislation introduced in place of divergent national rules provides Member States with a mechanism to maintain regulatory control over an area without infringing Treaty freedoms.[126] However, the ECJ has not been particularly aggressive in

---

[125] Stiglitz (2002: 222–24) notes that globalization has increased awareness of the need for global collective action in arenas where impacts are global.

[126] Generally on harmonization legislation as a 'lawful barrier': see McGee and Weatherill (1990).

outlawing national laws covering the area of financial services (Moloney 2002: 335–36), which means therefore that Treaty considerations cannot be viewed as a particularly strong force underlying the trend towards Europeanization of securities regulation.

There are also counter-considerations that will lead Member States sometimes to oppose securities laws proposals or to offer only conditional support for them. The reasons for Member States' opposition can vary and the consequences can be unpredictable. Sometimes the opposition may be rooted in Member States' concerns about the preservation of important national principles or institutions. On other occasions opposition may be a tactical step in intergovernmental bargaining across a range of different issues. The sorry tale of the Takeover Directive[127] provides examples of various motivations at work and serves as a graphic illustration of their potentially destructive impact. The Directive's progress was significantly impeded at key stages by Members States' substantive concerns about its potential impact on national arrangements (including British concerns about the potential threat to the self-regulatory status of its Takeover Panel, German concerns about the risk of the non-reciprocal opening up of German business to foreign ownership and the implications for employee involvement in corporate governance (Becht 2003) and Nordic country concerns about the threat to dual-class share structures that were used to keep the ownership of the largest Nordic listed firms concentrated in the hands of a few families and banks) (Hogfeldt 2003).

Unrelated issues that got thrown into the mix as States sought to strike bargains to protect their national preferences with regard to takeovers included the status of Gibraltar (Spain's support for a version of the Directive approved by the British at one stage becoming a pawn in complex Anglo-Spanish negotiations over the former colony's fate) (Wolf and Atkinson 1999), a Commission proposal on the rights of temporary agency workers (in a classic instance of horse-trading, a British–German deal was struck whereby Germany agreed to lend the United Kingdom its support in blocking the temporary workers proposal and in return the United Kingdom agreed to support the blocking of a version of the Takeover Directive that was objectionable to Germany) (Rudnick 2003), and the EU Common Agricultural Plan (in another deal Germany softened its opposition to reform of the CAP to secure French support for its objections to the Takeover Directive) (Evans-Pritchard 2003). The end result of these long periods of national intransigence followed by messy compromises was a severely emasculated measure characterized by

---

[127] Dir 2004/25/EC of the European Parliament and of the Council of 21 April 2004 on takeover bids, [2004] OJ L142/12.

multi-tiered optionality in respect of important provisions.[128] The deal to achieve this result was brokered by Member States in the Council of Ministers and was secured in spite of strong opposition from the European Commission.

The Takeover Directive in its final form is an embarrassment for the EU: so much time and effort spent to achieve so little. It manifestly fails to open up the market for corporate control by making the ownership of European companies more contestable.[129] As such it represents a victory for national protectionism. Furthermore, in the delicate power play between the various EU institutions, it is a sign of the Council's growing ascendancy over the Commission, a pattern that has also been evident elsewhere in the EU's activities.[130]

Does the Takeover Directive represent a failure for the Lamfalussy process? A simple answer to this question is 'no' because the Takeover Directive was not dealt with under the Lamfalussy process: indeed its origins long pre-dated the emergence of that process. And even had it been handled under the Lamfalussy process, strictly it would not have been a 'failure' because that process was not designed to override Member States' political objections to proposed new laws (had it been, the proposal to introduce it would surely have been a political non-starter) (McKee 2003). At the same time, it is indisputable that the Takeover Directive debacle has damaged the credibility of the Lamfalussy process because, in line with some predictions (Hertig and Lee 2003: 369), it has been tainted by association.[131] If Member States repeat the pattern of the Takeover Directive and, within the Lamfalussy process, regularly use their Level 1 powers to dilute or distort measures to the point where they are deprived of significant practical effect it is likely that the process will indeed become 'an ingenious but largely irrelevant footnote in history' (*Financial Times* 2003). But the Takeover Directive might be no more than an outlier, distinctive in part because of its convoluted legislative history and in part because of special deep sensitivities about

[128] Member States have the option of opting into the provision requiring shareholder approval for defensive measures by a target's board (Art 9) and the 'breakthrough provision' whereby any restrictions on voting rights and on transfer can be ignored in certain circumstances, for example by the bidder following a takeover (Art 11). In Member States that do not opt in, individual companies will be allowed to opt in, but they will be free to opt out again when faced with a bidder that does not apply the same provisions.

[129] Becht (2003) comments on the emphasis on reciprocity that, 'in view of the history of the Takeover Directive one could not fail to suspect a Machiavellian plot most foul; by asking for everything, the politicians pressing for reciprocity hoped to get nothing. To the extent that this is true, the plotters must be pleased with the result.'

[130] The Commission has been on the back foot since 1999 when, under the presidency of Jacques Santer, the College of Commissioners, its political arm appointed by Member States, was forced to resign amid charges of fraud and mismanagement within the Commission's operations: see Peterson (2002: 71–94).

[131] *Financial Times* (2003) lambasts the Takeover Dir as 'craven'.

the desirability of pushing continental European countries towards the Anglo-American model of widely-held corporate ownership (Becht 2003). The contribution made by the Lamfalussy process in moving forward other, more 'core' securities law proposals in the FSAP suggests that there remains room for optimism about its long-term significance.

V. AN ALTERNATIVE MODEL: A PAN-EUROPEAN SECURITIES REGULATORY (AND SUPERVISORY) AGENCY

An alternative model for securities rule-making and supervision within the EU would be to abandon the Lamfalussy process in favor of the establishment by the EU of a securities regulatory agency. Arguments for a central regulatory agency are that this would establish a machinery for the production of better laws more quickly, assist with the uniform implementation of rules on a pan-European basis, facilitate exploitation of economies of scale, provide a one-stop shop for investor complaints and concerns, diminish the risk of regulatory capture and provide at least the potential for improved transparency and accountability.[132] There are counter-arguments. Whatever its other deficiencies, the evidence to date strongly supports the claim that the Lamfalussy process has speeded up the legislative process. Advocates of the regulatory agency model who suggest that Lamfalussy might have the opposite effect (Avgerinos 2003a), are not on strong ground. True, there remain some politically-sensitive issues that can slow up the process considerably, particularly at Level 1, but it is unclear that Member States would even countenance delegating rule-making power in respect of the most controversial issues, such as take-overs, to a regulatory agency. Implementation takes place within a system, and crucial parts of the European system, particularly with regard to enforcement, remain fragmented along national lines. A single regulatory agency would thus face the quite daunting task of having to work with some 25 different judicial infrastructures, most of which would at any given time inevitably be unfamiliar to the single regulator's staff. It is not self-evident that this would lead to more uniform implementation of rules than is potentially achievable under Level 3 of the Lamfalussy process. Industry participants and consumers would still have to invest resources in understanding the different enforcement mechanisms available across the EU, so cost savings in that area might not be great. A supranational agency might indeed be less vulnerable to capture by national interest groups, but it does not follow that the risk of capture necessarily would be lower because supranational regulators would be susceptible to similar temptations to take advantage

---

[132] Avgerinos (2003a) provides a review of the issues.

of blandishments proffered by supranationally-active lobbyists. Even if it were true that a supranational agency would be less prone to capture because of its greater distance from regulated entities than a national agency, this could have harmful implications in another direction because its remoteness could make it less market sensitive and less able to engage constructively with market participants in mutual problem-solving. That a regulatory agency would deliver improvements in transparency and accountability is not assured (Harlow 2002: 75–78).

The arguments for and against an EU securities regulatory agency are not new, but they have recently begun to attract considerable attention in academic and policy circles, and also amongst market participants.[133] Superficially, views appear to split along national grounds, with the French leading the proponents[134] and the British leading the opponents (*Economist* 2001a; 2003; Green 2000; Lastra 2003: 54–55). However, closer examination suggests that reported French enthusiasm for a securities regulatory agency could be overstated (Parliamentary Select Committee on the EU 2003: paras 43–45). The European Commission has traditionally been opposed to the establishment of regulatory agencies, understandably so since this could entail an encroachment on its powers, but there are suggestions that blows to the Commission's prestige and influence in recent years are producing a change of attitude, as ambitious Commission technocrats look to the possibility of rechanneling their careers into independent agencies (Majone 2002a; 2002b).

In relation to securities market regulation, such a sea-change in the Commission's attitude is not yet apparent. Although the Commission has acknowledged (1999: 14) that the option of a single authority to oversee securities markets supervision may eventually emerge as a meaningful proposition in the light of changing market reality, for the moment it remains committed to the 'network'-based approach of the Lamfalussy process and has actively supported its extension into banking and insurance regulation (European Commission 2003f). A network approach to regulation, in which regulatory decisions are made on the basis of inputs from a range of sources rather than by a single, centralized body, is evident too elsewhere across the range of the Commission's policy-making activities (O'Keefe and Carey 2002: 15).

There are serious legal and practical obstacles in the path towards the establishment of an EU securities regulatory agency because this would probably require a Treaty change (although there is some difference of views on this point) (Avgerinos 2003a). Whether or not a Treaty change is

---

[133] See, e.g., Deutsche Bank Research (2003) strongly endorsing the case for a single EU regulatory and supervisory authority.
[134] Norman (2002b: 3) reporting results of a survey by the Paris-based Eurofi 2000 Association (Eurofi, *An Integrated European Financial Market* (Survey, November 2002)) and British reaction to it.

needed, were the idea of a pan-European securities regulatory agency to move up to the top of the policy agenda, the strong difference of views in Member States on its desirability would undoubtedly lead to long-running heated political debate and negotiations. For European policy-makers to risk getting sucked into a debate on an issue of such legal complexity and political tortuousness just at a time when the EU has established a workable alternative model for securities regulation and supervision could prove to be a serious mistake.

The timing is also wrong for another fundamentally important reason. The now-conventional thinking that underpins the concentration of regulatory and supervisory authority in a single agency is that this is economically efficient and effective because it achieves a neat match between regulatory infrastructure and market conditions. In the context of bringing together responsibility for different parts of the financial services industry, this argument is framed in terms of the blurring of sectoral distinctions that renders sectorally-fragemented regulation inappropriate. Blurring of sectoral boundaries is not an issue that is directly relevant to the European debate about a securities regulatory agency because, for the moment, EU regulation is still organized on a sectoral basis but the core of the thinking about unitary models of regulation—that regulatory systems should match the markets they are designed to regulate—is useful. It implies that a good starting point in thinking about whether an EU securities regulatory agency is appropriate is to ask whether the EU actually does have a single securities market. We do not find this in current European market conditions: wholesale financial markets are integrating and infrastructure providers such as exchanges are increasingly gearing up to operate transnationally but there is clear evidence that retail financial services in the EU are still fragmented along largely national lines (Ferran 2004: ch. 2).

Prospects for the future are that fragmentation is likely to increase rather than diminish following the enlargement of the EU in May 2004 to include the formerly Communist Eastern European and Baltic countries where securities market activity has lagged far behind the EU-15. From an economic perspective, therefore, it looks distinctly premature to push the case for a single regulatory agency when lack of market integration means that the expanding EU does not constitute a optimal area, in terms of its economic development, for its application (Alexander 2002). Regulatory intervention ahead of the market is always fraught with difficulty. In this particular situation, the uncertain benefits flowing from the establishment of a single securities regulatory agency do not warrant the very considerable risks of mistakes in infrastructure planning that could significantly impede progress towards a properly integrated securities market.

VI. CONCLUSIONS

This chapter has sought to consider whether post-Lamfalussy, the EU has in place a well-functioning securities regulatory machinery that is suitably designed for the delivery of high-quality legislation. Devising a regulatory system that is simultaneously efficient in substance (i.e. it delivers good rules), efficient in process (i.e. it works cost-effectively and promptly), legitimate and properly accountable raises major challenges whatever the legal environment. There are particular difficulties in a transnational context, such as that of the EU, because of strong perceptions of lack of legitimacy and poor accountability.

The broad conclusion is that, though not perfect, the Lamfalussy process is a step in the right direction. For the immediate future, the course of action that commends itself therefore is to concentrate on refining and upgrading the Lamfalussy process so as to enable it to work more efficiently and effectively. The Lamfalussy process has been openly described as one in which people are 'learning by doing' and CESR's chairman has publicly said that it is just 'a good beginning' (van Leeuwen 2003). Gathering more evidence on existing practices and approaches in Member States before legislative proposals are brought forward and using this evidence to conduct regulatory impact analysis have been suggested as disciplines that could enhance the operation of the Lamfalussy process (Securities Expert Group 2004: 10–11). Incremental improvements of this sort seem more likely to advance the cause of good regulation than more radical alternatives. The establishment of an independent regulatory agency in place of the Lamfalussy process would not guarantee the correction of the known deficiencies. Moreover, consideration of the agency model looks distinctly premature in the light of prevailing economic market conditions across the expanding EU.

The Lamfalussy process is best seen as a pragmatic solution to a difficult multi-dimensional problem. The regulatory challenge presented by the mismatch between slow-moving legislative machinery and dynamic securities markets is well known to securities market specialists. This challenge is encountered in an acute form in the EU because of the particularly cumbersome nature of its traditional legislative processes. Also familiar to securities market specialists is the fact that the issues that arise in relation to the regulation of technically sophisticated securities markets often require solutions that legislators, many steps removed from the markets, are not well equipped to deliver. This issue, too, acquires a distinctive flavor when considered in the broad context of the EU. Across the board new collaborative methods of governance, embracing dialogue and co-ordinated efforts at mutual problem-solving between the central institutions, national bodies, technical experts and other parties, are emerging in order to deal with the increasing complexity of the issues on the EU's policy agenda (Scott and Trubek 2002). At the same time, however, major policy questions are arising about the legitimacy of these new approaches (*ibid.*), as well as political battles over the position of the main EU institutions in emerging new governance structures. Against this background, the mere fact that a process that addresses the key, specialist problems—namely the need for a speedier and more technically sophisticated method of making regulation for securities markets—has gained a foothold rather than being submerged under a welter of policy concerns or bogged down in an inter-institutional power struggle can be counted as a significant achievement.

Giving a broad welcome to the Lamfalussy process implies not judging its deficiencies too harshly but, at the same time, it does not mean uncritical acceptance of how it operates. Foremost amongst its positive features is the establishment of a split between Level 1 and Level 2 legislation. In most fields of regulation there is a need for some form of executive, delegated rule-making machinery to fine-tune the regime and keep it broadly up to date; the need is acute in relation to securities markets because of their complexity and dynamism. The structure for controlling decisions about where to draw the line between Level 1 and Level 2 reflects political realities. As such, it seems inevitable that the line will sometimes be put in the 'wrong' place if judged from a detached, theoretical perspective but the system should be sufficiently robust to withstand some degree of misplacement. An optimistic prognosis is that misplacement problems will diminish as time goes on, as the Council and European Parliament become less wary of dropping matters down to Level 2 (and also to Level 3), and as CESR develops the capabilities to deal effectively with the resulting large workload.

The evidence to date suggests that separating 'technical' details from 'essential' elements has helped to speed up the initial rule-making process. Some speed/quality arbitrage has been spotted (Parliamentary Select Committee on the EU 2003: paras. 43–45; Norman 2003) but the root cause of this has been more to do with the FSAP deadlines (which pre-dated the Lamfalussy process) than with the process itself. Similarly, blame for poor-quality rules that were a fudged compromise concocted to satisfy sectarian national interests of Member States cannot strictly be laid at the feet of the Lamfalussy process, though it is unlikely to avoid becoming tainted by association.

A system that makes it easier to write and amend rules could also be a system that lends itself to the production of a regime that is of poor quality because it is overly prescriptive and legalistic. Although concerns have been voiced about this, the few Level 2 measures passed to date do not support claims that the emerging post-FSAP regime is already too detailed. Yet the potential is clearly present for regulatory excess, particularly at Level 2 and Level 3 of the Lamfalussy process. Whether this potential is kept in check depends of a range of variables, such as how well informed those who have power to make the rules are about regulatory needs and how disciplined they are (or are required to be) in taking heed of the information at their disposal. It is therefore appropriate to emphasize the need for evidence-based law-making, regulatory impact assessments and feedback statements, although the strain that such requirements may place on already stretched resources does need to be recognized and addressed.

The effective operation of a network-based approach to rule-making, where regulatory decisions are informed by evidence and expert advice, depends on openness and dialogue between all interested parties. The Lamfalussy process has brought more openness into the securities law-making process and has engendered more systematic use of consultation mechanisms. Refinements are needed, but the early signs as regards procedural fairness are broadly encouraging. A potential weakness is the unevenness of representation in the policy and rule-formation processes of investor groups as compared to industry lobbies. If left unchecked, in the longer term this could make the law-making process appear haphazard, if not unfairly selective.

The ties that bind the participants in the Lamfalussy process form a complex and delicate web. The interdependence of the various actors and the mechanisms by which they hold each other in check are still evolving. Indeed the whole Lamfalussy edifice presently rests on a shaky, temporary inter-institutional compromise over their respective involvement in the process and the mechanisms whereby they can control each other. The long term future may eventually be secured under the new EU Constitution but, in the meantime, the extension of the Lamfalussy process into banking and insurance regulation suggests that the controversy is dying down and that its place is becoming more secure on a de facto basis.

Within its specialist field, the Lamfalussy process can thus be seen as an ongoing attempt to reduce the tensions between the need for an efficient regulatory system characterized by speed, expertise and adaptability and the need for a system that is legitimate and properly accountable. The Lamfalussy process seeks to address some of the concerns about regulatory techniques that are expert-driven (such as the informality of networks and the lack of transparency about how they operate that can generate a sense of complexity and yield results that can appear arbitrary or tainted by self-interest) (Picciotto 1997). As such, its operation over time could usefully inform more wide-ranging assessments of possible solutions to contemporary problems of regulatory legitimacy and accountability.

REFERENCES

Alexander, K. (2002), 'Establishing a European Securities Regulator: Is the European Union an Optimal Economic Area for a Single Securities Regulator?' Cambridge Endovment for Research in Finance Working Paper No. 7, available via http://www.cerf.cam.ac.uk/publications/files/WP07-Kern%20Alexander2. prn.pdf.

Andenas, M. (1998), 'The Financial Market and the Commission as Legislator', 19 *Company Lawyer* 98.

Arlman, P. (2004), Speech by FESE Secretary General, at Globalisation 5, a FEAS/FESE Conference, Prague, 25 Feb. The text of this speech is available via http://www.fese.be/initiatives/speeches/2004/arlman_25feb2004.htm (last visited).

Arnull, A.M., Dashwood, A.A., Ross, M.G, and Wyatt, D.A. (2000), *Wyatt & Dashwood's European Union Law* (4th ed, London: Sweet & Maxwell).

Avgerinos, Y.V. (2002), 'Essential and Non-essential Measures: Delegation of Powers in EU Securities Regulation', 8 *European Law Journal* 269.

—— (2003a), 'EU Financial Market Supervision Revisited: The European Securities Regulator', Jean Monnet Working Paper 7/03, available via http://www.jeanmonnetprogram.org/papers/03/030701.pdf (last visited 18 Aug. 2005).

—— (2003b), *Regulating and Supervising Investment Services in the European Union* (Basingstoke: Palgrave Macmillan).

Baldwin, R. and Cave, M. (1999), *Understanding Regulation* (Oxford: Oxford University Press).

Barclays Bank (2003), *Response to Inter-Institutional Group* (July), available via http://europa.eu.int/comm/internal_market/en/finances/mobil/docs/lamf alussy/2003–07-comments-barclays_en.pdf.

Becht, M. (2003), 'Reciprocity in Takeovers', European Corporate Governance Institute Law Working Paper No. 14/2003, available at http://www.ssrn.com/abstract=463003 (last visited 18 Aug. 2005).

Black, J. (2001), 'Decentring Regulation: Understanding the Role of Regulation and Self Regulation in a "Post-Regulatory" World', 54 *Current Legal Problems* 103.

—— (2002), 'Mapping the Contours of Contemporary Financial Services Regulation' [2002] *Journal of Corporate Law Studies* 253.

Bolkestein, F. (2001), Letter (2 Oct.) from Frits Bolkestein, European Commissioner for the Internal Market, to Christina Randzio-Plath, Chair of the Economic and Monetary Affairs Committee, available via http://www.europarl.eu.int/comparl/econ/lamfalussy_process/ep_position/lt_bolkestein

Bradley, K.S.C. (1997), 'The European Parliament and Comitology: On the Road to Nowhere', 3 *European Law Journal* 230.

Braithwaite, J. and Drahos, P. (2000), *Global Business Regulation* (Cambridge: Cambridge University Press).

Brewer, J.H. (2002), 'PM Allows His Frustration to Show at the European Summit As the Day's Business is "Strictly for Anoraks"', *Sunday Express*, 17 March, p. 11.

British Bankers Association (2003), *BBA Comments on the Lamfalussy Process*, available at http://europa.eu.int/comm/internal_market/securities/docs/ monitoring/first-report/2003–07-comments-bba_en.pdf (last visited 18 August 2005).

Carr, R. (2003), 'EU Investment Services Directive Could Kill Off Execution-only Share Trading', *Investors Chronicle*, 25 April, p. 13.

CESR (2001), Public Statement of Consultation Practices (CESR/01–007c), available at http://www.cesr-eu.org (last visited 15 August 2005).

—— (2002), Standards for Alternative Trading Systems (CESR/02–086b, 2002).

—— (2004a), Annual Report 2003(CESR/03–396).

—— (2004b), The Role of CESR At 'Level 3' Under the Lamfalussy Process (CESR/04–104b).

Council of Economics and Finance Ministers (2001), Results of the Council of Economics and Finance Ministers, March, Stockholm, available via http:// europa.eu.int/comm/internal_market/en/finances/mobil/01-memo105.htm (last visited 19 August 2005).

Craig, P. (1999), 'The Nature of the Community: Integration, Democracy, and Legitimacy' in Craig and de Búrca (eds), *The Evolution of EU Law* (Oxford: Oxford University Press), pp. 42–50.

Dashwood, A. (2001), 'The Constitution of the EU After Nice: Law-Making Procedures', 26 *European Law Review* 215.

de Búrca, G. (1999), 'The Institutional Development of the EU: A Constitutional Analysis' in P. Craig and G. de Búrca (eds), *The Evolution of EU Law* (Oxford: Oxford University Press), p. 65.

Dehousse, R. (1997), 'Regulation by Networks in the European Community: The Role of European Agencies', 4 *Journal of European Public Policy* 246.

—— (1999), 'Towards a Regulation of Transitional Governance? Citizens' Rights and the Reform of Comitology Procedures' in Joerges and Vos (eds), *EU Committees* (Oxford: Hart Publishing), pp. 110–12.

Deutsche Bank Research (2003), 'Reform of EU Regulatory and Supervisory Structures: Progress Report', 4 *EU Monitor* (July) (Financial Markets Special) 10.

DG Internal Market Services (2003), *Implementation of Article 8 of Directive 2003/6/EC (Market Abuse)* (Working Document ESC 14/2003), http:// www.europa.eu.int/comm/internal_market/en/finances/mobil/docs/market abuse/esc-14–2003_en.pdf.

Dombey, D. (2001), 'EU Rejects Chance to Set Cross-border Takeover Rules', *Financial Times*, 5 July, p. 1.

—— (2004), 'Sarbanes-Oxley and Europe—US Legislation Finds a Friend Across the Water', *Financial Times*, 23 Apr., Understanding Corporate Governance Supplement, p. 9.

Dombey, D. and Sevastopulo, D. (2003), 'No Accord Yet Over European Auditors', *Financial Times*, 16 October, p. 8.

Dombey, D. and Skorecki, A. (2003), 'MEPs Clear Way For Deal on Borrowing', *Financial Times*, 27 June 2003, p. 8.

Economic and Financial Committee (2002a), *Report on Financial Regulation, Supervision and Stability* (Brussels, October 2002), available via http:// europa.eu.int/comm/internal_market/en/finances/cross-sector/consultation/ efc-eport_en.pdf (accessed May 2004).

—— (2002b), *Report on EU Financial Integration* (ECFIN/194/02-EN).

Economist (1997), 'Thatcherites in Brussels (Really)', 15 March, p. 25.

—— (2001a), 'A Ragbag of Reform', 3 March, p. 93.

—— (2001b), 'Labouring with Lamfalussy', 16 June 2001, p. 97.

—— (2002a), 'How to Protect Investors', 27 April, p. 81.

—— (2002b), 'Scrapping Over the Pieces—Laborious Efforts Towards a Single Market', 9 March, p. 85.

—— (2002c), 'A Bit of Give and Take: Another Transatlantic Row Over Financial Regulation', 19 October, p. 99.

—— (2003), 'Trojan Horses', 15 February, p. 77.

—— (2004), 'Actions Speak Louder than Words', *Economist Global Agenda*, 7 May 2003, via www.economist.com (accessed June 2004).

European Central Bank (2001), Opinion of the European Central Bank on a proposal for a Directive on the prospectus to be published when securities are offered to the public or admitted to trading (CON/2001/36), OJ 2001 No. C344/5.

—— (2003), Opinion of the European Central Bank on a proposal for a Directive on the harmonisation of transparency requirements with regard to information about issuers whose securities are admitted to trading on a regulated market (CON/2003/21) OJ 2003 No. C242/6.

European Commission (1998), *Financial Services: Building a Framework for Action*, available via http://www.europa.eu.int/comm/internal_market/en/finances/general/fsen.pdf (accessed May 2004).

—— (1999), Financial Services: Implementing the Framework for Financial Markets: Action Plan (COM (1999) 232).

—— (2001a), *European Governance White Paper* (COM (2001) 428).

—— (2001b), Proposal for a Directive of the European Parliament and of the Council on insider dealing and market manipulation (market abuse) (COM (2001) 281), explanatory memorandum, p. 5

—— (2001c), Proposal for a Directive of the European Parliament and of the Council on the prospectus to be published when securities are offered to the public or admitted to trading (COM (2001) 280),

—— (2002c), Action Plan 'Simplifying and Improving the Regulatory Environment' (COM(2002) 278), para. 1.1.

—— (2002a), Towards a Reinforced Culture of Consultation and Dialogue— General Principles and Minimum Standards for Consultation of Interested Parties by the Commission (COM(2002) 704).

—— (2002b), Proposal for a Directive of the European Parliament and of the Council on investment services and regulated markets, and amending Council Directives 85/611/EEC, Council Directive 93/6/EEC and European Parliament and Council Directive 2000/12/EC (COM (2002) 625).

—— (2003a), Main differences between the Commission draft regulation on draft implementing rules for the Prospectus Directive and the CESR advice (ESC / 42/2003-rev2).

—— (2003b), 'Provisional Mandate to CESR for Technical Advice on Possible Implementing Measures Concerning the Future Directive on Financial Instruments Mar-kets' (MARKT/G2 D(2003)), available via http://europa.

eu.int/comm/internal_market/en/finances/mobil/isd/docs/esc37-mandate_en.pdf (accessed May 2004).

——n (2003c), 'Investment Services Directive: Council Agreement is Major Step Towards Integrated EU Equities Market', Commission Press Release, 7 Oct.

—— (2003d), 'Financial Services: Commission to set up Expert Forum to Look at Policies from Users' Point of View (FIN–USE)', Commission Press Release, 25 July.

—— (2003e), 'EU Concerned About US Audit Registration Step', Commission Press Release, 24 April.

—— (2003f), *Financial Services: The FSAP Enters the Home Strait* (9th FSAP Progress Report, Nov.).

European Securities Committee (2003a), Summary Record of the Ninth Meeting of European Securities Committee/Alternates, 30 January 2003 (ESC 9/2003), available via http://europa.eu.int/comm/internal_market/en/finances/mobil/docs/esc/meeting-01–2003-report_en1.pdf (accessed May 2004).

—— (2003b), Summary Record of the 11th Meeting of European Securities Committee / Alternates 23 May 2003 (ESC 21/2003), available via http://europa.eu.int/comm/internal_market/en/finances/mobil/docs/esc/meeting-05–2003-report_en.pdf (accessed May 2004).

Evans-Pritchard, A. (2003), 'EC Fury at Franco-German Backroom Deal', *Daily Telegraph*, 13 June, p. 34.

Federation of German Industries (2003), *Lamfalussy Process—Statement on the First Interim Report of May 2003*, available via http://europa.eu.int/comm/internal_market/en/finances/mobil/docs/lamfalussy/2003-07-comments-bdi1_en.pdf (accessed May 2004).

Ferran, E. (2004), *Building an EU Securities Market* (Cambridge: Cambridge University Press).

Financial Services Authority (2003), Alternative Trading Systems: Policy Statement and Made Text (London: FSA).

Financial Times (2002), Lex Column, 'The Prodi Plot', 19 Nov., p. 20.

—— (2003), Leader Column, 'Concerns About the Lamfalussy Approach', 1 December, p. 18.

Forbes (2003), 'Bolkestein Sees EU–US Audit Firm Deal by Year End', Forbes.com, quoting Frits Bolkestein, European Internal Market Commission http://www.forbes.com/personalfi-nance/retirement/newswire/2003/10/09/rtr1103943.html.

Gillingham, J. (2003), *European Integration 1965–2003* (Cambridge: Cambridge University Press).

Green, D. (2000), 'Enhanced Co-operation among Regulators and the Role of National Regulators in a Global Market', 2 *Journal of International Financial Markets* 7.

Guerrera, F. and Norman, P. (2002), 'European Leaders Invested Heavily in Building a Single Capital Market to Rival the US', *Financial Times*, 4 December, p. 17.

Haas, P.M. (1992), 'Introduction: Epistemic Communities and International Policy Co-ordination', 46 *International Organization* [1].

Harlow, C. (2002), *Accountability in the European Union* (Oxford: Oxford University Press).

Heritier, A. (1996), 'The Accommodation of Diversity in European Policy-making and Its Outcomes: Regulatory Policy as Patchwork', 3 *Journal of European Public Policy* 149.

Hertig, G. (2001), 'Regulatory Competition for EU Financial Services' in D. C. Esty and D. Geradi, *Regulatory Competition and Economic Integration* (Oxford: Oxford University Press).

Hertig, G. and Lee, R. (2003), 'Four Predictions About the Future of EU Securities Regulation' 2003 *Journal of Corporate Law Studies* 359.

Hix, S. (1999), *The Political System of the European Union* (Basingstoke: Palgrave Macmillan).

Hogfeldt, P. (2003), 'The History and Politics of Corporate Ownership in Sweden', *European Corporate Governance Institute* Finance Working Paper No. 30/2003, ssrn abstractid=449460.

Hopt, K.J. (1976), 'The Necessity of Co-ordinating or Approximating Economic Legislation, or of Supplementing or Replacing it by Community Law—A Report', 13 *Common Market Law Review* 245.

IIMG (2003a), Inter-Institutional Monitoring Group for Securities Markets, First Interim Report Monitoring the New Process for Regulating Securities Markets in Europe (The Lamfalussy Process) (Brussels, May 2003).

—— (2003b), Inter-Institutional Monitoring Group for Securities Markets, *Second Interim Report Monitoring the Lamfalussy Process*) (Brussels, December 2003).

Inel, B. (2003a), 'Assessing the First Two Years of the New Regulatory Framework for Financial Markets in Europe', 18(9) *Journal of International Banking Law and Regulation* 363.

—— (2003b), 'Implementing the Market Abuse Directive', 8 *European Financial Services Regulation* 10.

—— (2004), 'Impact of Enlargement on the Wholesale Banking Markets', 14 *European Financial Services Regulation* 3.

Joerges, C. (1999), '"Good Governance" Through Comitology' in Joerges and Vos (eds), *EU Committees* (Oxford: Hart Pblishing), p. 318.

Joerges, C. and Vos, E. (eds) (1999), *EU Committees: Social Regulation, Law and Politics* (Oxford, Hart Publishing).

Lamfalussy Committee (2000), *The Regulation of European Securities Markets: Initial Report* (Brussels, 9 November), available at http://www.europa.eu.int/comm/internal_market/en/finances/general/lamfalussyen.pdf (last visited 2005).

Lamfalussy Committee (2001), *The Regulation of European Securities Markets: Final Report* (Brussels, 15 February), available at http://www.europa.eu.int/comm/internal_market/en/finances/general/lamfalussyen.pdf (last visited 2005).

Lastra, R.M. (2003), 'The Governance Structure for Financial Regulation and Supervision in Europe', 10 *Columbia Journal of Economic Law* 49.

Lewis, J. (2002), 'National Interests: Coreper' in Peterson and Shackleton (eds), *The Institutions of the European Union*, pp. 277–98.

Lisbon European Council (2000), Presidency Conclusions, 23–24 Mar., available at http://europa.eu.int/european_council/conclusions/index_en.htm (last visited 18 August 2005).

Macey, J. (2003), 'Regulatory Globalization as a Response to Regulatory Competition', *Emory Law Journal* 1353.

Majone, G. (1996), 'Regulatory Legitimacy' in Majone (ed), *Regulating Europe* London: Routledge), p. 300

—— (2002a), 'Delegation of Regulatory Powers in a Mixed Polity', 8 *European Law Journal* 319.

—— (2002b), 'Functional Interests: European Agencies' in Peterson and Shackleton (eds), *The Institutions of the European Union* (Oxford: Oxford University Press), p. 323.

Mazey, S. and Richardson, J. (2001), 'Interest Groups and EU Policy-making' in Richardson (ed), *European Union* (London: Routledge), 217–37.

McGee, A. and Weatherill, S. (1990), 'The Evolution of the Single Market—Harmonisation or Liberalisation', 53 *Modern Law Review* 578.

McKee, M. (2003), 'The Unpredictable Future of European Securities Regulation', 18 *Journal of International Banking Law and Regulation* 277.

Moloney, N. (2002), *EC Securities Regulation* (Oxford: Oxford University Press).

—— (2004), 'Confidence and Competence: the Conundrum of EC Capital Markets Law' 2004 *Journal of Corporate Law Studies* 1.

Norman, P. (2002a), 'A Tiny Committee with Considerable Reach', *Financial Times*, 7 November, p. 16.

—— (2002b), 'EU Urged to Mull Single Financial Watchdog', *Financial Times*, 27 November, p. 3.

—— (2003), 'EU Tries to Balance Quality and Haste', *FT.com*, 6 April.

Nugent, N. (1999), *The Government and Politics of the European Union* (4th ed, Basingstoke: Palgrave Macmillan).

—— (2002), 'The Commission's Services' in Peterson and Shackleton (eds), *The Institutions of the European Union* (Oxford: Oxford University Press), pp. 156–62.

O'Keefe, D. and Carey, N. (2002), 'The Internal Market and Investor Protection' in G. Ferrarini, K.J. Hopt and E. Wymeersch (eds), *Capital Markets in the Age of the Euro* (London, Kluwer Law International), pp. 1–16.

Parliamentary Select Committee on the European Union (2003), *Towards a Single Market for Finance: the Financial Services Action Plan* (45th Report, London, TSO).

PCAOB (2004), Final Rules Relating to the Oversight of Non-US Public Accounting Firms (PCAOB Release No. 2004–005, June).

Peterson, J. (2002), 'The College of Commissioners' in Peterson and Shackleton (eds), *The Institutions of the European Union* (Oxford: Oxford University Press), pp. 71–94.

Picciotto, S. (1997), 'Networks in International Economic Integration: Fragmented States and the Dilemmas of Neo-liberalism', 17 *Northwestern Journal of International Law and Business* 1014.

Reinhardt, N. (2004), *The Lamfalussy Process: A Guide and Evaluation* (Brussels: Houston Consulting Europe, April).

Revell, S. (2003), 'The Prospectus Directive', 14 *Practical Law for Companies* 14.

Richardson, J. (ed) (2001a), *European Union: Power and Policy-Making* (2nd ed, London: Routledge).

—— (2001b), 'Policy-making in the EU: Interests, Ideas and Garbage Cans of Primeval Soup' in Richardson (ed), *European Union: Power and Policy-Making* (2nd ed, London: Routledge), pp. 3–26.

Rudnick, D. (2003), 'Big Guns Voice Concern at Takeover Directive Amendments', *Daily Telegraph*, 6 November, p. 15.

Scott, C. (2001), 'Analysing Regulatory Space: Fragmented Resources and Institutional Design' [2001] *PL* 329.

—— (2002), 'The Governance of the European Union: The Potential for Multi-Level Control', 8 *European Law Journal* 59.

Scott, J. and Trubek, D.M. (2002), 'Mind the Gap: Law and the New Approaches to Governance in the European Union', 8 *European Law Journal* 1.

Securities Expert Group (2004), *Financial Services Action Plan: Progress and Prospects* (Final Report, Brussels, May), pp. 9–10. This report is available at http://www.europa.eu.int/comm/internal_market/en/finances/actionplan/docs/stocktaking/fasap-stocktaking-report-securities_en.pdf (last visited 2005).

Shackleton, M. (2002), 'The European Parliament' in J. Peterson and M. Shackleton (eds), *The Institutions of the European Union* (Oxford: Oxford University Press), pp. 95–117.

Skorecki, A. and Buck, T. (2004), 'Banks in EU Set for Share Trading Shake-up', *FT.com*, 24 Feb.

Slaughter, A.M. (2003), 'Global Government Networks, Global Information Agencies, and Dis-aggregated Democracy', 24 *Michigan Journal of International Law* 1041.

Snyder F. (1999), 'EMU Revisited: Are We Making a Constitution? What Constitution Are We Making?' in Craig and de Búrca (eds), *The Evolution of EU Law* (Oxford: Oxford University Press), p. 463.

Stigler, G. (1971), 'The Theory of Economic Regulation', 6(2) *Bell Journal of Economics and Management Sciences* 3.

Stiglitz, J. (2002), *Globalization and its Discontents* (London: Penguin).

Stockholm European Council (2001), The Council's Resolution on More Effective Securities Market Regulation in the European Union (Stockholm, 23 Mar.), available at http://ue.eu.int/ueDocs/cms_Date/docs/pressData/en/ec/00100-r1. per cent20ann-r1.en1.html (last visited 19 August 2005).

Thatcher, M. (2001), 'European Regulation' in Richardson (ed), *European Union: Power and Policy-Making* (2nd ed, London: Routledge), pp. 304–7.

Trefgarne, G. (2002), 'MEP Wins AIM Concessions', *Daily Telegraph*, 27 Feb., p. 39.

Tsoukalis, L. (2001), 'Economic and Monetary Union', in H. Wallace and W. Wallace (eds), *Policy-Making in the European Union* (4th ed, Oxford: Oxford University Press).

van Leeuwen, A.D. (2002), 'Interview with CESR Chairman', 7(3) *The Financial Regulator* 20.

—— (2003), Speech by Chairman of CESR, 'A Network of Regulators to Meet the Challenges of Regulating European Capital Markets' (Ref.: CESR/03–055), Guildhall, London, 6 Mar., text available via http://www.cesr-eu.org (accessed May 2004).

Villiers, T. (2003), 'Where Next for the ISD?' (3 Nov.) *The Parliament Magazine* 23.

Wallace, H. (2000a), 'The Institutional Setting' in H. Wallace and W. Wallace (eds), *Policy-Making in the European Union* (4th ed, Oxford: Oxford University Press), p. 6.

—— (2000b), 'The Policy Process' in H. Wallace and W. Wallace (eds), *Policy-Making in the European Union* (4th ed, Oxford: Oxford University Press).

Weatherill, S. and Beaumont, P. (2000), *EU Law* (London: Penguin).

Wincott, D. (2001), 'Looking Forward or Harking Back? The Commission and the Reform of Governance in the EU', 39 *Journal of Common Market Studies* 897.

Wolf, J. and Atkinson, D. (1999), 'Spain Rocks Takeover Pact', *Guardian*, 22 June, p. 20.

Young, A.R. and Wallace, H. (2001), 'The Single Market' in H. Wallace and W. Wallace (eds), *Policy-Making in the European Union* (4th ed, Oxford: Oxford University Press), pp. 98–102.

17

EC Company Law Directives and Regulations: How Trivial Are They?

LUCA ENRIQUES*

I. INTRODUCTION

IN A RECENT article on the dynamics of state competition for corporate charters in the United States, Mark Roe argues that Delaware's main competitor in making corporate law is the federal government (2003). Since 'Delaware players know that the federal government can take away their corporate lawmaking power in whole or in part,' (Roe 2003: 592) the federal government has a heavy influence on the state's corporate law (Roe 2003: 591). This intuition, that, as Roe argues, is confirmed by the history of Delaware law and federal politics, law, and regulation (Roe 2003: 600–34),[1] carries significant implications

---

* University of Bologna and ECGI (luca.enriques@unibo.it). For helpful comments to earlier drafts of this chapter, I wish to thank Riccardo Basso, Carmine Di Noia, Eilís Ferran, Matteo Gatti, Jeffrey Gordon, Harald Halbhuber, Niamh Moloney, Federico Mucciarelli, Katharina Pistor, Mark Roe, Bruna Szegö, Marcello Tarabusi, participants at the 11th CLEF annual meeting at ETH (Zurich), at the Conference 'EU Corporate Law Making: Institutional Structure, Regulatory Competition, and Regulatory Strategies,' held at Harvard Law School on 29–30 October 2004, and at the ECGI and Oxford Review of Economic Policy Conference on Corporate Governance, held at the Saïd Business School in Oxford on 28–29 January 2005, and especially Brian Cheffins, Gérard Hertig and Stefano Lombardo. I am also grateful to Bill Carney, who provided me with an unpublished appendix to an inspiring article of his, to Mette Neville, for a clarification on Swedish company law, and to Carlo Salodini for his valuable research assistance. The usual disclaimers apply. This chapter was previously published in (2006) 27 *University of Pennsylvania Journal of International Economic Law* 1–78. The permission of the *University of Pennsylvania Journal of Economic Law* to republish is gratefully acknowledged.

[1] Roe provides evidence supporting the view that the federal government 'can displace corporate law,' '[c]an [i]nspire [f]ear' in Delaware players, and 'deeply and directly affects the corporate internal affairs that Delaware seeks to regulate'). See also Bratton (1994: 418–25) who similarly provides evidence of the fact that the federal threat to intervene in the corporate law area affects Delaware law. For a strong critique of Roe's thesis *see* Romano (2005: 26–35).

for the debate on competition for corporate charters in the United States (Roe 2003: 634–43). And it is also relevant to the European debate on whether *Centros* and its progeny[2] can trigger regulatory competition within the EU (Roe 2003: 643–44). According to Roe (2003: 644),

> those who analyze the EU's *Centros* debate need to understand that the full parallel [with the American race] brings Brussels ... into the picture. Whether Brussels is effective, defective, or ineffectual affects the race.

While Member States are not now engaged in competition for corporate charters, and cannot be expected to engage in one in the near future,[3] the very presence of a centralized policymaker within the EU appears to play a role in determining the likelihood of a US-style scenario, and more generally in the evolution of corporate laws[4] within the Union. This chapter inquires into the role played by EC legislation in the sphere of corporate law. Parts II and III respond to the question of how far EC legislation actually shapes corporate laws in the various Member States, and, in short, how important it is for the governance and management of EU companies.

At first sight, the EC appears to play a central role in shaping EU corporate laws, here conceived broadly to include also accounting law and securities law regulating issuers. EC harmonization measures under Article 44(2)(g) of the EC Treaty,[5] now cover a number of areas, including formation of companies, distributions to shareholders, new issues of shares, mergers, divisions, accounting, auditing, mandatory disclosure, insider trading, takeovers, and so on.[6] The EC has also created a European legal form, the European Company, which any medium-to-large EU business may adopt.[7]

---

[2] See Cases C-212/97 *Centros Ltd v Erhvervs-og Selskabsstyrelsen* [1999] ECR I-1459; C-208/00 *Überseering BV v Nordic Construction Baumanagement GmbH* [2002] ECR I-9919; C-167/01 *Kamer van Koophandel v Inspire Art* [2003] ECR I-10155.

[3] See, e.g., Enriques (2004a) and Tröger (2004) each arguing that a scenario similar to the American one, in which one or more European States engage in chartermongering, is highly unlikely.

[4] The terms 'corporate law' and 'company law' are used as synonyms throughout this chapter. The same is true for the terms 'corporations' and 'companies.'

[5] Art 44(2)(g) of the Treaty establishing the European Community grants the Council the power to 'coordinate to the necessary extent the safeguards which, for the protection of the interests of members and other, are required by Member States of companies or firms within the meaning of the second paragraph of Art 48 with a view to making such safeguards equivalent throughout the Community.'

[6] App 1 below provides the list of all relevant EC Directives and Regulations.

[7] In 1985, the EC introduced another legal form, the European Economic Interests Grouping or EEIG (see Council Reg (EEC) 2137/85 of 25 July 1985). This legal form, which has been quite successful especially in France and Belgium (see http://www.libertas-institut.com/uk/uk_Vorlage.htm, whereby a list of 1447 EEIGs), will not be considered in here, because arguably it is not a company in any meaningful sense: Member States are free to 'determine

One may think that, in the face of EC's pervasive intervention in the field, the European corporate law landscape is indeed similar to the American as recently described by Mark Roe (2003); that is, that EC institutions in Brussels have a strong influence upon Member States' corporate laws and, by implication, upon EU companies, either because they have already intervened in the area or because they may do so in the future. But, as we shall see, this is not the case.

Quite the opposite, existing EC corporate law is mostly trivial, in the sense that, with due but limited exceptions, it has very little impact on the way companies, and especially medium and large ones, are directed, managed, and controlled: first of all, EC corporate law does not cover such core areas as fiduciary duties and shareholder remedies; secondly, it is under-enforced; thirdly, given the very sporadic judiciary interpretation of the European Court of Justice, EC corporate law tends to be implemented and construed differently in each Member State, i.e. according to local legal culture and consistent with prior provisions; fourthly, when it has introduced new rules, it has done so with respect to issues on which Member States would have most probably legislated even in the absence of an EC mandate; finally, most EC corporate law rules can be categorized as optional, market-mimicking, unimportant, or avoidable. As a result, EC Directives and Regulations play no significant role in addressing the agency problems stemming from the corporate form, because there is very little they prohibit or require or enable to do. By contrast, national corporate laws, as argued in Part IV.B, contain the core rules, which do have an impact upon EU companies' governance and management.

Of course, the triviality hypothesis which is tested in Parts II and III does not apply to European Court of Justice case law in the area of freedom of establishment. *Centros, Überseering,* and *Inspire Art*[8] have in fact made it somewhat easier for start-up and closely-held companies to engage in regulatory arbitrage,[9] already prompting national reforms of the regulation of such companies.[10] However, these case-law develop-

---

whether or not groupings registered at their registries, pursuant to Art 6, have legal personality' (Art 1, para 3); members' 'participations' in the grouping can only be transferred with the unanimous consent of other members (Art 22, para 1); and grouping's members are jointly and severally liable for the grouping's debts and liabilities of whatever nature (Art 24, para 1). On legal personality, free transferability of shares and limited liability as core features of corporations, *see* Kraakman *et al.* (2004: 6–11).

[8] See above n 2.
[9] See, e.g., Enriques (2004a: 1261).
[10] An overhaul of Dutch corporate law is currently at its final stage (see de Kluiver (2004: 132)), while in France, Loi No 2003-721 of 1 August 2003 got rid of the most apparent competitive disadvantage of French vis-a-vis English corporate law, i.e. minimum capital for (private) limited liability companies (*sociétés à responsabilité limitée*) (Art 1).

ments are beyond the scope of this chapter, which deals with *secondary* EC corporate law, i.e. Directives and Regulations.

Finding that, notwithstanding the steady stream of secondary EC corporate law rules over the last three decades, EC legislation is only marginally important for EU companies (other than smaller ones), Part IV qualifies the triviality thesis, by identifying exceptions to it and by highlighting the major impact of Directives and Regulations in this area: they raise the cost of doing business by making it compulsory or highly advisable to obtain the advice of some professionals, such as accountants and lawyers, thereby securing these professionals' rents. Further, EC corporate law does affect the evolution of European corporate laws and, to some degree, the dynamics of regulatory competition. Finally, it has developed as an industry itself, employing a number of EC and state officials and lobbyists, and creating occasions for rent extraction by politicians. Part V concludes.

II. THE TRIVIALITY THESIS (1): SCOPE, ENFORCEMENT, INTERPRETATION AND TIMING OF EC CORPORATE LAW RULES

Since 1968, the EC has adopted 37 Directives[11] and 10 regulations[12] in the area of corporate law,[13] and its output, after a decade or so of deep crisis,[14] has been significantly growing since 2001.

Undeniably, national corporate laws have changed as a consequence of the harmonization measures.[15] As the European Commission itself put it in a recent Communication,

---

[11] A Directive is a legislative act which, according to Art 249, EC Treaty, 'shall be binding, as to the result to be achieved, upon each Member State to which it is addressed, but shall leave to the national authorities the choice of form and methods.' National authorities have to transpose Directives, i.e. to introduce domestic laws and regulations consistent with them. In practice, the content of Directives is often so specific as to leave national authorities little or no choice of form and methods.

[12] A Regulation is a legislative act which, again according to Art 249, EC Treaty, 'shall have general application. It shall be binding in its entirety and directly applicable in all Member States.'

[13] Eleven (including the Takeover Directive) are 'core' corporate law Directives (10) or Regulations (one), while 18 measures deal with auditing and accounting issues (11 Directives and seven Regulations). The remaining eighteen measures are in the securities law area (16 Directives and two Regulations); of these eighteen securities law measures, 10 have been repealed by Directives consolidating or updating them. See App 1.A.

[14] See Hopt (2000: 127) describing the 'political and other difficulties with company law harmonization' experienced by the European Commission during the 1990s.

[15] See, e.g., Blaurock (1998: 383).

Table 1: Number of EC Company Law Directives and Regulations per year
(Updated to 31 December 2004. Years in which no Directives or Regulations were adopted are omitted)

1968	1	1989	4
1977	1	1990	3
1978	2	1992	1
1979	1	1994	2
1980	1	1999	1
1982	3	2001	4
1983	1	2002	1
1984	2	2003	8
1987	1	2004	9
1988	1	Total	47

[o]ver the years, the EU institutions have taken a number of initiatives in the area of company law, many leading to impressive achievements. ... [T]hese European measures have had an important impact on national company law.[16]

This view is also shared by some European legal scholars. For instance, according to the Danish author of an EC company law treatise, 'a quite comprehensive Community law regulation on most material aspects in the capital companies has been achieved' (Werlauff 2003: 100).[17]

Does this mean that EC rules have a real impact on the governance and management of EU corporations?[18] As this and the following part argue, the short answer is no: a closer look at the relevant Directives and

[16] See Modernising Company Law and Enhancing Corporate Governance in the European Union—A Plan to Move Forward. Communication from the Commission to the Council and the European Parliament 6 (COM (2003) 284(01)) (emphasis and footnotes omitted).

[17] See also Wouters (2000: 258–67) stating that 'what has been realized by the Community in the field of company and accounting law is impressive'; Gleichmann (1991: 3–4): 'the work of harmonizing national company law in the Community must be counted a success. This is shown not only by the number of Directives that are in force .... It is also true when measured by the importance of the areas of the law that have been coordinated').

Edwards (1999) describes as 'significantly realized' the prediction by Clive Schmitthoff according to which company law would 'emerge as a truly European law'; Davies (2003: 112) describes the impact of EC law on English company law as 'substantial'; Lecourt (2004: 225) argues that entire areas of company law are under EC influence and that harmonized rules have been an important factor of modernisation for European firms.

[18] Note that the question here is not whether EC secondary legislation in the corporate law area has helped achieve the objective of markets integration. For a sceptical assessment on EC securities law's role in the building of a single EU securities market, see Ferran (2004: 36–41).

Regulations reveals that EC corporate law, especially with respect to well established companies, is trivial, due to its scope, sporadic enforcement and parochial interpretation, because it usually covers areas on which Member States had already or would have legislated anyway, and, as the next part argues, given that most of its rules are optional, market-mimicking, unimportant or avoidable.

A. Scope of EC Corporate Law

The efforts to cover the core areas of corporate law have thus far failed. The Commission proposals on the corporate governance of companies and on company groups have never even been close to adoption,[19] nor is there any evidence that they have affected national legislation in any way.[20] As Harald Halbhuber (2001) notes, the Directives that have instead been approved 'do not purport to deal with crucial issues like fiduciary duties, exit, expulsion, and redemption, transfer of shares etc.' 'The legal rights and remedies of shareholders against the management of the company in the operation of the business, involving issues like derivative suits and directors' liability, and finally, the liability shield itself and ways to pierce it, remain matters of national law' (Halbhuber 2001: 1406).[21]

B. Sporadic Enforcement, Parochial Interpretation

The impact of EC corporate law on individual jurisdictions is lessened by the well-known fact that the enforcement mechanisms of EC corporate law are imperfect to say the least.[22] Even more fundamentally, one can doubt that anything really worth calling EC corporate law exists 'off the books.'

[19] See, e.g., Edwards (1999: 389, 391) describing the legislative work done on these proposals and reports that they have been abandoned.

[20] This is all the more true of the EC Commission's non-binding 'recommendations.' They are, in fact, usually ignored by Member States. See, e.g., Enriques (2003a: 917). To be sure, whenever national policymakers happen to have the same policy agenda as the Commission, a recommendation may help make the case for that policy choice, lending it a European flavour and hence make it more appealing. But whenever EC and national policymakers' agendas differ, the impact of recommendations is nil. This justifies our decision here simply to ignore them. For the same reasons, EC Commission's Communications in this area will be ignored.

[21] See also Timmermans (2002: 3) who similarly states that: 'attempts to harmonise classic issues of company law such as the institutional structure of the public company, minority protection, and directors' liability, failed'; Andersson (2003: 186) suggests that: 'the legislative efforts of the EU have to a large extent … been concerned with matters of lesser economic importance or at least with issues of relatively minor practical value.'

[22] See, e.g., Hopt (1999: 57).

1. *Underenforcement*

The Commission has traditionally lacked the resources to monitor Member States' compliance with corporate law Directives (Edwards 1999: 11);[23] and no significant enforcement 'from the bottom,' in the form of European Court of Justice (ECJ) preliminary reference procedures from national courts has ever made up for this. Thus far, the ECJ (which has no docket control) has decided upon no more than 25 preliminary reference procedures dealing with secondary EC corporate law.[24]

Of course, Member States do implement Directives, although often with considerable delay. However, major instances of implementing rules that are clearly at odds with the text of the Directives can be found throughout the EU. To mention but one, in implementing the Fourth Council Directive of July 25, 1978 (Fourth Directive),[25] Germany simply omitted a provision transposing Article 2, para 5.[26]

[23] See Wolff (1993: 24). Thus far, the European Court of Justice has decided on no more than 11 proceedings against Member States for failure to implement corporate law Directives (Lexis search of CELEX European Union Cases database, 2 January 2005. See App 2.A). Nine of them concerned failure to implement Directives within the deadline provided for in the Directives themselves. One of them concerned failure to transpose two articles in a Directive and only one dealt with the more substantive issue of whether the implementing rules had correctly transposed the Directive's provisions (see below text accompanying n 30). The EC Commission website reports nine infringement procedures in the area of 'Company Law and Financial Reporting' between 1998 and 2004 (of these, four were brought in 2004) (see http://www.europa.eu.int/comm/internal_market/financial-reporting/infringements_en. htm (last visited on 2 January 2005). No infringement proceedings are reported with respect to securities Directives and Regulations (see http://www.europa.eu.int/comm/internal_ market/en/finances/infr/index.htm (last visited on 2 January 2005).

[24] LexisNexis search of CELEX European Union Cases database, 2 January 2005. See App 2.B. The preliminary rulings had been requested by courts from Greece (nine requests, for a total of seven rulings: in two instances two cases were decided jointly); Germany (eight requests, for a total of seven rulings: in one instance two cases were decided jointly); the Netherlands (three); Austria (one); Belgium (one); France (one); and Spain (one). For comparison, just between 1998 and 2002 the ECJ decided upon or otherwise completed no fewer than 1129 preliminary reference proceedings. See European Court of Justice (2002: 158). It is also interesting to note that 16 out of the 25 cases involved proceedings between private parties on the one hand and the state on the other (as prosecutor or law enforcer in three cases, as bankruptcy administrator in eight of the nine Greek cases, as tax authority in two cases, as company register in two cases, and as regulator of auditors in one case).

[25] Fourth Council Dir 78/660/EEC of 25 July 1978 based on Art 54(3)(g) of the Treaty on the annual accounts of certain types of companies, [1978] OJ L222/11.

[26] See Alexander (1993: 64). See also Van Hulle (1997: 716): 'Some Member States (Germany, Austria, Finland and Sweden) were so unhappy about [the true and fair view concept] that they refused to fully implement it.'

Art 2, para 5, provides that '[w]here in exceptional cases the application of a provision of this Directive is incompatible with the obligation laid down in paragraph 3, that provision must be departed from in order to give a true and fair view within the meaning of paragraph 3. Any such departure must be disclosed in the notes on the accounts together with an explanation of the reasons for it and a statement of its effect on the assets, liabilities, financial position and profit or loss. The Member States may define the exceptional cases in question and lay down the relevant special rules.'

Germany decided not to introduce a provision expressly transposing Art 2, para 5, on the grounds that it was superfluous: such an implementing rule would only have stated explicitly

More insidiously, Member States have sometimes failed to enforce implementing rules. Again, Germany is a case in point with respect to the obligation to disclose annual accounts, as imposed by the Fourth Directive.[27] Although most private companies (GmbHs) failed to comply, no sanction ever followed, because rules on sanctions had been crafted in such a way as to make them practically impossible to apply.[28] Fifteen years after the deadline for the implementation of the relevant EC provisions,[29] the ECJ finally declared that Germany had failed to comply with its obligations under EC law.[30] Despite changes in the rules sanctioning the violation of the disclosure obligation so as to make it easier for sanctions to be applied,[31] many German companies still fail to disclose their accounts.[32] This warrants the suspicion (admittedly, only the suspicion) that the accounting rules implementing the Fourth Directive may also be commonly violated: in the absence of disclosure to the public, the incentive to draw true and fair accounts is definitely less.[33]

EC securities law, as the Lamfalussy Report recognized,[34] is also a field in which Member States have often violated Community law with very little subsequent EC enforcement.[35] It is too early to tell whether the new

what could be derived from the general principle in German law, according to which rules have to be construed consistently with the Directive's legislative intent as expressed in Art 2. See, e.g., Habersack (2003: 233 n 47) reporting that this view was endorsed by the Government commission in charge of drafting the rules implementing the Fourth Dir; Ordelheide (1993: 86): 'The so-called functional interpretation of the law can be regarded as an equivalent to the overriding property of the true and fair view of Art 2 (5)'.

Although, as is argued immediately below, it is impossible to tell what the content of an EC corporate law provision is until the ECJ decides upon it, it would be surprising if Art 2, para 5, were to be construed as simply meaning that the specific provisions of the Fourth Dir have to be construed according to the legislative intent. See Haller (2002): '[Art 2, para 5,] ranks professional judgement higher than codified rules or standards.'

[27] See Art 47.
[28] See, e.g., Edwards (1999: 26–27). Similarly, in Spain 'the law does not establish a penalty for not ... [depositing annual accounts in the Registro Mercantil] unless the company goes bankrupt. This implies that not all firms, especially the smaller ones, comply with this obligation ....' (Gutiérrez and Tribó 2004: 7).
[29] See Art 55, para 2(d), Fourth Dir.
[30] Case C-191-95 *Commission v Federal Republic of Germany* [1998] ECR I-5449.
[31] See, e.g., Habersack (2003: 69).
[32] *Cf* Höfner (2004: 476) stating that, despite the absence of statistical data, it is clear that the majority of the 100,000 German GmbH & Co KG—one of the legal forms available to German businesses to which the Fourth Dir applies—fail to disclose their accounts.
[33] Not to mention that in Germany annual accounts prepared according to company law rules are relevant also for tax purposes (see e.g. Haller (2002: 157), which of course does not encourage compliance with the true and fair view principle.
[34] See Wise Men (2001: 14–15).
[35] See, e.g., Lannoo (1999: 282) with specific reference to the first insider trading Directive and to Council Dir 88/627/EEC of 12 December 1988 on the information to be published when a major holding in a listed company is acquired or disposed of [1988] OJ L348/62; Moloney (2002: 153–54) with respect to Council Dir 80/390/EEC of 17 March 1980

wave of securities Directives,[36] together with the Lamfalussy architecture and especially its level 3 and level 4 regulatory tools,[37] will change this state of affairs.[38]

A process of 'intentional or unintentional erosion' (Buxbaum and Hopt 1988: 265) may also take place, by which new national laws modify rules implementing EC Directives in a way inconsistent with the latter, a phenomenon 'which may well occur without the Community authorities being aware of it or being in a position to evaluate its impact' (*ibid.*).

Good examples of erosion can be found in recent corporate law developments in Italy. The comprehensive corporate law reform of 2003 blatantly violates the Second Directive[39] in several respects. For instance, contrary to its Article 18, para 1, which bans subscription of own shares outright, Article 2357-*ter*, para 2, of the Italian Civil Code now provides that the shareholders' meeting may authorize the company to exercise the pre-emptive rights pertaining to its treasury shares and thus to subscribe its own shares.[40] Or, against the Second Directive's Article 13, the provisions on conversion of companies do not require an expert report assessing that the value of the net assets of a private limited liability company ('*società a responsabilità limitata*') being converted into a public

---

coordinating the requirements for the drawing up, scrutiny and distribution of the listing particulars to be published for the admission of securities to official stock exchange listing [1980] OJ L100/1. See also above, end of n 23. Katharina Pistor suggests (2004: 352) that accession countries may have adopted a 'comply but don't enforce strategy' with respect to EC corporate law measures such as Dir 88/627/EEC.

[36] For a complete list of these see below, App 1.

[37] Under the 'Lamfalussy Process,' 'the key objective of level 3 [is] to ensure consistent, timely, common and uniform implementation of Level 1 and 2 acts in member states, via enhanced co-operation and networking among EU securities regulators,' while '[a]t level 4, the Commission and the member states would strengthen the enforcement of community law' (Hertig and Lee 2003: 363). See below text preceding n 146 for a brief description of Lamfalussy approach's level 1 and level 2 measures.

[38] According to an experts group appraising the impact of the Financial Services Action Plan, 'at present, enforcement is not sufficiently effective, in particular because of lack of political impetus, infringement procedures that are too time-consuming and insufficient allocation of Commission resources' (Securities Expert Group 2004: 17).

See also Hertig and Lee (2003: 367) who express the view that the Lamfalussy method will fail to solve the problem of weak enforcement of EC securities law.

Similarly, it has been argued that the recent steps forward in EC accounting regulation, and especially the adoption of International Financial Reporting Standards, may have less impact than commonly expected, due to the fact that, as recent scandals in the US and in Europe have shown, proper enforcement of accounting rules is crucial and, at present, totally left to Member States. See Lannoo (2003: 352, 357).

[39] Second Council Dir 77/91 of 13 December 1976 on coordination of safeguards which, for the protection of the interests of members and others, are required by Member States of companies within the meaning of the second paragraph of Art 58 of the Treaty, in respect of the formation of public limited liability companies and the maintenance and alteration of their capital, with a view to making such safeguards equivalent [1977] OJ L26/1.

[40] See critically Portale (2003: 264). [See also *ibid.* for another example of erosion concerning the EC rules on divisions.]

company ('*società per azioni*') corresponds at least to the transformed entity's legal capital (Enriques 2003b: 112–13).

Finally, the fact that Directives have no 'direct horizontal effect' further dulls the impact of EC legislation on corporate law within the Member States. As the ECJ so frequently reiterated, Directives are addressed to Member States and private parties cannot invoke them in relationships with other private parties.[41] This means that national company laws that conflict with a Directive remain in effect as regards private parties until they are repealed by the national legislator, even if in the meantime the ECJ finds that they are in violation of the Directive. To be sure, the Court has also held that, in applying national law, national courts must construe the national law,

> *as far as possible*, in the light of the wording and the purpose of the Directive in order to achieve the result pursued by the latter.'[42]

In fact, as the *Marleasing* case shows, such a requirement may actually produce an outcome that closely resembles direct horizontal effect.[43]

2. Does Secondary EC Corporate Law Really Exist?

An even more fundamental question may be raised about EC corporate law. Is there any secondary EC corporate law at all, apart from the interpretation the ECJ has provided in the 19 rulings thus far issued on substantive grounds in this area?[44] Harald Halbhuber (2001: 1385) has convincingly shown that national doctrinal structures 'filter European legal materials,' so that one may question whether EC corporate law

---

[41] See, e.g., Case 152/84, *M. H. Marshall v Southampton and South-West Hampshire Area Health Authority (Teaching)*, [1986] E.C.R. 723, para 48. Directives may have a direct 'vertical effect,' i.e. be applicable to the relationship between a private party and a Member State, possibly giving a private party harmed by the failure to implement a Directive the right to claim damages from the state. See, e.g., Craig and de Búrca (2003: 115).

[42] Case C-106/89 *Marleasing SA v La Comercial Internacional de Alimentacion SA* [1990] ECR I-4135, para 8 (emphasis added).

[43] *Cf* Werlauff (2003: 66–67). In *Marleasing* (above n 42), the ECJ held that Art 11 of the First Dir (First Council Dir 68/151/EEC of 9 March 1968 on co-ordination of safeguards which, for the protection of the interests of members and others, are required by Member States of companies within the meaning of the second paragraph of Art 58 of the Treaty, with a view to making such safeguards equivalent throughout the Community [1968] OJ L65/43), at the time not yet implemented by Spain, required Spanish courts to de facto disregard the Civil Code provisions, otherwise applying also to the corporate contract, according to which contracts without cause (purpose), or whose cause is unlawful, are void (Art 11 contains an exhaustive list of grounds for a declaration of nullity of a company; lack of cause or unlawful cause are not included).

[44] Out of these 19 rulings (one provided in an enforcement action against Germany by the Commission, above n 30, and 18 in preliminary rulings proceedings: see below App 2.B), six (those given in the Greek cases) deal with the same question, while three deal with very specific questions concerning the Fourth Dir. See below n 48.

'means the same for lawyers from different Member States'. More specifically, he shows how German lawyers' national legal culture led them to 'misread crucial [ECJ] case law [on companies' freedom of establishment] ... for over a decade,' (Halbhuber 2001: 1386)[45] and to 'overstate the harmonization actually achieved' (Halbhuber 2001: 1407) through corporate law Directives.

A good example of this tendency to 'nationalise' EC corporate law can also be found in Italian corporate law scholarship. Italian legal scholars tend to construe the Second Directive's provision (Article 34) that '[t]he subscribed capital may not be reduced to an amount less than the minimum capital laid down in accordance with Article 6,' as adopting the recapitalize or liquidate rule[46] which the Italian Civil Code (Article 2447) imposes upon Italian companies,[47] while in fact the Directive's provision 'only forbids formal capital reduction below that threshold [by the shareholders' meeting]' (Enriques and Macey 2001: 1183).

Even apart from these nationalistic tendencies in the interpretation of EC corporate law, there are instances in which core provisions in the Directives themselves cannot reasonably be construed uniformly, because different versions in different languages are incompatible. The most prominent case is Article 2 of the Fourth Directive, adopting the overriding principle that

[t]he annual accounts shall give a true and fair view of the company's assets, liabilities, financial position and profit or loss' (para 3).

As accounting scholars have shown, not only are the English and the German versions of Article 2 in no way direct translations of one another, but they 'do not appear to say or mean the same thing' (Alexander 1993: 63). If this is the case, it is no wonder that interpretations of Article 2, perhaps *the* core EC accounting law provision, are different in the various countries.[48]

---

[45] See also *ibid.*: 1387–99 showing the authors' idiosyncratic interpretation of ECJ company law cases from *Daily Mail* (*The Queen v H.M. Treasury and Commissioner of Inland Revenue, ex parte Daily Mail and General Trust PLC*, [1988] ECR 5483) to *Centros*.

[46] See below text corresponding to nn 71–72.

[47] See, e.g., Denozza (1993: 323).

[48] See *Id., passim* (showing that the interpretation of the true and fair view principle is different in the UK, Germany, and France). See also Haller (2002: 157): the true and fair value concept 'has been implemented and/or interpreted in the individual national laws in different ways. This has led to various European perceptions of [true and fair view], resulting in the possibility that financial statements may provide a [true and fair view] in the perception of one country, whereas the principle is essentially violated in another country;' [footnotes omitted].

See further Hopt (1991: 299): '[the true and fair view principle] is beautifully incorporated into the German commercial law statute. But ... [e]verything is more or less like before. This is true even in the book. The new statutory text is generally interpreted in the light of the old legal situation' [footnotes omitted].

To conclude on this point, with the possible exception of the few interpretative issues clarified by ECJ rulings, and no matter what truly EC-minded and ECJ-educated legal scholars argue, the prevailing interpretation of any given Directive in each jurisdiction is, wherever possible, an interpretation compatible with the existing legal culture. In other words, tradition and pre-harmonization corporate law tend to prevail, trivializing EC corporate law.

C. The Problem of 'Hindsight Bias'

As Brian Cheffins (1997: 448) has argued, 'the EU has typically done little more than superimpose a series of measures on domestic regulations already in place'. While this may be true with respect to many corporate law issues,[49] one has to concede that at least in certain policy areas the EC has issued Directives before most of the Member States had legislation in place, prompting them to adopt new rules. The most prominent example of a proactive move by the EC is the first Directive on insider trading.[50] Its proposal dates back to 1987, at a time when, among the then 12 Member States, only three (France, the United Kingdom, and Denmark) had insider trading prohibitions already in place.[51] Recently, the European Commission came first in adopting a post-Enron policy agenda to respond to US corporate governance reforms and was quickly followed on the same path by many Member States (Enriques 2003a: 916–25), some of which, to be sure, have succeeded in converting their reform efforts

---

The ECJ, presumably well aware of the far-reaching implications of any broad guideline on how to construe Art 2, has provided very narrow holdings when asked for a preliminary ruling involving its interpretation (the two relevant cases are Case C-234/94 *Tomberger v Gebrüder von der Wettern* [1996] ECR I-3133, and Case C-275-97 *DE + ES Bauunternehmung GmbH v Finanzamt Bergheim* [1999] ECR I-5331). *Cf* also Edwards (1999: 135): '[in *Tomberger*, the ECJ] couch[ed] its ruling in terms which were both highly specific and extremely cautious.'

[49] Of course, this claim cannot be made with respect to accession countries, and especially transition ones, which have in fact had to deeply revise their corporate laws before joining the EU. See Pistor, Raiser and Gelfer (2000: 340): 'European harmonization guidelines have unleashed what some commentators have called a tornado of legislative activities in the countries wishing to join the EU'.

This does not imply that EC corporate law has been non-trivial for the 10 new accession countries. It only means that these new Member States have had to change their laws in order to introduce, as argued throughout this section, a set of trivial rules. *Cf ibid.*: 340–41: '[w]ithout a proper understanding of the imported legal concepts [i.e. of the imported harmonized EC rules]... their role in infuencing economic behavior in the transition may be limited'.

[50] Council Dir 89/592/EEC of 13 November 1989 coordinating regulations on insider dealing [1989] OJ L334/30.

[51] See, e.g., Warren (1991: 1040).

into law without waiting for the EC's implementation of the Commission's plans.[52]

Thus, EC institutions, at least at times, appear to play a proactive role within the EU, by setting the corporate law reform agenda. However, one should not overestimate the relevance of such proactive moves. In fact, it happens very frequently that corporate law reformers around the world work on the same policy issues at the same time. In the second half of the 1980s, this was the case with insider trading: pressure both from capital markets (Pitt and Hardison 1992: 201–3) and from US regulators (Colombatto and Macey 1996: 952)[53] prompted a global 'rush to prohibit insider trading, or to enforce dormant laws against the practice' (Pitt and Hardison 1992: 201). Arguably, the EC acted as a focal point for such pressures, but Member States were already considering a ban on insider trading at the time[54] and many of them would have adopted it even in the absence of the Directive. Admittedly, this claim is impossible to prove or disprove. But, for instance, Germany's adoption in the 1990s and at the beginning of the new century of a number of laws aiming to promote its financial center by adapting its legislation to international best practices strongly suggests that an insider trading prohibition would have been among those measures even in the absence of an EC mandate to implement the first insider trading Directive.[55]

One may counter that other Member States would never have banned insider trading. This may well be true, but then one should not fail to consider that in some Member States insider trading prohibitions are so little enforced,[56] that the implementation of the first insider trading

[52] Most notably, this is the case of France, which enacted the *'Loi de securité financière,'* a French equivalent of the Sarbanes-Oxley Act, in July 2003. See *ibid.:* 918.

[53] The SEC exerted pressure on states, such as Japan, Switzerland, and Germany, as well as on the EC itself, to criminalize insider trading.

[54] For instance, in 1989 the Italian Parliament (1989: 116–23) was already discussing three bills aiming to criminalize insider trading. Only one of them made a reference to the Directive proposal in its explanatory memorandum.

[55] *Cf* Standen (1995: 200–1) arguing that the strategic need to promote the German financial center (*'Finanzplatz Deutschland'*) had the greatest impact on the policymakers' choice to ban insider trading in 1994.

[56] See Bhattacharya and Daouk (2002: 81) who report data from 1999 showing that insider trading laws had never been enforced in Austria, Ireland, and Luxembourg. Since then, there has been one conviction for insider trading in Austria (e-mail from Martin Gelter to the author (30 November 2004) (on file with the author)) and one in Luxembourg (e-mail from Françoise Thoma to the author (30 November 2004) (on file with the author)), and no conviction yet in Ireland (e-mail from Niamh Moloney to the author (6 December 2004) (on file with the author)). See also Ferran (2004a: 33) reporting that 'only nineteen convictions for insider trading were achieved in Britain, Germany, France, Switzerland and Italy in the five years before 2002, contrasting sharply with the forty-six successful prosecutions achieved in the same period by a single district court in Manhattan'.

Directive may have changed virtually nothing for them and their market players.[57]

In sum, policy issues are often on every policymaker's agenda at the same time. In some instances EU institutions are able to adopt Directives ahead of Member States.[58] But this does not mean that such Directives significantly change Member States policymakers' course of action.

To conclude, some general features of secondary EC corporate law confirm the hypothesis that such law is trivial, i.e. the limited scope of its provisions, which do not cover core company law issues, the problem of under-enforcement, the parochial interpretation given to it within Member States, and its timing, since it either covers areas already de facto harmonized from bottom up or regulates issues that were also in Member States policymakers' agenda at the time of their adoption.

III. THE TRIVIALITY THESIS (2): NATURE AND CONTENT OF EC CORPORATE LAW RULES

This Part argues that the provisions laid down by EC corporate law Directives and Regulations are optional, market-mimicking, unimportant, and/or avoidable,[59] or, in other words, that, with the exceptions outlined in Part IV, they fail to contain any meaningful prohibition, requirement, or enabling rule.

---

[57] According to a recent study, the existence of an unenforced ban on insider trading may have actually made things worse for companies in those countries, at least until they enforce insider trading laws for the first time: see Bhattacharya and Daouk (2004) who find that the cost of equity rises when a country introduces an insider trading law, but does not enforce it.

[58] In other instances, they are not: at the end of the 1990s virtually everywhere was corporate governance reform an issue, and of course the European Commission also studied whether to issue policy proposals (see Lannoo and Khachaturyan (2004: 42)), but before the American and European corporate scandals came to light in the first years of the century, the Commission was only able to issue a comparative study of existing corporate governance codes (see European Commission (2002)).

[59] The classification of trivial rules as optional, market-mimicking, unimportant, or avoidable resembles that proposed by Bernard Black, who distinguishes between market-mimicking, avoidable, changeable, and unimportant rules (1990: 551–52). 'Changeable' rules are not included here for two reasons: first, in general, all rules are changeable, but this does not mean that they are trivial until they are repealed. And it is unreasonable to expect that they will soon be repealed in the absence of regulatory competition (see *ibid:*. 559: rules are trivial if they are changeable and they are changeable if jurisdictions compete); secondly, and more specifically, EC rules are less changeable than others, due to the well known petrification of Community law: once a Directive or regulation has been adopted, it is very difficult to amend it, let alone repeal it (see especially Buxbaum and Hopt (1988: 243).

A. Optional Rules

Optional rules are defined here as those that Member States can freely decide whether or not to implement, or that individual companies may choose whether or not to comply with, through opt-in or opt-out decisions. To be sure, opt-in provisions are not trivial, if they introduce a regime previously unavailable in one of the Member States and if companies in this state do opt into the new regime in significant numbers.[60] Most EC Directives contain optional rules or even allow Member States to choose from a menu of alternatives.[61]

Two prominent examples of optional rules are Articles 9 and 11 of the Takeover Directive.[62] As is well known, the EC succeeded in adopting a Directive on takeovers only after the Council and the European Parliament had agreed not to harmonize target companies' defensive tactics, i.e. the only politically hot issue in the Directive proposal and the one that had led to the European Parliament's rejection of the earlier proposal.[63]

The final text still contains two provisions laying down a modified passivity rule, according to which shareholders' meetings must authorize defensive tactics in advance (Article 9), and a breakthrough rule trumping restrictions on transfers of shares and providing for a one-share-one-vote rule in the meeting called to authorize defensive tactics and in the first meeting following the bid, provided that, in the latter case, the bidder holds 75 per cent of the shares or more following the bid (Article 11). Article 12, however, deprives both provisions of practical significance by allowing Member States not to require companies to apply them. The only condition for this course to be taken is that the Member State allow its companies to opt into the modified passivity and/or breakthrough regimes.

Of course, the modified passivity rule, although optional, might prove not to be completely trivial if, as suggested above, two conditions are met:[64] first, it allows companies to choose the new, supposedly

---

[60] Optional rules may also be non-trivial, if the default option is 'sticky,' i.e. if it is costly for firms to opt into the optional regime or to opt out of it. See Hertig and McCahery (2004). None of the examples provided in the text of EC corporate law optional rules appear to lead to a sticky outcome (perhaps with the exception of the provision granting pre-emption rights as regards widely held companies with active institutional owners). In fact, such rules usually allow companies to stick to their (or their Member States') previous practices.

[61] See critically Buxbaum and Hopt (1988: 235–36).

[62] Dir 2004/25/EC of the European Parliament and of the Council of 21 April 2004 on takeover bids [2004] OJ L142/12.

[63] See, e.g., Cioffi (2002: 384–85).

[64] As noted by Bianco and Szegö (2004: 125), the breakthrough rule only applies to companies having made contractual choices such as restricting the transfer of shares or voting rights, so that these companies may already opt into a substantially similar regime by abandoning those choices.

shareholder-friendlier regime, when this regime was unavailable under national law. This appears in fact to be the case in Germany: under German law public companies' (*Aktiengesellschaften*) statutes may not deviate from the allocation of powers among the different organs as determined by the law.[65] Therefore, a company statute may not require that frustrating actions, such as a defensive acquisition, falling under the scope of the management board's powers according to the law, be authorized by the shareholders' meeting. The second condition is that a non-trivial number of companies from jurisdictions previously precluding such a choice of regimes do opt into the Directive's new regime. It is easy to foresee that companies with dominant shareholders will have no incentive to do so, because granting the shareholders' meeting the power to decide on defences would be a useless and perhaps legally troublesome formality.[66] For obvious reasons, management-controlled companies are unlikely to opt into the shareholder-friendlier regime, unless coalitions of institutional shareholders prompt them to do so.

In the field of accounting, it is also well known that the Directives leave Member States with plenty of leeway on which accounting rules to impose upon their companies. In their current version, the Fourth and Seventh[67] Directives contain respectively 45 and 57 opt-in or opt-out provisions, while both also provide for further options for individual companies. Legal scholars agree that this menu of options has 'allow[ed] member states to preserve their accounting tradition' (Ebke 2000: 119; Wymeersch 2004: 166; Woolridge 1991: 13). However, one should add that at least in some countries, such as Italy and Spain, the Directives have significantly upgraded accounting practices (Russo and Siniscalco 1984: 64). For instance, before the Seventh Directive, only listed companies were required to prepare consolidated annual accounts in Italy (Campobasso 2002), while no such requirement existed for any company in Spain.[68]

---

[65] See generally, e.g., Schmidt (2002: 869–70). See also Bianco and Szegö (2004: 125) with specific reference to defensive tactics.

[66] It would be troublesome in countries, such as Germany itself, where shareholders may easily challenge the validity of shareholders' meetings resolutions in court. See, e.g., Noack and Zetzsche (2005: 18–19) discussing current reform initiatives aimed at restricting the often abused shareholders' right to challenge the validity of shareholder meeting resolutions in court.

[67] Seventh Council Dir 83/349/EEC of 13 June 1983 based on the Art 54(3)(g) of the Treaty on consolidated accounts [1983] OJ L193/1.

[68] See, e.g., Mora and Rees (1998: 681). See also Haller (2002: 156): 'group accounts … —which have been heavily neglected prior to the Seventh Directive in many Member States (e.g. Austria, Belgium, Italy, Greece and Spain)—have increasingly become recognized as a solid basis for investment decisions'.

Up to a point, even minimum capital and capital maintenance rules in the Second Directive can be described as optional.[69] There is nothing to prevent Member States from imposing a minimum capital as low as that prescribed by the Second Directive (25,000 euro)[70] nor individual companies from fixing a legal capital equal to the minimum and counting further contributions as share premiums.[71] As a matter of fact, the Second Directive does not require that the share premium account be treated as share capital or as a non-distributable reserve for capital maintenance purposes (Rickford 2004: 939–40). To be sure, if net assets fall below 25,000 euro a company will be unable to make distributions to shareholders.[72] Since a company may have negative net assets with no lower bound for an indefinite time (at least in theory, and unless of course the national company law has the recapitalize or liquidate rule),[73] this limitation may seem to be non-trivial. However, even in the absence of the Second Directive, often a company in such a situation would still be unable to distribute assets to shareholders due to covenants imposed by

[69] *Cf* Hertig (2004: 371) referring to capital maintenance rules as opt-in provisions. See also Schön (2004: 438–39) who similarly describes capital maintenance rules as opt-in provisions.

[70] Art 6, Second Dir. Consider also that the Second Dir only requires that at least one-quarter of the subscribed capital be paid up at the time of incorporation (Art 9).

[71] It is however true that most existing public limited liability companies' legal capital is much higher than the Second Dir's and even than the Member States' prescribed minimum, due to choices made in the past and possibly prompted by banks. It would be difficult for them to reduce their capital to the statutory minimum, unless of course banks agreed. For banks, it would mean to switch from a system in which the law, following a company's decision to have a high legal capital, provides a cap on distributions, to one in which they agree on a cap with each individual corporate borrower. For obvious reasons, they prefer to stick to the current system, which also managers and dominant shareholders like, because it allows and even requires them to retain more free cash (see Enriques and Macey (2001: 1202)). This appears to be a major qualification to the idea that legal capital rules are trivial (See also below text accompanying nn 139 and 147 for further qualifications). However, one should consider, first, that most Member States had legal capital rules already in place at the time companies chose to have a high legal capital (i.e., this was not the product of the Second Company Law Directive), and Secondly, that the repeal of legal capital rules would not change things significantly for existing companies with a high legal capital. Banks would most probably reserve a veto power on capital reductions, which managers and controlling shareholders, unless their interests are aligned with outside shareholders', will be willing to accept in order to control a larger pie. Finally, arguing that the overall impact of legal capital rules is trivial (with due qualifications) does not mean that they are anyhow justified from an economic point of view, because they impose some costs, however trivial for any individual company, while having no offsetting benefits, whether for creditors or society as a whole (see *ibid.*, especially at 1185–95).

[72] Note that the recent adoption of IASB's IFRS by the EC and the consequent obligation to treat stock options and pension scheme deficits as expenses (see *ibid.*: 948–50, 958–60) has no impact upon the Second Dir rules on distributions as a matter of EC law. In fact, according to Reg 1606/2002 of the European Parliament and of the Council of 19 July 2002 on the application of international accounting standards [2002] OJ L243/1, IFRS are only mandatory for consolidated accounts, while restrictions on distributions are related to the annual accounts of individual companies.

[73] See below text accompanying n 190.

sophisticated creditors,[74] so that legal capital rules of this kind can also be described as market-mimicking to some degree.

A cornerstone of the Second Directive is the shareholders' right (subject to exceptions) to pre-emption on newly issued shares (Article 29). As a matter of fact, this provision boils down to a default rule from which companies may opt out through a resolution of the shareholders' meeting to be taken every five years. The resolution must be taken at least by either of the majorities prescribed in Article 40 (two-thirds of the shares represented at the meeting or, if a majority of the shares is present, a simple majority of the shares present). This is indeed a protection for qualified minorities that may try to block the meeting's resolution if less than a majority of the shares are represented, but hardly an insurmountable obstacle for most companies,[75] at least in continental European countries, where ownership is concentrated.[76]

A further instance of an optional rule is in Article 9 of the First Directive. This article aims to protect third parties by 'restrict[ing] to the greatest possible extent the grounds on which obligations entered into in the name of the company are not valid.'[77] As the Swedish experience illustrates, this article 'formally only applies to company organs, i.e., in Swedish law, the board of directors and managing directors' (Anderson 2003: 191). What happens in Sweden is that in 'everyday business life it is common for major contracts to be concluded by an authorized signatory, and not by the board of directors as such or by the managing director. ... Since an authorized signatory is not a company organ, the old rule still applies, which is the same as in Swedish agency law. The result is that the old doctrine of ultra vires can still be invoked against a third party who acts in culpable bad faith' (*ibid.*).

In other words, it is common practice in Sweden to opt out of the EC-derived rule on companies' authority.[78]

---

[74] See generally Smith and Warner (1979: 131–35).

[75] *Cf* Davies (2003: 635): 'the statutory pre-emptive rights can be disapplied with relative ease and afford an individual equity shareholder precious little assurance that his existing pre-emptive rights will be preserved unless his shares carry sufficient votes to block the passing of a special resolution'.

[76] In the UK, institutional investors have agreed upon a strict policy with respect to proposals to disapply pre-emption rights, while companies think that pre-emption rights increase the cost of raising capital. See *ibid.*: 637–38: 'it would seem that the real issue is more to do with the level of underwriting fees and whether the fees connected with capital issues should go predominantly to the institutions, in their capacity as underwriters of rights issues, or to investment banks carrying out book-building exercises in connection with general issues, than with the inherent costs of rights issues as against general issues'.

[77] First Dir, Preamble.

[78] See Swedish Companies Act, Ch 8, § 35(2). One may counter that Art 9 is not trivial, since it dictates what the default rule is across the EU, thereby reducing the risks associated with the fact that companies can only act through agents and that it is often difficult, especially in cross-border settings, to find out what the law regulating companies' authority is. While this may be true for limits 'arising under the statutes or from a decision of the competent organs'

Another set of totally optional rules is the European Company Statute,[79] which introduced an additional legal form, regulated partly by the Statute itself, partly by national corporate laws. The impact of the Statute might prove to be non-trivial, if companies start using the new form as a means to implement cross-border mergers or to reincorporate in another jurisdiction (Enriques 2004b: 79–80). It is too early to predict whether this will be the case.[80] For certain, however, there are still tax obstacles that may make it practically impossible to use the new legal form for cross-border mergers or reincoporations.[81] And according to most observers, the legal regime of the European company itself is too complex and too rigid to make the new legal form attractive.[82]

Finally, rules on mutual recognition and more generally aiming to facilitate cross-border transactions, such as cross-border offerings and listings, are enabling rules, i.e. optional: they only apply when companies want to take advantage of them. Therefore, even these rules can be evaluated as trivial or not, depending on whether companies across the EU indeed take advantage of the newly available opportunities.

From this point of view, the new Prospectus Directive[83] is seen by many 'as a big step forward as compared to the previous measures in place' (Lannoo 2003: 346). The previous regime was in fact unanimously held to be a failure, since cross-border public offerings were extremely rare.[84]

(Art 9, para 2, First Dir), Art 9, para 1, itself, however, allows Member States to choose either of two regimes on *ultra vires*. *Cf* La Villa (1974: 347) who argues that Art 9 fails to provide 'a unitary principle which completely harmonizes the various legislations of member states [relating to the powers of the company's representatives]'. Further, the First Dir does not cover limits deriving from domestic laws nor does it harmonize rules on corporate agents' conflicts of interest, as the ECJ itself clarified. See Case C-104/96 *Cooperatieve Rabobank 'Vecht en Plassengebied' BA v Erik Aarnoud Minderhoud* [1997] ECR I-7211.

[79] Reg (EC) 2001/2157 of 8 October 2001 on the Statute for a European company (SE) [2001] OJ L294/1, and Dir 2001/86/EC of 8 October 2001 supplementing the Statute for a European company with regard to the involvement of employees [2001] OJ L294/22.

[80] The European Company Statute entered into force on 8 October 2004 (Art 70, Reg 2001/2157), but only five Member States had at the time already taken the necessary measures to allow European Companies to be founded on their territory. See European Commission (2004).

[81] See, e.g., Wymeersch (2003: 691).

[82] See, e.g., Pérakis (2003 : 229–31).

[83] Dir 2003/71/EC of the European Parliament and of the Council of 4 November 2003 on the prospectus to be published when securities are offered to the public or admitted to trading and amending Dir 2001/34/EC [2003] OJ L345/64.

[84] See Jackson and Pan (2001: 684); Lannoo (2003: 340); Moloney (2002: 140, 209–10) describes the obstacles faced by issuers willing to make a cross-border offering under the previous regime.

The Directives on listing conditions and particulars (Dir 80/390/EEC, above n 35, and Council Dir 82/121/EEC of 15 February 1982 on information to be published on a regular basis by companies the shares of which have been admitted to official stock exchange listing, [1982] OJ L48/26) are also commonly held to have been ineffective with respect to their

It is of course too early to tell whether the new regime will work, i.e. if the number of cross-border public offerings will significantly increase.[85] However, practitioners have already identified some features in the Prospectus Directive that could determine its failure: in short, it is suggested that, while it will be possible to make a cross-border public offering relying on a prospectus in English and, if the host or the home Member State so requires, on a translation in the local language of the summary only,

> the summary is required to contain a wording that 'it should be read as an introduction to the prospectus and any decision to invest in the securities should be based on consideration of the prospectus as a whole by the investor' (Bartos and Lippert 2003: 18).[86]

The problem is that it is impossible for an investor who does not speak English to base her decision on consideration of the prospectus as a whole. Further, the summary must have a maximum length, so that it will be impossible to incorporate 'a 10 to 15 page section on risk factors' (*ibid.*: 19). Putting two and two together, the risk of civil or criminal liability for publishing a misleading summary[87] might lead issuers either to translate the whole prospectus or to keep marketing their securities in their domestic market only (*ibid.*).[88] In other words, the practical outcome might be the same as under the previous regime.

B. Market-mimicking Rules

Market-mimicking rules are rules that most private parties would adopt even in the absence of statutory provisions imposing them. As Bernard Black acknowledges, it is hard to prove that a rule is market-mimicking (1990: 552):

purpose of facilitating multiple listings. And, in any event, they have become obsolete following market and technological developments: see Ferrarini (1999: 577) with specific regard to Dir 82/121/EEC, above.

[85] The new regime goes into force after 1 July 2005, the deadline for the Prospectus Dir's implementation by the Member States (Art 29). See, however, Ferran (2004a: 201) reporting that the 'informed market opinion [according to which] retail equity offerings that make use of the passport are likely to remain rare.'

[86] Bartos and Lippert are quoting from Art 5, para 2, of the Prospectus Dir (emphasis omitted).

[87] See Art 6, para 2, Prospectus Dir.

[88] Bartos and Lippert (2003) also doubt whether another enabling feature of the Prospectus Dir, incorporation by reference, will work. According to the two authors, in the absence of an integrated system of disclosure such as the one in place in the US, it will not.

The force of the arguments for why a particular rule is market mimicking will depend on analogies, on the background and prior beliefs of the reader, on guesses about transaction costs, and on the force of alternative arguments.

As examples of market-mimicking rules, Black cites those requiring approval by a majority of shareholders of major corporate changes, such as mergers and liquidations. Requiring a shareholders' vote on mergers and divisions, as Articles 7 and 5 of the Third and Sixth Directives[89] respectively do, can reasonably be categorized as market-mimicking.[90]

Rules granting creditors the right to obtain security for their claims or adequate safeguards in case certain transactions are undertaken, such as reductions of capital, mergers or divisions,[91] are in part market-mimicking and in part unimportant. They are (timidly) market-mimicking with regard to sophisticated creditors, who normally reserve the far more effective right to veto such transactions (usually in broader and more detailed terms) or insert an acceleration clause applying if these transactions are entered into (Smith and Warner 1979: 128–36). And they are unimportant with regard to other creditors, as explained below.[92]

Arguably, the fact that a rule is present in all of the US states' corporation codes is evidence of its market-mimicking character. In fact, although today in the United States the market for corporate charters is not particularly active,[93] it has been at least in the past, leading most states to converge on a very limited set of rules. Those surviving in each US jurisdiction are thus, intuitively, rules that very few corporations would not choose. William Carney has found that 13 EC corporate law provisions are adopted in all 50 US states.[94] Assuming that what is

---

[89] Third Council Dir 78/855/EEC of 9 October 1978 based on Art 54(3)(g) of the Treaty concerning mergers of public limited liability companies [1978] OJ L295/36, and Sixth Council Dir 82/891/EEC of 17 December 1982 based on Art 54(3)(g) of the Treaty, concerning the division of public limited liability companies [1982] OJ L378/47.

[90] To be sure, all of the provisions in the Third and the Sixth Dirs also fall under the category of avoidable rules. See below text accompanying n 169.

[91] See Art 32, Second Dir, Art 13, Third Dir, and Art 12, Sixth Dir.

[92] See below text accompanying nn 100–1.

[93] See Kahan and Kamar (2002); Bebchuk and Hamdani (2002). But see also Romano (2005: 12–25) who criticises the view that there is currently no regulatory competition in the corporate law area.

[94] Carney (1997: 320) provides a table according to which fourteen EC provisions are adopted by all US states; actually, the list of EC provisions that the author has kindly provided contains 13 such provisions. These are the provisions requiring (1) '[p]ublication of articles of constitution and amendments;' (2) '[p]ublication of identity of official agent;' (3) '[p]ublication of winding up of company;' (4) '[p]ublication of any declaration of nullity by the courts;' and those providing (5) that '[c]ompletion of formalities of incorporation is a bar to personal liability of agents;' (6) that '[l]imits on powers of organs (governing bodies) may not be relied on against third parties even if disclosed;' (7) that '[n]ames of companies shall be distinctive;' (8) that the '[a]rticles of incorporation must identify [the] [r]egistered office [and (9) the] [i]dentity of the incorporators; (9) that '[i]f reduction of subscribed capital by

market-mimicking in the United States is also in the EU, these 13 provisions can be categorized as such.[95]

C. Unimportant Rules

Black defines 'unimportant rules' as those that 'can be complied with at nominal cost, or involve situations that almost never occur' (1990: 560). Rules granting rights that will almost never be exercised also qualify as such.

Among rules that can be complied with at nominal (or at least negligible) cost is Article 17 of the Second Directive, according to which, when a company suffers

> a serious loss of the subscribed capital, a general meeting of shareholders must be called within the period laid down by the laws of the Member States, to consider whether the company should be wound up or any other measures taken.

Nothing appears to prevent Member States from requiring that this discussion take place at the next annual meeting at the latest, so that companies will not even have to incur the costs of calling an extraordinary meeting for the purpose.

Similarly, the cost of disclosing well-specified facts or documents such as the fact that a company has only one shareholder,[96] the articles of constitution and its amendments,[97] or the identity of the persons authorized to represent the company[98] will normally be trivial both in monetary terms and with regard to some hypothetical interest in keeping those facts secret.

Finally, the provision in the Twelfth Directive, that contracts between the sole owner and the corporation 'shall be recorded in minutes or drawn up in writing' (Article 5, para 1) can also be complied with at nominal cost.

---

compulsory withdrawal of shares is permitted, it must be authorized in the articles of incorporation before the shares are issued, and must be approved by the shareholders;' (10) that the '[r]ights and obligations of redeemable shares must be specified in articles of incorporation before issuance; (11) that [b]oard of directors must approve and publish an agreement and plan of merger;' (12) that '[n]otice of the merger must be published;' (13) that [t]he effect of a merger is to transfer all assets and liabilities to the surviving company.'
See also Carney (undated) with references to the relevant EC and US law provisions.

[95] Many of them also appear to be unimportant. See above n 94.
[96] Art 3, Twelfth Council Company Law Dir 89/667/EEC of 21 December 1989 on single-member private limited-liability companies [1989] OJ L395/40.
[97] Art 2, para 1(a), First Dir.
[98] Art 2, para 1(d), First Dir.

Rules that involve situations that almost never occur include provisions on the nullity of companies.[99] In Vanessa Edwards's words (1999: 46),

> [a] declaration of nullity was a rare occurrence even in those original Member States which recognized the concept, so that these provisions are relatively unimportant.

Among rules granting rights that will almost never be exercised are those entitling unsophisticated creditors to obtain security for their claims or adequate safeguards if certain transactions are undertaken, such as reductions of capital, mergers or divisions.[100] In fact, either such creditors have bargaining power vis-a-vis the company or they lack it. If they have bargaining power, but failed to contract for such protections at the outset, possibly because they are unsophisticated, they will be able to protect themselves against the negative consequences of such transactions without the need for a *right* to obtain those safeguards. If they have no bargaining power, they will be de facto unable to exercise their right, because the company would otherwise retaliate against them.[101] And in any event, should a creditor in fact exercise the right to obtain security or an adequate safeguard, the instances in which the resulting cost for the companies involved will be such that the transaction will not go through will be so rare as to make this hypothesis, again, trivial.

D. Avoidable Rules

Avoidable rules are, in Black's terminology, those that can 'be avoided through proper planning' (1990: 555). In our setting, the planning can take place at the company level, at the national level, or at both: at the company level, when it is private parties who carefully design transactions so as to avoid the application of a given rule; at the national level, when the planning is at the implementation stage as the result of choices made, whether implicitly or explicitly, by the policymakers transposing the EC rules.

To be sure, proper planning at the company level can be costly: as Black acknowledges (1990: 557),

---

[99] Section III, First Dir.

[100] See above n 91.

[101] *Cf* Enriques and Macey (2001: 1191) with specific regard to reductions of capital. Note that such provisions do not provide that the company must obtain creditors' consent to execute certain transactions. They require creditors to activate in order to obtain protection, thus making it less plausible that a bargaining problem connected with an endowment effect will arise.

> [t]he greater the costs of avoidance, relative to a rule's importance, the less avoidable the rule. … At some point, the cost of avoiding a rule is large enough so that we can't call the rule trivial.

As a matter of fact, avoidance costs may be high, especially in light of the legal advice which is normally necessary to obtain in the process. Since the costs of avoidance have a strong fixed component, avoidable rules may therefore prove to be non-trivial for smaller businesses, as conceded also in Part IV.[102]

An example of rules avoidable at the company level can be found in Article 11 of the Second Directive, according to which a special procedure has to be followed in order for a company to acquire any asset belonging to one of the company's founders for consideration of more than one-tenth of the company's subscribed capital within two years of incorporation. This provision is easily avoided by starting a business by acquiring an existing, possibly dormant, company incorporated more than two years before,[103] or 'by entering into one of the many kinds of … transactions that Article 11 of the Second Directive does not cover' (Enriques and Macey 2001: 1186).

True, there is the risk that Member States' laws will qualify such transactions as indirectly falling under the scope of the national provision implementing the Directive (Spolidoro 2004: 724–25). But it is far from certain that this will be the case, depending also on the care the company and its shareholders have taken in planning the transaction. And, more to the point, this treatment of evasive transactions will be an application of national laws and local judges' activism, not of EC corporate law.[104]

Similarly, the prohibition against the issue of stock in exchange for 'an undertaking to perform work or supply services'[105] does not impinge upon the validity of a contract by which the company reserves the right to pay workers' salaries or advisors' fees in shares. Once the work or service has been performed, the workers or the advisors will have a credit with the company. Pursuant to their previous agreement, the company will issue shares as payment for the services. Instead of contributing new money to the company, the workers or advisors will simply offset their debt to the company for the payment of their shares with the company's liquid and due debt for the performed work or services.[106] Such an

[102] See below text accompanying n 147.

[103] For a description of the various ways by which Art 11 can be circumvented *see* Spolidoro (2004: 724–25).

[104] See Case C-83/91 *Meilicke v ADV/ORGA*, Opinion by Advocate General Tesauro [1992] ECR I-4871, para 21. Member States in fact differ as to the reaction against evasive transactions. See Halbhuber (2001: 1406).

[105] Art 7, Second Dir.

[106] *Cf Meilicke v ADV/ORGA*, Opinion by Advocate General Tesauro, above n 104, paras 15–16 (Art 10 does not apply to contributions by waiver of a liquid and due debt).

arrangement would solve any cash constraint by start-up companies. Further, suppose there are two parties, a financier and an entrepreneur, who are willing to form a company in which the former will hold 49 per cent and the latter 51 per cent, and that the entrepreneur has no assets that can be validly contributed to the company according to the Directive. Leaving tax issues aside, nothing prevents the financier from paying up the entrepreneur's capital in her stead.[107] Once the company is formed the entrepreneur may enter, as the case may be, an employment relationship of some kind with the company.[108]

Proper planning will also allow avoidance of the Second Directive provision capping the number of own shares a company may hold at any given moment at 10 per cent (Article 19(1)(c)). In fact, a company having reached that cap may acquire further shares after reducing the share capital and cancelling the treasury shares in excess. This will of course be cumbersome, because a shareholder meeting will have to be convened to decide on this, but it is far from having a chilling effect.[109]

Article 23 of the Second Directive is perhaps the most telling example of an avoidable EC company law rule. This sweeping prohibition against firms providing financial assistance to those acquiring their shares is often said to render leveraged buyouts illegal.[110]

The sheer volume of private equity buyouts in Europe indicates that the hindering effect of Article 23 cannot be as great as is often contended:[111] In 2003, a total of 945 private equity buyouts were completed—24 per cent fewer than in 2002—for a total value of 61,691 million euro—8 billion less than the previous year,[112] while in 2004 '[a] record $40 billion of loans for leveraged buyouts have been arranged in Europe ..., compared with $29 billion for ... 2003' (*Bloomberg* 2004). In the last few years the European buyout market has grown even bigger than that of the United States. Since 2001 buyout activity in Europe has been 70 per cent greater than in the United States in terms of announced deal value.[113]

In the face of Article 23, how can this be? First, some Member States,

---

[107] See Spolidoro (2003: 209) with specific regard to Italian law.

[108] Art 11 does not apply to the employment contract, because it refers to 'asset[s]' (or *'élément[s] d'actif'* in the French version), while the credit for future work is not an asset from an accounting point of view.

[109] The provisions granting creditors the right to obtain adequate security in the process—as argued above text accompanying nn 91–93; 100–1—will be either market-mimicking or unimportant, having therefore no chilling effect either.

[110] See, e.g., Wymeersch (1998: 734).

[111] *Cf*, e.g., Rickford (2004: 945) ('The prohibition [on financial assistance] ... remains for public companies a major and costly impediment to wholly legitimate and desirable commercial transactions, for example leveraged buy-outs').

[112] See Initiative Europe Barometer Q4 2003 4, *at* http://www.initiative-europe.com/press/downloads/Q42003.pdf.

[113] See Smith (2004: 18) reporting data collected by JP Morgan.

and notably the United Kingdom, have introduced exemptions.[114] Secondly, in all Member States 'intricate ... evasion techniques have been invented by smart lawyers' (Wymeersch 2004: 177) which national courts, for better or for worse, have usually judged to be in line with the prohibition on financial assistance.[115]

Avoidable rules can be found in securities regulation as well. First, there are certainly ways around the obligation to disclose major holdings as required once by Directive 88/627/EEC[116] and now by Directive 2001/34/EC.[117] One is reported by Marco Becht and Ekkehart Böhmer (2001: 151): when a stake is held by a company, the disclosure obligation applies to owners exercising control over it. Since the definition of control does not include joint control,[118] in Germany

> shares held by unlisted firms with two 50 per cent-owners are never attributed beyond the level of the unlisted firm, because neither of the owners is deemed to be 'controlling.'[119]

A further example of avoidable rules can be found in the prospectus regime in place prior to the adoption of the Prospectus Directive. As Howell Jackson and Eric Pan report (2001: 681–82), it was common practice for issuers to offer their securities in other Member States to professionals only, relying upon the exemption for such offerings in the

---

[114] See, e.g., Ferran (1999: 391–92).

[115] Wymeersch (1998: 735, 738–39) reports arguments developed in various Member States in order to construe the prohibition restrictively. See also Bruno (2002: 814) who finds that no Italian court has ever declared the illegality of a merger leveraged buy out. A recent decision by the English Court of Appeal (*Chaston v SWP Group plc*, [2002] EWCA Civ 1999, [2003] 1 B.C.L.C. 675), however, failed to accommodate restrictive interpretations of the financial assistance prohibition. As Eilís Ferran notes (2004: 226), this decision has reminded corporate finance practitioners that they must 'continue to operate on the basis that financial assistance is a pervasive and serious problem and must grapple to find ways round it that have not been undermined by the case law. It seems inevitable that the processes involved in avoiding financial assistance problems will continue to involve significant costs. There is anecdotal evidence that many law firms have already consulted leading company law barristers for advice on the implications of *Chaston* and it seems reasonable to assume that this will be a continuing source of revenue for a few specialists. The amounts involved are necessarily a matter of speculation, but it is safe to say that the advice of leading members of the corporate Bar certainly does not come cheap.'

[116] Council Dir 88/627/EEC, above n 35.

[117] Dir 2001/34/EC of the European Parliament and of the Council of 28 May 2001 on the admission of securities to official stock exchange listing and on information to be published on those securities [2001] OJ L184/1.

[118] Art 87, Dir 2001/34/EC.

[119] *Ibid.* This will hold true also under Dir 2004/109/EC of the European Parliament and of the Council of 15 December 2004 on the harmonisation of transparency requirements in relation to information about issuers whose securities are admitted to trading on a regulated market and amending Dir 2001/34/EC [2004] OJ L390/38, whose provisions on major holdings will come into force on 20 January 2007. See Arts 2(1)(f) and 9.

relevant Directive.[120] The professionals would then resell the securities to retail investors (Jackson and Pan 1999: 688).[121] This was possible because neither Directive 89/298/EEC nor securities law of at least some Member States[122] imposed resale restrictions similar to SEC's rule 144.[123]

The new Prospectus Directive would appear to impose a prospectus for any resale which may fall under the broad definition of offer to the public provided for in Article 2(1)(d).[124] However, it is expected that the United Kingdom (and possibly other Member States) will include a carve-out in the definition of 'offer to the public' for communication in connection with screen trading on, inter alia, multilateral trading facilities.[125] If this is the case, it may prove easy for qualified investors to resell securities to retail investors through these trading venues without a prospectus. Further, each resale will be regarded as a separate offer,[126] so that 'a resale addressed to fewer than 100 persons, whatever their status, would fall outside the prospectus requirement for resales' (Ferran 2004a: 201, n 257).[127]

To be sure, the New Prospectus Directive is also a maximum harmonization measure. As such, it will definitely have an impact upon any offer to the public, by exclusively identifying what will have to be disclosed in the prospectus. However, as Eilís Ferran has suggested (Ferran 2004a: 145), Member States may

> side step the maximum harmonization effect of the Prospectus Directive by recasting disclosure requirements that are outside the Directive in the form of substantive criteria that must be satisfied by issues seeking admission to trading on a regulated market.

A good example of secondary EC corporate law rules that can be avoided by efforts at the national level are those in the Third and Sixth Directives on mergers and divisions respectively. The United Kingdom has in fact

---

[120] See Art 2, para 1(a), Council Dir 89/298/EEC of 17 April 1989 coordinating the requirements for the drawing-up, scrutiny, and distribution of the prospectus to be published when transferable securities are offered to the public [1989] OJ L124/8.

[121] See also generally Moloney (2002: 68) highlighting that 'the Securities Directives contain substantial escape opportunities for Member States from their harmonizing effects in the form of a network of exemptions, derogations, and generally worded obligations'.

[122] See, e.g., Costi and Enriques (2004: 59–60) stating that Italian securities laws impose no resale restrictions.

[123] 17 C.F.R. § 230.144 (2000).

[124] See Art 3(2).

[125] HM Treasury & FSA, UK Implementation of the Prospectus Dir 2003/71/EC. A Consultation Document 22 (October 2004) (at http://www.hm-treasury.gov.uk/media/DFE/27/DFE27339-BCDC-D4B3-16FD311B308ABF54.pdf).

[126] See Art 3(2).

[127] See also Ferran (2004a: at 200–1): 'Preventing seepage from wholesale to retail markets through resales of securities that were offered originally on an exempt basis remains an issue that EU policy-makers appear disinclined to address vigorously.'

implemented these Directives through provisions that cover a very limited set of transactions, de facto leaving parties free to achieve the same results as those normally sought through 'mergers' or 'divisions,' by choosing transactional structures not covered by the Directives (Davies 2003: 799–800; Edwards 1999: 91). The fact that at least one Member State was able to reduce the impact of these Directives practically to nothing, and apparently without breaching them, is evidence that they have no bite.

Some rules are avoidable thanks to planning both by the Member State at the implementation stage and by private parties. The best example of this kind of rule is perhaps the provision requiring Member States to have a mandatory bid rule in place (Article 5 of the Takeover Directive). This provision allows the measure to be implemented through easily avoidable rules. First, according to Article 4, para 5, '[p]rovided that the general principles set out in Article 3(1) are respected, Member States may grant derogations from the Directive's rules,' including the mandatory bid rule, 'in order to take account of circumstances determined at national level.' They may also grant their supervisory authority 'the power to waive national rules.'[128] Secondly, the Directive does not identify the threshold for the mandatory bid obligation (Article 5, para 1). It only states that the shares held have to confer on the acquirer 'the control of that company' (para 3). Nothing appears to prevent Member States from fixing the threshold at, say, 50 per cent plus one share, making it easy for control to change hands without triggering the requirement. Further, as I have argued elsewhere, the few, patchy provisions on the mandatory bid contained in Article 5 'leave plenty of room for more or less ingenious ways to avoid the requirement, depending of course on how national implementing rules are drafted and enforced' (Enriques 2004c: 776).

E. Conclusions

This Part and the previous one have provided arguments in favor of the triviality thesis. They have shown that such rules are trivial, i.e. have very little impact upon EU companies' governance and management: they do not cover core areas such as fiduciary duties and shareholder remedies; they are under-enforced and normally construed in such a way as to be

---

[128] As I have noted elsewhere (2004c: 774), 'unjustified or over-ample use of this power may constitute a breach of Article 3(1)(a) (protection of minority shareholders in case of control transfer), unless of course some other equivalent form of protection is provided. In any event, the grey area in which a reasoned decision may be judged to be consistent with the Directive is broad enough to leave Member State and local supervisory authorities considerable influence in the administration of the national mandatory bid regime.'

compatible with pre-existing national rules and practices. Finally, most EC corporate law can be categorized as optional, market-mimicking, unimportant, or avoidable. In other words, there is (almost)[129] nothing non-trivial that EC corporate law requires to do, forbids, or enables to do.

IV. SOME QUALIFICATIONS TO THE TRIVIALITY THESIS AND ONE POSSIBLE OBJECTION

It would be an overstatement to conclude that secondary EC corporate law is trivial without any qualification. This part provides the necessary qualifications to the triviality thesis and counters a possible objection to it, namely that the same kind of analysis would justify the conclusion that even EU national corporate laws are trivial.

A. Qualifications to the Triviality Thesis

A few qualifications have to be made to the triviality thesis. First, a few provisions or sets of rules are non-trivial. Secondly, EC corporate law has increased the regulatory burden of corporate laws across the EU, correspondingly securing higher rents for certain interest groups. Thirdly, EC corporate law plays a role in the evolution of corporate law within the EU, prompting pre-emptive changes in national corporate laws, creating the scope for excessive regulation, acting as a curb to experimentation, and making it somewhat less likely that a European Delaware will emerge. Finally, its production has become an industry itself, employing many EC and national functionaires and lobbyists, and creating occasions for rent extraction by politicians.

1. The Exceptions

The analysis in the previous parts has not provided an exhaustive list of the existing secondary EC company law provisions in order to show that each of them is trivial. Instead, it has provided some general reasons why secondary EC company law is trivial (Part II) and categorized most of its provisions as optional, market-mimicking, unimportant, or avoidable (Part III). However, one has to concede that a few specific rules or sets of rules have indeed had, or can be predicted to have, an impact on companies and their behavior.

First, we can cite the Takeover Directive provision granting a successful bidder the right to purchase shares from minority shareholders

---

[129] See below § IV.A.1.

(Article 15)[130]: unless Member States find ways to make this right de facto impossible to exercise, e.g. by making it extremely easy for minority shareholders to challenge the fairness of the squeeze-out price and/or block the squeeze-out procedure, one can predict that highly successful bidders will often exercise their squeeze-out right. One can also mention the Eighth Directive's[131] provisions defining the professional qualifications of persons in charge of the auditing of a company's accounts (as imposed by the Fourth and Seventh Directives),[132] because in comparison with the requirements until then in force in at least some of the Member States (e.g., Italy), the Directive's requirements involved an upgrade of the professional qualifications requested.[133]

Further, despite the optional character of most of the Fourth and Seventh Directives' provisions and the tendency to construe them according to local practices and traditions, the accounting Directives have had, and, in the case of the IAS Regulation, are already having, a significant impact on companies.[134] Of course it remains to be seen whether and how uniformly the international accounting standards will be enforced.[135]

Finally, one may argue that the mandatory disclosure rules in securities Directives have also implied an upgrade of national regulations. However, the enforcement issue in this area may be so serious as to make such rules trivial.[136]

Recent developments in securities law, with the EC's new approach to legislation and enforcement of securities laws, could increase the impact of EU action, although it is still too early to say whether this will indeed be the case.[137]

---

[130] The corresponding sell-out right provision (Art 16) appears to be at least as easily avoidable as the provision on mandatory bids (see above text accompanying nn 131–32) since it presupposes a voluntary or mandatory bid made to all the holders of the offeree company.

[131] Eighth Council Dir 84/253/EEC of 10 April 1984 based on Art 54(3)(g) of the Treaty on the approval of persons responsible for carrying out the statutory audits of accounting documents [1984] OJ L126/20.

[132] See Arts 51 and 37 respectively.

[133] Of course, the Eighth Directive contained grandfathering provisions for auditors in practice at the time of implementation and with lower qualifications than those required by the Directive itself. See Arts. 12-18.

[134] See Haller (2002: 159) describing the impact of the accounting Directives as 'enormous'.

[135] See above n 38.

[136] *cf* Nowak (2003: 432) reporting that in Germany 'disclosures [as mandated by the first insider trading Directive] have been misused by some issuers as a public relations tool, while many other issuers have not disclosed a single statement.'

To be sure, the author so continues: 'Nevertheless, *ad hoc* disclosure activity of domestic issuers increased sharply, rising from 991 notifications in 1995 to 5057 disclosures in 2000, and falling … to 3781 in 2002.'

[137] See Hertig and McCahery (this volume, ch 15) who doubt that the EU plays and will any time soon play any central role even in the areas of securities and accounting law; Hertig and Lee (2003: 359) doubt that EC action in the area of securities law will ever be meaningful until a European SEC is created. See also above n 38.

2. Impact on the Cost of Doing Business and on Professionals' Rents

As argued in part III, most corporate law rules are trivial in the sense that there is almost nothing meaningful that EC corporate law requires to do, forbids, or enables to do. The main qualification to this claim is that many EC corporate law rules impose a small burden on each company, by requiring it to pay for the services of a professional or of a public body. Examples are:

— the First Directive's requirement that 'the company statutes and any amendments to those documents ... be drawn up and certified in due legal form' (i.e. through public notaries in countries where this category of professionals exists), or must be subject to 'preventive control, administrative or judicial'[138];
— the First, Second, Third, Sixth, Eleventh,[139] and Twelfth Directives' provisions imposing publicity in the company register of certain facts or documents, because companies have no choice but to buy the 'disclosure services' provided by the relevant public bodies and will find it helpful to turn to professionals or corporate services firms in complying;
— the accounting Directives, that at least in some of the Member States have led to an upgrade of accounting rules and practices, thereby inflating the demand for accountants' services;
— the mandatory bid rule: given the sums at stake, potential acquirers will inevitably seek the help of a top law firm in order to avoid it, unless of course they want to acquire all of the target's shares for cash anyway.[140]

Even avoidable rules can induce companies to pay for professional services for compliance. When the compliance costs, including the fees for the professional services, are lower than the avoidance costs (again, including the cost of legal advice), avoidable rules will be complied with and the professional services acquired. Such is often the case, in practice, with the Second Directive's rules requiring an expert opinion for non-cash contributions.

While the burden of such rules is mostly trivial from the point of view of an individual company, and especially for well-established ones, in the

---

[138] Art 10, First Dir. In Spain, public notaries and especially Company Registrar's officials extract significant rents from the preventive control of the validity of company statutes. See Alfaro Águila-Real (2004: 456–67).

[139] Eleventh Council Dir 89/666/EEC of 21 December 1989 concerning disclosure requirements in respect of branches opened in a Member State by certain types of company governed by the law of another State [1989] OJ L395/36.

[140] See Enriques (2004c: 794–95) highlighting that the Directive potentially increases the scope for exemptions and price discounts and for national supervisory authorities' discretion in granting them.

aggregate, by inflating the demand for professional services, they secure significant rents for the professionals and public officials providing those services. Further, since the burden on businesses has a fixed component, these rules have a disproportionate impact on smaller firms. Therefore, their overall effect is to raise, if only marginally, the barriers to entry into the European markets, by making it more expensive to adopt the corporate form.

The same ultimate effect of increasing the cost of doing business derives of course from the Eighth Directive, which defines the pro-fessional qualifications of persons in charge of the compulsory auditing of a company's accounts[141] and therefore raises a legal barrier to entry into the market for auditing services, intuitively with an impact on the price for such services.

A general feature of EC corporate law also leads to higher costs: it undeniably increases the complexity of national corporate laws,[142] making them more institutionally differentiated.[143] Secondary EC corporate law adds two layers of rules to those at the national level. Member States' law must be consistent with EC Directives and Regu-lations, which in turn must be consistent with the EC Treaty.

Lawyers can reap economic benefits from the complexity of the law.[144] As Gillian Hadfield (2000: 995) aptly points out, complexity is one of the causes for the substantial deviation of the market for legal services from the competitive model. Among other things, complexity

> is responsible for the credence nature of legal services … mak[ing] price and quantity in the market predominantly the result of beliefs and wealth, rather than of cost (Hadfield 2000: 995).[145]

In the case of securities law Directives and Regulations adopted under the Lamfalussy approach, the picture is even more complex than in other corporate law areas. We have here two layers of secondary EC law and yet a third one of 'quasi-law:' framework (or level 1) Directives and

---

[141] Art 51 of the Fourth Dir and 37 of the Seventh Directive, with due exceptions, mandate the audit of annual accounts.

[142] *Cf* Cheffins (1997: 448): 'the changes that have taken place have often made it more difficult for a resident of a Member State to know what the situation is with his own legislation while doing little to inform him about what the law is in other EU countries.'

[143] Peter Schuck (1992: 3–4) identifies four features of a complex legal system: density, technicality, indeterminacy and, what is relevant to our purposes, institutional differen-tiation, i.e. the fact that a legal system 'contains a number of decision structures that draw upon different sources of legitimacy, possess different kinds of organizational intelligence, and employ different decision processes for creating, elaborating, and applying the rules.'

[144] See Halbhuber (2001: 1412): '[s]uch complexity is bound to benefit lawyers able to handle it.'

[145] See also Hadfiled (2000: 995–96) for further insights on the beneficial effects of legal complexity upon lawyers' welfare.

Regulations contain the main principles and rules; level 2 measures, i.e. Directives and Regulations contain more detailed provisions and, thanks to the smoother legislative process, can be modified more often to adapt to market and technological changes. In addition to these two layers, the Lamfalussy approach also provides for a third level, in which CESR issues guidelines for the implementation and uniform interpretation of level 1 and level 2 measures.[146] Arguably, the documents produced by CESR to fulfil its level 3 tasks also have to be taken into account by national securities regulators and, as a consequence, by lawyers when construing national rules. Note that here, not only is the law more complex because there are additional layers of rules, but since the legislative landscape is bound to change more often, keeping up with it will be a further justification for charging a higher price for legal advice: new rules always imply greater uncertainty, and hence a higher legal risk, due to the absence of precedents and widely shared interpretations.

Finally, Part III has shown that many EC corporate law provisions are more or less easily avoidable. When compliance costs (including lost profit opportunities) are higher than the avoidance costs, companies will avoid them. To do so, as hinted before, advice from a lawyer will be necessary and usually sufficient.[147] Therefore, avoidable rules too raise the cost of doing business and corporate lawyers' rents. On the margin, they may also raise the cost of some transactions to the point that it is not convenient to carry them out.

Secondary EC corporate law provisions such as those described can finally be seen as aiming to protect the rents extracted by interest groups in individual Member States by eliminating the risk of domestic companies' (re)incorporating in other EC jurisdictions without such rules (Carney 1997: 317).

To conclude, EC intervention in this area is like a cartel aiming to protect or increase the monopolistic rents of well-defined interest groups, especially professionals providing corporate-law-related services.

3. EC Corporate Law and the Dynamics of EU National Laws.

The presence of a centralized lawmaker affects how corporate law is produced and evolves within the EU in various ways.

---

[146] For a more detailed description of the Lamfalussy approach see Ferran (2004a: 61–84). See also *ibid*.: 100 for the prediction that level 3 standard, and guidelines will 'move into the foreground' once the level 1 and level 2 measures implementing the Financial Services Action Plan are adopted, possibly also extending to areas uncovered by secondary EC legislation.

[147] See also above n 115 and especially the quotation from Eilís Ferran's comment on *Chaston v SWP Group plc*.

a. Pre-emptive Changes of National Corporate Laws.   First of all, Member States have sometimes pre-emptively reformed their company laws so as to anticipate, guide, or in any event affect the outcome of, harmonization efforts. For instance, back in the sixties, Germany and France enacted their corporate law reforms also with the purpose of displaying more modern laws, from which the Commission, in their view, might have drawn inspiration for its first harmonization steps (Stein 1971: 92, 102).

More recently, a good example of a proactive move by a Member State with the clear purpose of affecting the outcome of harmonizing efforts at the EC level is that of Germany and its rules on takeover defences. In Jeffrey Gordon's reading (2004: 547), the anti-takeover provision in the German law on takeovers was

> a bargaining chip in a kind of trade negotiation, a raising of barriers designed to precipitate a crisis and force a new round of negotiations that would lower trade barriers—here, takeover protections—across the board.

Of course, an alternative and more straightforward reading is that the anti-takeover provision was a reaction to the Mannesmann takeover and to prior pro-takeover policy choices made by the German Government (Cioffi 2002: 385–87). Even in this perspective, however, the 2001 anti-takeover policy choice can at the same time be viewed as an effective way to contrast the Commission's attempt to adopt the modified passivity rule EU-wide, by credibly putting Germany's weight on a different policy choice.

In the United States, according to Roe's thesis (2003: 592), the federal authorities shape corporate law either by direct intervention or because 'Delaware players know that the federal government can take away their corporate lawmaking power in whole or in part' and therefore act in ways that federal authorities will not dislike (Roe 2003: 632). Something close to the reverse seems to be true in Europe, where Member States reform their corporate laws in order to affect the outcome of EC institutions' initiatives, let these adopt rules that they have already in place or that they would introduce anyway, and are usually able to block EC developments they (or better their businesses) dislike.[148] In other words, while in the United States, according to Roe, Delaware adapts to federal law and politics, in the EU it is the EC that adapts to Member States' laws and politics. In the interaction between Member States and the EC, however, national laws may change in anticipation of possible policy initiatives at the EC level, as takeover law developments in Germany suggest.

---

[148] See also below text accompanying nn 178–79.

b. EC Corporate Law as a Cartel. Further, EC corporate law can also be viewed as a cartel among national legislators.[149] Like any anticompetitive agreement, it may secure monopoly rents, increase consumer (societal) welfare, or have both effects. It is impossible to say whether EC corporate law provisions, as a whole or one by one, would stand scrutiny under a 'rule of reason' analysis. But at least three implications can be drawn from the characterization of EC corporate law as a cartel.

First, the risk exists that, like any cartel, EC institutions may abuse their monopoly power. What is taking place in the securities law area, with over-active EC institutions issuing level 1 and level 2 measures and level 3 guidelines every other month or so, with no realistic prospect that this is only a temporary phenomenon,[150] can be seen as an illustration of how the EC monopoly power may be abused by engaging in excessive innovation.[151] An ever-changing legal environment greatly increases the compliance costs of EC securities law. In fact, businesses and their consultants have to make the organizational and operational changes required by every regulatory update. Further, the Lamfalussy method may, as an outcome, worsen the already questionable quality of EC securities law. That is, if rules are easy to change, it may be seen as more acceptable for them to be badly worded, inconsistent or simply wrong. In other words, given the chance to legislate more swiftly, EC institutions, which are already prone to produce bad-quality rules, due to the complex art of reaching far-fetched political compromises and to the absence of regulatory competition restraining them, may just end up producing bad rules more often than before.[152] This risk may well balance the positive effect of greater changeability of rules, i.e. the fact that mistaken rules can themselves be repealed more easily.

Secondly, from a dynamic perspective, in areas covered by harmonization, experimentation with new regulatory solutions by single jurisdictions is more difficult, if not ruled out altogether (Romano 1993: 132). Poison pills provide a good illustration of this point. These defensive devices are said to be unfeasible under European corporate laws, due to the 'protection for pre-emptive rights and barriers to discriminatory issuances [which] ... are buttressed by the Second Company Law Directive' (Gordon 2004: 551, n 23).

---

[149] See above text following n 147.

[150] See *Financial Times* (2005) reporting the new Internal Market Commissioner's pledge not to issue important legislative proposals in 2005 in the financial markets area, but also citing a report by Houston Consulting, a company that tracks the Financial Services Action Plan, according to which '78 EU financial services measures are in the pipeline'.

[151] *Cf* Ayres (1995: 558–59) who suggests that Delaware may engage in excessive innovation of its corporate law thanks to its market power.

[152] *Cf* Ferran (2004a: 57) similarly highlighting the 'risk that a system that makes it easier to make laws could remove a *de facto* check on excessive legalism and increase the overall regulatory burden.'

Recent developments in Italian law show that there may be ways around such protections and barriers, depending on how broadly the Second Directive's provisions are construed. Under the 2003 Italian corporate law, companies may issue 'participating financial instruments,'[153] i.e. non-voting or limited voting securities with cash-flow rights possibly identical to those pertaining to shares, but explicitly not treated as shares according to the law.[154] Thus, a company's board of directors, provided that the company's charter authorized it do so, may issue such 'non-share shares' with no need to grant existing shareholders pre-emption rights and possibly in favor of shareholders holding less than a specified percentage of the company's capital.[155] They may also issue securities incorporating an option to purchase such non-share shares at a heavy discount and grant the board the power to redeem such rights. In a word, a device quite similar to a poison pill would now seem available to Italian companies. The most important difference would of course be that the general meeting, that is competent on charter amendments, would have to entrust the board with the power to adopt the Italian-style poison pill. However, this could be easily done at the IPO stage or before the dominant shareholder divests its controlling stake.

Yet, the risk of a court declaring the Italian-style poison pill illegal would be high, especially in light of the provision granting shareholders the pre-emption right on newly issued shares (Enriques 2005). In fact, Italian corporate law scholars and judges often tend to argue that mandatory corporate law rules should apply by analogy to cases similar to those explicitly covered.[156] The presence of an EC Directive imposing pre-emption rights would add further arguments in favor of the illegality of this defensive device, thus increasing the legal risk attaching to it. And this would be despite that, as a matter of EC law, it is far from certain that such a device would violate the Second Directive provisions on equality of treatment[157] and pre-emption rights,[158] as Belgian corporate law also

---

[153] Art 2346(6), C.c.

[154] See, e.g., Enriques and Sforzolini (2004: 79).

[155] *Cf* Gatti (2004: 360–63) considering the hypothesis of a new issue of shares and warrants similarly discriminating against a bidder and concluding that it would not violate the principle of equality of treatment of shareholders.

[156] See critically Enriques (2004d).

[157] Art 42 of the Second Dir provides that '[f]or the purposes of the implementation of this Directive, the laws of the Member States shall ensure equal treatment to all shareholders who are in the same position.' Arguably, if 'non-share shares' are not covered by the Second Dir's provisions on new issues of shares, then Art 42 does not apply to them. And, in any event, it is at least doubtful that the bidder and the other shareholders would be 'in the same position.'

[158] If the reasoning in Advocate General's opinion in *Meilicke* applies (see above n 106 and accompanying text), then it would be for the Member States to decide, according to their domestic laws, whether to strike down these 'poison pills' on the ground that the company, by issuing them, has avoided the rules granting shareholders equal treatment and pre-emption rights.

appears to suggest with regard to the latter.[159] To conclude, even avoidable EC company law rules may increase the legal risk attached to innovation in company law, thereby acting as a curb to it.[160]

Finally, even in a post-*Centros* world it is most unlikely that any Member State will become active in the market for corporate charters.[161] One reason why the Delaware-like scenario is unrealistic is that any Member State considering such a move must allow for the possibility that the EC would intervene to ban any corporate law feature that might actually attract incorporations.[162] So, the very existence of EC lawmaking power in the corporate law area—together with the fact that this power has been exercised fairly often over the decades—may work as a barrier to competition among jurisdictions.

This chapter's thesis that EC corporate law consists principally of rules designed to safeguard the rents of specific interest groups in part reinforces and in part weakens the claim that the EC's power to legislate in the corporate law area has a chilling effect on regulatory competition. On the one hand, should a Member State ever succeed in attracting reincorporations by devising rules that eliminate well-organized interest groups' rents (if there are any beyond those already secured by EC corporate law), there is a very good chance that the EC would step in to outlaw the attractive features of any such competing jurisdiction. On the other hand, the competing jurisdiction may be successful thanks to rules which attract businesses for other reasons (like a greater respect for private parties' determinations or even their pro-management tilt) without touching the interests of well-organized groups. In this case, provided that the chartermongering state succeeds in attracting a relevant number of companies, any attempt to rule out the attractive features of the competing jurisdictions would predictably fail, in light of the EC's inability thus far to win businesses' resistance against non-trivial harmonizing rules.

4. EC Corporate Law Legislation: a Flourishing Industry

Finally, no matter how trivial the outcome, legislation in the corporate law area is indeed something serious: its ever more active production machinery matters not only to those who are directly engaged in the supply of EC corporate law, but also to businesses and professionals,

---

[159] Under Belgian law, other than during a takeover, the general meeting may authorize the board to issue *parts bénéficiaires*, i.e. non-share shares, giving existing shareholders no pre-emption rights on them. See Cincotti (2004 : 229); e-mail from Christoph van der Elst to the author (14 February 2005) (on file with the author).

[160] *Cf* Grundmann (2004: 612–13) emphasizing the advantages of regulatory competition 'as a "discovery device".'

[161] See above text accompanying n 3.

[162] See, e.g., Enriques (2004a: 1269–70).

who, normally through their associations, lobby EC and national institutions for or against the adoption of new EC measures.

As Table 1 and Appendix 1 show, after a slow start in the 1960s and 1970s, the output of EC corporate law has been steady and is now increasing fast. EC legislation needs continuous updating and maintenance. Further, according to many, and especially according to the EC Commission, EC corporate law has to cover more areas and to become more important.[163]

In short, EC corporate law matters as an active and growing lawmaking enterprise, first and foremost to those involved in supplying it, and second to those who may gain or lose from new rules and therefore lobby for or against them.

The following are the groups involved in the supply of EC corporate law:

— politicians at the EC level (Commissioners and Members of the European Parliament), especially with regard to those rare policy issues that are politically sensitive, such as, recently, takeover defences;
— EC officials in charge of corporate law issues within the Internal Market Directorate General,[164] now together with officials working at the Committee of European Securities Regulators (CESR) in Paris;
— officials working on these issues within the European Council's Permanent Representatives Committee (COREPER);
— national politicians dealing with such issues, again especially with regard to politically sensitive issues;
— national public officials having a part in Council meetings, in their preparation and/or in the implementation of Directives once approved;
— lawyers and law professors involved as advisors to lawmakers at the EC level (when EC measures are drafted) and at Member State level (both when EC measures are drafted and when they are to be transposed);[165]

---

[163] See Modernising Company Law and Enhancing Corporate Governance in the European Union—A Plan to Move Forward. Communication from the Commission to the Council and the European Parliament, above n 22, at 24–26 (table displaying 14 legislative initiatives extending the scope of EC corporate law and three changing the existing framework).

[164] Directorate General G (Financial Markets) has a Unit in charge of 'Company law, corporate governance and financial crime,' a Unit in charge of 'Accounting and auditing,' and a Unit in charge of 'Securities markets and investment services providers.'

[165] The importance of lawyers and law professors in the debate and in the process of EC corporate law production can hardly be overestimated. Traditionally, the Commission has requested the advice of prominent corporate law professors and practitioners around Europe in drafting Directives and getting ideas on how to proceed towards more comprehensive harmonization. See Stein (1971: 316) reporting that already in the mid-1960s 'a number of national company law experts … was commissioned to prepare comparative studies on selected aspects of national laws. These studies would contain more or less specific

— Brussels-based lobbying professionals and people working for EC-level industry associations.[166]

EC corporate law matters to these groups in various ways. First of all, these groups (plausibly with the exception of lobbying professionals) usually share a genuine belief in the virtues of harmonization of EU corporate laws, seeing it as a tool both to achieve the objective of market integration and to have better corporate laws in place across the EU.

Secondly, and more cynically, all these groups also have an interest in keeping an active lawmaking process going and, even more, in expanding the areas covered by EC corporate law, whatever its content. This is the case of politicians and bureaucrats at the EC level, of lobbyists as a group,[167] and of lawyers and law professors involved as advisors.

suggestions as to which rules could or should be coordinated and in what way.' See also Van Ommeslaghe (1969: 498) describing the primary role played by such company law experts in the drafting of the early company law Directives. Most recently, the Commission renewed this tradition when it appointed the High Level Group of Company Law Experts, comprising seven leading European lawyers (see Report of the High Level Group of Company Law Experts on a Modern Regulatory Framework for Company Law in Europe, in *Reforming Company and Takeover Law in Europe*, above n 86, 925, 1058). The Group helped the Commission draft a new takeover Directive proposal (see Report of the High Level Group of Company Law Experts on Issues Related to Takeover Bids, *ibid.*, 825, *passim*) and then provided it with an ambitious agenda for post-Enron reforms and for the modernization of EC corporate law (see Report of the High Level Group of Company Law Experts on a Modern Regulatory Framework for Company Law in Europe, *ibid.*, 933–54). Unsurprisingly, the Group advocates the creation of 'a more permanent structure which could provide the Commission with independent advice on future regulatory initiatives in the area of EU company law' (*ibid.* at 961). See critically Hertig and McCahery (2003: 192). In October 2004, the Commission has created a European Corporate Governance Forum 'to help the convergence of national efforts, encourage best practice and advise the Commission' (Bolkestein 2004). More recently, the Commission has declared its 'intention to set up a consultative committee called the Advisory Committee on Corporate Governance and Company Law that would enable it to obtain technical advice on the implementation of the 2003 Company law and Corporate Governance Action Plan.' See Call for applications for the establishment of the Advisory Committee on Corporate Governance and Company Law, at http://www.europa.eu.int/comm/internal_market/company/docs/advisory-committee/call-applications-2004-12_en.pdf.

The centrality of lawyers is far from peculiar to EC corporate law making. The same is in fact true, for instance, of lawyers in the US: 'The driving force behind many corporate statutes is corporate lawyers' (Kahan and Kamar 2002: 705); in Germany: 'Law professors, through the participation on government appointed commissions, play a significant role in law reform in … Germany' (Kirchner *et al.* 2004: 11); and in Italy: Enriques (2004d: 11) reports that 33 out of the 35 components of the Commission in charge of drafting the Italian corporate law reform of 2003 were lawyers, and among them 24 were also law professors.

[166] See generally Vaubel (1994: 154).

[167] See generally (*ibid.* 153–54). Individual lobbyists will do their best to avoid EC legislation on behalf of their clients/employers and with a view to increasing the chances to be assigned the same work again later on in light of the EC Commission's insistence on its harmonization projects (as exemplified by the story of the Takeover Directive). As a group, however, Brussels lobbyists can only gain from an ever greater amount of EC legislation, because interest groups opposing it will sooner or later take action in order to have it repealed or changed and because EC legislation usually generates further legislation in the form of amendments, attempts to reach a higher level of harmonization, updates and so on.

Not only a greater scope for EC corporate law[168] but also a more active EC corporate lawmaking industry will increase the power and prestige of all these groups. This is also the case of national-level bureaucrats in charge of implementation and of lawyers and law professors serving as their advisors, often the same people following the legislative works leading to the adoption of the Directives for their respective countries. As a matter of fact, most changes in national corporate laws in the last 35 years have been the result of EC Directives, so that apparently EC corporate law production has inflated the national 'demand' for legislative work in this field,[169] leading in turn to greater support for new EC initiatives from national legislative bureaucracies and corporate law scholars. Some of the national bureaucrats, politicians, and advisors will also favor EC legislation so as to develop a pro-European reputation, with a view to being promoted to a position in Brussels.[170]

For lawyers and legal scholars involved in the production of EC corporate law as advisors to the Commission or to national Governments, the process itself may have a consumption-good component, such as

> the chance to reflect and consult with peers in a nonadversary setting about ideal statutory solutions to various problems—the counterpart of academic conferences (Carney 1997: 725).[171]

Politicians and bureaucrats at national and EC level alike will further favor EC legislation which allows specific interest groups to extract rents, the former to secure their votes and/or campaign contributions, the latter to increase their power and prestige among such groups, possibly with a view to jobs in the private sector later on.[172]

---

[168] As Majone (1989: 167) observes, 'the desire of the Commission to increase its influence [is] a fairly uncontroversial behavioral assumption.'

[169] This does not contradict the view that EC corporate law is trivial. It only shows that EC corporate law inflates the demand for corporate law reform services by requiring Member States to review their corporate laws, however trivially, more often than they would otherwise do.

[170] See generally Vaubel (1994a: 157); *ibid.* (1994b: 233).

[171] EC corporate law has a consumption good component for European corporate law professors in general, because it provides a common ground for research in this area of law. See Stein (1971: 193) reporting that even back in the 1960s '[t]he interest generated by the Commission's [early] work has led to what one may call a flowering of comparative company law studies in the universities and in the some forty new centers of European studies.'

EC company law also justifies (and helps find funding for) cross-border work and international conferences much better than mere comparative curiosity. Similarly, as Harald Halbhuber (2001: 1412) notes, '[f]ar from deploring the confusion created by Directives, some German authors praise it as an intellectual challenge, a veritable comparative lawyer's paradise that would see national lawyers competing for influence on the ECJ's interpretation of the Directives.'

[172] For anecdotal evidence see Stein (1971: 189–90) reporting the case of a German civil servant who joined the Commission staff in 1958, became 'director of the Directorate dealing with harmonization of company law ... [and] resigned in 1969 to become a member of the board of an insurance concern'.

National politicians and bureaucrats may also favor EC legislation in this area whenever it may raise the cost of doing business in other Member States to the same level as in their home state, thereby securing the rents extracted by the relevant national interest groups.[173]

Turning from the suppliers of EC corporate law to those who are bound to gain or lose from it, section IV.A.2 identified the interest groups that benefit most. These groups actively demand EC corporate lawmaking. Accounts of the legislative process leading to the adoption of corporate law Directives confirm that organized interest groups, such as accountants and their associations, have always played an active role in the production of EC corporate law,[174] consistent with the more general finding that interest groups play a prominent role in the EC lawmaking process.[175]

EC corporate law also serves lawyers' and law professors' interests,[176] not only thanks to the increased complexity of the legal framework, but also because it may reduce 'the regulatory surplus that parties could exploit by engaging in regulatory arbitrage' (Lombardo 2002: 1993). Lawyers' and law professors' human capital is heavily invested in their domestic corporate laws and deeply connected with the mastery of their native language. Should private parties massively decide to opt out of their domestic law, they would lose money and prestige (Halbhuber 2001: 1413; Lombardo 2002: 193). This helps explain why lawyers and law professors, quite aside from their genuine belief in the virtues of harmonization, usually favor it.[177]

Other groups, such as businesses and their associations or families

---

[173] See generally Vaubel (1994a: 158). Belgium and Italy, which already imposed the publication of annual accounts by their companies were among the most active proponents of a similar obligation at EC level (Van Ommeslaghe 1969: 498–9). See Stein (1971: 232) stating that Belgian and Italian experts pushed for immediate mandate of the obligation to disclose annual accounts.

[174] See (*ibid.*: 195–235), for an account of the legislative history of the First Dir highlighting how much the various interest groups were involved in the process. See also Edwards (1999: 118–19) on the proactive role of the German Institute of Public Accountants in the lawmaking process leading to the adoption of the Fourth Dir; Walton (1997: 722): 'In 1965 the Commission asked the accounting profession in the ... six member states ... to constitute an expert group to prepare a report on the harmonization of accounting for listed firms,' the work of which constituted the basis for the first draft of the Fourth Dir.

[175] See, e.g., Vaubel (1994b: 238); Medin and Fraga (1988: 154). See also Schmitthoff (1976: 100): 'The eventual form in which the Council of Ministers approves an important legislative measure has often, in fact, been agreed between the officials of the Commission and the representatives of interested circles in the Member States'.

[176] It is perhaps worth pointing out that lawyers (and law professors) play a two-fold role in (corporate) lawmaking, both on the supply side and on the demand side. See Ribstein (1994: 1014–15) with specific regard to Delaware's corporate lawmaking process.

[177] What is argued here is, again, not inconsistent with the claim that Directives and Regulations issued thus far are mostly trivial. First of all, they may be trivial due to the unsuccessful attempt to harmonize in a more effective way. Secondly, those advocating the adoption of corporate law Directives and Regulations plausibly perceive them to be less trivial than they are.

holding controlling blocks in EU companies, far from pushing for EC intervention,[178] have usually *resisted* EC's attempts to harmonize areas of law (in a non-trivial way).[179] As Parts II and III have shown, on the whole their resistance has been effective, leading, with few exceptions, to a fair amount of trivial EC corporate law.

The most common view, at least among lawyers, is that the EC's failure to harmonize EC corporate law more meaningfully is the outcome of a game in which a public-interest-minded European Commission attempts to improve the fairness and efficiency of corporate law within the EU, while Member States, captive to the interests of national businesses, block or water down the proposals. And it may well be that the resistance by dominant interest groups at the national level has always prevented the adoption of non-trivial EC rules.[180]

Once we take the interests of suppliers of EC corporate law into account, however, one may take a more cynical view at the EC company law production process. One may regard the EC institutions' failure to issue non-trivial rules as the result of a different game, in which EC politicians and public officials (no matter whether, as the case may be, in

[178] Desmond McComb makes this point (1991: 266, 283) with regard to accounting Directives: 'The accounting Directives have been a prime example of legislation from above in the almost total absence of evident social need or demand.'

[179] For instance, both the UNICE (the main association of European industrialists) and the *Fédération Bancaire* opposed most proposed rules to be inserted in the Second Dir, *see* Stein (1971: 319–26). See also *generally* Lannoo (1999: 292): 'Member States and businesses prefer to keep control over corporate control in their hands'; and, with specific regard to accounting Directives, Diggle and Nobes (1994: 330): 'Governments will also respond to strong lobby groups. ... These groups will be aiming to preserve the status quo, to maintain flexibility, to minimise costs, and so forth. One powerful example of the influence of corporate lobbyists is the inclusion of special Articles in the Seventh Directive that enable the unique consolidation practices of Unilever and Royal Dutch Shell to continue (Article 12 and 15).' One may see an exception to this in so-called global players' pressure for an EC regime allowing them to use the International Accounting Standards (see e.g., Haller (2002: 168). However, one should note that for global players the first best solution would have been simply to have EC accounting Directives scrapped so as to be able to use IAS, as opposed to the current EC regime in which individual accounts are still regulated by the Fourth Dir (unless Member States exercise the option Art 5 of Reg 1606/2002 grants them to have individual accounts drawn according to IAS), while consolidated accounts must be drawn up according to the IAS principles as endorsed by the EC. As a matter of fact, the adoption of IAS accounting principles by the EC mainly reflects the EC institutions' (and especially the Commission's) aim 'to keep itself in the game of taking future influence in international accounting harmonization' (*Ibid.*: 164), also in the face of Member States' pro-active moves to allow global players to use International Accounting Standards (for instance, in 1998 Germany allowed its listed companies to prepare consolidated annual accounts in accordance with internationally accepted accounting principles: see, e.g., Nowak (2003: 435).

[180] *Cf* Bebchuk and Roe (1999: 165): 'British managers, French and Italian controlling shareholders, and German codeterminated firms may each prefer a system of corporate governance that radically differs from that preferred by the others. But ... [t]hey might wish to preserve their positional advantage in their own firms and as such might all prefer to prevent European Union officials from imposing a common set of corporate rules.'

perfect good faith) propose controversial, non-trivial rules often with the tacit or explicit support of one or more Member States already having such rules in place, while politicians and bureaucrats from Member States in which the proposed rules would harm specific interest groups oppose them on those groups' behalf. Eventually, this is a game Member States will always be pleased to play: not only are they usually able to block any meaningful legislation in this area, thereby acting as champions of the organized national interests opposing the EC measure. But, should they fail to block it, they can always put the blame on the EC and on other Member States. While it is debatable whether the EU economies would be better off with more relevant EC corporate law rules in place, it is certain that, in the process, the interest groups resisting EC intervention will have spent time and money in national and European lobbying.[181]

A good illustration is the process that resulted in toothless rules on takeover defences. The EC first proposed a modified passivity rule clearly inspired by the English City Code. This was strongly opposed by corporate Germany, following the traumatic takeover of Mannesmann by Vodafone, and German Members of the European Parliament followed suit (Cioffi 2002: 384). The European Parliament's rejection led the Commission to raise the stakes and, on the advice of the High Level Group of Company Law Experts,[182] to propose even more controversial rules, which would hit dominant shareholders and incumbent managers around the EU unevenly, de facto prohibiting some structural defences against takeovers, while leaving others untouched.[183]

The European Parliament, following the advice of two academics (Lieb and Lamandini 2003), proposed amendments that would have extended the negative impact of the Directive to other structural defences, namely multiple voting capital structures, while again leaving others untouched.[184] The strong opposition from Member States with dominant shareholders and incumbent managers who might lose the quasi-rents stemming from their uncontestable control positions was finally successful: the rules were made optional, i.e. trivial.[185] In the meantime,

---

[181] *Cf* Kostel (1993: 2153–54): federal lawmaking involves greater lobbying expenditures by managers, while the legislative outcome will be at best no less pro-managers than state corporate statutes, the added expense of managerial lobbying at the federal level being thus 'pure waste.'

[182] See above n 165.

[183] See Art 11, Proposal for a European Parliament and Council Directive on takeover bids (COM(2002) 534) of 2 October 2002 which declares restrictions on the transfer of shares and on voting rights respectively unenforceable and ineffective during the bid and imposing the breakthrough rule; no provision in the proposal addressed structural defences such as pyramids, cross-holdings or even multiple voting structures.

[184] See European Parliament Report on the Proposal for a European Parliament and Council Dir on Takeover Bids, Final A5-0000/2003 (3 December 2003) which extends the breakthrough rule so as to neutralize multiple voting structures, but again addressing neither pyramids nor cross-holdings.

[185] See above text accompanying nn 62–66.

these groups conducted an impressive lobbying campaign both at the national and at the EC level.[186] In other words, they spent a lot of money and effort to obtain what they wanted—that is ... nothing.[187]

Undeniably, the one provided here is a cynical view of why EC corporate law matters. One may of course paint a more idealistic picture, in which what little has been achieved despite Member States' and businesses' resistance improved the quality of companies' disclosure, prevented companies from entering into value-destroying transactions, and, at the end of the day, improved the quality of Member States' corporate law, also to the benefit of their (often too myopic) businesses or, in any event, of their economies. In other words, the higher cost of doing business deriving from EC corporate law would be justified on efficiency grounds, the benefits more than offsetting the costs. This may well be. The point is that while the benefits of secondary EC corporate law, also in the light of the triviality of most of its rules, are debatable at best,[188] it is hard to deny that the cost of setting up a company and of carrying out certain transactions is higher as a consequence of EC law, that EC corporate law helps certain interest groups secure their rents, that the corporate law landscape is more complex than it would otherwise be, that EC corporate law has a curbing effect upon the dynamics of regulatory competition in this area of law, and finally that its lawmaking industry is busy and flourishing.

B. One Possible Objection: Are Member States' Corporate Laws also Trivial?

Before concluding, it may be worth countering a possible objection to our analysis thus far, i.e. that the same analysis with regard to individual Member States might well conclude that their corporate laws are no less trivial. Undeniably, many national provisions are trivial, but not all; and some of them do matter greatly for businesses.

First of all, in some jurisdictions rules implementing trivial EC corporate law provisions are non-trivial, simply because their

---

[186] See, e.g., Brown-Humes and Guerrera (2002: 10) giving voice to Wallenberg family's opposition to plans to extend the breakthrough rule to multiple voting shares and reporting that a member of the family and vice-chairman of the family holding company Investor AB, Jacob Wallenberg, would meet the Commissioner for Internal Market on that day.

[187] See generally McChesney (1997) who provides a theory of how politicians may threaten legislative action in order to appropriate private actors' rents or quasi-rents.

[188] As Part IV has argued, one of the few achievements of EC corporate law is the requirement that companies over a given size prepare annual accounts according to certain rules, have them audited and make them public. Brian Cheffins provides an excellent critique of the policy of imposing such requirements on smaller companies, mainly on grounds valid in general for closely-held companies (1997: 512–21).

policymakers, lawyers and judges take them seriously. This is the case of rules on contributions in kind, for instance, in Germany (Halbhuber 2001: 1406).

Secondly, though not technically part of corporate law, rules on co-determination do matter in countries that impose them, and it is no coincidence that no attempt to export co-determination through Directives and Regulations has ever succeeded.[189]

Thirdly, domestic rules and doctrines on structural and non-structural defences against takeovers are self-evidently relevant. Further, it is hard to deny that rules and doctrines on directors' duties and liability, related-party transactions and shareholder suits against directors and dominant shareholders are non-trivial.

The same is true of a rule found in some Member States, which Jonathan Macey and I have termed the 'recapitalize or liquidate rule,'[190] requiring that when losses push net assets below some specified minimum, the company must either recapitalize or reorganize as a company with capital requirement no smaller than its remaining net assets. If it fails to do so promptly, it must be wound up, and if the company is not liquidated, the directors are personally liable. Self-evidently, this rule plays a major role for 'asset-light' companies and especially for companies in the proximity of insolvency.[191]

To be sure, after the recent ECJ decisions on companies' freedom of establishment (*Centros* etc.), one may argue that State corporate laws have become trivial in the sense that companies may avoid national rules simply by (re)incorporating elsewhere.[192] For the present, however, legal, tax and other barriers to corporate law arbitrage, especially for already existing companies, are still high enough to preserve national corporate laws' relevance (Enriques 2004a: 1260–66). And in any event, the trivialization of national company laws due to the ECJ decisions would not itself make EC Directives and Regulations less trivial.

V. CONCLUSION

This chapter has argued that secondary EC corporate law has thus far been trivial, i.e. has had and is having very little impact upon EU corporations' governance and management. First, it fails to cover core

[189] See, e.g., Buxbaum and Hopt (1988: 259–62).

[190] See Enriques and Macey (2001: 1183–84) who cite such rules in place in Italy, France, Spain, and Sweden.

[191] *Cf* Weigmann (1997: 423) stating that loss of capital is the most frequent event of dissolution in Italy together with insolvency.

[192] *Cf* Black (1990: 556, 558) arguing that reincorporation renders avoidable every rule that is mandatory in one state and optional in another, provided that the costs of reincorporating are low enough.

corporate law areas, such as e.g., fiduciary duties and shareholder remedies. Secondly, the rules are under-enforced. Thirdly, in the presence of very sporadic judiciary interpretation by the European Court of Justice, EC corporate law tends to be implemented and construed differently in different Member States, i.e. according to local legal culture and consistently with pre-existing corporate law. Fourthly, when it has introduced new rules, it has done so with respect to issues on which Member States would have most probably legislated even in the absence of an EC mandate. Finally, most of its rules are optional, market-mimicking, unimportant or avoidable. This cannot be said of national corporate laws, which still regulate core issues, sometimes even in an intrusive way, as in imposing passivity upon managers of target companies during a takeover or requiring companies to recapitalize or liquidate as assets fall below some specified minimum.

There are, of course, due qualifications to the triviality thesis. First of all, a few rules or sets of rules indeed have had or are bound to have a meaningful impact on companies and their operations. Secondly, EC corporate law has increased the regulatory burden of corporate laws across the EU, correspondingly securing higher rents for certain interest groups. Thirdly, secondary EC corporate law has an impact on the evolution of European corporate laws and the dynamics of regulatory competition in various ways. In short, Member States interact with EC institutions in order to affect the outcome of its harmonization efforts and, in the process, alter their company laws to this purpose. EC institutions may abuse their monopoly power to impose rules on EU companies, especially by overfrequent legislative innovation; in areas covered by EC law (no matter how trivial), experimentation by (however mildly) competing jurisdictions is ruled out, or at least more difficult, especially when the EU measures involve comprehensive harmonization; the mere possibility of intervening in the area of corporate law may curb regulatory competition. Finally, its production has become an industry itself, employing many EC and national functionaires and lobbyists, and creating occasions for rent extraction by politicians.

EU institutions have recently become over-active in all areas of corporate law as defined here: in securities regulation, a number of level 1 and level 2 Directives and Regulations have been issued, that attempt to harmonize completely securities law and to ensure greater uniformity in its enforcement as well. In accounting law, the Commission is playing an active role in the shaping of international accounting principles[193] and

---

[193] See, e.g., Bolkestein (2004: 9) reporting that the EC Commission has interacted with the International Accounting Standard Board in order to obtain 'improvements' of the International Financial Reporting Standards. See also Commission Reg (EEC) 2086/2004 of 19 November 2004 (endorsing IAS 39, but carving out its 'full fair value option' and its hedge accounting provisions).

has proposed to reshape the regulation of auditing and accounting following the example of the Sarbanes-Oxley Act.[194] In core corporate law, an ambitious action plan is being transformed into Directive proposals.[195] Such activism might soon render the main thesis of this chapter obsolete. If the experience so far is of any guidance, however, the final impact of all these efforts on national corporate laws and EU companies may well prove to be weaker than expected. Further, whatever the final outcome of the new trend toward harmonization, this chapter provides a framework to assess whether the forthcoming wave of EC legislation can escape the destiny of triviality thus far characterizing EC company law Directives and Regulations.

APPENDIX 1: EC CORPORATE LAW DIRECTIVES AND REGULATIONS[196]

First Council Directive 68/151/EEC of 9 March 1968 on co-ordination of safeguards which, for the protection of the interests of members and others, are required by Member States of companies within the meaning of the second paragraph of Article 58 of the Treaty, with a view to making such safeguards equivalent throughout the Community, as amended by Directive 2003/58/EC of 15 July 2003.

Second Council Directive 77/91/EEC of 13 December 1976 on coordination of safeguards which, for the protection of the interests of members and others, are required by Member States of companies within the meaning of the second paragraph of Article 58 of the Treaty, in respect of the formation of public limited liability companies and the maintenance and alteration of their capital, with a view to making such safeguards equivalent, as amended by
Council Directive 92/101/EEC of 23 November 1992.

---

[194] See Proposal for a Dir on Statutory Audit of Annual Accounts and Consolidated Accounts and Amending Council Dirs 78/660/EEC and 83/349/EEC (COM/2004/0177 final), and Proposal for a Dir of the European Parliament and of the Council Amending Council Dirs 78/660/EEC and 83/349/EEC Concerning the Annual Accounts of Certain Types of Companies and Consolidated Accounts (at http://www.europa.eu.int/comm/internal_market/accounting/docs/board/prop-dir_en.pdf).

[195] See Modernising Company Law and Enhancing Corporate Governance in the European Union—A Plan to Move Forward, above n 16. For the first implementation steps, see Proposal for a Dir of the European Parliament and of the Council on Cross-Border Mergers of Companies with Share Capital (COM (2003) 703(01)), and Proposal for a Dir of the European Parliament and of the Council Amending Council Dir 77/91/EEC, As Regards the Formation of Public Limited Liability Companies and the Maintenance and Alteration of their Capital (at http://www.europa.eu.int/comm/internal_market/company/docs/capital/2004-proposal/proposal_en.pdf).

[196] Updated to 31 December 2004. In italics are measures that have already been cited in the App or which will be cited further below. In square brackets are measures that have been repealed.

Third Council Directive 78/855/EEC of 9 October 1978 based on Article 54 (3) (g) of the Treaty concerning mergers of public limited liability companies.

Fourth Council Directive 78/660/EEC of 25 July 1978 based on Article 54(3)(g) of the Treaty on the annual accounts of certain types of companies as amended by
Seventh Council Directive 83/349/EEC of 13 June 1983 (below);

Council Directive 84/569/EEC of 27 November 1984;

Eleventh Council Directive 89/666/EEC of 21 December 1989 (below);

Council Directive 90/604/EEC of 8 November 1990;

Council Directive 90/605/EEC of 8 November 1990;

Council Directive 94/8/EC of 21 March 1994;

Council Directive 99/60/EC of 17 June 1999;

Directive 2001/65/EC of 27 September 2001;

Council Directive 2003/38/EC of 13 May 2003;

Directive 2003/51/EC of the European Parliament and of the Council of 18 June 2003.

[Directive 79/279/EEC coordinating the conditions for the admission of securities to official stock exchange listing, as amended by
Council Directive 82/148/EEC of 3 March 1982;

Council Directive 88/627/EEC of 12 December 1988 (below); and as repealed by
Directive 2001/34/EC of the European Parliament and of the Council of 28 May 2001 (below).]

[Council Directive 80/390/EEC of 17 March 1980 coordinating the requirements for the drawing up, scrutiny and distribution of the listing particulars to be published for the admission of securities to official stock exchange listing, as amended by
Council Directive 82/148/EEC of 3 March 1982;

Council Directive 87/345/EEC of 22 June 1987;

Council Directive 90/211/EEC of 23 April 1990;

Directive 94/18/EC of the European Parliament and of the Council of 30 May 1994; and as repealed by
Directive 2001/34/EC of the European Parliament and of the Council of 28 May 2001 (below).]

[Council Directive 82/121/EEC of 15 February 1982 on information to be published on a regular basis by companies the shares of which have been admitted to official stock-exchange listing, as repealed by
Directive 2001/34/EC of the European Parliament and of the Council of 28 May 2001 (below).]

Sixth Council Directive 82/891/EEC of 17 December 1982 based on Article 54(3)(g) of the Treaty, concerning the division of public limited liability companies.

Seventh Council Directive 83/349/EEC of 13 June 1983 based on the Article 54(3)(g) of the Treaty on consolidated accounts as amended by
Eleventh Council Directive 89/666/EEC of 21 December 1989 (below);

Council Directive 90/604/EEC of 8 November 1990;

Council Directive 90/605/EEC of 8 November 1990;

Directive 2001/65/EC of 27 September 2001;

Directive 2003/51/EC of the European Parliament and of the Council of 18 June 2003.

Eighth Council Directive 84/253/EEC of 10 April 1984 based on Article 54(3)(g) of the Treaty on the approval of persons responsible for carrying out the statutory audits of accounting documents.

[Council Directive 88/627/EEC of 12 December 1988 on the information to be published when a major holding in a listed company is acquired or disposed of, as repealed by
Directive 2001/34/EC of the European Parliament and of the Council of 28 May 2001 (below).]

[Council Directive 89/298/EEC of 17 April 1989 coordinating the requirements for the drawing-up, scrutiny and distribution of the prospectus to be published when transferable securities are offered to the public, as repealed by
Directive 2003/71/EC of the European Parliament and of the Council of 4 November 2003 (below).]

[Council Directive 89/592/EEC of 13 November 1989 coordinating regulations on insider dealing, as repealed by
Directive 2003/6/EC of the European Parliament and of the Council of 28 January 2003 (below).]

Eleventh Council Directive 89/666/EEC of 21 December 1989 concerning disclosure requirements in respect of branches opened in a Member State by certain types of company governed by the law of another State.

Twelfth Council Company Law Directive 89/667/EEC of 21 December 1989 on single-member private limited-liability companies.

Directive 2001/34/EC of the European Parliament and of the Council of 28 May 2001 on the admission of securities to official stock exchange listing and on information to be published on those securities, as amended by
Directive 2003/6/EC of the European Parliament and of the Council of 28 January 2003 (below);

Directive 2003/71/EC of the European Parliament and of the Council of 4 November 2003 (below).

Directive 2004/109/EC of the European Parliament and of the Council of 15 December 2004 (below).

Regulation (EC) 2001/2157 of 8 October 2001 on the Statute for a European company (SE).

Directive 2001/86/EC of 8 October 2001 supplementing the Statute for a European company with regard to the involvement of employees.

Regulation (EC) 1606/2002 of the European Parliament and of the Council of 19 July 2002, as implemented by
Commission Regulation (EC) 1725/2003 of 29 September 2003 and Annexes, adopting certain international accounting standards in accordance with Regulation 606/2002/ EC, as amended by
Commission Regulation (EC) 707/2004 of 6 April 2004;

Commission Regulation (EC) 2086/2004 of 19 November 2004;

Commission Regulation (EC) 2236/2004 of 29 December 2004;

Commission Regulation (EC) 2237/2004 of 29 December 2004;

Commission Regulation (EC) 2238/2004 of 29 December 2004.

Directive 2003/6/EC of the European Parliament and of the Council of 28 January 2003 on insider dealing and market manipulation (market abuse) as implemented by

Commission Directive 2003/124/EC of 22 December 2003 implementing Directive 2003/6/EC as regards the definition and public disclosure of inside information and the definition of market manipulation;

Commission Regulation (EC) 2273/2003 of 22 December 2003 implementing Directive 2003/6/EC as regards exemptions for buy-back programmes and stabilisation of financial instruments;

Commission Directive 2004/72/EC of 29 April 2004 implementing Directive 2003/6/EC as regards accepted market practices, the definition of inside information in relation to derivatives on commodities, the drawing up of lists of insiders, the notification of managers' transactions and the notification of suspicious transactions.[197]

Directive 2003/71/EC of the European Parliament and of the Council of 4 November 2003 on the prospectus to be published when securities are offered to the public or admitted to trading and amending Directive 2001/34/EC, as implemented by
Commission Regulation (CE) 809/2004 of 29 April 2004 implementing Directive 2003/71/EC of the European Parliament and of the Council as regards information contained in prospectuses as well as the format, incorporation by reference and publication of such prospectuses and dissemination of advertisements.[198]

Directive 2004/25/EC of the European Parliament and of the Council of 21 April 2004 on takeover bids.

Directive 2004/109/EC of the European Parliament and of the Council of 15 December 2004 on the harmonization of transparency requirements in relation to information about issuers whose securities are admitted to trading on a regulated market and amending Directive 2001/34/EC.

APPENDIX 2: ECJ CASES INVOLVING SECONDARY EC CORPORATE LAW ISSUES

A. Proceedings Concerning Failure by Member States to Implement Directives

C-136/81, *Commission v Republic of Italy* [1982] ECR 3547 (failure to transpose Second Directive);
C-148/81, *Commission v Kingdom of Belgium* [1982] ECR 3555 (failure to transpose Second Directive);
C-148/81, *Commission v Grand Duchy of Luxembourg* [1982] ECR 3565 (failure to transpose Second Directive);
C-151/81, *Commission v Ireland* [1982] ECR 3573 (failure to transpose Second Directive);

---

[197] Dir 2003/6/EC is also implemented by Commission Dir 2003/125/EC of 22 December 2003. The latter Directive, which implements the former 'as regards the fair presentation of investment recommendations and the disclosure of conflicts of interest,' does not deal with corporate law issues and is therefore not included in the list.
[198] See also CESR's Recommendations for the Consistent Implementation of the European Commission's Regulation on Prospectuses No 809/2004, February 2005 (CESR/05/054b) (available on CESR's website), a Lamfalussy-approach level 3 measure.

C-390/85, *Commission v Kingdom of Belgium* [1987] ECR 761 (failure to transpose three securities law Directives);

C-17/85, *Commission v Republic of Italy* [1986] ECR 1199 (failure to transpose Fourth Directive);

C-157/91, *Commission v Kingdom of the Netherlands* [1992] ECR I-5899 (failure to transpose two Articles of Eighth Directive);

C-95/94, *Commission v Kingdom of Spain* [1995] ECR I-1967 (case removed from the register);

C-191/95, *Commission v Federal Republic of Germany* [1998] ECR I-5449 (failure to transpose First and Fourth Directives by failing to provide appropriate penalties as prescribed by those Directives);

C-272/97, *Commission v Federal Republic of Germany* [1999] ECR I-2175 (failure to transpose Directive 90/605/EEC);

C-185/98, *Commission v Hellenic Republic* [1999] ECR I-3047 (failure to transpose Directive 92/101/CEE).

B. Preliminary Rulings

C-32/74, *Friedrich Haaga GmbH* [1974] ECR 1201.

C-136/87, *Ubbink Isolatie BV v Dak- en Wandtechniek BV* [1988] ECR 4665 (First Directive);

C-38/89, *Ministère public v Guy Blanguernon* [1990] ECR I-83 (Fourth Directive, but generally holding that national law implementing a Directive has full force, even if other States have failed to implemented it yet);

C-106/89, *Marleasing SA v La Comercial Internacional de Alimentacion SA* [1990] ECR I-4135 (First Directive, but generally holding that national law has to be interpreted consistently with EC law);

C-381/89, *Syndesmos Melon tis Eleftheras Evangelikis Ekklissias and others v Greek State and others* [1992] ECR I-2111 (Second Directive);

C-19/90 and C-20/90, *Karella and Karellas v Minister for Industry, Energy and Technology and Organismos Anasygkrotiseos Epicheiriseon AE* [1991] ECR I-2691 (Second Directive);

C-83/91, *Meilicke v ADV/ORGA F. A. Meyer AG* [1992] ECR I-4871 (decided on procedural grounds);

C-134/91 and C-135/91, *Kerafina-Keramische-und Finanz Holding AG and Vioktimatiki AEVE v Hellenic Republic and Organismos Oikonomikis Anasygkrotissis Epicheirisseon AE.* [1992] ECR I-5699 (Second Directive);

C-441/93, *Pafitis and Others v TKE and Others* [1996] ECR I-1347 (Second Directive);

C-234/94, *Tomberger v Gebruder von der Wettern GmbH* [1996] ECR I-3133 (Fourth Directive);

C-42/95, *Siemens AG v Henry Nold* [1996] ECR I-6017 (Second Directive).

C-97/96, *Verband deutscher Daihatsu-Handler eV v Daihatsu Deutschland GmbH* [1997] ECR I-6843 (First and Fourth Directives);

C-104/96, *Cooperatieve Rabobank 'Vecht en Plassengebied' BA v Erik Aarnoud Minderhoud* [1997] ECR I-7211 (First Directive);

C-367/96, *Kefalas and Others v Elliniko Dimosio (Greek State) and Organismos Oikonomikis Anasygkrotisis Epicheiriseon AE (OAE)* [1998] ECR I-2843 (Second Directive);

C-275/97, *DE + ES Bauunternehmung GmbH v Finanzamt Bergheim* [1999] ECR I-5331 (Fourth Directive);

C-373-97, *Dionysios Diamantis v Elliniko Dimosio (Greek State) and Organismos Ikonomikis Anasygkrotisis Epicheiriseon AE (OAE)* [2000] ECR I-1705 (Second Directive);

C-28/99, *Criminal proceedings against Jean Verdonck, Ronald Everaert and Edith de Baedts* [2001] ECR I-3399 (first Insider Trading Directive);

C-306/99, *Banque internationale pour l'Afrique occidentale SA (BIAO) v Finanzamt für Großunternehmen in Hamburg* [2003] ECR I-1 (Fourth Directive).

C-182/00, *Lutz GmbH and Others* [2002] ECR I-547 (decided on procedural grounds);

C-167/01, *Kamer van Koophandel v Inspire Art* [2003] ECR I-10155 (Eleventh Directive).

C-435/02 and C-103/03, Axel Springer AG v Zeitungsverlag GmbH & Co. Essen KG and Hans Jürgen Weske [2004] ECR I-(9.23.2004) ((First and Fourth Directives).

C-255/01, Panagiotis Markopoulos and Others v Ypourgos Anaptyxis and Soma Orkoton Elegkton [2004] ECR I-(10–7–2004) (Eleventh Directive).

REFERENCES

Alexander, D. (1993), 'A European True and Fair View?', 1 *European Accounting Review* 59.

Alfaro Águila-Real, J. (2004), 'Lowering Legal Barriers to Entry Through Technology Without Touching Vested Interests: The Spanish Sociedad Limitada-Nueva Empresa', 5 *European Business Law Review* 449.

Andersson, J. (2003), 'The High Level Group and the Issue of European Company Law Harmonisation—Europe Stumbles Along?' in *The Regulation of Companies. A Tribute to Krüger Andersen* 183 (Mette Neville & Karsten Engsig Sørensen eds)

Ayres, I. (1995), 'Supply-Side Inefficiencies in Corporate Charter Competition: Lessons from Patents, Yachting and Bluebooks', 43 *Kansas Law Review* 541.

Bartos, J. and Lippert, M. (2003), 'Why Europe's New Prospectus Regime May Fail', *International Financial Law Review*, Aug. 2003, at 18.

Basedow, J., Hopt, K.J. and Kötz, H. (eds.), (1998), *Festschrift für Ulrich drobnig zum siebzigten Geburtstag* (Tübingen: Mohr Siebeck).

Bebchuk, L.A. and Hamdani, A. (2002), 'Vigorous Race or Leisurely Walk: Reconsidering the Competition over Corporate Charters, 112 *Yale Law Journal* 553.

Bebchuk, L.A. and Roe, M.J. (1999), 'A Theory of Path Dependence in Corporate Ownership and Governance', 52 *Stanford Law Review* 127.

Becht, M. and Böhmer, E. (2001), 'Ownership and Voting Power in Germany', in *The Control of Corporate Europe* 128 (Fabrizio Barca & Marco Becht eds) (Oxford: Oxford University Press).

Bhattacharya, U. and Daouk, H. (2002), 'The World Price of Insider Trading', 57 *Journal of Finance* 75.

—— (2004), 'When No Law is Better than a Good Law' (June), available at http://ssrn.com/abstract=558021.

Bianco, M. and Szegö, B. (2004), 'Le riforme del diritto societario e dell'OPA a livello europeo', in *La governance dell'impresa tra regole ed etica* 101 (Fabrizio Carotti *et al.* eds) Milan: Il sole 24 ole).

Black, B.S. (1990), 'Is Corporate Law Trivial?: A Political and Economic Analysis', 84 *Northwestern University Law Review* 542.

Blaurock, U. (1998), 'Steps Toward a Uniform Corporate Law in the European Union', 31 *Cornell International Law Journal* 377.

Bloomberg (2004), 'Record Debts in European Buyouts Spur "Credit Bubble" Concerns', Bloomberg.com (29 Dec.), available at http://www.bloomberg.com/apps/news?pid=10000085&sid=arzvgEO2dYs4&refer=europe#.

Bolkestein, F. (2004a), 'Corporate Governance in the European Union' (18 Oct.), available at http://www.europa.eu.int/rapid/pressReleasesAction.do?reference=SPEECH/04/460&format=HTML&aged=0&language=EN&guiLanguage=en.

Bolkestein, F. (2004b), 'End the Carping over Accounting Standards', *Financial Times (Europe)*, 9 Nov., at 9.

Bratton, W.W. (1994), 'Corporate Law's Race to Nowhere in Particular', 44 *University of Toronto Law Journal* 401.

Brown-Humes, C. and Guerrera, F. (2002), 'Wallenberg Attacks EU over Takeover Proposals', *Financial Times (London)*, 31 January, at 10.

Buxbaum, R.M. and Hopt, K.J. (1988), *Legal Harmonization and the Business Enterprise* (Berlin: de Gruyter).

Buxbaum, R.M. *et al.* (eds) (1991), *European Business Law. Legal and Economic Analyses on Integration and Harmonization* (Berlin: de Gruyter).

Campobasso, G.F. (2002), *Diritto commerciale, 2, Diritto delle società* 473 (5th ed) (Turin: Utek).

Carney, W.J. (undated), App A, *Adoption or Rejection of EC Company Law Directives in US* (unpublished manuscript, on file with the author).

—— (1997), 'The Political Economy of Competition for Corporate Charters', 26 *Journal of Legal Studies* 303.

CESR (2005), Recommendations for the Consistent Implementation of the European Commission's Regulation on Prospectuses No 809/2004, Feb. 2005 (CESR/05/054b)

Cheffins, B.R. (1997), *Company Law. Theory, Structure and Operation* (Oxford: Oxford University Press).

Cincotti, C. (2005), 'L'esperienza delle parts *bénéficiaries* belghe e gli strumenti finanziari partecipativi di cui all'art. 2346 c.c.', Banca Borsa Titoli di Credito, 221.

Cioffi, J.W. (2002), 'Restructuring "Germany Inc.": The Politics of Company and Takeover Law Reform in Germany and the European Union', 2002 *Law and Policy* 355.

Colombatto, E. and Macey, J.R. (1996), 'A Public Choice Model of International Economic Cooperation and the Decline of the Nation State', 18 *Cardozo Law Review* 925.

Committee of Wise Men (2001), Final Report of the Committee of Wise Men on the Regulation of European Securities Markets (Brussels, 15 February).

Costi, R. and Enriques, L. (2004), *Il mercato mobiliare* (Padova: CEDAM).

Craig, P. and de Búrca, G. (2003), *EU Law. Text, Cases, and Materials* (3rd ed) (Oxford: Oxford University Press).

Davies, P. (2003), *'Gower & Davies' Principles of Modern Company Law* (7th ed).

de Kluiver, H-J (2004), 'Inspiring a New European Company Law?', in 1 *European Company and Financial Law Review* 121.

Denozza, F. (1993), 'Le società', in 1 *I cinquant'anni del Codice Civile* 321.

De Tilla, M., Alpa, G. and Patti, s. (eds.) (2003), *Nuovo diritto societario* (Rome: Italia Oggi).

Diggle, G. and Nobes, C. (1994), 'European Rule-making in Accounting: The Seventh Directive as a Case Study', 24 *Accounting and Business Research* 319.

Ebke, W.F. (2000), 'Accounting, Auditing and Global Capital Markets', in *Corporations, Capital Markets and the Business in the Law. Liber Amicorum Richard M. Buxbaum* 113 (Theodor Baums *et al.* eds) (Oxford: Oxford University Press).

Edwards, V. (1999), *EC Company Law* (Oxford: Oxford University Press).

Enriques, L. (2003a), 'Bad Apples, Bad Oranges: A Comment from Old Europe on Post-Enron Corporate Governance Reforms', 38 *Wake Forest Law Review* 911.

—— (2003b), 'Spunti in tema di strumenti finanziari partecipativi e ibridi e di azioni correlate e riscattabili (con un caveat sulle trasformazioni elusive da S.r.l. a S.p.a.)', in *Nuovo diritto societario* 107 (Maurizio de Tilla *et al.* eds).

—— (2004a), 'EC Company Law and the Fears of a European Delaware', 15 *European Business Law Review* 1259.

—— (2004b), 'Silence Is Golden: The European Company As a Catalyst for Company Law Arbitrage', 4 *Journal of Corporate Law Studies* 77.

—— (2004c), 'The Mandatory Bid Rule in the Proposed EC Takeover Directive: Harmonization As Rent-Seeking?', in G. Ferrarini *et al* (eds.), *Reforming Company and Takeover Law in Europe* (Oxford: Oxford University Press).

—— (2004d), 'Uno sguardo cinico sulla riforma del diritto societario: più rendite; meno rigidità?', Working Paper Indret (July), available at http://www.indret.com/rcs_articulos/cas/231.pdf.

—— (2006), 'Quartum non datur: appunti in tema di "strumenti finanziari partecipativi" in Inghilterra, negli Stati Uniti e in Italia', forthcoming in *Banca Borsa Titoli di Credito* 166.

Enriques, L. and Macey, J.R. (2001), 'Creditors Versus Capital Formation: The Case Against the European Legal Capital Rules', 86 *Cornell Law Review* 1165.

Enriques, L. and Scassellati Sforzolini, G.S. (2004), 'Adeguamenti statutari: scelte di fondo e nuove opportunità nella riforma societaria', 2004 *Notariato* 69.

European Commission (2002), 'Comparative Study of Corporate Governance Codes Relevant to the European Union and Its Member States', at http://www.europa.eu.int/comm/internal_market/company/docs/corpgov/corp-gov-codes-rpt-summary_en.pdf (27 March).

—— (2004), Company Law: European Company Statute in Force, But National Delays Stop Companies Using It (press release by the European Commission, 8 Oct. IP/04/1195, available at http://europa.eu.int/rapid/pressReleasesAction.do?reference=IP/04/1195&format=HTML&aged=0&language=EN&guiLanguage=en).

European Court of Justice (2002), Annual Report for Year 2002, available at http://curia.eu.int/en/instit/presentationfr/rapport/stat/st02cr.pdf.

European Parliament (2003), Report on the Proposal for a European Parliament and Council Directive on Takeover Bids, Final A5-0000/2003 (3 December).

European Union (2004), Call for applications for the establishment of the Advisory Committee on Corporate Governance and Company Law, at http://www.europa.eu.int/comm/internal_market/company/docs/advisory-committee/call-applications-2004–12_en.pdf.

Ferran, E. (1999), *Company Law and Corporate Finance* (Oxford: Oxford University Press).

—— (2004a), *Building an EU Securities Market* (Cambridge: Cambridge University Press).

—— (2004b), 'Corporate Transactions and Financial Assistance: Shifting Policy Perceptions But Static Law', 63 *Cambridge Law Journal* 225.

Ferrarini, G. (1999), 'The European Regulation of Stock Exchanges: New Perspectives', in 36 *Common Market Law Review* 569.

Financial Times (2005), 'Editorial, When in Doubt Just Do Nowt', in *Fin. Times (Europe)*, 24 Jan., at 10.

Gatti, M. (2004), *OPA e struttura del mercato del controllo societario* (Milan: Giuffré).

Gleichmann, K. (1991), 'Perspectives on European Company Law', 14 *Forum Internationale* 3.

Gordon, J.N. (2004), 'An American Perspective on Anti-Takeover Laws in the EU: The German Example, in Reforming Company and Takeover Law in Europe', above n 86, 542, 547.

Grundmann, S. (2004), 'The Structure of European Company Law: From Crisis to Boom', 5 *European Business Organization and Law Review* 601.

Gutiérrez, M. and Tribó, J.A. (2004), Private Benefits Extraction in Closely-Held Corporations: The Case for Multiple Large Shareholders (Oct.) (ECGI Working Paper No 53/2004), at http://papers.ssrn.com/sol3/papers.cfm?abstract_id=302756.

Habersack, M. (2003), *Europäisches Gesellschaftsercht*, (2nd ed) Munich: Beck).

Hadfield, G.K. (2000), 'The Price of Law: How the Market for Lawyers Distorts the Justice System', 98 *Michigan Law Review* 953.

Halbhuber, H. (2001), 'National Doctrinal Structures and European Company Law', 38 *Common Market Law Review* 1385.

Haller, A. (2002), 'Financial Accounting Developments in the European Union: Past Events and Future Prospects', 11 *European Accounting Review* 153.

Hertig, G. (2004), 'Efficient Fostering of EU Regulatory Competition', 2004 *Schweizerische Zeitschrift für Wirtschaftsrecht* 369.

Hertig, G. and Lee, R. (2003), 'Four Predictions about the Future of EU Securities Regulation', 3 *Journal of Corporate Law Studies* 359.

Hertig, G. and McCahery, J.A. (2004), 'Revamping the EU Corporate and Takeover Law Agenda—and Making it a Model for the U.S.' (23 February), available at http://repositories.cdlib.org/cgi/viewcontent.cgi?article=1104&context=berk eley_law_econ.

Höfner, K.D. (2004), 'Die Offenlegungsplicht bei der GmbH & Co. KG erneut auf dem Prüfstand', 2004 *Neue Juristische Wochenschrift* 475.

Hopt, K.J. (1999), 'Company Law in the European Union: Harmonisation and/or Subsidiarity', 1 *International and Comparative Corporate Law Journal* 41.

—— (2000), 'Common Principles of Corporate Governance in Europe?', in *The Clifford Chance Millennium Lectures* 105 (Basil S. Markesinis ed).

Hopt, R.J., Menjueq, M. and Wymeersch, E. (eds.), (2003) *La Société européenne, Organization juridique et fiscale, intérêts, perpectives* (Paris: Dalloz).

Initiative Europe (2003), Barometer Q4 2003, available at http://www.initiative-europe.com/press/downloads/Q42003.pdf.

Italian Parliament (1989), 'La disciplina dell'insider trading in Italia', 1989 *Rivista delle società* 116.

Jackson, H.E. and Pan, E.J. (2001), 'Regulatory Competition in International Securities Markets: Evidence from Europe in 1999—Part I', 56 *Business Lawyer* 653.

Kahan, M. and Kamar, E. (2002), 'The Myth of State Competition in Corporate Law', 55 *Stanford Law Review* 679.

Kirchner, C. *et al.* (2004), 'Regulatory Competition in EU Corporate Law after Inspire Art: Unbundling Delaware's Product for Europe', available at http://papers.ssrn.com/sol3/papers.cfm?abstract_id=617681.

Kostel, M.E. (1993), 'A Public Choice Perspective on the Debate over Federal Versus State Corporate Law', 79 *Virginia Law Review* 2129.

Kraakman, R. *et al.* (2004), *The Anatomy of Corporate Law* (Oxford: Oxford University Press).

'La disciplina dell'insider trading in Italia', 1989 *Rivista delle società* 116.

La Villa, G. (1974), 'The Validity of Company Undertakings and the Limits of the E.E.C. Harmonization', 3 *Anglo-American Law Review* 346.

Lannoo, K. (1999), 'A European Perspective on Corporate Governance', 37 *Journal of Common Market Studies* 269.

—— (2003), 'The Emerging Framework for Disclosure in the EU', 3 *Journal of Corporate Law Studies* 329.

Lannoo, K. and Khachaturyan, A. (2004), 'Reform of Corporate Governance in the EU', 5 *European Business Organization and Law Review* 37.

Lecourt, B. (2004), 'L'avenir du droit français des sociétés: que peut-on encore attendre du législateur européen?', 2004 *Revue des sociétés* 223.

Lieb, B.D. and Lamandini, M. (2003), The New Proposal of a Directive on Company Law Concerning Takeover Bids and the Achievement of a Level Playing Field, European Parliament Working Paper 57, available at http://www.jura.uni-duesseldorf.de/dozenten/noack/texte/sonstige/study.pdf.

Lombardo, S. (2002), *Regulatory Competition in Company Law in the European Community* (Berlin: de Gruyter).

Majone, G. (1989), 'Regulating Europe: Problems and Prospects', in *Jahrbuch zur Staats- und Verwaltungswissenschaft 1987/88* 159 (Thomas Ellwein *et al.* eds).

McChesney, F.S. (1997), *Money for Nothing: Politicians, Rent Extraction, and Political Extortion* (Cambridge, Mass.: Harvard University Press).

McComb, D. (1991), 'Accounting. A. Report, in European Business Law: Legal and Economic Analyses on Integration and Harmonization'.

Medin, J.A.F. and Fraga, P.P. (1988), 'A Framework for a Public Choice Analysis of the European Community', 1988 *Economia delle Scelte Pubbliche* 141.

Moloney, N. (2002), *EC Securities Regulation* (Oxford: Oxford University Press).

Mora, A. and Rees, W. (1998), 'The Early Adoption of Consolidated Accounting in Spain', 7 *European Accounting Review* 675.

Noack, U. and Zetzsche, D. (2005), 'Corporate Governance Reform in Germany: The Second Decade' (14 Jan.) available at http://papers.ssrn.com/sol3/papers.cfm?abstract_id=646761

Nowak, E. (2003), 'Investor Protection and Capital Market Regulation in Germany', in *The German Financial System* 425 (Jan P. Krahnen & Reinhard H. Schmidt eds) (Oxford: Oxford University Press).

Ordelheide, D. (1993), 'True and Fair View: A European and a German Perspective. A Commentary on "A European True and Fair View?" by David Alexander', 2 *European Accounting Review* 81.

Pérakis, E. (2003), 'SE: Une société pour quelles entreprises?', in *La Société Européenne. Organisation juridique et fiscale, intérêts, perspectives* 227 (Klaus J. Hopt *et al.* eds).

Pistor, K. (2004), 'Enhancing Corporate Governance in the New Member States: Does EU Law Help?', in George A. Bermann & Katharina Pistor (eds.), *Law and Governance in an Enlarged European Union* (Oxford: Hart Publishing) 339.

Pistor, K., Raiser, M. and Gelfer, S. (2000), 'Law and Finance in Transition Economies', 8 *Economic Transition* 325.

Pitt, H.L. and Hardison, D.B. (1992), 'Games Without Frontiers: Trends in the International Response to Insider Trading', 55 *Law and Contemporary Problems* 199.

Portale, G.B. (2003), 'Riforma delle società di capitali e limiti di effettività del diritto nazionale', 2003 *Le Società* 261.

Ribstein, L.E. (1994), 'Delaware, Lawyers and Contractual Choice of Law', 19 *Delaware Journal of Corporate Law* 999.

Rickford, J. (ed) (2004), 'Reforming Capital: Report of the Interdisciplinary Group on Capital Maintenance', 15 *European Business Law Review* 919.

Roe, M.J. (2003), 'Delaware's Competition', 117 *Harvard Law Review* 588.

Romano, R. (1993), *The Genius of American Corporate Law* (Washington, D.C.: American Enterprise Institute Press).

—— (2005) *Is Regulatory Competition a Problem for Corporate Governance?*

Russo, A. and Siniscalco, F. (1984), 'The Fourth Directive and Italy', *in EEC Accounting Harmonisation: Implementation and Impact of the Fourth Directive* 63 (S.J. Gray and A.G. Coenenberg eds).

Schmidt, K. (2002), *Gesellschaftsrech* (Köln: Carl Heymanns Verlag).

Schmitthoff, C.M. (1976), 'The Success of the Harmonization of European Company Law', 1976 *European Law Review* 100.

Schön, W. (2004), 'The Future of Legal Capital', 5 *European Business Law Review* 429.

Schuck, P.H. (1992), 'Legal Complexity: Some Causes, Consequences, and Cures', 42 *Duke Law Journal* 1.

Securities Expert Group (2004), Financial Services Action Plan: Progress and Prospects. Final Report (May), available at http://www. europeansecuritisation.com/pubs/FSAP_Stocktaking_Report.pdf.

Smith, C.W. and Warner, J.B. (1979), 'On Financial Contracting: An Analysis of Bond Covenants', 7 *Journal of Financial Economics* 117.

Smith, P. (2004), 'Buy-out Groups on the Spree in Europe', in *Financial Times (Europe)*, 21 Aug., at 18.

Spolidoro, M.S. (2003), 'Conferimenti e strumenti partecipativi nella riforma delle società di capitali', I *Diritto della Banca e del Mercato Finanziario* 205.

—— (2004), 'Gli acquisti pericolosi', in 1/3 *Trattato delle società per azioni* 679 (Giovanni E. Colombo & Giuseppe B. Portale eds).

Standen, D.J. (1995), 'Insider Trading Reforms Sweep Across Germany: Bracing for the Cold Winds of Change', 36 *Harvard International Law Journal* 177.

Stein, E. (1971), *Harmonization of European Company Laws* (Indianapolis: Bobbs-Merrill).

Timmermans, C.W.A. (2002), *Company Law As Ius Commune?* in W. Dervoe and D. Droshout (eds.), *First Walter van Gerven Lecture 2002* (Antwerp: Intersentia).

Tröger, T.T. (2004), 'Choice of Jurisdiction in European Corporate Law: Perspectives of European Corporate Governance' (24 July), available at http://ssrn.com/abstract=568782

Van Hulle, K. (1997), 'The True and Fair View Override in the European Accounting Directives', 6 *European Accounting Review* 711.

Van Ommeslaghe, P. (1969), 'La Première Directive du Conseil du 9 Mars 1968 en Matière de Sociétées', 5 *Cahiers de Droit Européen* 495.

Vaubel, R. (1994a), 'The Political Economy of Centralization and the European Community', 81 *Public Choice* 151.

—— (1994b), 'The Public Choice Analysis of European Integration: A Survey', 10 *European Journal of Political Economy* 227.

Walton, P. (1997), 'The True and Fair View and the Drafting of the Fourth Directive', 6 *European Accounting Review* 721.

Warren, M.G. (1991), 'The Regulation of Insider Trading in the European Community', 48 *Washington and Lee Law Review* 1037.

Weigmann, R. (1997), 'Società per azioni', in 14 *Digesto Discipline Privatistiche, Sezione Commerciale* 338.

Werlauff, E. (2003), *EU-Company Law. Common Business Law of 28 States* 100 (2nd ed) (Copenhagen: Danmarks Jurist).

Wolff, G. (1993), 'The Commission's Programme for Company Law Harmonisation: The Winding Road to a Uniform European Company Law?', in *E.C. Financial Market Regulation and Company Law* 19 (Mads Andenas & Stephen Keynon-Slade eds) (London: Sweet and Maxwell).

Woolridge, F. (1991), *Company Law in the United Kingdom and the European Community: Its Harmonization and Unification* (London: Athlone Press).

Wouters, J. (2000), 'European Company Law: Quo Vadis?', 37 *Common Market Law Review* 257.

Wymeersch, E. (1998), 'Article 23 of the Second Company Law Directive: The Prohibition on Financial Assistance to Acquire Shares of the Company', in *Festschrift für Ulrich Drobnig zum siebzigsten Geburtstag* 725 (Jürgen Basedow *et al.* eds).

—— (2003), 'The Transfer of the Company's Seat in European Company Law', 40 *Common Market Law Review* 661.

—— (2004), 'About Techniques of Regulating Companies in the European Union', in *Reforming Company and Takeover Law in Europe* 145 (Guido Ferrarini *et al.* eds) (Oxford: Oxford University Press).

Index

3Com, 84

ABN Amro, 207
accounting
  see also auditors; financial reporting
  accountants see accounting profession
  Enron fraud, 1–2, 4–5, 15
  EU law, impact, 671
  incentives to manipulate, 8–9, 221
  information gaps, 4–7
  Italy, 656
  politics, 326–8
  profession see accounting profession
  regulatory responses, 14–15
  Sarbanes-Oxley Act, 14, 135, 143, 156,
      267, 319–30
  Spain, 656
  standards see accounting standards
  UK companies, 396
  wave of fraud, 1, 4
accounting profession:
  European Union, 470–1, 681
  United States
    auditors' fees, 301–2, 307, 308–9, 323,
        328–30
    cartel behaviour, 299–304, 315–18
    demand for rules, 283–4
    further reforms, 330–6
    gatekeeping function, 304–5
    industry concentration, 296–9
    non-audit services, 296, 304–15
      conflicts of interest, 269, 431
      effect, 315–18
      further reforms, 332–3
      post-Sarbanes-Oxley, 323, 470
      tax services, 324, 334
    non-price competition, 304
    oligopoly, 295–336
    post-Sarbanes-Oxley, 323–30
    Sarbanes-Oxley Act, 296, 319–23
    scandals, 282
    self-regulation, 303
    staff, 308
accounting standards
  see also US GAAP
  audit failures, 270–9
  Enron, 15, 270, 274–9, 447
  European Union, 267, 447, 555, 585, 656
  flexibility, 287–90
  rules v principles, 266–70, 285–90
  transparency, 286–7
Ackermann, Josef, 361

actions en comblement du passif, 467
Adecco, 225
Adelphia, 1, 129, 230
Agrawal, A., 321
Ahold, 3, 545
Alexander, D., 651
Alexander, K., 628
Alstom, 3
American Bar Association, 246, 248, 256
American Institute of Certified Public
      Accountants, 303
American Institute of Public Accounting,
      319
analysts:
  access to information, 79–80
  conflicts of interest, 2, 53–4, 79, 81, 418n9
  Enron, 418n9
  EU regulation, 477–8
  Italy, 191
  limitations, 78–81
  and market fraud damages, 107–10
  and noise trading, 100–4
  Parmalat, 165–6, 168
  policy debate, 98–104
  selective disclosure to, 68–9, 92–104
  unfairness of disclosures, 92–5
  US regulation, 92–104
Andenas, M., 623
Andersen see Arthur Andersen
Anderson, J., 658
Anderson, K.L., 219
Anglo-American model see dispersed
      ownership systems
arbitrage:
  agency costs, 45–6, 51
  hedge funds, 45
  market efficiency limits, 5–6, 40–6, 49–50,
      77–8
  Modigliani-Miller propositions, 33
  and noise traders, 40, 41, 45–6, 49
  pricing model, 37
  rational arbitrage, 69
  regulatory arbitrage, 279, 503, 504, 518
Arden, Mary, 3
Areeda, P.E., 302n18
Argentina, 164, 190
Arlen, J., 563
Arlman, P., 615
Armour, John, 13, 21, 497–536
Arnull, A.M., 590
Arsht, Samuel, 139
Arthur Andersen: